STEREOSCOPIC LAW

In this unique book, Alexander Lian, a practicing commercial litigator, advances the thesis that the most famous article in American jurisprudence, Oliver Wendell Holmes's "The Path of the Law," presents Holmes's leading ideas on legal education. Through meticulous analysis, Lian explores Holmes's fundamental ideas on law and its study. He puts "The Path of the Law" within the trajectory of Holmes's jurisprudence, from earliest scholarship to *The Common Law* to the occasional pieces Holmes wrote or delivered after joining the US Supreme Court. Lian takes a close look at the reactions "The Path of the Law" has evoked, both positive and negative, and restates the essay's core teachings for today's legal educators. Lian convincingly shows that Holmes's "theory of legal study" broke down artificial barriers between theory and practice. For contemporary legal educators, *Stereoscopic Law* reformulates Holmes's fundamental message that the law must be seen and taught three-dimensionally.

ALEXANDER LIAN practices commercial litigation in Miami, FL. Since 2008, he has been a solo practitioner. His publications include numerous contributions to the ABA's Litigation Ethics Newsletter and a chapter in the recently published collection, *The Pragmatism and Prejudice of Oliver Wendell Holmes, Jr.* (2019).

Stereoscopic Law

OLIVER WENDELL HOLMES AND LEGAL EDUCATION

ALEXANDER LIAN

CAMBRIDGE
UNIVERSITY PRESS

CAMBRIDGE
UNIVERSITY PRESS

University Printing House, Cambridge CB2 8BS, United Kingdom

One Liberty Plaza, 20th Floor, New York, NY 10006, USA

477 Williamstown Road, Port Melbourne, VIC 3207, Australia

314-321, 3rd Floor, Plot 3, Splendor Forum, Jasola District Centre, New Delhi - 110025, India

103 Penang Road, #05-06/07, Visioncrest Commercial, Singapore 238467

Cambridge University Press is part of the University of Cambridge.

It furthers the University's mission by disseminating knowledge in the pursuit of education, learning and research at the highest international levels of excellence.

www.cambridge.org
Information on this title: www.cambridge.org/9781108465441
DOI: 10.1017/9781108640589

First published 2020
First paperback edition 2022

A catalogue record for this publication is available from the British Library

Library of Congress Cataloging in Publication data
NAMES: Lian, Alexander, 1964– author.
TITLE: Stereoscopic law : Oliver Wendell Holmes and legal education / Alexander Lian
DESCRIPTION: Cambridge, United Kingdom ; New York, NY : Cambridge University Press, 2020. | Includes bibliographical references and index.
IDENTIFIERS: LCCN 2020014093 (print) | LCCN 2020014094 (ebook) | ISBN 9781108474740 (hardback) | ISBN 9781108465441 (paperback) | ISBN 9781108640589 (epub)
SUBJECTS: LCSH: Law–Study and teaching–United States. | Law–United States–Methodology, | Holmes, Oliver Wendell, Jr., 1841–1935–Influence.
CLASSIFICATION: LCC KF272 .L53 2020 (print) | LCC KF272 (ebook) | DDC 340.071/173–dc23
LC record available at https://lccn.loc.gov/2020014093
LC ebook record available at https://lccn.loc.gov/2020014094

ISBN 978-1-108-47474-0 Hardback
ISBN 978-1-108-46544-1 Paperback

FOR PAUL K. CONKIN

with lasting appreciation

If I am right it will be a slow business for our people to reach rational views, assuming we are allowed to work peaceably to that end. But as I grow older I grow calm. If I feel what are perhaps an old man's apprehensions, that competition from new races will cut deeper than working men's disputes and will test whether we can hang together and can fight; if I fear that we are running through the world's resources at a pace that we cannot keep; I do not lose my hopes. I do not pin my dreams for the future to my country or even to my race.

Oliver Wendell Holmes, Jr., "Law and the Court"

Contents

Preface

As the initial motive for this book lay in legal pedagogy, and since I am by profession not a legal educator – I mainly litigate civil and commercial cases – I should try to describe briefly the various circumstances that led to its writing. In late 2012 I decided to write a biography of a federal case that I had successfully brought to conclusion after trial and appeal (including oral argument). The point of that book was to present to the interested reader, mainly law students I assumed, an integrated account of how litigation worked in the United States. It had taken me a number of years after law school to understand how the many pieces fit together so I thought a book like mine might help shorten the learning curve for others. Of course, my presentation was meant to be only one solo practitioner's take.

I thought it would be of interest for two reasons. First, the case had brought within its orbit most of the principal court branches of both the federal and the Florida state system. It didn't make it to the United States Supreme Court, so I didn't have a cherry to top off the sundae. But it, or the primary issue it presented, involved a federal district court and a court of appeal, a bankruptcy court, several state trial courts, a state court of appeal, and the state supreme court (which, incidentally, ended up nullifying the effect of the federal district court's ruling that the federal appellate court had upheld).

The second and secondary reason I thought the book would be of interest to law students arose from the eventful fact that I had taken this case – a contingency suit for the recovery of a pre-construction deposit for a luxury condominium unit – only a couple of months or so after setting up my own law practice. I had gone solo in the summer of 2008 with little more than five years of professional experience to draw upon. It was not a propitious time to be embarking on such a venture, but circumstances had left me little alternative. The travails of setting up and maintaining a law practice magnified every step and misstep in a case that was not my only case but which quickly became the one to consume much of my attention.

The case ended in 2011 and by late 2012, as mentioned, I decided that the story had the potential to put the central pieces of the litigation puzzle together in an informing and interesting way. By the beginning of January 2016 I had written over half the book and had in the preceding years become quite well versed on the background and purpose of the federal rules of civil procedure. But I began to realize as I thought and wrote more and more about the law – instead of merely using law for a specific professional purpose – that I had no framework to draw upon. I could write accurately about details and context but I had no bigger, bigger picture to help me understand. I determined to develop my theoretical sophistication and thought a good way to do that was to return to a famous essay in American jurisprudence that had piqued my interest in law school.

I had read that essay in law school but on my own time. I attended two law schools, and neither of them to my knowledge put much emphasis on jurisprudence or on helping students think about the law philosophically. In tone the two law schools were quite different and – at the risk of oversimplifying – the bigger picture offered to help organize the many details at one was "morality" and at the other "economics." I am writing in shorthand of course. Whether or not these descriptions are accurate, it is the impression that has remained with me. It was at the second school's bookstore where I came across Judge Richard Posner's *The Essential Holmes*. The first sentence of the introduction caught my attention: "Oliver Wendell Holmes is the most illustrious figure in the history of American law."[1] I had no idea.

I had run across Holmes's name before but only in passing. In my first year's contract course I recall reading excerpts with his name attached on the topic of consideration. Prior to law school I had enrolled in graduate school to study American Intellectual History and had bumped into Holmes, here and there, mainly in connection with my study of William James and his famous piece "The Will to Believe."

I had never actually fully read anything by Holmes, so when I further learned from Posner's introduction that Holmes's "The Path of the Law" "may be the best article-length work on law ever written" I was sold. I bought the book, took it home and began reading "The Path of the Law." It took more than one attempt to finally get through it. I did not find it easy reading. But the piece caught my attention. Since I was in law school I was especially keen on understanding his recommendations on how to study law, but much of it went past me. I looked at a few articles to help me understand the piece but none of them seemed to focus on the point that I felt Holmes was driving at – the study of law.

I conceived a vague notion of writing an article on "The Path of the Law" as an effort in legal pedagogy but soon the demands of graduation, the bar exam, and learning to practice like a lawyer took my full attention. It was not until over a decade later, when the disquiet over my lack of theoretical sophistication hit me

[1] Richard A. Posner, *Introduction*, in THE ESSENTIAL HOLMES ix (Richard A. Posner ed., 1992)

unawares – the hidden tax one pays for being a student of intellectual history – that I decided to take a short break from my biography of a case project and go back to Holmes and "The Path of the Law."

What I initially thought would be a six-month hiatus to write an article has stretched to almost four years and a lengthy book. As my kind and patient editors (John Berger and Matt Gallaway) will confirm, I am particularly bad at estimating completion dates. When I began I had no sense of, (1) the extensiveness of the literature on "The Path of the Law," (2) the necessity of understanding Holmes's thought as a whole to appreciating what he wrote in "Path," and (3) the sorry state of so much of what passes for legal scholarship. The months accumulated as I waded through the literature, struggled to understand Holmes, and tried to keep in balance the "searching" and the "thinking" that goes into any project of this type.

Parenthetically, I should say I have relied mainly on Holmes's published works. On occasion I delved into the Oliver Wendell Holmes Digital Suite's holdings, usually to find a cited document. I did not conduct any original research or read through its extensive collections or ferret through the Harvard University Archives. I tended to rely on Holmes's public statement of his positions in articles and addresses. I read a fair number of his opinions but not nearly all – or even most – of them. I also did not delve into the free speech cases or his opinions on economic matters. Possibly many of the interesting things he said to Richard T. Ely might have been brought into the discussion but I could not afford the year or two it would take to become sufficiently versed in the political economy of that era to say something intelligent and integrate it into the main topic, legal education.

Besides, I had a practice to maintain. I do most everything myself as I find it less stressful, after almost a dozen years of running a practice, to do it myself than to hand it off to someone else. Clients are also hiring me, not someone else, to do the job and the client is always the priority. There are problems of scale with this model but it has worked for me, especially when my entire life has ping-ponged between Holmes and the practice.

In no particular order since 2016 I have handled, (1) an ongoing constellation of lawsuits (trial level and appeal) that took seven years and involved various opposing law firms over the entitlement of a parent denomination to the property of its former member church (I represented the parent); (2) multiple enforcement actions on behalf of a Fortune 100 company for unpaid invoices usually totaling in the six figures, some of which involved pre-judgment or post-judgment writs of garnishment or attachment; (3) the defense of a multifamily property owner against allegations of violating migrant housing laws prosecuted by a state agency but under the auspices of a local quasi-judicial board; (4) the defense of a marine contractor for unpaid invoices brought by a marina for the use of two docking slips; (5) a long-standing foreclosure defense against a securitized asset trustee over a residence in Key West that dragged on for ten years, went to trial and appeal – we lost both – and that ended up, unexpectedly, with the owner managing to hold on to the property through a restructured loan; (6) a defense to a suit brought by, and a counterclaim against, a prominent Miami law firm in a particularly unpleasant, protracted dispute over unpaid legal bills; and (7) contingency lawsuits that did not always turn out exactly as one hoped. One on behalf of a commercial broker who got stiffed on the commission and another on behalf of an estate trying to recover a substantial pre-construction condominium unit deposit paid quite a few years before the decedent's unexpected death.

These are not all the matters I have handled since January 2016 but it gives a fair representation. And since the practice was mine and not someone else's I had the ongoing challenge that every business owner faces of staying in the black and not letting the tedious let-someone-else-deal-with-it problems build up and submerge the enterprise. The practice of law has now a reality to me very different from when I began as an associate.

This "reality of the practice" enlarged the imaginative reach at my disposal to understand Holmes, just as Holmes enlarged my ability to become increasingly self-reflexive. Unexpectedly, the practice itself became more interesting, less draining. It was the unpleasant and in many respects thankless aspects of litigation that had initially driven me to seek solace in and through nonfiction writing. But now, after spending so much time with Holmes, I began to see the law, and lawyers, with new eyes and, perhaps not coincidentally, found that my initially very vague notion back in 2001 that Holmes wrote the "The Path of the Law" as an exercise in legal pedagogy had been substantially correct.

Acknowledgements

Looking back as such a consuming project as this one draws to a close presents the challenge, not unlike that of selecting those causes which merit the label "proximate," of bringing together for special mention those people who I tend to feel have really helped make this accomplishment possible. This book stands at the intersection of two main highways: my early career as a student of American Intellectual History and my current one as a practicing litigator. Neither the paths taken nor their intersection is, broadly speaking, unique. At least not in any important way. I never went through the tremendous gulf of a dark, dying-man's solitude in pursuing this study, at least I don't think I did, but I did find that my decision to devote all my available time to work on Holmes and not look for ways to expand my practice and keep full the pipeline drew many puzzled looks and queries from colleagues ("So, how much money will this book make?"). That incredulity never really affected me deeply because deep down, I now realize, I still self-identified as an academic. But when midway through this project I discovered and excitedly signed up for a conference at Stanford Law School celebrating the work of Robert W. Gordon – both he and some of the listed participants had written extensively on Holmes – I also ended up discovering much to my consternation that the academic lawyers did not consider me an academic. I was a practitioner.

And I was a practitioner without a sterling resume or blue-chip academic credentials. Reflection on that experience and further insight into how the dynamic of "enmity and amity" continues to do its unholy work within the American legal profession helped steel me against further onslaughts against my self-identity and, by the same token, made me more appreciative of both those practitioners and those academic lawyers who were willing to take the time to respond to selected parts of the manuscript or to write an endorsement for the book. In particular I thank, on the academic side, Stephen M. Feldman and Bruce Kimball for penning endorsements. I also thank John Henry Schlegel for providing a hard-to-find piece written by Walter Wheeler Cook and, more importantly, for reading the manuscript and providing feedback. I very much appreciated his courtesies to a fellow scholar. On the practitioner side I must give especial thanks to Frederic Kellogg and Daniel Kornstein. Both also happen to be accomplished authors. Fred's encouragement in the early stages of the project was invaluable. And Dan, whom I contacted much later, after I discovered his book on Holmes, *The Second Greatest American*, graciously read the manuscript and had kind words to say. That meant a lot and helped keep me going.

Six months into this project I trashed everything I had done in frustration and started over. Holmes was a much harder nut to crack than I had imagined. Like the hero of my younger days, the intellectual historian Perry Miller, I had begun to feel that perhaps my voices had misled me and this field had indeed been fully threshed, even thrashed. Maybe there was no field at all. What field? What path? What law? Discouragement began to shadow me and sometimes it became a relief to fight with opposing counsel over something truly annoying but tangible – like whether opposing party witness depositions would be taken seriatim or alternating between one side and the other (it took the judge to decide and my side, the seriatim side, lost).

At such moments kinder voices than one's own provide a much-needed reprieve and for that I am most grateful. The voices of friends stretching past many years came to life in a new way when I undertook this project, especially those who are still part of an academic or educational community. I want to say thanks to Gary Chartier and Paul Gasparini, who each sought to provide tangible support as I battled through the work. Gary especially listened to long, incoherent monologues as I worked my way through Holmes, especially at the beginning, when I was certain that I did not understand him but had begun to become suspicious that many others didn't either.

Longtime friends Lance Cantos and John Haworth provided a welcome break from the rigors of the task during our annual meet-ups. I've always appreciated their friendship and their encouragement. Similarly, I've appreciated my long friendship with my graduate school roommate Bruce Harvey. Bruce now works as a professional consulting historian and documentation photographer based in Syracuse, New York. He was kind enough to use his expert photography skills to produce the art for the book's cover.

The one person who prophesied from the earliest of days that law lay in my future was my mother, Faride Jalube. She herself would have liked to become a lawyer so the disappointment was probably deeper than I could have comprehended when I blithely told her that I wanted to be a history professor instead. She accepted the news without enthusiasm and said nothing more about the law until the day, about twelve years later, when I told her I had decided to apply to law school. "See, I told you so," she said, pausing, not to emphasize the point, but to get enough breath to provide an exquisite summary of the many missed opportunities. For that reason I really had no idea how she would react when I informed her of my decision to cut back on the practice and start writing. She thought it was a very good idea. I wasn't sure at first how to take this burst of approval, especially when tangibly followed by books she sent on writing by writers. Perhaps her motherly wisdom had led her to see my need for some respite, or perhaps, more likely, her gift for knowing what ought to be done, and when, led her to provide unstinting support. I am of course unfailingly grateful, not only for her love and encouragement in this instance, and the lifelong dedication I have received, but also for her helping me understand a bit better the nature of that wisdom that lies behind practical judgments.

The disappointments associated with this Holmes project have in some ways cut deeper than any of the disappointments with court rulings or client decisions that have adversely affected my practice. Or even the disappointments I experienced in my academic half-life. Every writer wants her or his work to be taken seriously. In fact, one of the major points this book attempts to drive home is that without this "taken seriously," jurisprudence in America will not progress to the next level. It begins simply enough, with taking the time to read. People who I thought ought to be interested in the project, who might be interested, who might be induced to be interested were in fact indifferent. If a good man is hard to find, to paraphrase Flannery O'Connor, I can assure you that even harder to find is a good reader. For that reason I owe a special thank you to my sister, Michelle Reid, who alone took time from her hectic life to read carefully a manuscript far removed from her work and preoccupations and provide strong editorial feedback and well-placed questions.

Books are hard on personal relationships. In this case, no amount of contextualizing or poeticizing or reinscribing will conceal the fact that attention and energy are being directed to what is essentially a solitary pursuit. One who is not a writer, or one who wants to write a book but has not yet written one, has little inkling of what is in store. Martha Nino had little idea what she had signed up for when this project began and I could not do much more than provide periodic bulletins filled with promises of forthcoming certainty in increasingly vague terms. The situation more often than not bordered on the intolerable. Yet she persisted. It seems grossly disproportionate to acknowledge her steadfastness and love with just my heartfelt gratitude. She deserves so much more.

Newly minted lawyers arguing their first tort cases quickly learn the rhetorical value of the so-called but-for cause. But for x, y would not have happened. It may be quite persuasive in many instances, but if used unthinkingly it proves fallacious and susceptible to attack. It was Nicholas St. John Green who pointed out the many pitfalls that the background image of the "chain of causation" laid for the unwary and it took decades for other members of the profession to recognize and acknowledge the power and brilliance of his critique. One of the unexpected pleasant surprises in embarking on this study of Holmes was that it introduced me to Green. I read a number of his articles and what I could find about his life. The man had a powerful mind and personality. Even though he died relatively early, he had already shown tremendous critical capacity. The combined presence of people like Green and Holmes and other talented colleagues – from Adams to Ames to Bigelow to Gray to Langdell to Thayer – is the main reason I think modern American law was founded in Boston in the last quarter of the nineteenth century.

I may have also been attracted to Green because something about him – the breadth of learning, the synthetic reach, the incisiveness and precision obtained – reminded me of my mentor, Paul K. Conkin. Many of Conkin's colleagues, as did Green's contemporaries, recognized an unusual assemblage of mental powers. But because historians, by and large, are not forced as often as are legal professionals by circumstance to inspect their reasoning – mainly because the consequences of their conclusions are usually indirect and unseen – the profession, or at least the small part with which I was once intimately familiar (American Intellectual History), has no developed, institutional capacity to absorb and implement the combined talents people like Conkin have to offer.

Again, that is not to say that many historians did not admire and respect Conkin's work. He obtained professional prestige, and prominent colleagues would not infrequently describe him as the "most versatile as well as the most clearheaded of American Intellectual Historians[,]" or as "the foremost intellectual critic among American historians." But his drive for clearer, more precise language to convey better-grounded, more nuanced depictions of the past, whether of events or formalized thought, found few followers. I can personally attest he set an exceedingly high bar. So I can also understand some of the hesitancy.

His educative influence on me was profound, mainly by the persistence and dedication with which he went about the task of thinking, rather than any direct connection in terms of style or manner of approach. Conkin is Conkin. As graduate students we used to entertain newcomers or ourselves by swapping Conkin stories. After beginning this project I found out that he and James Willard Hurst had been friends when Conkin taught at Madison. They often rode the morning bus in together. I didn't learn much more about Hurst in that conversation but the image has stayed with me.

My tenure as a graduate student at Vanderbilt's history department was never secure, and without Conkin's support it would have ended sooner than it did. When I now think back on that long unhappy period I am struck by the anomaly that the most prominent member of the department, a master of the craft, and a man who did everything due next week two months ago, found somewhere the patience to bear with me. He did more than simply bear with me – he taught me much, he mentored, he instructed, he helped when needed; he never actively blocked what must have struck him as low-yield endeavors. He was also not above joining in the decision to fail me on my qualifying exam for doctoral candidacy (I passed on the second attempt), or assigning an F++ to a ten-page response to a preliminary exam question in the history of American religion. F++!! Yet through it all he bore with me. But for that commitment this book would not have been written. For that reason I offer him my profound thanks by way of dedication.

Introduction

The most famous speech in American jurisprudence strode into the lecture hall without title or name. Prominent members of the profession had gathered on an overcast Friday afternoon to celebrate the twenty-fifth anniversary of the Boston University School of Law. The clock soon struck half past two. Slated to deliver the keynote address, the tall, handsomely attired man with the imposing soldier's mustache silently sat back, expressionless perhaps, and waited his turn at the podium as encomia and pieties plied the thick air.[1]

The School's honored former professors, oblivious to the passing minutes, quietly contemplated the ceremony from portraits hung on freshly painted, cream-colored walls.[2]

The celebration featured a dedication for a new hall, Isaac Rich Hall, where the event took place. The hall occupied the top floor of a building recently bought and renovated; Bostonians had for fifty years called it the Mt. Vernon Church. The renovators kept the grand classical Greek façade and redid most everything else. The revamped upstairs space now filled with law students, faculty, and distinguished guests, including the presidents of Harvard and Tufts and the dean of the Harvard Law School.[3]

According to the *Boston Evening Transcript*, attendees took careful note of Massachusetts Supreme Judicial Court Associate Justice Holmes's address. Holmes himself later remarked that he had sleepy eyes pretty much wide-awake after he began.[4] He probably had good reason to be self-congratulatory since before he stood and addressed the audience the second of three scheduled speakers, a prominent alumnus, William V. Kellen, former Reporter for the

1 The Boston Evening Transcript, January 8, 1897 (Last Edition), at 3. *See also* David J. Seipp, *125th Anniversary Essay: Holmes's Path*, 77 B.U. L. Rev. 515, 545–46 (1997).

2 Bos. Evening Transcript, *supra* note 1, at 3.

3 *Id.*

4 Seipp, *supra* note 1, at 546.

Supreme Judicial Court, recounted in lengthy detail the history of the School of Law and its teaching methods.[5]

Mr. Kellen's programmatic discourse on the evils of an impoverished legal education – which included his lauding the merits of a sequenced curriculum "tied to no [pedagogical] system" that required the passing of "due test examination" before the pupil could advance to a degree – managed to adroitly sidestep acknowledging the School's debt to Christopher Columbus Langdell, Harvard Law School's renowned former dean.[6] At the same time it nicely continued the School of Law's heritage of protest – of using for instruction "every known method, device, and appliance" – against Langdell's ignominious single-minded "case method,"[7] even if the passing of years and the making of casebooks had subdued the protest's once impassioned resolve.

Dean Langdell, who began teaching at Harvard Law School in 1870, pioneered both the "case method" and the new graduation requirements for those Kellen called "embryo lawyers," the future "advisers to clients" and "assistants to juries and judges." They had to study for longer terms and pursue a sequenced program of courses. A student also had to pass examinations in each year's courses before advancing to the succeeding year or obtaining a degree. But Boston's, not Harvard's, had been the first law school in the country to extend formally the term of study to three years, a fact the speaker did not shy away from pointing out in 1897.[8]

The case method of instruction Langdell first wrought upon Harvard's law students eventually found literary notoriety in a fine and funny novel, *The Paper Chase*, published 100 years after the start of Langdell's tenure.[9] *The Paper Chase* also inspired an equally well-regarded movie and television series of the same name. The schooling of lawyers had by then become the country's most infamous rite of passage into an established profession.

The revolt against Langdell began from the beginning. His lampooned case method added incentive for Boston University to open its School of Law in 1872.

5 Bos. Evening Transcript, *supra* note 1, at 3.

6 *Id.* at 3.

7 *See* Robert Stevens, Law School: Legal Education in America from the 1850s to the 1980s 74 (1987) (noting that Boston University Law School was founded in 1872 by those who disagreed with the appearance of the case method at Harvard); Lawrence M. Friedman, A History of American Law 470 (3d ed. 2005) ("The Boston University Law School was founded in 1872 as an alternative to Harvard's insanity."). *But see* David J. Seipp, *A Short, Incomplete, and Opinionated History of the BU Law School* (April 7, 2019), www.bu.edu/law/about/history-of-the-school (noting that the assertion Boston University School of Law was founded as an alternative to Harvard is nothing more than "the standard Harvard history").

8 Bos. Evening Transcript, *supra* note 1. On Langdell's pedagogical reforms and contributions to legal education in the United States see Bruce A. Kimball, The Inception of Modern Professional Education: C.C. Langdell, 1826–1906 19–30, 218–28 (2009); William LaPiana, Logic and Experience: The Origins of Modern American Legal Education 7–15 (1994); Friedman, A History of American Law, *supra* note 7, at 467–68.

9 John Jay Osborn, Jr., The Paper Chase (1971).

It welcomed into its inaugural class disgruntled law students who sought refuge from what a later historian dubbed "Harvard's insanity."[10] Former Reporter Kellen graduated in 1876.[11]

The *Transcript* correspondent for the January 8, 1897 event made no mention of these hidden skirmishes. He dutifully devoted a few column inches to Kellen's solemn recital of the School of Law's accumulated glories before providing a remarkably accurate summary of the featured address. Holmes's address, the reporter once again prefaced, was "followed with the closest attention by the distinguished assemblage."[12]

> The study of the law is the study of the means of predicting cases in which the public force will be brought to bear upon the person concerned. The general propositions of the law, the so-called legal rights and duties, are only prophecies as to such cases. It is well to look at the subject from the point of view of the bad man who cares only for the practical consequences of his conduct. In this way we avoid one of the great fallacies which beset the subject – the confusion between law and morals – or between law and what we think ought to be the law. This confusion is felt in the common reasoning as to the rights of man, and as to the nature of duty in the legal sense.

Thus reads the opening paragraph of one newspaper's report to the Boston community of what Holmes said. In hindsight this paragraph, especially its first sentence, captured the gist of the opening sections of Holmes's address better than many subsequent full-length articles. The reasons for the disparities in comprehension are as curious as they are opaque.

Certainly Holmes must bear some of the fault himself. He sent his address into the world without a title.[13] Upon publication, both in this country and abroad, the nameless discourse assumed various guises. Boston University first published it as a pamphlet with the not very eye-catching title, "Address Delivered at the Dedication of the New Hall of the Boston University School of Law, January 8, 1897."[14] Students at the School of Law published the address the following February in the Boston Law School Magazine. They anointed it, "The Path of the Law."[15] The *Harvard Law Review* used the same name when it published the piece in March 1897.[16]

[10] FRIEDMAN, *supra* note 7. *See also* LAPIANA, *supra* note 8, at 92–93.

[11] BOS. EVENING TRANSCRIPT, *supra* note 1.

[12] *Id.*

[13] It appears Holmes may have omitted a title out of courtesy. According to David Seipp, Holmes wrote to the Boston University president and indicated that as the event belonged to the School of Law "that alone should appear on the title page without any special indication of the address." Seipp, *supra* note 1, at 549 (*quoting* Letter From Oliver Wendell Holmes to William Fairfield Warren, Jan. 21, 1897) (citations omitted).

[14] *Id.*

[15] *Id.*

[16] Oliver Wendell Holmes, *The Path of the Law*, 10 HARV. L. REV. 457 (1897).

Scotland's prestigious *Juridical Review* also published it in 1897, but anonymously and under a different title: "Law and the Study of Law." It advised its readers in a footnote that "[t]his discourse was pronounced at the dedication of the New Hall of the Boston University School of Law on 8th January, 1897. The author has kindly consented to its publication in the *Juridical Review*."[17]

When preparing the address, Holmes had variously referred to it as a discourse on "Legal Education," "The Principles of Legal Study," or "The Theory of Legal Study."[18] Given how Holmes described the address, one would expect to find among the reams of articles devoted to interpreting, critiquing, praising, or damning "The Path of the Law" – especially its infamous homunculus, the bad man – or among those simply using the piece as a foil for the scholar's analytical virtuosity or philosophical commitments, at least a significant subset devoted to the more mundane task of explicating the theory of legal study expressed within it. But no, that expectation would be disappointed.

The matter is curious.

"The Path of the Law" may be esoteric but cryptic it is not. The address itself did not hide Holmes's intent. One prominent commentator, considering an interpretation that cut across conventional lines, weighed the possibility that the "speech delivered to law students, is not about how to practice law, but how to study law." He further noted: "The first four words are 'When we study law,' and Holmes reminds us of his topic no fewer than ten times."[19] Despite this auspicious start, the commentator declined to pursue this line of inquiry.[20]

Of the numerous articles by contemporary legal scholars that have discussed or dissected "The Path of the Law," only William Twining in a pair of pieces separated by almost twenty-five years has persisted in the contention that "The Path of the Law" is not a "contribution to general jurisprudence, it was intended first and foremost as a discussion of legal education."[21]

[17] [Oliver Wendell Holmes], *Law and the Study of Law*, 9 JURIDICAL REV. 105, 105 n.α (1897).

[18] Seipp, *supra* note 1, at 549. *See also* MORTON J. HORWITZ, THE TRANSFORMATION OF AMERICAN LAW 1870–1960 143 (1992).

[19] David Luban, *The Bad Man and the Good Lawyer: A Centennial Essay on Holmes's The Path of the Law*, 72 N.Y.U. L. REV. 1547, 1550 n.21 (1997) (contending this concern for pedagogy did not surpass Holmes's primary intent to deliver a vocational address).

[20] *Id.* at 1550–51.

[21] William Twining, *Bad Man Revisited*, 58 CORNELL L. REV. 275, 276 (1973) (noting that the bad man personifies a standpoint that combines a certain vantage and the tacit knowing found in legal practice); William Twining, *Other People's Power: The Bad Man and English Positivism, 1897–1997*, 63 BROOKLYN L. REV. 189, 207–12 (1997); *see also* WILLIAM TWINING, KARL LLEWELLYN AND THE REALIST MOVEMENT 15–20, 390–91 (1973). More recent scholarship has also mentioned without much elaboration the inclusion of legal education in "The Path of the Law." *See, e.g.*, H. L. POHLMAN, JUSTICE OLIVER WENDELL HOLMES & UTILITARIAN JURISPRUDENCE 15 (1984); GERALD J. POSTEMA, LEGAL PHILOSOPHY IN THE TWENTIETH CENTURY: THE COMMON LAW WORLD 70–73 (2011).

Part of the purpose of this book is to continue along the course that Twining first took. I also recognize Hessel Yntema as a forerunner. Yntema in his 1931 "Mr. Justice Holmes' View of Legal Science" expressly identified "The Path of the Law" as containing "canons of dogmatic study," that directly connected to Holmes's theory of legal history and his scientific ideal.[22] Regrettably, Twining does not attempt to connect Yntema's insights with his own. Yet Yntema took an intriguing tack, and in like manner I will also try to bring the different sections of "The Path of the Law" – which Twining described as diffuse and rambling, filled with aperçus and obiter dicta[23] – into a tolerable working relationship. I do not contest Twining's observation that "Holmes never worked out in detail the implications of his pronouncements on legal education."[24] And only demur from Twining's contention that Holmes's "prescriptions were scattered and vague, and he dropped only a few very general hints about his view on educational priorities."[25]

Twining also suggested that Holmes in "The Path of the Law" put forth an "alternative philosophy of legal education to that which was prevailing at the time[.]"[26] Twining believes this alternative philosophy to be proto-realist and that Holmes probably did not realize the tremendous difficulties involved in implementing his suggested approach. Again, while I believe Twining to be on the right track I go in a different direction. My objective in this book, though, is not merely to point out how Twining got it wrong, or less than right, or how others missed the boat entirely, but to tackle some fundamental questions about "The Path of the Law." If Holmes's most famous discourse contained, at least in his mind, the rudiments of a theory of legal education then it seems to me worthwhile to inquire deeply into the subject.

In 1973 Twining made an interesting comment:

> Although the main focus of "The Path of the Law" is on legal education, it does not follow that the significance of the piece is limited to that relatively parochial topic. Worthwhile discussions of legal education often lead directly to the questioning of accepted theoretical assumptions, and Holmes's address is not a unique example of provocative jurisprudential statements stimulated by educational concerns. There has been, especially in America, a close connection, both historical and analytical, between legal theory and legal education.[27]

I happen to think legal education a less parochial topic than Twining did when he wrote this paragraph. The ways aspiring lawyers are brought into the profession in the United States has clearly discernible consequences for the practice of law, the

[22] Hessel E. Yntema, *Mr. Justice Holmes' View of Legal Science*, 40 Yale L.J. 696 (1931).
[23] Twining, *Bad Man Revisited*, *supra* note 21, at 278.
[24] *Id.* at 298.
[25] *Id.*
[26] Twining, Karl Llewellyn and the Realist Movement, *supra* note 21, at 19.
[27] Twining, *Bad Man Revisited*, *supra* note 21, at 278–79 n.6 (citing Note, *Legal Theory and Legal Education*, 79 Yale L.J. 1153 (1970)).

quality of the legal system, and for the social bonds that underwrite both the practice and the system. How to understand those social bonds is a question of the utmost importance. But, as Holmes often liked to say, let's not get the cart before the horse.

This book seeks to make a contribution to both American legal history and legal theory. It seeks to build on Twining's comment that in the United States there is a close connection, both historical and analytical, between legal theory and legal education. My basic argument, in one respect following Yntema, is that Holmes in "The Path of the Law" articulates a theory of legal study that depends upon, in ways not immediately obvious, his previous body of work. And that he further extends his most important insights in an essay that came two years later, "Law in Science and Science in Law."

Thus, on one level, this book is a work of intellectual history that describes and explicates certain of Holmes's ideas. But standpoint matters a great deal. My standpoint is that of a practicing lawyer. I think this matters because standpoint orients a discourse. I have also become convinced, after a prolonged immersion in Holmes's writings, that he shared a similar standpoint, that much of what he wrote he did for the purpose of improving the profession.

Think back for a moment to the Boston University School of Law event. The challenge implicit in a seasoned lawyer and judge addressing a group of budding professionals, the law students in the audience, arises from a disparity in experience. On one side of the podium stands a person well versed in the subject matter and practiced in its employment. On the other side sit novices. How does one convey to these students important lessons of professional experience in a manner pithy and memorable? How does one describe the professional path they ought to take?

Holmes rose to the challenge by crystallizing his convictions – he had, as of 1897, spent over thirty years in the profession, as student, practitioner, scholar, professor, and judge – and by conveying them in a style best described as the opposite of cant. "The Path of the Law" is not an exercise in plain speaking. It is too compressed for that description to work. Yet neither is it overly formal and sententious, in the style one might expect of a typical nineteenth-century vocational address. It conjoins the realism of hardened expectation with a hint of revelatory exclamation; it exhibits a distinctive habit of mind, a novel way of taking and talking about legal issues. My interpretation of "The Path of the Law" is premised on the belief that its rhythm, cadence, and movements match the vibrancy of a life lived in law as law existed in Boston (and probably beyond Boston) in the final quarter of the nineteenth century. It is also premised on the conviction that Holmes sought to rise a bit above that life, his here-and-now, not to repudiate it, but to give philosophical expression and extension to the vibrancy.

The most important sentence in "The Path of the Law" is the first: "When we study law we are not studying a mystery but a well known profession."[28] Throughout

[28] Oliver Wendell Holmes, *The Path of the Law*, *in* III The Collected Works of Justice Holmes: Complete Public Writings and Selected Judicial Opinions of Oliver Wendell Holmes 391 (Sheldon Novick ed., 1995) [hereinafter CW].

the address it stays visible, often a wavering watery image hovering in the distance to be sure, but no matter where in the text the reader is this sentence makes its presence felt. "When we study law we are not studying a mystery but a well known profession." The sentence seems latched; it's not. It begs a series of questions: why do we study "law" and not "the law"? To whom would it occur to say law is a mystery? And this profession the law student studies when he or she studies law – for what is it well known? Are we talking about members of America's so-called aristocratic class – as Tocqueville referred to the legal profession in the nineteenth century – or a collection of "pettifoggers and vipers," a long-lived description of legal practitioners in Anglo-American history? Or both? The questions the first sentence elicits are ranging but the point in focus is not. The center of attention, as the address reveals, is the what, how, and why of legal study.

Holmes also sought to encourage his established colleagues in the audience (the practicing lawyers and law professors) to employ a more refined, disciplined intelligence in resolving society's disputes and assisting in its ordering than that employed by those who had not taken the path of the law. If students of law aspired to be more than practitioners of a trade or members of an occupation – if law itself were to mature into a productive discipline – it demanded the development of certain skills. These included the twin abilities to understand the ends law had served in the past, and to use that nuanced awareness of past ends to formulate the necessary inquiries to ground future law.

As a judge, Holmes preferred to view current legal issues in a manner that respected the present course of the law. Yet he also wanted other members of the profession to share his interest in visualizing alternative directions, maybe even comparing new wants to past ends long forgotten. He also encouraged, as many people have pointed out, a more realistic or scientific approach to society and its problems. Holmes valued what his predecessors in the profession had accomplished – as befitting a jurist who authored a classic text on the common law – but he shied away from giving them too much credit. Though he never said it, he seems to have drawn a lesson from the unstated fact that law, unlike other inspired intellectual and artistic endeavors in the ancient world, had no recognized muse.[29] It drew its inspiration from sources less divine.

This study, then, as a work of intellectual history, will take the liberty of bringing into the twenty-first century a message intended for the twentieth. It takes its stand on my belief that Holmes intended "The Path of the Law" to be a primer on legal education. For that supposition to work successfully one must re-envision "The Path of the Law" against the backdrop of Holmes's pre-1897 jurisprudential and

[29] *See* Holmes, *Daniel Richardson, in* III CW 482–83 ("Their true monument is the body of our jurisprudence, – that vast cenotaph shaped by the genius of our race, and by powers greater than the greatest individual, yet to which the least may make their contribution and inscribe it with their names. The glory of lawyers, like that of men of science, is more corporate than individual.").

extra-jurisprudential writings. One must look carefully at *The Common Law* and the articles that came before and after it. One must ponder the collection of addresses contained in his *Speeches*. The majority of the forthcoming pages will focus on bringing to the fore and clarifying the cardinal ideas that ultimately find articulation in "The Path of the Law" and Holmes's later article "Law in Science and Science in Law." Though we will comment on these pieces along the way, they will not receive their fullest exposition until the last part of the book, Part V. In true Holmesian fashion we will seek to discern the pathways of thought from which "The Path of the Law" itself emerged and the direction toward which it tends.

The effort to discern and articulate the direction of Holmes's jurisprudential thinking that goes beyond "The Path of the Law" serves as the second aim of this book. In this respect the book moves from intellectual history toward legal theory. It seeks to build on Holmes's work, to articulate a theoretical foundation for legal education. One that ties teaching and learning to practice, practice to scholarship, and scales each of these endeavors according to their avowed purpose. That avowed purpose I take to be perfecting professional judgment.

Holmes had a unified sense of life that enabled him to grasp law as a purposive social activity.[30] The activity of law – its self-conceptualizations, its procedures and doctrines, its self-understood aims and justifications – has its own history within the broader culture. This study proposes that Holmes looked ahead toward a time when law would undergo a paradigm shift. I do not see that paradigm shift as the supersession of law.[31] Instead, I see it as dissolution of law's traditional conceptual architectures. That will fully happen when sufficient legal professionals in this country recognize the importance of law's three-dimensionality. Once they become adept at viewing law in this manner they may be able to construct, from that standpoint, a usable metric of the law. This task of constructing a metric is not easy to describe. It is not simply a matter of selecting one feature of experience – utility, for example – and using it to measure or gauge all other aspects. For now, let me just say that construction depends on a three-dimensional perspective. It will require legal professionals to determine the best means to coordinate various dimensions of American experience (such as sequence and context), and map certain features (such as specific iterations of liberty or equality) that once found, or continue to find, expression in and through law.

Viewing American law in three dimensions is such a counterintuitive notion I should try to explain what I mean. Especially since much of the following

30 Max Lerner believed Holmes to be "perhaps the most complete personality in the history of American thought." Max Lerner, *Introduction, in* THE MIND AND FAITH OF JUSTICE HOLMES: HIS SPEECHES, ESSAYS, LETTERS, AND JUDICIAL OPINIONS vii (Max Lerner ed. 1943). *See also* Richard A. Posner, *Introduction, in* THE ESSENTIAL HOLMES xxii (Richard A. Posner ed., 1992) (observing that Holmes had a personal philosophy and system of jurisprudence unmistakably his own).

31 RICHARD A. POSNER, THE PROBLEMATICS OF MORAL AND LEGAL THEORY 206–11 (1999).

exposition is an extended effort to both clarify (the intellectual history part) and extend (the legal theory part) Holmes's work by showcasing this one idea. And, as I will shortly discuss, the book's structure also contributes to the development of this idea by laying the analytical and historical framework necessary to bring "The Path of the Law" into 3D. We go from initial static delineations in the early parts to subsequent depictions that have increased dynamism and directionality.

For the purposes of legal pedagogy, teaching a student to view law in three dimensions means that the student must enter into what Holmes called "the purely legal point of view." The spatial imagery is important to our purposes because knowing one's way around law proper – as one tacitly knows one's way around one's hometown or neighborhood – leads to better-informed, on-point decision-making. To say it another way, professional knowledge and personal knowledge must be deliberately tied into each other so professional judgment may grow and mature.

Most of us, unassisted, cannot view law in three dimensions. We need to enhance our natural and acquired capabilities with artificial aids. To emphasize the point I have chosen to put on the cover of this book a photograph of a hand-held stereoscope that Holmes's father, Oliver Wendell Holmes, Sr., invented, but did not patent, in 1859. The replica I was able to find on eBay sits on a small stand. The plate on the stand's base identifies the viewer as "THE HOLMES STEREOSCOPE."[32]

A stereoscope is a device that mechanically reproduces what the human eyes do naturally. It takes two individual images, both similar but not identical, and merges them together to create a three-dimensional image. It artificially creates depth within a visual field. The resulting image is a *tertium quid*, a third something, that brings together into harmony two distinct photographic images. Two Holmes sentences first alerted me how I, as a practicing attorney, saw law – as I had been taught to see it – was shockingly superficial, flat.

> When I began it was not so easy as it is now to see that law, looked at through the stereoscope of history, is the story of our growth. It was not easy to put to oneself even the vaguer proposition that as the facts of the law are facts of the universe they are worthy of their share of the only intellectual interest there is, – the interest of being seen in their universal relations.[33]

These two sentences do much to bring Holmes's intellectual life into focus. They are from an unpublished and provisional farewell address he gave at the Boston Tavern Club after being nominated to the United States Supreme Court but before confirmation. In this after-dinner speech he eloquently, insightfully, but circumspectly commented on the life education he had received from over sixty years of

[32] *See* George E. Hamilton, Oliver Wendell Holmes: His Pioneer Stereoscope and the Later Industry 10–15 (1949).

[33] Oliver Wendell Holmes, *Address at Tavern Club Dinner*, *in* III CW 533–34.

living in Boston. Though barely two pages, it stands as a counterpoint to a much, much larger and more famous work, *The Education of Henry Adams*. From this speech we also learn, incidentally, that what Holmes considered to be the greatest moral experience of his life was not what many scholars have thought. It was not the Civil War, that he called the second greatest moral experience of his life. It was entering the legal profession.[34]

This revelation changed how I saw Holmes and how I understood his relationship to the legal profession. In my effort to understand what he meant by the "stereoscope of history" I stumbled upon the happy fact that his father had invented the wildly popular and economical hand-held viewer. It contributed to a boom in stereographs, the cards upon which the paired images were placed; all of a sudden, Victorian America's drawing rooms burst with photos of exotic peoples and locales. It was not lost upon me, though, that Holmes does not gush about the wonders of the stereoscope but almost off-handedly uses the device to suggest how historical study has the power to bring law to life.

But more than historical study is needed to make law three-dimensional. The stereoscope provided depth to images that were otherwise flat; that is, they already had height and width. That height and width corresponds to law existing in the unreflective present. The stereoscope becomes useful when joined with the analytical power to clarify issues, understand consequences, and make ever-finer discriminations from a specific standpoint. The legal mind that studies the law's past for the sake of applying law to the present and providing guidance to the future must be both perceptive and analytical. The more sophisticated and informed its discriminations the better because the better it will be able to communicate, in narrative or propositional form, the values that law either sought to protect, seeks to protect or, more fundamentally, uses to structure and energize itself.

Dimensionality in the way I am using it requires temporal perspective. Temporal perspective, in turn, unbolts the trapdoor of the present, the here-and-now; it gives one a greater feel and sense for the different actualities embedded in our lives. It works mainly through positioning and contrast. It may also on occasion lead one to question, or push against, the felt necessities of the present. These terms are admittedly vague. I hope that in the course of this book their meanings will become clearer. I also hope it will become evident why Holmes believed American law had to turn in on itself; it had to become self-reflexive. He also believed that the most truthful, intelligent, and most carefully proportioned story of law's growth would fortify a young and expanding democracy. Such a story might protect the country against the pressing social and cultural crosscurrents that threatened to wreck it.

Three-dimensionality forces into position and into relief what otherwise is free-floating, undefined, gray, amorphous, and concealed in seemingly definite, meaningful, and robust-sounding abstract words or general propositions. Three-dimensionality also

[34] *Id.*

makes it possible to coordinate what Holmes called "intellectual interest" and "the facts of the law." It also has the potential to lead to a needed legal positioning or navigational system (what I have also called a metric), one that would, in turn, permit a finer and richer canvassing of disputed cultural values than currently possible. At the very least, it can become an effective heuristic for developing professional judgment.

I take Holmes's pedagogical program as stated in "The Path of the Law" to be an outline for developing professional judgment. It begins with the basics and leads, progressively, to more difficult challenges. The law student must learn the rudiments of professional judgment, the working lawyer must develop and perfect it, the judge must enact it, the law professor must enhance it. That professional judgment, though, is not a series of disconnected "its" but a complex of thought and behavior seen from different angles. Once the body of working legal professionals in this country has assimilated this way of thinking about professional judgment then perhaps a philosopher of genius would come along and validate the whole endeavor. Holmes thought that philosopher might turn out to be him; he suffered, though, from more than his share of doubt.

Let me now explain how the book is structured and how it is meant to progress, both as a work of intellectual history and as a contribution to legal theory. A more detailed synopsis to each part follows that part's title page. The overview here has less detail but provides a wider scope.

Though this book is a study of Holmes, I do not begin Part I, "Law and the Legal Profession," with his work. I begin with a brief look at a book closer to my chronological present, A. W. Brian Simpson's *Invitation to Law*. I use Simpson's book, published in 1988, as a portal into the nineteenth century. The reason I begin with Simpson is because I believe Holmes would agree wholeheartedly with a maxim that Simpson brilliantly formulated or wisely repeated (I am not sure which): Law is for lawyers.

The idea that "law is for lawyers" leads me to an era in American history, not the only one to be sure, during which that very assertion was hotly disputed. From the beginning of his legal career in the 1860s Holmes justified the profession in professional terms. It took deep learning and much practice to fully understand law; it was not intuitive. That learning began for lawyers with a single, intertwined question: "What is (the) law?"

The effort to understand this intertwined question, which I liken to a DNA double helix, led me to analyze the strands separately – "What is the law?" and "What is law?" – and then as a single entity. On the one hand, the analysis required canvassing how practitioners, and those who wrote materials to guide them, thought law ought to connect to various factual situations. "What is the law?" always began as an empirical question, but Holmes, for one, did not believe it should end there. He saw much virtue in fully exploring the other part of the problem, "What is law?" That dual approach led him to develop a sophisticated conception of how the common law established jurisprudential boundaries, or what John Austin called the "province of jurisprudence." That section of Part I is akin to storyboarding a script. Part I also features detailed examinations of both the legal relationship we call "duty" and the consequence we call "penalty," without which the common law would not exist as we know it.

On the other hand, Holmes recognized, as do I, that jurisprudential boundaries changed over time, as did the manner in which judicial authorities punished or did not punish, or otherwise encouraged or discouraged, the behavior brought to their attention. Duties had seen and unseen histories. One must become aware of these histories; integrated correctly they created a more expansive horizon and furthered nascent positioning capacities within the law. Holmes used a distinctive mode of argumentation – emphasizing apperception and triangulation – to explore these and related topics in *The Common Law*. He believed this mode best fit the distinctive characteristics of the cultural power we call law. Bringing out that distinctiveness is the goal of Part II, entitled "The Inner Path of the Common Law."

For the sake of exposition it is often easier, for both writer and reader, to separate a complex, intertwined question, such as "What is (the) law?" into its static and dynamic aspects. I attempt to do that in Parts I and II. The harder endeavor is then bringing them back together. In that effort I am much indebted to James Willard Hurst's singular book, *Justice Holmes on Legal History*. I have adopted Hurst's terminology of sequence and context and have thought long and hard on what he has written. Meditating on Hurst has led me to pinpoint where he and I diverge in either our understanding of Holmes or in how each has chosen to envision and extend Holmes's project. Like *Justice Holmes on Legal History*, this book works both with and against Holmes's thought: "against" in the sense of grappling or wrestling with what Holmes meant on this or that issue or what he thought best for the future of law in this country; "with" in the sense of learning to think in sync with those Holmesian formulations too powerful to contest successfully (*e.g.*, "The life of the law has not been logic: it has been experience.").

Hurst made my own struggle both easier and harder. Easier because I could, and did, learn a lot from him. I could also draw some useful conclusions why academic lawyers have not devoted much attention to his study on Holmes and history. Harder because I had to take care not to supplant Holmes with Hurst. The whole matter became more manageable when I realized that Hurst had not been as deeply affected as I was by the notion, which Holmes first articulated in *The Common Law*, of a "purely legal point of view."[35] Perhaps that was because Hurst did not practice law for a living and I do. Regardless, the purely legal point of view as Holmes describes it in *The Common Law* I take to be the first iteration of the point of view of the bad man made infamous in "The Path of the Law."

Part III draws on *Justice Holmes on Legal History* to establish the necessary perimeters for the purely legal point of view. Holmes used the position of the legal

[35] Oliver Wendell Holmes, *The Common Law, in* III CW 277.

professional to center that viewpoint, but, apparently, was not satisfied merely to have discerned by that means the liminal point where past and present meet. He wanted to entrench that point of view, to make it self-determinative; to give it increased height, width, and depth. Philosophical or theoretical justifications provide invaluable assistance in such endeavors; they structure insights and bind aperçus. Though Holmes never completed the task to the extent he probably wished, he did leave us with "Law in Science and Science in Law." That 1899 article contained the pithiest statement of his fundamental theorem of the law: "as to any possible conduct it is either lawful or unlawful."[36]

One main thesis of this study is that Holmes's theorem of law restates in formal terms the insight he first had in *The Common Law*. The purely legal point of view makes increased intraprofessional awareness – another description for three-dimensionality – possible. That, in turn, provides the needed conditions for establishing a metric of the law. This metric, in my use, is a single mode of differentiation and integration. It provides the necessary means to increase law's (that is, the work that legal professionals do) intelligence and intelligibility, or, in equivalent terms, perspicuity and transparency. It enables law to become more *knowable*. Part III ends by exploring this paradoxical claim that through our own dedicated purposiveness, formalized and implemented through the idea of a metric, we can increase the capacity of the law to be known.

The very long Part IV is the hardest to explain. In a sense, it forms its own distinct unit, as do Parts I–III, on the one side, and Part V on the other. Entitled, "Thirteen Ways of Looking at the Bad Man," it reviews and analyzes selected interpretations of the bad man and "The Path of the Law" from the turn of the twentieth century to the present time. Yet its progression is not exactly chronological. My best defense – beyond any historical interest or value it may possess – is that it is an effort to show how one brings dimensionality, vividness, proportion, and depth into the scholarly study of law. I have tried to demonstrate how one begins to create a three-dimensional perspective by bringing to the fore, and setting into relief and juxtaposition, the manner in which many different legal scholars have conceived the identity of the bad man and Holmes's point for introducing him in "The Path of the Law."

In the limited exploration of this one issue, what stands out are not the many divergences of interpretation, or the more-or-less extreme one-sidedness, or the repeat instances of self-induced ignorance, but a widespread, practically institutionalized incapacity – the inability of one legal scholar to care about the thought of another. Indifference is endemic. I do not mean "care" in the sense of footnote acknowledgment or surface critique; I mean good faith study; hard thinking, probing, interaction, and reflection. Critical to the creation of a three-dimensional view of law, as well as to a viable jurisprudence, is the de-flattening of the concerns, opinions, beliefs, and rationales that have no immediate, innate hold on our own.

[36] Oliver Wendell Holmes, *Law in Science and Science in Law*, *in* III CW 416.

In our new era of limits we cannot continue blithely to disregard our co-thinkers or predecessors; to do so is wasteful and unproductive. We must learn to think through them, and they through us, not to achieve the same effect as a bullet, but to measure our thoughts against each other. Part IV in this respect attempts to add the placements of people and the directionalities of thought needed for depth and movement to the relatively static study of law contained in Part I, and to those elements of increased length (sequence) and width (context) and their interaction found in Part II.

The final part, which is even longer than Part IV, attempts to bring together the various topics addressed, and a few others, for the ultimate goal, not of synthesis, but of positioning Holmes's theory of legal study within his own vision of American law as I have come to understand it. That vision recognizes American law as an actual, ongoing, dynamic enterprise, one that attempts to control the different rates of movement that affect the different scales at which the law operates.

Bringing those scales into congruence may have been a long-cherished hope of Holmes. Politics and legality form in his eyes their own magnetic polarity. One had to measure movement, draw lines, and slowly, through patient, collective endeavor, turn law into a self-realized dimension of existence. In a way, this proposed endeavor provides a mode for natural evolutionary processes to become self-conscious. One had to understand the constitutive role of legal procedure. One had to become more sensible to the legal profession's synchronic and diachronic dimensions. One had to become more clear-eyed about the surreptitiousness of the past. One had to understand the fundamental role of professional judgments, how they worked off each other to build and inform a working profession.

A three-dimensional view of law helps to advance all those goals. It also becomes a way to extend perception and build-out knowledge of those legal acts Holmes believed dispositive, those that led to the temporal harm law sought to prevent or redress. That building-out may not be doable in the way Holmes imagined, systematically, but one could do it through topographical representations. Regardless of how one sought to depict the knowledge had or perception gained, Holmes believed uniquely American law began with practicality and he thought legal education should begin there as well. But it should not stay there. To bring into unison the different dimensions of American law required a new and different type of perspective, one purely legal. That perspective recognized law as a distinctive form of knowledge, a unique discipline – especially in the American context – of power.

PART I

Law and the Legal Profession

SYNOPSIS

Part I, "Law and the Legal Profession," presents the main theme of "The Path of the Law" – that law is for lawyers – and it does so from two different standpoints.

First, it approaches the theme from the more recent past. In Brian Simpson's 1986 *Invitation to Law* one finds an excellent sketch of the many facets of the legal profession, written from the perspective of an historian and sometime analyst of the common law who taught law for many years in both England and the United States. Simpson published his book the better part of a century after the publication of "The Path of the Law" and so draws attention both to the continuing persistence of a certain line of thought – that law is for lawyers – and its operative meaning in societies, such as England and the United States, with long-standing common law institutions and practices.

Part I also surveys a few nineteenth-century American challenges to legal learning, the common law, and lawyers. It uses those challenges to create one possible backdrop to Holmes's earliest extended articles on legal topics. Whether the study of law had any social value – and, if so, what? – and whether the study itself could be justified as a pursuit of knowledge posed issues to which the refrain "law is for lawyers" became in Holmes's hands the favored resolute response. This refrain also signaled Holmes's lifelong position on the social value of a legal education: lawyers provided an invaluable service to society by providing mechanisms and means for the clarification and achievement of social goals, the resolution of disputes, and, at their best, a heightened sensitivity to the different viewpoints that law had the ability to coalesce.

Yet their special professional role in American society also laid upon lawyers a mandate to further organize themselves internally. Lawyers had to become more self-conscious and clear-headed about their subject, law. Lawyers asked a perennial question whenever faced with a concrete legal problem – "what is the law?" For

Holmes lawyers must also learn to ask, "what is law?" These two questions, and the connections between them, formed the double helix of the legal profession.

Holmes attended to both questions in his early work. As is well known, he sought to organize and systematize law by categorizing duties. A better organizational framework would reduce, he believed, the perceived chaos of the common law. He also sought to clarify the nature and extent of law through an analysis of John Austin's definition of law. Holmes especially focused on the meaning of a legal penalty. Through this avenue Holmes demarcated law from other social phenomena. He used John Austin's analytic definition of law to create a boundary for jurisprudence, but in a sociological sense (as in what a court would or would not do and the attendant consequences), not as a postulate for insular legal reasoning.

1 LAW IS FOR LAWYERS

In the first chapter of A. W. Brian Simpson's outstanding textbook *Invitation to Law*, we find the following peculiar sentences:

> We often think of law as a body of rules, rather like school rules, telling us all, as citizens, how to behave, and what will happen if we do not. But this is not the way lawyers primarily think of their law. For lawyers the function of law is to tell *them* how to behave in settling what people's rights and duties and obligations and liabilities are. The elaborate body of general principles, the more detailed rules and exceptions to them, the definitions of terms and significant distinctions, the practices and conceptions which to lawyers constitute the law, are there to provide lawyers with ways of analyzing problems, and ways of rationally justifying decisions as to what is to be done by courts about them. Law is for lawyers.[1]

I've practiced law as a litigator for some time now and it would never have occurred to me, before reading Simpson's book, to explain the abstract term "law" as ultimately comprising a set of directives or pointers meant for me.[2] The phrase, "law is for lawyers," is evidently a synoptic one. This formulation, especially in Simpson's capable hands, has immediacy. It is fresh. It creates a personal connection between law and the student of law often lacking in the typical introductory text to legal study.

[1] A. W. B. Simpson, Invitation to Law 15 (1988) (emphasis in original).

[2] At the same time a law should not be understood as simply providing direct instructions to a lawyer (or a judge). *Id.* at 117 ("Passing a law, just like writing a symphony, cannot be understood simply as giving a set of instructions.").

Simpson's alliteration – "law is for lawyers" – brought to mind, after a bit, the "The Path of the Law's" opening: "When we study law we are not studying a mystery but a well known profession."[3]

This profession, whose members we in the United States simply call judges and lawyers, is well known because it's been around for a long time. Maybe not quite as long as law itself has been around, but still a long time. Simpson devotes the sixth chapter of *Invitation to Law* to "Lawyers," the chapter's title.[4] There we find out that those men who acted as intermediaries between the court and the person began to self-identify as a distinct group in England around the late thirteenth century. They claimed to possess specialized knowledge of law and special access to the seats of power.

Nothing fundamental in this respect has changed in the intervening hundreds of years because Simpson in the latter part of the twentieth century describes lawyers as:

> people who claim, frequently truthfully, to possess expert knowledge of the law, and practical skill in its working, and who earn money by selling their expertise either to the public generally, or to some particular person or institution which is prepared to employ them.[5]

In another part of the book Simpson points out that lawyers continue to function as the needed intermediaries since no other group in society is as well positioned to make the reality of the living legal system conform as much as possible to its guiding ideal: the rule of law.[6]

Simpson includes judges as part of the group. This inclusion makes sense in common law jurisdictions. Unlike their civil law counterparts, judges do not form a radically distinct lot. In most common law societies most judges train and practice as lawyers before becoming judges. They are members of the profession.[7]

If the rule of law functions as the reigning ideal – encapsulated in the modern notion that government officials should obey prescriptive limits on their power[8] – then lawyers in such a society train, or should train, to recognize and, when necessary, test those limits. They are bound, as a group, to make the rule of law available to their fellow citizens.[9]

3 Oliver Wendell Holmes, *The Path of the Law, in* III THE COLLECTED WORKS OF JUSTICE HOLMES: COMPLETE PUBLIC WRITINGS AND SELECTED JUDICIAL OPINIONS OF OLIVER WENDELL HOLMES 391 (Sheldon Novick ed., 1995) [hereinafter CW].

4 SIMPSON, *supra* note 1, at 142–72.

5 *Id.* at 142.

6 *Id.* at 41–46, 163 (noting that respect for the ideal of rule of law is a mechanism for protecting individuals from uncontrolled power).

7 *Id.* at 166–72.

8 *Id.* at 163–64.

9 *Id.* at 45, 163 ("There is no point having the rule of law but not letting people get at it.").

The term lawyer describes the people who willingly take on the task of negotiating, for themselves and for their clients, an ongoing deal between "Legal Ideals and Sordid Realities."[10] Those five words serve as the title for chapter II, which follows "The Pervasiveness of Law" and precedes the chapter on "Legal Systems and Legal Traditions."[11]

Simpson, we begin to see, progressively informs the invitee of the basic set-up – law is pervasive in modern societies – and of its fundamental orientation for Americans and most members of the British Commonwealth: Western European, secular, legalistic. And of the source of its primary mode of identification and implementation: English common law. Simpson believes that deliberately becoming part of the tradition, and learning to operate within the prevalent legal system, equips the invitee to engage in what he repeatedly calls the "special business of lawyers … the resolution of disputes and the ordering of social life[.]"[12]

Evidently the life of a lawyer involves a lot of mental shuttling: between the present exigent problem and the established and applicable rules, primarily. And, if the matter requires it, between recognized principles and foreseeable, probable outcomes. It also involves, if we read aright this task of "ordering social life," the ability to understand, formulate, and express in a concrete, effective way specific vital interests. This aptitude or skill is a necessary one, especially at the social or cultural margins, where such interests are not already interwoven into the commonweal.[13]

I would summarize Simpson's main advice to the invitee as follows: focus on the profession you wish to join; learn the profession's language, its habits, traditions, and goals; be prepared to habituate to its mannerisms and customs; constantly seek to understand how you might influence the opinion and actions of its other members.

Secondarily, keep in mind the social and economic constraints inherent in the practice of law as well as the relevant enticements, the ethical gray areas, the opportunities for enterprising behavior – if you are a person inclined to that type of behavior – and those points where self-directed goal-driven behavior passes beyond the pale.[14]

Ironically, the modern law student, whether in England or the United States, must attempt to follow all this advice (or much of it) not as an apprentice – the

[10] *Id.* at 28–52.

[11] Other principal chapters include "The Divisions of the Law" (IV), "The Sources of Law" (V), "The Academic Study of Law" (VII), and "The Future of Law" (VIII).

[12] SIMPSON, *supra* note 1, at 56.

[13] *Id.* at 23–25.

[14] My summary, though based on the book as a whole, extrapolates directly from this interesting sentence: "[L]aw exists in the rational collective consciousness of expert lawyers, just as culture may be viewed in this understandable if also puzzling way." *Id.* at 125.

reigning model for legal education in the United States until the advent of Langdell and the modern law school – but by hitting the books.[15]

This appears to be the takeaway from Simpson's text: law is for lawyers and if one wants to become a successful lawyer – in the sense of becoming an adept participant in the profession – one must first study law. Simpson may not have stated this exact point – it appears embarrassingly truistic – but it also appears to me to be a sound, if obvious, inference from his dictum that law is for lawyers.

The notion that to study law as written in casebooks, outlines, hornbooks, textbooks, and various other student aids to the legal arcana prevalent in a common law jurisdiction will, by some means, induct the hapless student into the profession is somewhat counterintuitive. If "studying law" equals "studying the profession," then why not head back in the direction of apprentice style learning?[16]

The law student is called upon to study law as an act of faith. The study of legal texts, supplemented by various drills – in the arts of legal drafting or advocacy, for example – promises to take the student beyond basic competence in legal concepts.

Proper study promises to reveal the profession to the student.

Somehow the very act of studying a textbook, or a collection of cases and the associated commentary – perhaps under the tutelage of the instructor, perhaps not – will assist in the transformation of the student's mind – help turn her into a fully fledged professional – if she simply remembers Holmes's admonition that she is not studying a "mystery" but "a well known profession." That is the cardinal point.

The student, ultimately, is asked to believe that the bit of law received in the classroom can stand in for the profession as a whole, can, in a sense, embody the group dynamics of the people who according to Simpson have a special role – due to their specialized knowledge and training – in resolving a society's disputes and assisting in its ordering.[17]

Becoming part of the profession primarily means one commits oneself to resolving social problems through predominantly legal means. The origin of legal problems in social life led Justice Holmes to declare that the study of law did not involve any essential mystery. All those arcane concepts, the esoteric terminology, ultimately arose from, and added to, the complexities of social life. But we – those alive in 1897 or 1988 or 2020 – are so far removed from the common law's oracular genesis

[15] On the apprenticeship as the dominant model of legal instruction in the United States throughout much of the nineteenth century see JAMES WILLARD HURST, THE GROWTH OF AMERICAN LAW: THE LAWMAKERS 256–76 (1950) ("In terms of what was accomplished, until the 1870's legal education in the colleges and universities was part of the era of apprentice training and proprietary schools."). Simpson also discusses the benefits of apprenticeship. SIMPSON, *supra* note 1, at 142–44.

[16] SIMPSON, *supra* note 1, at 142–44.

[17] *Id.* at 56; *see also* HURST, *supra* note 15, at 25. ("Law represents an effort – however short of the ideal – to order men's affairs according to a rational weighing of values and the means of achieving them[.]").

that we do best to focus our attention on its present revelation: the actual body of those living legal practitioners who ply the craft, make the money, engage the ideal.

2 NINETEENTH-CENTURY AMERICAN CHALLENGES TO LEGAL LEARNING, THE COMMON LAW, AND LAWYERS

Before a law student became a law student she or he most likely lived in a law-governed society. That law is omnipresent Simpson illustrated in the opening pages of his book, even if he wrote primarily of modern English society. This ubiquity of law, in England or America, led Simpson to wonder whether one really needed to pen a formal introduction to that part of social life with which everyone, or almost everyone, has a firsthand acquaintance.[18]

It is a nice question whether what is taken as self-evidently true in the late-twentieth or early twenty-first centuries holds also, without qualification, for the late nineteenth. Scholars concur that during the twentieth century American society witnessed a veritable proliferation of law and of laws. Lawrence M. Friedman has called it the period in American history when "Leviathan came of age."[19]

Holmes's career spanned the cusp of this transformation. He wrote "The Path of the Law" at the midpoint of his professional life. He also wrote it as one who recognized that American law was still in the stage of chrysalis. He believed in the virtues of thinking forward; he also believed in the importance of looking back.

Thus to appreciate the substance of Holmes's address we too must step back into an era when law had begun to play a different role in American society and the profession had begun to regain lost moorings. In Part V we will return to the issues of how a law student should learn law and why, when we discuss the substance of Holmes's advice in "The Path of the Law" and compare it to Simpson's. For the remainder of this part, and in Part II, we will do the historical and analytical spadework needed to understand Holmes's message to his audience at Isaac Rich Hall. Much of that spadework will be directed toward uncovering what Holmes called "the purely legal point of view." Parts III and IV will then seek to develop this notion of a purely legal point of view. They will do so by, first, clarifying the idea and then by establishing its contours in an unusual manner: through a depiction and juxtaposition of how some other legal scholars have seen its leading personification, the "bad man."

[18] *Id.* at 1–4. *See also* William Twining, Globalisation and Legal Theory 1–4 (2000) (observing that students quickly recognize that law is pervasive in society); H. L. A. Hart, The Concept of Law 2–3 (2d ed. 1994) (noting that most people are able to cite, with ease and confidence, examples of law).

[19] Lawrence M. Friedman, A History of American Law 503–37 (3d ed. 2005); *see also* Looking Back at Law's Century (Austin Sarat, Bryant Garth, and Robert A. Kagan eds., 2002).

i *Overcoming the Slur against Legal Learning*

From the vantage point of Boston, January 1897, the legal profession in the United States had made definite strides. In the preceding quarter-century it had managed to surmount what many had viewed as an existential crisis.[20] Its very raison d'être as a learned profession had come under attack during the preceding era of American history, commonly referred to as the Age of Jackson, or what one scholar has called with greater precision "the egalitarian interregnum."[21]

Whether the practice of law required learning, whether law should still be considered a learned profession – as opposed to an occupation or trade – naturally elicited varied reactions from practitioners and observers. A spectrum of opinion and attitude naturally evolved that still persists.

At one end were those who regarded legal practice as a trade or business – simply providing some type of service called legal to people called clients for compensation. Moving toward the center we find those who viewed it as an honorable occupation that required skill and craftsmanship; and still others who believed in it as a learned profession, the more fervent the belief – in either the learning itself or as a dedicated profession or both – the more it took on the trappings of a vocation. Until finally, at the other end, were those very few, like Holmes, who felt law, at its highest reaches, permitted glimpses into some of life's greatest mysteries.[22]

Oddly enough, each of these attitudes finds a voice in "The Path of the Law."

One sees this unique aspect of Holmes, this multivalency, in his earliest extended writings on law, those written before the publication of *The Common Law* in 1881. Almost from the beginning of his legal studies Holmes took a deep and scholarly interest in law.[23] He also found further support for this interest when, as a young practitioner, he complained, as young lawyers frequently do, about his lack of professional experience. He wanted to see more of what practicing lawyers actually did inside and outside the courtroom. He wanted to do more than sit behind a wooden desk researching and drafting. His mentor George Shattuck's advice: "The business of a lawyer is to know law."[24]

Holmes never forgot this piece of advice.

[20] Samuel Haber, The Quest for Authority and Honor in the American Professions, 1750–1900 91–116 (1991) (arguing that in terms of organizational power and effectiveness the mid-1800s were the nadir of the professions in America).

[21] *Id.*

[22] *Id.* at 109–12; Oliver Wendell Holmes, *The Use of Law Schools, in* III CW 475–76 (Lawyers are specialists "because they have undertaken to master a special branch of human knowledge – a branch, I may add, which is more immediately connected with all the highest interests of man than any other which deals with practical affairs.").

[23] Mark DeWolfe Howe, Justice Oliver Wendell Holmes: The Shaping Years 1841–1870 176–207 (1957).

[24] Holmes, *supra* note 22, at 479.

He never doubted that the profession, as a profession, should continue its devotion to studying law.[25] In one of his first articles Holmes wrote an extended assessment of how law could be put on a philosophical footing.[26] That same article also, in a roundabout way, addressed the substantive challenges directed at the vaunted "learning" of a historically learned profession.[27]

In "Codes, and the Arrangement of Law" Holmes deplores the lack of clear organizing principles for categorizing the state's substantive law, especially as presented in the many treatises, manuals, guides, and handbooks routinely published for practitioners and students.[28] This want of rational organizing principles made plausible the charge from the no-need-for-legal-learnin' crowd that law differed little from an occult science.[29] Its institutions and complex procedures self-evidently favored the initiated few against the uninitiated (and fleeced) many. Law, as practiced, had become an impediment to justice; that was the common complaint.[30]

If on the one side of the divide lay the radical conviction that the natural inheritance of each person – they generally said "man" in the nineteenth century – included a residual sense of natural justice and the corresponding ability – unaided by legal learning or lore – to discriminate legal right from legal wrong, on the other stood the more cautionary position that the common law heritage simply needed a good working over.[31] The development of legal codes – part of the era's codification movement – would instill the desired rationality into the traditional legal superstructure, eventually eradicating useless embellishments.[32]

Holmes agreed that law needs to be systematized clearly and intelligently – as he says, philosophically – but disagreed with the suggestion that the way of the legal code bested that of the common law. He begins "Codes, and the Arrangement of Law" with the somewhat odd gambit of extolling the merit of the common law practice of first deciding cases and only afterwards determining the principle of decision.

[25] *Id.* ("I fear that the bar has done its full share to exalt that most hateful of American words and ideals, 'smartness,' as against dignity of moral feeling and profundity of knowledge.").

[26] Oliver Wendell Holmes, *Codes, and the Arrangement of Law, in* I CW 212–21.

[27] *Id.*; *see also* Perry Miller, The Life of the Mind in America: From the Revolution to the Civil War 105–16 (1965) (recounting "the widespread hostility of ordinary Americans to the very concept of law and more specifically their bitter antagonism to the Common Law.").

[28] Holmes, *supra* note 26, at 212–13.

[29] Miller, *supra* note 27, at 187 ("In their inarticulate fashion, they suspected, what Tocqueville had concluded, that the American lawyer 'resembles the hierophants of Egypt, for like them he is the sole interpreter of an occult science.'") (citations omitted).

[30] *Id.* at 186–98.

[31] Friedman, *supra* note 19, at 65–71.

[32] *Id.* at 66. *See also* Stephen N. Subrin, *David Dudley Field and the Field Code: An Historical Analysis of an Earlier Procedural Vision*, 6 Law and Hist. Rev. 311 (1988); Charles M. Cook, The American Codification Movement: A Study of Antebellum Legal Reform 12–13 (1981); Gunther A. Weiss, *The Enchantment of Codification in the Common-Law World*, 25 Yale J. Int'l L. 435, 498–514 (2000).

In Holmes's formulation, a case is not simply a case but a "given state of facts." The given facts form the minor premise of an Aristotelian syllogism. The conclusion is the decision. Not uncommonly the decision makers know how the matter ought to be decided (the conclusion) given the facts (the minor premise). They just aren't sure of the major premise (the governing rule or precedent). Holmes adds that one should not unduly wonder that lawyers (he says lawyers, not judges)[33] like other people instinctively know – especially in matters of first impression – how they should decide, how they should respond to this "given state of facts," without "being very clear as to the *ratio decidendi*."[34] He seems to consider the presence of this psychological truth inherent in adjudication as simply one more of the many charms of the common law.

He calls the procedure by which common law judges sought to obtain clarity on the reasoning behind a series of decisions the method of "successive approximations" or "continual reconciliation of cases."[35] A decision is reached in the first case. Subsequent decisions in similar cases usually lead to the need to reconcile the cases. At each stage the effort to fully clarify the vaguely felt, semi-articulated principle continues. The method of "successive approximations" – the intellectual version of groping in the dark for the doorknob – permits, over time, a court "by true induction to state the principle which has until then been obscurely felt."[36]

And even then the process is not complete: further adjudications of "given states of facts" lead to the principle's modifications until the previously unfathomed "abstracted general rule takes its final shape."[37]

The decision-making procedure of simply applying a provision of a code to a given state of facts, without more, could not match the common law for logical subtlety, finesse, insight, and nuance. Holmes is especially attuned to the vibrancy of court decisions, especially when a principle, once hazy, had broken clearly across the horizon:

33 Friedman has pointed out that in the nineteenth century and even into the present a judgeship "was and is an offshoot of the bar – of that part of the bar active in political affairs." FRIEDMAN, *supra* note 19, at 90.

34 Holmes, *supra* note 26, at 212–13; *See also* FRIEDMAN, *supra* note 19, at 89 (quoting Chancellor James Kent: "My practice was, first, to make myself perfectly and accurately . . . master of the facts . . . I saw where justice lay, and the moral sense decided the court half the time; and I then sat down to search the authorities until I had examined my books. I might once in a while be embarrassed by a technical rule, but I most always found principles suited to my views of the case[.]"); Oliver Wendell Holmes, *Review of* A Selection of Cases on the Law of Contracts by C. C. Langdell, *in* I CW 243 ("We must mention here that we have been struck with the confirmation here afforded to a remark made on the first page of this volume of the *Law Review*, that judges know how to decide a good deal sooner than they know why.").

35 Holmes, *supra* note 26, at 213.

36 *Id.*

37 *Id.*

> A well settled legal doctrine embodies the work of many minds, and has been tested in form as well as substance by trained critics whose practical interest it is to resist it at every step.[38]

To this interplay between particulars, between the particular and the general, between a given state of facts and an emerging principle or rule of law, code-based legal thinking offered little more than a (drop-down) menu of categories. It offered little practical or theoretical guidance for assimilating the new into the old or the old into the new. For Holmes an overarching legal code and the style of reasoning it represented could not, from a legal point of view, do justice to the issues present in the novel case. That is to say, a legal code regime had no genuine method for assimilating the new or unexpected "given state of facts" into the existing body of law, or, on the other hand, for restating the existing body of law from a point of view different from those which initially informed the code.[39]

Holmes's defense of common law methods borders the ingenious, even if it leaves something wanting to those who believed in the power of human intelligence to crystallize illuminating legal principles able to withstand unmodified the tests of time. His defense rests on his sense for the reality of historical change or what many people in his era often called evolution. He appears to have found vitality in the common law method of reasoning to a legal principle – it served as a well-wrought, time-tested means for navigating through changing circumstances.

A code, on the other hand, did not in Holmes's opinion have the same circumnavigating capability. If a code simply stated a legal rule – which a court may amend as needed – then "the code is not law, but a mere text-book recommended by the government as containing all at present known on the subject."[40]

To this criticism of purpose Holmes adds a second regarding form. He disagrees with the oft-expressed wisdom that a code should be short:

[38] *Id.*

[39] *Id.* Holmes makes a similar point when, around eight years later, he observes the consequences of German legal scholars falling under the sway of Roman law: "In fact the Roman law, as fixed in the books of Justinian, may be called the common law of Germany; and every reader of German writers must be struck with the despotism which a system thus arrested at a particular stage of its development still wields over their modes of thought." Oliver Wendell Holmes, *Possession, in* III CW 46.

[40] *Id. See also* Oliver Wendell Holmes, *Review of* The Code of Iowa; Report of Commissioners to Revise Statutes of State of Iowa; *and* Codification in India and England a Speech *by Mr. Fitzjames Stephen, in* I CW 319–20 ("The best draughtsman that ever lived can feel a ground of decision more accurately than he can state it. Suppose he succeeds in stating a rule that would have sufficed for the correct decision in all past cases, it is in the highest degree probable that some future case will require some more refined discrimination not allowed by the words of the code . . . . A written rule of statute law is stated in but one form, and can only be construed from its own four corners. For, we repeat, that if more than that is allowed, the code is nothing but a text-book.").

> Another mistake, as we cannot but think, is that a code is to be short. This probably springs from the thoroughly exploded notion that it is to make every man his own lawyer, and would hardly be worth mentioning did not the makers of both the New York and Canada Civil Codes seem to entertain it. A code will not get rid of lawyers, and should be written for them much more than for the laity.[41]

The key sentence in this paragraph is of course the last: "A code will not get rid of lawyers and should be written for them much more than for the laity." To the common nineteenth-century idea that law belonged to all Americans as part of their birthright Holmes counterpoises the same point of view we subsequently find in Simpson: law is for lawyers.

ii *What Is (the) Law?*

It is difficult to conclude from "Codes, and the Arrangement of the Law" that Holmes believed in the wisdom of a code as the ultimate statement of United States law – similar to the role the Napoleonic Code played in France, other parts of Europe, and great stretches of Latin America[42] – but he certainly appears to have conceded that codification, perhaps limited to classifying the common law and to the arrangement of statutes, would advance legal thinking.[43]

The great benefit of constructing a code lay in intelligent categorization. Government needed to do the job because it could ignore the constraints of the marketplace. Legal topics could be arranged in categories that made sense, that followed some internal logic, and not simply in the manner of textbooks and manuals that tracked custom and pandered to practitioners. As he put it:

> If such a code were achieved, its component treatises would not have to be loaded with matter belonging elsewhere, as is necessarily the case with text-books written to sell. Take up a book on sales, or one on bills and notes, or a more general treatise on contracts, or one on domestic relations, or on real property, and in each you will

[41] *Id.*; *see also* HABER, *supra* note 20, at 126 ("Governor Andrew Jackson, an erstwhile lawyer with a hankering to somehow make law and morality the same, took up the cause of codification under the startling slogan, 'Let all restraints and barriers be removed.' The distinction between law and equity he thought should be abolished; cases at law were to be tried on their 'naked merits'; the courts would always be open so that a litigant could enter 'without a cent's cost and have his relief instantly'. There would be little or no preparation of a case for hearing and the skillfulness of counsel would be much less necessary. The parties themselves could state their case, be examined, and have justice done at once.").

[42] James Herget provides an illuminating discussion of what he calls "The Drive for Classification, 1870–1924." The Napoleonic code inspired parallel movements in other countries. Beyond that, many lawyers, including Holmes, wanted the common law to be more than a "ragbag" of cases. JAMES HERGET, AMERICAN JURISPRUDENCE: 1870–1970 63–81 (1990).

[43] Holmes, *supra* note 40, at 320.

> find discussion of the incapacities of infants and married women. A code would treat once and in the right place.[44]

A further advantage in a comprehensive mapping of law lay in bringing to the surface analogies hidden in the customary groupings. If "the old-fashioned English lawyer's idea of a satisfactory body of law was a chaos with a full index[,]"[45] the modern lawyer recognized the importance of discerning and enunciating underlying legal principles.

The index need not be full, merely well thought out.

Not incidentally, a well-wrought code would further the cause of legal learning.

> A well-arranged body of law would not only train the mind of the student to a sound legal habit of thought, but would remove obstacles from his path which he now only overcomes after years of experience and reflection.[46]

In the quoted sentence we see an initial articulation of the same point Holmes would make over twenty-five years later when he told the story, in "The Path of the Law," of the Vermont justice of the peace – presumably not a lawyer – who, when called upon to decide a suit against one farmer by another for the breaking of a churn, decided for the defendant after a diligent search in the Vermont statutes because he could find nothing specifically regarding churns.[47]

[44] Holmes, *supra* note 26, at 213–14.

[45] Oliver Wendell Holmes, *Review of* Essays upon the Form of the Law, *in* I CW 223.

[46] Holmes, *supra* note 26, at 214; *see also* HERGET, *supra* note 42 at 66 ("One could learn about animals by studying them alphabetically (albatross, ape, aphid, and so on), but a system of organization based on general characteristics of the subjects to be classified (that is, into kingdoms, phyla, classes, and so forth) would not only expedite learning but improve its quality because of the possibility of logical comparison and contrast."); Mathias W. Reimann, *Holmes's* Common Law *and German Legal Science*," in THE LEGACY OF OLIVER WENDELL HOLMES, JR. 72, 77–78 (Robert W. Gordon ed., 1992) ("He also made clear what he conceived to be the benefits of a well-organized law. Legal education would become better and more effective (and, one might add, less frustrating than his own) because students could master the law more easily and quickly if they could study in a logical arrangement.").

In addition, as David M. Rabban noted, in the 1870s leading legal scholars, such as William Hammond, believed that the changes in the transmission of legal knowledge – the rise of the modern law school – required a concerted rethinking of the law itself. *See* DAVID M. RABBAN, LAW'S HISTORY: AMERICAN LEGAL THOUGHT AND THE TRANSATLANTIC TURN TO HISTORY 225 (2013) ("Like Holmes and his friends at the Harvard Law School, Hammond tied the study of fundamental legal principles to the transformation of legal education. 'I have long been convinced,' he wrote Holmes, 'that the growth of our law schools, and the marked change of the method of professional training from mere office-work to systematic instruction must logically involve a re-formulation of the law itself.'") (citations omitted). *See also* G. EDWARD WHITE, TORT LAW IN AMERICA: AN INTELLECTUAL HISTORY 20–62 (Expand. ed. 2003).

[47] Oliver Wendell Holmes, *The Path of the Law, in* III CW 403.

"The same state of mind," lamented Holmes, "is shown in all our common digests and text-books."[48] It is an outlook that wrongly focuses on "dramatic incidents," instead of learning to abstract from the given facts the legally relevant acts.

In hindsight we can see that in the 1870s Holmes tackled a problem that had both practical and theoretical significance: mapping the (common) law. The practical importance lay in the assistance it provided to every practitioner – not unlike the Vermont justice of the peace – who faced the problem of finding "the law" applicable to the difficulty presented.

Holmes alludes to the challenges that the overturning – mainly in the 1840s and 1850s – of traditional pleading practices had created when he notes the likelihood that "forms of action and the distinctions between law and equity are to wholly pass away, and the courts are [simply] to enforce duties on the plain statement of facts out of which they arise[.]"[49] The removal of an antiquated pleading system may have had its benefits but it created challenges for understanding how an issue should be presented and decided.[50] Hence the steady and strong market in practitioner paraphernalia and student aids.

Holmes deplored the convenient solution of using intuitive or customary headings to categorize cases. Common sense said: cases regarding churns should be categorized under a heading entitled, "Churns." An intelligent, disciplined jurisprudence, on the other hand, sought to bypass the common, unsophisticated assumption, and categorize the substance of the dispute between the two farmers under a legal heading that found its origins in a distinct legal conception. The theoretical problem lay in formulating legal conceptions that encompassed comprehensive categories.

To go from organizing legal phenomena – statutes and the decided cases – to systematizing those same phenomena on the basis of articulated and distinct headings required a change in approach. One moved from asking, "what is the law?" to the more philosophical question: "what is law?" The trick, though, for someone of Holmes's inclination – who did not want to see the connections between the two questions abolished – lay in allowing each question to check and balance the other on the basis of function and practicality.

[48] *Id. But see* Frederick Schauer, *Prediction and Particularity*, 78 B.U. L. Rev. 773, 774–77 (1998) (defending the Vermont justice of the peace on the basis of a certain "size" and type of legal categorization).

[49] Holmes, *supra* note 26, at 221.

[50] *See* Reimann, *supra* note 46, at 76 ("While the common law had never been very systematic, at least the old forms of action and pleading and the separation of law and equity had provided some organization, though along procedural rather than substantive lines."). *See also* David M. Rabban, *The Historiography of* The Common Law, 28 Law & Soc. Inquiry 1161, 1167 (2003) ("In writing his book [*The Common Law*], Holmes sought to address the widespread sense in the Anglo-American legal world that a new conceptualization of the common law was needed to replace the collapse of its traditional organization around procedural forms of action.").

For lawyers bred in common law ways of thinking, the question "what is the law?" became second nature. In a legal system in which precedent ruled, the decided case, the longstanding rules, the hoary principles derived ultimately from custom or nature and mediated through longstanding habit, oriented the practitioner faced with a current-day legal issue or dispute, even if the immediate matter involved the interpretation and application of a statute. Especially in early nineteenth-century America many practitioners found their bearings in the common law tradition, mainly via Blackstone, when faced with the chaos of a legal order that had, in many states, precious little semblance of order. What practitioners take for granted today – finding the law that applies – presented formidable barriers to predecessors who did not have the benefit of sophisticated systems for organizing or easily retrieving the states' authoritative legal materials.[51]

Yet in the English tradition existed a counterpoint to the common law we often associate with the names Jeremy Bentham and John Austin. It sought to provide an alternative to the perceived chaos of the common law and its seemingly ad hoc methods of adjudication. The alternative rested not only on a clear, logical organization of existing law – Bentham advocated codification – but also on the developed use of formal reason in law: careful, analytic, deductive thinking employed to connect legal premises with legal conclusions. To this end arose a different guiding question: "what is law?"[52]

Holmes showed an interest in both questions, and at the same time. We see this in "Codes, and the Arrangement of Law." After clarifying some of the advantages and disadvantages of developing a legal code, he submits the first of many attempts to draw up a grand schema. As is well known, Holmes eventually gave up the effort to construct a legal taxonomy.[53] An enthused young Holmes, however, believed the answer to the problem of categorization lay in perceiving duties as the law's ultimate conceptions, not rights.[54]

On this point, that "duty" not "right" functioned as the generative legal conception for the profession, he never wavered.

[51] *See* Cook, *supra* note 32, at 24–35 (reviewing the chaos of session laws that existed in many states and the unavailability or inaccessibility of court decisions).

[52] Michael Lobban has pointed out that Austin had a much more favorable position on the uses and merits of the common law than did Bentham, who advocated a wholesale rejection. Michael Lobban, A History of the Philosophy of Law in the Common Law World, 1600–1900 155–87 (2007).

[53] *See* Frederic R. Kellogg, Oliver Wendell Holmes, Jr., Legal Theory, and Judicial Restraint 7–72 (2007); Herget, *supra* note 42, at 41 (stating that Holmes's flirtation with the expository tradition was short-lived).

[54] Oliver Wendell Holmes, *The Arrangement of the Law – Privity*, *in* I CW 303 ("In a former article [*Codes, and the Arrangement of Law*] we expressed the opinion that a sound classification of the law was impossible, except on the basis of the ultimate conception of *duty*, instead of the derivative notion, *rights*, which is the foundation of existing systems.").

"Duties precede rights logically and chronologically," the young Holmes avers.[55] As typically the case with Holmes, he explains his meaning through examples not exposition. The key to understanding his use of the term legal duty is to grasp that a duty, in his usage, involves a restriction or limitation on action or inaction. Within a recognizable legal system a sovereign declares certain groupings of facts to be unacceptable within the municipality, that is, the territory under its control. A legal duty describes the restraints that the sovereign imposes upon those under its sway. It also describes the related restraints the sovereign seeks to maintain against those over which – such as other sovereigns – it may have little direct control. Duties are logically primary; in the absence of legal duties a people or a person may do as they desire subject only to natural or social restraints. A natural restraint differs from one legal in that the latter operates through infliction of vigorous penalties. It seeks to enforce either imposed or agreed-upon desires to establish a certain course of conduct.

Given this line of reasoning, one might assume that a legal right exists when a legal duty is absent and one may do as one desires. But in "Codes, and the Arrangement of Law," Holmes specifically forecloses this option. Using the common law doctrine of possession as an example he says: "The so-called right of user in the owner is not derived from the law. Any man, unless restrained, may use any thing he can lay his hands on, in any way he can devise."[56] The legal right, unlike moral or political rights in certain moral or political philosophies, is not primary. It is derivative of the duty or duties that give shape and color to it and direct its claim against interference or inaction.

Holmes also asserts in this article that legal duties arose in connection to "facts outside the law."[57] He uses the legally imposed requirement to respect a pre-existing relationship between a person and an object as an example of how one moved from facts outside the law to facts inside the law.[58] This tracing of law's borders in the context of property law had both an expository and heuristic intent. One sees the common law most clearly as *law* in circumstances relating to possession because these circumstances help one see how certain facts lead to specific legal descriptions (such as property and ownership) when the force of sanction fuses them together. The corresponding legal right does not arise from the possession itself but from the legal duty to respect it (i.e., not to interfere with its enjoyment).

[55] Holmes, *supra* note 26, at 214.

[56] *Id.* at 216; *see also* Frederic Kellogg, The Formative Essays of Justice Holmes: The Making of an American Legal Philosophy 25 (1984) ("The scope of possible social conduct had nothing to do with the phenomenon called law. It could be engaged in anyway, and was neither created by nor dependent upon some hypothetical legitimating substance.").

[57] Holmes, *supra* note 26, at 216.

[58] *Id.* at 216 ("[T]he primitive elements [of property or ownership] are possession, which is a fact or situation outside the law, and a duty imposed on the rest of the world to respect it"; *id.* at 220, referring to, "[T]he true duty to respect possession which is enforced by the action at trover").

In taking this tack, Holmes seeks to present the common law – its layout and content – from within: unlike the philosopher who approaches the law from the outside, "[t]he business of the jurist is to make known the content of the law; that is, to work upon it from within, or logically, arranging and distributing it in order from its *summum genus* to its *infima species*."[59] This same basic orientation will reappear, without the taxonomical references, in his last major philosophical statement on the law, the 1899 article "Law in Science and Science in Law."[60]

Much of "Codes, and the Arrangement of Law" focuses on dividing duties into their respective categories (duties of sovereigns to each other, duties to one's sovereign, duties of all to all, duties of all to those in a particular relation, duties of those in a particular relation to each other) and showing the implications of doing so for existing legal doctrine.[61] Yet before he takes on this difficult task Holmes thinks it important to tackle first the question, "what is law?"

He begins by acknowledging the practical usefulness of John Austin's definition: that law is an enforceable command from an identifiable political superior to people competent to understand the command to do or forbear from doing certain types of acts upon pain of sanction.[62] Holmes thinks the definition adequate for the law that lawyers call law. But it had its evident limitations as a philosophical statement.

First, it failed to capture relevant features of the social world in which Holmes lived. He objects to the notion that only a delimited political authority can declare law, especially when one could not easily discern who, or what, constituted this supposed authority. As he noted: "who has the sovereign power, and whether such a power exists at all, are questions of fact and of degree."[63]

Second, it paid too much attention to the supposed source of the command and not enough to its "definiteness of expression" and "Certainty of being enforced."[64] In elaborating on this second criticism, Holmes asks rhetorically:

> In the nature of things, which is most truly law, the rule that if I am invited to a dinner party in London I must appear in evening dress under the penalty of not being asked to similar entertainments if I disobey; or the statute against usury in New York, which juries do not decline to carry out simply because they are never asked to do so?

[59] Holmes, *supra* note 39, at 47; *see also* Holmes, *supra* note 54, at 303 n.** ("[t]he end of all classification should be to make the law *knowable*; and that system best accomplishes that purpose which proceeds from the most general conception to the most specific proposition or exception in the order of logical subordination." [emphasis in original]). *See also* MARK DEWOLFE HOWE, JUSTICE OLIVER WENDELL HOLMES: THE PROVING YEARS, 1870–1881 217 (1963).

[60] Oliver Wendell Holmes, *Law in Science and Science in Law*, *in* III CW 412–13.

[61] Holmes, *supra* note 26, at 215–20.

[62] *Id.* at 215.

[63] *Id.*

[64] *Id.* ("Certainty" is capitalized in the original).

In the viability of sanction Holmes finds a living truth in Austin's analytic definition of law. The source of what a person recognized as law could easily be indefinite. To the objection that an "indefinite body cannot directly signify a command" he rejoins, "the rules of judge-made law are never authentically promulgated as rules, but are left to be inferred from the cases."[65]

One purpose of a penalty is to encourage obedience to the enforced command. Or, in other terms, a penalty supports recognition of, and conformity to, a duty (an ordered limitation or restraint) to others under the control of the same sovereign. In Holmes's formulation, the court stood as the primary enforcement body. Laws not enforced, regardless of the name, lacked an important defining feature: the certainty of enforcement.

Courts, in turn, gave rise to lawyers, that is, those people preoccupied with the study of the rules the courts may enforce.

> Rules not enforced by them [the courts], although equally imperative, are the study of no profession. It is on this account that the province of jurisprudence has to be so carefully determined.[66]

This statement posits that 'law' is a subclass of imperative (i.e., enforced) rules. The sociological fact that a political body enforces this subclass distinguishes it from other categories of rules. The specific enforcement body, the courts, is not the sovereign. Courts, except perhaps in matters pertaining specifically to the legal profession, do not have the power or authority to generate commands (in Austin's sense). For directives, they must look internally – to their own precedents – or externally, to other entities or participants in the legal system or to the norms and beliefs of the legal system itself. The rules the courts will enforce, the circumstances in which the courts will enforce them, and how, constitute the study of the legal profession.

On the other hand Holmes qualifies this statement by observing that international law, so-called, fails to meet Austin's definition of law – no super-national political authority exists – just as there were no courts in 1870 to enforce the commands of this nonexistent super-national political authority. Holmes concedes lawyers have "little to do professionally with rules falling outside Austin's division," but still study international law.[67] He concludes: Austin's definition had a practical convenience – no more, no less.[68]

Here we see firsthand Holmes's efforts to keep open and supple the links between the questions "what is the law?" and "what is law?"

On one side lies the practical-minded practitioner who wants to find and apply the actual rules in play. For Holmes this question – what are the actual rules in

65 *Id.*
66 *Id.*
67 *Id.*
68 *Id.*

play? – begins as an empirical one, a factual issue,[69] but he hopes it does not end there. He hopes a practitioner would do more than simply, and simple-mindedly, turn to the law books searching for the chapter titled, "Churns," or claim, as Austin did, that international law did not exist because it had no visible, unitary enforcement authority.

On the other side lies the more theoretical-minded practitioner who constantly seeks to think more inclusively about the actual rules in play in light of the given states of fact, who, that is to say, searches for guiding legal principles. Legal principles assist legal professionals in resolving legal disputes (or to accomplish other legal objectives) for which the actual rules in play provide scant direction. They do this by elucidating the basis in social fact for the corresponding or perhaps emerging rule of law.

At the end of "Codes, and the Arrangement of Law," Holmes winds his way back to the subject of duties. "A duty, strictly so called, is only created by a command which may be broken at the expense of incurring a penalty."[70] The importance of the use of the descriptive "so called" in the sentence may be to demarcate duties (perhaps moral or customary) that exist outside the law from those the law creates through command (even in the absence of a commander). The essence of a legally recognized duty is the presence of a legally enforceable penalty.

This point is a subtle one, but one interwoven throughout Holmes's thinking on the law. "That which the law directly compels, although it may onerously affect an individual, cannot be said to impose a duty upon him."[71] In these words Holmes

[69] It is in this context, of a practitioner first looking to see what the law is, that I understand Holmes's opaque remark that "Law is not a science, but is essentially empirical." *Id.* Holmes makes this comment in the course of discussing whether it makes more sense, when treating standard legal topics, to do so from the point of view of duty (which he advocated) or from that of right (the established practice). He thinks the issue partly one of convenience. Two pages later in the article he says, "But as we have said already, the side of the shield [the point of view of right or duty] contemplated is unimportant, if it is not suffered to become a source of delusion." *Id.* at 217. The implication of saying that "law is not a science" is that the mode of organization and course of exposition may not be as critical to its cogency as in other sciences (*e.g.*, chemistry or physics).

The empirical method, though, remains essential. A judge as much as a practitioner must take initial steps to inquire, as a matter of fact, what is the law the judge must enforce. *See id.* at 214; *see also* Oliver Wendell Holmes, *The Theory of Torts*, *in* I CW 328–29 ("Before law can act, however, either upon the private citizen or the judge, when, as in civilized communities, it is not directly addressed to the individual by the sovereign, a preliminary investigation of fact has to be made." And: "[T]hey [judicially noticed facts] may not even owe their compulsory power to their recognition by the courts, although they do not generate rules of law in the empirical sense in which lawyers use the phrase, unless they induce the judges to decide in the way they suggest."); Oliver Wendell Holmes, *Notes to* Kent's Commentaries, *in* II CW 196–98. *But see* G. EDWARD WHITE, JUSTICE OLIVER WENDELL HOLMES: LAW AND THE INNER SELF 128–29 (interpreting the phrase in a more behavioristic sense).

[70] Holmes, *supra* note 26, at 220.

[71] *Id.*

highlights a difference between being forcibly coerced and being ordered, a distinction that the word "command" often elides.[72]

Duties encompassed a wider gradation of acts and of options to act than rights. The study of duties took one straightaway to factual situations, to a compendium of acts and their boundaries. One in good common law fashion began with the facts and stayed with the facts.[73] The facts took on legal meaning, or, conversely, the facts became legally significant when a certain constellation focused the attention of the courts. The attention to duties, for Holmes, helped direct the legal mind in every factual circumstance to the individual strands of the fundamental legal double helix: "what is the law?" and "what is law?" It also enabled Holmes to circumscribe the province of jurisprudence from the rest of social life.

iii *Jurisprudential Boundaries*

Fields of study typically have their own content, method, form, and purpose.[74] For a young Holmes the content of jurisprudence – understood as the study of the common law – began with duties. He calls them "ultimate conceptions."[75] Why duties – in the sense of obligations to do or to forbear – had this privileged status Holmes never fully elucidates in his early scholarship. Duties are incidents to certain factual situations, but why recognized and imposed obligations to do or to forbear are connected to certain groupings of facts and not to others is left unexplained.

It appears duties initially arose as mandated responses to certain primary relationships (*e.g.*, the possessor and the thing possessed). The manner in which Holmes recurs to these primary relationships and the responses to them (*e.g.*, enforced respect) suggests that for him they did not exist as simply artificial constructs – a Hobbesian state of nature, for example – but as historically conditioned realities, perhaps with unascertainable beginnings and endings,

72 On this point see Gerald J. Postema, Legal Philosophy in the Twentieth Century: The Common Law World 9–13 (2011).

73 In this respect, Holmes's comments on the limitations of the civil law are apropos:

> We doubt the wisdom of making the civil law part of the course to be studied by beginners who intend to practice at the common-law bar. There is ground for suspicion that it tends to encourage a dangerous reliance of what Mr. Choate would have called glittering generalities, and a distaste for the exhaustive analysis of a particular case, with which the common law begins and ends.

Oliver Wendell Holmes, *Misunderstandings of the Civil Law*, *in* I CW 260.

74 *See, e.g.*, Paul K. Conkin & Roland N. Stromberg, Heritage and Challenge: The History and Theory of History 134 (1989) ("Four interrelated issues help distinguish one empirical discipline from another: subject matter, methods of inquiry, the form taken by the acquired knowledge, and the possible uses of such knowledge.").

75 Holmes, *supra* note 54, at 303.

but which a disciplined inquirer could trace throughout the history of the common law.[76]

From this ocean of primary relationships and the required responses to them, Holmes teases into existence an archipelago of duties that the courts have habitually enforced. These, he believes, demarcated and formed what he calls, in Austin's language but not with Austin's meaning, the "province of jurisprudence."[77]

In "Codes, and the Arrangement of Law," he makes two corollary points: duties, to be enforceable, need not be traced to an original determinate source. That is to say, directives regarding impermissible acts – acts that would incur a penalty – were intrinsic to any society (large or small) and required no certificate of origin to be effective (witness the swift justice of elegant Londoners against the perpetrator of a fashion faux pas). And, second, the specific subset of duties that concerned lawyers – that bounded the study of their profession – were those duties the violation of which took the violator outside the protection of the law.

I concede this second point is not clearly stated in the text of "Codes, and the Arrangement of Law," but must be inferred as something Holmes wanted to say in that article and actually did say in subsequent texts.[78] It is worth dwelling on this second point at some length because the boundary between the legal and the extralegal, between being inside the law or outside the law, set law off, for Holmes, from custom and morality or from social or individual expectation.

Two years after publishing "Codes, and the Arrangement of Law," Holmes uses his prerogative as the *American Law Review*'s principal book reviewer to expound his own further developed views on the demerits of Austin's definition of law after reading Frederick Pollock's piece, "Law and Command," on the same topic. In this short essay Holmes elaborates and refines the brief critique he made in "Codes, and the Arrangement of Law" of Austin's response to the question, "what is law?"[79]

Austin's response had three main parts: (1) a political authority or sovereign; (2) a command to political inferiors or subordinates to do or to forbear to do certain types of acts; and, (3) the imposition of a penalty or sanction in case of disobedience.

[76] See Frederic R. Kellogg's compatible hypothesis:

> The better explanation is what I have cautiously called a proto-Hegelian move – recasting the Hobbesian ethos as a product of history – although in detail quite unlike Hegel. It was rooted not in the *Zeitgeist* or the innate force of ideas but in a maturation of the process of resolving concrete and particular conflicts. Compared with Hobbes, Holmes's theory provided a more a naturalistic historical foundation for the objective rule of law, without which a coherent and robust order was inconceivable.

KELLOGG, *supra* note 53, at 87.

[77] Holmes, *supra* note 26, at 215.

[78] As the forthcoming discussion will indicate, those texts are Oliver Wendell Holmes, *Comment on* The Law Magazine and Review, *in* I CW 294–97 [hereinafter *The 1872 Jurisprudence Essay*], The Arrangement of Law – Privity, *supra* note 54, at 303–17, and *The Theory of Torts, supra* note 69, at 326–35.

[79] Holmes, *1872 Jurisprudence Essay, supra* note 78, at 294–97.

Holmes's critique alternates between sociological criticisms and philosophical ones. That is to say, in some instances – as in criticizing Austin's conception of sovereignty – Holmes points to real-world examples that show, he argues, that the source and deployment of political will and political power in society is much more variegated than Austin's theory allowed.[80] At other points Holmes questions the adequacy of Austin's command theory at a more fundamental level. He doubts its inherent adequacy and effectiveness as a working model for delimiting, arranging, and comprehending legal phenomena.[81]

Many of Holmes's criticisms focus on what he perceives to be the command theory's lack of flexibility. The rigid, vertical, top-down approach that analogized law to a direct command of a king to a subject on pain of sanction for disobedience failed to take into account countervailing social realities such as custom, popular opinion, and pressing moral or cultural sentiment. It also could not, as a mental pattern centered on rights, provide the theoretical power needed for an enlightened but practical jurisprudence. It was too static.[82]

Holmes shifts the focus from the source of law to its enforcement. He again introduces the concept of a "lawyers' law," by which he means what the chief enforcers of the sovereign's will say the law is. The chief enforcers are the courts – the judges – and it becomes the primary business of lawyers as professionals to understand and predict which of many possible motivations may prevail with a judge or judges in a specific case.[83]

The importance of Holmes's "1872 Jurisprudence Essay" does not lie in its perceptive criticisms of the command theory's shortcomings: law had many sources; the power to sanction arose in many of life's circumstances whether or not one connected the penalty to a recognizable law; the courts, not an indefinite sovereign, bore the authority to state and enforce the law in a particular case. Nor does it lie in its initial articulation of what came to be called the "prediction theory of law," or in how it advanced the conceptualization of law from unitary command to a rationalized complex of procedures professionals oversee. The "The 1872 Jurisprudence Essay's" main significance lies in the concentrated attention Holmes gives to the third part of Austin's theory, the nature of the imposed penalty.

Holmes tersely states the vital point: "A legal duty cannot be said to exist if the law intends to allow the person supposed to be subject to it an option at a certain price. The test of a legal duty is the absolute nature of the command."[84] The patient reader who has followed Holmes to this last part of the essay undoubtedly stops short in confusion at these sentences. One thought Holmes had discredited the idea of law

80 *Id.*
81 *Id.*
82 *Id.*; *see also* KELLOGG, *supra* note 53, at 92–93.
83 Holmes, 1872 *Jurisprudence Essay*, *supra* note 78, at 294–97.
84 *Id.* at 296.

as command from a sovereign. But here he is saying that the acid test for a legal duty is the "absolute nature of the command."

The resolution lies in understanding law as command, not in its source, but in its effect.[85] It is command not in origin but in application. From A to Z are twenty-four other letters; that is to say, many possibilities and pathways for interpretation, argument, posturing, and gamesmanship. As a practitioner, Holmes knew full well the many pitfalls that may befall: a precedent may not be followed; a statute may be emptied of content by construction; or a statute, effective initially, is repealed without a savings clause.[86] These hazards may be statistically low, but they existed, and a practitioner would do well to keep them in mind. But at the end a decision is made, the court rules.

To the extent the law declared leads to a penalty that deprives the person to whom the penalty is addressed of future legal options or support – in other words, expressly lowering that person's legal status – it approaches an absolute command.

Regardless of the command theory's many deficiencies, Holmes kept alive its sense that law invoked raw power. Law, however one may define it, directed power to specific ends. "The object of the law is to accomplish an external result."[87] Power in this strong sense meant more than incentives, or coercions; it meant something other than compulsion; it meant at times inaction, depriving a person of legal protection.[88]

To develop this distinction between being inside and outside the protective ambit of the law, Holmes had to distill the idea of a penalty. Distilling the idea of penalty, in turn, meant sharpening the notion of a legal duty. The logic of the terms seemed straightforward. An absolute command creates a legal duty. The breach of the legal duty leads to a penalty. He had said almost as much at the end of "Codes, and the Arrangement of the Law," – "A duty, strictly so called, is only created by commands

[85] H. L. A. Hart found this notion, of a command without a commander, to be inconceivable. H. L. A. Hart, The Concept of Law 113 (2d ed. 1994) ("But this last should perhaps have no more serious claims to our attention than the notion of a nephew without an uncle."). Without going into a full-length discussion, Hart's comparison seems misaligned.

[86] Holmes, *1872 Jurisprudence Essay*, *supra* note 78, at 295.

[87] *Id.* at 296.

[88] Holmes recognized that the phrase "outside the protection of the law" carried a different weight in his day from that of much earlier times. Oliver Wendell Holmes, *The Common Law*, *in* III CW 242 (noting that a defendant who did not peaceably submit to the jurisdiction of the court might be put outside the protection of the law so that any man might kill him on sight); *see also* Palmer v. Gordon, 173 Mass. 410, 412 (1899) ("A trespasser is not *caput lupinum*.") (per Holmes, J.); Stoffela v. Nugent, 217 U.S. 499, 501 (1910) ("But a man by committing a fraud does not become an outlaw and *caput lupinum*.") (per Holmes, J.); Derrick v. Wallace, 112 N.E. 440, 442 (N.Y. 1916) ("Anciently an outlawed felon was said to have a wolf's head (*caput lupinum*) so that anyone might kill him as he would a wolf. Later and until recently the convicted felon was disqualified as a witness.") (internal citations omitted).

which may be broken at the expense of incurring a penalty."[89] But now he sharpened his proposition by adding the adjective absolute to the noun command.

If the courts impose a penalty then one, it seems, could infer, all other things being equal, that, in the court's judgment, a duty that an absolute command created had been broken. The critical question resolved into: what counts as a true penalty?

A penalty had to be something more than an option to pay money. A penalty qua penalty had to lie in the legal opprobrium that became part of the conduct once it incurs the penalty. Holmes put it this way:

> If a statute subjects a person to a penal action in case of certain conduct on his part, but such conduct is protected and treated as lawful in all other connections in which it may come before the court, an option is in fact allowed . . . . The imposition of a penalty is therefore only evidence tending to show that an absolute command does not exist – penalty or no penalty – unless a breach of it is deprived of the protection of the law, which is shown by a number of consequences not accurately determinable in a general definition[.][90]

Holmes finishes the last sentence by using the example of the defense of invalidity of contract to do a forbidden act under the rule of *in pari delicto potior est conditio defendentis*: the law will not do anything to provide relief to the plaintiff for a cause of action – say breach of contract – that rests, at least in part, on the plaintiff's own illegal act.[91] Under the *in pari delicto* rule quoted, the law favors the status quo – the party in possession or the defendant – when both parties are equally in the wrong. The law does not permit the court to change the existing situation.

In Holmes's view, the legal *meaning* of the penalized conduct – and so of a legal duty – lay in what he called the "collateral consequences," which, and this is an important point, are "not accurately determinable in a general definition."[92] This point extends Holmes's insights, expressed in "Codes, and the Arrangement of Law," regarding the primacy of duty and the fundamental relationship between the one who has the duty and those charged to enforce the law.[93]

For example, the law against committing fraud through a Ponzi scheme does not in its general definition – something like "do not swindle Peter and Mary to pay Paul

[89] Holmes, *supra* note 26, at 220.

[90] *Id.* at 296.

[91] *Id.*

[92] *Id.*

[93] *See also* Holmes, *supra* note 69, at 86–87 ("An act cannot be called illegal unless it is absolutely prohibited and put outside the protection of the law in all connections, which is shown by such consequences as the invalidity of contracts to do the act in question, the rule *in pari delicto potior est conditio defendentis*, and the denial of relief when the illegal act is part of the plaintiff's case."); Nat'l Bank & Loan Co. v. Petrie, 189 U.S. 423, 425 (1903) ("[A] person does not become an outlaw and lose all rights by doing an illegal act.") (per Holmes, J.). Mark DeWolfe Howe notes the advances Holmes's conception of duty made over that of Austin's, but does not recognize the possibilities inherent in Holmes's conception for demarcating the province of jurisprudence. Howe, *supra* note 59, at 76–80.

and do not swindle Paul and Peter to pay Mary" – state that the court will *not* assist you, the Ponzi schemer, if the bank where you deposited the ill-gotten money negligently permitted your accomplice to make off with all the funds. But that would be the net result should you try to sue the bank for negligence and breach of contract.[94]

If the courts refuse, because of the penalized conduct, to assist or protect the penalized but aggrieved actor in the same or other proceedings, then by this test one knows that an absolute command has been broken.[95]

The logic of Holmes's terms leads to the counterintuitive conclusion that one may be liable but not have a strict legal duty.[96] The word doing all the heavy lifting is "duty" and it helps to keep in mind that Holmes, in his early writings, used "duty" to signify a complex of meanings regarding the interlacing and sequencing of beliefs and actions that fell within the domain called law.

First, the rudiments of what we call duty consist in certain mandated reactions to primary relationships. If one is called upon to respect a factual situation outside the law – the relationship between the possessor and the thing possessed,[97] for example – then certainly a component of that respect is noninterference and the awareness of certain reprisals should one interfere. The question then arises regarding the source of these reprisals. If the person interfered with retaliates against the interferer then one cannot really say under Holmes's terms that the duty not to interfere is a legal duty. It may be the law of the jungle but it is not law in Holmes's sense. Law in Holmes's sense signifies the strong desires of the sovereign power – which may or may not tie to a visible sovereign – as enforced through the courts. Duties represent a called-upon course of conduct. That which did the calling was the existing regime of law, that is, already enforced duties. The sovereign as a word denoting a specific seat of power had become in Holmes's hands a superfluous abstraction for the purposes of analyzing law.

The rudiments of duty, then, are both outside (the fact situation) and inside (called upon to respect) law proper.

94 *See generally* Bateman Eichler, Hill Richards, Inc. v. Berner, 472 U.S. 299 (1985).

95 In this connection, Holmes makes the following interesting observation:

> It remains, then, to seek for some ground for the protection of possession outside the Bill of Rights or the Declaration of Independence, which shall be consistent to the larger scope given to the conception in modern law. The courts have said but little on the subject. It was laid down in one case that it was an extension of the protection which the law throws around the person, and on that ground held that trespass *quare clausum* did not pass to an assignee in bankruptcy.

Holmes, *supra* note 88, at 223.

96 *See* Holmes, *supra* note 69, at 326 ("Mere liability to what is called a penalty by the statute imposing it may not create a duty, it was shown, and *a fortiori* such is not the direct result of the liability to a civil action.").

97 Holmes, *supra* note 26, at 216 (noting that the primitive elements of property are possession, a fact or situation outside the law, and a duty imposed on the rest of the world to respect it).

Second, the existence of a duty naturally suggests through the normal legal use of the word (if we can even say that "duty" has a normal legal use) that someone ought (is legally required) to do – or not do – something. Holmes seems to acknowledge this meaning when he refers to Austin's suggestion that a duty "is only created by commands which may be broken at the expense of incurring a penalty." The assertion expresses the point that a command creates a duty – the thing to be done or the required restraint – which carries with it a penalty for failure to comply. Yet Holmes undercuts this commonsense reading when he follows that sentence by saying: "The law addresses itself to the thing to be done, not to the person affected, and does not punish his failure to co-operate."[98]

It is worth dwelling on this latter sentence because if we understand what Holmes is driving at it will clarify much of his later thought and forestall interpretive dead ends.

For example, Mark DeWolfe Howe in his searching examination of Holmes's thinking on the topic of duty sees a decided shift between "Codes, and the Arrangement of Law," and the "1872 Jurisprudence Essay." Howe believes the former article's classificatory scheme depends on the Austinian conception of duty – that a duty may be found when a penalty has been prescribed – and supports this view by noting that at that time (1870) Holmes did not question the orthodox view that one who enters into a binding contract agrees to perform according to its terms – that is, has a duty to perform – and nonperformance leads to liability and the associated penalty.[99]

By the time of the "1872 Jurisprudence Essay" Holmes changed his mind, Howe says, due to his sophisticated criticisms of Austin's theory of duty.[100] The existence of a penalty (or, equivalently, a sanction or tax) did not serve as an infallible index to the existence of a legal duty. Holmes propounded an alternative conception, one that, again according to Howe, formed the basis for Holmes's infamous paradox, propounded in *The Common Law*, that a contracting party had no duty to perform its promises, only a duty to pay damages for nonperformance.[101]

98 *Id.* at 220.

99 Howe, *supra* note 59, at 68–83.

100 *Id.*

101 *Id.* at 233–40. Frederic Kellogg, in his The Formative Essays of Justice Holmes, argues against Howe's notion that Holmes, in the early part of his career, was sharpening and clarifying Austin's notion of a legal duty. Kellogg believes Holmes was beginning to jettison the concept of duty completely. "These early doubts would eventually grow into his wholesale rejection not only of the scheme of analytical ordering but of moral language itself as an accurate symbol for the conceptual content of law." Kellogg, *supra* note 56, at 268 n.12. *See also* Sheldon M. Novick, Honorable Justice: The Life of Oliver Wendell Holmes 450–51 n.9 (stating that in "The Path of the Law" Holmes abandoned the framework of "duties" to which he had stubbornly clung during the years he was preparing *The Common Law*).

I don't think Holmes ever saw the duties of which he wrote as anything other than legal duties. I think Howe was correct in his initial account of how Holmes analyzed duty, and even in connecting that analysis with Holmes's eventual introduction of the bad man, but Howe

Howe reasons as follows. "Austin had asserted that the command which is law – the command, that is, which brings into being a legal duty – may always be identified as such by the sovereign's threat that a penalty or sanction will be imposed if a certain course of conduct is followed."[102] Holmes, Howe says, criticizes Austin's formulation because it suggests that a penalty (or sanction or tax, in short, a negative consequence) serves as an infallible index to the existence of a legal duty. Not so. The existence of a negative consequence functions as a rule of construction to determine whether a true duty exists. The infallible indicia to a true legal duty lay in what Holmes calls the collateral consequences. Thus, even when a law carries with it no express negative consequences one must still look at other law to determine if the collateral consequences of infringement signal the existence of true legal duty – the breach of which leads to a drop in a person's legal status.

Howe finds an unexplained inconsistency in how Holmes criticizes Austin's definition of legal duty on the one hand but on the other continues to use that definition in his efforts to categorize existing law.

> Friends and critics alike were misled, perhaps, not only by Holmes's failure to redefine his terms but by the unquestionable fact that while as lecturer he was denying the philosophical validity of Austin's conception of duty, as essayist he was contemporaneously building his classification on that conception and showing no hesitation to include the promisor's [contractual] obligation in his schedule of legal duties.[103]

Though Howe may have had good reason to dwell on the evident problems arising from Holmes's criticisms of Austin's formulation and his apparent use of that same formulation as a classificatory tool, this particular set of problems are more apparent than real. And they have little to do with Holmes's distinctive formulation of contractual duties.

As suggested above, Holmes through refining the Austinian formulation seeks to mark off what he conceives as the borders or province of jurisprudence. The conception of duty, which Howe describes as one of "such extreme narrowness that it could not possibly become the basic element in a serviceable classification of law,"[104] had, in a sense, to perform a double duty: it had to conceptually limit the field of study *and* mark the different divisions within that field. If we are charitable toward Holmes we see, once again, his effort to keep strong the connections between the two important questions, "what is law?" (restated as "what is a duty?" restated as "what is a true penalty?") and "what is the law?" (restated as "what are the

evidently had a hard time himself adopting the bad man's perspective, that of the purely legal point of view.

[102] Howe, *supra* note 59, at 76.

[103] *Id.* at 77–78.

[104] *Id.* at 79.

applicable duty or duties?" restated as "what are the direct or indirect negative consequences?").

Yet even Howe, who has written as penetrating a study as any Holmes scholar on this topic, does not appreciate fully the keenness of the logic of Holmes's argument. We see the first hints in the sentence already quoted from "Codes, and the Arrangement of Law": "The law addresses itself to the thing to be done, not to the person affected, and does not punish the failure to co-operate."[105] Then in the "1872 Jurisprudence Essay" Holmes further elaborates: "The word [duty] imports the existence of an absolute wish on the part of the power imposing it to bring about a certain course of conduct, and to prevent the contrary."[106] These quotes lead one to ask: what is the logic of a duty when seen from the point of view of the enforcement power? The answer plainly lies in the connection of events, in the enforcement power's ability to turn physical circumstances into legal causes through the imposition of legal consequences.

It is true, as Holmes says, that the enforcement power seeks to work through motives – law can ill afford to dispense with the carrot and the stick – but that is a secondary objective. The main objective is to assure that when one social event occurs, another social event under the control of the enforcement power follows ineluctably. The law's primary concern is with what may be called legal events – to distinguish them from social events – and the internal order of these legal events, not expressly with the persons involved. Duty itself resolves into a fact or group of facts connecting to a prior fact or group of facts. The two facts or groups – the legal consequence and the legal cause – when fully connected through legal meaning constitute in their sequence a legal event.

Howe fails to appreciate how Holmes began to conceptualize law as an ongoing accumulation of interconnected legal events because he keeps, perhaps inadvertently, smuggling into the concept of duty a moral or social element. He is evidently unhappy that Holmes will not back off from his formulated so-called paradox that a contractual promise does not impose upon the promisor a duty to perform. Howe understands this to imply that the promisor only has a duty to pay damages if he does not perform.[107] But Holmes's formulation, as we will see in a later part, is subtler. A contractual promise, as Holmes defines it, is an assurance that a certain event will come to pass. If the event which the promisor has assured will come to pass does not happen then the enforcement power will, upon request and to the extent possible, ensure that another event will come to pass, in most instances a transfer of the promisor's property (often reduced to money) to the promisee. The promisor's assurance, or what others see as the duty, is merely a signal both for lawyers and the enforcement power that one event will follow another. The enforced sequence

[105] Holmes, *supra* note 26, at 220.

[106] Holmes, *supra* note 78, at 296.

[107] Howe, *supra* note 59, at 233–40.

takes on that distinct type of social meaning called law. In other words, a legal event has come into being.

The problem with the use of such terms as "duty," "sanctions," "penalties," and "consequences" is that they invariably take on moral coloration. They occlude the fundamental fact, at least for Holmes, that the enforcement power wants to see come to pass what it wants to see come to pass. Desires and beliefs agreed upon, and with recourse to adequate means of physical power, often take on the title law but do not become law, in any substantive sense, until they have in time entrenched themselves and begun to integrate and order life events other than those initially within their purview.

In sum, Holmes believes rights derived, both historically and logically, from duties. A lawyer should begin the study of law by studying law – and that for Holmes in the early stages of his career meant, among other things, understanding the different types of legal duties. Simply cataloging or reciting the cases on the basis of surface similarities (Mrs. Quickly's "dramatic elements"[108]) is not enough.

Second, duty – in the strict jurisprudential sense – meant the obligation to act in conformity with a command that Holmes calls absolute. One differentiated absolute commands from commands not absolute by looking at the penalty a violation incurred. If a penalty deprived a violator of the law's protection – as shown through the collateral legal consequences of the violation – then one knew the courts considered the command absolute.

Perhaps because Holmes packed into the word duty such an intricate complex of meaning, and because he probably well understood that he would be misunderstood, he began to look for other ways to explain his meaning without using the word. In his article "Possession" he purposefully avoids using the word and offered instead this lengthy paraphrase:

> [T]he direct operation of the law is to limit freedom of action or choice on the part of a greater or less number of persons in certain specified ways [i.e., duty]; while the fact that the power of removing or enforcing this limitation is generally confided to certain other private persons is not a necessary or universal correlative [i.e., right].[109]

In reviewing the reach of Holmes's conceptualization, one is struck by his effort to infuse rationality into the existing chaos of the common law. In his early writings he wanted to elucidate the law's actual operations, develop instructions to help guide the operators (lawyers and judges), and to perform both tasks in a way that preserved the appellation of "learned" to the profession.

The chief business of law, of judges and lawyers, lay in understanding legal duties and their enforcement. It meant knowing the law in two senses: the actual rules in play ("what is the law?") and the gradation of actual enforcement options – and their

[108] Holmes, *supra* note 47, at 391.
[109] Holmes, *supra* note 39, at 47.

consequences – that connected to various types of duties ("what is law?"). It also implied – something Holmes would soon expressly recognize as he began to delve more deeply into the history of the common law – that duties exemplified those social desires and beliefs both evident to the mind and those pressing but of which the mind was not fully cognizant. That is to say, one could not simply understand law as a static, isolated, and purposive system of duties. Duty stood in relation to law as did a flower to a plant – necessary and instrumental to the plant's reproduction but not the plant itself.

Holmes's efforts to draw jurisprudential boundaries in the early stages of his career amounted to a regimental plan for the profession. It supported the profession's claim to learning; it recognized the dangers of those who believed most people were naturally endowed with the needed faculties to discern, unaided, legal right from legal wrong. And it sought to order the ranks internally by stressing that proficiency in law required more than tradecraft competence.

One certainly had to become a competent lawyer. Becoming a proficient lawyer meant more than mastering esoteric legal terms or the profession's lore. Holmes never ignores the needs of the practitioner. He does not underestimate the importance of the prosaic, "what is the law?" But if the study of law does not transcend the practical needs of the practitioner it would lose its power to continue – as Simpson put it – ordering society.[110] This task requires, as new situations arise and awareness of their complexity grows, the constant intelligent re-asking of the question, "what is law?"

[110] James Willard Hurst puts the idea of "ordering society" this way: "As historian and as judge he [Holmes] recognized that the growth of this society had taken a distinctive character from its development of more and more intricately interdependent organization. This trend made the adjustment of relations a prime business of law, and a job which demanded sophisticated realism for its effective handling." JAMES WILLARD HURST, JUSTICE HOLMES ON LEGAL HISTORY 66–67 (1964).

PART II

The Inner Path of the Common Law

SYNOPSIS

This part revisits Holmes's effort to map the common law but from a different angle. Holmes's new approach expressly recognizes the dynamic nature of the common law as a legal system and attempts to develop a positioning mechanism that goes beyond taxonomy and analysis. The first section, "The Way of the Common Law," shows how Holmes adopts an attitude reminiscent of William Blackstone: law need not – as some early American legal thinkers wanted – primarily encapsulate the moral norms dominant, or seeking dominance, in an emerging post–revolutionary war society. Some laws one could in good conscience break as long as one was willing to pay the associated penalty. But unlike Blackstone Holmes did not see in the entirety of the common law a providential dispensation. Nor did he believe it manifested in time a moral or aesthetic symmetry – the so-called fearful sublimity of divine power and majesty.

Subsequent sections in Part II – "The Transmutation of Facts and Law" and "Lawyers' Law and Its Modes" – focus on Holmes's concern with the intuition a judge may have of how a case ought to be decided and how that judge seeks to give reason to that intuition. These visceral predicates, not necessarily contrary to reason, served as a necessary reference point for understanding the why and how of law. Holmes at times employs the artist's technique of linear perspective to visualize law's historical movement. He seems in his work to draw an implicit comparison between the manner in which a legal historian, looking backward, may try to understand the genesis and growth of a legal doctrine and how a judge, looking forward, attempts to articulate and connect an intuition of how a case ought to be decided to a viable legal form.

Recognized movements and recognized stabilities foster the creation of temporal dimensions of legal thought and action. Holmes seeks in *The Common Law* to point up, without ever using the phrase, law's three-dimensionality. He uses the techniques of historical perspective to bring into relief law's actuality or what James Willard Hurst calls the living legal order. Holmes's extensive discussion of liability in *The Common Law* reveals not only his urge to theorize and bring into line principles for discriminating fault, but also his effort to impress on the minds of his contemporaries the mode by which law modified and transformed itself. The law's ability to capture and array into a working order different viewpoints impressed Holmes and led him to attempt to replicate on paper what he thought happened in real life.

In reviewing his accomplishments in the early chapters of *The Common Law*, what stands out is Holmes's effort to trace the movements of legal thought and feeling that formed the environs of the common law world that he knew firsthand. In review of his work we single out his effort to do consciously what had beforehand happened naturally, that is, without conscious, purposive intent. Historical perspective provides the needed cultural position to understand Holmes's attempt to triangulate viewpoints and bring further order and direction to the common law. On this suggestion that the triangulation of viewpoints accounts for Holmes's hypothesis of how the external standard arose from an internal one, Part II concludes and makes way for a discussion of what Holmes calls "the purely legal point of view."

INTRODUCTION

It appears in retrospect that "The Path of the Law" attempted to restore an attitude regarding "law" and "duty" characteristic of a bygone era of common law practitioners or at least of the common law's most prominent eighteenth-century commentator, Sir William Blackstone. This attitude emerges most clearly in "The Path of the Law" when Holmes speaks of a person who "commits a contract," a locution strange to ears accustomed to expressions extolling the sanctity of contract.[1]

It also, through juxtaposition to the phrase "commits a tort," jars our sensibilities because it exposes how we have customarily drawn a line between these two descriptions of acts with legal consequences. More: it shows how we have vivified these descriptions through our significations and the place those significations have in the broader canvas of meaning that dominates American legal culture.

One of the great virtues of Holmes's work lies in his effort to bring to light the inner meanings that structure certain legal conceptions – such as duty, possession, liability, and contract. By analyzing this endeavor we best capture the distinctive quality, the flavor, of Holmes's scholarship in *The Common Law*. Unless we come to terms with this important work many of the nuances in subsequent writings, such as "The Path of the Law," will slide right by.

In this part, we will discuss another set of answers Holmes gave to the questions "what is the law?" and "what is law?" We will show Holmes's interest in developing his understanding of lawyers' law from a different perspective – through the lens of what he called "experience" – and not only through a relatively fixed form of reasoning, a method of inference summed up in the word "logic." Just as the province of jurisprudence had its changing borders it also had a dynamic interior

[1] Oliver Wendell Holmes, *The Path of the Law*, *in* III The Collected Works of Justice Holmes: Complete Public Writings and Selected Judicial Opinions of Oliver Wendell Holmes 394 (Sheldon Novick ed., 1995) [hereinafter CW].

region that secular professionals had to administer. This obligation pointed up the need for lawyers to become more self-conscious of how lawyers' law works. Law understood both as an ongoing activity and as an open system had its own direction and cumulative force as a cultural institution.

In this respect *The Common Law* represents the culmination of Holmes's effort to map the law. But instead of using categories and tables he attempts something far more ambitious: to establish the necessary points of legal reference and the means of construing relations between them so as to create dimensionality in the law. Through various techniques, including that of historical perspective, Holmes attempts to call forth out of the chaos of the common law a living, three-dimensional legal order. This objective required that Holmes understand the mode in which the common law had grown and the habit of mind (apperception) that interrelated existing vibrant elements of meaning, form, and circumstance with what Holmes believed to be certain universal psychological characteristics – revenge for instance.

This part concludes with a discussion of how Holmes through the triangulation of viewpoints articulated the external standard of liability. The move from the internal to the external standard represented the work of law (of lawyers and judges and other participants) as a fundamental ordering activity in society. It turned desiderata into intelligible forms that carried the threat of sanction. Law as an ordering activity worked through the dynamic created by the two interrelated questions fundamental to lawyers' law, "what is the law?" and "what is law?"

1 THE WAY OF THE COMMON LAW

Holmes may have admired the analytic power of John Austin's mind – after all, he made a version of Austin's command theory the centerpiece of what he calls "lawyers' law"[2] – but in "The Path of the Law" he lamented Austin's lack of legal learning. "The trouble with Austin," he says, "was that he did not know enough English law."[3] Holmes's friend Frederick Pollock thought that assessment too kind:

> Thanks for the fresh copy of the Boston Address. I am a little bit disappointed that you only say that Austin did not know *enough* law. The truth is that his law is thoroughly amateurish – his Roman law worse than his English – and this is why he has a reputation among half-educated publicists.[4]

[2] Oliver Wendell Holmes, *Comment on* The Law Magazine and Review, *in* I CW 295 [hereinafter *The 1872 Jurisprudence Essay*].

[3] Holmes, *supra* note 1, at 403.

[4] I The Holmes–Pollock Letters: The Correspondence of Mr. Justice Holmes and Sir Frederick Pollock, 1874–1932 94 [hereinafter Holmes–Pollock Letters] (Mark DeWolfe Howe ed., 2d ed. 1961) (emphasis in original).

Holmes made his comment in the context of criticizing writers who, in analyzing legal ideas, "have been confused by striving for a useless quintessence of all systems, instead of an accurate anatomy of one."[5]

In this last clause we have a clue to Holmes's self-appointed task and orientation: the accurate anatomy of the common law as a system.[6] We have shown in Part I how Holmes drew the borders for jurisprudence – through his formal analysis of duty – even as he attempted, at the same time, to map the interior by classifying the range and types of duties.

Holmes also commented on the intuition, or tacit knowledge as we might say today, openly acknowledged as a source of common law decision-making. Judges and lawyers often knew how a case should be decided before they knew why. In this respect they were not unlike Lord Mansfield's businessman who would most times get the decision right but the legal reasoning wrong.[7]

Holmes may not have attempted in his early writings to analyze the source of the intuition that sensed the result before it understood the reasoning, but he knew that it had something to do with careful attention to the facts.

One who wanted to learn the common law had to pay close attention to the facts underlying decisions. And: they had to learn which facts were worth paying attention to.[8] Presumably, Lord Mansfield's businessman knew firsthand what the parties to a lawsuit should have done in certain circumstances. He probably had a sense of what the court should do to rectify the problem. Legal knowledge often involved connecting proposed court action in the present circumstance with court action in previous similar circumstances on the basis of cogent reasoning. Since the businessman qua businessman presumably did not know the articulated legal principle or the rules for its deployment, he would most likely get the decision right but the legal reasoning wrong.

Initially, Holmes seems to have viewed the common law as a system casuistic in nature. It involved the self-conscious application of reason to facts within a tradition that favored the limited use of state power. In this mode, disputes that made their way before a court presented ethical questions encapsulated in two "shoulds": Within the range of options available, should the court do anything? If so, which option should the court take?

5 Holmes, *supra* note 1, at 403.

6 For a recent discussion of Holmes's efforts to systematize the common law without undermining its pragmatic style of procedure see Gerald J. Postema, *Law's System: The Necessity of System in Common Law*, N.Z. Law Rev. 69, 70–74 (2014).

7 Oliver Wendell Holmes, *Codes, and the Arrangement of Law, in* I CW 212–13.

8 Holmes made the same point after he had been a judge for many years. Oliver Wendell Holmes, *Law in Science and Science in Law, in* III CW 412 ("The man of science in the law is not merely a bookworm. To a microscopic eye for detail he must unite an insight which tells him what details are significant. Not every maker of exact investigation counts, but only he who directs his investigation to a crucial point.").

The task of convincing the court fell mainly on the litigants' lawyers. From the point of view of the parties, the dispute merited – or did not merit – court intervention. From the point of view of the court, it had already become involved upon the filing of the petition or suit. At every step, a range of options presented themselves to the court. It could go forward or it could stop. The existing body of law – procedural and substantive – along with unwritten norms guided the institution. Given the complexity of the common law, the court invariably had an administrative function that differed in degree, and sometimes in kind, from the ideal function of dispensing justice.

In recognizing, however dimly, the difference between administering the law and dispensing an ideal justice, the student of the common law began to comprehend the institutional side to lawyers' law. That is to say, the stringency of the penalty both demarcated the boundaries of jurisprudence and helped structure within jurisprudence's borders the most evident institutions of law enforcement – from police and sheriffs to state attorneys to judges to wardens to probation officers (to use current examples).

We see a similar point of view in Blackstone even if the language is a bit different. In a passage that unnerved one of the earliest distinctly American legal thinkers, Judge Nathaniel Chipman, Blackstone commented on the institutional significance of the difference between acts *malae in se* and acts *mala prohibita*:

> [W]hen the law has determined the field belongs to Titius, it is matter of conscience no longer to withhold or invade. So also, in regard to natural duties, and such offences, as are *malae in se*. Here we are bound by superior laws, before those human laws were in being, to perform the one and abstain from the other. But in regard to those laws, which enjoin only positive duties, and forbid only such things, which are not *malae in se*, but *mala prohibita* merely, annexing a penalty to non-compliance, here I apprehend conscience is no farther concerned, than by directing a submission to the penalty, in case of our breach of those laws. For otherwise the multitude of penal laws in the state, would not only be looked upon as impolitic, but would also be a very wicked thing, if every breach of such laws were made a snare for men's consciences. But in these cases, the alternative is offered to every man, either to do this, or submit to the penalty, and his conscience is safe, which ever side of the alternative he sees fit to take.[9]

[9] *See* Perry Miller, The Legal Mind in America: From Independence to the Civil War 19–30 (1962) (providing a selection from Nathaniel Chipman's *Sketches of the Principles of Government*, 1793, in which Blackstone is quoted and criticized, and which broaches the fundamental problem of how, and on what basis, law in the new nation should be implemented); *see also* Daniel J. Boorstin, The Mysterious Science of the Law: An Essay on Blackstone's Commentaries 158 (1941) ("The *Commentaries*, moreover, went on and proved that in England not only was the individual free to make laws; he was actually in a sense free to disobey them."). This attitude also comports well with the standard natural law view that on many and various civil matters natural law is indifferent and positive law has much latitude.

Blackstone's attitude regarding the violation of positive duties, those merely *mala prohibita*, struck Judge Chipman as enervating the moral worth of law itself.[10] The institutional significance of Blackstone's pronouncement lay in its implied recognition of law's administrative function. Under this view, courts existed to resolve many disputes that had nothing to do with natural duties or acts offensive to the conscience of the community.[11]

A person could, according to Blackstone, in good conscience violate a positive legal duty as long as the person was willing, in equally good conscience, to submit to the annexed penalty.[12]

This Old World common law attitude disgusted many post-revolutionary, morally fervent Americans. For them, laws founded on the right principles of a democratic republic did not exist, nor were they enacted, simply to be broken. Thus ran the antiphony.[13]

Holmes, writing in the century after Judge Chipman lodged his objections to Blackstone's latitudinarianism, invokes Blackstone's sensibility in his discussions of the common law as a legal system as well as in his investigations of specific legal doctrines. Holmes, in effect, reorients the view of those acts classed as *malae in se*. The focus, for the student of the common law, centered not so much on the perceived nature of the act itself as on the enforcement consequence. The acts Blackstone considered violations of natural duties Holmes sociologically reformulates, through Austin's analytic, as contraventions of an absolute command.[14]

The practice of the common law – viewed as a developed approach to handling and reasoning about legal problems and not simply as a substantive, if disorganized, set of maxims and rules – required its practitioners, and those who lived under its

[10] MILLER, *supra* note 9, at 21–30. For an evaluation of how Chipman fits within the broader sweep of American legal history, see STEPHEN M. FELDMAN, AMERICAN LEGAL THOUGHT FROM PREMODERNISM TO POSTMODERNISM: AN INTELLECTUAL VOYAGE 80–81 (2000).

[11] On this point, see Holmes's interesting discussion of how the preventive theory of punishment justifies different enforcement options for acts *malum in se* and those *malum prohibitum*. Oliver Wendell Holmes, *The Common Law*, *in* III CW 138.

[12] MILLER, *supra* note 9, at 21–22.

[13] PERRY MILLER , THE LIFE OF THE MIND IN AMERICA 105–16 (1965).

[14] For one vibrant example from later in Holmes's career of his insight into how social changes (changes in perceptions and attitudes) including those expressed in dominant moral codes affect legal conceptions of duty and the attendant enforcement response, see his remarks regarding the recounting in Bradford's *History of Plymouth Plantation* of the ministers' discussion of whether a man should be executed for what appears to have been the crime of bestiality. Holmes notes how the "law of fashion," even in morals, affects the enforcement consequence against an unlawful act. In contrast to the seventeenth-century Pilgrims, many residents of that same part of the earth in the late nineteenth century would find the described acts repulsive ("disgust of normal men"); a curious few as an indicator of an abnormal physiology. Holmes acknowledged that the law of Massachusetts in 1899 still considered the acts the seventeenth-century divines discussed a "serious crime, but which is no longer often heard of in court." Holmes, *supra* note 8, at 407; *see also* WILLIAM BRADFORD, HISTORY OF PLYMOUTH PLANTATION 386–98 (Charles Deane ed., 1856).

sway, to inculcate a sense of proportionality in the use of the enforcement power. Even more to the point: we may postulate that Holmes recognized early in his career that the common law legal system, which most likely had developed from specific juristic practices, not overarching principles, had not emerged, or grown, in an aesthetically symmetrical or orderly fashion. Holmes did not emphasize, as Blackstone did, the classical beauty or the architectonic sublimity of the common law.[15]

The common law might be described in many ways; elegant should not be one of them. Blackstone notwithstanding, the common law did not display in its history a providential ordering.[16] It was more robust, down to earth; as a legal system, it reflected what Holmes calls expediency and employed what Holmes calls form.[17] In Holmes's view, the common law primarily requires of its thoughtful practitioners an attitude that brings to bear on specific legal questions considerations both intellectual and practical. He does not applaud the approach of the logically, morally, or philosophically proficient but unrealistic and practically inexperienced legal connoisseur.

2 THE TRANSMUTATION OF FACTS AND LAW

What kind of person do we want the study of law to create? "The business of a lawyer is to know law."[18] Holmes took this advice to heart and sought to learn not only what we call the black letter law, but also to understand how laws – defined broadly as rules of conduct connected to legal support or sanctions – formed, reformed, transformed, or fell into desuetude. Continuities and discontinuities, when recognized, lead one back to the question, "what is law?" Holmes undertook the challenge of understanding law and its transmutation from within the "well known profession" of common law lawyers and not through the use of extraneous heuristics such as the Roman civil code.

He sought in his many writings – most notably *The Common Law* – to verbalize the common law's inherent dynamics. By the time he delivered his 1897 address at Boston University Holmes had transposed the major and minor themes of his earliest scholarship. The drive to classify and achieve analytic clarity now took second place to the effort to uncover and elucidate what one may call the magistrate's intuition.[19]

[15] *See* Boorstin, *supra* note 9, at 85–105; Richard D. Cosgrove, Our Lady the Common Law: An Anglo-American Legal Community, 1870–1930 19 (1987) (noting that in the opinion of many late nineteenth-century American legal thinkers a major virtue of the common law lay in its lack of symmetry).

[16] Boorstin, *supra* note 9, at 62–84.

[17] *See* James Willard Hurst, Justice Holmes on Legal History 62 (1964) ("The life of the law represents no homeostatic, functionally self-adjusting process, but the product of the qualities and defects of men's will, imagination, and feeling.").

[18] Oliver Wendell Holmes, *The Use of Law Schools*, *in* III CW 479.

[19] By "magistrate's intuition," I refer to the ability to sense and discern what Holmes calls "the grounds of public policy." That is, the pressing motivations, the sense of right or "good sense"

Initially, Holmes had sought to organize and elucidate the legal heritage.[20] We saw this effort in "Codes, and the Arrangement of Law," and subsequent articles in which he tackled fundamental legal conceptions (*e.g.*, duty, succession) and laid out the boundaries of jurisprudence. Despite his avowed attempts to bring order and clarity to the "ragbag" of the common law, Holmes kept in mind that the common law, as evinced through the decisions of its judges, had a substratum of sentiment impervious to logical overhaul. This substratum revealed itself episodically in a judge's reflexive sense as to what ought to be done given a certain state of facts even when the judge did not know exactly why.

One could describe the "substratum of sentiment" as unrealized feelings and background referents. These feelings and connected referents reveal themselves only retrospectively, through some type of historical study or meditation.

In this alternate plot line, a judge many times had a "gut instinct" as to what action the presented facts, after the judge thoroughly understood them, called forth in response. Chancellor James Kent called it a "moral sense."[21] Holmes does not use that language. He uses the language of expediency and policy. Law, to keep its vitality as an ordering principle, simply could not bless an individual judge's moral intuitions or even unconscious policy convictions. That is why legal thinkers had to find a way to bring the intuitions and convictions to light. Law, as a practical activity, had to retain its capacity to direct attention, to provide pointers. Less self-assured judges than Chancellor Kent looked to law for education and guidance, not merely for justification of an already formed opinion.

For the common law dynamic to work, different parts of the legal enterprise had to retain the integrity of their position and roles. In his 1873 "The Theory of Torts" we can see the beginning of this change in Holmes's emphasis from ordering and classifying legal conceptions to limning and understanding the role of visceral predicates.

In this short piece, celebrated for its categorization of unintentional torts, Holmes begins by summarizing the legal duty analysis he had developed in earlier writings. A court-imposed tax on a certain course of conduct does not necessarily lead to the

that arose from and referred back to the life of the relevant community. Holmes, *supra* note 11, at 169 ("In such a matter no authority is more deserving of respect than that of Chief Justice Shaw, for the strength of that great judge lay in an accurate appreciation of the requirements of the community whose officer he was. Some, indeed many, English judges could be named who have surpassed him in accurate technical knowledge, but few have lived who were his equals in their understanding of the grounds of public policy to which all laws must ultimately be referred. It was this which made him, in the language of the late Judge Curtis, the greatest *magistrate* which this country has produced." (emphasis in original)). For a good overview of Shaw's career and a list of reasons why he merited Holmes's praise see Leonard W. Levy, *Lemuel Shaw: America's 'Greatest Magistrate'*, 7 VILL. L. REV. 389 (1962).

20 Oliver Wendell Holmes, *Introduction to* The General Survey, *in* III CW 440 ("When I began, the law presented itself as a ragbag of details.").

21 LAWRENCE M. FRIEDMAN, A HISTORY OF AMERICAN LAW 89 (2005).

inference that a duty has been violated; liability does not equate to culpability.[22] Holmes thought it important to re-emphasize this point because of the confusion he observed in modern (nineteenth-century) practice in pleading negligence. "[T]he abolition of the old forms of action has allowed pleaders to state their case according to their own views of its essential elements. What does modern negligence mean?"[23]

To answer this question, Holmes performs an interesting two-part preliminary analysis. First he sketches how the common law develops, or as he says, grows. Yet this "growth" of law is curiously static, determined through its own internal logic that cannot quite solve all its problems. He frames the development of law by initially positioning endpoints that served as polar opposites. "Two widely different cases suggest a general distinction, which is a clear one when stated broadly." Cases gathered at and framed the opposite ends of the line, but as they began to approach each other the original distinctions became increasingly difficult to trace. Beyond the evident analytical impasse, the evident perplexity sometimes suggested a vanishing point. Dormant partialities often took charge. "[T]he determinations are made one way or the other on a very slight preponderance of feeling, rather than of articulate reason[.]"[24]

Courts may draw what Holmes calls a "mathematical line," but he acknowledges that such lines though practically necessary are intellectually arbitrary. It then happens that the formerly clear distinction between two different kinds of cases begins to fade, not into the past, but into the present: new emerging cases – what Holmes calls "nice cases" – create perplexity as the formerly clear distinctions shade imperceptibly into each other. In such circumstances the only guide or source of law a judge may have is the previously quoted "very slight preponderance of feeling."[25]

Holmes in these passages insightfully conjectures on the role of feeling in judicial lawmaking. He would, in the fertile period between writing of "The Theory of Torts" and the publication of *The Common Law*, extend and fortify this insight through historical and anthropological investigation and study. He eventually arrives at the conclusion – which one can discern in *The Common Law* – that how a

[22] Oliver Wendell Holmes, *The Theory of Torts, in* I CW 326.

[23] *Id.* at 327.

[24] *Id.*; for a specific example of how a vanishing point may come into being see Oliver Wendell Holmes, *Possession, in* III CW 52 ("[I]f the peculiar doctrines of agency are anomalous, and form, as the writer believes, the vanishing point of the service status, it may well happen that common sense will refuse to carry them out to their farthest applications."). *See also* Holmes, *supra* note 11, at 233. Holmes's way of seeing the law evinced an artistic sensibility. On this topic Daniel Kornstein has provided a uniquely perceptive portrait and discussion in his book on Holmes, *The Second Greatest American*. DANIEL KORNSTEIN, THE SECOND GREATEST AMERICAN loc. 2471–679 (2017) (ebook) ("This artistic attitude animates his legal writings and judicial opinions. Holmes was an artist, expressing the spirit of the common law[.]" at loc. 2659. And: "As Cezanne is considered the hinge to modern art, the point of departure, Holmes too, by the same token, is the hinge to modern law." at loc. 994).

[25] Holmes, *supra* note 22, at 327.

common law judge may decide what we call a difficult case had similarities to how a legal historian working in nineteenth century Anglophone cultures might understand and frame the growth of a legal practice or doctrine.

The two modes of inquiry in many ways mirror each other. The legal historian works backwards following his or her professional conscience until he or she reaches a vanishing point,[26] that is, the point where the existing answer to the question "what is the law?" beaches on the shore of an ultimate, unifying reference point: perhaps some kind of shared feeling, or a natural response to a social fact, perhaps a sentiment subtle, perhaps one strong or hard (*e.g.*, a "felt necessity") that expressed itself through direct action under the auspices of the relevant community's approbation. The historian, in sum and at the risk of oversimplifying, proceeds from form to generative feeling.

In the circumstances presented by the difficult case, the common law judge, also following his professional conscience, embarks from the shore of discernible feeling in a boat called suitability until he finds a dock: that is, a way to connect the experienced "very slight preponderance of feeling" to an existing answer to the question "what is the law?" (a prevailing legal form). The sense of suitability allows

[26] In this respect, it is interesting to see how Holmes described his scholarly endeavors to James Bryce in 1879 before delivering the Lowell Lectures:

> I console myself by studying towards a vanishing point which is the center of perspective in my landscape – but that has to be done at night for the most part and is wearing, and my articles though fragmentary in form and accidental in order are part of what lies as a whole in my mind – my scheme being to analyze what seem to be the fundamental notions and principles of our substantive law, putting them in an order which is a part of or results from the fundamental conception.

Mark DeWolfe Howe, Justice Oliver Wendell Holmes: The Proving Years, 1870–1882 25 (1963). He made a similar comment, though more broadly stated, in a letter to William James years earlier:

> And the winter has been a success, I think, both for the simple discipline of the work and because I now go on with an ever increasing conviction that law as well as any other series of facts in this world may be approached in the interests of science and may be studied, yes and practiced, with the preservation of one's ideals. I should even say that they grow robust under the regimen, – more than that I do not ask. To finish the search of mankind, to discover the *ne plus ultra* which is the demand of ingenuous youth, one finds is not allotted to an individual. To reconcile oneself to life – to simply apprehend that this dream disturbing the sleep of the cosm [*sic*] is not the result of dyspepsy but is well – to suspect some of the divine harmonies, though you cannot note them like a score of music – these things, methinks, furnish *vanishing points* which give a kind of perspective to the chaos of events. Perhaps I am fortunate in what I have often made a reproach to myself.

Catherine Drinker Bowen, Yankee from Olympus: Justice Holmes and His Family 246 (1944) (quoting letter from Oliver Wendell Holmes to William James (Dec. 15, 1867) (on file with Harvard University – Harvard Law School Library / Howe, Mark DeWolfe. Research materials relating to life of Oliver Wendell Holmes, Jr., 1858–1968. General Correspondence, General, Group II: Box 16, Folder 18, James, William, correspondent, 1867–1907) (emphasis added).

the "slight preponderance of feeling" to express itself in a concrete decision that connects to other concrete decisions. It often connects to the existing law through policy rationalizations.[27]

The judge, in these specific circumstances, goes from feeling to form.

We see an example of the historian's approach in *The Common Law*.[28] In the opening chapters of that book Holmes tells a story of how various manifestations of

[27] In this respect, it is perhaps not inapposite to connect "policy rationalizations" – whether by a judge or a lawyer – to what Holmes calls "the spontaneous action of intelligence." Holmes uses this latter phrase to describe how lawyers understood or explained the doctrine of tacking in property law (it added the previous owner's time of possession to the buyer's to arrive at the needed time of possession to maintain the use of a right of way). The spontaneous action of intelligence, as a rationale for the formulation of legal doctrine, gave little attention to the mode of reasoning that the existing legal framework inculcated. How lawyers and judges reasoned from analogy, or what Holmes terms a "way of thinking," led to more credible explanations for specific legal doctrines than simply citing "the spontaneous action of the intelligence." Holmes was careful, however, to differentiate between the desirable advantages a doctrine provided and the habit of mind that led to its formulation. Oliver Wendell Holmes, *Primitive Notions in Modern Law, No. II, in* III CW 21, 29; *see also* Sheldon Novick's discussion of how Holmes conceptualized the mechanism of evolution, Sheldon Novick, *Introduction, in* I THE COLLECTED WORKS OF JUSTICE HOLMES 45–46 (Sheldon Novick ed., 1995) ("As society and its circumstances changed, the older forms of language and the law persisted. But ignorance of the past, and the process of rationalization, allowed judges slowly to infuse new ideas and purposes into old forms, and these incremental departures from precedent compelled law to evolve, at every stage reflecting, within the limits of precedent, the judges' unconscious perceptions of public policy, of what was to the advantage of the community from which the judges were drawn."). Novick's assessment emphasizes legal evolution as a matter of establishing continuities, what a prior generation called the "genetic method," but it does not recognize, as Holmes did, the unaccounted-for breaks or discontinuities. The standard work on legal evolution is Peter Stein's *Legal Evolution: The Story of An Idea*. He writes: "I have used the term legal evolution to describe a group of theories which claim to explain legal change not merely in historical terms but as proceeding according to determinate stages, or in a certain predetermined manner. In their fully developed form, such theories were essentially a nineteenth-century phenomenon and did not long survive the end of the century." PETER STEIN, LEGAL EVOLUTION: THE STORY OF AN IDEA 122 (1980). Interestingly, Stein's book contains no discussion of Holmes.

[28] I understand that for many scholars Holmes underperformed as an historian in *The Common Law*, or, worse yet, violated the most sacred canons of that profession. Robert Gordon, for example, notes that "an authentically historicist approach would try to understand why it might be *meaningful* to a particular people to treat trees and oxen ceremonially as human beings. Holmes's approach here does the opposite: His uses of history and anthropology lead him back through sociobiology to as reductionist a psychology as any of the classical ones." David Rabban in an extensive discussion of *The Common Law*'s historical sections repeatedly charges that Holmes "manipulated history to serve analytical goals," "sacrificed historical accuracy," and that the book is replete with historical errors.

Gordon's criticism amounts to the peeve that Holmes should have written a different book than the one he wrote. He should have written a book for scholars, historians or anthropologists primarily, not lawyers. In writing a book for the legal profession Holmes had to find a way to connect in exposition what he believed had happened in real life: that what nineteenth-century lawyers understood as the common law system had its antecedents in the early practices of so-called primitives. I think he was aware that much of the meaning of the primitive practices is opaque, at best, to moderns and most likely inaccessible. To have written a book examining the

liability, both for intentional and unintentional harms, had originated in revenge. Revenge – an example of a felt necessity outside the law – served as the vanishing point that organized and structured the story of liability's manifestations within the law.[29] Revenge signified both an opinion of wrongdoing and a feeling of blame.[30] It could not be directly seen, or touched, or heard; the word described the meaning of a unified, interrelated series of purposeful acts. Revenge provided the historian with the basis for a perspective on the past that did not depend on chronology. It ordered the historical story of liability's manifestations so that the elements made sense in relation with, and in proportion to, each other.[31]

In like manner a judge's "very slight preponderance of feeling," even if only evoked when the supposed dividing line between two species of cases had

meaningfulness of certain practices would hinder his ability to bring the past into the present and use history as a critical tool. That is why, I speculate, he demarcated his field of research through the overlap of passions he believed primitives and moderns shared. That still doesn't allow him to escape the full force of Gordon's criticism but it hints that he may have recognized the problem.

I have a harder time judging the merits of Rabban's criticisms, mainly because I don't have the skills necessary to review the original documents upon which Holmes relied. But it doesn't appear that Rabban does either. He relies on reports second- and thirdhand (for example, on Mark DeWolfe Howe who cites C. I. Fifoot). My main problem with the weight that Rabban gives his arguments regarding Holmes's dismal performance as an historian in *The Common Law* – manipulating the historical record, sacrificing historical accuracy for the sake of a thesis, and making many factual mistakes – is that it does not easily fit with the high praise other historians (which Rabban also recognizes) accorded to Holmes's book. Mark DeWolfe Howe began his introduction to the John Harvard Library edition of *The Common Law* by noting Maitland's remark that "for a long time to come [it] will leave its mark wide and deep on all the best thoughts of Americans and Englishmen about the history of their common law." Mark DeWolfe Howe, *Introduction*, *in* Oliver Wendell Holmes, The Common Law xi (Mark DeWolfe Howe ed., 1963) (citations omitted). Such high praise from that generation's acknowledged leading historian of English legal history is difficult to square with Rabban's criticisms. Howe himself explained in what sense Maitland's praise should be understood and how one should understand Holmes's historical work. *Id.* at xx–xxi. Rabban does not. He makes little effort to explain why Maitland would lavishly praise one who, at least according to Rabban, had so flagrantly violated the canons that guide historians. Nor does he attempt to explain why a leading historian of the common law in the succeeding generation, Theodore F. T. Plucknett, would continue to see Holmes as an eminent predecessor and pathbreaker. Indeed, Rabban does not even cite Plucknett's *Holmes: The Historian* in his book. *See* Robert W. Gordon, *Holmes's Common Law As Legal and Social Science*, *in* Robert W. Gordon, Taming the Past: Essays on Law in History and History in Law 50–74, 60 (2017) (emphasis in original); David M. Rabban, *The Historiography of* The Common Law, 28 Law & Social Inquiry 1184–93 (2003); David M. Rabban, Law's History: American Legal Thought and the Transatlantic Turn toward History 215–68 (2013); Theodore F. T. Plucknett, *Holmes: The Historian*, 44 Harv. L. Rev. 712, 712–16 (1931).

29 Holmes, *supra* note 11, at 115–34, 134 ("My aim and purpose have been to show that the various forms of liability known to modern law spring from the common ground of revenge.") *See also id.* at 136 ("Others, without this logical apparatus [Hegel's], are content to rely upon a felt necessity that suffering should follow wrong-doing.").

30 *Id.* at 116.

31 *Id.* at 115–34.

disappeared, could structure the law going forward because either the same or similar intuition of some embedded value might lead others to analogous judgments. Or, in other instances, succeeding judges might treat the first decision as authoritative. It may, in fact, initiate the development of a new legal polarity with its own distinctive yet unfathomed vanishing point.

We have to remember that for Holmes the purpose of the practice of law is to fashion rules of conduct or, perhaps better put, to clarify legally enforceable duties in the context of a given state of facts. The purpose of law as an enforcement activity is to achieve a certain objective.

As part of his effort to explicate modern negligence Holmes provides in "The Theory of Torts" a brief prolegomenon to how judge-made law in a common law system develops in the face of novel circumstances. He recognizes feeling or sentiment as a source of law – perhaps in some instances a primary but not exclusive source of law. He still, at this point, has not acquired a sense for how such feelings attained durability and depth. He simply observes that in those "nice cases" where the preponderance of feeling might move the needle, common law judges also had recourse to jurors who represented the average opinion or common sense of the community. The jury in these instances had to assist the judges' efforts to articulate a rule of law.[32] Holmes still viewed law in only two dimensions, not three. He had not yet unified his sense of history with his sense of law.

The second part of Holmes's brief preliminary analysis in "The Theory of Torts" moved from a description of the morphology of law to a description of the activity of law finding as an instituted practice. Here Holmes shifts to a viewpoint internal to lawyers' law.

> Law as law is an agent, influencing conduct by motives, and applying consequences. Before law can act, however, either upon the private citizen or the judge, when, as in civilized communities, it is not directly addressed to an individual by the sovereign, a preliminary investigation of fact must be made.[33]

Holmes describes those facts to be found as the class of facts that suggest a rule of law.[34] It is the court itself seeking to answer the question, "what is the law?" Holmes observes how through usage and precedent certain facts of this class – say, certain customs – no longer require judicial inquiry, "the courts simply satisfy themselves from the precedents that their predecessors have laid down a rule of law."[35]

The instituted court practices for ascertaining the applicable rule of law had over time, Holmes notes, regularized themselves to economize on judicial resources.

[32] Holmes, *supra* note 22, 328–31. That is, by making certain findings of fact the jury assisted the court in converting a given state of facts into a corresponding rule of law.

[33] *Id.* at 328.

[34] *Id.*

[35] *Id.* at 329.

Judges approached cases of negligence by first looking to see where the authoritative, and commanding, rule of law lay:

> In some cases the fact, the belief of which controls the action of judges, is an act of the legislature; in others it is public policy, as understood by them; in others it is custom or course of dealing of those classes most interested; and in others where there is no statute, no clear ground of policy, no practice of a specially interested class, it is the practice of the average member of the community – what a prudent man would do under the circumstances – and the judge accepts the juryman as representing the prudent man. But still the function of the juryman is only to inform the conscience of the court by suggesting a standard, just as when the finding is on a custom.[36]

In Holmes's rendition of how the common law develops, the main judicial function of the jury is not to decide what are commonly called "issues of fact" – that is, issues of credibility, of deciding which assertion, the plaintiff's or the defendant's, is more likely to be true – but to suggest a rule of conduct to the court.[37] Or, as Holmes memorably and importantly puts it: "to inform the conscience of the court." It is the court's belief that the "practice of the average member of the community" carries weight that puts the outcome of the jury's deliberations on par with an act of the legislature.

In viewing the jury's role in this way, Holmes projects at least one insider's view of how the common law developed and, more to the point, should continue to develop. His refusal to define negligence solely in terms of culpability (in the sense of moral blameworthiness) reflected a professional bias as much as an historical and philosophical objection.

Culpability, though necessary to the criminal law and to some extent for the law of torts, could at times hamper criminal or tort law's development because it directed focus to an individual mindset or disposition and not to an external standard. Or, more accurately, culpability, as the counterweight to the fact of an experienced injury, directed the sufferer's attention – or the attention of the victim's proxies – through a series of inferences regarding the injury's source.[38] Historically

[36] *Id.* at 330; *see also* Oliver Wendell Holmes, *Notes to* Kent's Commentaries, *in* II CW 196–98 ("When there is no definite fact, such as a statute, a precedent, a custom, or a rule of public policy, a belief in which determines the action of judges, they sometimes accept what would be the conduct of a prudent man – meaning thereby of the jury – as their standard.").

[37] Holmes, *supra* note 22, at 330–31 ("If it [negligence] means simply that in certain cases it is not exactly determined what overt acts will make a man liable, the function of the jury is in theory continually vanishing.").

[38] The relation between the terms "revenge" and "culpability" in Holmes's articles written before *The Common Law* and in *The Common Law* itself has caused confusion. G. Edward White professes to find an utter incompatibility if not reversal in Holmes's argument. Clearly, there is some inconsistency of usage (see *infra* n. 39). Yet part of the problem is the lack of clear language, in Holmes's writings and in subsequent commentators', as to what "revenge" or "culpability" means or meant or could have meant. More to the point, it is possible that early

speaking, Holmes argues in "The Theory of Torts," the external facts were primary in the common law, not intent.[39] Culpability, like revenge, functioned best when it remained a limit condition.

Between "The Theory of Torts" and *The Common Law* Holmes engaged in an intensive course of study that ultimately resulted in a series of carefully written, concentrated articles that developed ideas, themes, and points of view that eventually found fuller expression in *The Common Law* and later writings.[40] The most well known of his ideas, the common law's tendency, evident in various of its departments, to shift from an internal standard of liability to one external, depended for its fullest articulation on Holmes's own nuanced historical and psychological investigations for how groupings of established facts became law.

Holmes showed an abiding fascination for how social facts – that is, interrelated actions or human conduct and behavior as opposed to natural events – became law (acquired concrete legal meaning) and how law, in turn, became the preferred cultural avenue by and through which a society controlled its growth and expansion. At the same time law itself as a culturally instituted practice also expanded. But it had done so through fits and starts, lurching this way and that, propelled unaware by the crosscurrents of experience. To orient itself the American legal profession, in these circumstances, had to become more self-aware, more self-conscious of its own lawmaking capabilities. It had to realize the deficiencies of its preferred form of reasoning, logic. It had to acquire a sense of historical depth.

Part of this newfound awareness included the developed appreciation for how given states of facts, whether inside or outside institutional practice, transmuted, over time, through law into institutional habit or into an authoritative rule of conduct. Holmes made this point succinctly, if opaquely, at the end of lecture I of *The Common Law*:

antecedents to conceptions of blame, as Holmes saw it, had what we would call genetic connections to later full-blown conceptions. Holmes says that revenge "imports" (signifies or brings in) both a feeling of blame and an opinion of wrongdoing. White found this assertion unfounded and on the whole misleading. I do not. I think part of the problem is that Holmes is trying to find a way to make what he calls the "savage mind" comprehensible to a sophisticated late nineteenth-century sensibility (the "modern mind"). The hermeneutic objective presents a difficult, perhaps impossible task. Even more so for Holmes who did not excel in expository communication. *See* G. Edward White, Justice Oliver Wendell Holmes: Law and the Inner Self 155–57 (1993); Oliver Wendell Holmes, *Primitive Notions in Modern Law, No. I, in* III CW 9 (stating that "the savage mind well represents the childish [or primitive] stage"); *see also* Howe, *supra* note 26, at 186–87 (noting that Holmes repudiated an earlier opinion that some liabilities in tort had always been absolute).

39 Holmes, *supra* note 22, at 326 ("The old writs in trespass did not allege, nor was it necessary to show, any thing savoring of culpability.") *But see* Holmes, *supra* note 11, at 117 ("But whatever may have been the early law, the foregoing account shows the starting-point of the system with which we have to deal. Our system of private liability for the consequences of a man's own acts, that is, for his trespasses, started from the notion of actual intent and actual personal culpability.").

40 *See* White, *supra* note 38, at 128–29.

> It remains to be proved that, while the terminology of morals is still retained, and while law does still and always, in a certain sense, measure legal liability by moral standards, it nevertheless, by the very necessity of its nature, is continually transmuting these moral standards into external or objective ones, from which the actual guilt of the party concerned is wholly eliminated.[41]

The resulting forms or usages may be different in each context (institutional or more broadly cultural) but the transformations bore striking similarities. The job of lawyers – or, more broadly, the law's job in society – lay in consciously regulating these transformations. Regulating might mean furthering them along – self-consciously advancing the transmutation of facts into law through the articulation of legal principles and social goals – or the opposite. The opposite would be an activity akin to deracinating: established law torn up by the roots and examined. Or, in a less organic and more conceptual metaphor, deconstructing the magistrate's intuition.

In Holmes's view lawyers should be trained to do both.

3 LAWYERS' LAW AND ITS MODES

Law's prevalence in the twentieth century, of which Simpson made especial note,[42] seems to have differed in kind or perhaps in degree from what had in the previous century been the norm in the United States. It is hard to speak with any precision on this topic, however. If we use Holmes's own assertions as indicators it seems that even when custom, usage, and ad hoc common law or equity decisions predominated the felt pervasiveness of law in society may have been hardly different in terms of conscious effects than in an era heavy with legislation, regulations, and rules.[43]

The focus of Simpson and other commentators on the law's prevalence draws attention to the increased ambit of conscious legal action. Scholars such as Lawrence Friedman have used a wide-angled lens to show how legal institutions in American history have functioned in the service of mainly economic and political interests.[44] That law – in the sense of case decisions, formal enactments, or administrative regulations – displays an instrumental quality – as a means toward an end – few, including Holmes, would dispute.

[41] Holmes, *supra* note 11, at 134.

[42] A. W. B. SIMPSON, INVITATION TO LAW 1–27 (1988).

[43] *See* William J. Novak, *Law, Capitalism, and the Liberal State: The Historical Sociology of James Willard Hurst*, 18 LAW & HIST. REV. 97, 134 (2000) ("Indeed, one of the most important (if often overlooked) of Hurst's discoveries about nineteenth-century American law was the extensive use of regulatory powers that imposed 'substantial burdens upon individuals for the sake of group interests.'") (quoting HURST, *supra* note 17, at 72).

[44] *See* FRIEDMAN, *supra* note 21; LAWRENCE M. FRIEDMAN, AMERICAN LAW IN THE 20TH CENTURY (2002).

Holmes is of course credited for bringing to the fore this instrumental quality of law and using it as evidence that more is involved in legal decision-making than drawing logical inferences from precedent or first principles. One is invariably led to quote from the opening paragraph of *The Common Law*: "The life of the law has not been logic: it has been experience."[45] The juxtaposition of law's instrumentalism with its prevalence has contributed to an ongoing awareness of law's extension as a mode of social manipulation and control that finds its genesis not in the dictates of reason but in the necessities of experience.

The awareness of law's extension as a mode of social control is just one step away from the realization that regularities in the manner of control permit prediction. Thus arises, one might think, the prediction theory of law. H. L. A. Hart famously criticized the prediction theory of law (what the court or law enforcement officials would do in fact) as an external viewpoint that had no cognizance of the internal point of view.[46]

According to Hart, the observer who employs the external point of view treats the red traffic light as a "sign" – a "natural *sign that* people will behave in certain ways, as clouds are a *sign that* rain will come[.]"

> In so doing he will miss out on a whole dimension of social life of those who he is watching, since for them the red light is not merely a sign that others will stop: they look upon it as a *signal for* them to stop, and so a reason for stopping in conformity to rules which make stopping when the light is red a standard of behaviour and an obligation .... For them the violation of a rule is not merely a basis for the prediction that a hostile reaction will follow but a *reason* for the hostility.[47]

Apart from questioning the soundness of the foregoing criticism, the student of Holmes notes two points of overlap with Holmes's theory of legal study: the notion of law as a "dimension of social life," and Hart's recognition of the existence of, if not the constant interaction between, different points of view.

i *The Dimensions of Lawyers' Law*

Early in his scholarship Holmes compared the social expectation that one wear an evening dress when dining with sophisticated Londoners with a dormant New York statute prohibiting usury and asked: "[i]n the nature of things, which is most truly law[?]"[48] The answer to Holmes's rhetorical question under the operative terms that Holmes articulated is neither. The social rule is not law, even if enforced, because the ultimate enforcement body is not a court, and the dormant New York usury

45 Holmes, *supra* note 11, at 115.

46 H. L. A. Hart, The Concept of Law 88–90 (2d ed. 1994) (emphasis in original).

47 *Id.* at 90 (emphasis in original).

48 Holmes, *supra* note 7, at 215.

statute is not law because the prosecuting authority (or aggrieved private litigant) either does not ask or finds it nearly impossible to convince a court to enforce it.

Holmes uses the viability of court enforcement to draw attention to a recognized legal duty and its connected penalty as law's most pronounced aspect. Working from this insight he employs his scholarship to scale the various dimensions of what he calls "lawyers' law"[49] – the thinking and practice internal to the profession – into a relatively unified whole.

Scholars have recognized that in *The Common Law* Holmes broke with the customary ways of writing a study in jurisprudence.[50] Holmes brought to bear on the book an historical awareness and sensibility reminiscent of German scholarship, analytic tools drawn from the English tradition, and a preoccupation with "theories of legislation" or "public policy" that would become the hallmark of American legal scholarship in the twentieth century.[51] *The Common Law* is learned but not obviously elephantine in erudition. It is unified; it is angled and directed; it develops a theme; it triangulates a point of view. It provides proportionately minimal support in relation to the boldness of its claims. Its chief value lies not in its scholarship but in how it models a three-dimensional conception of law. It is written not for philosophers or historians but primarily for practicing judges and lawyers and legal scholars, the bench, the bar, and the emerging legal academy.[52] It is an extended argument, a

[49] Holmes, *supra* note 2, at 295.

[50] Frederic Rogers Kellogg, The Formative Essays of Justice Holmes: The Making of an American Legal Philosophy 7 (1984) ("The unique contribution of *The Common Law* clearly lies in a break from European legal scholarship."); White, *supra* note 38, at 193 ("The result is that *The Common Law* evades any effort, even that of contemporary reviewers, to make it into a stereotyped or even 'representative' late nineteenth-century work of scholarship. Its historicist emphasis may ultimately be subversive of its 'scientific' orientation, and its policy imperatives may overwhelm its treatment of historical evidence . . . . His vivid, cryptic, but at the same time cautious and qualified language makes it extraordinarily difficult to locate the book in time.").

[51] *See* Thomas C. Grey, *Holmes and Legal Pragmatism*, 41 Stan. L. Rev. 787, 805–15 (1989). Grey appreciates the innovation Holmes undertook in writing from viewpoints that focused on law as experience, logic, and prediction. He does not think Holmes successfully performed the feat in *The Common Law*, which Grey believed to be a book "deeply flawed by sentimental legalistic antiquarianism."

[52] Holmes, who practiced law for a number of years before becoming a judge, recognized the contributions that both lawyers and judges made to legal decision-making. Oliver Wendell Holmes, *The Law*, *in* III CW 469 ("But if not of the Bench, shall I speak of the Bar? Shall I ask what the court would be, unaided? The law is made by the Bar, even more than by the Bench[.]"). *See also* Gerald J. Postema, Legal Philosophy in the Twentieth Century: The Common Law World 57–64 (2011) (observing that Holmes's positivism "still moved within a basically common-law jurisprudential framework and the focal point within that framework is the courts; the jurisprudential perspective was that of lawyers and judges working within the practice of law, not social scientists standing outside it."); White, *supra* note 38, at 195 ("Its [*The Common Law's*] arguably greatest contribution – Holmes' recognition that the law is simultaneously influenced by internal professional and extralegal factors, and that legal doctrine is the product of a complex interaction between those sets of factors – was not emphasized by contemporary reviewers and has been largely ignored or oversimplified by

brief if you will, for the profession to instill in its members a clearer sense of and a deeper feel for law and its practice.[53]

Given the conditions of late nineteenth-century society – the many problems related to expanding and diverse populations, shifts in cultural and political power, the increase of economic wherewithal and economic disparity, and within the legal profession a reorientation of procedure and practice – *The Common Law* seeks to restate the common legal heritage in a manner fitting to the circumstances.[54] How the profession should proceed, how lawyers' law should be studied and practiced, especially at a time when many traditional markers – forms of common law pleading, for example – had disappeared or diminished in importance, are the unstated but pertinent issues. To the hurly-burly of everyday legal practice, Holmes counterpoises a methodological principle – a way of thinking about law – that recognizes how law, as he said, by the very necessity of its nature transmutes facts into rules, and how rules, in turn, become new facts.[55]

The obscurity of Holmes's statement lessens when one bears in mind Holmes's fundamental difficulty: how to keep strong law's vitality and legitimacy as an ordering principle (for instance: how to prevent court action from degenerating into naked command) in a society buffeted by, and which has become acutely conscious of, the struggle and contest among and between varied interests. Many commentators believe Holmes simply lauded, or acquiesced to, the predominance of brute political power. That opinion may be partly correct; but it often ignores

subsequent commentators."); Howe, *supra* note 26, at 158 ("Doubtless Holmes's call for a realistic analysis of the judicial process was inspired by his philosophical proclivities and antipathies, yet it could stir enthusiasm in minds less hostile than was his to metaphysical abstraction. His words had force and meaning not merely to philosophers but to practitioners and judges – to lawyers who cared little for history and less for philosophy but who sought for generality that was true to their own experience."); Mark DeWolfe Howe, *The Positivism of Mr. Justice Holmes*, 64 Harv. L. Rev. 529, 540 (1951) (noting that *The Common Law* was written for sophisticated and mature lawyers); Hessel E. Yntema, *Mr. Justice Holmes' View of Legal Science*, 40 Yale L.J. 696, 702 (1931) ("It is not to be forgotten that the subject of the lectures of *The Common Law* was not legal history but the common law system, and the principal addresses were to the profession – to law students and lawyers, not to scientists.").

53 As Hurst put it: "To insist [as Holmes did] that legal history be written to show what relevance events bore to meaningful questions was to insist that it be written to enlarge theoretical knowledge of the content and processes of social experience." Hurst, *supra* note 17, at 6.

54 Sheldon Novick sees the book's key theme leading to a restatement "of the whole body of common law as an instrument of social purpose – in this case, to avoid needless harm." Novick, *supra* note 27, at 45. David Rabban provides a more nuanced interpretation: "The pervasiveness of objective and external standards is the analytical theme that emerges most clearly from Holmes's book." Rabban, *supra* note 28, at 1184 (2003).

55 Thomas C. Grey notes the parallels between Holmes and John Dewey regarding the ends-means continuum. Grey did not expressly connect this philosophical perspective to Holmes's mode of analysis in *The Common Law* but it seems to me to fit. Grey, *supra* 51, at 850–63.

Holmes's undying faith in his profession, in lawyers' law, and his belief in the ultimate strength of the philosophic insight it could provide.[56]

The idea of liability connects *The Common Law* with Holmes's previously published articles. It also points forward to his subsequent jurisprudential writings, including "The Path of the Law."

Liability sums up several prominent features of law as a type of cultural behavior. In Holmes's use it synthesizes legal responsibility or fault. The synthesis can be instantaneous or the result of a drawn out procedure. Holmes is far from clear; but in keeping with his theory of how ancient German and Roman proto-legal procedures and institutions lay behind much of the common law he traces a type of apperception that primarily works off cultural similarities and seemingly natural, intuitive connections.[57] He employs this mode of analysis in imagining the progression of liability as an operative legal premise. From the "germ" (or seed) of revenge – which comprised socially acknowledged feelings of anger and hatred and a desire for vengeance along with socially understood opinions of wrongdoing or blame – arose legal procedures and doctrines for satisfying the demand for revenge and grafting upon the manner of resolution other important interests.[58] At the source existed what still is intuitively understood today: the implacable hurt, pain, or loss.

[56] Two examples: "Nor will his [the lover of the law] task be done until, by the farthest stretch of human imagination, he has seen with his eyes the birth and growth of society, and by the farthest stretch of reason he has understood the philosophy of its being." Holmes, *supra* note 52, at 469; And: Lawyers are specialists "because they have undertaken to master a special branch of human knowledge, – a branch, I may add, which is more immediately connected with all the highest interests of man than any other which deals with practical affairs." Holmes, *supra* note 18, at 476. *But see* Postema, *supra* note 52, at 46–48 (arguing that there is no coherent social or political philosophy in Holmes; his lauding of power and his savage skepticism regarding the human ability to bridge differences regarding different conceptions of the good masked his own unwillingness to think deep or hard about the issues).

[57] In an essay published almost twenty years after *The Common Law*, Holmes wrote of his continued fascination with morphology and transformation of ideas in the law. He explained it thus: "Surely a flower is not more unlike a leaf, or a segment of a skull more unlike a vertebra, than the executor as we know him is remote from his prototype, the saleman of Salic law. I confess that such a development fills me with interest, not only for itself, but as an illustration of what you see all through the law – the paucity of original ideas in man, and the slow, coasting way in which he works along from rudimentary beginnings to the complex and artificial conceptions of civilised [*sic*] life." Holmes, *supra* note 8, at 408.

[58] Holmes, *supra* note 11, at 132 ("We have now followed the development of the chief forms of liability in modern law for anything other than the immediate and manifest consequences of a man's own acts. We have seen the parallel course of events in the two parents, – Roman law and the German customs, – and in the offspring of those two on English soil with regard to servants, animals, and inanimate things. We have seen a single germ multiplying and branching into products as different from each other as the flower from the root. It hardly remains to ask what that germ was. We have seen that it was the desire for retaliation against the offending thing itself."); *see also* Oliver Wendell Holmes, *Agency I*, *in* III CW 344 ("So, framing a historical hypothesis, if the starting-point of the modern law is the *patria potestas* [paternal power], a little study will show that the fiction of identity is a natural growth from such a germ.").

Just as Holmes had used the concept of a legal duty to demarcate the outer reach of jurisprudence – to distinguish facts inside from those outside the protection of the law – he used liability to illustrate law's development within the established jurisprudential boundaries. Liability typified the mode of transmutation: "the story will also afford an instructive example of the mode in which the law has grown, without a break, from barbarism to civilization."[59] If in the province of jurisprudence duty worked synchronically as an orienting concept, liability did so diachronically.[60]

History provided the pivot point for understanding the relation between the two types of conceptions. Holmes cautions early in *The Common Law* that one should not expect too much or too little from history.

> I shall use the history of our law so far as it is necessary to explain a conception or to interpret a rule, but no further. In doing so there are two errors equally to be avoided by both writer and reader. One is that supposing, because an idea seems very familiar and natural to us, that it has always been so. Many things which we take for granted have had to be laboriously fought out or thought out in past times. The other mistake is the opposite one of asking too much of history. We start with man full grown. It may be assumed that the earliest barbarian whose practices are to be considered, had a good many of the same feelings and passions as ourselves.[61]

It takes some reflection to understand the complementarity of the two errors that Holmes identifies. On the one side lies the too little: one undervalues and leaves untapped the enormous potential of historical investigation for self-knowledge, either writ small or large, knowledge, that is to say, that decodes the instruments and materials available to the legal reasoner. The decoding may be needed most precisely when a legal ideal, conception, principle, method of reasoning, or mode of procedure carries the heavy patina of familiarity.

The mistake of asking too much of history is, one may assert, less often encountered, either in Holmes's time or our own. The expectation that history – either as an established discipline or as a watchword for evolution – would divulge the inner secrets of civilization seemed to Holmes to transform history from a genus of inquiry into a species of religion. How a barbarian understood the meaning of his suffering

59 Holmes, *supra* note 11, at 117.

60 Gerald Postema attempts to explain the relationship between the static and dynamic aspects of Holmes's thought – understood as the synchronic and the diachronic – in his chapter on Holmes. Postema, *supra* note 52, at 57–70. Postema's explanatory framework for Holmes's jurisprudence, though similar to that advanced in this study, shows little feel for the dialogic, inquisitive attitude that characterizes how Holmes thought lawyers must interact with the relevant past. Postema's style is too analytic and too disengaged from the legal profession to adequately convey the liveliness of Holmes's thought. His analysis would have benefitted from a close reading of *Justice Holmes on Legal History*. In that able and perceptive exploration of Holmes's thought, Hurst more productively, as will be seen in Part III, describes the diachronic elements as "sequence" and the synchronic as "context." Hurst, *supra* note 17, at 21–86. Postema, like most other scholars who write on Holmes, makes no mention of Hurst's valuable study.

61 Holmes, *supra* note 11, at 115.

became less important to Holmes than that he understood his suffering had a concrete source. It came down to how much trust, or faith, the historical inquirer could have in the existing artifacts and the available modes of inference to reveal the actual course of the past. Holmes thought it prudent to limit the category human to the overlapping feelings and passions that he believed both barbarians and moderns shared.[62]

Thus Holmes's contention that in the pre-legal world revenge informed liability fits squarely between the two errors he identified in the use of historical investigation and reflection. Revenge described a natural reaction to deliberately caused harm or injury. The anger and the passion for vengeance were understandable because they still existed; moderns felt revenge, perhaps not as acutely as their barbarian ancestors, but felt it they did. Both the opinion of a wrong done and the simultaneous feeling that held the perpetrator blameworthy motivated retaliation. Revenge, at one and the same time, established belief regarding the cause of the hurt, pain, or loss and determined the needed response.

Without delving into the psychological or anthropological accuracy of Holmes's assertions and assumptions, we can see that, jurisprudentially speaking, a society began to move from the pre-legal to the legal when it began to develop and enforce procedures for the manner in which a member or members of the society could seek revenge against another member or members. How a society developed and enforced specific procedures, and under what circumstances, are all questions of fact. How participants understood that enforcement's significance might not be a question a modern inquirer can answer with any assurance. To expect historical inquiry to answer fully questions of this kind may be asking too much of the discipline. But lawyers and judges are ordinarily not scholars. What they needed, in Holmes's view, was a defensible, sustainable working supposition that could clarify the legal mind by elucidating its dominant habits, and its principal instruments and materials.[63]

How does one do this? Holmes does it by first recognizing the reality of historical change, not merely at the surface of society, in political change or in assessments of cultural progress or decline for example, but at a deeper level of consciousness.[64]

[62] Novick sees a resemblance between Holmes's depiction of "human beings" as having basic psychological structures and the view of a structuralist such as Claude Lévi-Strauss. *See* Novick, *supra* note 27, at 45–46. *But see* Louis Menand, *The Principles of Oliver Wendell Holmes, in* Louis Menand, American Studies 35 (2002) (observing that Novick's conclusion that Holmes was a structuralist is one that can be called in many respects unique).

[63] As Hurst put it: "To insist that legal history be written to show what relevance events bore to meaningful questions was to insist that it be written to enlarge theoretical knowledge of the content and processes of social experience." Hurst, *supra* note 17, at 6.

[64] In this respect, Holmes commented on the inability of the great Roman jurists to provide sound explanations for certain legal rules they inherited: "The Roman lawyers, not looking beyond their own system or their own time, drew on their wits for an explanation which would show them that the law as they found it was reasonable." They had no awareness of a prior stage in human history when the "personification of inanimate nature common to savages and children[,]" must have been more prevalent. The movement out of such a mindset requires, for the lack of a better expression, a modification of consciousness that signals a deeper transformation than

He, for instance, criticizes a French legal historian, Claude Joseph Tissot, for his lack of "historical perspective" – that is, not realizing that changes in the modes of legal reasoning pointed to underlying transformations of human consciousness.[65]

Whether these underlying transformations or stages are instinctual or spiritual or some primal amalgamation of the two Holmes does not say and he does not need to for his purposes. He stays at the surface, surveying the terrain, recognizing that some of its features may be indicative of deeper geological changes.[66] If the legal mind is to acquire any depth of perspective it must disabuse itself of the notion that what is familiar today existed, in the same way and for the same reasons, yesterday and the day before yesterday. That is one point. The second is that the awareness of difference is of marginal use unless the difference itself can be positioned.[67]

One must understand the importance of cultural positioning to appreciate the significance of what Holmes wrought in *The Common Law*. He still believed duty the fundamental legal conception when he wrote the book. The sustained effort to control physical power through fixed, legitimated consequences permitted the development of a legal order. In this respect court enforcement – "what the court would do in fact" – provided the beginnings of a three-dimensional grid for the plotting of a legal order in a common law world.

Duty, as stated above, set the jurisprudential boundary. But for such a formal conception to be truly fundamental it had to prove itself efficacious. This required

simply fixing a failure to reason aright. Holmes, *supra* note 11, at 119–20. *See also* Holmes, *supra* note 38, at 9 ("Even among full-grown civilized Europeans, as Mr. Gote appositely remarks, 'the force of momentary passion will often suffice to supersede the acquired habit, and even an intelligent man may be impelled in a moment of agonizing pain to kick or beat the lifeless object from which he has suffered.' In such matters, the savage mind well represents the childish stage."). These comments put into question Saul Touster's assertion that *The Common Law* was a "failure" and that Holmes sacrificed jurisprudential breadth for the narrow intellectual securities of case law. Saul Touster, *Holmes a Hundred Years Ago: The Common Law and Legal Theory*, 10 HOFSTRA L. REV. 673, 685, 692–93 (1981).

65 Holmes, *supra* note 38, at 9 ("Tissot, however, from lack of historical perspective, did not sufficiently distinguish between the law of the Twelve Tables and that of Justinian; nor did he seem to recognize the descent of his second and third stages [proceeding against an animal symbolically; then abandoning that in favor of indemnity] from his first [animism that endowed an animal or the inanimate object with "life" and treated it accordingly]. He did not realize that the earlier institutions were not arbitrarily introduced as a matter of policy, or that the decemvirs were incapable of the comparatively civilized reasoning of Ulpian.").

66 For an excellent discussion of the "romantic" elements in Holmes's thought, especially relating to his sensitivity to the role of the instincts and unconscious, see Anne Dailey, *Holmes and the Romantic Mind*, 48 DUKE L.J. 429 (1998).

67 As Holmes put it in 1886, "They [the law professors at Harvard] have said that to make a general principle worth anything you must give it a body; you must show in what way and how far it would be applied actually in an actual system; you must show how it has gradually emerged as the felt reconciliation of concrete instances no one of which established it in terms. Finally, you must show its historic relations to other principles, often of very different date and origin, and thus set it in the perspective without which its proportions will never be truly judged." Holmes, *supra* note 18, at 477. One wonders to what extent the Harvard law professors actually said anything close to this in 1886 but Holmes did.

understanding how it played out in real life circumstances. It is not that Duty becomes operationalized as duties but that duties, for the sake of the development of the jurisprudential enterprise, become formalized as Duty. Understanding how duties played out required, in turn, that one understand the various interactions between the enforcement body and those called upon to obey.

Holmes models such interactions in *The Common Law*, especially the early chapters, through the same technique by which he framed the development of case law. He first posits a clear, indisputable instance, say, one person directly and intentionally harming another. The harm done was immediate and manifest. All the ancient legal materials at his disposal indicated that in such a circumstance the person harmed blamed the person who committed the intentional act. On this basis the person harmed sought vengeance. Whether the ascription of blame was justified does not matter because the question of moral signification's value is in many ways unanswerable. The ascription becomes in Holmes's use a postulated fixed point that seems plausible, especially given his limit condition of humans exhibiting similar feelings and passions.

Holmes then sets up the other endpoint, the clearly unintentional, accidental act that leads to some kind of injury: "even a dog distinguishes between being stumbled over and being kicked."[68] Thus we have two clear conceptions: the deliberate act and the accidental movement. We also have harms or injuries of varying extent. Holmes argues that the initially simple interaction, from intentional harm to the passion for revenge against the perpetrator to a socially recognized and approved way of retaliating (*e.g.*, the blood feud or the composition) and thus quieting the passion, extended – or grew or developed or evolved – into a more, from the legal point of view, complex interaction. The simple became complex as it moved away from the initial endpoints (an intentional grievous harm, an accidental but slight injury) toward less easily classified instances.[69]

But before turning to what Holmes in another context called "nice cases," let us pause and consider how Holmes presented the early forms of liability in *The Common Law*. He admits that his attempt to formulate a general theory of civil and criminal liability results from what he calls a study of tendencies.[70] It presents an interpretive thesis. It seeks to justify a novel interpretation of existing legal materials. Holmes approaches the common law as one steeped in its history and yet alert to topics of current concerns and modern points of view.

[68] Holmes, *supra* note 11, at 116; *see also* Oliver Wendell Holmes, *Trespass and Negligence*, *in* III CW 86 ("But vengeance is founded on the thought that a wrong has been done, and the feeling of blame, however much the opinion may be distorted from the truth by passion. Even a dog can distinguish between being stumbled over and being kicked.").

[69] *See* Holmes, *supra* note 20, at 439 ("As we follow it [history] from century to century, we see logic at work attempting to develop the concrete cases given in experience into universal rules, and the struggle for life between the attempted generalizations and other competing forms. We watch the metamorphosis of the simple into the complex.").

[70] Holmes, *supra* note 11, at 115–16.

In regards to liability – understood as both the manner in which harm is attributed to a source and the way in which that source is subjected to a concerted response – Holmes found the passion for revenge instrumental. When he says that "[o]ur system of private liability for the consequences of a man's own acts, that is, for his trespasses, started from the notion of actual intent and actual personal culpability[,]"[71] he is referring to what the person or people who felt the passion for revenge inferred from the occurrence of their hurt, pain, or loss and made real through their belief. Without the ability to attribute an actual cause, the victim's desire for revenge would flounder. For this reason Holmes insists on the importance of vengeance as both the "ground" of legal procedure and as the "principle" of early forms of liability. It imputes an interrelation. It gives meaning to an otherwise meaningless disorienting pain. Holmes repeats twice in the opening lectures that vengeance "imports" – in the sense of "signifies" or "brings in" – an opinion that "its object is actually and personally to blame."[72]

If vengeance is subject to the sway of belief, then when Holmes highlights the notions of actual intent and actual personal culpability he is referring to operative conceptions, insofar as they can be reconstructed, from which the modern system of private liability emerged. Or, to put it another way, if later scholars deem actual intent and actual personal culpability to have been the bases of liability they must also recognize that liability, as a legal form, melded the passion for revenge with other vital interests. The passion for revenge did not exist in a social vacuum; it depended on the prevailing mentality for its coherence and on those with enforcement oversight to modulate its vehemence.

Holmes, in essence, invites us in the opening chapters of *The Common Law* to consider the nature of a legal form – its emergence, its instantiation and definition – and how such forms become both the materials and means of legal reasoning. The legal mind, if one may use that expression, comprises congeries of attitudes, sentiments, rationales, purposes, and specialized modes of thought tied to specific institutions and forms. Liability, viewed in historical perspective, displays the multivalency inherent in its manifestations as well as an overall orientation. Such a perspective points up the wrongheadedness of taking a part (logic) for the whole.

Beyond revaluating the use of logic in the application of law, Holmes dwells on the fallacy inherent in ahistorical, presentist thinking that, seemingly naturally and

[71] *Id.* at 117.

[72] *Id.* at 116, 135. *But see* Gordon, *supra* note 28, at 50–74. Gordon believes Holmes undermined the potentialities of a historicist approach through the use of a reductive psychology:

> But an authentically historicist approach would try to understand why it might be *meaningful* to a particular people to treat trees and oxen ceremonially as human beings. Holmes's approach here [in the opening chapter of *The Common Law*] does the opposite: His uses of history and anthropology lead him back through sociobiology to as reductionist a psychology as any of the classical ones.

Id. at 60.

spontaneously, articulates the reasons or policies that support a legal rule. Holmes's target in the opening pages of *The Common Law* is not so much the formalist bogeyman, à la Langdell, as the habit of mind that prizes its own ingenuity and its own capacity to formulate justifications and policies with scant awareness of a legal rule or doctrine's background in time or sources in consciousness. Lawyers trained in "smartness" would rarely become masters of the profession or learn to appreciate fully its dignity.[73]

Holmes effectively uses the rhetorical device of antithesis to set the stage for the examination to follow. He first states the rule then the prevailing rationale:

- An animal of ferocious habits escapes from its owner and harms a neighbor. The owner proves that the animal's escape was not due to negligence but is still held liable. *Rationale*: Liability is justified even though the owner was not negligent at the moment of escape because the owner acted in a manner that merited legal liability at a prior moment in time, that is, when he first obtained custody of the animal.
- An employee driving a cart in the course of employment hurts a pedestrian. The employer is held liable, even though the employee, an independent person, caused the injury. *Rationale*: Liability is justified, according to both the Roman and analytic jurists, because the employer did not properly vet the suitability of the employee for the employment before hiring. If the employer responds by affirming he took all possible precautions, the jurists shift to an additional ground, that the employer ought to insure the public against the acts of his employees or that the public should have available a viable remedy.
- In 1851 Congress limited the liability of the ship owner to the ship and its freight. *Rationale*: The legislators justified the enactment on the grounds that liability should be limited to the amount ventured. An argument, Holmes noted parenthetically, also recited to support the use of the corporate form.
- Under English law an indictment for homicide must indicate the value of the instrument used. *Rationale*: According to Blackstone, the instrument of death is an "accursed thing," and should be forfeited to the king.[74]

Holmes shows that these different points of law, despite their purported rationales, may be traced to a single originating source. They exist as outgrowths of a single primitive notion – the desire for vengeance against the thing that did the damage.[75]

[73] Holmes, *supra* note 18, at 476 ("I fear that the bar has done its full share to exalt that most hateful of American words and ideals, 'smartness,' as against dignity of moral feeling and profundity of knowledge.").

[74] Holmes, *supra* note 11, at 117–18; *see also* Holmes, *supra* note 38, at 5.

[75] In *Primitive Notions in Modern Law, No. I*, he says: "Here is a medley of rules gathered from the four corners of the law, each with its more or less adequate reason, and each certainly showing no trace of connection with any other, yet all of which, with many others, as we shall

Holmes infers the underlying operative belief to be that liability actually inhered in the offending thing. The key descriptive term regarding both intent and culpability is "actual." Actuality, in the sense that Holmes uses it, often reveals itself through full-bodied strictures that spring up unbidden. It involves more than an isolated or insulated psychological event. To describe the experienced sense of actuality in the context of law Holmes coins the perfect phrase: "felt necessity."[76]

An intelligence – like Holmes's – alert to historical transformations, to psychological and sociological dynamics invariably laments the thinness of spontaneous rationales.[77]

Sustained reflection on forms of liability led Holmes to develop his thesis on the relations between form and occasion in the development of the common law. A rule or formula, said Holmes, arises in response to a need, custom, or belief. The rule or formula persists long after the circumstances that called it forth have passed from view. It partakes of what appears to be an eternal present. Indeed, the common law had traditionally located itself in the manifold of time through the phrase "the memory of man runneth not to the contrary."[78] But with the aid of artifacts and the honing of inference, inquirers learned that the presumed eternal present is specious, and one could begin to delineate the progression of a legal principle – typically not linear – by identifying what Holmes calls survivals. Oftentimes these take the form of a legal fiction, "which shadows, as fictions so often do, the facts of an early stage of society, and which could hardly have been invented had these facts been otherwise."[79]

Armed with this technique, Holmes supplements his previous analysis of the development of case law. In addition to identifying the relevant polar opposites, Holmes now believes he found the right combination of history and psychology to replicate on paper what he thinks happened in real life. In other words, he begins to position a "nice case" against background referents to determine the unknown – and to participants, perhaps unknowable – pressure points at work. If there were subconscious inclinations at work in rule formulation or justification – and it is difficult to know how to identify and measure such inclinations – then only by comparing different fundamental rules from different areas of the law could one perhaps reveal those inclinations.

Yet historical investigation and reflection did more than simply bring to light how a universal psychological attribute, the passion for vengeance, informed a specific

presently show, may plausibly be referred for their origin to the primitive notion [that liability attached directly to the thing doing the damage]." Holmes, *supra* note 38, at 5.

[76] Holmes, *supra* note 11, at 115.

[77] Holmes, *supra* note 8, at 414 (stating that inflated and unreal explanations are part of the danger of inventing reasons off-hand for whatever we find established in the law).

[78] For an interesting discussion of the provenance and uses of this phrase see Kunal Parker, Common Law, History, and Democracy in America, 1790–1900 28–35 (2011).

[79] Holmes, *supra* note 11, at 291.

cultural sensibility. It helped one develop a basis for viewing law with depth and perspective.[80] We come back to the topic of positioning.

In the opening pages of *The Common Law* Holmes wanted to understand how people in the past dealt with harms that did not fall within the two paradigmatic cases (a person's actual intent or accidental movement). Let us look at his first example, the ferocious animal that escaped and injured a neighbor. The fact is taken as established that the animal's escape was not due to the owner's negligence. Yet the neighbor looks to the owner for redress. What legal principle supports the neighbor's claim? The owner did not intentionally and directly cause the harm. The ferocious animal did. Why is the horrible event not simply accounted to accident, chance, fate, the will of God, or a turn of misfortune? Because, says the analytic jurist or the policy rationalizer, the owner acted negligently when he first captured the animal and brought it to where people live. And, those who act negligently should pay for the injuries due to their act.

In making these presumably sound arguments the jurist shows little sense for, or susceptibility to, a legal principle's peregrinations. The original legal principle in this case – the owner must give up the object that caused the harm – governed the imputation of fault. Fault or blame may be concentrated or dissipated. Revenge concentrates feeling and action toward a single endpoint: the ostensible source of harm. The opposite of revenge – for which we have no good words, except perhaps forgiveness or acceptance – dissipates feeling and unnerves action. The one who suffers simply buries her sobbing head in her hands or turns his face toward the stars and stares.

Holmes argues that a thoughtful scrutiny of the early legal traditions of different societies showed that the iteration of vengeance as an attempt to concentrate feeling and action depended as much on the broader cultural sensibility as the individual incident.

"And in curious contrast with the principle as inverted to meet still more modern views of public policy, if the animal was of a wild nature, that is, in the very case of the most ferocious animals, the owner ceased to be liable the moment it escaped, because at that moment it ceased to be owner."[81] This interesting juxtaposition of what Holmes identifies as a modern view, and, curiously, a "still more modern view" of public policy that led to the inversion of the principle of liability, captures Holmes's technique for fathoming the social and cultural origins of legal principles. Once he discerned that good sense must be latent in the principle that when an owner of a truly ferocious animal lost ownership upon the animal's escape –

[80] As James Willard Hurst noted: "Mr. Justice Holmes urged that we cannot understand the dynamics or measure the full dimensions of a legal order unless we look at it in time." And: "[T]o understand law's relations to men's social existence we need to recognize that a legal order has dimensions in time which determine its character, impact, and direction." Hurst, *supra* note 17, at vii, 3–4.

[81] Holmes, *supra* note 11, at 119.

however done and due to whatever cause – the owner no longer had liability for what the animal did, Holmes had in place a legal landmark (or, from another angle, an indicator of a vanishing point).

A legal principle initially encapsulated a particular policy, which, presumably, imported or signified the assumptions, presumptions, and interests of an entire society or, more often the case, of subgroups within the society with enough power to have their interests taken into account by those charged with formulating and enforcing law.

The intelligent use of history for the purpose of understanding law depended on constructing legal landmarks by which the felt necessities – of varying intensity – that existed in the present could be self-consciously recognized and measured.[82] Legal landmarks – we might even call them legal totems – structured the domain of law from the self-conscious point of view of the present. Conscious orientation to a landmark, or conscious opposition to it, existed as two ever-present possibilities. But every so often, when faced with nice cases, members of the profession had to think more deeply about the meaning of the landmarks and their value for the here and now. This type of thinking required the controlled use of history. Holmes sought to demonstrate the controlled use of history in *The Common Law*. He wrote for the legal profession, not for cultural anthropologists (more interested in the issues of cultural change and transmission) or professional historians (often more concerned with establishing the historical facts and their interrelations). He wrote for those charged to facilitate the ordering of a society.[83]

Holmes evidently thought it useful for lawyers and judges to consider the background referents for the legal principles or rules brought into play in deciding cases. On the one hand, they would not fall into the fallacy of merely justifying the principles or rules with on-the-spot policy rationales. Or simply follow an existing rule blindly. On the other hand, they would also recognize that inferences from precedent, even when defensible logically, often proved historically unsound – conclusions grafted on culturally discordant premises that appeared unified to the unaware because of fossilization.

82 *See* Holmes, *supra* note 8, at 412–13 ("The true science of the law does not consist mainly in a theological working out of dogma or a logical development as in mathematics, or only in a study of it as an anthropological document from the outside; an even more important part consists in the establishment of its postulates from within upon accurately measured social desires instead of tradition.").

83 In this respect, note Holmes's praise of W. S. Holdsworth's history of English law: "The line between antiquarianism and knowledge of practical importance is kept with tact. Enough is told to gratify disinterested philosophic curiosity, yet not more than should be read by any one who desires to understand his art." Oliver Wendell Holmes, *Review of* A History of English Law, *in* III CW 435. *See also* Howe, *supra* note 26, at 121 (noting that Holmes, and perhaps because of Holmes his generation, turned history toward emancipating rather than dogmatic uses).

Better, more sophisticated decision-making and argumentation required a more educated sense and feel for the domain of law and its history. At the rudimentary professional level practitioners must learn to discern, for instance, the different procedural or evidentiary rules that stood behind certain precedents.[84] Or, at a more macro political level, to recognize many personal beliefs or cultural opinions for what they were – the outpourings of individual or group proclivities. Members of the profession had to become more self-conscious of their own existence and place within the common law tradition. Holmes shows in *The Common Law* that a conscious awakening to and realization of law's depths did not necessarily lead, à la Blackstone, to aesthetic appreciation or acquiescence before law's majesty. He wants to make the common law come alive by showing its three-dimensionality. He then shows how it lives in the moment.

He reveals how, for example, when it came to adjudging the liability for a ferocious animal, or a slave or an employee, or even an inanimate object, like a ship, the motive force of revenge played a strong if unseen and vestigial role. It reached beyond its own endpoint of actual, intentional trespasses and influenced how the formulators and enforcers of law treated a person (the owner) whose action relative to the matter at hand could, from the opposite endpoint, be seen as slightly more than accidental.

The owners of the animal or ship or lethal instrument, or the employer of a worker, found themselves ensnared in law because vengeance had such a strong subterranean position in the culture. Yet, in time and through circumstance, the other endpoint made its presence felt: the recognized accidental movement – the unsuccessful caging of a ferocious animal; the inattentive employee; the object that proximately caused harm – that alleviated at times the stridency of revenge. New landmarks formed (eventually called composition or indemnification) that bowed to revenge but served, as well, the needs of the moment, what Holmes did not hesitate to call the greater good.[85]

[84] For example, in *Common Carriers and the Common Law*, Holmes twice comments in footnotes about the difficulties, when analyzing early decisions, of "distinguishing between principles of substantive law, and rules relating only to procedure." And: "so that the student is often at a loss to make up his mind whether the language of the court is merely relevant to the form of an action or the scope of a general issue, or whether it establishes a rule for the conduct of life." Oliver Wendell Holmes, *Common Carriers and the Common Law*, *in* III CW 67 n.*; 73 n.**.

[85] *See, e.g.*, Holmes, *supra* note 11, at 137, 138 ("If it be true, as I shall presently try to show, that the general principles of criminal and civil liability are the same, it will follow from that alone that theory and fact agree in frequently punishing those who have been guilty of no moral wrong, and who could not be condemned by any standard that did not avowedly disregard the personal peculiarities of the individuals concerned." And: "If this is a true account of the law as it stands, the law does undoubtedly treat the individual as a means to an end, and uses him as a tool to increase the general welfare at his own expense.").

ii *The Triangulation of Viewpoints*

For one bred in the common law the topology of law does not exist in the heavenly city of the legal philosophers. Nor does it mainly arise from decisions made daily in the chambers and anterooms of county or small claims courts. It exists within the ambit of the legal profession. Law as practiced, law as lived, law reasoned and reasoning, law as institution and as text, law as – in Simpson's terms – pointers for lawyers, or, in Roberta Kevelson's succinct phrase, "law as a system of signs," exists within, and for, the collective expertise of dedicated practitioners.[86]

The modern reader of Holmes may find interesting Holmes's repeated use of such laden words as "marks" or "imports" or "prophecies" when discussing law. We come back to Holmes's sensitivity to the multivalency – the often multiple and overlapping meanings and their shifts – expressed through specific legal terms and phrases within the circumstances in which they are, or were, articulated and enforced.

Holmes appears to have equated "tendencies" in the common law with the mode and direction of change in legal meaning.[87] It takes some instrumentation to navigate the opening chapters of *The Common Law*, especially in trying to understand how the system of private liability's origins in revenge – the paradigmatic style for ascribing actual intent and culpability (an internal standard) – morphed into a regime that seemed to favor what Holmes calls an external standard.[88]

Commentators have repeated, with approval, Hart's remark that *The Common Law* "resembles a necklace of splendid diamonds surprisingly held together at certain points by nothing better than string." The diamonds are the book's "marvelous insights into the genius of the Common Law and the detailed explorations of the dynamic of its growth[,]" while, on the other hand, "the string is the sometimes obscure and hasty argument, the contemptuous dismissal of rival views, and the exaggerations with which Holmes sought to build up the tendencies which he found actually at work in the history of the law into a tough, collective philosophy of society."[89]

86 Roberta Kevelson, The Law As a System of Signs 3–12 (1988).

87 Holmes, *supra* note 11, at 154–55 ("The law did not begin with a theory. It has never worked one out. The point from which it started and that at which I shall try to show that it has arrived, are on different planes. In the progress from one to the other, it is to be expected that its course should not be straight and its direction not always visible. All that can be done is point out a tendency, and justify it. The tendency, which is our main concern, is a matter of fact to be gathered from the cases.").

88 Frederic R. Kellogg, Oliver Wendell Holmes, Jr., Legal Theory, and Judicial Restraint 84 (2007) (stating that vengeance is the primitive "moral" standard of liability, later replaced by externality, or the prevailing community standard of prudent conduct under the relevant circumstances).

89 H. L. A. Hart, *Diamonds and Strings: Holmes on the Common Law*, *in* H. L. A. Hart, Essays in Jurisprudence 278 (1983) (*Diamonds and Strings* orig. pub. 1963). *See also* Postema, *supra* note 52, at 48 n.9; Hurst, *supra* note 17, at viii ("Most tantalizing, in his writing he offered only fragmentary insights or hypotheses concerning interactions of law and the general life. The

Hart and other commentators on Holmes often write of Holmes's tough-mindedness, or that he was hard-nosed and unsentimental, and through these descriptions often point to personal traits they consider cold, impersonal, and unappealing. Invariably, they draw lines connecting Holmes's outlook to his time fighting in the American Civil War. The brutality and harshness of that fratricidal conflict apparently reinforced the sneering, unsympathetic qualities of Holmes's personality.[90]

As a counterpoint to this opinion one is tempted to set up a thought experiment: if the Civil War had never happened, and Holmes had never fought in a real battle, and suffered injuries, and watched his comrades and friends die, but in all other respects his life stayed more or less the same and he still pursued the study of the common law with the same fervor and single-minded dedication as he did after leaving the battlefront, would he have arrived at different convictions or arguments regarding the development of the common law and its tendencies? My own response is probably not.[91]

My answer has less to do with what Emerson called the "iron wire" of temperament than it does with the intrinsic nature of the subject matter.[92] The study of the common law, in the way a serious student of law studies it, is not a pretty business.[93] An intensive study of not only the early history of the common law but also that of

reader who is not a specialist remembers his principal book chiefly for these flashing fragments; yet, they are only fragments.").

90 *See, e.g.*, Postema, *supra* note 52, at 46–48. John M. Kang refers to the common opinion among those who have written on Holmes that the Civil War decisively changed his outlook as the "Civil War Thesis." Kang thinks it has been overblown, especially in the hands of such people as Louis Menand. Kang believes that Holmes's moral ideal of manliness endured the Civil War and became stronger thereafter. This fixation on manliness, not his wartime experience, best explains certain features of Holmes's thought and personality. John M. Kang, Oliver Wendell Holmes and the Fixations of Manliness 62–77 (2018).

91 My initial hunch found confirmation when I subsequently ran across Holmes's November 1902 Address to Boston's Tavern Club. Oliver Wendell Holmes, *Address at Tavern Club Dinner*, *in* III CW 534. *See also* Susan-Mary Grant, Oliver Wendell Holmes: Civil War Soldier, Supreme Court Justice 114 (2016) ("Undoubtedly Holmes saw life as a battle, the law as the rules of engagement, but the fact of his having been a soldier may not have informed this perspective to the degree sometimes assumed.").

92 Ralph Waldo Emerson, *Experience*, *in* Essays and Poems by Ralph Waldo Emerson 237 (Peter Norberg ed., 2004) ("Life is a train of moods like a string of beads, and as we pass through them, they prove to be many-colored lenses which paint the world their own hue, and each shows only what lies in its focus .... Temperament is the iron wire on which the beads are strung.").

93 Kellogg, relying on Gerald Postema's study of the common law, points out how Holmes's notorious skepticism had an alternate source than his Civil War experiences or his temperament: It "was part of the strategy of traditional common law theory in challenging the defenders of the centralized state in their problematic reliance, like that of Hobbes, on sovereign natural reason." Kellogg, *supra* note 88, at 102 (citing Gerald J. Postema, Bentham and the Common Law Tradition 60–71 (1986)).

other legal traditions (mainly Roman and of medieval Catholicism) or of what nineteenth-century writers called "primitive times" leads one straightaway to epochs and eras of human history where the means for lawfully avenging a wrong or enforcing an obligation seem heinous to a modern, sensitized sensibility.

Holmes knew he lived during a time when the "social instincts of man" had not yet grown to control "his actions absolutely, even in anti-social situations."[94] Perhaps this "time" of which Holmes speaks would be a permanent feature of human experience, perhaps not. Regardless, Holmes determined to be true to his beliefs – that is, to say or do what appeared right to him and his particular assortment of "can't helps" – and, just as important, to recognize the activity of law for what it was and what it should be.[95] "[R]ules of law are or should be based upon a morality which is generally accepted, no rule founded on a theory of absolute unselfishness can be laid down without a breach between law and working beliefs."[96]

To this "positivism" of approach Holmes adds the nuance and insight only achieved through intense immersion in the intricacies of the subject matter.[97] For him the key question centered on the viability of the internal standard as a measure of both criminal and civil liability. Holmes believed due to his historical and psychological studies that revenge had indelibly impressed the internal standard with its marks. He also believed that when viewed as a whole the legal materials at his disposal – the cases, the medieval and modern treatises and legal guides – supported the strong inference that those in the past who thought about and administered the legal rules to which Americans looked for guidance had begun to enunciate principles for liability that did not find their ultimate source in revenge.

It is often difficult for us to follow Holmes because our intellectual priorities are different and our intellectual training, broadly speaking, is so out of step with his. Holmes grew up learning Greek and Latin.[98] He grew up in a social environment that valued broad learning and prized the creation and fortification of a refined cultural sensibility. This educational style valued tradition even if at various points it rebelled against the received wisdom. Many commentators on Holmes do not possess the language skills he had nor have they cultivated the same breadth of

94 Holmes, *supra* note 11, at 137.

95 Oliver Wendell Holmes, *Ideals and Doubts*, *in* III CW 443 ("When I say that a thing is true, I mean that I cannot help believing it. I am stating an experience as to which there is no choice. But as there are many things that I cannot help doing that the universe can, I do not venture to assume that my inabilities in the way of thought are inabilities of the universe. I therefore define truth as the system of my limitations, and leave absolute truth for those who are better equipped. With absolute truth I leave absolute ideals of conduct equally on one side.").

96 Holmes, *supra* note 11, at 137.

97 On this topic one must quote Hurst: "The younger Holmes spent himself unstintingly to reduce the crude ore of the Yearbooks and Reports to the pure metal of *The Common Law*." Hurst, *supra* note 17, at 33–34.

98 Howe, *supra* note 26, at 141 ("His education in the classics made it easy for him to work in the materials of Roman law.").

understanding and perception.[99] Scholarly apparatus normally mitigates these handicaps in other areas of study. A well-versed scholar, or group of scholars, usually provides relevant translations, background references, explanations, and annotations that seek to bridge the intellectual divide between author and reader.

It comes as something of a shock, then, to the untutored student of Holmes when the realization sets in that the scholarly apparatus for the oeuvre of the person Morton J. Horwitz described as America's only great legal thinker is so woefully underdeveloped.[100] Critical editions of *The Common Law* and of Holmes's earlier scholarship, for example, do not contain translations of his many quotes from medieval or early modern authorities.[101]

Be that as it may, one also senses that part of the reason for the lack of appreciation for Holmes's scholarly style is because many commentators do not share Holmes's strong commitment to keeping open and supple the bonds between the two questions that form the double helix of the profession: "what is the law?" and "what is law?"

Holmes's firm, uncompromising attention to this legal double helix suggests how his mind moved as it developed the needed reference points to support his thesis of the shift from an internal standard of liability to an external one. After establishing in lecture I the correspondence between the passion for vengeance and the internal standard, he asks, in the opening pages of lecture II, the following:

> The question is whether such a standard [the internal standard] is still accepted either in this primitive form, or in some more refined development, as is commonly supposed, and as seems not impossible, considering the relative slowness with which the criminal law has improved.[102]

As Holmes considers this question he first zooms in on the historic importance of using punishment – in the sense of inflicting pain for the sake of pain and for no

[99] David Rabban comments that Holmes was part of that "founding generation of professional legal scholars" who were more "cosmopolitan, more learned, and more internationally respected than many of the people who have misrepresented or neglected them." Rabban, *supra* note 28, at 1.

[100] Morton J. Horwitz, *The Place of Justice Holmes in American Legal Thought*, *in* The Legacy of Oliver Wendell Holmes, Jr. 31 (Robert W. Gordon ed., 1992). By same token, David Rosenberg calls Holmes "the most illustrious jurist in American law." David Rosenberg, Hidden Holmes: His Theory of Torts in History 1 (1995).

[101] For this reason, one understands why many commentators may find fitting Hart's likening of Holmes's argumentation, in places, to a dinky string holding together his diamonds of insight. Even though Hart himself, who studied classics at Oxford, would presumably have had enough skill in the relevant languages to make sense of what Holmes wrote. *See, e.g.*, White, *supra* note 38, at 132 (remarking that modern readers are left disabled in assessing much of Holmes's argument when the proof for his claims takes the form of long quotations in the original languages without accompanying translation). On this point, one wonders why the Permanent Committee for the Oliver Wendell Holmes Devise does not attempt to rectify the problem.

[102] Holmes, *supra* note 11, at 135.

greater social or moral end – to satisfy, at times even gratify, the desire for vengeance. As Holmes tersely put it: "The prisoner pays with his body."[103]

The realization that gratification of the desire for revenge has built-in limits, especially when it comes to punishing wrongs that do not elicit the required intensity of desire, leads Holmes to slowly zoom out and consider a broader issue: what is the purpose of punishment? Holmes canvases this issue by evaluating the three leading responses – that its purpose is to reform the criminal, or to deter the criminal from committing similar crimes, or to enact retribution. Of the three he believes only the second, the preventive theory, had the needed vitality and plasticity to subsume all instances of punishment, or even quasi-punishments, across the field.

> Prevention would accordingly seem to be the chief and only universal purpose of punishment. The law threatens certain pains if you do certain things, intending thereby to give you a new motive for not doing them. If you persist in doing them, it has to inflict the pains in order that its threats may continue to be believed.[104]

If he is correct in his analysis, Holmes maintains, then the conclusion is inescapable that the "law does undoubtedly treat the individual as a means to an end, and uses him as a tool to increase general welfare at his own expense."[105] It is exactly at this point that Holmes begins to shift the lens of vision to a new angle. The prevailing point of view is no longer that of the sufferer, or the sufferer's kin, hell-bent on revenge but that of a new, broader viewpoint or viewpoints that reflect a different social and cultural stance.

Holmes contends the criminal law operated from this new viewpoint or viewpoints, what he calls that of the "general welfare." He supports this contention by noting two important legal doctrines. The first recognized self-defense (or self-preference as he puts it) as an exception to the general prohibition against murder. The hoary principle that ignorance of the law is no excuse for breaking it serves as the second supporting legal doctrine. In both cases Holmes insists they exemplified that "[p]ublic policy sacrifices the individual to the general good."[106]

The cloudiness in Holmes's argument lies in the identification of the law's point of view with an unspecified broader social interest or general welfare. One certainly gets the sense that Holmes recognized the many evident or incipient tragedies inhering in the position "that liability to punishment cannot be finally and absolutely determined by considering the actual personal unworthiness of the criminal alone."[107] And perhaps for that reason he added the comment, "[t]hat consideration

[103] *Id.* at 136.
[104] *Id.* at 138.
[105] *Id.*
[106] *Id.* at 139.
[107] *Id.* at 139–40.

will govern only so far as the public welfare permits or demands."[108] Holmes was well aware of life's tragedies but did not, evidently, possess a tragic sense of life.

Though Holmes did not dwell on the nature and historic sources of the "law's point of view" we can surmise that for him it would have ultimately implicated the profession, or the same people that Simpson referred to as law's intermediaries. It is worth pointing out, parenthetically, that Holmes's most important piece of evidence that the criminal law encapsulated a point of view that overcame that of vengeance lay in the doctrine that ignorance of the law is no excuse. It is evident that without this operative fiction the ability of the legal profession to exist and function as a profession would be imperiled. It served as a necessary operative fiction to the professional mindset that finds the question "what is the law?" meaningful.[109]

Exactly how the criminal law achieved a viewpoint that overcame that of vengeance Holmes leaves for the most part unexplained. Even the internal standard, as Holmes depicts it, did not hesitate on occasion to sacrifice the individual, or at least the individual's property, on the altar of an overriding interest.[110] That the ox was stoned or the ship seized as a deodand presumably had a direct effect on those owners who harbored no evil intent. The real problem with the internal standard was its limited ability to absorb new facts and transmute them into sufficient grounds (working beliefs) for the application of combined social action (law).[111] Holmes alluded to this limitation when he spoke of the restricted reach of revenge's intensity.[112]

Consequently we can begin to see the situation that Holmes faced. If the internal standard lay in the background of two related (and related because of the standard) but contrary positions (actual intent, accidental movement), and if the internal standard had became unusable once, as Holmes put it, civilization reached a certain height, then the question became whether through the pressure of circumstance (new given states of fact) those who decided cases began to move toward a different standard, or whether, in almost equivalent language, the internal standard itself began to shift.

We need not immediately jump to the conclusion that the new standard would be what Holmes called an external one. It simply needed to be a standard of liability

108 *Id.*

109 Holmes, *supra* note 22, at 328–29 ("The fundamental fiction of the law is that all are presumed to know it and it follows that whatever facts are necessary preliminaries to such knowledge may not only be judicially noticed by the courts which declare the law, but must be found out at their peril by those who are called on to obey it.").

110 Holmes, *supra* note 11, at 127 ("It did not matter that the instrument forfeited belonged to an innocent person.").

111 Holmes, *supra* note 20, at 439 ("Beliefs, so far as they bear upon the attainment of a wish (as most beliefs do), lead in the first place to a social attitude, and later to combined social action, that is, to law.").

112 Holmes, *supra* note 11, at 136.

less exclusively internal, that is, a standard that did not paradigmatically correlate with the passion for revenge and its ascription of direct wrongdoing. The natural temptation is to view Holmes's articulated external standard as one that he posited simply in opposition to the one he called internal. And Holmes says a great deal to support this reading. The alternative is to wonder whether Holmes used a more sophisticated means – more sophisticated than simply positing an antithesis to an articulated thesis – by which to reveal and name a new orientation for measuring liability.

In other words: to uncover a tendency in the common law, and not simply superimpose on the sequence and range of historical cases a theory that purports to explain, or justify, both criminal and civil liability, Holmes had to find a fixed reference point by which the shift necessitated by the internal standard's incapacity to handle the increasing permutations of factual patterns could be explained. Through a type of cultural triangulation the legal inquirer would uncover an emerging point of view that had the capacity to bring into line the range of extant factual permutations and affixed consequence with his or her strong sense of the present.

"The law," Holmes said, "did not begin with a theory. It has never worked one out. The point from which it started and that at which I shall try to show it has arrived, are on different planes. In the progress from one to the other, it is to be expected that its course should not be straight and its direction not always visible."[113]

[113] *Id.* at 154–55. Incidentally, comments like this one demonstrate, in my opinion, Holmes's unique approach in *The Common Law*. The notion of separate, distinct planes in the overall progression of the common law – if "progression" is the right word; perhaps movement is better – distinguishes Holmes's unique ideas from those of such famous scholars as Henry Sumner Maine and Frederick Karl von Savigny. Many commentators, though, roll their eyes at Holmes's protestations of originality. Howe recognizes merit to Holmes's self-assessment but still points out where he believes Holmes has gone too far. For example, Howe finds Holmes to be way too coy regarding the influence of Henry Maine's *Ancient Law* upon the approach taken in *The Common Law*. He points out that chapters in *The Common Law* mimicked the headings Maine used in *Ancient Law*. Howe, *supra* note 26, at 148–49 n.31. This same point has found its way into discussions by Neil Duxbury (NEIL DUXBURY, PATTERNS OF AMERICAN JURISPRUDENCE 34 n.99 (1995)), G. Edward White (WHITE, *supra* note 38, at 194), and David Rabban (RABBAN, *supra* note 28, at 218–20). More important, commentators are virtually unanimous in finding the source of Holmes's historical methodology in Maine and Savigny. *See, e.g.*, WHITE, *supra* note 38, at 151–53; Mathias W. Reimann, *Holmes's Common Law and German Legal Science*, *in* THE LEGACY OF OLIVER WENDELL HOLMES JR. 98–99 (Robert W. Gordon ed., 1992) (noting the basic congruence of purpose between Holmes and Savigny despite what Reimann characterizes as Holmes's misleading and unfair polemical attack on Savigny and German legal science). But, to my knowledge, one will not find in either Maine or Savigny the equivalent of Holmes's notion of a "leap" from one plane of experience to another. Maine's *Ancient Law* relies on the historical and comparative methods to establish and illustrate the operative successions or stages of law as it develops in human societies or, on the other hand, using the successive developments in what is recognized as law as a clue to broader changes in society and culture. The stages for Maine proceed in ordered regularity – through designated instruments of change: legal fictions, equity, and legislation – following a natural course of development. Maine in the first four parts of *Ancient Law* provides a historical

We see in these sentences Holmes admitting that even with the tools he has available – certain psychological structures, an identified mode in which the law had grown (adaptation of primitive survivals), and the habit of apperception that links the unknown or unfamiliar with the known or familiar – he cannot provide an adequate explanation for how law moved from the internal standard to the external one. He understands that human beings may have gone through sociological stages – theological, metaphysical, and the positivistic in Comte's terms – but he is unable to capture the movement of mentality red-handed.[114] He comes closest when discussing the developing law of common carriers, but even then one gets the sense the movement existed on the same plane rather than manifesting a leap from one plane to another.[115]

Even so, the effort to bring depth to the historical record, to create a sense of historical perspective, played an important part in his endorsement of the external standard as the one fitting to the modern world. The fixed reference point (or, in artistic terms, the vanishing point, the point of convergence) that made it possible for Holmes to triangulate to a self-aware, present perspective regarding criminal and civil liability – what he calls the external standard – had to be the conscience of the court.[116]

and philosophical prolegomenon of sorts to his account of law in primitive society and its subsequent changes in various departments. HENRY SUMNER MAINE, ANCIENT LAW 1–141 (reprint. ed., Dorset Press 1986) (orig. pub. 1861). *See also* FREDERICK POLLOCK, INTRODUCTION AND NOTES TO SIR HENRY MAINE'S 'ANCIENT LAW' viii (1906) (arguing that Maine's greatest accomplishment lay in creating the natural history of law); Alan Diamond, *Introduction, in* THE VICTORIAN ACHIEVEMENT OF SIR HENRY MAINE: A CENTENNIAL REAPPRAISAL 1–4 (Alan Diamond ed., 1991); Calvin Woodard, *A Wake (or Awakening) for Historical Jurisprudence, in* THE VICTORIAN ACHIEVEMENT OF SIR HENRY MAINE at 217–37.

Savigny's concept of the law evolving organically over time became fundamental to the German historicist approach. It recognized no important breaks in the prevailing legal consciousness, or perhaps less strongly, that it was always possible to recapture the elemental German sensibility and that pursuit, in an ideal formulation, may have been the primary cultural goal of scholarship and of being a scholar in nineteenth-century Germany. Law's undying immanence – recognized by the presence of certain generative jural forms – signaled its origins in the primal sentiments and values and "turn of mind" of the German people. Savigny believed Roman law provided the best and most developed formal apparatus for expressing the genius peculiar to the German people. Mathias Reimann, *Nineteenth Century German Legal Science*, 31 B.C.L. REV. 837, 851–58, 880–84 (1990); *see also* FREDERICK KARL VON SAVIGNY, OF THE VOCATION OF OUR AGE FOR LEGISLATION AND JURISPRUDENCE 137–40 (Abraham Hayward trans., Littlewood & Co. Old Bailey 1831) (orig. pub. 1814) (note, flyleaf shows Savigny's first and middle name as Frederick Charles rather than Frederick Karl).

114 Toward the end of *The Common Law* he remarks: "In the first Lecture of this course the thought with which we have to deal was shown in its theological stage, to borrow Comte's well-known phraseology, as where an axe was made the object of criminal process; and also in the metaphysical stage, where the language of personification alone survived, but survived to cause confusion of reasoning." Holmes, *supra* note 11, at 309–10.

115 *Id.* 207–20.

116 We infer this connection from, among other things, Holmes's comments that the purpose of the jury was to inform the conscience of the court. Holmes, *supra* note 22, at 328–31. White

The conscience of the court in this sense is not the term of art often used in equity proceedings or as a test for punitive damages. Without suffering too much loss of nuance and descriptive power one may also refer to it, in modern terms, as the ethos of the profession.

Before the court as an institution or the "well known profession" of law existed, at least as we recognize it, members of communities had to have some approved means for avenging perceived wrongs that occurred within the community. As many scholars before him, Holmes found the rudiments of law in procedure. The approved procedure for righting a wrong – whether approved by fiat or custom or consensus or as something that just was or "in the air" as Maine would say[117] – concentrated the sentiment both of the community and of those members who felt the keen thirst for revenge.[118] The action took place in the first person, whether we are talking of the blood feud or the ancient appeal. In nonparticipants' approbation of the aggrieved parties' action lay the beginnings of what Holmes calls the conscience of the court or what we refer as the ethos of the profession.

As Holmes adumbrated the shift of the internal standard he also needed to postulate a reference point by which to recognize and plot its movement. If on the one side the internal standard imputed actual will and knowledge onto the offending object, and if on the other the instituted procedure for exacting revenge recognized and gave (a judicial) voice to this universal passion, then the shift to a new standard required that it somehow line up with both of these points. The new, emerging standard (the external standard) did line up with both of these points. It did so through an "ideal being," which Holmes christens as the prudent, reasonable average man.[119]

The prudent, reasonable average man of torts fame bore a faint resemblance to the internal standard – the prudent man functioned a bit like a survival from this new perspective – because the prudent, reasonable average man, as an "ideal being," directed the imputation of blameworthiness, as had the internal standard in the epochs in which societies projected malevolent intentions onto creatures

likewise notes the importance of the "internal" or "intraprofessional" perspective running throughout *The Common Law*. WHITE, *supra* note 38, at 179, 181, and 195. "Holmes had shown, in *The Common Law*, that searching legal analysis of legal subjects required both an internal and external perspective." *Id.* at 179.

[117] MAINE, *supra* note 113, at 6.

[118] In this respect, Howe connects procedure to vengeance with what he calls Holmes's principle of responsiveness:

> Holmes did not, I think, advocate the law's responsiveness to the felt necessities of a society merely because it would provide egoism with legal sanction. He found that the principle of responsiveness provided a helpful guide in the interpretation of legal history. It cast light, for instance, on the law's decision to meet the clamor for vengeance by affording public processes of prosecution.

HOWE, *supra* note 26, at 174.

[119] Holmes, *supra* note 11, at 141, 170–71.

and things.[120] It did so indirectly, however. It did so indirectly because of an expanded awareness of causes and consequences. Gone was the direct correlation between the hurt and the liability vested in the hurt's immediate, proximate source. The prudent, reasonable average man also set the new terms for procedure. Fault now became, in most instances, an issue of proving the failure of the defendant to act as the prudent, reasonable average man would have acted under the known circumstances.[121] In this sense the prudent, reasonable average man also faintly reflected, as a reverberation, the voice procedure had given to vengeance.[122]

The prudent average man became in Holmes's hands a new stereoscopic viewpoint that could only be understood as a stereoscopic viewpoint retrospectively. If the internal standard represented one point of view, and the development of a procedure to permit the internal standard its own direct expression – by exerting its will on the offending thing – another, the prudent, reasonable average man became the new triangulated point of view after the pressure of circumstances rendered the internal viewpoint and its associated procedure relatively unworkable.

What is left unsaid in this analysis, what Holmes does not discuss, is the sense of human dignity – the sense of spiritual moment that accompanied the venting of the passion for revenge – that found gratification and exultation in lavishing pain on the offending thing.[123] To suggest such actions were permitted for the sake of peace and the public weal is to bring in a later valuation, one that actually justifies the external standard. It is an attempt to foist this justification upon an earlier, different sense of joy in the face of misery, an almost irrepressible glee uprising from a sense of vitality. Holmes never made this error. The vitality of an ancient way of life that left trace elements in the present impressed itself on his sensibilities even if he could never quite explain how we got here from there.

[120] *Id.* at 140.

[121] *Id.* at 140, 170–71.

[122] Southern Pacific Co. v. Jensen, 244 U.S. 205, 222 (1917) (Holmes, J., dissenting) ("The common law is not a brooding omnipresence in the sky but the articulate voice of some sovereign or quasi-sovereign that can be identified[.]"). *See also* Holmes, *supra* note 11, at 291 (noting that legal fictions often shadow the facts of an early stage of society and could hardly have been invented had these facts been otherwise).

[123] In a 1902 article, John Dewey made similar observations in a different context – that of the occupation of hunting – regarding the "savages" (aborigines) in Australia: "The savage's repugnance to what we term a higher plane of life is not due to stupidity or dullness or apathy – or to any other merely negative qualities – such traits are a later development and fit the individual only too readily for exploitation as a tool by 'superior races.' His aversion is due to the fact that in the new occupations he does not have so clear or so intense a sphere for the display of intellectual and practical skill, or such opportunity for a dramatic play of emotion. Consciousness, even if superficial, is maintained at a higher intensity." John Dewey, *Interpretation of Savage Mind*, 9 PSYCH. REV. 217, 223 (1902).

What Holmes could do, though, and did, was to advocate for increasing the range and power of law as an organizing principle of social life. This goal required dissipating the vitality of what Holmes called the internal standard of liability and redirecting its motive force toward the formation of an external one. He believed the common law had already, by the latter part of the nineteenth century, begun on this path. He wanted to do his part to further it along.

PART III

The Purely Legal Point of View

SYNOPSIS

Understanding Holmes's notion of the purely legal point of view depends on appreciating the temporal dimensions of the legal order. This part begins by showcasing James Willard Hurst's *Justice Holmes on Legal History*. An artful meditation, Hurst's book translates Holmes into an idiom that expresses the actuality of law, or law as embedded in social reality. Hurst isolates sequence and context – which he analogizes to length and depth (sequence) and width (context) – as the dimensions of experience that the perspective of time on legal events reveals. Even if Holmes never expressly formulates his ideas in the way Hurst suggests, Hurst believes this manner of identifying and extending Holmes's insights into how history works in the context of experience – history understood as both a subject and a method of inquiry – brings to the fore Holmes's perceptions on the value of history, and its limitations, for the legal profession.

Hurst's insights into how sequence and context reveal dimensions in experience paves the way for one to better appreciate Holmes's attempts to bring a sense of three-dimensionality into law. Given his own painstaking studies as a young man, Holmes could hardly do other than take a deep view of the law. Law understood as a field of entrenched values with their own impetus and momentum, generative capabilities and inherent conflicts, led Holmes to search for a perspective uniquely legal that took these multifaceted living realities as they existed in the present into account. Eventually, two years after delivering "The Path of the Law," he would articulate a "theory of the law" – the philosophical idea that any possible conduct is either lawful or unlawful.

This deceptively simple theory takes legal study beyond analytical precision and historical description. It depends on a viewpoint intrinsically legal. Holmes's "bad man" represents this purely legal point of view. The bad man debuts not in "The Path of the Law" but in *The Common Law*, in the section where Holmes discusses conditions precedent in the law of contracts. Part III reviews Holmes's discussion, and then comments on the significance the purely legal point of view has for legal knowledge. In sum: it has the potential to create the circumstances needed to render law more knowable, that is, to expand the law's capacity to be known. Part III concludes by suggesting that the direction of Holmes's thought leads to the strong inference he was searching for a fundamental metric of the law.

INTRODUCTION

The life of the law has been experience. Though "The Path of the Law" does not include this sentence, or a direct variation, it does include its proxy as the opening line: "When we study law we are not studying a mystery but a well known profession."[1] And just as Simpson does in his *Invitation to Law*, Holmes highlights the social function of lawyers as designated intermediaries in the article's second sentence: "We are studying what we shall want in order to appear before judges, or to advise people in such a way as to keep them out of court."[2]

But then Holmes takes an unexpected step, probably more unexpected to an 1897 audience than a 2020 one, and explains that the profession of law is a profession, not because lawyers are learned or aspire to service, but because people will pay lawyers to advise them on how to avoid unwanted entanglements with the judicial arm of the state. The object of legal study, then, is prediction – "prediction of the incidence of the public force through the instrumentality of the courts[.]"[3]

This part will place the most important notion in "The Path of the Law" – the bad man intent on predicting what the courts will do in fact – within the trajectory of Holmes's thought. It will show how the "bad man" as an idea connects with the "longitudinal" and "lateral" elements contained in Holmes's conceptualization of law as an interactive cultural activity.[4] This part will also construe the address itself

[1] Oliver Wendell Holmes, *The Path of the Law*, *in* III The Collected Works of Justice Holmes: Complete Public Writings and Selected Judicial Opinions of Oliver Wendell Holmes 391 (Sheldon Novick ed., 1995) [hereinafter CW].

[2] *Id.*

[3] *Id.*

[4] The words "lateral" and "longitudinal" refer to Holmes's sectional studies of the law. In *The Arrangement of the Law – Privity*, Holmes distinguishes it from his previous article, *Codes, and the Arrangement of the Law*, by saying that while *Codes* provided a look at a "lateral section of the law, – at duties contemplated as existing [at] a given instant of time; it remains to make a

as part of Holmes's overarching, if unrealized, ambition of creating the equivalent of a positioning system, a metric of the law. Through this positioning system Holmes sought to advance what he regarded as the quintessentially professional obligation to bring out of the chaos of the law an order useful to implementing social goals.

The sophisticated manner in which Holmes broached these objectives requires that one acquire an equally nuanced understanding of how Holmes took a deep view of the past, or, in other words, how he viewed his present with historical perspective. That effort proved key in making law three-dimensional. Understanding his use of "experience" and "history" facilitates the task of exposition on this point.

"The Path of the Law" also engaged the then current debates regarding the proper way to train aspiring lawyers. It sought to reorient those debates. The leading issues should not be wrangles over the mechanics of study or problems of professional competence. Law had its own dignity; its study, properly done, deepened and widened the mind. Holmes had long escaped his fear that what Edmund Burke had said might be true: that the study of law sharpened the mind by narrowing it.[5]

Part V will explicitly focus on Holmes's theory of legal study as reflected in "The Path of the Law" and other pieces Holmes wrote during the same period, including "Law in Science and Science in Law." The analysis will turn on the notion that the study and practice of law has the capacity, in a manner of speaking, to turn lead into gold. Holmes did not explicitly say this but he acted as if it were true. If the legitimate use of the public force had a power unequalled in the social world, then those charged with directing and justifying its deployment had to learn how to measure and control it. In short, they should keep in mind the basic interrelated question that structured the profession's DNA: "what is the law?" – "what is law?"

Apart from its social and cultural power, law as generally practiced and understood evinced an implicit professional ideal. In this respect, "The Path of the Law" represents, along with "Law in Science and Science in Law," Holmes's most considered statement on this implicit ideal. Advancement of the professional ideal depended on practitioners recognizing law's status as a discipline – that it has its own content, form, method, and purposes. Those directly practicing in the discipline (scholars and teachers) should in turn be self-aware. They should reflect upon how the discipline ties into and works within the dynamic, formative power law exerts in the social world as an ordering, sustaining principle of social life.

Advancement in understanding for Holmes required uncovering the purely legal point of view. This point of view or perspective rested on an acute awareness and sophisticated perception of law's power to reshape behavior and turn it into conduct.

longitudinal section, that is, to show them as continuing in time." Oliver Wendell Holmes, *The Arrangement of the Law – Privity*, *in* I CW 304. At the time of *Privity* Holmes had not yet articulated the form–substance dynamic that would inform *The Common Law*.

5 Holmes, *Introduction to* The General Survey, *in* III CW 440 ("One saw people whom one respected and admired leaving the study because they thought it narrowed the mind; for which they had the authority of Burke.").

1 EXPERIENCE AND HISTORY

Experience and history are both laden words, especially in the corpus of Holmes's work and the many studies that have tried to construe an overall understanding of Holmes. They both in different ways obviously implicate the past. In his unjustly overlooked meditation on Holmes's work as an historian James Willard Hurst generates from Holmes's thoughts and insights a *tableau vivant* of the roles law enacted on the canvas of the American past.[6] Hurst studies Holmes from the perspective of one interested in the part law – through institutions, participants, embedded values, and articulated ideals – played in the epic of the nation's formation.

History looms large in the endeavor. As does experience as a basic category of thought and analysis.[7] Though Holmes may not have been always clear and consistent in his usage, we would do well to follow Hurst's suggestion and treat, for the sake of analyzing and understanding Holmes's theory of legal study, experience and history as two different concepts.[8]

Experience, the broader and more fundamental of the two, conjoins what from other angles may be seen as disparate events or phenomena into a living whole. In *The Common Law*'s opening paragraph we see Holmes alluding to this joinder of times in experience, the coexistence of past, present, and future in a single juxtaposed whole:

6 James Willard Hurst, Justice Holmes on Legal History (1964). David Rabban, who has written knowledgeably and extensively on Holmes's use of history, notes that Hurst is the only scholar of the many who have written on Holmes to focus primarily on the topic of Holmes and history. Curiously, Rabban sidesteps discussing Hurst's book, either in his article on *The Common Law* or in his major work, *Law's History*. Rabban says he wants to concentrate on *The Common Law* to investigate how Holmes practiced and theorized about history. For that reason he does not address *Justice Holmes on Legal History*. *See* David M. Rabban, *The Historiography of* The Common Law, 28 Law & Social Inquiry 1161, 1162 (2003). Even so, one would assume that Hurst's goal of drawing on Holmes to make "serviceable tools for the historian's workshop" demands a fairly intimate knowledge of Holmes's approach to history, both as a dimension of human existence and as a craft. And a close reading of Hurst's book bears this supposition out.

7 According to Louis Menand, Holmes "meant it [experience] as the name for everything that arises out of the interaction of the human organism with its environment: beliefs, sentiments, customs, values, policies, prejudices – what he called 'the felt necessities of the time.' Our word for it (in many ways less satisfactory) is 'culture.'" Menand identifies three features of Holmes's conception of experience of particular importance: (1) experience is not reducible to propositions; (2) it is not individual and internal but collective and consensual, social not psychological; and, (3) experience contains inherently imprecise, uncertain, and indeterminate elements. Louis Menand, *The Principles of Oliver Wendell Holmes*, *in* American Studies 38–46 (2002); Thomas C. Grey suggests that Holmes used "experience" to mean "an indefinite mixture of habit, instrumental reason, and the search for internal coherence." Thomas C. Grey, *Holmes and Legal Pragmatism*, 41 Stan. L. Rev. 787, 814 (1989).

8 Hurst, *supra* note 6, at 3–17.

> The law embodies the story of a nation's development through many centuries, and it cannot be dealt with as if it contained only the axioms and corollaries of a book of mathematics. *In order to know what it is, we must know what it has been, and what it tends to become.* We must alternately consult history and existing theories of legislation. But the most difficult labor will be to understand the combination of the two into new products at every stage. The substance of the law at any given time pretty nearly corresponds, so far as it goes, with what then is understood to be convenient; but its form and machinery, and the degree to which it is able to work out desired results, depend very much upon its past.[9]

Plainly the imperative of the book is to expand the capacity of the law to be known. Traditional logic, understood as a formalized system of reasoning, either deductive or inductive, is not sufficient, in and of itself, to increase the range of the law's capacity to be known once the inquirer views law as both encapsulating and emerging from dynamic, interactive cultural activity. For that task one must adopt a different stance and use, along with logic, an assortment of other clarifying and investigative tools.

Holmes's curious inversion of the steps to be taken – first know *what the law has been* and *what the law tends to become* to know, then, *what the law is* – leads to a perplexity: how does knowledge of the law-in-the-past and of law-in-the-future lead to knowledge of law-in-the-here-and-now? We are led back to Holmes's sense of actuality, or what Hurst called "living law."[10] The law that is operative and real, that functions in, and molds values for, an existing society or community does not arise from atemporal axioms or corollaries. The necessary premises, or grounds of action, are rooted in the temporal dimensions of experience.

In other words: living law does not arise from a dead postulate.

But if the law is living it must be ready and able to meet the test of new facts. A test successfully met modifies overtly, or sometimes subtly, the nature of law itself. A law that successfully meets the test of new facts becomes a law that has successfully met the test of new facts, that is, a law that continues to generate order. Facts of greater complexity successfully subsumed, via keener principles, permit the applicable law to regenerate – become stronger, more vigorous, or in Hurst's words, more durable. And, of course, laws self-evidently not able to meet the tests of new facts – construed broadly as tests of experience – degenerate, lose vigor and vitality and eventually fall into desuetude.

9 Oliver Wendell Holmes, *The Common Law*, *in* III CW 115 (emphasis added).

10 Hurst, *supra* note 6, at 11; *see also id.* at 6 ("To focus thus upon the *living reality* of a particular system should not make study parochial in concept.") (emphasis added); *id.* at 13 ("Study of a *living legal order* soon enforces on our attention that time has another dimension besides sequence. We think, feel, and exercise will differently than we might otherwise, not only because we experience events or situations in sequence, but also because we experience them as coexisting or concurrent. This is to say that context is a dimension in time of key significance to legal order.") (emphasis added).

To know the part law-in-the-past plays in experience requires preliminary investigation. That is where history, understood as a mode of inquiry, comes in. On the other hand, to know law-in-the-future requires understanding "existing theories of legislation." At this point, given Holmes's usage, an interesting ambiguity arises: existing now or then? The answer appears to be both, in the present and in the past. Though one can never be sure with Holmes, what he seems to mean by "existing theories of legislation" are the justifications or rationales, or what we now call policy arguments, that anchor a given rule in the mind of its adherents.

"Existing theories of legislation" also encompass what Holmes calls "good sense."[11] Good sense makes an able judge able.[12] It propelled Judge Lemuel Shaw to the top rank of magistrate. Shaw mastered law. Good sense keeps logic in its proper place. As Holmes put it in a pair of lectures on agency he prepared after publishing *The Common Law*: "the whole outline of the law, as it stands to-day, is the resultant of a conflict between logic and good sense – the one striving to carry fictions out to consistent results, the other restraining and at last overcoming that effort when the results become too manifestly unjust."[13] The law of agency – and perhaps in other areas as well – exhibited this ongoing struggle between logic and good sense because the participants had lost sight of the meaning of the original rule of law – "for whenever a rule of law is in fact a survival of ancient traditions, its ancient meaning is gradually forgotten, and it has to be reconciled to present notions of policy and justice, or to disappear."[14]

It would seem, then, that the task of the inquirer is to separate the form from the substance or, in terms of *The Common Law*, to understand the paradox of form and substance. On the one side is a historically given form (rule of law), on the other substantive theories of legislation that differ from those which originally gave meaning to the form. Logic deals mainly with form; one must reach substance through other means, primarily through historical investigation and a better grasp of human psychology. The substance involves the "secret root from which the law draws all the juices of life," that which is "expedient for the community concerned."[15] The substance consists of variegated sentiments and beliefs, some clear and distinct to the mind of those who hold them, others less so. The form the law assumes in a given state of facts aligns those prevailing beliefs with definite, concerted, direct, outward action.

This way of depicting law's dynamic, how lawmakers weave the past into the present and the present into the past, while finding support in Holmes's writings,

[11] Hurst suggests yet another possibility for what "theories of legislation" may mean: "expressions, primarily, of what we see as indicated by the contemporary context of affairs." *Id.* at 13.

[12] Holmes, *supra* note 9, at 133 (stating that law is administered by able and experienced men who know too much to sacrifice good sense to syllogism).

[13] Oliver Wendell Holmes, *Agency I* and *Agency II*, *in* III CW 340–71, 364.

[14] *Id.* at 370.

[15] Holmes, *supra* note 9, at 132–33.

misses the element of perspective – the sense of depth crucial to the law's three-dimensionality – that structures Holmes's manner of projecting legal history. The fundamental error lies in taking a part for the whole, history for experience. The likely source of confusion lies in Holmes's ambiguous use of the phrase "existing theories of legislation." Existing when? And how? Without the needed temporal markers the inquirer cannot develop a feel for the historical distance that may exist between different and perhaps opposing theories.

For law to expand its capacity to be known, inquirers had to become more self-conscious of their use of legal methods and materials. There lies an imperative at the heart of *The Common Law*, an appeal to the nascent intellectual conscience of practitioners. And here we arrive at the distinctive contribution of that landmark in legal thought called *The Common Law*. The book, carefully and thoughtfully read, opens the door to a new way of seeing the activity of lawmaking. The intermixing of form and substance, or the interweaving of past and present, could no longer operate in the shadows, under the guise of fictions and unheralded survivals. The maturity of history as a discipline had made it impossible for legal practitioners to continue naively in the game of artificial reason.[16]

History as a discipline, and as a perspective, provided the means to counteract the pressure of circumstances that exists in lived, present immediate experience: instead of countenancing blithely but confidently mouthed, historically naive policy rationales one could, as Holmes attempted, advance the meaning of law as a human endeavor by establishing a positioning system to orient the activity of lawmaking. If categorization failed to do the trick, one needed an alternate means to position oneself in what would otherwise be something similar to a legal chaos – with or without an index. Holmes controlled his use of history in *The Common Law* because his goal lay in using history, along with psychology and logic, to fashion a perspective of (and in) experience distinctly legal.

2 THE PERSPECTIVE OF LAW: SEQUENCE AND CONTEXT

Hurst's lectures on Holmes and legal history developed Hurst's insights into Holmes's thought that, in all likelihood, arose after a very long immersion in Holmes's writings. From these insights Hurst formulated the categories of depiction and analysis he used in presenting Holmes's ideas on the roles of law in the past and present. Hurst is at pains to distance Holmes from responsibility for the categories'

[16] Holmes, *supra* note 5, at 440 ("Now, a man can start with the knowledge that he starts fair – that the best of Europe, as well as of this country and England, are before him. And those results are so illuminating that diligence alone is enough to give him an understanding of how the law came to be what it is.").

origination or use.[17] Nevertheless, one cannot shake the feeling that Hurst believed Holmes to have been a direct predecessor in the endeavor to survey and map law's roles in nineteenth- and early twentieth-century American society and culture, even if Holmes's main preoccupation had been to bring an internal order to law as an ongoing practice.

Hurst believed Holmes's overall approach too narrow, too court focused.[18] It lacked a certain amount of sophistication if looked at as a strictly scholarly enterprise. Hurst widened the angle to include other institutional actors, and to provide the historical and sociological facts for which Holmes apparently did not have the patience or inclination.[19]

Holmes's strength went the other way. He worked at the level of perception; he offered careful discriminations and explanations of the legal conceptions he chose to set against the panorama of social life. He was an artist of thought who used law as his medium.[20] It is difficult to convey the manner and intent of Holmes's subtle evocations of law to readers taught to whittle law down to its instrumental use. We come back to the question, "what kind of person do we want the study of law to create?"

The business of a lawyer is to know law.[21] For Holmes, to know law in a large way or to master it required that the student understand the immediate objective – to advise clients or to advocate for them – and the less immediate but no less pressing long-range objective. That objective one may describe as ensuring that law as a dedicated pursuit retained its vitality as a principle of order. This endeavor seemed to Holmes particularly crucial in a time when it appeared to many thoughtful observers, both in the British Isles and in America, that the foundational pillars of traditional civilized life had begun to disintegrate. Social arrangements, hoary creeds, basic beliefs in God or in what, for the lack of a better phrase, may be called the order of things, had all shifted, seismically one could say, and the aftershocks have continued into the present.

Law stood for the mode in which behavior became acts, legal or illegal, because of lawmakers' capacity to impute and elicit – to and from experience – both meaning and purpose. Legal forms did something other than exist to become survivals. Holmes believed the font of meaning lay always and everywhere in the present. The job of the legal intellect, legal intellect's role in a growing and

[17] HURST, *supra* note 6, at viii ("The present essays offer some hypotheses for the pattern and content of which I take responsibility, appraising by the logic of our experience the life of the law within the United States.").

[18] *Id.* at 5.

[19] *Id.* at 33–34, 40–41, 60, 91.

[20] As Holmes wrote to Harold Laski in 1919: "it has been my business to know the movement of thought in one of its great expressions – the law – and my pleasure to try to know something of its movement in philosophy[.]" *Id.* at 119 (citing I HOLMES–LASKI LETTERS: THE CORRESPONDENCE OF MR. JUSTICE HOLMES AND HAROLD J. LASKI 210 (Mark DeWolfe Howe ed., 1953).

[21] Oliver Wendell Holmes, *The Use of Law Schools*, *in* III CW 479.

expanding society, included the tiresome work of excavating the present and bringing into line with our sense of the now – what is real and actual and takes strong hold of our attention and interest – a nuanced and justified understanding of the past and an even more nuanced and justified sense for the future, of the relative worth and scope of existing ends felt and thought desirable.

Thus to appreciate Holmes's efforts to fashion a distinctly legal perspective one must begin where Hurst thought the most charitable reading of Holmes would lead one: to the time dimensions of experience.

i *Experience As Sequence*

"To understand law as a system which has more significant dimensions in time than in logic is not merely to see more clearly the elements of will involved, but also to energize the mind to command will to better effect."[22] Thus writes Hurst in the chapter that opens his study of Holmes and history. It emphasizes Holmes's commitment to understanding how law as an activity fit into a distinctly American setting. Hurst's sentence focuses on an objective that, if it did not inform Holmes's many initial forays into a legal history that stretched far beyond the American past, became in time an additional justification for those youthful forays.

That objective involves – and I will sidestep for the moment the question whether Holmes would have acceded to this description – enduing an ability to draw philosophical sustenance from the least nourishing elements of human experience. Here the word "experience" refers to the substance of things undertaken or undergone, their outcomes, and the person who has, or the people who have, undertaken and undergone. I offer this description of Holmes's objective tentatively, as a suggestion to help bring into sharper view Hurst's somewhat indistinct contention that understanding the legal order through the dimensions of time serves to "energize mind to command will to better effect."

Hurst himself believed that for Holmes historical perspective energized the mind in two ways. First, it did so by releasing humans from the bondage of the past, the chains of custom and familiarity. Second, by showing the "changing variety and growth in men's experience"[23] it taught "wisdom and courage to reject absolute premises and to exercise the scope which life offers to achieve fresh meaning."[24] These lessons are certainly worthy in and of themselves, but the brute question remains whether they are sufficient for a life lived in, and committed to, law.

Aside from how an historical perspective might energize the inquiring mind, Hurst found sufficient reason for Holmes employing this perspective in the opposition between history, the realm of will and emotion, and logic the realm of timeless

[22] HURST, *supra* note 6, at 9.
[23] *Id.* at 10.
[24] *Id.*

relations of form. "Dealing with timeless relations of form, logic does not identify or measure emotion, which grows in time."[25]

The notion that emotion grows in time is not self-evident. It takes many whirs of the internal hard disk before one connects Hurst's observation to Holmes's opening salvo in *The Common Law*. There Holmes had attributed the "life of the law" to experience – that is, a complex of ideas, perceptions, policy intuitions, purposes, felt necessities, or, in much less sophisticated language, a lot of stuff existing together at what seems like the same time that appears to have some role in laying down the existing law. Or, one could in contrast simply understand Holmes's use of the term experience in the typical classically conservative manner: to indicate the customs, usages, knowledge and know-how that accumulated over time in dealing with disputes. Adherents then passed along these practices as learning and lore from generation to generation.

Holmes's interest in the growth of law as an aspect of the general growth of culture was secondary however. He was primarily, keenly, interested in understanding the "life of the law" from the internal perspective, that is, that of a professional practitioner. The life of the law, then, in his own terms, must mean the life of "beliefs . . . [that] lead in the first place to a social attitude, and later to combined social action[.]"[26] On Hurst's view historical perspective permitted the inquirer, among other things, to study the growth of emotion or feeling in time. That much seems correct. But it also did the opposite. It permitted the acute inquirer, such as Holmes, to observe how in time and in the context of law an emotion or feeling wilted and shrank.

If we accept the results of Holmes's laborious investigations in *The Common Law* at face value we can little doubt that revenge – which I will assume is an emotion or a complex of emotions – played a smaller role in the law of thirteenth-century England than it had in the same part of the earth 600 years earlier but in all probability a larger one than it would play in that same part of the earth 600 years later.

For reasons indicated in the Part II, a legal regime in which revenge played a significant role could not continue in the face of social complexity and cultural advancement. That does not mean revenge, as an emotional state or as an act, would die out any time soon.[27] It does mean that as its social vitality diminished so did its cultural importance. The lessening of revenge – its reduced role as a social and cultural fact – must have, one speculates, created the needed space in the law for other emotions, perhaps nascent, to grow and intertwine and eventually flourish.

[25] *Id.* at 11.

[26] Holmes, *supra* note 5, at 439.

[27] It would not die out for Holmes because he understood it as part of human psychology. It existed in both barbarians and those civilized. This permanent, or structural, feature of the human makeup sat uneasily, but perhaps necessarily, with dynamic elements of growth and modification.

Holmes did not directly tease out these conclusions from the premises he provided in the opening chapters of *The Common Law*, but Hurst certainly found enough in that book and in Holmes's other writings to put forward the supposition that in the time dimensions of experience lay the necessary catwalks and tunnels to understanding Holmes's fundamental orientation.

> If, then, we look to understand a given legal order by passing beyond manipulation of logic to examine its history, we need to define the dimensions of experience which the perspective of time reveals. At least for legal history, these dimensions are two: sequence (analogous to length and depth), and context (analogous to breadth).[28]

In parsing the idea of sequence in experience, Hurst sought to flesh out Holmes's assertion that to know what the law is one must know what it has been and what it tends to become. Given his own historical and sociological interests, Hurst glossed Holmes's assertion "to know what the law is" by inserting "the role of" between what and is – "in order to know what [the role of law] . . . is."[29] It is at this point that we see Hurst swerve to his own emphases on the sociological and economic bases of law, but that orientation does not hinder one from profiting from Hurst's trenchant analysis of how the notion of sequence captures a range of historical realities Holmes used to backdrop his prescriptions for the study of law.

Hurst's concept of sequence resembles the idea of path dependency.[30] But it is more variegated and more attuned than that idea to the interchange between past

[28] HURST, *supra* note 6, at 11. Hurst's way of categorizing experience into sequence and context somewhat resembles Morton White's use of historicism and cultural organicism as the two guiding ideas to explain the "revolt against formalism" which focused the energies of such leading late nineteenth- and early twentieth-century American thinkers as Holmes, Dewey, Veblen, Robinson, and Beard. White terms historicism "the attempt to explain facts by reference to earlier facts." Cultural organicism means the effort to find explanations and relevant materials for understanding the object of study in related social sciences. MORTON G. WHITE, SOCIAL THOUGHT IN AMERICA: THE REVOLT AGAINST FORMALISM 12 (1976 ed.) (orig. pub. 1947).

One may even trace the lineage of this analytical scheme to Frederick Karl von Savigny. Mathias Reimann argues Savigny united the historical method and systematic method, as the two methods pursued the same goal of detecting unity and order in apparent variety and chaos. According to Savigny,

> [t]he given variety of law . . . is twofold, namely in part contemporaneous, and in part successive, which necessarily requires a twofold scientific treatment. The reduction of the contemporaneous variety to its inherent unity is the systematic method . . . . The treatment of the successive variety, however, is the truly historical method.

Mathias Reimann, *Nineteenth Century German Legal Science*, 31 B.C. L. REV. 837, 855–56 (1990).

[29] HURST, *supra* note 6, at 13.

[30] On the idea of path dependency and its relation to Holmes *see* Richard A. Posner, *Path Dependency, Pragmatism, and Critique of History in Adjudication and Legal Scholarship*, 67 U. CHI L. REV., 573, 583–88 (2000). Posner focuses on inertia, the continuity and persistence of a given starting point due mainly to habituation, and the lack of good information needed to

realities and present wants and convictions. Hurst finds the effects of sequence – that "items in experience" follow one another – manifested in a "living legal order" through the conscious realizations of past commitments, current trends, and the dynamics of change (the pace and interplay between continuity and discontinuity). Hurst uses words like *momentum* and *impetus* to describe the felt reality of certain patterns of behavior that self-evidently exist in the present and shape the future but with loci that exist in the past.[31]

Hurst believes the cumulative aspect of sequence captured most of Holmes's attention. From his prolonged and deep studies in far-flung legal materials, one infers, Holmes developed a feel for trends that escaped the conscious perception of participants. The revelatory power of historical study impressed upon him the force of those currents of conscious life that originate not in the depths of the individual mind but at the unseen wellsprings of a shared social and cultural life.

As Hurst put it:

> If it fulfills man's individual and social nature, that events and men's thoughts and emotional responses to events derive impetus from their place in sequence, this effect of sequence derives also from men's limitations. Their lives are short, their individual stores of imagination and will subject to exhaustion, the variations of concrete experience infinite. Much that happens, therefore, proceeds by trend – by the cumulation of human responses and of impersonal events in patterns which at a given point or span in time men take as given facts. There are 'events' which take three hundred years to happen . . . . These are realities of our lives all the more because they tend to shape perception and will beyond our awareness of their effect. It is only in the historical dimension that we probe these depths of our being.[32]

It would be a mistake to think that only history, understood as a formal discipline of study, has the capability to reveal those aspects of sequence concealed in the historical dimension of time.[33] Psychology presents an alternate path.[34] One could

create a more efficient and supple legal system; *see also* Clayton P. Gillette, *The Path Dependence of the Law*, *in* THE PATH OF THE LAW AND ITS INFLUENCE: THE LEGACY OF OLIVER WENDELL HOLMES, JR., 245–77 (Steven J. Burton ed., 2000).

31 HURST, *supra* note 6, at 21–52; *see also* Morris R. Cohen, *Justice Holmes and the Nature of Law*, 31 COLUM. L. REV. 352, 357 (1931) ("But Holmes has been wise enough to realize the historical truth that certain phases of human life have remained relatively constant for long periods and that elements of the law may be the same today as in ancient Rome.").

32 HURST, *supra* note 6, at 22.

33 As Hurst put it: "Holmes would trace roots of legal history deep in the cumulative sequences of experience which bring values and institutions to definition." *Id.* at 25.

34 On the role of psychology and the limits of historical explanation *see* Oliver Wendell Holmes, *Review of* Essays in Anglo-Saxon Law, *in* III CW 19 ("It must not be forgotten that there is a limit to historical explanation, as it is called. Some things (the origin of the notion of property, for instance) receive more light from an analysis of human nature.") *See also* MARK DEWOLFE HOWE, JUSTICE HOLMES: THE PROVING YEARS 1870–1882 147–48 (1963).

In regard to this topic, Hurst makes the interesting suggestion that human psychology may have represented for Holmes with "those psychological factors which, if not inherent and

even imagine the relatively timeless dimension of logic providing entrée at the right moments. The point is that without the tools of history a flashing psychological insight or the apprehension of an antinomy would have no staying power, little or no ability to connect with the living, breathing tissue of full-bodied conscious experience.

ii *Experience As Context*

If sequence gave dimensions of length and depth to temporal experience, what Hurst calls context provides the needed dimension of breadth. Context involves that temporal slice of experience, past or present, which directs attention, first, to "the functional integrity and efficiency of certain social institutions and processes," and then to "the continuing achievement of acceptable balances of power among competing interests."[35]

Context does not complement or supplement sequence. It mainly provides another angle of focus on what is always, already present in experience, or on what one may less obliquely call the total situation. As Hurst points out, sequence (fixed commitments, trends, continuities and discontinuities) are partly constitutive of context even as context (social function and balance of power) frames and elicits the patterns of thought and behavior that become earmarked as sequence.

"In contrast to analytical social science," history, said Hurst, using the word to indicate the intent of the historian, "tries to grasp human phenomena as wholes." It "studied to grasp the whole event." An unobtainable goal Hurst concedes; but the synthesis that historical study attempts "might add dimensions to understanding which more abstract studies did not uncover."[36]

Holmes the historian, and even Holmes the judge, paid less attention to the dynamics of context than he did to that of sequence. Hurst illuminatingly compares Holmes to Brandeis:

> As much as Holmes, the author of *Other People's Money* knew that to give meaning to events one must place them in time. It was the sequence (and especially the trend) aspects of time which most engaged Holmes's imagination. But it was time as context (that is, the functional and balance-of-power aspects of time) which from the outset of his public career chiefly engaged Brandeis's interests.[37]

Perhaps Holmes's disinclination to study social facts in the same way that Brandeis did made him susceptible to self-deception or romanticism regarding the power of

unchanging in the species, are at any rate subject to such a slow rate of change as to reach beyond ordinary conceptions of history." HURST, *supra* note 6, at 70.

35 HURST, *supra* note 6, at 55–56.

36 *Id.* at 58–59.

37 *Id.* at 34.

the nascent social sciences to quantify and measure social action. In Hurst's opinion Holmes had too much unwarranted confidence in the power of economics or social statistics to orient and guide public affairs.[38]

As Hurst perceptively noted: "Indeed, where public policy was poorly made, the defect often derived from the fact that decisions had been taken upon a calculus which was too abstract because it included too few variables. In this aspect, acute historical perspective might be more useful for good policy making than propositions from more analytical studies."[39]

Even so, Holmes showed his awareness of the importance of context in occasional remarks referencing the needs of the present. These "needs" or the "pressures of context" brought to the fore the appositions of present experience and the opportunities they offered for legal institutions to transmute pressing hindrances or out-of-step behavior into legally significant facts. Holmes recognized that the heritage of the United States gave special content to the social roles of law.[40] What Hurst called the "middle-class viewpoint" and the "constitutional ideal" led this society to "emphasize the organization, dispersion, and responsible interaction of public and private centers of decision making."[41]

Thus the awareness of the temporal dimensions of experience, understood in Hurst's terms as sequence and context, makes possible a perspective on the past distinctly legal. That is to say, a perspective that viewed considered court action or inaction against a past and in light of a future that contained correlated potentialities for meaning once new questions arose. The cumulative trends upon which Holmes tended to focus had a life history of their own. Bringing these life histories into the open simultaneously gave shape to, and deepened one's sense of, the present. One achieved a fuller sense of context.

In like manner, the recognition of experience's temporal dimensions sharpened one's sense of the future. Ends received the type of clarification that could only come from a cultivated historical sensibility supplemented with the necessary empirical spadework and analytical sifting. For this reason Holmes took pains to distinguish the acquisition of historical knowledge needed for the refined understanding of law from the raw erudition of the master historian or the doctrinaire learning of the single-minded legal scholar. In the study of law history had its place. So did the study of incidents, outcomes, and consequences. Historical learning had an integral use but one that an experienced legal intelligence should control.

38 *Id.* at 59–60.
39 *Id.*
40 *Id.* at 60–65.
41 *Id.* at 65.

3 THE PERSPECTIVE OF LAW: THE BAD MAN

i A *Troublesome Fire*

The most troubling passage in "The Path of the Law" for the argument of this study – that Holmes sought to establish a perspective purely legal that brought into view and made use of law's three-dimensionality – comes early in the address. The predictions with which the students of law must busy themselves are not, Holmes says, unmanageably large. He continues:

> They present themselves as a finite body of dogma which may be mastered within a reasonable time. It is a great mistake to be frightened by the ever increasing number of reports. The reports of a given jurisdiction in the course of a generation take up pretty much the whole body of the law, and restate it from the present point of view. We could reconstruct the corpus from them if all that went before were burned. The use of the earlier reports is mainly historical, a use about which I shall have something to say before I have finished.[42]

Holmes's effort to soothe those law students in his audience who may have felt overwhelmed by the sheer volume of reported cases takes an unforeseen rhetorical twist when he, in a manner perhaps slightly avuncular, shrugs off the possible effects on legal learning and practice if all the reports prior to those that the existing generation produced went up in smoke.

It takes a moment or two for this comment to sink in.

We must keep in mind that the man making this remark is an associate justice of the Massachusetts Supreme Judicial Court. We must keep in mind that the most prominent member of the Boston faculty in attendance, Melville Bigelow, earned his international reputation through his painstaking work in English legal history.[43] We must keep in mind that Holmes's former colleague, both in law practice and at the Harvard Law School, the patient James Bradley Thayer, also in the audience, had done groundbreaking work in the history of the jury.[44] Later in the address Holmes acknowledges the contributions to historical scholarship of both these men, as he does of James Barr Ames, also a noted historian of the common law and the then current dean of the Harvard Law School. Yet less than five minutes into the speech here is the author of *The Common Law* – who spent years of his youth studying the opaque records of primitive and early law, scrutinizing the medieval Year Books, digesting Glanvill and Bracton, Coke, Hale, and Blackstone, growing pale and gaunt from the toll of editing Kent's *Commentaries* – telling over 100 law students in the audience that if thousands and thousands of pages of reported

[42] Holmes, *supra* note 1, at 391–92.

[43] On Bigelow's accomplishments as a legal historian see David M. Rabban, Law's History: American Legal Thought and the Transatlantic Turn to History 204–32 (2013).

[44] *See id.* at 286–306 for a recounting of Thayer's career.

English and American cases shriveled up and turned into ash the net effect on this well-known profession would not be catastrophic!

At such moments one can almost understand Grant Gilmore's well-known suspicions of the man, especially his considered pronouncement that *The Common Law* amounted to little more than an "elaborate joke."[45]

Nature and history may on occasion have their wry fun with the gullible and the wise, but there is no reason to think that a young man hoping to make his mark by forty had any of the needed double- or triple-mindedness to pull off a stunt of the magnitude Gilmore suggests. It may have been different as Holmes approached his fifty-sixth year. I, for one, would not be shocked if it turned out that Holmes was not above every now and again pulling the tail of the cosmos instead of giving it a twist.[46]

The currents that run through "The Path of the Law" find their source in the above quoted passage, in Holmes's assurance that even in the face of an apocalyptic fire the legal corpus could be reconstructed. The phrases seem carefully placed. The reports of a given jurisdiction – say, Massachusetts – in the course of a generation – every twenty-five years or so I assume – take up pretty much the whole body of the law – laws of crime, torts, contracts, property, inheritance and succession – and restate it from the present point of view.

This last phrase – "restate it from the present point of view" – more than any other in "The Path of the Law" connects it to *The Common Law*. In that work Holmes did exactly what he now describes: restate the existing body of law from the present point of view. Restate means to say again. But one must do so in a clearer, more accessible way and, especially, in a convincing manner. It is not merely to repeat or reiterate. The term "present point of view" is harder to define but points up what Hurst labeled "context." In Holmes's language the present point of view would include what he called "felt necessities," currents of meaning and calls to action subjectively felt and obeyed even if not always objectively recognized.

In other words, the present point of view as Holmes uses the phrase already indicates a consciousness of historical change, that we in the present may have a different view of life – of what elements are most important or needful and pressing – than those who bequeathed to us this body of law meant to guide us as we collectively govern our behavior and determine our conduct. Restatement of the law is then the lot of the profession. This fundamental perception guided Holmes throughout the work that culminated in *The Common Law* and reached its fullest

45 *See* Sheldon M. Novick, *Introduction*, *in* I CW 6; *see also* GRANT GILMORE, THE AGES OF AMERICAN LAW 47 (2d ed., new foreword and final chapter by Phillip Bobbitt 2014) (orig. ed. 1977).

46 Cohen remarks that Holmes's "youthfulness that expresses itself in delightful tricks and pranks – 'We will twist the tail of the Cosmos until it squeaks' – expresses itself also in the willingness to doubt one's own first principles." Felix S. Cohen, *Holmes–Cohen Correspondence*, 9 J. HIST. IDEAS 3, 45 (1948).

expression not in "The Path of the Law" but in his next major piece, "Law in Science and Science in Law."

The real eye-opener is Holmes's contention that the full corpus of law could be reconstructed from a given jurisdiction's reports spanning a generation. The relevant question is how? And, for that matter, what constitutes the entire "body of law"?

We have to consider the possibility that this sentence may be a throwaway. Holmes later reported that he was pleased to have slumbering student eyes widen in attention. Holmes may have been doing a sly bit of grandstanding with his reference to torched cases. I tend to think though that he meant what he said and what he said encapsulated a lifelong effort to bring order out of the chaos of the common law.

The phrase "body of law" upon careful consideration turns one's attention to Holmes's prior efforts to categorize existing law on the basis of duties. He never gave up his youthful determination that it was better to organize and understand law upon essential facts of legal significance and not on dramatic incidents. As we noted earlier in this book, it is in "The Path of the Law" where he expresses the hope that a farmer upset about his churn will not be stymied in his search for redress because the justice of the peace cannot find a heading in the Vermont statutes entitled "Churns."

The body of law as Holmes uses the phrase probably comprises the duties he had identified early in his career – from all to the sovereign, from all to all, from those in a particular situation to all, from all to those in a particular situation, from those in a particular situation to those in a particular situation. The list may not be exhaustive or sufficiently fine-grained but we are talking loosely of a body of law, not of a set or series of logical sets.

Understanding his use of the term "reconstruct" proves more daunting than construing "corpus" or "body of law" because it forces one to think through how gaps in the corpus might be filled. The gaps may be one of two kinds. Either the gap exists because the needed precedent has gone up in smoke, or it is because the factual issue under consideration presents what Holmes had called a "nice case," that is, one for which no direct precedent exists or existed and which requires a more careful discrimination of the applicable legal principles, maxims, or rules. We are concerned with the lack of existing precedent or persuasive authority, not the problem of first impression, with reconstruction not construction. The question then becomes: by what means of inference does one fill out the body of law from the extant reported decisions or, more broadly, from "the finite body of dogma which may be mastered in a reasonable time[?]"

The question becomes complex because of the presence of the phrase "finite body of dogma." "Finite body of dogma" obviously connects to the phrase "body of law" in the same paragraph but it is not certain that by both phrases Holmes means the same thing. Because he describes the "finite body of dogma" as "the number of our predictions" that have been "generalized and reduced to a system," some commentators have been led to conclude that for him, as for Langdell, the law fundamentally consists of cohering principles.[47] But Holmes's lifelong protest against the use of glittering generalities (*e.g.*, freedom of contract) either to teach law or to justify decisions causes one to demur from this conclusion and leads one to draw a line between a "finite body of dogma" and a "body of law."

The difference between the two in a common law jurisdiction lies in the facts by which the generalized predictions take meaning. The law for Holmes as a working system began with specific court action in a particular case. The cases that set the groundwork and prove commanding through subsequent use lead to legal principles because of the human ability to review, scrutinize, and generalize. One may for pedagogical purposes, or for utility, or for providing legal advice extract a developed and guiding principle, or less grandly a specific rule, but isolated principles collected and systematized into a "finite body" did not a legal corpus make. This point will become clearer when we focus in Part V on Holmes's interesting use of the word "dogma" and its connection to legal study.

We return to the problem of reconstruction and wonder what alternative is left if the gaps within the extant body of law cannot be closed solely through logical inference. Or, to be more precise, when the belief prevails that logic alone is an inadequate tool for forming the necessary connective tissue because its inherent limitations are all too evident.

In Holmes's own terms a generation so tasked would still have recourse to the dynamics created by its own conflicts and disagreements over values and right outcomes. It would still have recourse to its own good sense and collective expertise (its "well known profession"). It would bring into the present a heritage of value, sentiment, and will, a set of prepossessions that ground legal action. The materials for re-creation and reconstruction are in fact ever present to – in a different metaphor – seal the cracks the extant cases and logical inference alone cannot cover. The body of law would in time fill itself out even if all that came before disappeared because each generation has recourse to its own experience.

For this interpretation to work, the constraints Holmes set in place must be observed. The task is reconstruction, not construction. What has been preserved must be enough from which to extrapolate what has been lost. That the endeavor is not purely far-fetched Holmes demonstrated through his own work as a legal historian. In commenting on a historical work published many years after *The Common Law* he noted with pride that the new study "showed that I had pretty well reconstructed the fish from a bone and scale." A phrase, Howe notes, that "aptly characterized much of Holmes's achievement as analytical historian."[48]

47 *See, e.g.*, Grey, *supra* note 7, at 816–26.

48 HOWE, *supra* note 34, at 278–79; *see also* Felix Frankfurter, *The Early Writings of O. W. Holmes, Jr.*, 44 HARV. L. REV. 717, 718 (1931) (observing that Holmes revealed in his work the imaginative gift that in a great scientist reconstructs the extinct species from a single vertebra).

Thus Holmes's little eye-opening introit to the main substance of the Boston University School of Law address reinforces the impression that history – understood as prior court decisions – is only one means by which the past may be self-consciously brought into the present. Historical scholarship provides another avenue. Recognition of the multifaceted role of experience in the decision-making process is yet a third.

The present understood as the here-and-now, the actuality that one faces, the conflicts from which one cannot escape, the case one must decide or the client one must advise, exists, for the profession, within what Hurst describes as the temporal dimensions of experience. Law understood in the manner that Holmes understands it deprives the present of its sense of ultimacy. A temporally informed legal perspective sees the possibility of constructing a legal metric because it recognizes law's three-dimensionality. Three-dimensionality arises when the ambit within which legal professionals work is brought into tighter juxtaposition, greater relief. A legal metric depends, in other words, on recognizing law's three-dimensionality for its full articulation.

ii *The Theory of the Law*

"The Path of the Law" may contain Holmes's most sustained reflections on the prerequisites for legal study but the most important sentence on that topic comes from "Law in Science and Science in Law."

> When he has discovered that the difference is a difference of degree, that distinguished extremes have between them a penumbra in which one gradually shades into the other, a tyro thinks to puzzle you by asking where you are going to draw the line, and an advocate of more experience will show the arbitrariness of the line proposed by putting cases very near to it on one side or the other. *But the theory of the law is that such lines exist, because the theory of the law as to any possible conduct is that it is either lawful or unlawful.*[49]

The simplicity of the last sentence astonishes one because of the way in which Holmes states it. On the one hand it seems obvious that from the point of view of the law conduct is either lawful or unlawful. On the other hand, the statement once made forces one to reflect upon the perspective from which this statement makes the most sense and which this statement illuminates. The provenance of that perspective has an Hegelian resonance: the perspective of the law comes into being when (recognizable) legal professionals reflect on what is already (recognizably) law, that is, on what is more than caprice or what Holmes once referred to as the blandishments of the emperor's wife.[50]

49 Oliver Wendell Holmes, *Law in Science and Science in Law*, *in* III CW 416 (emphasis added).

50 Oliver Wendell Holmes, *Comment on* The Law Magazine and Review, *in* I CW 295 [hereinafter *The 1872 Jurisprudence Essay*].

The logical conclusion: the perspective of the law cannot come into being if law does not already exist.

Without embroiling ourselves in an illusory chicken-or-the-egg problem, the fundamental theorem that all conduct is either lawful or unlawful turns on the recognition that there must already exist mandated conduct and the concerted effort to extrapolate a pattern out of prior determinations. In essence, a necessary precondition for the theory of law as Holmes expresses it is the co-existence of already mandated and un-mandated conduct from which further series of actions denoted unlawful or lawful are derived. Holmes's fundamental theorem of law begins *in medias res* and, most important, stays *in medias res*. One cannot draw legal lines self-consciously and intelligently if initial lines, or least points, did not already in some sense exist. At the same time, the theory admits no conduct that cannot be classified as either unlawful or lawful and implicitly recognizes that conduct may be reclassified.

We can see in retrospect that the idea Holmes enunciated with such compactness and clarity in 1899 he had been searching for since his earliest articles, "Codes, and the Arrangement of the Law," the "1872 Jurisprudence Essay," and "The Theory of Torts." He had now developed a point of view distinctly legal and distinctly philosophical that took as its fundamental standpoint that of the legal professional. He did not attempt, as did John Austin, to philosophically systematize universal features of law by starting from a fundamental proposition – the command of the sovereign. Holmes uses the same starting point but understands the philosophical goal and approach differently. It requires the extension of existing concepts or the formulation of new ones through a greater attentiveness to social facts, their variety, their relevant pasts and anticipated futures.

What exactly are the distinguishing features of legal concepts or principles, or how one should describe precisely the reasoning process that leads to new, subtler generalizations Holmes does not explain. Holmes simply sketches his position and provides pointers for those who care to follow along. He states the overriding concern in the opening sentence of the paragraph right before the one that contains the above quotation. It is education. "The growth of education is an increase in the knowledge of measure."[51]

Education in this sense means substituting quantitative for qualitative judgments. The specific challenge for the jurisprudential critic – one who understands and reflects upon the workings and directions of an operative legal system and seeks to clarify what Holmes calls the magistrate's intuition – differs from that facing, say, the art critic or the music critic. But the challenges coincide in the common pursuit for greater sophistication. Holmes uses examples from these two fields to show the difference in the quality of judgments between a critic and an amateur. The latter, for instance, reacts to a statue by exclaiming, "It is grotesque!" The technically

[51] Holmes, *supra* note 49, at 415.

trained critic agrees and says: "That statue is so many heads high, instead of the normal so many heads."[52] The trained critic has achieved a level of understanding and of explanatory precision through the use of quantitative terms that renders the amateur comparatively dumb.

Holmes wants at least a few legal professionals to be more like technically trained sophisticated critics than gifted amateurs. He wants them to adopt the language of what he calls quantity – of number, measurement, magnitude, and proportion. He acknowledges the impending difficulties. Yet an unbiased review of his life's work reveals an abiding passion for clear thinking on the relations between how much of this and how much of that.[53]

Lest we get lost in the fog of abstraction let us consider, first, his word choices. He shows a predilection for words describing magnitude and quantity. He speaks of setting jurisprudential boundaries, of drawing lines and determining degrees, and, most vividly, of counting claws and teeth to gauge the captured dragon's strength.[54]

Second, consider how in "Law in Science and Science in Law" he vests specific ends with a lineage and an approbation (or disapprobation) that distinctively marks them off as social. "Well, in the law we only occasionally can reach an absolutely final and quantitative determination, because the worth of the competing social ends which respectively solicit a judgment for the plaintiff or the defendant cannot be reduced to number and accurately fixed."[55] In this sentence we see Holmes's view that what stands behind any particular plaintiff or defendant's specific interest – a *sine qua non* for that interest to gain traction in the legal process – is the agreement of other people that the specific interest represents or directly implicates dearly held values or beliefs.

But if competing social ends cannot always be quantified and measured, does that stymie the effort to improve legal practice? Not for Holmes. He laments any retreat, any "slackening in the eternal pursuit of the more exact."[56] The quest continues. He observes that a social goal's worth – which he defines as "the intensity of competing desires" – varies with the ideals of the time. He continues: "if the desires were constant, we could not get beyond a relative decision that one was greater and one was less."[57]

52 *Id.*

53 One example: "The trouble with general or literary historical works is that they deal with premises or conclusions that are both unquantified. We readily admit their assumption that such and such a previous fact tended to produce such and such a later one; but how much of the first would be necessary to produce how much of the last, and how much there actually was of either, we are not told." Holmes, *supra* note 5, at 439.

54 Holmes, *supra* note 1, at 399. Holmes says the dragon is a hoary rule of law that must be gotten "out of his cave on to the plain and into the daylight" where the claws and teeth can be counted. *Id.* The counting I take to be a way of discerning from these indicators (claws and teeth) the dragon's strength, that is, to determine its present power and vitality.

55 Holmes, *supra* note 49, at 415.

56 *Id.*

57 *Id.*

In these brief phrases Holmes broaches the most important postulate of his theory of law. It is this: the concerted action we call law is subject to a higher law, the law of fashion. "The law of fashion is the law of life."[58] The congeries of sentiments and desires that can call upon sufficient power to achieve an external result are always subject to revaluation. By whom? The people who later in time reflect upon, or react to, what they or others before them have done. Historical awareness reveals desires competing and shifting. It brings to light varying levels of intensity and duration in the pursuit of ends, terms that indicate commitment, value or worth. Because the desires are shifting and competing – that is to say, some win and some lose – and because over time even the winners can lose vitality (become less real or actual, have less ability to draw forth attention and life-commitment),[59] the angle of vision that historical awareness provides creates the possibility for measurement. Precisely because varying desires at varying times became law – seen in retrospect from a specific angle of historical vision – these desires are not binary or uniformly relative. The potential for measurement exists.

The possibility for measurement is not measurement itself. From the beginning of his career Holmes revealed a fascination for finding ratios between conflicting interests. He never stopped searching for the right words to articulate his idea of a legal metric, that which would enable and facilitate the formulation of such ratios. His turn toward history opens the door to more material, a larger number of instances of imposed or thwarted desire, additional opportunities to make comparisons and adduce relationships between different regimes of the good. It also allows him to recognize the prevalence of what Hurst calls "drift" and the omnipresence of imitative behavior. Finally it permits him to formulate his fundamental theory of the law – a theory about which we shall have more to say in Part V – that establishes its own intrinsic perspective on experience. It is a perspective historically derived but not one primarily historical. It is a perspective that leads to a distinctive discipline – a field of inquiry – regarding the use and justification of that specific type of social power that renders conduct lawful or unlawful.

iii *The Bad Man Appears*

Jerome Frank, Mark DeWolfe Howe, and David Seipp all noticed that the famed bad man of "The Path of the Law" first appeared, in a slightly different guise, in a section of *The Common Law* where Holmes discusses contractual conditions.[60]

[58] *Id.* at 406.

[59] Karl Llewellyn uses the word "vital" in a similar way in his legal analysis. *See* Karl N. Llewellyn, *What Price Contract? – An Essay in Perspective*, 40 YALE L.J. 704, 728 (1931) ("by 'vital' I mean a concept which had vigorously influenced men's actions").

[60] HOWE, *supra* note 34, at 238 n.38; Jerome Frank, *Mr. Justice Holmes and Non-Euclidean Legal Thinking*, 17 CORNELL L. REV. 568, 570 n.4 (1932); David J. Seipp, *125th Anniversary Essay: Holmes's Path*, 77 B.U. L. REV. 515, 525 (1997). More broadly, David Rosenberg has correctly

In an analysis on the nature and role of conditions in contracts – where he took more than one swipe at Langdell – Holmes contends that contractual conditions, properly understood, did more than simply encase a promise. They also had a more important function than choreographing the pleadings.

He does not deny the (limited) usefulness of the standard formulation: "The conditions which a contract may contain have been divided by theorists into conditions precedent and conditions subsequent. The distinction has even been pronounced of great importance."[61] Pronounced by whom? Well, by Langdell for one in his A *Summary of the Law of Contracts*.[62] Holmes acknowledges that for the purposes of determining the existence and viability of a cause of action given the applicable procedural rules, such delineation as Langdell's seems legitimate and logical.

But then Holmes takes a philosophical stab at the issue in his trademark manner. He creates a polarity. "In one sense, all conditions are subsequent; in another, all are precedent." It depends, he says, from what point one looks at the legal event we call a contract.

All conditions may be taken as subsequent "to the first stage of the obligation." He provides the following example: "Take for instance, the case of a promise to pay for work if done to the satisfaction of the architect. The condition is a clear case of what is called a condition precedent. There can be no duty to pay until the architect is satisfied." But a contract exists before the occurrence of the agreed upon event – the satisfaction of the architect – "because the determination whether the promisor shall pay or not is no longer within his control. Hence the condition is subsequent to the existence of the obligation."[63]

Langdell had defined a condition precedent as an event that precedes in time the promisor's obligation to perform.[64] Holmes considers Langdell's division somewhat arbitrary, perhaps driven more by the rules of procedure, by the march of the pleadings, than by anything intrinsic to the law of contracts. Where Langdell recognizes an obligation to perform that arises only after the occurrence of the agreed upon event, Holmes sees the obligation and the performance as stages of a broader sequence (the formation, progression, and terminus of the contract) that began when the promisor and promisee agreed that the promisor would pay the promisee when the architect expressed satisfaction with the promisee's work. That is when the contract came into existence. Langdell's obvious rejoinder is that that may

pointed out that the perspective that Holmes intended the "bad man" to represent was present in Holmes's work from the very beginning. DAVID ROSENBERG, THE HIDDEN HOLMES: HIS THEORY OF TORTS IN HISTORY 196 n.48 (1995).

61 Holmes, *supra* note 9, at 276.

62 CHRISTOPHER COLUMBUS LANGDELL, A SUMMARY OF THE LAW OF CONTRACTS 33–35 (2d ed. 1880).

63 Holmes, *supra* note 9, at 277.

64 LANGDELL, *supra* note 62, at 33–35.

be when the parties formed the contract but the promisee cannot enforce it until the agreed-upon event occurs and the promisor does not perform.

Holmes's main point is that simply viewing conditions in terms of their position in time – whether occurring before or after performance of the obligation – does little to advance the law of contracts. A contract, according to Holmes's notion of "committing a contract," of a contract defined not simply as promise but as the "taking of a risk," signifies an action with the legal consequence of liability already attached. If the thing that is supposed to happen does not happen the promisor – the one who took the risk of the thing happening – is taken to know at the time of the contract's formation the probable legal consequences.[65] Unlike in torts, where often an inquiry is needed to determine if the complained of act constitutes a civil wrong (an act with certain legal consequences attached), in Holmes's rendition of contract law no initial inquiry is required. Or it's required only rarely, when the parties dispute the existence of a contract.

At the inception of the legal event, upon commencing "the first stage of obligation," the actor understands, or is taken to understand, that she or he is acting under circumstances that lead to directly foreseeable legal consequences. That is what Holmes means by "committing a contract."

Based on the foregoing reasoning – that committing a contract sets one on a trajectory toward foreseeable legal consequences – one can easily comprehend how Holmes sets up the other end of the polarity. If in one sense all conditions after the initial stage of obligation are conditions subsequent – coming after the decisive, formative legal acts or "special facts" (such as promise and consideration)[66] – then in an equivalent manner those same conditions are precedent to what Holmes refers to as "the incidence of the burden of the law."[67] The "burden of the law" as Holmes uses the term is, I take it, the enforcement authority's specific impositions upon the actor for the non-happening of the circumstance for which the actor assumed liability when he or she contracted.

Holmes explains his point that "every condition subsequent is precedent to the incidence of the burden of the law" this way:

> If we look at the law as it would be regarded by one who had no scruples against doing anything which he could do without incurring legal consequences, it is obvious that the main consequence attached by law to a contract is a greater or less possibility of having to pay money. The only question from the purely legal point of view is whether the promisor will be compelled to pay. And the important moment is that at which that point is settled. All conditions are precedent to that.[68]

65 Holmes, *supra* note 9, at 268–72.

66 For a good discussion of this point, *see* Patrick J. Kelley, *Critical Analysis of Holmes's Theory of Contract*, 75 Notre Dame L. Rev. 1681, 1720–29 (2000).

67 Holmes, *supra* note 9, at 277.

68 *Id.*

The man called bad makes his first appearance in Holmes's published corpus in 1881 as "one who had no scruples against doing anything he could do without incurring legal consequences." The main consequence he seeks to avoid, when it comes to contracts, is the possibility of having to pay money. Sixteen years later, when he makes an appearance in "The Path of the Law," he has not changed in his fundamental attitude or interests. He still wishes to avoid encounters with the public force. He still "cares nothing for an ethical rule which is believed and practiced by his neighbors," but "is likely nevertheless to care a good deal to avoid being made to pay money, and will want to keep out of jail if he can."[69]

If we take Holmes's unscrupulous bad man as personifying a point of view – what Holmes calls "the purely legal point of view" – we see from how Holmes employs him in both *The Common Law* and "The Path of the Law" that the focus of the bad man's (and Holmes's) attention is on the likely terminus of a legal event. That terminus, as we pointed out in Part I, lies in both the evident, easily foreseeable consequences and those collateral consequences that may not be immediately obvious.

In regard to contractual conditions, all conditions of whatever type are precedent "in this extreme sense" to enacted legal consequences. Thus the endpoints that Holmes creates regarding contractual conditions – all are subsequent to the moment the obligation is created and precedent to the legal authority taking concrete, material action – serve to frame an analysis of contractual conditions that bypasses Langdell's distinction between conditions that must be satisfied before a promise can be broken and those which discharge a liability after the obligation has accrued. Holmes thinks such distinctions to be "of the slightest importance."[70]

Clearly Holmes did not think it helpful to isolate certain necessary steps that may be part of the legal event called contract, a legal event that may eventually include an enforcement stage, and call them conditions when it appeared to him that they had more the character of stipulations. "It is much more important to mark the distinction between a stipulation which only has the effect of confining a promise to certain cases, and a condition properly so called."[71] What, then, is a condition? Holmes says it is an occurrence that gives, when it happens, one of the parties the option of treating "the contract as if it had not been made[.]"[72]

He then adds this significant gloss: "When a condition operates as such, it lets in an outside force to destroy the existing state of things."[73] The nature of a condition as Holmes defines it reinforces the notion that a contract is a legal event with its own beginning point, trajectory, and terminus. A condition in Holmes's sense permits the party in whose favor it operates the option of disrupting or short-circuiting the

69 Holmes, *supra* note 1, at 392.
70 Holmes, *supra* note 9, at 277.
71 *Id.*
72 *Id.*
73 *Id.* at 278.

contract. That party, at its choosing, may continue along the contractually agreed upon path and sue the counter-party for breach or void the contract altogether and seek its due remedy outside the confines of the contract. As Holmes says, these remedies are mutually exclusive.[74]

Holmes's introduction of the bad man fits with his habit of analyzing law through a dialectic of viewpoints. Each viewpoint has its associated interest or interests. The bad man's concern that he may have to pay money showed the artificiality of Langdell's contractual conditions. Contractual conditions, commonly called, may have their own administrative sequence, but unduly elevating that administrative sequence ran the danger of turning the law of contractual conditions into a function of procedure. Contracts are acts that should be understood philosophically. Those who stand in a special relationship to each other do so by virtue of their mutual anticipation regarding a future state of affairs.

To better understand Holmes's position, let's return to his example of the promise to pay for work if done to the satisfaction of the architect. The promise, or "accepted assurance," from the promisor to the promisee is that the promisor will pay once the work is done to the architect's satisfaction. Holmes believed this point initiated the legal event because "the determination whether the promisor shall pay or not is no longer within his control." That is to say, the formation of the contract brought into the parties' relationship an external or objective reference point (represented in this example by the architect's satisfaction) that would direct the parties either away from or toward the connected legal consequences.

Dissected, Holmes's example reveals the following. The promisor no longer has the power to decide whether the promisee's work is sufficiently satisfactory to merit payment. The promisor has taken the risk that she may have to pay even if she is not satisfied with the work done. All that matters is the architect's satisfaction. The promisor may have to pay for and actually be stuck with defective work. The promisee, on the other hand, has taken the risk that the architect will find his work unsatisfactory. He will then not be paid for the work done, and he may have to do additional work. The promisee has taken the risk of working for free. He has taken the risk of having to labor until the architect is satisfied. Still another foreseeable consequence is that the promisee may be found to have breached the contract if the architect is never satisfied. He may then be liable to the promisor for contractual damages.

The promises made by both sides (to pay upon the architect certifying satisfaction, to perform the work according to the satisfaction of the architect) lead to nothing more than a delineated legal event. As Holmes would much later insist to Pollock: "I stick to my paradox as to what a contract was at common law: not a *promise* to pay damages or, etc., but an act imposing a liability to damages *nisi* [unless]. You commit a tort & are liable. You commit a contract and are liable

[74] *Id.*

unless the event agreed upon, over which you may have no, and never absolute control, comes to pass."[75]

This notion of giving up control (and becoming presumptively liable) is what separates Holmes's view of how the common law treated contracts from other prominent views existing at the time.[76] The point, to return to the example above, is not that the architect has the power to decide. One or the other party may believe the architect certifying satisfaction, or the architect's unwillingness to certify satisfaction, to be unreasonable. The dispute may then land in front of a legal authority that must then determine if the architect acted reasonably (if that is the prevailing legal test). The point is the loss of control.

Holmes's opinion that the common law presumed contractual liability until shown otherwise is the opposite of the currently common opinion that a contract simply means one has promised to perform or to pay damages. A contract, by definition, committed the contractors to certain legal consequences.

Legally speaking there is no separate duty to keep a promise. The legal duty and the associated penalty are already built into a contractual promise. In the same manner, to see a contract as providing an option to either perform or pay damages – efficient breach theory – is to break up into distinct analytical categories what Holmes viewed as a single legal event. It is an attempt to take control of the legal event. But the essence of contract, for Holmes, was, to a lesser or greater degree, a giving up of control. There is simply a duty (so-called) to make good unless the promised act or circumstance happens.[77] That is the so-called penalty the law annexes.[78] Yet even then the so-called penalty may not be forthcoming if an agreed upon occurrence – called a condition – upends the relationship called a contract.

Through his reflections on the nature of contractual conditions Holmes continued to demonstrate the power that knowledge of concrete circumstances had in creating the necessary links of legal cause and effect. In keeping with his external standard, the knowledge may be actual or imputed. Certain groupings of facts gave rise to legal events. Other groupings upended them. Still other groupings failed to meet the relevant legal tests. To understand the operative differences and distinctions between and among the groupings and the connected legal consequences one had to adopt, in Holmes's words, "the purely legal point of view."

[75] 1 The Holmes–Pollock Letters: The Correspondence of Mr. Justice Holmes and Sir Frederick Pollock 1874–1932 177 (Mark DeWolfe Howe ed., 2d ed. 1961) (emphasis in original). *See also* Joseph M. Perillo, *Misreading Oliver Wendell Holmes on Efficient Breach and Tortious Interference*, 68 Fordham L. Rev. 1085, 1086–90 (2000).

[76] Kelley, *supra* note 66, at 1694–1714.

[77] Holmes, *supra* note 9, at 269 ("The only universal consequence of a legally binding promise is, that the law makes the promisor pay damages if the promised event does not come to pass. In every case it leaves him free from interference until the time for fulfillment has gone by, and therefore free to break his contract if he chooses.").

[78] I write "so-called" because the penalty and duty are not "absolute" as discussed in Part I.

4 THE PERSPECTIVE OF LAW: INCREASING LAW'S CAPACITY TO BE KNOWN

The great challenge for someone of Holmes's ilk in the late nineteenth century lay in finding the best way to draw out from the immense range of natural phenomena – which includes human phenomena – the formulations of legal cause and effect (how much of this and how much of that) that met the prevailing criteria of intelligibility and proof. In his own work Holmes rarely wavers from his primary purpose of shaping the common law according to how he comprehends the prevailing criteria, and extending the common law's fundamental mode of operation.

Could he draw from such a study a portrait of law's actuality? He thought so. The portrait of something born in history cannot be done well without a subjective responsiveness to the life it once had and may continue to have.[79] Life in this sense equals persistence or what Holmes calls tendencies. Tendency in this strong sense is more than the excavated scale and bone of a long extinct fish. It exists in the present and pushes toward the future. One wonders if Holmes understood his own recognition of certain tendencies in the common law as a sign of his present, as the actuality of the law as it existed in his here-and-now. Holmes had learned through his historical investigations that the present of which one is not aware takes shape retrospectively through conscious effort. Conscious effort in this sense, in regard to law, is called legal thinking. It involves more than logic. It exemplifies the abilities to analyze legal subjects; to feel and understand the different motives at work; and to tease out from circumstances (a conjoined past, present, and future) new meanings for legal action.

Holmes sought to further order the common law by bringing to light certain of its distinctive operations; he would reveal salient features that corresponded to the needs of his present. Such features could then further orient lawmakers' conduct. To the extent one understands the common law as a "system" this required, in the terms in which and through which Holmes worked, increasing – however minutely – through one's own effort the capacity of the common law to be known.

We have apparently entered the realm of paradox. On the one hand we assert Holmes's lifelong intent to bring order out of the existing chaos of the common law, to make the common law more knowable; and, on the other hand, we suggest that to make the common law more knowable, as Holmes wanted to do, one must expand

[79] On this point it is worth noting John T. Noonan's perceptive comments on what he calls the "alliance of law and history." JOHN T. NOONAN, JR., PERSONS AND MASKS OF THE LAW: CARDOZO, HOLMES, JEFFERSON, AND WYTHE AS MAKERS OF THE MASKS 152–67 (2002 ed.) (orig. pub. 1976). *Id.* at 164 ("We are bound to the past, that is, to the past participants. Within the context of the community they have made we are in dialogue with them; and law is a form of the dialogue.").

the capacity of the common law to be known.[80] It may seem counterintuitive to speak of increasing the capacity of the law to be known in this way. If, for instance, law as we know it ultimately resolves into a set of principles then it seems odd to suggest that their capacity to be known, or to be knowable, can be extended.

What does that mean? Does it mean we understand how a principle applies to more instances? That would indicate greater appreciation for the principle's formulation, greater adroitness in realizing its implications and ramifications – how it fits within the broader scheme of which it is a part – and that, in turn, would extend one's ability to put the principle to practical use. But such pragmatic knowledge, in one use of the term pragmatic, simply equates knowledge of the principle with its uses and potential uses for solving problems or answering questions. It bespeaks experimentation, tallying up results and looking for productive outcomes.

Alternately, expanding the capacity of the law to be known may be Holmes's way of bringing to light the genesis of law in the cohesion of desire, belief, purpose, and power. The cohesive element we might call reasoning, and reasoning taken beyond the purely instrumental we might call philosophical. Philosophizing worked best in the common law when it took in a range of phenomena and organized it from the standpoint of single generative fact. From that broader range, one then drew out further commonalities – similar features of experience – and fortified them into an active synthesis or abstraction.

An abstraction, such as duty, took its power from the actuality of fact. In the case of duty the force of the concept arose from the actuality of exile, of complete loss of recognized legal status. One was thrust back into a pre-legal and perhaps even pre-political status; one became an outlaw. The abstraction, nascent in the mind of a

[80] We should distinguish at this juncture different senses of the word "knowable." Holmes uses it in a footnote in his "The Arrangement of the Law – Privity" to indicate that a better classification of the law – per duties, not rights – would reveal an underlying rationale between divisions and subdivisions and frame the overall system. The use of systematic categorization takes the law from the realm of topical, customary groupings to that of a progressive logical order (from the most general conception to the most specific proposition or exception). David Rosenberg believes Holmes's general theory of torts, reflecting Holmes's anti-formalist jurisprudential orientation, has the power to make law knowable in a different way. Holmes's general theory of torts employs for Rosenberg a principle – that of choice predicated on foreseeability of harm – that helps one make better sense of the extant tort cases and of future ones because it clarifies the main presumption as to any given circumstance: people should make choices to avoid foreseeable harm. That is, the presumption applies unless there is no preexisting duty to avoid foreseeable harm (as in economic competition) or unless they are privileged from complying with an existing duty (for example, to not disparage another's reputation). The word "knowable" in the sense in which I am using it connects to Rosenberg's use but goes one step beyond by seeking to elucidate a framework and a method conducive to the formulation of principles of the type that Rosenberg discerned in Holmes's general theory of torts. Thus, human activity itself becomes the subject and the means for human knowledge – warrantable assertions that extend the human power to infer consequences, predict, and transmute actualities into meaningful propositions that, in turn, transmute actualities. *See* Holmes, *supra* note 4, at 303 n**; ROSENBERG, *supra* note 60, at 57–61.

conceiver, became real, that is became a recognized element of experience, when other people began to treat the conception as real. They found meaning in it. The meaning elicited or imposed may or may not equate with the original state of affairs (*e.g.*, exile), but to that original state of affairs the developed and emerging meanings had a genetic connection. Abstracting in this sense, as Frederic Kellogg has pointed out, works from subtle but often illusive notions of similarity (*this* is basically just like *that*).[81] The abstraction then gains actuality through the habit of apperception.

Take for example admiralty law. The conception of the deodand did not originate the law of the sea but gave that law its initial shape. The pressure of circumstances and the needs of a developing society led to changes in its configurations. In his analysis of how the deodand shaped admiralty law, Holmes started with the fundamental insight that a ship endowed with characteristics recognizably human led to a certain rule of liability. Understanding, in turn, how that rule of liability adjusted to changing circumstances and needs at first pressing and then in time less demanding helped one make sense of the particular features of admiralty law and why it persisted in the shape that it had.

To the fundamental law of fashion Holmes added a notion reminiscent of Spinoza, the corollary of conatus – continuous self-preserving and self-enhancing movement.

But in what sense would such patient deconstruction of law in terms of past consciousness(es) that, despite transfigurations, may still have vital trace elements in the present lead to an expansion of law's capacity to be known? The importance of an insight or an aperçu, Holmes believed, lay in its ability to structure an entire field of knowledge. The insight itself led one to adopt a certain position and from that point extend the insight's power through the further organization of phenomena.

In respect to law the fundamental insight that law originates in social beliefs and attitudes that eventuate in combined social action led Holmes to this observation:

> The philosophers teach us that an idea is the first step toward an act. Beliefs, so far as they bear upon the attainment of a wish (and most beliefs do), lead in the first place to a social attitude, and later to combined social action, that is, to law. Hence, ever since it has existed, the law has expressed what men most strongly have believed and desired. And, as the beliefs and desires of the Western world have changed and developed a good deal since the days of the Twelve Tables and the Law of the Salian Franks, I thought it dangerously near a platitude to say, a dozen years ago, that the law might be regarded as a great anthropological document. But, as a gentleman prominent at the bar of one of the States professed difficulty in understanding what I meant, it is evident that the rudiments need eternal repetition. Any man who is interested in ideas needs only the suggestion that I have made to realize that the history of the law is the embryology of a most important set of ideas, and perhaps more than any other history tells the story of the race.[82]

[81] Frederic R. Kellogg, Oliver Wendell Holmes Jr. and Legal Logic 36–53 (2018).

[82] Holmes, *supra* note 5, at 439.

Holmes's suggestion that the law "might be regarded as a great anthropological document" reminds one of his comments in "The Path of the Law" that the law "is the witness and external deposit of our moral life. Its history is the history of the moral development of our race."[83] It also leads one by natural progression to his most definite articulation in "Law in Science and Science in Law" of the ideal toward which he aimed:

> The true science of the law does not consist mainly in a theological working out of dogma or a logical development as in mathematics, or only in a study of it as an anthropological document from the outside; an even more important part consists in the establishment of its postulates from within upon accurately measured social desires instead of tradition.

"[A]n even more important part consists in the establishment of its postulates from within upon accurately measured social desires instead of tradition." This is the critical clause. What does it tell us? It tells us that the key formulated insights (the postulates) of the common law – in torts, property, contracts, and in rules of inheritance for instance – must be established from within the law, that is, from within the law's own perspective or what Holmes also calls the "purely legal point of view."

That is the first point. If we are correct that the necessary postulates are the fundamental insights that generate continued order – repetitive enforcement of behavior that exhibits some type of regularity or pattern – then the second point, that these insights must be established on accurately measured social desires instead of tradition, tells us less concerning the inherent vitality of the existing postulates than about how they should be grounded. Holmes wants the grounding to be intelligence, not custom or authority.

To accurately measure social desires it appears one must ascertain the social desire being measured and then develop the appropriate metric. It has seemed to some scholars that at this juncture Holmes took a turn toward utilitarianism. And there may be some support for that contention.[84] But Holmes's terms for justifying an individual good or even the good of the many did not arise from a generalized notion of utility. It arose from his recognition that humans pursued different types of values at different times, and the order and internal relation of the values pursued led to different overall assessments of relative importance. In modern terms, we could say that the activity of law often takes place in a field of competing and incommensurable goods. Trade-offs are necessary. Or, as Holmes liked to say, there's always a bill.

The importance of Holmes's position did not lie in the common view that trade-offs are omnipresent. It lay in his recognition that each entrenched social desire

[83] Holmes, *supra* note 1, at 392.

[84] *See* H. L. Pohlman, Justice Oliver Wendell Holmes & Utilitarian Jurisprudence (1984).

seeks to crowd out the others and all of them often join to fight off newcomers. Conflict is endemic.[85] For that reason, any social desire sufficiently strong to have law on its side will initially prevail. It will forcefully manifest itself as an external result. But its persistence over time, especially as values change and reorder themselves and leaps in consciousness lead to transfigurations of existing arrangements, may be due less to law's capacity to order and command and more to an array of hidden negative capabilities.

Legal forms persist for many reasons. On the one side lie such common traits as indolence, inattention, the propensity to take the path of least resistance, recourse to the known and the familiar, and on the other what the anthropologist Claude Lévi-Strauss terms bricolage, the ability to manipulate existing forms to serve new unforeseen ends.[86] The liability of a ship that had caused injury or death may find its roots in a consciousness for which the law of the deodand had significant effect; but its transformation in time into a rule of limited liability protecting the ship's owners or its operators served other ends and fit within different legal assumptions.

Lévi-Strauss uses bricolage to distinguish what he calls the savage mind from a mind understood as supposedly scientific, perhaps even modern, that finds its métier in concepts. Such a division, Lévi-Strauss argues, misunderstands both the nature of mind and the nature of science. Both the so-called savage mind and the modern mind operate in a scientific manner. They simply do so on different planes. The relevant distinction lay in the reach and potency of abstractions conceived as concepts, that is, ideas with great power to synthesize features of experience that, in turn, become the basis for more encompassing extensions of intelligence. The savage mind operated more through signs (icons) that had a more direct relationship with the concrete, the here-and-now.[87]

If one views Holmes within the terms that Lévi-Strauss made popular, then the simplest way to explain Holmes's overriding intellectual ambition is to say that he wanted to move the legal mind of his time from the savage plane, which operated at the level of bricolage,[88] and past the plane of modern scientific concepts, to a plane

85 Frederic R. Kellogg, Oliver Wendell Holmes, Jr., Legal Theory, and Judicial Restraint 111 (2007); *see also* Hudson Water Co. v. McCarter, 209 U.S. 349, 355 (1908) ("All rights tend to declare themselves absolute to their logical extreme. Yet all in fact are limited by the neighborhood of principles of policy which are other than those on which the particular right is founded, and which become strong enough to hold their own when a particular point is reached.") (per Holmes, J.).

86 Claude Lévi-Strauss, The Savage Mind 16–22 (1966) (orig. pub. 1962).

87 *Id.* at 35–39.

88 Bricolage has made itself useful in the hands of American students of jurisprudence. Nathalie Hull employs it as an orienting concept, along with the idea of a network or community of discourse, to illuminate the professional lives of Roscoe Pound and Karl Llewellyn. In their search for a specifically American jurisprudence each of these thinkers made some headway by cobbling together bits and pieces of prior thought along with new concepts or instruments of social analysis but, in Hull's opinion, never accomplished the ultimate goal of articulating a jurisprudence that did full justice to the reality of American life. At least that is my best guess of

that supported a new inner sense of both the flux of experience and its relatively invariant elements. The plane, that is to say, where one recognized and believed in the possibility of infusing greater intelligence and dimensionality into legal acts, of increasing the transparency of legal power.

That overriding objective rested on the recognition that the common law at its origins and in its development exhibited a more-or-less dense opacity one sought to diminish through historical investigation and psychological argument. Whether Holmes's specific assertions and inferences met the best tests of truth available in his time or our own is less important (though not unimportant) than whether the presuppositions they elaborated or the premises they offered had the capacity to create a field of knowledge or, in short, a discipline. The law constituted a specific mode by which humans studied themselves. The form of the human did not exist ready-made but grew in time. We recall Jose Ortega y Gasset's dictum that humans do not have a nature, only a history.[89] From that point it is not inordinately difficult to grasp Holmes's vision of discovering the fundamental metric: the coordinated dimensions of experience that make effective and productive legal analysis possible. By this fundamental metric the capacity of the law to be known could be expanded.

The expansion of law's capacity to be known required the ability to measure social desires both diachronically and synchronically. We have to understand them in the fullness of their length, depth, and breadth. We are back to Hurst's ideas of sequence and context. It stands to reason then that when Holmes writes of trade-offs, of knowing what a luxury will cost, he has in mind not only current rates of exchange – those that exist synchronically – but also those that exist diachronically, corresponding between past, future, and present. Or as Holmes once blithely put it to his friend Pollock, one may lose James Hill (1838–1916 AD) but gain Aeschylus (525/524–456/455 BC).[90]

what Hull means by an "American jurisprudence." N. E. H. Hull, Roscoe Pound & Karl Llewellyn: Searching for an American Jurisprudence 1–16 (1997). Jack Balkin uses it to explore how cultural structures – including those we call law – come into being and change. J. M. Balkin, Cultural Software: A Theory of Ideology 23–41 (1998). Neither of these scholars noticed that Lévi-Strauss intended *bricolage* to signify an anterior scientific mindset (he did not want to use the word *primitive*) to the one we tend to recognize as modern. It had its own manner of ordering and of signifying. The philosopher Daniel Dennett usefully pinpoints the contrast when he notes that for Lévi-Strauss the tinkerer "is willing to be guided by the nature of the material, whereas the engineer wants the material to be perfectly malleable – like the concrete so beloved by the Bauhaus architects." Daniel C. Dennett, Darwin's Dangerous Idea: Evolution and the Meanings of Life 225–26 (1995).

89 Jose Ortega y Gasset, History As a System and Other Essays toward a Philosophy of History 217 (1941).

90 I Holmes–Pollock Letters, *supra* note 75, at 167. *See also* Oliver Wendell Holmes, *Remarks at a Dinner of the Alpha Delta Phi Club*, *in* III CW 540 ("There would be compensations even if we had to drop from James Hill to Aeschylus and Aristotle.").

Evidently Holmes took the long view. But a view no longer than the law itself – who is to say whether law's persistence in social life dictated its own representations to an inquiring mind? That possibility necessitated historical investigation. Yet if historical investigation succeeded in disaggregating beliefs, in splitting what the passage of time and the presence of passive capabilities had fused, what should one do with the results? In contemporary terms, how should one splice and edit the reams of footage left over from so many different reels?

We come back to Holmes's ideal: the establishment of the law's postulates from within upon accurately measured social desires. That is the true science of the law, one that the purely legal point of view makes possible. It begins by establishing a system of coordinates within a carefully circumscribed realm of human activity. It recognizes that human activity began in want and perception but did not become recognizably human until belief separated itself from the want–perception dyad and established its own separate footing. Beliefs when shared guided social action. If sufficiently strong to prevail against counter-forces such beliefs became law within the broader social ambit. Granted much of this may be speculation but for Holmes these notions, or similar notions, took root for heuristic purposes in the focal point of revenge.

In Part II we attempted to account for the movement from the internal standard to the external standard. We suggested it had to do with the triangulation of viewpoints and noted, in passing, that Holmes saw what had occurred in the history of the common law – the jump from the internal to the external standard – but knew enough to know that he could not explain it in a way that made sense to him. What is really most important about Holmes for our present day is his sense of intelligibility and his efforts as a judge and jurist to articulate that sense in the idiom of his time. It was, of course, his misfortune to carry the burden of a message for which there was no audience. The well-known profession of his era had little taste or talent to appreciate what he had to offer.

We now draw the inference – one tempered by the lapse of over a century since Holmes published his most vital writings – that his sense of intelligibility kept pushing against the limits that the sensibility of his era imposed on his search for knowledge. Holmes had made it his business to know law, and the pleasure he took in philosophy – in the search of the most general yet meaningful conceptions of which humans were capable – redounded to his legal work. He never stopped looking for inspired utterances that could further reveal the law's inner workings.

He took it as a given that law could only truly be known from within, by one practiced in its workings, by one who felt and recognized the systolic and diastolic movement of the central inquiry ("what is the law?" – "what is law?"). Why? Because the cases upon which the axe would fall – when and how the power of the law would strike – always reflected the power of certain living postulates in the here-and-now over others. That is to say the point of view of the law, shown through the conduct it would judge lawful or unlawful, shifted over time. Thus to satisfy a Holmesian sense of intelligibility the fundamental theory of the law had to connect with the fundamental reality of the law, that many enforced social desires wax and wane, and to do that it needed to establish its own organizing metric.

This route brings us back to Holmes's bad man. The bad man represents the purely legal point of view partly because his interest is expressly not moral or social (remember he is without scruples and cares not for the opinions of his neighbors), nor, just as important, is it political (the bad man is not primarily concerned with the legitimacy of public power or the preferences of those in power as expressed through policy). The bad man simply cares to know what legal consequences will attach to his actions. If a policy preference directly and overtly connects to a legal consequence then the bad man cares. Yet even this formulation does not fully capture the importance of the bad man as a projection of the law because from one point of view it is not difficult to ascertain the most obvious legal consequences – you pay money or you don't, you go to jail or you stay out.

The inadequacy of this external viewpoint leads to the second reason why the bad man represents the purely legal point of view. It is because the bad man's interest in knowing what legal consequences will attach to his actions – what the courts will do in fact and will continue to do in fact once the initial consequences are attached – requires the bad man to adopt the court's outlook to surmise how the court will determine and adjudicate the legally relevant facts. But we know once the bad man looks back on his own projected conduct in the way a court would he has to see it against the backdrop of already established law. The purely legal point of view stays ever focused on established law and the pressure it exerts.

In Holmes's succinct formulation, for the bad man to predict what the court will do in fact he must understand what the court has already done in fact. We will in Part V explore further what this "in fact" means. The bad man must, among other things, understand the circumstances in which the court has acted in the past. He first asks the question, "what is the law?" If he sees that his proposed conduct does not fall within the scope of circumstances already legally established, he must then proceed to the second step of the inquiry, "what is law?" In other words: "how will the courts array my proposed action (or inaction) against existing law and current concerns?" Ideally he must, in Hurst's terms, understand the sequence and context that enmesh his proposed conduct if he hopes to answer intelligently this question. From that complex hypothesis the bad man then infers the risk to his legal status that his proposed conduct may impose.

Holmes's use of the bad man is hard to understand without comprehending first Holmes's conception of duty.[91] For now we do well to note the genius of Holmes's bad man device. It functions both as a propaedeutic for beginners and as a lodestar

[91] Howe pointed this out in 1963. HOWE, *supra* note 34, at 238 n.38.

for those more experienced in the practice. It also lights a path for those charged with the task of litigating and deciding a nice case.

Its methodological importance arises from the recognition that presently held strong beliefs backed up by strong action occupy the same dimension of experience, legally speaking, as a common law decision from the thirteenth century. The challenge is to find a way to include both on the same coordinated three-dimensional grid despite recognized differences in space and time and in human consciousness.

Though Holmes did not articulate the metric of the law as an idea fundamental to his theory of legal study, many of his most important insights point towards it. The inferences line up. Past rules of law evincing beliefs no longer strong or desirable or immediately comprehensible must become part of the extant primary facts looking for new groupings.[92] For the law of the future, present deciders must determine new factual relations and their legal consequences. They must approach legal disputes with the depth of perspective. The cohesive that binds these primary social facts together into legally relevant groupings must come from conceptions internal to the profession but mediated through the social life that exists external to the profession. The needed reference points for the "best" or "right" decision do not merely come from morality or logic or history or psychology or sociology or economics or even the most persuasive policy rationales. They come from a constructed metric able to coordinate and thus provide a means to measure the panoply of social beliefs and desires prominent in law.

Should such a legal metric come into existence it would then be possible to expand the capacity of the law to be known because each new legal problem would bring forth recognition of congruencies and conflicts with previously established points of law. New relations would ensue. Perhaps new lines would need to be drawn, new degrees calculated, unexpected proportions between existing quantities noted. Such a coordinate system would further map the law and enhance the ability – which is now mainly intuitive – to position rules of law or declared principles within a dynamic three-dimensional system.

As Holmes expresses the hope in "Law in Science and Science in Law," such a metric would establish legal postulates upon accurately measured social desires.

[92] According to Philip P. Wiener, Nicholas St. John Green was the first to recognize the importance of reestablishing and repositioning past law through inductive reasoning. Inductive reasoning for Green included both historical and analytical methods. As Wiener noted, "Green's pragmatic historicism does not prevent him from following Austin's logical procedure of systematizing the common law, which was 'a mass of details,' for, like all English law, 'it has none of those large coherent principles which are a sure index to details.' *The 'details,' however, are not simply the mass of law but its shifting historical contexts with its diverse expression of the public will.*" Philip P. Wiener, Evolution and the Founders of Pragmatism 155 (Harper Torchbook 1965) (orig. pub. 1949) (emphasis added).

Social desires and beliefs expressed through law, measured against one another and emplotted within a three-dimensional coordinate system derived for that purpose, would make it possible to take into account their comparable duration, scope, relative strengths and weaknesses, their benefits and costs.

This coordinate system would presumably, as it develops, make likely further insights into those beliefs and desires and thereby render law increasingly knowable.

PART IV

Thirteen Ways of Looking at the Bad Man

SYNOPSIS

After providing a recapitulation of Parts I–III, Part IV seeks to bring into relief the purely legal point of view. To that end, it sketches portraits of varying lengths and extent. The focus is the various positions and ideas that have achieved currency regarding Holmes's bad man. It brings together realists, natural law proponents, pragmatists, and certain moralists and legal philosophers who have written either on Holmes or "The Path of the Law." There may be one or two surprises. People like John Zane or Francis E. Lucey, for example, usually do not receive extensive treatments in books on Holmes. But as the goal of this part is to bring the purely legal point of view into 3D, it became necessary to not only range deeply into the ideas but also bring out the sensibilities or temperaments that underlay them. And to accurately portray those emotions and attitudes – ranging from reverence of Holmes to contempt – that give definition and character to the various stances described.

Another purpose of this part is to provide one example of how one may go about creating dimensionality in the law. The technique I have chosen brings the legal scholars discussed into an arrangement, a composition. At one time in the annals of intellectual history the technique might have been described as recreating the conversation. But it is more than that. It is actually attempting to enliven a discourse, to form a full-fledged background, middle ground, and foreground that give it dimensionality and depth. It seeks to create the necessary legal space for the active inquirer, the participant in the legal process who wants to know, "What is (the) law?"

In modeling a three-dimensional view of law, this part attempts to define the subject matter of law through the give-and-take of historical placement and philosophical analysis. It recognizes that historical and philosophical approach as necessarily participatory and dialogic. The end governs the means, and the end in this case is bringing to the fore Holmes's conception of the bad man. He is the "remote conception," the projection that makes the purely legal point of view possible.

RECAPITULATION

One frequent problem with many Holmes studies is the tendency to treat his entire publicly accessible writings – book notes, law notes, longer law articles, notes to *Kent's Commentaries*, *The Common Law*, speeches and after-dinner remarks, the wide-ranging published correspondence, his hundreds and hundreds of opinions – as a single integrated volume from which a commentator may quote at will. Holmes's concentrated, at times epigrammatic style facilitates this scholarly sin; this amassed volume becomes a bible of texts or catchphrases. Many become pretexts for a commentator's chosen position without too much or any punctiliousness for the text's context or audience or place within the trajectory of Holmes's thought.

Sadly enough, I cannot say I have been able to avoid entirely this transgression. To atone allow me to recapitulate the course taken and describe Holmes's main trajectory of thought along with one or two changing emphases.

We began by equating the first sentence of "The Path of the Law" with Brian Simpson's declaration, in his *Invitation to Law*, that "law is for lawyers." Simpson's declaration, and Holmes's averment that "When we study law we are not studying a mystery but a well known profession[,]" served to delimit legal study to a specific range of pointers – in Simpson's terms that which tells a lawyer what to do to safeguard a client's interests – and the practices of which these pointers or signs are an integral part.

These pointers and practices exist and function within a broader social body. Simpson comments repeatedly in *Invitation to Law* on the pervasiveness of law in the modern world, an observation that other commentators have reiterated. Holmes does not make the same point, or at least not in the same way. He does, however, note that law in the sense that Austin used the term – what Holmes calls lawyers' law – is a subset of the broader commands or compulsions that serve to orient human behavior within the larger society. We may, for the sake of convenience, refer to the entire range of overt social commands or inner compulsions to obey internal commands as *duties*, in the loose sense, and identify those duties as legal that lead to a strict penalty for the contravention of what Holmes calls an absolute command. The other types of duties we could for convenience categorize as spiritual, social, and moral.[1]

The common thread in both Holmes and Simpson is that law, broadly construed, while pervasive is not co-extensive with any other array of internal or external restraints that exist within a functioning society. Law, as Holmes understands it, has a point of focus, or more accurately, a locus, and that locus is the courts.

Holmes identifies law's operative scope within the cultural range of duties that exist in a delimited sovereign territory. He then sets the whole range of duties against encompassing social currents and undercurrents that manifest themselves in the continuous flows of desire and belief, purpose and power. He at times refers to these social currents and undercurrents as experience. It is the life of the law, as it is of every other type of duty. Holmes's reflections on law's social and cultural reality tie to the basic understanding he shared with his peers that legal practices, institutions, and their justifications and purposes evolve, albeit at different rates. That was the essential baseline.

This essential baseline – that permeable cultural conditions are often embedded in what we think about, how we think about it, and the point of view that brings both of these activities home to us – had ramifications for how Holmes conceives the task for legal thought. A legal thinker's objective is to first verbalize and then conceptualize the ongoing interaction between existing laws – durable social beliefs and attitudes enforcing preferred conduct through state-sanctioned means – and existing (or projected) conduct that is not or should not be sanctioned. These two intertwined aspects of social experience one may further conceptualize as bounded by two interconnected inquiries: "what is the law?" and "what is law?" Holmes's many investigations and studies focus on one or the other of these queries or the movements between them.

From an existing social and cultural matrix – old England – certain rules for the deployment of state force became fixed and embedded through usage and conviction. The governing authority's need to employ these rules in an increasing number of situations, some new and varied, led, historically speaking, to the formation of a professional group knowledgeable in their substance, scope, and use. Thus not only did the substance of existing legal rules require intense learning, so did the manner

[1] Analytically, and without doing too great an injustice to Holmes, one could categorize duties as a system of restraints that exist under four headings: spiritual (sense of dignity); social (sense of civic comportment, familial and social expectation); moral (sense of ethical conduct, especially to others with whom we have no preexisting close relationship); and legal (commands that must be obeyed upon pain of sanction). For the distinction between the "spiritual" and the "moral" in establishing frameworks of the good, I am indebted to CHARLES TAYLOR, THE SOURCES OF THE SELF: THE MAKING OF THE MODERN IDENTITY 3–52 (1989).

and mode of their implementation. One could not be profitably studied without the other.

From his earliest scholarship Holmes found himself curious as to the mechanisms by which, in a continuously existing state regime or legal tradition, existing legal rules changed or new rules came into being. He became convinced from an early date that the common law's mode of adjudication – its primary emphasis on the facts of a dispute – rendered it superior to any other competing mode precisely because of this emphasis on the facts. Close attention to particulars permitted flexibility of approach and the necessary openness to new experience; it enabled lawmakers to navigate the contours of circumstance. One kept looking to the decided cases – established facts and their no-longer-in-doubt immediate legal consequences – for a principle, a *ratio decidendi*, that would encapsulate what was important from prior groupings of facts and make possible new extensions of legal meaning, new cohesions of facts and their legal consequences.

How successive fragments of social experience solidified into law, and how law, in turn, refashioned itself according to different prevailing strictures of intelligibility – or, as Holmes notes, sometimes even in the absence of effective strictures[2] – fascinated the scholar who saw in law's history the stratigraphy of human development. Imagine, then, the transcendent burst of sunlight this scholar feels in his inner being when he realizes the process by which fragments of social experience become transmuted into law is not simply localized in some hoary artifact but exists as an ever-present observable reality.

Revenge existed; and it still exists.[3]

That changed legal consequences may have, along with other social and cultural factors, modified the observable quality of this primary human emotion tells a story interesting to those willing to invest the time to read it. The present suddenly acquires a dimension of depth, both historical and psychological. Transformed by this insight, Holmes sees new living meaning in an observation he repeated more than once in his early writings: "It is the merit of the common law that it decides the case first and determines the principle afterwards."[4]

2 Oliver Wendell Holmes, *Primitive Notions in Modern Law No. II*, *in* III The Collected Works of Justice Holmes: Complete Public Writings and Selected Judicial Opinions of Oliver Wendell Holmes 30 (Sheldon Novick ed., 1995) [hereinafter CW] ("The answer is to be found not in reasoning, but in a failure to reason.").

3 Holmes encapsulates the moment of awareness in these sentences: "In such matters, the savage mind well represents the childish stage. The wild native of Brazil would bite the stone he stumbled over, or the arrow that wounded him. Such a mental condition may be traced along the course of history, not merely in impulsive habit, but in formally enacted law." Oliver Wendell Holmes, *Primitive Notions in Modern Law No. I*, *in* III CW 9. And: "We might expect, therefore, that in this case [that of a ship], if anywhere, there was room for the operation of that way of thinking which we have already described, and which is shown by manifold instances to be by no means extinct at the present day." *Id.* at 12.

4 Oliver Wendell Holmes, *Codes, and the Arrangement of the Law*, *in* I CW 212.

If someone other than Holmes – especially the historical Holmes, America's only great jurist – had written this sentence one's initial reaction might well be skeptical. Why is it the common law's *merit* to decide first and then in the decision's aftermath, perhaps long afterwards, articulate the governing principle? That successive cases involving the same or similar subject matter collectively reveal what will finally become the operative principle which, until its articulation, has been only vaguely felt, points up what Holmes evidently believes to be the congruence between the natural development of enforceable duties and the instituted lawmaking social practice called the common law. The incessant looping of present into past and past into present weaved now-new-law into courses of conduct already determined and vice versa. It functioned as a *techne*, a developed craft. Or as Holmes once unforgettably put it: "When I think of the law, I think of a loom."[5]

Holmes had little desire to bring in wholesale the equivalent of industrial techniques of manufacture to supplant the ancient craftsmanship and the way of life that sustained it. He showed little interest in following the footsteps of a David Dudley Field. Yet living with progress and its progeny was the lot of the modern, and the *techne* of the law should not fear to embrace it or them. What did that mean for Holmes? It meant recognizing and emphasizing the importance of Austin's suggestion that jurisprudence have its own province. It was part of the secular order; the human-made city, not what Augustine called the City of God. Law concerned itself only with temporal damage, not with the infractions of duties from provenances other than the legal. It functioned in a realm as distinct from politics as from morals. It had its own subject matter, its own favored methods of investigation, analysis, and inference, its own internal problems, its distinctive enchantments, its specific uses and forms, it claimed certain drudgeries and exasperations peculiarly its own, and if its practitioners thought like Holmes and followed his lead they would hardly ever in their day-to-day work utter the word justice. That would be déclassé.[6]

All these potentialities of thought and meaning lay entwined and folded within the merit of the common law. It took a strong burst of sunlight at just the right angle for this seed to germinate and sprout. The *techne* of the law might yet transcend its

[5] As reported in Walton H. Hamilton, *The Legal Philosophy of Justices Holmes and Brandeis*, 33 Current History and Forum 654, 660 (1931); *see also* Oliver Wendell Holmes, *The Law*, *in* III CW 469 ("When I think thus of the law, I see a princess mightier than she who once wrought Bayeux, eternally weaving into her dim web figures of the ever-lengthening past, – figures too dim to be noticed by the idle, too symbolic to be interpreted except by her pupils, but to the discerning eye disclosing every painful step and every world-shaking contest by which mankind has worked and fought its way from savage isolation to organic social life."); Silas Bent, Justice Oliver Wendell Holmes 12 (1931).

[6] *See* Justice Oliver Wendell Holmes: His Book Notices and Uncollected Letters and Papers 201 (Harry C. Shriver ed., 1936) ("I have said to my brethren many times that I hate justice, which means that I know if a man begins to talk about that, for one reason or another he is shirking thinking in legal terms."). *But see* Robin L. West, Teaching Law: Justice, Politics, and the Demands of Professionalism 43–92 (2014) (lamenting that legalism has marginalized the formal study of justice in the legal profession).

artificial reason and its dark arts of cavil, deception, and misdirection, and become something philosophical, something worthy of a philosopher, something that even Emerson might be proud to claim as the heritage of the active thinker. The question was how?

In putting forward this question we are not claiming that Holmes thought in exactly these terms. But as this part and the next will show, there are pronounced resonances between what we are saying here and what Holmes wrote well over 100 years ago. That itself is no major announcement since this is self-evidently a study of Holmes's thought. But we must also keep in mind that in between what Holmes wrote then and what we are writing now sit layers of commentary and disquisition that are part of the meaning of Holmes and integral to the dominant legal mindset that has taken shape in the United States.

Misunderstandings of Holmes abound, but that is simply part of nature's profligacy. "The Path of the Law" has become the cynosure of critique; its brief against the unwarranted imposition of moral terms upon legal categories of thought attracting the most rejoinders. The whole controversy invariably takes the historically informed reader back to Judge Chipman's broadside against Blackstone. Yet the connotations do not end there. That the common law has an inner path, that its vitality depends on certain sentiments and aspirations, on certain subjective preferences and passive capacities, Holmes as much as anyone in the common law's modern history brought home and he did so as both messenger and message. Law may be a social tool to unify interests and corral viewpoints; but so is money. The pursuit of law understood as a pathway to knowledge has a dignity that the pursuit of money cannot match. On that point, parenthetically, Holmes found reason enough to praise the railroad magnate James J. Hill, who in his own realm pursued knowledge as avidly or more so than he did money.[7]

Law looks to actualities. It relies on sequence to help determine context and vice versa as James Willard Hurst so ably demonstrated. One has to look to history. One has to understand that social facts transmuted in the crucible of strong belief into external legal consequence. The process could not go on blindly forever, trusting solely to random outcomes, adventitious possibilities for growth and development. The creed which Holmes shared, a creed that looked to intelligence and will, that upheld the singular transparency of the universe – had not the great Emerson written a hymn to the great eyeball? – marked the path upon which the student of the law must travel. The journey requires vision. The wayfarer prays for insight. And, of course, for many of our nineteenth-century cultural forebears nothing was worth doing if it did not also demand immense reservoirs of fortitude and strength.

[7] See especially chapter VI, "Industrial and Railroad Consolidations," in James J. Hill, Highways of Progress 114–39 (1910); Michael P. Malone, James J. Hill: Empire Builder of the Northwest 192–96 (1996). For Holmes's comments see, 1 The Holmes–Pollock Letters: The Correspondence of Mr. Justice Holmes and Sir Frederick Pollock, 1874–1932 at 166–67 (Mark DeWolfe Howe ed., 2d ed. 1961).

Bringing a sense of depth to the common law, in the same way in which the eighteenth- and nineteenth-century quest for the astral parallax brought a sense of depth to the night sky, must certainly count as one of the great accomplishments of *The Common Law*. From a sense of relative distances perspective took hold. Stars that to the naked, untutored eye appeared right next to each other turned out to be hundreds of light years apart from each other and from the observer.[8] Centuries of patient inquiry bore a new way of seeing; the imagined night sky no longer took on forms reminiscent of flattened Byzantine iconography. We eventually got Van Gogh's starry hallucinations instead.

Less evocatively then Van Gogh, the working astronomer began to develop a different feel than predecessors for the dimensions of the universe. Investigations of time, space, and relative distances began to reveal a distinct, and more precise, sense of the universe's scale. The newly measured distances seemed vast and the space between them visually empty. Perhaps to many the universe suddenly seemed cold and unfeeling – a lament Joseph Wood Krutch would in time utter passionately and disconsolately[9] – but only because the universe had become literally deep as well as metaphorically dark.[10]

We exist in the universe; it does not exist within us. Holmes repeated this minted truism more than once.[11]

If temporal perspective brought form to the chaos of the common law, one needed much insight to bring that perspective to bear upon the present and for it to become the basis of well-wrought disciplined legal inquiry. Such insights mainly come from the doing and the participating, not from the observing and the commenting on incidents and consequences related to the doing and the participating.

8 On the search for the astral parallax and the new awareness of the depth and scale of the universe, see Alan W. Hirshfeld, Parallax: The Race to Measure the Cosmos (2001).

9 Joseph Wood Krutch, The Modern Temper (1929). And even as Krutch was writing his book, physicists were unraveling the implications of Einstein's work for their understanding of the structure of the universe.

10 Holmes well understood Krutch's feeling: "And the whole, if there is a whole, would be I know not how much other, if an atom were subtracted from it, but I do not believe a shudder would go through the sky if our whole ant heap were kerosened. But then it might – in short my only belief is that I know nothing of it." Felix S. Cohen, *Holmes–Cohen Correspondence*, 9 J. Hist. Ideas 3, 9 (1948); *see also* The Holmes–Einstein Letters: Correspondence of Mr. Justice Holmes and Lewis Einstein 1903–1935 50 (James Bishop Peabody ed., 1964) ("I doubt if a shudder would go through the spheres if the whole ant-heap were kerosened.").

11 As reported by Dean Acheson: "At the outset of our philosophy we must take a step of supreme faith – we must admit that we are not God. When I admit you, I announce that I am not dreaming the universe but am existing in it as less than it." Dean Acheson, Morning and Noon 63 (1965) (reporting from a transcript of Holmes's conversation with a young law clerk) (quoted in Sheldon M. Novick, *Justice Holmes's Philosophy*, 70 Wash. U. L.Q. 703, 713–14 (1992)). And: "If I am in the universe, and not it in me, I am in something that contains intellect, significance, ideals." *Id.* at 716 (quoting letter from Oliver W. Holmes to Felix Frankfurter, Feb. 16, 1912). Holmes also expressed these ideas formally in at least two important articles "Ideals and Doubts" and "Natural Law." Oliver Wendell Holmes, *Ideals and Doubts, in* III CW III 442–44, and Oliver Wendell Holmes, *Natural Law, in* III CW 445–48.

And thus we come to one of Holmes's greatest insights, that of the bad man, the purely legal point of view. The multifarious stars of the common law, its cases, become in their measured, relative distances an universe for us, us lawyers, us practitioners, us legal thinkers who are acquainted firsthand with the inner machinations of a profession that is certainly well known, and not in any substantive sense opaque or mysterious, but still, paradoxically, unknown to itself in ways that mattered to Holmes or to anyone who holds the law in reverence, not because it manifests God's will or the hidden destiny of freedom, but because the law has become a new path to the grandeur of knowledge and its terrible joys.[12]

Terrible joys are hard to fathom in the twenty-first century and perhaps the conditions conducive to their firsthand acquaintance have begun to recede from the present. The grandeur of knowledge somehow still stands as a living ideal; the many tremendous advances it inspired camouflaging losses and costs. Even so, law as a *techne* still needs much development to fulfill the end that Holmes foresaw, for it to approach ever closer to his ideal. Holmes groped for the language to describe his vision of law-in-the-future, of erecting what we have called a fundamental metric of the law. In light of this end, lifelong students of law must try to direct and control nature's inveterate profligacy and bring all available resources to bear to continue the work Holmes began almost single-handedly.

INTRODUCTION

We ended the last part by discussing how Holmes took the point of view of the man he characterizes as having no scruples in *The Common Law* and equated that standpoint to what he calls the purely legal point of view. In "The Path of the Law" he uses a similar literary technique but with a new name, the bad man. In continuing our effort to explicate the leading ideas found in "The Path of the Law" it now becomes necessary to add chiaroscuro to our analysis. We seek to put the purely legal point of view itself into greater relief, to give it volume and depth as it

[12] Sheldon Novick makes similar observations in respect to *The Path of the Law*, though for him Holmes sought mainly for wisdom:

> Filled with self-confidence and pleasure in his work, he gladly accepted an invitation to talk to the law students at Boston University, where Melville Bigelow, once his companion in the Social Law Library, was now dean. Holmes painted in rapid uncorrected brushstrokes his vision of law as a science. Law study began with what seemed sordid and unpromising materials. But when pursued with scientific, even religious, devotion, it became a way to wisdom.

Sheldon M. Novick, Honorable Justice: The Life of Oliver Wendell Holmes 223 (1989); *see also* Mark DeWolfe Howe, *Introduction*, to Oliver Wendell Holmes, The Common Law xvii (Mark DeWolfe Howe ed., 1963) (noting that Holmes looked upon the common law with something approaching reverence); Oliver Wendell Holmes, *Walbridge Abner Field, in* III CW 497 ("with a kind of desperate joy we go back to the fight").

were. We propose to do that through composition, by creating a gallery of people and their ideas.

All the legal scholars directly discussed in this part devoted effort, some more intensively than others, to understanding Holmes or "The Path of the Law." Almost all of them understood Holmes or "The Path of the Law" differently than we do. They provide a great opportunity to measure differences in conception and approach as Holmes himself continues to recede in time. We have chosen to focus on the bad man because more often than not that figure centered the discussion. And because for us the bad man is the purely legal point of view personified. By positioning the thirteen ways of looking at the bad man into one composition we hope to add greater depth and dimensionality to our study. Fair warning: this part is very long because we have depicted in some detail these different ways. The details are important because the ideas matter. Granted, none of the commentators reviewed, except Hessel Yntema, understood "The Path of the Law" as primarily a discourse on legal education. But that permits our depictions to take on greater resonance, as the bad man becomes a Rorschach test of sorts. How legal scholars perceive the bad man and the article in which he made his first formal appearance has done much to create and maintain the legal cultures in which we now live. With due apologies to Wallace Stevens we proceed.[13]

1 INTROIT

We begin with the basic descriptions – this personified man has no scruples, is bad, and "cares nothing for an ethical rule which is believed and practiced by his neighbors."[14] The bad man may be surrounded by twenty neighbors who all hear and abide by the same still voice of conscience, yet that voice he does not hear, of conscience he has no conscience, and in the still silent room the only things moving are the eyes of the bad man. They will not shut.

2 SHELDON NOVICK

Learning the law requires understanding the law's limits. Early in his career Holmes had sought to delimit the province of jurisprudence through his concept of duty. In this sense, the province of jurisprudence reflected law as a municipal ideal, law internal to a sovereign territory that secured for its members a minimally protected

[13] Robert Gordon says that Holmes in "The Path of the Law" was not suggesting a new theory of law "but rather (to paraphrase Wallace Stevens) 'thirteen ways of looking at' law[.]" I think Holmes was suggesting a new theory though not in the traditional sense. Robert W. Gordon, *Law As a Vocation*, *in* The Path of the Law and Its Influence: The Legacy of Oliver Wendell Holmes Jr. 13 (Stephen J. Burton ed., 2000).

[14] Oliver Wendell Holmes, *The Common Law*, *in* III CW 277; Oliver Wendell Holmes, *The Path of the Law*, *in* III CW 392.

status, a secure ambit for activity and for redress. The breach of a strict legal duty led to a drop in legal status. Holmes believes that many times the breach of duty and the attendant drop in status only become evident through what he calls the collateral legal consequences. Law withdraws its protection. It will through its agents do to a person, or permit others to do, things that would have been unwarranted to one who kept his or her legal status intact. The power of the state is great, in its active and in its passive side. Holmes alludes to this when he says: "People want to know under what circumstances and how far they will run the risk of coming against what is so much stronger than themselves, and hence it becomes a business to find out when this danger is to be feared."[15]

Thus, the first line, a boundary, is drawn. It is between those inside the protection of the law – those within the municipality, the city – and those outside its protection. Historical allusions, as well as political and religious ones, flood the mind upon the mention of this imagery of a "city" but Holmes, severe in his single-mindedness, stays focused on the mental discipline required to predict "the incidence of public force through the instrumentality of the courts."[16]

The established boundary creates its own objective. The means of study are set, "the body of reports, treatises, and of statutes."[17] The question is clearly posed: what actions or inactions, given the surrounding circumstances, will lead the courts to determine, upon the request of the government or of a private party, that the party indicted or sued has violated a strict legal duty?

The Boston Brahmin who first articulated this query well understood that in actual social life ostracism takes many forms and for many reasons. A malady peculiar to the modern is self-ostracism, the deprivation of self-esteem that corresponds to a diminution of one's own dignity or to the all-too-prevalent situation of possessing no viable sense of self-worth. A strong sense of dignity leads to a strong sense of duty, as Sheldon Novick so well portrayed in his biography of Holmes. Novick's firm opinion that Holmes pursued the virtues of the gentleman led to Novick's peculiar interpretation – it summarized a life-code, the "way" of a dedicated craft – of "The Path of the Law."[18]

Other duties, from those reflecting a sense of social obligation and comportment to those moral, strictly called, may have their own isolating consequences when

[15] Holmes, *The Path of the Law*, *supra* note 14, at 391.

[16] *Id.*

[17] *Id.*

[18] NOVICK, *supra* note 12, at 450–51. Novick assumes the title, "The Path of the Law," is "probably a conscious reference to the Tao, a term that connotes both a path to understanding and a way of life; as in Bushido, the Way of the Warrior, a term Holmes almost certainly knew." *See also* Novick, *supra* note 11, at 703, 708 (noting that Holmes's table of duties was taken not from the Bible, but from the code of chivalry).

intentionally disregarded.[19] The visible and invisible lines of punishment for the breach of each type of duty do not always coalesce. To recognize the nature, scope, and reach of the specific duty that concerns those involved in the practice and enforcement of law one must understand the basic terms of reference, that is, the line between action or inaction that led to acceptable or required state-mandated conduct and that which did not.

The bad man, therefore, who fears neither God nor social opinion but only the judges before him, and who derives a sense of self-worth from sources opaque, must keep in mind the duties that others call good, whether of dignity, basic sociality, or those specifically owed to other members, near and far, of the commonweal and commonly understood as moral. The bad man must keep his presence of mind because those duties labeled legal – though analytically separate from the others, which one may group for convenience under the rubric moral – may at any given time be affected by the other three, or a combination thereof. Legal duties can and do change. But the lines between the types of duties still exist. The bad man must adopt at least three other simultaneous perspectives, three other mindsets, to ensure as much as possible he stays out of harm's way.

3 JAMES TUFTS

James Tufts, who reviewed Holmes's *Collected Legal Papers* in 1921, began his remarks by comparing them to the recently published *Letters* of William James.[20] He suggested both thinkers shared the same basic orientation:

> [G]rowing to maturity at a period when evolutionary philosophy was at once giving new interest to the genesis of mind and institutions and at the same time shaking the authority of the past as past, both thinkers made deep-going analyses of assumptions and logic in their respective fields.

Tufts considered James a fighter against absolutist systems, whether in the natural sciences or in religious thought. Holmes, Tufts added, "has as firmly set himself against the block universe of legal conceptions and rigidly fixed social order. He sought to give man room to express his advancing needs in an orderly progressing society."[21]

One may well wonder if Tufts's last sentence describing Holmes's aims did not already reflect the emerging myth of Holmes the staunchly progressive liberal. Such a view would be hard to square with what Tufts understands as the "somewhat

[19] For an interesting discussion of the difference between acts expressing altruism or other social instincts and those that fall under the domain of duty, understood in moral terms, see RICHARD A. POSNER, THE PROBLEMATICS OF MORAL AND LEGAL THEORY 30–38 (1999).

[20] James H. Tufts, *The Legal and Social Philosophy of Mr. Justice Holmes*, 7 A.B.A. J., 359, 359 (1921).

[21] *Id.*

cynical doctrine that law may be regarded as nothing more or less than prediction and that to get a clear view of law as law it must be emptied of moral implications."[22] With these words Tufts introduces the bad man and, he believes, the morally deadening view that legal duties, understood solely as the predictions of likely ensuing legal consequences upon failure of performance, have no authoritative claim to respect.

> If we take all moral implications out of the law and regard it as a system of predictions, similar, let us say, to the meteorological forecasts of frosts and storms, can we maintain the respect for the authority of law which we all agree that members of other groups than our own should maintain?

Tufts's formulation comes after a series of examples involving a duty to keep a contractual promise (or pay damages), a duty to drive within the speed limit (or pay a fine), a duty to submit an accurate inventory to the tax assessor (or get into trouble). The removal of "all moral implication out of law" – or as he quotes Holmes, "to wash it with cynical acid" – brings into law, Tufts claims, an intellectual perspective reminiscent of the one that Hobbes and Machiavelli brought into political theory.

Tufts has little doubt such a perspective may lead to clearer legal thinking – though he does not specify what, exactly, would be clarified or how – but he does not think the potential gains worth the cost to the integrity of the social order. A substratum of goodwill, an inclination to obey the law because it is law must exist, Tufts believes, for law to garner the required respect to function effectively within a society. To separate morals from law in the manner that Holmes suggests carries real dangers: "It is indeed the danger that besets every professional point of view in so far as it is scientific and therefore abstract."[23] The myopic employment of a purely technical and scientific point of view turns institutions thus administered into social obstacles instead of enabling them to advance the purposes for which they were originally created.

For this reason, Tufts can't bring himself to believe that Holmes meant what he wrote: "And I do not think that Justice Holmes would wish to have the law studied purely from the bad man's point of view."[24]

In Tufts's reluctance we see a well-known division of opinion regarding the nature of law and its purposes: either it is a distinct, autonomous realm of experience which may be studied on its own terms to the exclusion of moral and other matters, or it necessarily implicates in its generative concepts and in the logic of their development moral values. In Tufts's remarks we also note a common confusion regarding the starting and endpoint of legal learning that corresponds to the division just described.

[22] *Id.* at 362.
[23] *Id.* at 363.
[24] *Id.*

On the one side, Tufts praises Holmes for his Jamesian refusal to tolerate a block universe of legal conceptions. But when Holmes draws from the presumed evolutionary context the needed starting point or points for understanding legal phenomena, Tufts protests, not to its logic, but to its ramifications. It is Tufts, not Holmes, who describes the bad man's point of view as emptying law of all moral implication. Perhaps it is just a matter of word choice, but Holmes expresses his desire in "The Path of the Law" that "every word of moral significance could be banished from law altogether," which, to my mind, is substantially different from suggesting law be emptied of all moral implication. The latter suggests sealing law off from morality. That would be a decided impossibility. The duties that constitute law are in constant contact and connection with all the other requirements of social life, especially those other duties (moral, social, and spiritual) we have grouped together under the rubric moral.

On the other side, Tufts fails to understand that the bad man's predictions of what the courts will do in fact are predictions within the existing legal system. His comparison to the weather system is inapposite. The legal system exists within the dynamics of the social order and has, over time and at least in the United States, become itself a prime mover within that social order. The legal system – to the extent we can use the word 'system' in this context – changes constantly, in small ways and large, and its changes are often responses to purposive behavior. The bad man as a perspective focuses, by necessity, on isolated legal events taken out of the existing social currents and crosscurrents.

It is certainly true, in the majority of cases, that the duty not to speed means that if one speeds and is ticketed one must pay a fine. That is an isolated legal event that may have a different beginning or endpoint depending on a variety of factors: for example, whether this is the driver's first speeding infraction in the year or the tenth; or on the difference between the ticketed speed and the posted speed limit – a significantly higher rate in many jurisdictions will land one in jail; or because as a result of the speeding another vehicle was hit and a person died. One may face a charge of vehicular manslaughter and still get a speeding ticket.

When one understands that legal events – the basic units of legal study – are only isolated for heuristic purposes, to educate attorneys and courts by indicating the direction (if any) the established line of conduct leads, the temptation to embed them in the block universe of legal conceptions disappears. They eventually meld back into the newsprint of daily life until another legal occasion calls them forth. Otherwise, as the old song has it, the beat goes on. Never for a moment do the newsfeeds stop – the political battles rage, public opinion sways, and the digital loop refreshes every few seconds. If social life has become a never-ending pantomime displayed on a 360-degree big screen, the bad man is its ever-faithful watchful audience of one.

4 JEROME FRANK

Jerome Frank in 1932 repeated the comparison Tufts had made between Holmes's bad man and Machiavelli in part I of his "Mr. Justice Holmes and Non-Euclidean Legal Thinking."[25] Modern intelligent study of governmental processes began with Machiavelli, says Frank.[26] "Machiavelli, in his description of the ways of rulers, 'proceeds in a calm unmoral way, like a lecturer on frogs.'"[27] This unbiased attention to actualities is what Frank prizes. And it is what Holmes brought to the legal scene in America.

> In the latter part of the nineteenth century in America, Oliver Wendell Holmes, Jr., a keen-minded idealistic lawyer, disgusted with the muddle-headed character of customary ways of dealing with the judicial process, and doubtless with the 'wicked' Machiavelli in mind, spoke these words: *If you want to know the law and nothing else, you must look at it as a bad man*[.][28]

Frank apparently chose his words carefully. Holmes is keen-minded and yet "one of the finest idealists of our time."[29] The keenness lies in the recognition that "law is not pure mathematics; that the so-called self-evident truths of the traditional jurisprudence are not self-evident; and that many axioms of legal thinking do not appear on the surface but are concealed and must be dug out for inspection."[30] That is non-Euclidean legal thinking.[31]

The idealism apparently resides in the hope that a clearer, more realistic understanding of how legal processes work will lead to the an improvement in those processes and, through refraction, in the people who administer them.[32]

One sees in Frank's latter assessment a prime example of the common tendency among those early twentieth-century legal thinkers who looked to Holmes as a guide – often called legal realists – to turn the bad man's point of view into the realist's point of view. By this I mean that the bad man's perspective (the purely legal point of view) transforms in their hands into a sharpened angle of vision and into a scholarly program for investigating how participants in the legal process actually behave. Frank credits Holmes for advancing beyond Machiavelli by perceiving that actual behavior includes the pursuit of ideals (people's "hopes and desires"), and for

25 Jerome Frank, *Mr. Justice Holmes and Non-Euclidean Legal Thinking*, 17 CORNELL L. REV. 568, 568 (1932).

26 *Id.*

27 *Id.* at 569 (no citation given in original for internal quote).

28 *Id.* (emphasis in original).

29 *Id.* at 570 n.5.

30 *Id.* at 571.

31 For an excellent discussion of the vogue of the non-Euclidean in the 1930s, and of Frank and other legal realists' efforts to bring the non-Euclidean into legal theory, *see* EDWARD A. PURCELL, JR., THE CRISIS OF DEMOCRATIC THEORY: SCIENTIFIC NATURALISM & THE PROBLEM OF VALUE 47–94 (1973).

32 Frank, *supra* note 25, at 570 n.5.

recognizing the power of ideals for changing existing behavior (turning *ought* into *is*).[33] Even more pointedly, Holmes did not fall into a tar pit as did Machiavelli: "he did not advise the good man to adopt the conduct of the bad man, he merely advised him to learn from the observant bad man what is actually going on."[34]

And what is actually going on in the realm of law circa 1932 is the overthrow of Euclidean thinking understood as self-evident axioms anchoring deductive chains that support ineluctable legal conclusions. "*Holmes*," Frank states with great fanfare, "*can fairly be said to have invented non-Euclidean legal thinking*."[35]

Frank's analysis is robust and sophisticated. He recognizes that for Holmes the articulation and application of effective legal axioms or postulates involves more than logical or philosophical clear-headedness in stocking and exploiting a store of legal dogma. He also recognizes that, again for Holmes, the ultimate formulation of a rule of conduct that proves valuable over time may require many attempts. He applauds Holmes's admonition to the profession that it become more self-aware, even more self-critical, of its own practices, its guiding ideals, its faith in the viability of the materials and means at its disposal for accomplishing the social ends that justify its existence as a profession.

Frank like Tufts includes Holmes in the generation that first grappled with the consequences of Darwinian evolution. Darwin's theory included chance as part of its statement of natural interactions. But unlike Tufts he finds in Holmes's conception of the bad man a point of view that liberates and ennobles the practice of law:

> Holmes with his bad man pointed out the error in the old axiom that legal rights and duties could be logically deduced from so-called legal rules. As Copernicus caused men to drop a geo-centric notion of the universe and to take up a helio-centruction [*sic*] notion, so Holmes' bad man will, sooner or later, compel all intelligent persons to acknowledge that the center of the legal world is not in the rules but in specific court decisions (*i.e.*, judgments, orders and decrees) in specific lawsuits. Because of Holmes' clear vision we are able to see that what any specific man may and must lawfully do and not do is discoverable not in books but in some actual lawsuit which has occurred or may occur in a court-house, – a lawsuit relating to some acts or words of that specific man.[36]

33 *Id.* at 570.

34 *Id.* at 571.

35 *Id.* at 572 (emphasis in original). Of course, given Frank's proclamation, one cannot help but quote from Holmes's Feb. 3, 1919, letter to Morris Cohen: "How I wish I knew what the non-Euclidean geometry is!" Cohen, *supra* note 10, at 14.

36 *Id.* at 578. Novick makes what appears to be an analogous observation: "Holmes's idea that the common law was the result rather than the cause of judicial decisions was epochal; in law it was comparable (and in some ways similar) to the impact of relativity on physics. Holmes's insight seems correct and now seems almost too obvious to mention." Sheldon M. Novick, *Introduction*, *in* I The Collected Works of Justice Holmes 118–19 (Sheldon M. Novick ed., 1995). And: "In *The Common Law*, there was a fundamental shift in his view, like the 'paradigm shift' in physics that followed the theories of relativity: the fundamental question was not the rule of conduct but the circumstances under which the judge would impose liability.

Frank ends his summation with the exclamatory note, "Holmes' bad man may be compared with that most precocious of children who, as the Emperor passed by, admired for his clothes by the assembled crowd cried out, 'But he has nothing on at all!'"[37]

In Frank's hands, Holmes's bad man loses his 'badness' and becomes an astute, acute social observer, one who does not hesitate to puncture pretense, to unveil facts, and to think only in terms of the actual and achievable. For Frank the postulates or axioms that focus inquiry have their locus in the present. His investigations of these axioms or postulates – which often in his rendition sound like maxims of the law – take a predominantly psychological turn with hardly any consciousness of history.[38] If on the one hand Frank's mode of inquiry points up Holmes's sometimes facile melding of two distinct perspectives – the psychological and the historical – on the other hand it lacks Holmes's sense for the law's depth and dimensionality. The point of view the bad man personifies arises from a refined and self-aware sense of history, of the movements of human consciousness, of relative distances between and among informed perceptions of what the law at any given time found or finds desirable.

It is not a point of view a child, no matter how precocious, can attain.

Frank, for all his astuteness, did not quite realize that the perspective of the bad man joins a sense of present actuality and an awareness of the immense reach of self-interestedness with a sense of historical variety and movement. A feel for history, as the Italian philosopher Giambattista Vico noted long ago, converts the raw behaviorism of the present – to use the lingo of the realists – into a civilizing moment. Or to say it as poetically as Wallace Stevens did: "A man and a woman and a blackbird [bad man] are one."

5 JOHN ZANE

Frank's insistence that "Holmes' bad man will, sooner or later, compel all *intelligent persons* to acknowledge that the center of the legal world is not in the rules but in specific court decisions ... in specific lawsuits[,]"[39] brings to mind the classic Woody Allen gibe about intellectuals – they only kill their own.

In this case the likely target is one John Zane who launched a two-pronged assault on Holmes in 1918. Frank refers to the "absurd attack" on Holmes in Zane's 1918 article, "German Legal Philosophy."[40] Zane also in that same year issued a fairly stunning broadside against Holmes, a sitting associate justice of the United States

The focus of Holmes's investigation shifted away from political society as a whole and narrowed to the judge's courtroom." *Id.*

[37] Frank, *supra* note 25, at 568, 578 n.28.

[38] *Id.* at 579–99.

[39] *Id.* at 578 (emphasis added).

[40] *Id.* at 570, n.5.

Supreme Court – which Frank does not cite – that accuses Holmes of perpetuating a cleverly disguised, damnable "legal heresy" in one of his opinions.[41]

The indomitable Zane, who like Holmes takes the entire horizon of law within his field of vision, and who, as Holmes, is learned in the classic languages and tosses off like popcorn Latin quotes from his teeming brain, first lights into Holmes – or as Holmes put it to Pollock, "walks into me"[42] – in his article on "German Legal Philosophy," which, incidentally, is not so much about German legal philosophy as it is a learned, lengthy tour of the development of law and legal thinking (ninety dense pages' worth) from inchoate beginnings in the social mind to the last year of World War I.[43]

In "German Legal Philosophy" Zane does not mention the bad man –whether he knew about him is hard to say: the collection of Holmes's legal writings that include "The Path of the Law" is not published until 1920 – but he does direct his considerable ire at this well-known declaration of Holmes: "Law is a statement of the circumstances in which the public force will be brought to bear upon men through the courts."[44]

Zane believes, and states so in print, that Holmes cynically, and with "concealed amusement," foisted this definition of law on his philosophically naïve Supreme Court brethren.[45] The latter, guiled into concession in the 1909 case of *America Banana Co.* v. *United Fruit Co.*, righted themselves the following year and effectively overruled Holmes in *Kuhn* v. *Fairmont Coal Co.*[46]

Holmes's dissent in *Kuhn* v. *Fairmont Coal Co.* Zane considers a relic of legal barbarity:

> If a man desires to see where the idea that the courts make law lands a rational mind, let him analyze the dissenting opinion. If he think it sound, he may be absolutely certain that he does not know what law is.[47]

41 John Zane, *A Legal Heresy*, 13 ILL. L. REV. 431 (1918–19).
42 II HOLMES–POLLOCK LETTERS, *supra* note 7, at 3.
43 John Zane, *German Legal Philosophy*, 16 MICH. L. REV. 287 (1918).
44 *Id.* at 345 (citing America Banana Co. v. United Fruit Co., 213 U.S. 347, 356 (1909)).
45 *Id.* at 345.
46 *Id.*; Kuhn v. Fairmont Coal Co. 215 U.S. 349 (1910).
47 *Id.* at 346 n.79. Zane tones down the criticism in his 1927 book *The Story of Law*. There he simply says:

> A celebrated judge in this country has defined law as "a statement of the circumstances in which the public force will be brought to bear through the courts," but this definition makes an immaterial matter the substance of the definition and ignores altogether the idea that law is a rule. Law would exist without public force applied, for long before there were courts there was a great body of law that a man was bound not to violate and that was generally obeyed. The fact is that no one can go any further than to say law is a part, and only a part, of the now large body of rules that govern men in their relations and conduct toward one another in the social organization to which they belong.

JOHN ZANE, THE STORY OF LAW 1 (1927). Reading this paragraph in light of our own analysis of how Holmes demarcated the duties called legal from the other types of duties that map and

This tiny but incendiary verbal grenade presumably occasioned Frank's murderous retort years later that sooner or later all *intelligent persons* would be compelled to admit that the courts and the cases and not the rules are at the center of the legal universe.

Zane did not limit his diatribe to Holmes's definition of law in *America Banana Co. v. United Fruit Co.* He also aimed a few rounds in the direction of Holmes's friend, John Chipman Gray, whose *The Nature and Sources of Law* Holmes cites approvingly in his dissent.[48] And then in a subsequent article, "A Legal Heresy," Zane drops the following shell. It must have, one imagines, gotten the old soldier's dander up.[49]

> In one of the Year Books of Edward I, a sergeant-at-law, arguing to the court, was driven by the exigencies of his case to assert that a female serf, who had become free by marrying a freeman, was remitted to her servile status as soon as she became a widow. "That is false," sharply interrupted one judge. "Worse than false, it is a heresy," added Justice Staunton. A statement of law that was both false and heretical was then a professional misdemeanor. In the case of a judge at this day we may venture to say that it is at least an indiscretion, but when it lends support to the atrocious German theory of law and justice which has desolated much of the world, it becomes a duty to expose its hollowness.[50]

What probably made this opening to "A Legal Heresy" even harder for Holmes to bear was Zane's turning on Holmes a few pages later the same type of cold clinical scrutiny – "to study him as a human document"[51] – that Holmes had successfully employed for most of his life, at least since his abolitionist-leaning days, for cutting through cant.

Holmes, Zane admits, had penned a classic in *The Common Law*[52] and had in various addresses uttered remarkable words, perhaps some of the best spoken in the

guide social life, one is tempted to agree with Holmes's surmise that Zane in his 1918 articles "means a different thing from what I do by law and the fight is more about words than he thinks. But there is a real difference expressed by him in a tone of dogmatism upon which I should not venture, although I think I could smash him if he would say what he thought and not only what he didn't believe." II HOLMES–POLLOCK LETTERS, *supra* note 7, at 3.

48 Kuhn v. Fairmont Coal Co., 215 U.S. 349, 370–71 (1910).

49 Zane foreshadowed his "A Legal Heresy" argument in "German Legal Philosophy." Zane, *supra* note 43, at 349 n.83. Undoubtedly the fact that Zane's "A Legal Heresy" was part of a celebratory publication commemorating John Wigmore's twenty-five years of service at the Northwestern University School of Law only rubbed salt in the wound. Holmes's friend Frederick Pollock wrote the lead essay. *See generally* 13 ILL. L. REV. Issue 2 (1918–19). The placement of the Zane essay in the Wigmore festschrift, along with Holmes's absence as a participant, may help explain why Zane rankled Holmes as much as he did. *See* G. EDWARD WHITE, JUSTICE OLIVER WENDELL HOLMES: LAW AND THE INNER SELF 371–77 (observing that Zane uniquely got under Holmes's skin).

50 Zane, *supra* note 43, at 431.

51 *Id.* at 438 n.23.

52 Though in "German Legal Philosophy" he laced his compliment with a hint of arsenic: "*The Common Law* of Holmes was exceedingly good if it had been true, but it had at any rate the rarest and best of all things, charm and inspiration and faultless diction." Zane, *supra* note 43, at 355.

United States about the profession of law. His was clearly an adroit mind, well stocked, catholic in its interests, discriminating in its tastes, a mind belonging to a man who was never merely a lawyer but always a man of letters.[53] Zane notes the liveliness of Holmes's style, both in life and in opinion writing; and regarding the latter he singles out Holmes's talent for epigrams, which, Zane cannot refrain from adding, are unfortunate nullities, neither truths nor half-truths.[54]

Whether as a matter of genuine disappointment, or merely as a rhetorical ploy, Zane's vignette of a judge who betrayed his own best promise transitions subtly from tones light-gray to gray upon gray to something a shade darker without any definite border – Holmes the new kind of judge, erudite, urbane, worldly-wise; Holmes the master judicial craftsman, drafting powerfully worded opinions with astonishing ease and sure-handedness; Holmes the hare eyeing sidewise the tortoises at the gate; Holmes the crafty legal philosopher whose doctrine of "irresponsible state power" – that is, state power that has no obligation to respond to anything outside itself – lends credence to a malignant German absolutism; Holmes the misguided follower of Austin's hollow theory of state sovereignty; Holmes the proponent of the pernicious belief that courts can and do make law; Holmes the purveyor of popular legal nostrums – such as use of the police power in favor of "strong and preponderant opinion" – that purposely disregard constitutional limitations and undermine the Fourteenth Amendment.

Apparently Holmes's much vaunted productivity set Zane's teeth on edge. The sheer speed and the evident upwelling of a mind that appears to mint its own maxims – a mind that often disarms the unwise and causes the novice to gape in great surprise – cast, for Zane, the darkest shadows, the umbras, whenever a truly complex issue wends its way to the court: it "shows one defect of his mind, and that is that he works with such celerity that he does not think through a difficult matter to the end, nor does he always examine his authorities with scrupulous care[.]"[55]

Zane professed bewilderment; he claimed to be unable to find any thread of cogent legal reasoning running through Holmes's many opinions until he came across *Lochner*.

> I confess that his varied and Protean phenomena, constantly shifting with his wide and omnivorous reading, were baffling until I found in one of his dissenting opinions, *Lochner v. New York*, 198 U.S. 45, 76, this statement, which absurdly enough has been selected by Mr. Frankfurter for special commendation: '*General propositions do not decide concrete cases. The decision will depend on a judgment or intuition more subtle than any articulate major premise.*' Since only legal judgments that are given are in concrete cases, it follows that he asserts that lawsuits are not to

[53] Zane, *supra* note 41, at 439 n.23 (continued).

[54] *Id.*

[55] *Id.* at 440 n.23 (continued).

be decided by general propositions of law, but by means of a 'more subtle intuition.' This sounds like the unconscious self-satire of the Biglow Papers:

> 'Ez to my princerples, I glory
> In hevin' nothin' o' the sort.'

At last we can strike our finger on the place and say:

> "Thou ailest here, thou dost not know what justice is.'[56]

Justice for the principled Zane means deciding a case according to a general proposition of law applicable to all similar cases.[57]

On this same point Zane criticizes Gray's *The Nature and Sources of Law*. Gray, Zane asserts, confuses rules about thinking with rules regarding the ascertainment of a rule of law and its application to a concrete case. Gray's query, "what was the law in the time of Richard Coeur de Lion on the liability of a telegraph company to the persons to whom the message was sent," classifies as rank nonsense because "it is mentally impossible to conceive a rule of law governing non-existent human conduct."[58] It is a psychological absurdity.[59] Zane's reasoning is opaque on this point, but he appears to be linking the conceptual possibility of an extant governing rule with the actuality of the conduct sought to be governed. General rules of law are ascertainable, he maintains, and through deductive reasoning one may bring them to bear on the particulars of a dispute. Zane believes the history and sociology of law provide ample support for this contention. The existence of a sovereign, or that courts enforce law through sanctions, are expendable parts of law's administrative machinery – ones that vary from time to time and from place to place.[60]

Finally, we come to Holmes's damned and damnable heresy. It is this: "there can be no legal right as against the authority which makes the law on which the right depends."[61] Holmes cites, among others, Thomas Hobbes and Jean Bodin in support of this proposition. Zane expends much effort to demonstrate that Holmes's proposition of law lacks theoretical coherence and does not even have the support he claims in the authorities he names. Zane then closes: "at the cost of no little labor

[56] *Id.* at 440–41 n.23 (continued) (emphasis in original).

[57] *Id.*; *see also id.* at 435 ("Theoretically we know that this whole social existence and fabric of humanity is impossible without the evolution and dominance of the sentiment and idea of justice. The concept of justice … postulates *jural freedom*, i.e. equality before the laws, or to put it another way, justice requires pre-existing rules of law applicable to all alike and impartially applied in adjudication.").

[58] Zane, *supra* note 43, at 346.

[59] *Id.*

[60] *Id.* at 346–48.

[61] Zane, *supra* note 41, at 432 (quoting Kawananokoa v. Polyblank, 205 U.S. 349, 353 (1907)).

I have demonstrated that Justice Holmes' rule that the government is not bound by the laws cannot be supported except on some 'subtle intuition' of his own, which is not so 'articulate' as ever to have become the major premise of any other jurist."[62]

It requires little perspicuity to note that what Holmes said and what Zane damned do not match up. In many respects Frank correctly describes Zane's arguments, or at least their evident rhetorical implications, as absurd. Even so, Zane's angle of reproach, though it never mentions the bad man, brings the bad man into full view in all but name. Take the three propositions against which Zane takes especial umbrage:

1. There can be no legal right against the authority which makes the law on which the right depends;
2. That law is the statement of the circumstances in which the public force will be brought to bear upon men through the courts; and,
3. General propositions do not decide concrete cases. The decision will depend on a judgment or intuition more subtle than any articulate premise.

In these three propositions we can see the outline of the purely legal point of view that Holmes first articulates in *The Common Law*.

First, legal duties take logical and chronological priority over legal rights. One who has a legal right has an enforceable claim, backed by the state authority, against another who has failed in the applicable duty's performance. Those legal duties that have corresponding rights, and not all do, are the duties that those who control the enforcement power recognize. Thus a legal right depends on a legal duty and for one to have a legal right against the state authority it must be sustained by a legal duty the enforcement power is willing to impose against itself and its agents. Other (social or moral) grounds for calls against the state authority or its agents may exist and may prove powerful in gathering support and directing action, but they are not, strictly speaking, legal rights, though they may in time lead to expressed legal rights predicated on recognized legal duties.

Second, based on this understanding of municipal law – the function of what he sometimes calls the territorial club – Holmes argues that many gradations exist between acts that are clearly outside the pale – outside the protection of the law – and those that unquestionably fall within. Law in this view becomes a social practice, a *techne*, which operates by ascertaining facts and judging their relations against each other and against certain limits. A case or a statute is as much a part of the circumstances included in a statement of law as the admitted evidentiary facts, the ultimate facts the tribunal finds operative, and those generalizations encapsulated in an abiding rule or principle of decision.

If the first two propositions project a perspective that uses the notion of an "absolute command" as an instance of a vanishing point, and the successive

[62] *Id.* at 459.

gradations of enforcement options as a way to position legal events relative to each other and to multiple vanishing points, the third proposition electrifies and animates the entire cinematic field of vision. It recognizes that law lives. Each movement in the present has repercussions on how legal events future and past are perceived, understood, felt.

To vary the image: in the circuitry of a common law legal system – especially that of the United States – the courts act as transformers of the enforcement power. Controlled conduction of that power is as much art as science; intuitive know-how is part of any *techne*, even one, such as law, that also requires the ability to reason clearly and distinctly. The articulated major premise may not fully capture all the grounds – the felt reactions, the sense of what is needful and what is right and proper – but it may enunciate many of the most evident and serve as a pointer to those that elide verbalization.

The purely legal point of view sustains itself on the recognition that lawmaking powers must become cognizant of their own intrinsic dynamic, their inherent transformative capacities. The fundamental theory of the law, we recall, suggests that law, understood as a *techne*, may render any conduct lawful or unlawful. If Darwin could postulate and frame the natural mechanisms of speciation, Holmes saw no reason why a similar hypothesis and analysis could not elucidate that realm of social activity that eventuated in those specialized marks we call law.

Zane still operated from a predominantly mentalist framework. One that privileged the idea of equality under law, law understood as evolving, self-reinforcing jural relations grounded in collective sentiment and guided by a broadly envisioned ideal. Naturally Zane would, as is unmistakable in the passages quoted above, find little to his liking in the legal philosophy of one who refused to see in law the progressive working out of a realizable ideal.

Presumably for Holmes Zane's *civitas* reeked too much of *elegantia juris*, of logical cohesion of part to part.

A distinctly legal perspective is all-important for understanding law and developing a mastery of it as a practice; but a legal perspective, no matter how pure, is still just a perspective, one of many, limited and fallible and fated.

Zane saw little innuendo in the inflections of what he thought could properly be called law. Holmes, even if he granted Zane's premises, pondered little else.

6 HESSEL YNTEMA

Frank and Zane in their different ways express skepticism about any "science" of law.[63] Hessel E. Yntema, a legal scholar who did not share that skepticism,

[63] Frank, *supra* note 25, at 579 n.30 ("Thus the present writer disagrees with some of the non-Euclideans as to the possibility of developing a 'science of law.'"); Zane, *supra* note 47, at 2

published a perceptive piece in 1931 entitled, "Mr. Justice Holmes' View of Legal Science."[64]

Yntema professes to admire the prophetic Holmes from afar.[65] He believes Holmes had early in his career come to opinions and conclusions regarding law and its operations far ahead of his time. A more prominent jurist, Roscoe Pound, makes the same observation, though from a different angle.[66]

Yntema identifies the three main strands of the Holmesian idea of legal science – advanced in *The Common Law* and Holmes's two most important essays, "The Path of the Law," and "Law in Science and Science in Law" – as follows: a theory of legal history, canons of dogmatic study, and the rational or scientific ideal. "Roughly speaking," says Yntema, "the basic structure is the theory of legal history as outlined in the first lecture of *The Common Law*; this, enriched by judicial experience and projected upon contemporary legal study, becomes the canons of dogmatic study in *The Path of the Law*."[67] The rational or scientific ideal that informs both "The Path of the Law" and "Law in Science and Science in Law" further capitalizes Holmes's vision of a legal science.

i *The Theory of Legal History*

For his account of Holmes's theory of legal history Yntema relies on the opening chapter of *The Common Law*. He, like other commentators, recognizes what Howe calls the emancipatory uses to which Holmes directed his historical research and reflection. It is, Yntema asserts, a "vigorous conception of historical study, which has little sympathy for mere antiquarianism."[68] He further states that the study of the present by reference to the past invites a theory of legal evolution.[69] By this latter phrase Yntema seems to emphasize the question that all who seek to clarify the present by recourse to the past must try to answer: how did the then become the now?

In Yntema's opinion, Holmes's hypothesis of the paradox of form and substance in law seeks to articulate the reality of historical change as seen through the eyes of the law. In other words, one interested in understanding the use of legitimized power to

("The science of law, if there is a such a science, is but one of the several sciences that are concerned with men living in a social state.").

64 Hessel E. Yntema, *Mr. Justice Holmes' View of Legal Science*, 40 YALE L.J. 696 (1931).

65 *Id.* at 696 ("Both scholar and judge have the same marks of genius: nowhere a clearer, more prophetic vision of the realities of law.").

66 Roscoe Pound, *Judge Holmes's Contributions to the Science of Law*, 34 HARV. L. REV. 449, 449 (1921) ("His ideas have so thoroughly entered into the substance of our legal thought, and the papers and addresses in which they are set forth are so buried in the periodical literature of the law that the epigoni [*sic*] could easily forget whose armor they were wearing and whose weapons they were wielding.").

67 Yntema, *supra* note 64, at 696–97.

68 *Id.* at 697.

69 *Id.*

obtain social ends wants to know how discrete acts of power – court decisions, for example – are connected to each other and to other legal events. Are they connected by something other than sheer will or authority? In a common law system one invokes the principle of *stare decisis* and singles out the human power to reason logically from the extant decision or decisions to the present case. For Holmes this favored, though not exclusive, explanation of what the courts are doing (present tense) did not suffice to account for what historical research into past court records and other artifacts revealed – what the courts had *actually* done.

The italicizing of 'actually' reinforces its adverbial effect: the clash between what practitioners said, or believed, and what relatively unadulterated thinking buttressed by facts showed. The feeling of incongruity arises and becomes strong, strong enough to eventually engender a mood of skepticism. Without this adverbial effect no semantic nuance exists between what is done and what is actually done. Done is done.

Yntema does not gloss what he calls Holmes's hypothesis of the paradox of form and substance with the sort of observations we have just made. As befitting a legal scholar who recognized the importance of empirical study of law-related behavior,[70] Yntema applauds the adverbial effect of *actually* wherever it appears in Holmes's writings. For this reason Yntema believes what he calls Holmes's hypothesis is fundamental to Holmes's conception of legal science:

> The substance of the law at any given time pretty nearly corresponds, so far as it goes, with what is then understood to be convenient; but its form and machinery, and the degree to which it is able to work out desired results, depend very much on its past.

Yntema notes that Holmes introduced this hypothesis in 1881, the publication year of *The Common Law*,[71] and, incidentally, fifty years to the month (March 1931) in which Yntema published his short article.[72] In the interim, Holmes had become a distinguished judge and through his many decisions sought to give body and breath to his jurisprudential insights. Yntema believes the hypothesis's most evident implications still reflect the patina of truth for the study of law and its history.

The first implication of Holmes's hypothesis suggests that law "must found itself on actual forces" because it is a "practical thing." It is what we have called in equivalent language a *techne*.[73]

[70] *See* John Henry Schlegel, American Legal Realism & Empirical Social Science 147–210 (1995); N. E. H. Hull, Roscoe Pound & Karl Llewellyn: Searching for an American Jurisprudence 284 (1997).

[71] Holmes first expressly formulated what Yntema calls the hypothesis of the paradox of form and substance in "Common Carriers and the Common Law," published in 1879. Oliver Wendell Holmes, *Common Carriers and the Common Law*, *in* III CW 75–76.

[72] Yntema's article is part of the special edition of the *Yale Law Journal* dedicated to Justice Holmes in honor of his ninetieth birthday.

[73] Yntema, *supra* note 64, at 698.

The second major implication recognizes that the contention "in substance the growth of law is legislative" applies to both the law's content and its grounds. In distinguishing between legislative content and legislative grounds Yntema makes an extremely important observation. One can almost hear his forefinger tapping the page. Because law is legislative in its grounds, it makes eminent sense to highlight the significance, as Holmes does, of "the felt necessities of the time, the prevalent moral and political theories, intuitions of public policy, avowed or unconscious, even the prejudices which judges share with their fellow-men." We are back to the first page of *The Common Law*. But then Yntema adds this clause to the passage just quoted: "in the interpretation and adaptation of ancient rules or the creation of new."[74]

Yntema's distinction between legislative content and legislative grounds encapsulates the gist of Holmes's argument in lecture I of *The Common Law*. Yntema has artfully connected "felt necessities" from the opening section of lecture I with Holmes's summation at lecture I's end of the significance of his research into how the common law develops: "in substance the growth of law is legislative. And this in a deeper sense than that what the courts declare to have always been the law is in fact new. *It is legislative in its grounds*."[75]

The second major implication of Holmes's hypothesis of the paradox of form and substance in Yntema's opinion directs attention to the radical equivalence Holmes asserts between what is typically understood as the ground of a legal rule – traditionally labeled the facts, acts of omission or commission – and those features of human behavior less easily concretized or objectified into facts. Or those aspects that legal professionals typically do not acknowledge as being part of the pertinent factual circumstances. These are, Holmes maintains, the "very considerations which judges most rarely mention, and always with an apology[.]" These considerations are "the secret root from which law draws all the juices of life." Holmes then quite uncharacteristically explains what he means:

> I mean, of course, considerations of what is expedient for the community concerned. Every important principle which is developed by litigation is in fact and at bottom the result of more or less definitely understood views of public policy; most generally, to be sure, under our practice and traditions, the unconscious result of instinctive preferences and inarticulate convictions, but none the less traceable to view of public policy in the last analysis … But hitherto this process has been largely unconscious. It is important, on that account, to bring to mind what the

[74] *Id.*

[75] Holmes, *The Common Law*, *supra* note 14, at 132–33 (emphasis added). Novick notes that Holmes corrected the second-to-last sentence quoted to read: "And legislative not merely in this sense that rules which the courts declare to have always been the law are in fact new." *Id.* at 134 n.13.

actual course of events has been. If it were only to insist on a more conscious recognition of the legislative function of the courts[.][76]

By this explanation Holmes effectively broadens the working conception of "facts" operative in the law and, at the same time, levels the field. The existing form – an established doctrine, a working rule – is not eradicated or rendered relatively unimportant but demoted from the intellectual high ground it formerly occupied. That is to say, dogmas and doctrines, axioms and rules – the authority of authority or the authority of reason – lose their formerly high status as untainted manifestations of will or thought. Or, as the 1930s Jerome Frank might puckishly say, the earth no longer stood still.

The recognition that the features of experience Judge Richard A. Posner has grouped together (undoubtedly with a touch of irony) under the word "priors"[77] are ever a part of the total factual situation from which a court-issued rule takes its shape led Yntema to the third major implication of Holmes's hypothesis. It is the secondary significance of logic.[78] Here we encounter once again the famous line – "the life of the law has not been logic: it has been experience" – and the deficiencies of logic are connected to its limited perspective: "failure of all theories which consider law only from its formal side."[79]

Logic still had its place. But based on Holmes's understanding of the course of legal history its role is reduced in proportion to its actual importance. Though Yntema does not mention it, the inference is clear that one consequence of logic's downsized role for practitioners is an attenuated confidence in logic's monitoring and regulative capabilities. If the syllogism is not as potent an intellectual force as once believed, to what could a practitioner appeal to counteract the blandishments of the emperor's wife?

That historical study and reflection required the reconsideration of the value of existing legal forms – those which Holmes calls primitive survivals – describes the fourth major implication. In a legal system that purports to follow precedent this implication has far-reaching consequences for the study and practice of law.

The final implication of Holmes's hypothesis, according to Yntema, focuses on the "desirability of an actualistic [*sic*] description of the [legal] process[.]"[80] This focus involves bringing to the foreground of attention the legislative function of the courts, and "the progressive measurement of human conduct by more 'external or objective' and less moral, legal standards."[81]

76 *Id.* at 133.

77 *See, e.g.*, Richard A. Posner, Divergent Paths: The Academy and the Judiciary 17–18 (2016).

78 Yntema, *supra* note 64, at 698.

79 *Id.*

80 *Id.*

81 *Id.*

What might entail a "progressive measurement" Yntema unfortunately does not explain. We assume that Yntema in this sentence is alluding to Holmes's ideal of founding a "true science of the law" on the "establishment of its postulates from within upon accurately measured social desires instead of tradition."[82] Progressive measurement probably refers to the slow build-up of knowledge based on careful review of legal events and their consequences, or to the outcome of research into different types of social behavior – including legal behavior – and the standards by which the results would be evaluated depend less on existing moral or legal criteria than criteria slowly constructed from an intelligent assessment and reassessment of relevant effects and their antecedents (ongoing experience).

For Yntema, Holmes's theory of legal history begins and ends in actual experience. It is empirical; it looks to actual forces; it recognizes the actuality of historical experience and how that experience is transmuted into the working beliefs that underlie the present. It resituates logic, and expands legislative grounds to expressly include the less obvious but no less vital elements that inform individual and group proclivities and decision-making. Its manner of framing the effects of the past on the present directly leads to a program of legal study. Yntema refers to this program as the canons of dogmatic study, the second main element of Holmes's view of legal science.

ii *The Canons of Dogmatic Study*

The canons of legal study are in effect, Yntema says, "the application of the theory of legal history to contemporary professional legal study."[83] As one might expect, what Yntema calls the canons of dogmatic study are analogous to the main propositions of Holmes's theory of legal history that Yntema identifies. Yntema distinguishes six canons, but it is to the second that we should first direct our attention.

The second canon recognizes that law conceived as a body of dogma or systematized prediction must be objective. "The study is 'of the law as a business with well understood limits, a body of dogma within definite lines.' Hence to avoid confusion, the necessity of the distinction between law and ethics, of a 'bad man' attitude toward law."[84]

After quoting the relevant passage from "The Path of the Law" that directs the novice to look at the law as a bad man and not as a good man who finds his reasons for conduct, either inside or outside the law, in the vaguer sanctions of conscience, Yntema says: "It should be noted that this canon of professional study does not deny ethics or its fundamental relation to law."[85]

82 Oliver Wendell Holmes, *Law in Science and Science in Law*, *in* III CW 412–13.
83 Yntema, *supra* note 64, at 698.
84 *Id.*
85 *Id.* at 699.

What then is the point of calling the bad man bad and advocating his attitude of looking at the law? For Yntema this outlook serves as a wedge to split apart what exists as an encompassing whole in the experienced present. It separates the objective from the subjective. It does so by objectifying law as a means by which and through which prediction occurs.

The first canon conceives the subject of legal study as a type of dogma – that is, authoritative systematized teachings or truths – which enables the student, when rightly comprehended, to predict the likelihood of future legal consequences. Prediction is the objective – in the sense of point or purpose of study – and Yntema finds this objective to be "practical, realistic." It has the significance of being real and effective, of being founded on "actual forces."[86]

We again run into the adverbial effect of actuality. Law-related activity under this conception is pervasive; it manifests a potentially overwhelming immanence. In this environment, legal study and analysis function as carefully crafted steps toward the ultimate end of understanding how to subsume and, to the extent possible, control sovereign power. Prediction as a pedagogical goal in Yntema's hands creates its own internal dynamic. As part of Holmes's theory of legal history it finds a locus in the past and partakes in the cumulative sequences of experience. On the other side, as a term of art in the natural sciences and the burgeoning social sciences it encapsulates an ideal of scientific knowledge. The best test of a scientific hypothesis is its predictive power.

To predict – how? by what means? and for what end? – becomes an overriding objective that conceals the significance of the underlying stance one takes toward the law itself. In its most sophisticated formulation, law, understood in this context as a developed and justified body of decisions and pronouncements (judicial or legislative) regarding the use of the sovereign power, should either reflect recurring (cultural, psychological, economic, political) beliefs rooted in perceived social regularities or encapsulate the best, most rigorous, most up-to-date results of intelligent investigations into law-related activities and behaviors.

Yntema leans toward the latter endpoint of this spectrum. Yet, this depiction of the means by which the "factors that condition the law [are] to be ascertained, analyzed and evaluated[,]"[87] obscures those filaments of experience (nascent goods and bads) of which Holmes seems at times preternaturally aware. Holmes alludes to them through his use of the word prophecy, a word that oddly – given Yntema's own recognition of the prophetic character of Holmes's work – does not once appear in Yntema's analysis. The significance this term has for revealing Holmes's subtle handling of legal phenomena we will address in both Section 13 and the next part.

[86] *Id.* at 698–9.
[87] *Id.* at 700.

The forms of analysis that Yntema superimposes on Holmes's writings (how he organizes, connects, and conveys Holmes's overall message), while perceptive and incisive, leave out what may in the long run be most vital, the sense of depth and dimensionality that Holmes brings to his understanding of law. In Yntema's hands the bad man serves to ward off predominantly subjective understandings of law, law interpreted in primarily personal or moral terms. It also serves as a means to objectify legal phenomena and create the type of mindset needed for social scientific objectivity.[88] The enjoinder to look at the law as a bad man, who cares only about the material legal consequences, and not as a good man, who pays heed to those vaguer sanctions of conscience, unless emplotted into the course of law's history within the relevant territorial borders, remains singularly artificial in its employment, static, unable to assimilate into the intuitive good sense of the living legal order.

Even so, we cannot deny Yntema's astuteness in conveying the essential lineaments of Holmes's theory of legal history and its corresponding canons of legal study. To the canons of understanding the practical objective of such study – prediction – and the importance of demarcating legal dogma from subjective moral or ethical concerns – that is, emphasizing the objective nature of the body of law that exists – Yntema adds the means and material of such study – the third canon: especially the reports of cases, the oracles of the law stretching back 600 years – and the jurisprudential work of clarifying and extending the law through analysis and generalization, what he calls the fourth canon of dogmatic study.

Yntema finds the fifth canon, the rule that the method of prediction is not primarily logical or mathematical in form, to be the most far-reaching since it establishes the sixth canon of legal study:

> [T]o discover from history how it has come to be what it is; and, finally, so far as you can, to consider the ends which the several rules seek to accomplish, the reasons why those ends are desired, and whether they are worth the price.[89]

This sixth and final canon of dogmatic study, Yntema observes, essentially recapitulates Holmes's theory of legal history as it once again emphasizes the critical use of historical research and reflection for evaluating the worth of existing legal forms.

iii *The Rational or Scientific Ideal in Law*

Yntema's exposition of the canons of dogmatic study tracked Holmes's 1897 address. By expressly connecting those canons to Holmes's understanding and exposition of

[88] Later in his career Yntema abandoned "the distinction between 'is' and 'ought' for purposes of legal science." Hessel E. Yntema, *American Legal Realism in Retrospect*, 14 VAND. L. REV. 317, 325 (1960).

[89] Yntema, *supra* note 64, at 700 (quoting Holmes, *The Path of the Law*, *supra* note 14, at 398–402).

the dynamics of historical change, Yntema initiated a line of commentary similar to our own. The reality of legal change and its inherent dynamics within the municipality set the limits of legal study. More exactly: what Yntema calls the canons of dogmatic study could only function usefully as canons within the constraints that Holmes's theory of legal history articulated. As the what, how, and why of legal study all interconnected, one would expect that the method and means of study would be congruent with Holmes's conceptualization of law as a subject of study.

Without expressly questioning how Holmes proposed to match the method and means with law's subject and purpose, Yntema quotes this important passage from "Law in Science and Science in Law":

> I sometimes tell students that law schools pursue an inspirational method combined with a logical method, that is, the postulates are taken for granted upon authority without inquiry into their worth, and then logic is used as the only tool to develop the results. It is a necessary method for the purpose of teaching dogma. But inasmuch as the real justification of a rule of law, if there be one, is that it helps to bring about a social end which we desire, it is not less necessary that those who make and develop the law should have those ends articulately in their minds.[90]

We note in this paragraph an odd, unexpected incongruity in educational method: what Homes calls the amalgamation of an "inspirational method" with a "logical method." The oddity increases when one notes the unsuitability in many respects of each method as a way to study the subject matter called law as Holmes conceives it. Holmes has effectively identified how the case method – which he believes comprises both an "inspirational method" and a "logical method" – fails to advance the purpose of law (to clarify and enact social ends).

The incongruities in the quoted passage do not capture Yntema's attention. To these incongruities we will return in the next part. What does hold his attention is Holmes's notion of the rational or scientific ideal in law. This orienting ideal arises, in Yntema's opinion, from how Holmes has set up the fundamental tension in the law:

> The formulation of the legal process as logical in form but legislative in substance – in other words, essentially in terms of public policy, social ends and the weighing of interests – states the crucial problems of a realistic jurisprudence: How are the factors that condition the law to be ascertained, analyzed and evaluated?[91]

As he has done in the previous two sections, Yntema outlines Holmes's "suggestive rather than detailed" responses to the topic. First, Holmes rejects the reliance on tradition when it comes to determining the worth of legislative grounds and goals. "The present," Holmes writes, "has a right to govern itself so far as it can."[92]

[90] *Id.* (quoting Holmes, *supra* note 82, at 418).

[91] *Id.* at 700.

[92] *Id.* at 700–01 (quoting Holmes, *supra* note 82, at 492).

Second, the study of history, while necessary to the rational study of legal rules, must be kept in check.

Third, the legal science of the future will rely more on quantitative than qualitative judgments. This goal is in keeping with Holmes's vigilant pursuit of the more exact.

Taken in unison these elements, for Yntema, point toward Holmes's overarching rational or scientific ideal. As he sums it up:

> Thus, both in dogma and in practice, the basis of law is to be scientific. Holmes' view looks beyond formal traditionalism, past even prevailing standards of professional dogmatic study, to the development of a rational legal science, more empirical and less historical, directed to the more exact measurement of social ends.[93]

Yntema repeats toward the article's end that Holmes's vision of legal science, even after fifty years, is still prophetic. He considers Holmes's formulation of legal evolution in terms of social ends a thesis more profound, trenchant, and universal than Maine's celebrated theorem of "status to contract" or the nowadays less known "law of imitation" of Gabriel Tarde. "Its great virtue," he says in words pregnant with meaning, "is to turn historical study upon tradition and thus to suggest a basis for a more rational consideration of legal problems."[94]

Yntema finds Holmes's view of legal science also notable for its practical quality. He sees limitations in this as well – as providing fodder for narrow antiquarian minds, or restricting the necessity of reaching beyond the confines of professional education to the study of legal institutions in their sociological and other contexts – but in the main he believes that Holmes's view attributes to the practical "the penetration of a profound and realistic philosophy of enlightened skepticism."[95] This redounding assertion, like others that Yntema uses, is both enticing and lamentably opaque.

Reading Yntema on Holmes reminds one of that peculiar intellectual lament found in the Christian New Testament – of seeing through a glass, darkly. Almost alone among his peers Yntema senses the importance that *The Common Law* had for "The Path of the Law."[96] He also recognizes Holmes's express commitment to the scientific ideal. He perceptively intuits that what Holmes is saying is still vital for the future of the profession. He can comprehend the words; he can even provide astute readings; he cannot, it seems, shake the feeling he's missing something.

93 *Id.* at 701.
94 *Id.* at 702.
95 *Id.* at 702–03.
96 John Henry Schlegel points out that the realists most actively engaged in empirical research generally ignored the disciplines of history and historical sociology. SCHLEGEL, *supra* note 70, at 235–37.

7 WALTER WHEELER COOK

The year 1941 ushered in a new decade. Holmes has been dead going on six years. In retrospect this moment in chronological time, as measured by the Western calendar, makes a surreal impression. The memory of Holmes, still strong for his admirers, begins to undergo a weird transmogrification. From the minds of those inheritors of New England's historic sense of historical destiny the Yankee from Olympus springs forth fully robed. His mustachios luxuriously waxed and regal, eyes even, gaze studied, lips softly set, mouth unsmiling, teeth un-shown, hands free of any evident implement of war: Greek and Puritan antecedents notwithstanding, might this not be the nation's first native (Hindu) god?

Holmes bequeathed his money and his library to the United States of America. His alma mater, Harvard, received his papers, thousands upon thousands of letters, many notebooks, the famous so-called Black Book[97] – which contained Holmes's handwritten notations of the books he read over a lifetime – and annotated copies of his early articles and essays. Professor Felix Frankfurter took charge of the Holmes brand (as we would say nowadays), recognizing its value for the political and social causes he cared about. In this mission Harold J. Laski aided and abetted from London. Frankfurter eventually recruited one of Holmes's last secretaries (today called law clerks), his mentee Mark DeWolfe Howe, to amass the great justice's far-flung correspondence and the other materials needed to stock the archival store from which the perceptive, literate, and hardworking Howe would eventually produce an authorized biography.

The first two volumes of Howe's uncompleted monument lay far in the future. It has been reported that both Howe's early death and his growing antipathy to Holmes's personality ultimately distracted him from finishing the job. I don't query the effect of the death but do wonder about the alleged antipathy.

But at the dawn of the 1940s one imagines Howe pulling hard at the oar. The great Holmes has died, Britain is facing the German firestorm, Japan ranges through the eastern borders of the Asian continent like a hungry tiger, that tremendous economic downturn that gave new meaning to the word depression lingers like a nagging, troubling cough, FDR proclaims America's faith in the four freedoms, communism still manages to simultaneously inspire dread and hope in the American polity, and those intelligences attracted to historical questions begin to pour renewed energy into investigating and expounding the distinctively "American" features of their high octane civilization.

In the tiny annals of jurisprudence one observes the same stirrings of Emersonian pride, anxiety, and curiosity – what dishes would, or could, American lawyers and legal thinkers bring to what had been an almost exclusively European cuisine? Appropriately entitled *My Philosophy of Law*, a volume published in 1941 brought together the

[97] *See* MICHAEL H. HOFFHEIMER, JUSTICE HOLMES AND THE NATURAL LAW 16 n.58 (1992).

jurisprudential credo of sixteen American legal philosophers.[98] The editors declared themselves motivated in part to show that legal philosophy is not some "foreign disease."[99] I, for one, snickered and then felt saddened when I read that.

Of the sixteen participants only John Dewey's name will garner – as these things are measured – widespread recognition in today's world. Perhaps among lawyers Roscoe Pound will come in a close second, but probably not. Very few names or ideas last more than twenty or twenty-five years as Holmes noted in a different context. The other names have for the most part faded into the binary nooks and crannies of dissertation depositories.

The editors arranged the credos alphabetically. Why I'm not sure but we can all make a good guess. Credo number three belongs to one Walter Wheeler Cook. He is sandwiched between Morris Cohen and John Dewey. Unlucky for him as both of these men, professional philosophers, were better known at that time than he. But Cook had his admirers. None other than Charles E. Clark, judge of the Second Circuit Court of Appeals, former dean of the Yale Law School, and principal drafter of the Federal Rules of Civil Procedure, wrote in a 1944 tribute after the man had passed that he regarded Cook, with the exception of Holmes himself, as the nation's earliest and preeminent legal realist. He considered Cook's place assured in the history of American legal thought.[100]

As did other participants, Cook begins his entry with the complaint that the space allotted was hardly sufficient to expound one's legal philosophy. Even so, he gamely put forward his basic conviction:

> [T]he primary aim is to examine the problems of the lawyer, the judge, the law teacher, and the legal investigator from the point of view of the logic of inquiry developed by modern science.[101]

Cook thinks legal critics have persistently misunderstood his fundamental proposition because they have in mind outmoded understandings of the scientific enterprise and scientific procedure.

> What has been pointed out in these earlier discussions is that thoughtful scientists today no longer adopt the dogmatic views of the Victorian scientists that final truth about the physical world has been reached, but recognize instead that scientific 'knowledge' consists of what John Dewey has recently called "warranted assertions" about the world, and that even our most trusted generalizations are working hypotheses which are theoretically subject to revision as experience widens.[102]

98 My Philosophy of Law: Credos of Sixteen American Scholars [hereinafter My Philosophy of Law] (1941).
99 *Id.* at vii–viii.
100 Charles E. Clark, *Walter Wheeler Cook*, 38 Ill. L. Rev. 341, 341–44 (1944).
101 My Philosophy of Law, *supra* note 98, at 51.
102 *Id.* at 52.

It is hard to know how seriously to take Cook's claim in 1941 that less-than-thoughtful scientists still adhered to the "dogmatic view" that "final truth had been reached." Perhaps by "scientist" he intends to include knowledge seekers or professional inquirers beyond those who study only nature and its observable objects.

What increasingly becomes evident as one proceeds through the piece is Cook's belief that one could study legal phenomena, however identified and circumscribed, scientifically; that is, by employing certain steps in a certain way. Following Dewey he identifies the required procedure or algorithm as a logic of inquiry.[103]

Cook argues, "that the logical structure of scientific inquiry is the same, whether one studies physics and chemistry or biology and the social sciences."[104] In other words, the subject matter of inquiry does not call for a fundamentally different series of intellectual steps for investigating the specific subject, formulating questions, developing plans of action, or putting doubts to sleep. Law, as one of the human sciences, or those inquiries ultimately concerned with value, would undoubtedly benefit from a less doctrinaire, more empirical and more self-consciously experimental approach.

True to form, Cook speaks less often of law and more often of the work of lawyers, judges, law teachers, and legal investigators. Law is what lawyers, judges, law teachers, and legal investigators do. And I'm sure he did not mean the list to be exhaustive. To the common criticism that this way of looking at matters leaves ultimate, normative oughts flapping in the wind Cook makes this reply:

> What is asserted is that same 'logic of inquiry' developed in connection with the physical sciences can be utilized in developing a theory of 'values'. More specifically, the proposition is that the same general techniques of carrying on intelligent inquiry can furnish us, not only with a 'descriptive science' of acts of valuation by human beings, but also with the means to evaluate acts of value, and so with a 'normative' science if one likes to call it that.[105]

Cook clarifies that by "'normative'" he means no more than the provisional sense of intellectual satisfaction, the (temporary) feeling of fit or rightness that sometimes arises when from competing proposals one selects the one that best addresses the "needs and lacks" of a specific, existing situation. He seems to take for granted the plans of action dictated by different, frequently opposing, ultimate ends may not cohere. These so-called ultimate ends are typically encapsulated in such glittering generalities as justice, honor, happiness, goodness, or, as Holmes would probably say in this connection, property, sanctity of contract, freedom of speech, and the general welfare.[106]

[103] *Id.* at 57–59.
[104] *Id.* at 52.
[105] *Id.* at 62.
[106] *Id.* at 61–65.

Cook's drive to infuse into the workings of law the spirit of scientific empiricism did not begin and end in with a single defined logic of inquiry. He recognizes that different subject matters might require different applications or modifications of the same overarching technique. More than a specific program he advocates a point of view he calls scientific. His particular version subtends a vision of experience that takes into account the constancy of change or what Holmes refers to as the law of fashion. From this premise the conclusion naturally arises that the inquirer into legal phenomena (certain types of acts of value) must employ specific steps in the spirit of inquiry – that is, the inquirer's approach must reflect the preference for warranted assertions that extend beyond isolated, unchecked, and thus unbalanced and disproportionate individual or group proclivities.

The point here is a subtle one. On the one side Cook wants to avoid those who believe that truth is fixed, that initially warranted assertions formulated as absolutes can retain their high intellectual status under all conditions, through all conjunctions of events. On the other side Cook pulls back from a naked subjectivism that emphasizes more the 'I' than the 'think' in the phrase "I think best."

These expressly philosophical commitments find, for Cook, their métier in the law through a more profound awareness of the context that law, as an assembly of interrelated activities, creates or can still create for an expansive and expanding social life. Legal activities, at their best, clarify, conceptualize, and contextualize aspects of a shared social existence – that which some thinkers use the word experience to describe – as part of the ongoing self-imposed task of making life progressively both more individualized and more communal. The present and the past are brought to bear, one upon the other. To further these ends, Cook believes that legal professionals must take an approach self-consciously scientific.

In 1935, when Holmes died, Cook paused from his obligations at the United States Department of the Treasury, where he had found temporary employment, to compose, at the invitation of the editor of the *American Bar Association Journal*, a short tribute to the man whom he owed such a great intellectual debt. He entitled it, "Oliver Wendell Holmes: Scientist."[107]

Cook begins this short piece by pinpointing what he believes to have been the general point of view that Holmes, as a young ambitious legal scholar and thinker, had long sought and finally found.[108] He deems it enshrined in the words, "all life is an experiment." "Are not," says Cook, "[the] implications and assumptions [underlying this sentence] essentially identical with those of every true scientist, of every

[107] Walter Wheeler Cook, *Oliver Wendell Holmes: Scientist*, 21 A.B.A. J. 211–13 (1935).

[108] *Id.* Cook quotes from Holmes's 1900 speech given to the Boston at a reception in his honor as the new chief justice of the Massachusetts Judicial Supreme Court. In that speech, Holmes reminisces about his life and says: "One begins with a search for a general point of view. After a time he finds one, and then for a while he is absorbed in testing it, in trying to satisfy himself whether it is true." *See* Oliver Wendell Holmes, *Speech at Bar Association of Boston Dinner, in* III CW 499.

believer in the application of the scientific habit of thought in all fields of human endeavor?"[109]

Cook takes the phrase "all life is an experiment" from Holmes's 1919 dissenting opinion in *Abrams* v. *United States*. Underlying this summation is the realization that "time has upset many fighting faiths." From this sense of how the passage of time in the modern world tends to upend cherished beliefs and implacable convictions, Cook discerns the source of Holmes's willingness to permit legislatures to engage in social and economic experiments.

While Yntema emphasizes the role of history as a technique or mode of inquiry in Holmes's thought, Cook sees in Holmes's recognition that beliefs and convictions – as intentional, active motivations – have a limited life span a distinctive manner of bringing history, understood as the realized or realizable past, into the scientific ambit.

The many years Holmes spent delving into cases on trespass or trover or the source of rights against bailees or the duties of a common carrier had, in other words, instilled in him a habit of mind. This habit of mind revealed itself in Holmes's manner of approaching and assessing human action and belief. He recognized both the partiality and the necessity – the necessity to life itself – of perspectives or, in the equivalent language of Nietzsche, of horizons.

Cook sees in the attitude expressed in the phrase "all life is an experiment" the spirit of the true scientist. We cannot derive from this short piece on Holmes whether Cook believes that attitude a sufficient description of the practicing scientist or, more likely, simply a good starting point. All life may be an experiment – but who is the experimenter, what is the objective, and how are the results to be gauged and tallied?

The sense that one is fallible may provide incentive to some needed second-guessing of first convictions, especially in a court of law or equity, but for the logic of inquiry to be relevant and pragmatic in that setting one must have the ability to recognize when one has reached a (provisional) stopping point. The "needs and lacks" of a specific situation, say the culmination of a suit hard-fought and protracted, the sort that Holmes would often hear in the United States Supreme Court, require a developed feel for the legal rationales that will meet the existing situation and those policy concerns that extend beyond it.

Holmes's approach was not quite as open-ended as Cook suggests in the opening section of his tribute. Lines still had to be drawn and measured. The concrete borders of the municipality still set the perimeters for the less-concrete jurisprudential boundaries. Cook senses this when he draws attention to the second aspect of Holmes's thought that he believes bolsters Holmes's scientific bona fides.

This second aspect involves Holmes's separation of law from morals. After quoting the relevant sentences on this topic from "The Path of the Law," Cook observes:

[109] Cook, *supra* note 107, at 211.

"Precisely so: if one would study law like a scientist, he must for certain purposes – note the limiting phrase – isolate and study it *as a system*."[110] Cook further notes that for Holmes law, unlike mathematics, is not a "closed system," but a series of predictions about legal consequences.

Cook does not further elucidate in what sense for Holmes law is a "system," or why, exactly, isolating it and viewing it as a system is scientific. Cook evidently thinks Holmes made a step of the first importance when, for pedagogical reasons, he defined law as a domain apart from morals. On this point he recounts an interesting exchange he had with the justice regarding the latter's notion of committing a contract.

In a letter to Holmes dated February 22, 1919, Cook had objected to *The Common Law*'s statement that, "a contractor is free to break his contract." In reply Holmes wrote:

> On the other point I agree that in one sense it is not desirable to express the position of a contractor as I expressed it. Of course it is not the theory of the common law that he has an option. I dare say it even might be proper to describe the breach as illegal, although early in my legal studies I was perplexed to discover the difference between illegality and conduct that merely was taxed or had to be paid for. I asked myself what is the difference between the mill acts and conversion, for which latter as in former case you simply have to pay the value of the thing taken. *To know law one must be cynical and disregard ethics that find no legal expression.* The only legal differences that I could discover were that a contract to do the act called illegal was void and that there was no contribution between wrongdoers. The reasons that I thought and still think my mode of statement useful (though the majority of the profession no doubt would view it with repugnance) is that no contract depends for its performance solely on the will of the contractor and that apart from special objections to wagers a man may contract for a future event that is wholly outside of his power but the non-occurrence of which will be a breach, none the less. I restated my view in *Globe Refining Co. v. Landa Cotton Oil Co.* 190 U.S. 540, 543 where on the latter page I say "when a man makes a contract". I wanted to say "commits a contract" but thought it would not quite do. There again I endeavored to indicate the bearing of my mode of statement on general theory. I say that at common law a contractor simply is taking the risk of a future event.[111]

[110] *Id.* at 212 (emphasis in original).

[111] *Id.* at 212–13 (emphasis added). I have quoted the relevant section of Justice Holmes's reply letter in full. Cook in his article leaves out the sentences between the one ending in "none the less" and the last sentence. *See* letter from Oliver Wendell Holmes, Jr. to Walter Wheeler Cook (Feb. 25, 1919) (on file with Harvard University Holmes Digital Suite. Mark DeWolfe Howe's research materials on Holmes, 1858–1968. Finding Aid, General Correspondence, General Group II: Box 14, Folder 18, Cook, Walter Wheeler, correspondent, 1919–1931); *see also* MARK DEWOLFE HOWE, JUSTICE OLIVER WENDELL HOLMES: THE PROVING YEARS, 1870–1882 237 (1963).

In Justice Holmes's correspondence to Cook we find confirmation of the suggestion made earlier that one should, for the sake of understanding Holmes and for the purposes of legal analysis, recognize the existence and interplay of different types of duties – spiritual, moral, social, and legal. As did Cook, we note in Holmes's admonition, "[t]o know law one must be cynical and disregard ethics that find no legal expression[,]" the substance of the section in the "The Path of the Law" that urges law students to adopt in their studies the perspective of the bad man. Holmes realized early in his studies that the domains of morals and law were not coextensive. The "ethics" (moral duties) that found expression in law – doubtlessly fortified through physical power – had acquired a different level of importance and therefore a different status than those moral duties that had not achieved this level of expression.[112] This distinction had helped Holmes understand the exact nature and reach of the law of contracts. He then assumes, as many of us would, that what aided him in deepening his understanding of law would help the younger generation as well.

Cook emphasizes the scientific aspects of Holmes's approach. He takes this tack partly to counter the suggestion that Holmes "had improperly divorced law and morals, and taken the cynical position that law ought to be considered without regard to ethics[,]"[113] and partly to reinforce his own recommendations that the study of law be put on an explicitly scientific footing. It would take us too far afield to evaluate the extent to which Holmes's approach to visualizing, verbalizing, clarifying, and conceptualizing law is 'scientific' in the manner that Cook advocates. One certainly finds in Holmes an effort to enhance comprehension and deepen understanding of judicial acts within the boundaries of these United States. Perhaps that is science enough.

Cook, though, clearly grasps the weight Holmes places on collateral consequences for understanding a specific point of law. He shows this by restating and explaining Holmes's idea of committing a contract. In his rendition he connects the contractor's beach of the contract with the contractee's duty to mitigate damages.[114] He then concludes the section by saying,

> Whether Mr. Justice Holmes's view is right or wrong I am not concerned at the moment to establish, but rather to call attention to how it was reached, namely, in a manner truly scientific: Careful observation of the data, that is to say, of the phenomena of judicial decision as they occurred; the elimination of the irrelevant, such as ethics which had found no expression in the law, and which one might read

[112] *See also* Holmes, *supra* note 82, at 407 ("It is proper to resort to it [historical explanation] to discover what ideals of society have been strong enough to reach that final form of expression [that is, law].").

[113] Cook, *supra* note 107, at 212.

[114] *Id.* at 213. But there is little indication that Cook appreciates how Holmes visualized the emergence of a legal duty.

> into the law unless he used adequate analytical tools in the shape of carefully defined concepts of legal right, legal duty, primary right, etc., etc.[115]

The final, very short section of "Oliver Wendell Holmes: Scientist" Cook devotes to quoting the passage from "The Path of the Law" in which Holmes urges upon his listeners the importance of jurisprudence. "Was it not," Cook rhetorically asks, "one of the things which distinguished Holmes from most of his colleagues and made him stand preeminent among them, that his adequate equipment in the field of 'theory' and jurisprudence enabled him to 'look through all the dramatic incidents and discern the true basis of prophecy?'"[116]

May it be something more than coincidence that both Yntema and Cook, each a designated realist, come close to finding in Holmes's mode of assembling, categorizing, and explicating the work of common law judges a vestige of the ancient theological art of scrutinizing oracular messages? Of course neither would put it quite this way. And Holmes said it first. But realists, by definition, have little professional concern with the unreal. Yet the real or the actual – to use the words interchangeably – might, in a manner legal investigators may not quite ignore, incorporate the unreal: the imagined, the desired, the superstitious, even that personal welter of deeply held beliefs, unwarranted, unsubstantiated, unassailable. Why do some moral duties find, in Holmes's words, legal expression while others do not? And from what sources do the moral duties themselves arise? From the customary and the social? Or do we take that step called Nietzschean and find their ultimate genesis in the spiritual dialectic between the flavored few and the unflavored many?

The question is not an easy one. For Holmes the legal arts he employed knew few boundaries. He admired Dewey. He also admired Emerson and James Hill. He didn't read the newspapers much but he paid extremely close attention to the cases before him. Each told its own unique tale of fact and law. He took his stand in the law. He was always willing to look across the horizon and reach toward any high and glittering edge of golden thought, but he stood firm on the grounds of his chosen profession, settled in the conviction that from the grass at his feet green shoots would continue to sprout.

8 FRANCIS E. LUCEY

The year 1941 also marked the beginning of a concerted Jesuit campaign against Holmes's reputation. In retrospect it is something to behold. If Zane "walked into" Holmes in 1918, the Jesuits in the 1940s came at him in waves, like a succession of biblical plagues. Thanks to the recent recovery of what two law professors label "the forgotten jurisprudential debate" – between Catholic scholars and those law

[115] *Id.*
[116] *Id.*

professors and judges known as "legal realists," mainly from the 1920s through the early 1950s – we have a better sense of the circumstances in which the Jesuit attack took place.[117]

Attack is not too strong a word. That characterization has as much to do with the Jesuits' tone as with the substance of their criticisms. Prior to 1941 other legal scholars committed to Thomism (views derived from the grand medieval synthesis of St. Thomas Aquinas) and hoping to integrate its teachings into contemporary legal education had called into doubt Holmes-inspired positions on the nature of law, the analytic separation of law and morals, and the role of the judge's personal and professional proclivities in the decision-making process.[118] Professors Breen and Strang in their article draw attention to the best known of these scholars, William Kennedy, another contributor to *My Philosophy of Law*, as well as to the less-known Miriam Theresa Rooney, whose 1937 published dissertation, *Lawlessness, Law, and Sanction*, directly challenged in Thomas Aquinas's name some of the recently deceased justice's most hard-won insights.[119]

But the tone at least with respect to Holmes had been respectful, mostly. The rattlesnake venom that flowed through Zane's words didn't pour as readily from identifiably Catholic pens and presses. That began to change as the 1930s drew to a close and the 1940s began. It's hard from the vantage of this writing to appreciate the intellectual temper of the times and the exact pitch of the noetic animus, but it seems to have involved the existence or nonexistence of something called natural law.[120]

The first intrepid Jesuit to break through the vale of admiration that ensconced Holmes and come to fathom the danger that Holmes posed to the American polity was the longtime regent of Georgetown University's School of Law, Francis E. Lucey. Lucey remarked in 1951, a decade after he fired the initial salvo, that his

[117] John M. Breen and Lee J. Strang, *The Forgotten Jurisprudential Debate: Catholic Legal Thought's Response to Legal Realism*, 98 Marq. L. Rev. 1203 (2015). The authors rightly note that the use of the descriptive phrase "legal realism" or its cognate, "legal realists," is contested. They attempt to provide the requisite meaning by listing what they consider to be the core claims of the most prominent legal realists. *Id.* at 1219–224.

[118] *Id.* at 1227–238. For a review of the ultimately unsuccessful efforts to institute a law school curriculum based upon a Catholic legal pedagogy see John M. Breen and Lee J. Strang, *The Road Not Taken: Catholic Legal Education at the Middle of the Twentieth Century*, 51 Am. J. Legal Hist. 553 (2011).

[119] Breen & Strang, *supra* note 117, at 1234 ("Rooney described a falling-away over the centuries [from the Scholastic concept of sanction] giving rise to Justice Holmes's influential claims."); *see also* Miriam Theresa Rooney, Lawlessness, Law, and Sanction 114–36 (1937).

[120] The best introduction to the temper and the issues is Purcell, *supra* note 31, at 159–78; *see also id.* at 141 ("For the events of the thirties – the depression and the threat of totalitarianism – strained the resources of American thought and challenged the best minds in the nation."). G. Edward White provides an overview of the Jesuit attack on Holmes in his *The Rise and Fall of Justice Holmes*, 39 U. Chi. L. Rev. 51, 65–68 (1971) ("If the passions of the war-scarred 1940s stimulated some of the most savage evaluations of Holmes, they also generated some of the most mature.").

detractors might be surprised to learn that he too, in the late 1920s and early 1930s, had been a "great admirer" of Justice Holmes.[121] He had found the man's style seductive, taken in by "the novelty of his expression and his uncanny ability to turn a phrase that was pregnant with significance."[122]

Beyond style stood cardinal points of law and equity that Lucey believed Holmes upheld. In Holmes's best-known dissents Lucey saw a true champion of the spirit of American democracy, a judge solicitous for the inviolable dignity of the individual and maybe even filled with a bit of sympathy for life's unfortunates. But Holmes's striking of certain discordant notes made him uneasy. Some things Holmes said bothered Lucey. He determined to investigate the source of the dissonance. He reports that he committed himself to "reading everything judicial and non-judicial that Holmes had written. My spare time in the next few years was devoted to the task of reading and re-reading until I became certain that I fully understood the so-called great jurist."[123]

He then recounts:

> After the middle thirties the question mark in my mind was gone. But so too was the idol. In digging into that idol I discovered a philosophical skeleton of life and law, of man and morals, that was horribly deformed. The bones formed a well articulated whole, but the whole in relief was ugly and menacing. By 1936 I knew that, sooner or later, something had to be done about it.[124]

Even if the imagery is hard to visualize – the bones formed a well-articulated whole yet the skeleton itself was horribly deformed – it pointedly expresses Lucey's recoil from what he ultimately uncovers. He is horrified by his realization of what he now sees as Holmes's true thoughts and sentiments. Horror, we suddenly grasp, is not a trope limited to movies or novels or Edvard Munch–inspired graphic art. It has its uses in jurisprudence. It grounds and informs – gives shape and texture to – Lucey's intellectual and emotional assault against the memory of Holmes.[125]

The felt need to do *something* about the perceived Holmesian menace became increasingly intense as the latter half of the decade progressed and Lucey watched Holmes's influence on the legal profession expand. By the end of the 1930s he determined he could no longer remain silent and when the opportunity presented itself in 1941 to strike hard at the king he took it.[126] As he recalled, "I showed by

[121] Francis E. Lucey, *Holmes – Liberal – Humanitarian – Believer in Democracy?*, 39 Geo. L.J. 523, 524 (1951).

[122] *Id.*

[123] *Id.*

[124] *Id.*

[125] Francis Biddle, in commenting on this passage, blandly notes that it "partakes of the rhetorical; but in spite of its ineptness we do get a sense that Father Lucey was upset." I imagine Biddle made a formidable, if exasperating, opponent in the courtroom and in the bedroom. Francis Biddle, Justice Holmes, Natural Law, and the Supreme Court 44 (1961).

[126] Lucey, *supra* note 121, 525.

excerpts from his writings that his philosophy was akin to Hitler's and that if adopted it would be the death knell of our democracy. I was not exaggerating nor overemphasizing as this article ['Holmes – Liberal – Humanitarian – Believer in Democracy?'] will, I am certain, demonstrate."[127]

That after a full decade Lucey continued to believe – given all he knew in 1951 about Hitler and the Nazis he probably did not know in 1941 – Holmes's philosophy "was akin to Hitler's" shows how deeply the horror impregnated his mind.

He began his July 1941 article, "Jurisprudence and the Future Social Order," with the hard-to-miss prophecy, "[a]ll thinking persons realize that things are not going to be what they used to be when this war is over whether we become actively involved or not. There is an uneasy stir in the atmosphere."[128] The "uneasy stir" made itself evident in the questions that arose concerning the future of American society and its predominant political and social values. "Will democracy survive?," Lucey queried. Or was America heading on the path that Germany had already trod? Was something like Nazism lying in wait for the American republic?[129]

Lucey hastened to add that whatever was wrong with Nazism could not be attributed to its science. By "science" he appears to mean the ability to frame social problems and to engineer a solution. As he noted: "I cannot think of any progressive measures which we have adopted which Germany did not have before we adopted them, some of them even long before Hitler's time."[130]

So, what was the problem?

> It is the philosophy of the nature of a human being, of a man. It is the false philosophy of life, law and government; that philosophy of healthy, warm, well-sheltered and well-trained animals, mighty lions with the dignity and independence that a cage provides, a philosophy that divorces itself from the moral dignity of man. Why did the Nazis adopt this system? Because their philosophy is the philosophy of the deification of the state and social interests, claims and demands, and the philosophy of what is useful and works; realism, utilitarianism, and pragmatism.[131]

From these sentences we begin to glean that Lucey's controversy with some of the prevailing social philosophies in the United States circa 1941 had little do with the manner of thinking that they engendered, their techniques for addressing social issues. The critical problems lay in the justificatory ends, in the subtle message that social institutions, arrangements, and interests took precedence over the "moral dignity" of the individual. Perhaps we could even infer that the main failing for Lucey lies in the unarticulated assumption that whatever "moral dignity" an

[127] *Id.*
[128] Francis E. Lucey, *Jurisprudence and the Future Social Order*, 16 Int'l Soc. Sci. Rev. 211 (1941).
[129] *Id.*
[130] *Id.*
[131] *Id.*

individual possesses derives from existing and transitory social arrangements and interests. It does not arise from something beyond the social and the historical, something permanent, everlasting, and embedded in "nature," conceived either as a whole (natural law) or as a part (natural rights).

Lucey equated this moral dignity of the individual with the "theory of natural rights which brought our nation and our democracy into being."[132] The social philosophies circulating throughout the legal profession, especially in its law schools – venues that, Lucey noted, had in the previous fifty years acquired a dominant role in shaping judicial and legislative thought[133] – worked together to devalue the individual and overvalue so-called social interests, either of specific groups or of the state as a whole.[134]

As did the Catholic authors that followed Lucey's lead, Lucey emphasizes the deviations of current moods and convictions from those of the country's founders. To Catholic critics natural rights and natural law meant something. Natural law stood above and beyond transitory circumstances, political winds, the social and economic needs of the moment as a transcendent measure of right and wrong, good and evil. Most important, it regulated the state. The state was not omnipotent. The state did not mint basic legal rights, any more than it did rights fundamentally moral.

The drift of Lucey's argument in the opening sections of "Jurisprudence and the Future Social Order" is clear even if specific terms beg further elucidation and the overall historical argumentation seems facile and tendentious. As the paragraphs quickly advance, Lucey warms more and more to his theme until his vehemence climaxes with this pronouncement:

> The functional approach, with the pragmatic test of what works, as the sole criterion of what makes right, sounds very much like what must have been the theme song of the Nazi storm troopers in the regimentation of Germany and the subsequent experiments in Czechoslovakia, Poland, Denmark, Norway, Holland, Belgium, France and the Balkan countries. Any sharp analysis of pragmatism, utilitarianism,

[132] *Id.* at 212.

[133] Lucey would later gloss this observation with this interesting comment:

> An increasing number of our Judges, lawyers and legal scholars are the product of our modern law schools. Many of our Judges were members of the faculties of these law schools. For many years these law schools have been teaching by the case method. Although the case method properly used has distinct advantages, it is accompanied by a grave peril. It is very easy for one to jump from a case method to a case philosophy. The case easily becomes the 'all' of law study, and likewise the 'all' and 'is' of the law. Principles of law imbedded in the case, are first, disregarded in the method and then in the philosophy of law. It seems more than a coincidence that most of the outstanding 'Is' Realists were law-school professors, who used this method.

Francis E. Lucey, *Natural Law and American Legal Realism: Their Respective Contributions to a Theory of Law in a Democratic Society*, 6 Geo. L.J. 493, 526 n.67 (1942).

[134] Lucey, *supra* note 128, at 212.

Hegelianism, or realism, as applied to law discloses one inescapable consequence, namely, that might makes right.[135]

His theme established, Lucey slows the tempo and introduces Holmes in the second movement of his article. He refers to Holmes as the "so-called great liberal." He further describes him as an agnostic, a skeptic, and an experimentalist. He then strikes a by now recurring note: "Being all three he had no patience with the jurisprudence of the founding fathers."[136]

Holmes's impatience boiled down to a disbelief in absolute values and "in the importance and dignity of the individual."[137] The latter point really subsumes the former, so after all the swirling and the intellectual upheaval we end up at a point of contact seemingly far removed from Holmes's jurisprudence as thus far described in this book. The point of contact and the source of horror that shocked Lucey lie in this notion of the inviolability of individual dignity. Lucey believes it a transcendent truth. He claims Holmes held it in utter disregard. The way of Holmes led to an odious totalitarianism. Zane had made a similar argument many years before except he called the horror "German absolutism." Perhaps not so coincidentally in the same year Zane larded Holmes with calumny, 1918, Holmes wrote one of his last published pieces, "Natural Law," an essay that only incited his Jesuit critics to torrid extremes.

The neuralgic point of contact between Holmes and the Jesuits lay in the meaning and scope of human dignity. That much is clear. Not that the Jesuits limited their critiques to this score. In extensive articles published in 1942 and 1943 other members of the order besides Lucey ranged across Holmes's writings and provided a full-scale critique of what they conceived to be the essentials of his jurisprudence.[138] Holmes did not in every single instance appear in a false light; the construals and evaluations they offered, however, were not overtly favorable and only rarely charitable.[139]

To Lucey we owe the initial articulation of a starch antipathy, the forceful expression of a deep-seated opposition to Holmes that, according to one historian,

[135] *Id.* at 213.

[136] *Id.* at 214.

[137] *Id.*

[138] *See, e.g.*, John C. Ford, *The Fundamentals of Holmes' Juristic Philosophy*, 11 FORDHAM L. REV. 255 (1942); Paul L. Gregg, *The Pragmatism of Mr. Justice Holmes*, 31 GEO. L.J. 262 (1943); *see also* James B. O'Shaughnessy, *Justice Holmes and Chancellor More*, 3 CATH. U. L. REV. 145 (1953). O'Shaughnessy may not have been a member of the Society of Jesus.

[139] Not a member of the Society of Jesus but apparently inspired by their articles is the author of some of the least charitable pieces on Holmes, Ben W. Palmer. *See* Ben W. Palmer, *Hobbes, Holmes and Hitler*, 31 A.B.A. J. 569 (1945) and Ben W. Palmer, *The Totalitarianism of Mr. Justice Holmes: Another Chapter in the Controversy*, 37 A.B.A. J. 809 (1951).

is partly responsible for the continued interest in and controversy over Holmes's legacy.[140] Lucey followed up his 1941 piece with a much more extensive 1942 analysis entitled "Natural Law and American Legal Realism: Their Respective Contributions to a Theory of Law in a Democratic Society." In this article Lucey reveals he is capable of more than florid invective: he provides in some respects as keen a reading of Holmes as would Holmes's most polished interpreter, Mark DeWolfe Howe.[141]

Lucey begins the article by tracing the vogue of legal realism to the writings of its two most well-known progenitors, Holmes and Roscoe Pound. He finds Holmes the more intellectually consistent man, and more open and frank regarding the source of his views and in stating his personal opinions. Of course, much of that openness and frankness had to do with the publication, after Holmes's death, of his letters to such correspondents as John C. H. Wu and Frederick Pollock.

Lucey effectively uses the published personal correspondence to enmesh Holmes's formal writings, post *The Common Law*, into a superimposed ideology of sheer will and power. It all gets condensed in the catchphrase "might makes right."[142] But might expressed in law typically requires a more intricate mechanism than when expressed in politics, or more simply and brutishly, in war. Lucey clearly has limited inclination for such intricacy. He does not spend much time scrutinizing particulars. He oddly enough does not mention *Buck* v. *Bell*, the 1927 decision concerning the constitutionality of a Virginia statute permitting the forced sterilization of a so-called unfit ("feebleminded") woman. Its majority opinion contained Holmes's most infamous line: "Three generations of imbeciles are enough."[143]

Lucey's fixation on the Holmesian horror darkens the coming day; the apocalyptic beast he must slay eclipses the risen sun.

He believes it comes down to what gives the binding force of law its ability to bind. "Holmes saw clearly that the binding force in law had to be either a moral ought or physical force. He would have nothing to do with the moral ought. That meant a God, and all that was against his taste."[144] That assessment fails to recognize that for Holmes a people's respect for law played a critical role in the formation of

[140] David H. Burton, *Justice Holmes and the Jesuits*, 27 Am. Juris. 45 (1982) (stating that the Jesuit onslaught generated continued scholarly interest in Holmes); *see also* White, *supra* note 120, at 67 ("The association of Holmes with totalitarianism sparked a debate that was, in its ramifications, to preoccupy legal scholars in America for a further decade. At the core of the debate was the question whether the American legal system embodied any absolute moral principles or whether it merely exemplified contemporary social norms.").

[141] Albert W. Alschuler remarks that Lucey and the other Jesuits who wrote on Holmes "understood Holmes better than the lawyers and scholars who viewed him as a liberal hero. Some of them, however, did not enhance their credibility when they denounced Holmes's agnosticism and linked him with Hitler." Albert W. Alschuler, Law without Values: The Life, Work, and Legacy of Justice Holmes 204 n.21 (2000).

[142] Lucey, *supra* note 133, at 495–97, 512–13.

[143] Buck v. Bell, 274 U.S. 200, 207 (1927) (per Holmes, J.).

[144] Lucey, *supra* note 133, at 498.

society, but it does pinpoint the importance of taste – or fashion when applied to a group – in Holmes's outlook.

Lucey then proceeds to round out his analysis:

> Holmes, faithful to his three fundamentals, physical force, tastes in place of reason, and functional approach, proceeded with perfect consistency, to divorce law from morals, to reduce morals also to mere dominant tastes or prejudices, namely, imperfect social generalizations expressed in terms of emotion, to reject principles absolutely, because these are only "I can't helps," "*Ich kann nicht anders*," not "*mann kann nicht anders*," *i.e.*, in our tastes; and finally to approach everything with skepticism for it may all be just a bad dream.[145]

How Lucey conglomerates Holmes's beliefs oddly limns an existentialism that would become current and intellectually stylish in the immediate postwar years. 1942, coincidentally, saw also the publication of Albert Camus's *The Myth of Sisyphus*. The surprise in the assemblage is not the implied Jesuit challenge to the sense of unreality and diminution of thought and being that any good Catholic believes follows in the wake of Martin Luther's *ich kann nicht anders* – "I can do no other" – words Luther reportedly said after taking his stand against certain fundamental tenets of Catholic doctrine and theology at the 1521 Diet of Worms. It is rather Lucey's juxtaposition of a "we can do no other" to Holmes's individual "can't help." Lucey refers to "our tastes," and careful thought on the context and manner of his exposition leads to the realization that "tastes" in this usage extends far beyond a preference for crimson-red wine instead of stout beer.

How far? Far enough for tastes to comprise senses of the good that include the moral and the social and that hard-to-define sense of the worth of the self that exists apart from social location or moral evaluation. For lack of more precise terms we may refer to the latter "hard-to-define sense of worth" as the spiritual source of a recognized duty, that which constitutes a prevalent sense of dignity, that to which Lucey appends the word moral as in the phrase, "the inviolable moral dignity of the individual."

If we are correct in our premises we are led to the conclusion that for Lucey the inviolable dignity of the individual depends on more than personal preference, it connects to group tastes – a composite but unified sense of what is real and vital and good – which, in turn, itself rests on a deeper ground or dovetails with a higher, larger whole. It's hard to know from this angle the stream's source. Either way, we are talking about God, the guarantor of the really real and of that individual dignity that the really real, for Lucey, logically entails.

Lucey believes one must take on faith that it – presumably the "it" being a conjunction of felt and acknowledged actualities, what we often just call life –is not a bad dream, and the percolating sense of the surreal or the unreal often

[145] *Id.* at 500–02.

seemingly present in modern life, either infused throughout the whole or nibbling at the edges of consciousness, is not a deadening finality. Holmes also took it on faith but refused to surmise a guarantor. Lucey treats this refusal – as do so many other commentators – as indicative of a personal failing, a lack of humanity on Holmes's part. Lucey did not realize, probably because beyond his ken, that Holmes's skepticism and agnosticism – not simply concerning God language but about endowments to the really real (Holmes calls it the universe) – did not arise because of a personal failing but for the exact opposite reason. Holmes's sensibility, intelligence, diligence, and sustained forays into the past had awakened him to beforehand unimaginable shifts in the sense of actuality – what is felt and thought and believed as real and vital – that have occurred in the course of human history. Historical study creates its own sense of the unreal when the actuality of the present cannot enfold that of the past or vice versa.

Holmes sums up his awareness of these tectonic shifts in cultural life and their potentially debilitating effect upon the disciplined inquirer by declaring that the law of fashion is a law of life.[146] Never had such a single gossipy, trivial word, fashion, captured and conveyed such a momentous awakening. It fused the travails of consciousness to the whims of the moment.[147]

Oblivious to the deeper reaches of Holmes's thought, but led by an unyielding feeling that something was amiss, Lucey continues his journey into the heart of darkness. The bad man, he says, is the "man who runs counter to the dominant groups' completely changeable tastes."[148] Compare this statement to Holmes's opening sentence in his 1918 essay, "Natural Law": "It is not enough for the knight of romance that you agree that his lady is a very nice girl – if you do not admit that she is the best that God ever made or will make, you must fight."[149]

In both statements taste informs sentiment and directs action. Demand for agreement regarding tastes also, oddly, plays a role in both. Lucey could not accept the intrinsic supremacy of taste because it went counter to his beliefs in God and in

[146] Holmes, *supra* note 82, at 406.

[147] In an insightful piece, economist Walton H. Hamilton notes a curious sense of timelessness in Holmes's intellectual life, especially as revealed in his correspondence with Frederick Pollock, but does not fully understand the source or its effect on Holmes. He ends up depicting Holmes in a manner not dissimilar to how Holmes depicted Henry Adams: as an old cardinal with a gift for turning what is alive into ashes. Walton H. Hamilton, *On Dating Mr. Justice Holmes*, 9 U. Chi. L. Rev. 1, 28 (1941).

[148] Lucey, *supra* note 133, at 503.

[149] Holmes, *Natural Law*, *in* III CW 445. Despite Holmes's evident critique of "natural law" in this article – however one may define or understand the meaning of the term – one scholar, Michael H. Hoffheimer, has maintained in a book-length study the thesis that "[r]ecognition of Holmes's continuity with transcendentalist and natural law tradition contributes to a more complete understanding of his life and thought." Hoffheimer, *supra* note 97, at 15. *See also* Daniel J. Boorstin, *The Elusiveness of Mr. Justice Holmes*, 14 New Eng. Quart. 478, 485–87; Allen Mendenhall, *The Natural Law Theorist*, *in* The Pragmatism and Prejudice of Oliver Wendell Holmes Jr. 87–115 (Seth Vannatta ed., 2019).

transcendent values; values, that is, not limited by time or place or other congeries of circumstance that delimit and direct the human powers to be aware, to feel, to think, and to choose. Holmes, for his part, sees in this insistence on the rightness of one's opinion of what is best or most preferable, and the attendant willingness to fight, a symptom of what he describes as the inborn demand for the superlative.[150]

If agreement cannot be reached, and if the matter is sufficiently momentous to make disagreement intolerable, one must fight. One possesses what Holmes called in another context the sacred right to kill.[151] This hard saying of Holmes becomes even harder to understand when one strips from it the luminosity of Holmes's genius; it then becomes further grist for Lucey's feverish attack. The case, as the litigators like to say, is at issue: who is more constrained by an unappealable, arbitrary taste, the dominant group that creates its own enforceable norms and seemingly changes them at will or the jurist who believes he has found the "criteria of universal validity which he collects under the head of natural law?"[152]

While we cannot canvass the issue and sub-issues here, it bears noting that Holmes supports his position with the averment that "Certitude is not the test of certainty."[153] What then is the test of certainty? It is precisely where sufficient different, distinctive, and weighty "can't helps" meet and effectively draw a line with which they can all live. It lies in the set sequences of action and reaction. "Can't helps" help create events and imbue them with meaning. One may be tempted at this point to connect this way of putting the matter with Holmes's notion of the morphology of law: "Beliefs, so far as they bear upon the attainment of a wish (as most beliefs do), lead in the first place to a social attitude, and later to combined social action, that is, to law."[154] Lucey certainly makes this connection when he denounces the prevalence and dominance of group tastes in Holmes's thought – curiously eroding his earlier criticism that Holmes is too individualistic in his "can't helps" – but he misses the main point that the warrant of enforcement action does not lie for Holmes in the superlative. It does not lie in demanding conformity of taste – be it body, heart, mind, or soul or all of these together – to some overriding justified beatific object of desire.

The warrant lies in both containing such unrelenting demands and, conversely, in protecting and preserving the life that would diminish should those unrelenting demands have their way ("A dog will fight for his bone."). That social action which contains, protects, and preserves Holmes calls law. Its justification lies not in some

[150] Holmes, *Natural Law*, *supra* note 149, at 445–46.

[151] Holmes used the phrase "a sacred right to kill" in a train conversation with Judge Learned Hand on June 19, 1918. *See* Frederic R. Kellogg, *Learned Hand and the Great Train Ride*, 56 Am. Scholar 471, 480–82 (1987); Thomas Healy, The Great Dissent: How Oliver Wendell Holmes Changed His Mind – and Changed the History of Free Speech in America 21 (2013).

[152] Holmes, *supra* note 149, at 446.

[153] *Id.*

[154] Oliver Wendell Holmes, *Introduction to* The General Survey, *in* III CW 439.

abstract, transcendent "good" but in a series of collated, pressing desires and wants that a certain style of life should persist or a certain ideal implicit in that life become manifest. Holmes recognizes that styles of life present and potentially competing within a certain jurisdiction are multifarious. But the point where they agree – the intersection of dominant social or personal interest, emotional attachment, and moral preference – becomes a cultural and legal pivot, a node of cultivated living.

Holmes does not include such heavy terms in his "Natural Law" essay. He is too fine an artist, too careful a judge. Instead, he merely comments that the "jurists who believe in natural law seem to me to be in that naïve state of mind that accepts what has been familiar and accepted by them and their neighbors as something that must be accepted by all men everywhere."[155] The key term in this sentence, as evidenced by its repetition, is "accept." Without delving into the psychological and sociological dynamics at play, we note that Holmes shrewdly turns the tables on the natural law jurists and uses this reiterated acceptance and demand for acceptance to redefine in terms intelligible to him what transcendent means.

"It is true that beliefs and wishes have a transcendental basis in the sense that their foundation is arbitrary. You can not help entertaining and feeling them, and there is an end of it."[156] Holmes broadens traditional transcendental categories beyond the – not necessary but probable – conditions of thought or of thinking, or the existence of a thought's object, to include those everyday aspects of life that normally do not find a place in philosophical analysis – the granite rocks upon which one played as a child or the barberry bush that bewitched one's eager eye. The formative power of antecedents, historical and otherwise, becomes unquestioned. And upon this realization all these antecedents become the subject matter for inquiry and reflection.[157] Our interests and purposes, even those felt but hardly comprehended demands, are electrified with the current of the present. It is all here, all now, all potential grounds for subsequent line drawing and redrawing. What occurs occurs – it is felt and entertained – and that includes the inborn demand for the superlative. The ideal is always part of the mix. But doubt too beckons at the door.[158] Holmes views the

[155] Holmes, *supra* note 149, at 446.

[156] *Id.* at 446–47.

[157] In what may be a similar analysis, but in a different key, Herbert W. Schneider sees Holmes manifesting in his own work the same type of "radical empiricism" that marked William James's study of psychology. Schneider's analysis is too brief and opaque to be sure of its direction. *See* Herbert W. Schneider, A History of American Philosophy, ch. 41, "Empirical Radicalism," 561–63 (1946) ("Holmes applied James's 'anti-gnosticism' to the common law . . . . With such empiricism as a point of departure, he formulated in 1897 his famous pragmatic definition of law as 'the prediction of the incidence of public force through the instrumentality of the courts.'").

[158] On this point see Holmes, *supra* note 11, at 442–44 ("But I have found it a help to clear thinking to try to get behind my conventional assumptions as a judge whose first business is to see that the game is played according to the rules whether I like them or not. To have doubted one's own first principles is the mark of a civilized man. To know what you want and why you think that such a measure will help it is the first but by no means the last step towards intelligent legal

superlative as intrinsically a "demand" because it, for him, no longer retains an atmospheric, universalistic, extra-human divinely ordained quality. The ideal no longer functions as a portal to the transcendent beyond. It has fallen from the region of extra-human actuality to that of phenomenological fact. It has become thinkable, understandable – a manageable ideal.

Almost without question – though I cannot cite a specific passage in support – Lucey knew Holmes had stacked the deck against him – 'him' referring to believers in God or natural law – but he had little ability to counteract the Holmesian menace head-on because he had no direct sense of, or feel for, those reaches of experience from which Holmes spoke. His acuity led him to discern the interplay between the bad man and dominant group tastes. But because he had no firsthand knowledge of how actuality can and does transform he fails to appreciate the intricate mechanisms at work in lawmaking.

In returning to Lucey's interpretation of the bad man one is struck by Lucey's insight that Holmes unabashedly uses the bad man as a device to create a dynamic between competing tastes. This observation is important, and in some ways similar to how a later commentator, Catharine Wells, would explain the meaning of the bad man.[159]

Wells writes in 2000:

> If we take this seriously [that law is the organized force of the community], it follows that equating the bad man to the lawbreaker means that Holmes's bad man is not necessarily bad. The bad man is simply someone who does not share in the ideals that the law represents. The bad man could, for example, be a feminist, a religious fundamentalist, an abolitionist, a black separatist, a gay activist, or even a Moonie. Or course, he (or she) could also be a psychopath, a murderer, or a bigot. Whoever the bad man is, his opposition to legal values and his consequent violations of law do not by themselves make him truly evil. He is a lawbreaker and nothing more. His violations may include acts that many of us would morally censure, but this is not the point. The law is not about morality; it is about regulating conduct for the benefit of the entire community.[160]

The critical difference between Wells and Lucey is that Wells situates the dynamic in more directly conflictual terms than does Lucey. She also merges the bad man into an existing lawbreaker. The bad man for Wells does not share the ideals of the lawmaking majority; for Lucey, in contrast, the bad man does not think or act in terms of ideals at all. He thinks in terms of wants. Lucey's view veers in a

reform. The other and more difficult one is to realize what you must give up to get it, and to consider whether you are ready to pay the price.").

[159] Catharine Pierce Wells, *Oliver Wendell Holmes, Jr., and William James: The Bad Man and the Moral Life*, *in* THE PATH OF THE LAW AND ITS INFLUENCE: THE LEGACY OF OLIVER WENDELL HOLMES, JR. 211–30 (Steven J. Burton ed., 2000).

[160] *Id.* at 225.

different direction than Wells's, and to appreciate the contrast it is worth quoting his description of the bad man in context:

> Since for Holmes the binding force in law is nothing but physical force applied through decisions of courts to the bad man, namely the man who runs counter to the dominant groups' completely changeable tastes, the only important thing in law is to try to predict how public policy, *i.e.*, dominant tastes will change, and in changing change decisions. The smart judge should keep his eye on fast developing tastes and write a minority opinion based on the same, betting that some day that minority taste will be the dominant taste and public policy.[161]

Lucey's description retains Holmes's prospective emphasis; it focuses on the termination of legal events. But he collapses events into capricious or arbitrary sequences that rarely connect or connect haphazardly. We are, in effect, back to the blandishments of the emperor's wife, the singularity of motives that the young Holmes thought would make prediction practically impossible.[162]

Lucey has little sense for the differing timescales of legal events, or for the deep-seated cultural continuities that predated the founders of the country, or for the inner complexity of most legal actions. In Lucey's rendition the bad man is canny, quick thinking – as is the judge who brought him to being – one who finds it relatively easy to plot events and manipulate outcomes in anticipation of shifting tastes. Curiously, we see hovering over Lucey's analysis a sentiment similar to what we first saw in Zane: the blatant distrust of Holmes, a feeling that he is a deceiver and a disguised social menace; that he is an omen of horror, in other words.

Lucey refers to Holmes as a "smart judge" – using the word "smart" to describe intellectual qualities Holmes himself disparaged – and repeats later in the article his denigrating comment about Holmes's guile:

> And so the good Realist lawyer must watch the 'becoming' in social stimulants. If he can get at the 'begin of the beginning,' he can place a long range bet and be a real Bettabilitarian as was his idol Holmes. If the Realist lawyer ever becomes a judge, he will, like his idol Holmes, laugh at those spurious rationalizations called legal principles and keep his eye steadfastly on such 'begin of begins' in social stimulants as are coming up fast on the track of social institutions. Then he too can write a daring minority opinion, and place a bet that one day it will be a majority view; not that it is of any object or eternal importance in itself, or as far as Society or mankind is concerned.[163]

Plainly, Lucey weaves sharp conduct into the meaning of Holmes's phenomenological approach to law. Sharp conduct requires sharp thinking which, of course, produces something perilously close to the ill-famed legal sharpster. Lucey takes this

[161] Lucey, *supra* note 133, at 503.
[162] Oliver Wendell Holmes, *Comment on* The Law Magazine and Review, *in* I CW 295 [hereinafter *The 1872 Jurisprudence Essay*].
[163] Lucey, *supra* note 133, at 512.

corrosive cynical mentality as the end-all and be-all of the Holmesian attitude toward law. It is thin and self-serving. From Lucey's perspective it appears to be indicative of, and presumably closely related to, a disposition and an intelligence he would probably not hesitate to describe in other contexts as diabolical.

Finally, as does Zane, Lucey taunts Holmes's mature understanding that "[l]aw is a statement of the circumstances in which the public force will be brought to bear upon men through the Courts."[164] Again, he displays an unerring eye for the lineaments of Holmes's legal thought even if he is befogged and horrified by the ultimate picture:

> The descriptive statement of the events or circumstances, expressed by decisions of the courts, in which Society punishes or has been punishing individuals is what is meant by law. The civil law does not punish consequences but sequences of events of a certain type. Society by application of its physical force is punishing certain types of human events or behavior today. There is no ought that Society should punish these particular types. It just *is* doing so today. Tomorrow it may leave unpunished the events or behavior punished today and punish what today is unpunished. Honesty may be a crime or grounds for a tort tomorrow . . . . If there are no ultimate permanent objective values and no moral oughts, of course, anything which Society capriciously enforces is law, and Society can capriciously brings its force to bear in any direction.[165]

Despite glimpsing the importance of sequence in Holmes's thought – "civil law does not punish consequences but sequences of events of a certain type" – Lucey cannot comprehend how a legal philosophy that seems to advocate tacking according to society's evolving tastes could ever draw from its own self-imposed constraints the social meaning needed to inscribe value into the determined legal sequence.

Or, to put it another way, how could such a legal philosophy lead to the same compass of real being and translucence that he and others like him find in natural law? It cannot. Lucey sees no intrinsic transcendent goodness or beauty in humanity. For him Holmes mirrors the horror of the human-all-too-human. For that reason he cannot fathom how Holmes, who never forgot the radiant granite or the burgundy barberry of his youth, could knowingly speak in his arch Bostonian accent of catching an echo of the infinite.[166]

[164] American Banana Co. v. United Fruit Co., 213 U.S. 347, 356 (1909).

[165] Lucey, *supra* note 133, at 508 (emphasis in original).

[166] The phrase to "catch an echo of the infinite" is found in the last sentence of "The Path of the Law." Holmes *supra* note 14, at 406. In 1922 Holmes reprises the refrain in a letter to Judge Learned Hand: "I assume that your ambition, like mine, cannot be satisfied by office or anything resting in the will of others but only by the trembling hope that you have hit the *ut de poitrine*." Quoted in MARK DEWOLFE HOWE, JUSTICE OLIVER WENDELL HOLMES: THE SHAPING YEARS 1841–1870 280–81. *Ut de poitrine* refers, I believe, to the very difficult-to-reach note of high C sung from the chest. Incidentally, "trembling" is a very important word for Holmes. *See* Oliver Wendell Holmes, *The Puritan*, *in* III CW 471 ("And of many a man who

9 LON FULLER

Around the same time that the good Rev. Lucey determined he would reveal the grotesquery that was Justice Holmes to the reading public of American lawyers, a newly hired Professor of Law at the Harvard Law School published a series of lectures with the quaint, faintly psychological sounding title, *The Law in Quest of Itself*.[167]

To go from Lucey and the other Holmes-bashing Jesuits – especially Father Gregg[168] – to the cultivated Lon Fuller is to change the channel from UFC Ultimate Fighting to Wimbledon tennis. Fuller is undeniably steely and unrelenting in his volleys; he executes with feline wit and more than a modicum of grace. Like the Jesuits he finds much to criticize in the program of the so-called legal realists – mainly Jerome Frank, Karl Llwelleyn, Joseph Walter Bingham, Walter Wheeler Cook, and Underhill Moore[169] – but unlike them he does not vent his spleen or trash-talk Holmes. Even so, Fuller finds deeply troubling Holmes's divorce of law and morals. His entire jurisprudential critique, at least as articulated in *Quest*, centers on the impossibility of separating the *ought* from the *is*.

It helps in thinking through Fuller's overall argument in *Quest* to refer to his contribution in *My Philosophy of Law*. There he announces his "dissent from certain accepted conceptions of law and legal study . . . current in this country[.]"[170]

The literary tradition in law is the first of the two prevalent attitudes from which he demurs. Fuller intends this unexpected phrase, "the literary tradition," to encompass "the conception of law which brings to legal study a complex of attitudes and emotions" closely resembling those that students of literature bring to the study of classical literature.[171] These "attitudes and emotions" harbor an essentially cabined, constrained critical stance and orientation. They do not necessarily suppress criticism; rather, the underlying disposition reveals itself in an "orientation it gives to criticism, and in the things away from which it directs criticism."[172]

One of the things from which criticism is diverted is the proper scope of legal study. The literary tradition has its established *corpus juris*, the classic materials of the law classroom. These materials set the boundaries of legal study, and have done

now hears me, whether a member of his church or not, it may be said, as it was said of Thomas Shepard by Cotton Mather, 'So the character of his daily conversation was a trembling walk with God.'"); and Oliver Wendell Holmes, *Law and the Court, in* III CW 505 ("it is only in rare moments like this that there comes a pause and for half an hour one feels a trembling hope"). *See also* Benjamin N. Cardozo, *Introduction: Mr. Justice Holmes, in* MR. JUSTICE HOLMES 19–20 (Felix Frankfurter ed., 1931).

[167] LON L. FULLER, THE LAW IN QUEST OF ITSELF (1940).

[168] Gregg, *supra* note 138, at 262–95.

[169] *See, e.g.*, Lon L. Fuller, *American Legal Realism*, 82 U. PA. L. REV., 429, 429–62 (1934).

[170] MY PHILOSOPHY OF LAW, *supra* note 98, at 113.

[171] *Id.* at 114.

[172] *Id.*

so, Fuller avers, for the past "three or four decades in this country." Only recently have scholars – presumably the legal realists – "seriously threatened" this course, or curriculum, of materials and study.[173]

The almost ubiquitous distaste adherents to the literary tradition have against redrawing the established boundaries of legal study melds into a strong propensity against examining "critically the fundamental conceptions underlying the body of learning it considers as its proper object." This "disinclination derives not so much from articulate premises as from a general spirit."[174]

Plainly, the criticisms Fuller levels against the literary attitude are pretty pointed. And it does not take much reading between the lines to see that Fuller aims his reproach at many of his own colleagues. He finds them unwilling to reconsider the traditional materials and course of legal study. This conservative unwillingness is further aided and abetted by the case method, which in its standard employment creates an artificial universe of the legally relevant and, not unexpectedly, fortifies the professor's intellectual authority. Professorial commitment to the literary tradition has an additional incentive Fuller dryly adds. It "makes the giving and grading of examinations easy." It is much easier to judge a student's competence and originality when "tested against a background of accepted premises." For these reasons he dissents; and notes for the record that his colleagues are averse to reconceptualizing or critiquing the standard justifications for what is studied, and how, and why.[175]

The other attitude that fills Fuller with misgiving is one that "sees the salvation of the law in a pervasive application of the methods of natural science."[176] It is less common but strongly held. Here he takes direct aim at those in the legal academy who, at the other extreme of the literary tradition, are pushing for wholesale change in how law is seen, understood, and studied. They want the endeavor to become more "scientific." Fuller does not think scientific methods, as applied to singularly legal materials or problems, will materially contribute to heightened comprehension or provide specific legal resolutions. A specifically legal resolution he describes as one that helps answer how "we are going to distribute functions among the members of the society and how we shall divide the common product."[177]

How Fuller frames the overriding legal problem shows that his controversy with the proponents of scientific methods lacks the clear contour line of contrast that shaped his criticisms of the literary tradition. His discussion meanders. On the one hand, he believes the fashionable mode in which the purported scientific methods are being implemented – the survey and the questionnaire, for instance – are inherently unsuited to resolving the concrete legal issues that increasingly integrated

173 *Id.*
174 *Id.* at 115.
175 *Id.* at 116–18.
176 *Id.* at 118.
177 *Id.* at 118–19.

economic and other social activities create. On the other hand, he wants to affirm his belief in rationalism. A rationalist, must, he suggests, accept the limits and resistances inherent in the forms used and in the stuff (legal thinking and action) one seeks to shape.[178]

Fuller accepts irrationality as part of life. The methods called scientific, primarily understood as distinct sets of logical procedure, have their proper role in legal study. He does not want to limit their function to mainly that of a logical dam, controlling through sluicegates the onrush of vivid or vehement arguments. Fuller maintains that logic has a creative role, one that brings to light hidden but important implications existing within any body of knowledge including law. These implications, when revealed, "have the force of new facts." Yet logic alone cannot reveal all such facts. "The imperfectly rationalized" is ever a part of existence, existing not in the categories (forms) of thought or in the ravenous maw of raw, undigested experience, but in the liminality between the thought and the un-thought.[179]

Fuller closes his contribution to *My Philosophy of Law* with a brief discussion on the importance of seeking balance between contending social forces and, using the example of contract, with this observation:

> But I will venture the prediction that no society will reveal a real and lasting vitality which is not founded upon institutions which, like contract, reconcile man's need for form with his need for freedom. This means in the end that the way in which the individual views his relation to the universe is not something irrelevant to society but its very keystone. We must have a good metaphysics before we can have a good politics. And a good metaphysics is one which gives form to life without stifling it.[180]

From this short selection it is possible to discern one of Fuller's favored intellectual tools for analysis and exposition, that which Morris Cohen designated the "principle of polarity."[181] The principle of polarity leads a thinker to define and relate terms to their opposites on the premise that each implies the other. It recognizes a constant state of tension between them. Fuller uses the polar terms form and freedom in a manner reminiscent of another important mid-twentieth-century

[178] *Id.* at 118–21.

[179] *Id.* at 121–22. ("By imposing his own sharp dichotomy on Western thinking, Kant caused it to lose the more primitive and valid insight of Leibniz, that the progression from things unclear to things clear is a matter of degree and of indefinite development. By suppressing this simpler and saner view, Kant paved the way for the sterile excesses of modern positivism and for the violent excesses of modern romantic irrationalism.")

[180] *Id.* at 125.

[181] Fuller, *supra* note 169, at 452–53; Lon L. Fuller, *Reason and Fiat in Case Law*, 59 HARV. L. REV. 376, 381 (1946). On Morris Cohen's use of the principle of polarity and its influence on legal scholars like Fuller see DAVID A HOLLINGER, MORRIS COHEN AND THE SCIENTIFIC IDEAL 78–79, 188 (1975).

American thinker, Reinhold Niebuhr.[182] In the context of his contribution to *My Philosophy of Law*, it leads him to criticize the literary tradition in law on the grounds of deficient form. And in regard to those legal scholars susceptible to the blandishments of the natural sciences, we find basically the same criticism: the misguided effort to study law solely along the formal strictures of recognized scientific methods. Too restrictive form, not enough play; even more to the point for Fuller, not enough attention to the creative element in life, that is to say, to the mode of legal reasoning best suited to elicit an effective unity from a ranging (sometimes raging) multiplicity.

If we turn with these thoughts in mind to *Quest*, we may better understand Fuller's comments regarding the bad man and understand, also, why he misses the mark.

Let us begin with the first and most obvious question: what does Fuller mean by saying that the law is in *quest* of itself? Or with different emphasis: the law is in quest of *itself*? Fuller tells us what he means: "As the title of these lectures suggests, this review [of the chief schools of legal positivism] will involve a study of the law's quest for some exclusive hegemony of its own, for some *Ultima Thule* where its existence can be free from the complications of ethics and philosophy."[183]

Ultima Thule means some unknown region, the extreme limit of travel and discovery, that which exists in the northernmost part of the world. In Fuller's use it points up an imaginary element or quality that gives shape to the positivists' ideal. He further says, "[b]asically the quest of positivism is for some test which will designate plainly the law *that is* and distinguishes it from the law that is merely becoming or merely ought to be."[184] This ideal has especially mesmerized the dominant American school of positivists, the realists. "These men represent that direction of legal positivism which seeks to anchor itself in some datum of nature, which considers that the law's quest of itself can end successfully only if it terminates in some tangible external reality."[185]

How is it, Fuller wonders, how is it that this situation arose in American jurisprudence, that legal scholars expend so much more effort in obtaining empirical data,

[182] *See, e.g.*, Reinhold Niebuhr, Moral Man and Immoral Society (1932), and Reinhold Niebuhr, The Nature and Destiny of Man (2 vols. 1943).

[183] Fuller, *supra* note 167, at 16–17.

[184] *Id.* at 34 (emphasis in original).

[185] *Id.* at 47. *See also* Lon L. Fuller, *Book Review of Jerome Hall's* Readings in Jurisprudence, 87 U. Pa. L. Rev., 625, 627 n.2 (1939) (Fuller distinguishes between three senses of legal positivism: (1) that used by Austin, which focuses on law as that which humans will; (2) that used by Comte, which focuses on observed and unembroidered facts and excludes metaphysical entities; and (3) that most common in Fuller's day, that which "stands in opposition to the view that law is something which cannot be talked about without being altered in the course of being talked about. It asserts a faith in the existence of a raw datum of law which can be sought out, examined, and defined, and it asserts that the quest of this Pure Fact of Law is an undertaking important enough to call for the expenditure or [*sic*] great quantities of human energy.").

in extrapolating the behavior patterns of judges, than applying reason to human relations, than meditating on the ends of law and the nature of justice?[186]

He traces positivism's appeal to certain emotional attitudes. "Today," he says, "it is still positivism which is the sophisticated view .... It alone has purified its truths by a thorough washing in cynical acid."[187] The phrase "cynical acid" is a direct quote from "The Path of the Law." The suspicion that Holmes had something to do with this sad state of affairs is borne out some pages later. The "enormous influence" of Holmes, we learn, "has been particularly significant because it most strongly affected those who by temperament would otherwise be most likely to contribute to the creation of a new common law."[188]

Fuller recognizes that Holmes in his own work "did not always remain faithful to the program for a rigid separation of law and morals laid down in his early essays." Holmes at times spoke eloquently of human aspirations in law ("there is in all men the demand for the superlative"). But these very lapses from a foolish consistency gave, paradoxically, greater credence to positivism's program of isolating morals from law because of the philosophic wisdom that seemed to imbue Holmes's words.[189]

Fuller focuses on Holmes in *Quest* as part of his broader effort to define the issue between legal positivism and natural law. Despite different formulations, the problem of whether, and if so how, law and morals should be separated, or at a more rarified level, the nature of the relation between the *is* and the *ought*, structures the book and reveals the dimensions of Fuller's thinking. If legal positivists look to impose ever more refined discriminations – as to both "law" and "fact" – then natural law, in Fuller's never fully articulated version,[190] denies the possibility of absolute demarcation at any level of analysis or use. His insistence on the fundamental integration or coalescence of the *is* and the *ought* earned him censure from Morris Cohen, who found, in his judgment, the lack of intellectual discipline in the book as troubling as Fuller's inaccuracies about Holmes.[191]

In his review of *Quest* Cohen drew the following conclusion:

> One who denies a sharp distinction between the law that is and the law that ought to be, obviously cannot, even if he professes to believe in natural law, draw a clear distinction between good and bad laws. Something like this leads Professor Fuller to deny the obvious truth of Justice Holmes' statement that a bad man can use the

[186] FULLER, *supra* note 167, at 2–8; *see also* Lon Fuller, *Review of Roscoe Pound*, The Formative Era of American Law, 34 ILL. L. REV. 372, 372–74 (1939).
[187] FULLER, *supra* note 167, at 104.
[188] *Id.* at 117–18.
[189] *Id.* at 117–18, 109.
[190] On the difficult topic of Fuller and natural law see Kristen Rundle, *Opening the Doors of Inquiry: Lon Fuller and the Natural Law Tradition*, *in* THE CAMBRIDGE COMPANION TO NATURAL LAW JURISPRUDENCE 428–56 (George Duke and Robert P. George eds., 2017).
[191] Morris R. Cohen, *Should Legal Thought Abandon Clear Distinctions?*, 36 ILL. L. REV. 239, 239–46 (1941).

law for his own evil purposes, a denial that seems to me a veritable *reductio ad absurdum* of our author's position.[192]

This criticism as stated probably reveals more about Cohen's intellectual commitments than the coherence and cogency of Fuller's position. Fuller's refusal to admit a clear conceptual distinction between the *is* and the *ought* finds a parallel – if not a justification – in what at least one commentator views as Holmes's emphasis on the basic indeterminacy of experience.[193]

Be that as it may, Cohen's assertion that Fuller denies the "obvious truth of Justice Holmes' statement that a bad man can use the law for his own evil purposes" distorts what Fuller actually says in *Quest* about the bad man.

Fuller starts by asking whether legal positivism could be "useful" and still retain its "positivistic integrity" (that is, maintain a clear-cut separation between the *is* and the *ought*). He addresses the argument of those who point to the "art of predicting judicial behavior" as best combining the positivist injunction to ignore the *ought* with the eminently practical task of advising a client concerning the potential legal consequences of proposed action or inaction.

"But is it so clear," Fuller asks, "that the practitioner is unconcerned with natural law?"[194] He proposes to "test" this question by considering Holmes's figure of the bad man. He accurately describes how Holmes presents the bad man in "The Path of the Law," as one indifferent to intrinsic good or evil, or to approbation or censure, but still keenly attuned to legal penalties he may incur. Fuller finds Holmes's figure "very convincing" and even "plausible" as a working projection for positivism as a legal theory, but ultimately finds fault with it because it is an "abstraction."[195]

One wants to give Fuller the benefit of sympathetic understanding when he states the obvious – that the bad man is an abstraction – as if it could be otherwise – but the charitable impulse begins to wane as Fuller explains what he means. He thinks the bad man a peculiar kind of abstraction because, first, it's an odd sort of bad man that worries "about a fine of two dollars but apparently not about the possible loss of friends and customers."[196] Second, the bad man as Holmes presents him appears to determine the legal risks associated with a specific line of conduct without any inquiry whatsoever. In other words, Fuller claims that Holmes "assumes that his bad man has already reached a conclusion concerning legal risks," so much so that Holmes supposedly "neglects to inquire into the process by which this man would actually arrive at such a conclusion."[197]

[192] *Id.* at 243 (internal citations omitted).

[193] *See* Louis Menand, *The Principles of Oliver Wendell Holmes, in* American Studies 38–46 (2002).

[194] Fuller, *supra* note 167, at 92.

[195] *Id.* at 92–95.

[196] *Id.* at 93.

[197] *Id.* at 93–94.

One who has both read "The Path of the Law" and admired Fuller's intellectual finesse cannot help but be momentarily startled by his analysis in *Quest* of Holmes's use of the bad man. It is decidedly poor. The most obvious rejoinder to Fuller's first musing about the so-called peculiarity of the bad man – worrying about the two-dollar penalty without much concern about loss of friends and customers – is that it ignores the very constraints Holmes used to construct the bad man. The bad man by definition has no social conscience and is concerned only with material legal consequences. Asking whether the bad man might lose customers highlights an inhibition connected to a certain perceived consequence, but this in itself does little to advance one's understanding of the inner workings of the law.

As for Holmes assuming the bad man can magically know the probable legal consequences of his acts or omissions without any inquiry, that is the sort of statement that rightly falls into what Cohen identified as the absurd reaches of Fuller's thought. It soon becomes evident that Fuller makes this statement, not because he read "The Path of the Law" with any extraordinary care, or sought to genuinely understand its elliptical wording within the context of Holmes's thought, but because it offers a lead into his main argument. That holds that prediction of what a court (or judge) will do is impossible unless moral or ethical factors are taken into account. The bad man must consider how his actions will be viewed by third parties and what effect that will have on the ultimate legal outcome. This requirement inevitably leads to moral considerations.

"In short," says Fuller, "our bad man, if he is effectively to look after his own interests, will have to learn to look at the law through the eyes of a good man. To be a good positivist, he will have to become a natural-law lawyer."[198]

Comparing Fuller's analysis to Cohen's remark about the bad man illuminates how both are unsatisfactory. Cohen reads Holmes as saying that the bad man can use "law for his own evil purposes." This statement, taken as a generic descriptive, is unobjectionable. Undoubtedly real live bad women and men exist who undoubtedly use law to accomplish their evil purposes. One would be shocked if it were not so. Much of American procedural law is designed with these adverse interests in mind. Fuller cannot be taken to deny this assertion as a general truism about life in a modern law-bound society.

The real curiosity is why Cohen reads Holmes this way. It appears to be that Holmes, for Cohen, advanced legal thinking through his distrust of "ideas or principles that are not embodied in the actual decisions of the courts enforced by the power of the State."[199] Holmes drew attention to the winding razor wire edges of the enforcement power and Cohen believes that at least some of these razors stay

[198] *Id.* at 94–95.

[199] Morris R. Cohen, *A Critical Sketch of Legal Philosophy in America*, *in* 2 Law a Century of Progress 1835–1935: Contributions in Celebration of the 100th Anniversary of the Founding of The School of Law of New York University, 301 (1937).

ever conceptually sharp and rust-free under all conditions and environments. On Cohen's likely view, the bad man uses his knowledge of law mainly for evasion, for not coming into contact with these very sharp discouragements; not primarily to learn the inherent compressive and tensile strength of this omnipresent alloy of will and ideal.[200]

Fuller, in contrast, is interested how ideas or principles become embodied in actual court decisions enforced by state power and the many other ways he believes law becomes visible in social life. He is curious about the actual process. That makes his approach intriguing and insightful, but ultimately disappointing because of his unwillingness to recognize – at least within the context of *Quest* – that for one to understand the transmutation of the moral into the legal (or the reverse) one has to be able to distinguish methodically between these two (and other important) sources of duty in a historically conscientious way. Fuller's fixation on the presence of the *ought* in personal and social life, sometimes using the term in a conventionally moral way and sometimes using it to signify the effort to act competently and professionally, or to denote the drive to improve performance or outcomes according to internally accepted criteria, or to reveal the aesthetic or moral form-creating capability that he thinks underwrites human striving, made him prone to facile argumentation and whistling-in-the-dark non sequiturs.

I do not mean to be unduly harsh on Fuller. His attention to how the bad man must engage in the task of prophecy, especially when the threat of legal sanction wobbles like a star in the distance, bears similarities to the perspective we advance in Section 13. The problem with Fuller lies mainly in how his polemical bent at times undercuts some of his own best insights.[201] It is also how he analyzes Holmes's use of the bad man, not so much the conclusion he reaches, that merits pointed criticism.

In writings after *Quest* Fuller kept up the fusillade against those who upheld the separation thesis (the philosophical importance of maintaining a conceptual separation between law and morality). We see clear evidence in notable articles published before his 1964 masterwork, *The Morality of Law*. In "Reason and Fiat in Case Law," for example, he again singles out Holmes as the person most responsible for American jurisprudence's deviation from what should have been its natural course as part of an expanding and growing civilization.[202] He finds troubling Holmes's sly denigration of natural law as a "brooding omnipresence in the sky," and Holmes's efforts to "cut the law loose from the ethical considerations that have shaped it or, in other words, from its underlying reasons."[203] Holmes personifies the deep flaw of

[200] My understanding of Cohen's legal philosophy is much indebted to David Hollinger. *See* HOLLINGER, *supra* note 181, at 165–99.

[201] On Fuller's penchant for polemics see Nicola Lacey, *Out of the Witches' Cauldron?: Reinterpreting the Context and Re-assessing the Significance of the Hart–Fuller Debate*, *in* THE HART–FULLER DEBATE IN THE 21ST CENTURY 20 (Peter Crane ed., 2010).

[202] Fuller, *supra* note 181, at 394–95.

[203] *Id.* at 379, 384.

legal positivism: its attempt to restate law purely in terms of power relations without any reference to ethical determinants.[204]

Fuller maintained the same critique against legal positivism's arch-exemplar in the twentieth century, H. L. A. Hart. In their famous debate Fuller hammered away at what he took to be legal positivism's glaring weakness, its inability to live up to its own professed ideal of fidelity to law. In the measure and application of this ideal he deems the issue joined between legal positivists and those who dissent from their prescriptive ethos. After a lengthy exposition, he concludes –

> I do not think it is unfair to the positivistic philosophy to say that it never gives any coherent meaning to the moral obligation of fidelity to law. This obligation seems to be conceived as sui generis, wholly unrelated to any of the ordinary, extralegal ends of human life. The fundamental postulate of positivism – that law must be strictly severed from morality – seems to deny the possibility of any bridge between the obligation to obey law and other moral obligations.[205]

And with this riposte Fuller momentarily turns his attention again to Holmes, but this time in the context of the question whether positivism, as a legal philosophy, played a non-negligible role in the rise of the Nazi dictatorship.

Granted, Hart had put the general issue on the table.[206] But he had not mentioned Holmes. Fuller takes the opportunity to remind his readers that "[d]uring the last half century in this country no issue of legal philosophy has caused more spilling of ink and adrenalin than the assertion that there are 'totalitarian' implications in the views of Oliver Wendell Holmes, Jr." Even the gentlest criticisms, he goes on to say, "seem to stir the reader's mind with the memory of past acerbities."[207]

It does no good, he adds, to attempt to blunt the force of the criticism by suggesting that Holmes may not have realized the implications of his own thought: "this is merely to substitute one insult for another." Neither does it help, Fuller further laments, to recall James's observation that Holmes is "composed of at least two and a half different people rolled into one, and the way he keeps them together in one tight skin, without quarreling any more than they do, is remarkable."[208]

Fuller says no more about the matter; he ends with the quote from James. But the inference is evident that he does not necessarily disagree that there might be something to the whole "totalitarian" argument. He writes this in 1958. We are about twenty years from when Lucey first sounded the alarm. Yet even a decade earlier, in 1946, Fuller had written about the urgency of discrediting a legal

[204] *Id.* at 387.

[205] Lon L. Fuller, *Positivism and Fidelity to Law – A Reply to Professor Hart*, 71 HARV. L. REV. 630, 656 (1958).

[206] H. L. A. Hart, *Positivism and the Separation of Law and Morals*, 71 HARV. L. REV. 593, 615–21 (1958).

[207] Fuller, *supra* note 205, at 657.

[208] *Id.* at 657–58.

philosophy essentially "alien to the American spirit."[209] Fuller may not have been a mid-twentieth-century God-fearing, Holmes-whacking Jesuit living in the United States, but in this phrase he certainly struck a note similar to theirs.

I am not aware of any indication of what may have been Mark DeWolfe Howe's reaction to these specific comments regarding Holmes in Fuller's response to H. L. A. Hart. Fuller and Howe were colleagues at Harvard. One can only assume that Howe either read or was apprised of what Fuller wrote. That Fuller directed these comments toward Howe is a fair inference given that the only citation provided in these paragraphs, other than the source of the James quote, is to Howe's 1951 article "The Positivism of Mr. Justice Holmes."[210]

The debate on the ramifications of Holmes's thought had, it seems, come full circle. We will turn to "The Positivism of Mr. Justice Holmes" in the next section. As will become clear, Howe directs most of his arguments at Fuller, especially at how Fuller presented Holmes in *Quest*. Howe contends Fuller did an injustice to Holmes and Howe is correct.

At the same time, Howe does not quite explicitly recognize what Fuller saw all too clearly in *Quest* – that Holmes's prestige endorsed a certain style of thought which, in turn, made it inordinately difficult for gifted students of a certain temperamental stamp to follow a different path. Ideas mattered to Fuller. He wanted the study of law to be more than a rite of passage to an amoral but lucrative profession. He attacked the idol that was Holmes for the same reasons he criticized the prevailing "literary tradition" and the then current fascination with scientific methods. In their different ways they stifled creativity; they blocked inquiry and increased the likelihood that those who studied law would become so engrossed with the prevailing rules or their conceptualization and explication that they would never develop the capacity to look at the existing social order in any other way. Or even realize that there were other ways or other incipient orders.

10 MARK DEWOLFE HOWE

The travails Mark DeWolfe Howe endured to write the authorized biography of Holmes have not, even to this day, been fully appreciated. Howe served as Holmes's Supreme Court secretary in the 1933–34 term. Howe owed the honor to Felix Frankfurter, who had taken over from John Chipman Gray the task of selecting the Harvard Law graduate sent to clerk for Holmes each year. Frankfurter, whom Holmes in his final years had selected to be his official biographer, then prevailed on the young Howe in 1937 to quit private practice and take an academic post at the new law school at the University of Buffalo so as to better assist Frankfurter in the

[209] Fuller, *supra* note 181, at 394.
[210] Mark DeWolfe Howe, *The Positivism of Mr. Justice Holmes*, 64 Harv. L. Rev. 529 (1951).

enormous task of gathering the voluminous letters and other documents that pertained to Holmes's life.[211]

Eventually Howe became the designated authorized biographer. That did stop Frankfurter, now himself a member of the Supreme Court, from barraging his former – no longer young – pupil to stay on task and to remain vigilant in protecting the deceased justice's reputation.[212] Howe probably did not need Frankfurter's prodding. By 1951 he had been a professor at Harvard Law for six years, had earned military medals recognizing his valiant service in World War II, and had mastered the intellectual history of the late nineteenth-, early twentieth-century transatlantic legal community.

It is hard to know from the published volumes Howe's ultimate opinion on Holmes. Howe's unexpected death left uncompleted the authorized biography. One has no reason to think that Howe shared his subject's indifference to twentieth-century social causes. He was after all a Frankfurter protégé. The opposite is actually the case. The record shows he worked hard to promote civil rights for black Americans.[213] Howe duly notes Holmes's indifference to most social and civil rights causes but that is not the theme that stands out in the two published biographical volumes. Nor is it ambition, though that too is duly noted. Howe seems to have been struck by Holmes's deep belief in effort, though not in the effort to do or be good or to be pious – to be in a right relationship with God – in the New England Puritan sense. Holmes did not believe in God.

Holmes, Howe suggested in his biographical volumes, dedicated his conscious life to the effort to think profoundly and to achieve insight. And he sought to do both in and through law. In the process Holmes transformed law – that farrago of principles, precedent, and practices by which Americans sought to govern themselves – into a vocabulary fit for philosophical talk about the ends of life and the (un)common good. Holmes transformed the common law into a literature that concentrated a community's intricate historical experience with legal power and its recognized sources – no tiny feat.

This interpretation of Howe on Holmes finds justification in Howe's work but Howe does not in any single passage express his take on Holmes in the same language that I have used.[214] I have made some necessary inferences that take into account the scope of Howe's work within the context of my own study of Holmes and what I have been able to glean about Howe. Howe did more or less the same type of thing during the period of his active scholarship on Holmes. Though he did it on a much larger scale.

[211] Holmes and Frankfurter: Their Correspondence, 1912–1934 xxix–xxxviii (Robert M. Mennel and Christine L. Compson eds., 1996).

[212] *Id.*

[213] Paul Freund, *Mark DeWolfe Howe*, 79 Proceedings of the Massachusetts Historical Society, Third Series 197–99 (noting Howe's commitment to civil rights).

[214] *See, e.g.*, Howe, *supra* note 111, at 135–59, 280–83.

Howe also had to meet some fairly high expectations. His mentor, sometime patron, and now Justice Frankfurter, had, along with Harold Laski, turned Holmes into a champion of progressive liberalism. Frankfurter currently held Holmes's former seat on the Court (seat 3).[215] Jerome Frank had once proclaimed Holmes the most completely adult jurist of his generation. Frank now sat on the United States Court of Appeal for the Second Circuit. Senior scholars Hessel Yntema and Karl Llewellyn traced the origin of the "realist" way of looking at law to Holmes and "The Path of the Law." Former Harvard Law dean, Roscoe Pound, believed the American jurists who followed in Holmes's footsteps were mostly epigone.[216]

More broadly, Catherine Drinker Bowen saw much merit in fellow writer Elizabeth Shepley Sergeant's proclamation that in Holmes one found "a Yankee, strayed from Olympus."[217] For Bowen Holmes's life made an incredibly important statement about the heeded virtues of America. Her novel, *Yankee from Olympus: Justice Holmes and His Family*, which recounted three generations of Holmeses, arrived in numerous mailboxes across the country as a featured April 1944 Book-of-the-Month Club selection.[218] That in turn helped create an audience for Emmet Lavery's popular 1946 Broadway play, *The Magnificent Yankee*. Lavery's play became a Hollywood movie of the same title in 1951, the year our hero, Howe, published his response to Fuller's *Quest* in the *Harvard Law Review*. According to filmography website IMDb, *The Magnificent Yankee* also came out in the United Kingdom under the title, *The Man with Thirty Sons*, and in Brazil as *Nobre Rebelde* ("A Noble Rebel"). In 1965 the film was remade for TV as a Hallmark Hall of Fame production.[219]

But the wave of acclamation didn't stop with *The Magnificent Yankee*. In 1956, *Mr. Justice Holmes* by renowned children's author Clara Ingram Judson was published.[220] The cover of the copy I have shows that it received the Annual Children's Book Award for Special Excellence from the Thomas Alva Edison Foundation. The book was also a runner-up for the Newbery Medal, which recognized annually the author of "the most distinguished contribution to American

[215] For seat information *see Felix Frankfurter*, Oyez, www.oyez.org/justices/felix_frankfurter (last accessed April 7, 2018).

[216] Pound, *supra* note 66, at 449.

[217] Elizabeth Shepley Sergeant, *Justice Touched with Fire*, *in* MR. JUSTICE HOLMES 183–211 (Felix Frankfurter ed., 1931).

[218] Saul Touster mentions that *Yankee from Olympus* was a Book-of-the-Month Club selection in his *Holmes a Hundred Years Ago*: The Common Law *and Legal Theory*, 10 HOFSTRA L. REV. 673, 674 n.7 (1981). In addition, a copy of the book that I purchased includes a reprint of Henry Seidel Canby's review from the April 1944 edition of the *Book-of-the-Month Club News*.

[219] *The Magnificent Yankee*, www.imdb.com/title/tt0042702/releaseinfo?ref_=tt_dt_dt#akas (last accessed Apr. 7, 2018); Laura Krugman Ray, *Judicial Fictions: Images of Supreme Court Justices in the Novel, Drama, and Film*, 39 ARIZ. L. REV. 151, 159, 163–66 (1997).

[220] CLARA INGRAM JUDSON, MR. JUSTICE HOLMES (1956).

literature for children."[221] And in 1968 the United States Postal Service issued its bright maroon-on-white fifteen-cent Oliver Wendell Holmes stamp as part of its Prominent Americans Series.

These were some of the currents. The crosscurrents noticeably began with the Jesuits, though in retrospect one can see the first significant stirrings of intellectual animosity in Zane. These crosscurrents gathered energy within the legal profession from the publication of Ben W. Palmer's articles in the *American Bar Association Journal* in 1945 and 1946 (including the notorious "Hobbes, Holmes, and Hitler").[222] Palmer connected Holmes with the noetic conditions that made possible the rise of totalitarianism and the concomitant erosion of natural law even as he began by acknowledging that "[a]ll Americans, even the most conservative, are proud of Mr. Justice Holmes. For his career was intensely American."[223]

California lawyer Harold McKinnon followed Palmer and published "The Secret of Mr. Justice Holmes" in the April 1950 issue. McKinnon began by squarely facing the Sphinx. Two facts about Holmes cried out for reconciliation: "[h]e had a very bad philosophy. Yet he ranks among the greatest men of our time." "His very name," McKinnon added, "has become a symbol of what is implicitly felt to be something characteristic of American life." McKinnon proposed to reveal the secret of the riddle that was Holmes, "a thinker who in his cosmic appraisals rejects what are the very foundations of our society but who is nevertheless honored as few other men of his time."[224]

The revelation lay in the unvarnished truth that in Holmes America had its "agnostic prophet to an agnostic age." It helped too that this particular agnostic prophet had an abundance of charm, good looks, family fame, legal talent, and real literary ability. But McKinnon, quoting Max Lerner, ultimately views Holmes's fame as an index to the times:

> The fact is that Holmes's 'bad man' standard, his rejection of natural law, and his definition of law as what the courts will in fact do, were all congenial to the mood and quality of a pragmatic America in whose practical business life the realm of fact had elbowed out the norms of morality.

While the liberal Lerner may have found some solace that the same social forces that brought Holmes to prominence also lifted William James and John Dewey (declared champions of the individual's sanctity), the conservative McKinnon lamented the prevailing moral complacency that could without much compunction reject the Judeo-Christian tradition and the natural law heritage. Americans

[221] www.ala.org/alsc/awardsgrants/bookmedia/newberymedal/newberymedal (last accessed April 8, 2018).

[222] Palmer, *Hobbes, Holmes and Hitler*, *supra* note 139, at 569–73; Ben W. Palmer, *Defense against Leviathan*, 32 A.B.A. J. 328, 328–32, 360 (1946).

[223] Palmer, *Hobbes, Holmes and Hitler*, *supra* note 139, at 569.

[224] Harold R. McKinnon, *The Secret of Mr. Justice Holmes: An Analysis*, 36 A.B.A. J. 261, 261–64, 342–46 (1950).

(or at least the subgroup who attended law schools) had to get past Holmes and once again accept the proposition that "law is not a product of irresponsible will but a branch of ethics because its whole purpose lies in being an instrument for the common good."[225]

Into this maelstrom of opinion jumps Howe. Though the feeling against Holmes had been seething for a decade, it appears that the decision of Westbrook Pegler – a nationally known two-fisted wordsmith – to call out Holmes as "the God of an evil cult," a "cynical and senile brutalitarian" who "had no more morals than a pig" in the December 18, 1950, edition of the *Boston American* was more than our man Howe could stand.[226]

Howe began his "The Positivism of Mr. Justice Holmes" by musing on the tremendous distance opinion regarding Holmes had traveled from the beginning of the 1930s – when such talented and erudite minds as Justice Benjamin N. Cardozo's had referred to Holmes as one of jurisprudence's greatest philosophers and seers – to twenty years later when the "mountebank" Pegler could without much trepidation write for print such "delicate words." Howe was nothing if not a Boston Brahmin.[227]

True to form, though acknowledging the slurs of the Jesuits and the popgun pops of Palmer, Howe begged off any direct engagement with these adherents of the "Catholic philosophy of law." He would not square off against Fathers Lucey or Ford or even attorney Palmer – who another member of the Minnesota bar had already rebutted in the pages of the *American Bar Association Journal* ("Justice Holmes Was Not on a Ladder to Hitler").[228] Howe took the fight directly to the only man of the bunch he considered a worthy antagonist, Lon Fuller.

> I am strongly persuaded that Professor Fuller has expressed in his writing on Holmes a point of view which many lawyers have come, perhaps unconsciously, to share – a feeling not only that Holmes' philosophy of law was inconsistent with the highest traditions and aspirations of Western thought, but that his scale of moral and political values was badly suited to measure the needs of a progressive and civilized society.[229]

Howe had good reason to focus on Fuller. Even Max Lerner, in his well-regarded *The Mind and Faith of Justice Holmes* – dedicated to Justice Frankfurter – had conceded that Fuller was right "that much of the attractiveness of the positivist, or

[225] *Id.* at 345. The Lerner quote is from THE MIND AND FAITH OF JUSTICE HOLMES: HIS SPEECHES, ESSAYS, LETTERS, AND JUDICIAL OPINIONS 369 (Max Lerner ed. 1943).

[226] Howe, *supra* note 210, at 530 n.4 (1951); *see also* Fred Rodell, *Justice Holmes and His Hecklers*, 60 YALE L.J. 620 (1951); Westbrook Pegler, *Fair Enough*, BOS. AM., Dec. 18, 1950, at 34, 45.

[227] Howe, *supra* note 210, at 529–30.

[228] Charles W. Briggs, *Justice Holmes Was Not on a Ladder to Hitler*, 32 A.B.A. J. 631 (1946).

[229] Howe, *supra* note 210, at 531.

hard-boiled, conception of law for us may be traced to the glamour and sense of philosophic breadth with which Holmes invested this view."[230]

Few today would be able to immediately grasp how Holmes, or anyone else for that matter, would be able to invest a "hard-boiled" conception of law with a sense of philosophic breadth much less glamour. Those were indeed some heady intellectual times. If we take positivism in American law to mean what Howe took it to mean, first, a separation of law and morality and, second, the opinion that law does not simply encapsulate norms of good and evil, or an ethic of right and wrong, but, rather, it is that which justifies "an informed and prophetic judgment as to what the courts will do in fact[,]" then we are in a much better position to appreciate the charge that Holmes's "scale of moral and political values was badly suited to measure the needs of a progressive and civilized society."[231]

Howe's article is a tour de force both for Holmes studies and broader histories of American intellect and culture. Yet he does not really explain his point in diagnosing the discomfort many lawyers supposedly felt about the lack of fit between Holmes's scale of moral and political values and the pressing needs of a progressive and civilized society.

To put it another way: Howe interprets Fuller as a spokesperson for the point of view that finds Holmes's scale of values wanting. Fuller identified the essence of the problem in the unwarranted and unwarrantable separation of the *is* from the *ought*. That is why, for instance, Fuller had argued that H. L. A. Hart betrayed the fundamental value of fidelity to law through his positivistic analysis and determination of what type of rules constituted legal rules or law. Fidelity itself arose from a norm that was not legal. It came from an *ought* (normative belief) that suffused and encompassed the *is* (recognizable legal rules) as a kind of luminiferous ether.

For Fuller, according to Howe's interpretation, a progressive and civilized society – meaning, I think, a society that had progressed from a morally barbaric stage and remained intent on continuing to progress and to retain its hard-won goods – found little or no guidance in a scale of values that originated in a deep seated skepticism. Holmes's skepticism manifested itself in two ways: first, as a moral skepticism – one that disaffirms unchanging intrinsic or natural or God-mandated moral goods or ends – and, second, as an intellectual skepticism that found its genesis in the conviction that certitude is not the test for certainty. For a society intent on retaining its moral and political goods and adding to the store, the realization that the beliefs that once had underwritten these goods no longer had the necessary underwriting capacity – God had become disastrously overexposed – left that society's most culturally alert minds in the lurch. Once the society's lawyers

[230] The Mind and Faith of Justice Holmes, *supra* 225, at 368–69.

[231] Howe, *supra* note 210, at 531.

arrived at the same conclusion the game – as another Holmes, Sherlock, might well have said – was no longer afoot.

Fuller had put Howe in a really tight spot. Howe had his own moral and political commitments and a sophisticated understanding of the trajectory informed beliefs about morality and law had taken since Holmes's birth in Boston, 1841. Howe's father had written a biography of Holmes's father, and Howe himself could trace his New England lineage back many generations. Howe had also edited the collection of letters between Holmes and Pollock published in 1941. He then witnessed the use of those letters to cast aspersions on Holmes as a man – whom, by all indicators, Howe sincerely respected – and to support arguments for the reinstatement of attitudes and beliefs Howe thought impossible to reinstate. The God of Howe's (and Holmes's) New England forebears had died.

Apart from the life or death of a divine being that had at one time in New England's history underwritten moral commitment, stood the issue of whether one could discern through ratiocination or determine through reflection on past social action the permanent regulative principles of conduct. Fuller appeared to think that one could and damned Holmes for making state-sanctioned force and not those regulative principles the basis from which to determine the rightness or wrongness of legal action. More directly, he essentially lambasted Holmes for refusing to even countenance the possibility – "postulate" in the language of the early twentieth century – that the task could be done.

Fuller, I further suggest, found Holmes's unwillingness to postulate the existence of relatively untrammelled, untouched moral principles upon which an ethic could be founded and against which laws themselves judged as good or bad to be the most repellent feature of Holmes's thought. It retarded the further development of civilization, understood as the increased spread and infusion of human goods including moral ones. Holmes's unwillingness to believe in these goods as the medieval knight believed in the unmatched beauty of his damsel effectively cut the tendons of the many hands that took Holmes very seriously but still wanted to spread the good news.

Howe's response to Fuller indicated that he had a sense of what Fuller was driving at and that he himself had wrestled in the wee hours of the dawn with the same problem. On the other side of the coin, he was Holmes's authorized biographer and if Holmes had stood for anything it was the need to make legal decision-making more rational. How that injunction had been understood and acted upon takes us to the history of various movements in American law from the beginning of the twentieth century to its midpoint. Howe came to the conclusion that Fuller was conducting a rearguard action. Howe further decided to take the fight directly to Fuller, not by downplaying what may have appeared to be the most troubling element of Holmes's thought – his positivism – but by repositioning and foregrounding that positivism against a backstory that placed Holmes's scale of values and consequent separation of law and morality into a new sequence.

Howe begins by drawing attention to Holmes's 1895 Memorial Day speech, "The Soldier's Faith." Howe believes the words Holmes uttered that day gave tone and color to Fuller's opinion that Holmes's "Civil War experience bred in the young soldier a sentimental enthusiasm for the heroism of obedience, which, in the mature philosopher became blind respect for authority as such."[232]

> I do not know what is true. I do not know the meaning of the universe. But in the midst of doubt, in the collapse of creeds, there is one thing I do not doubt, that no man who lives in the same world with most of us can doubt, and that is that the faith is true and adorable which leads a soldier to throw away his life in obedience to a blindly accepted duty, in a cause which he little understands, in a plan of campaign of which he has no notion, under tactics of which he does not see the use.[233]

Howe concedes this passage "reflects most significantly the mixing of skepticism and romanticism in Holmes' faith."[234] But to read it as the creed of an authoritarian, as Fuller and many others seem to do, "is totally to disregard its context; to suggest that he there was saying that might makes right, that the *is* is more important than the *ought*, distorts his thesis beyond recognition."[235]

What is Holmes's thesis? For Howe it is a thesis that arises from a pronounced skepticism in both faith and morals. In faith because scientific thought had overturned the ancient verities, and in morals – pertaining more to the conviction of right than to its execution – because of the Civil War and Holmes's realization that those who fought and died alongside him and against him had convictions no less sacred than his own. Yet as to the thesis itself Howe does little more than repeat the words of Holmes – as one might sing the refrain of a song – "that the faith is true and adorable which leads a soldier to throw his life in obedience to a blindly accepted duty, in a cause which he little understands, in a plan of campaign of which he has no notion, under tactics of which he does not see the use." These lines do not form a "cynical or complacent answer to the problem of intense experience" but affirm an original truth, not of proposition or argument, but of Holmes's life.[236]

Howe then proceeds in his article to connect his interpretation of Holmes's intellectual development – comprising two decisive stages of growth, the abandonment of a religiously imbued faith and a recognition of the irreducible sense of actualities that underlies morality – to Holmes's theory of law. Before proceeding to that important topic let us pause for a moment to consider this truth or faith of Holmes. Howe contextualizes it by overlaying Holmes's Civil War experience upon

[232] *Id.* at 532.
[233] *Id.*
[234] *Id.*
[235] *Id.* at 537.
[236] *Id.*

Holmes's upbringing among the vanguard of Boston's (and nearby Cambridge's) social thinkers, those who increasingly looked to science and not to tradition as their primary guide. He does so to counter Fuller's authoritarian slant on Holmes. Yet through his adroit contextualization Howe stifles the power of Holmes's faith to resonate.

In the "The Soldier's Faith" Holmes's eloquence reaches the perfection of its pitch. Included in his *Speeches*, a collection of addresses Holmes published in successively enlarged editions from 1891 to 1913, "The Soldier's Faith" reprises all the important themes of power, effort, feeling, want, reliance, destiny, duty, democracy, and country that work their way through Holmes's mediations on the two topics that seemed to hold his greatest interest, the value of life and the worth of law. It is Emersonian through and through.

"To be a soldier or descended from soldiers, in time of peace to be ready to give one's life rather than to suffer disgrace, that is what the word has meant; and if we try to claim it at less cost than a splendid carelessness for life, we are trying to steal the good will without the responsibilities of the place. We will not dispute about tastes. The man of the future may want something different."[237] The man of the future would reappear almost two years later in "The Path of the Law." But for now Holmes speaks of a soldier as the early Christians spoke about themselves. They coined the term "pagan," a civilian, one not a member of what eventually became the great army of Christ. Nietzsche, it seems, was not the only late nineteenth-century thinker to spoil the Christians as the Israelites once spoiled the Egyptians, or as the early Christians, in turn, had spoiled the ancient philosophers.

Holmes goes beyond Emerson or Nietzsche or even Dostoyevsky in communicating the intensity of the feeling that opened up to him the urgency of life, the "unspeakable, somewhat" that makes a soldier "capable of miracle, able to lift himself by the might of his own soul, unaided, able to face annihilation for a blind belief."[238] The moment comes when the "cynic force" of common sense has spent itself, when a "dumb animal" faith emerges, blind, in a stupor, but filled with the fiercest resolve to crash against the surf.[239]

Denuding Holmes's oratory leaves us with a perplexity: can we speak intelligibly of an instinct for something supervening sheer survival? The bond that takes a soldier to the grave, that supersedes the common impulse to run or to hide, that underwrites the willingness to face annihilation for a cause disbelieved or to engage in tactics not understood, but solely for the dignity of duty, for the sake of an ideal – "the divine folly of honor" – that encompasses self-devotion, can this bond to others and to one's self, these intricately interconnected circuits of human energy, be

[237] Oliver Wendell Holmes, *The Soldier's Faith, in* III CW 487.
[238] *Id.* at 487–88.
[239] *Id.*; *see also* Oliver Wendell Holmes, *Memorial Day, in* III CW 462–67.

adequately or intelligibly depicted as contributing to the formation or re-formation of a recognizable culture-making power?

I do not feel confident I have been able to convey the force and gravity of the insight into life that molded Holmes's very being. Yet he was remarkably open about it so one does not feel quite as awed as Henry Adams says he felt when standing before the Dynamo or as some people today tend to feel when reading Heidegger's *Being and Time*. The language of Holmes is not the language of war but of a war-torn culture. It is the expression of a culture that finds buoyant the question, "Is life worth living?"

Howe may have understood the significance and currency that question had in the America of 1895. That was the year of "The Soldier's Faith" and also when William James published his well-known essay, "Is Life Worth Living?" Howe probably understood too that Holmes's resounding answer, that the joy of life lay in the living, in exerting one's powers with all one's passion and might, would fail to appease the demand of thinkers who believed that power should serve *oughts* and *oughts* could never be *oughts* unless reason, not authority, backed them up.

In retrospect one sees that these oppositions – is/ought, reason/authority – do little to communicate the inherent dynamics of Holmes's thinking. The limits they suggest do not accurately reflect his interests and aims. The movements between the denoted values are too dispersed. Holmes's insight on the value of living points toward an immense, elemental, almost primal compression of will and belief; it is indicative of the will-to-power-for-an-unseen-end. Not content with the paradox of enduing the spiritual with the most unspiritual of reflex arcs, the blatant struggle and tear for life, Holmes adds to his readers' bewilderment by claiming that the Civil War was the *second* greatest moral experience of his life.

He presumably calls the Civil War a moral experience because of how the "unspeakable, somewhat" fused to a half-articulated, half-hidden ideal and thereby laid the needed social ground for the eventual pronouncements of future articulated goods and bads. The sacrifice of blood and the death of boon companions taught him that passion (intensely dedicated effort) when most concentrated, as in war, operates, as we might say today, like a naturally designed collider. The tremendous impact of conflicting, powerfully held convictions or wills in compressed, high-velocity circumstances, seeking incompatible ends, bared to him the basic constituents of cultural matter and ultimately reworked them. This astounding insight also revealed that the same death-and-life combustion that the war magnified a thousand-fold – magnified enough, that is, for it to become detectable to consciousness, for the insensible to become for an instant sensible – operated similarly though much less perceptibly at larger scales.

That insight into the continuity of the culture-making power takes us to what Holmes eventually recognized as his greatest moral experience, the law.

> The change from those barren surroundings to today is inseparably identified in my mind with the change from boyhood to age. In either aspect the beginning was a weary time, even though mitigated by Henry Bowditch's teachings in the rudiments of crime – ringing doorbells and playing devil's tricks at back doors – a weary time – a time of waiting for 'some divine, far-off event.'
>
> The event came. There was more than one. I am thinking now more of spiritual than of external changes. College gave one atmosphere. The war was a great moral experience. The first five or ten years of one's profession was another, and perhaps a greater one.[240]

To bring together fighting in war and training in law as transformative moral experiences bring us face-to-face with Holmes's uncanny ability to poeticize the depths of his personal experience into a lucent prose. This ability proves itself in the manner in which it espies in experience tiny little bonds; in the faith that these bonds may be espied, brought to the fore, and expressed in ever-enlarging contexts.

Howe was right to praise Holmes for giving neither the "cynical nor the complacent answer to the problem of intense experience."[241] Instead Holmes honored the dedication and devotion of the soldier. Howe should have gone one step further, however, and recognized that the frame of mind or attitude that Holmes honored was one he articulated out of the reaches of his own desires as they realized themselves in colliding with the brutal realities of fighting the war and studying and practicing the law. In the firestorm of his being, Holmes found customary social and cultural partitions shattered. He was able to recognize some of the slivers that came together in the rebuilt kaleidoscope: Puritan, American, thinker, soldier, lawyer, writer, judge. He accepted them as the operative facts of his life and dedicated himself to tracing out their interconnections to each other and to those elements of existence that vibrated at the edges of his awareness. Through that ruminative process Holmes sought to bring that which was not self-evidently part of his life into his life. That's how he enlarged the web of his perceptions and matured his insights.

And that's also how he came to see how his experience in war, when life hung by a single red thread, bore strong similarities to his experience in learning the law and its practice. It was not solely that both were intense, transformative experiences. That interpretation smacks too much of an insulated aestheticism. Holmes came to see that each event revealed to him an aspect of how the culture-making power worked. To adapt his well-known phrase to his own experience: through the Civil War at the subatomic level and in the common law at the interstices of precedent, through myriad motions from the molecular to the molar.[242] The world was actually woven

[240] Oliver Wendell Holmes, *Address at Tavern Club Dinner*, *in* III CW 534.

[241] Howe, *supra* note 210, at 537.

[242] *See* "Death by Molar or Molecular Motion," in The Mind and Faith of Justice Holmes, *supra* note 225, at 122–23; Southern Pacific Co. v. Jensen, 244 U.S. 205, 221 (1917) (Holmes, J., dissenting).

and weaving even though it appeared torn. It took him years, and much heartache and intense soul searching to find the strength and will to realize that one fact.

It might seem these thoughts on Holmes's intellectual path and orientation have little to do with his legal theory or with how Howe seeks to place "The Soldier's Faith" within the events of Holmes's life. Yet neither "The Soldier's Faith" nor Holmes's theory of law is fully understandable without taking his intellectual sensibility and orientation into account. Howe stops at the threshold of "The Soldier's Faith." If he had not, he would have recognized the importance in 1951 of the sentences that Holmes wrote immediately before the oft-quoted refrain and after his saying that the man of the future may want something different.

> But who of us could endure a world, although cut up into five-acre lots and having no man upon it who was not well fed and well housed, without the divine folly of honor, without the senseless passion for knowledge out-reaching the flaming bounds of the possible? I do not know what is true. I do not know the meaning of the universe . . . .[243]

Holmes was a soldier in the war and in the law. He learned to fight; he was not afraid to kill. He sought honor in fighting for his country and in pursuing what lay beyond the charged outer fences of knowledge. It was an uncommon combination and an even less common sequence.

Howe understood the sequence in a more programmatic manner. First, as Holmes's loss of religious faith ("he had shaken off the religious faith on which so many of the assumptions of the world around him were based"), and, second, the subsequent realization, inspired by the war, that "personal taste in morals does not establish universal or objective truth in ethics."[244] Howe believed these two skepticisms informed Holmes's study of law, though it would be more accurate to say that his study of law provided him the substantive matter for their fullest articulation. For Howe they fueled Holmes's intellectual ambition for "creative speculation." That drive found its outlet in the Herculean task of cleansing the stables of nineteenth-century law, in aerating a heavy deadening must. Revamping the law, Howe says, required Holmes to subject its analytical traditions "to the same rigorous and skeptical inspection to which science subjected theology." Likewise, the law's "moral postulates, imbedded in the old complacency," had to be utterly and fearlessly reexamined.[245]

Critics like Fuller failed to understand the prevailing atmosphere of belief that permeated sophisticated opinion about law and its study during the era in which Holmes came to intellectual maturity. It took the strong historical arm of Sir Henry Maine to crack the ancient mindset's Potemkin facade, and a scientific approach

[243] Holmes, *supra* note 237, at 487.
[244] Howe, *supra* note 210, at 537.
[245] *Id.* at 538–39.

reminiscent of Darwin's to make the break irreparable. Holmes took to the task with gusto in *The Common Law*.

Howe identifies two overriding achievements in *The Common Law*. To Coke's "reason is the life of the law," Holmes counterpoised his "the life of the law has not been logic; it has been experience." To the prevailing sense of an immanent, immutable, and integrated governing morality Holmes introduced a new element, that of dynamic, quasi-directionless change.

> The other achievement, less apparent though it may have been, was no less significant. It was to call attention to the fact that though moral conceptions had been of predominant importance in the initial formulation of rules of law, time and experience had given to the language of morality as it survives in law, a meaning substantially different from that which it originally possessed.[246]

Holmes had noticed the tendency of moral concepts to transmute over time: "As time passed, however, the words lingered in the law, still laden with the deceptive implications of morality, but infused with new meaning and new purposes." Holmes then inferred from this historically manifested transformation that "the terms of subjective morality had acquired in the law an objective meaning quite different from that which they had at first possessed."[247]

Howe's argument is that for Holmes words like fraud, malice, and negligence had, in their initial use, relatively coherent and overlapping subjective and objective meanings. They reflected the prevailing moral and legal sentiments and evaluations of the community. Yet as the law progressed – new cases arose, new decisions announced – the legal meaning of these terms (what Howe calls the objective meaning) began to shift and over time the moral meaning (the subjective meaning) and the legal meaning began to operate on different frequency bands within the community's spectrum of duties. At certain points they divided because the legal meaning shifted further away from the moral meaning or vice versa. Holmes not only sought to bring this legal evolution to the attention of the profession, he sought too to develop in his book a style of thinking capable of recognizing and bringing to present purpose the perceived shifts in meaning and value.

Howe then forcefully argues that critics like Fuller who see Holmes as an avatar of positivism – as one who asserts the law must "concern itself exclusively with the *is* and never bother itself with the *ought*" – never cite *The Common Law* to support that thesis. They mainly rely on (and condemn) "The Path of the Law." Yet, "The Path of the Law" says nothing that was not already said in *The Common Law*. The message was the same. Only the emphasis had changed because Holmes intended *The Common Law* for "sophisticated and mature lawyers" and "The Path of the Law" for students.

246 *Id.* at 539.
247 *Id.*

> Each effort, however, was the expression of the same philosophical concern of which I have already spoken. In talking to students, Holmes asked them at the outset to look behind the surface of traditional definitions to the stuff of law. For generations, students had been told that law is 'a system of reason' and had been charged by their elders to remember that it is a 'deduction from principles of ethics.' We may have forgotten the words of Rufus Choate, but, to the audience that Holmes addressed, the suggestion that the invisible and omnipresent law was the 'whispered yet authoritative voice of all the past and good' still had persuasive eloquence. Read with appreciation of the circumstances in which the address was delivered, "The Path of the Law" is anything but the formulation of a totalitarian creed. It is a philosopher's plea that theory should be founded in fact; an historian's argument that experience tells more of truth than does eloquence.[248]

Howe demonstrates his sophistication by recognizing the atmospheric cultural shift that Holmes portended. The "invisible and omnipresent law" had lost its cloak of invisibility; Holmes did more than anyone else to bring to the profession's attention the exposed interstices of the law, and instead of merely reasoned eloquence one learned to expect the agon of right(eous) vs. right(eous).

But Howe still had to deal with the bad man. Holmes used this "dramatic image," Howe insists, to dispel the prevailing confusion between law and morality. To Howe Holmes's use of the bad man as a teaching device for students was obvious: "Such a man, Holmes indicated, might have a more accurate understanding of the meaning in law of such words as 'fraud,' 'malice' and 'intent' than a student nurtured in the pieties of Rufus Choate."[249] Since Howe believed Holmes had simply reiterated *The Common Law* thesis in "The Path of the Law," he pointed out that neither Fuller nor the other Holmes critics had argued that Holmes "was mistaken in saying that the language of morality when used in the law loses much of its ethical content."[250]

Howe came to the conclusion that Fuller's argument that for Holmes law was a solely a matter of fiat, and that Holmes had no interest in the *ought* only the *is*, revealed not simply a misunderstanding of Holmes but a deliberate ("willful") misreading. "It is my thesis," Howe concluded, "that Holmes never laid down the program which Professor Fuller ascribes to him, that from first to last he insisted that the ultimate source of law is the moral judgment of the community. He felt, however, that understanding of the law would be more perceptive than it had been if one saw morality as its source rather than its content."[251]

Howe unfortunately does not elucidate on the difference it would make to view morality as the source of law rather than its content. If the content of law is not

[248] *Id.* at 541; On the continuities in Holmes's thought see Richard A Posner, Overcoming Law 282–83 (1995) (observing that the continuity of Holmes's thought is more remarkable than its eddies).

[249] *Id.*

[250] *Id.*

[251] *Id.* at 541–42.

morality, then what is it? One can imagine Fuller putting his finger right on this sentence and arguing that what Howe gave with his right hand he took away with his left.

Howe may have overextended his argument but he was right in the fundamentals. Over time legal notions had migrated in different directions than moral ones. Law students had to disabuse themselves of the idea that what felt or seemed intuitively "right" in the moral sense and what the law mandated or prohibited had anything other than a circumstantial relationship and sometimes not even that. One was not invariably deducible from the other. Howe, however, did not quite realize that these movements did not occur on the same plane; vertical gaps existed. That is to say, he did not fully see how Holmes had through his melding of analytical and historical arguments created lenses through which to project an integrated, relatively unified common law. The resulting image, like a map, had been scaled to the proportions best suited to meet professional needs.

Or, to change the metaphor, Howe did not see that Holmes wanted legal professionals in the United States to work toward creating a metric – in the sense of a defined, artificial space, as in topology, in which the units that serve to define a continuous space one also uses to measure movement within it. Holmes sensed breaks in experience (experience understood as perceived antecedents, both subjective and objective, to present lawmaking) that historical techniques were powerless to portray. There had been occasional leaps in mentality from one plane to another as well as minute migrations along the planes themselves. But only in retrospect could one surmise that those mental planes even existed. By recurring to psychology he downplayed the radical implications of the breaks. He believed that law, to move forward, had to dialogue with its own past. Yet for law to be aware of and in dialogue with its past, in any strong sense, and still effectively function as *law* in the present required – though Holmes never quite put it this way – the conscious creation of a three-dimensional space in which intelligent fact gathering, adept historical formulation, sophisticated value comparison, and prudent legal decision-making could take place. Learning to see the law in 3D would lead to the creation of the necessary metric, the tool needed for law to develop intelligently.

Howe was aware of both the dynamic and static elements in Holmes's thought but did not understand how Holmes had wanted to find a way to unite them into a single operative framework. For that reason he could articulate a strong defense against Fuller's charge that Holmes delinked law from morality, or that Holmes premised fiat over reason, but he could not quite fathom the purpose behind the bad man.

If Holmes had put forward the dramatic image of the bad man to teach to students the same lessons that he had sought to teach to more mature audiences in *The Common Law*, then Howe admitted it was probably an artistic failure. Still, the carping of Fuller and others on what may have been no more than a bad rhetorical ploy on Holmes's part to bolster their arguments about the substantive defects in Holmes's thought appeared to anger him. They did not see, as he did, that Holmes understood the law as the means by which morality threw off its swaddling and through developed and developing external standards became embedded in the very institutions of a growing, complex society. Howe was right as far as he went but he did not go far enough. The modern world had not decentered Howe's spiritual core to the same extent as it had Holmes's.

Consequently, despite his valiant effort to point out how Holmes's critics had misguidedly interpreted the purpose of the bad man – as a dramatic figure it was not intended to foster cynicism or teach lawyers to become bad people or underhanded, diabolical actors – Howe could still begin "The Positivism of Mr. Justice Holmes's" concluding section on what seems to be a distinctively un-Holmesian note.

> If my efforts thus far have met with any success, I trust that I have demonstrated that Holmes did not deny that a primary source of law is the realm of moral standards in which society has its being, and that he considered the first responsibility of the lawyer and judge to be that of bringing the law into conformity with those moral standards.[252]

In the terms which have guided this study, we would query Howe's use of the phrase "realm of moral standards in which society has its being." Is it within the realm of moral standards that society has its being or is it in the realm of faith? Maybe something similar to The Soldier's Faith? It's hard to say. But we don't have to resolve that issue to note how Howe struggles to find the proper way to describe the relationship in Holmes's thought between morality and law. He did not consider Holmes a positivist in the sense in which that term was bandied about mid-century. But he well understood that Holmes was not a traditional moralist-in-the-law as were, for instance, Joseph Story, James Kent, or Rufus Choate.

Howe ultimately erases the same horizon line that Holmes had in his essay, "Natural Law." Human values were human values; they did not have cosmic significance. Their absolute yearning for the absolute – absolute assurance, absolute conviction, absolute certitude and certainty – had impassioned many of Holmes's detractors. Fuller, who may not have been a traditional advocate of the absolute, was no less disposed against Holmes. The evidence, as Howe suggests, led one to think that Holmes's real offense for Fuller was not his positivism but his moral skepticism.

The question, says Howe, came down to this:

> Are we intellectually willing and emotionally able to accept that total skepticism which led Holmes to question whether man has a cosmic significance 'different in kind from that which belongs to a baboon or a grain of sand'? There are many

[252] *Id.* at 544. Patrick Atiyah rightly expresses reservations on Howe's "insistence that Holmes recognized the importance of morals in the assessment of law as it ought to be." P. S. Atiyah, *The Legacy of Holmes through English Eyes*, 63 B.U. L. Rev. 343, 345 n.22 (1983).

indications that our stomachs are not strong enough to accept the bitter pill which Holmes has tendered us.[253]

And so, without ever admitting it, Howe circles back to the Jesuits, and to Palmer, and even to people behind the scenes like Mortimer Adler (who in 1931 had written that Holmes lived in a "phantasy world of his own construction" and had lamented his "unfortunate and evil influence" on the legal profession).[254] They all, one way or another, upheld the banner of Natural Law. Even Fuller, "who has given to the concept of natural law a meaning substantially different from that which history has given it," sought shelter beneath the "deceptive security of a phrase."[255] Howe fully understood the intellectual travails of the times inhered in the pressing anxiety that the skepticism of Holmes ineluctably led to the unvarnished cynicism, and even worse traits, of a Hitler.

"We have begun to ask ourselves whether, despite Holmes, there are not some standards of decency so fundamental and so permanent that they may properly be described as absolute."[256]

Clearly the issue bothered him. But he threw his lot in with Holmes. He decided to stand by both Holmes's skepticism and how he understood Holmes's faith. At the same time he acknowledged "the never-ending problem of determining through what process and by what standards the influence of morality on law is to be made effective" remained as vital as when Holmes considered the question.[257]

It stands out in retrospect that Howe romanticized Holmes's deep-seated faith in the power of passionate effort. Romanticized in the sense of interpreting Holmes's faith in "the fruitfulness of struggle and action" in terms of vitality, passion, élan, in evincing the spiritually replenishing power of commitment and ardor.[258] Romanticized, also, in how action and drive take on added significance as means for expressing and bringing to realization feelings and ideas and proto-sensibilities that would otherwise remain unexpressed and unrealized. We have interpreted Holmes's faith a bit differently. Instead of the traditional romantic elements we have emphasized the peculiar concentration of drives that the will to survive manifests when fused to belief; how for Holmes the passionate intensity of the effort to overcome danger in war for the sake of duty and honor revealed the culture-making power in its sub-atomic state.

[253] *Id.* at 545.

[254] Fred Rodell remarks that Mortimer Adler, of *The Great Books* fame, reprinted McKinnon's "The Secret of Mr. Justice Holmes" as a pamphlet and added a laudatory foreword. Fred Rodell, *supra* note 226, at 621. For Adler's remarks see Mortimer J. Adler, *Legal Certainty*, *in Symposium*, Law and the Modern Mind, 31 COLUM. L. REV. 97, 107 (1931).

[255] Howe, *supra* note 210, at 545.

[256] *Id.*

[257] *Id.*

[258] For a similar take on the romantic elements in Holmes's self-imposed injunction to live greatly see Ruth Gavison, *Holmes's Heritage: Living Greatly in the Law*, 78 B.U. L. REV. 843, 847–56 (1998); *see also* Anne Dailey, *Holmes and the Romantic Mind*, 48 DUKE L.J. 429, 491–93 (1998).

We also emphasized how the greatest moral experience of Holmes's life, learning the law and its practice, revealed to him the continuity of the culture-making power. What the war magnified the court uniquely beheld. "We all, whether we know it or not, are fighting to make the kind of world that we should like."[259]

Howe did not discuss in "The Positivism of Mr. Justice Holmes" how Holmes's passionate belief in effort and drive worked itself out in the law. He took the fight to Fuller on the issue of skepticism but, strangely, said nothing about how those that believed Holmes had said something vitally important for American law had sought to implement the message. For many legal scholars at mid-century "The Path of the Law" had obtained its eminence precisely because many of their prominent predecessors believed it put a brake on unwarranted, unwarrantable assertions. It had become a commonplace in the preceding era to separate "fact" from "value" and to direct legal scholarship toward the study of fact – ascertainable behavioral patterns or "law in action."

Fuller believed the whole endeavor misguided and incoherent. One could not fully disentangle the *is* from the *ought*. And he laid the blame for this misstep squarely on Holmes. Accordingly, if the editors at the *Harvard Law Review* saw fit to publish a rejoinder to Howe's strong defense of Holmes and equally strong rebuke of Fuller, one would have expected Fuller the polemicist to provide eagerly some steely, serrated words. Steely words came but not from him. Two months after Howe's article, his colleague Henry M. Hart, Jr. – "a former President of the *Review*," dropped the editors in their introductory précis – published his weighty reply.[260]

i *Henry Hart Responds to Howe*

In a chapter from *Patterns of American Jurisprudence*, fittingly entitled "Finding Faith in Reason," Neil Duxbury mentions the mutual intellectual inspiration Henry Hart and Fuller found in each other. Fuller clearly appreciated Hart's (and Hart's collaborator, Albert Sacks's) project, *The Legal Process*, and they in turn gratefully acknowledged his effort to put American jurisprudence on a new footing.[261] However it came to be that Hart would answer Howe – whether Fuller or someone else requested or he volunteered – his article, curiously entitled "Holmes' Positivism – An Addendum," took on a gravelly if collegial tone.[262]

After initial, very brief, academic pleasantries Hart took a Solomonic course. Literally. He split the baby. Well, not exactly split as he cut "The Path of the

[259] Holmes, *supra* note 11, at 446.
[260] Editors, *This Month*, 64 Harv. L. Rev. vii, vii–viii (1951).
[261] Neil Duxbury, Patterns of American Jurisprudence 232–33 (1995).
[262] Henry M. Hart, Jr., *Holmes' Positivism – An Addendum*, 64 Harv. L. Rev. 929 (1951); Robert Summers tells us that Henry Hart and Fuller were particularly close friends. Robert S. Summers, Lon L. Fuller 6, 14 (1984).

Law" into two unequal parts. The first part, consisting roughly of the beginning one-third, ends with Holmes expressing the faint desideratum that perhaps banishing every word of moral significance from the law would result in a net gain. The second part, that begins with the sentence, "So much for the limits of the law[,]" Hart found "intellectually satisfying." The first part he did not.[263]

Nor did he find particularly successful Howe's attempt to stitch together the mismatched pieces. Hart connected the first part of "The Path of the Law" with those legal scholars who believed it vital to focus on what legal officials *do* as opposed to what they say in justification of their action. Hart points to Joseph Walter Bingham, Walter Wheeler Cook, Karl Llewellyn, and, especially, Felix Cohen as representative of those who have taken that first part (using the bad man's point of view) as a guide and would blithely lead others into "the deadly bog of behaviorism."[264]

The reference to behaviorism takes us to the dispute current at that time regarding the proper subject matter for legal study. Even that way of formulating the issue – "proper subject matter for legal study" – is unhelpful because it does not distinguish between *who* wants to study law and *how* and *why*. Howe took pains to point out that Holmes addressed "The Path of the Law" to students. Hart, less interested in its setting, focuses on how Holmes's "positivistic followers," have, given Holmes's prestige, used the first part to impress a behavioristic program on the legal academy. In his criticism we hear echoes of Fuller's objection to the realist program more than a decade earlier.

Oddly, Hart does not footnote or mention Morton White's recent (1947) book, *Social Thought in America: The Revolt against Formalism*.[265] He twice in his "Addendum" uses the word "revolt" to describe the way Howe portrays Holmes's intellectual reaction to certain elements of his culture – a word, incidentally, that Howe does not use.[266] Other than this admittedly weak hint nothing else suggests that he read or knew about White's work. That was unfortunate because in *Social Thought in America* White sees the same paradox or apparent contradiction in "The Path of the Law" that Hart finds and which Hart also believes Howe downplays.[267]

What is the apparent contradiction? It arises from Holmes's refusal to "consider the right or duty as something existing apart from and independent of the consequences of its breach, to which certain sanctions are added afterwards." Hart saw that as the key thesis of the first part of "The Path of the Law," one which supported

[263] Hart, *id.* at 929–31.
[264] *Id.* at 932.
[265] Morton White, Social Thought in America: The Revolt against Formalism (1976 ed.) (orig. pub. 1947).
[266] Hart, *supra* note 262, at 929, 937.
[267] Frederic Kellogg has also noted that Fuller, Henry M. Hart, and Morton White made parallel criticisms of Holmes. Frederic Rogers Kellogg, The Formative Essays of Justice Holmes: The Making of an American Legal Philosophy 58–61 (1984).

Holmes's insistence that law is nothing more than the prophecies of what the courts will do in fact. The gist of the second part lay in the "eye-opening" conclusion that legal professionals should fix their "attention on the purposes of law and 'spend our energy on a study of the ends sought to be attained and the reasons for desiring them.'"[268]

> A modern logician might say that Holmes was denying two things: (1) that the rules of law could be deduced from the principles of ethics, (2) that the concepts of law could be defined in terms of ethics. But curiously enough one of the reasons he gives for denying (1) *seems* to reintroduce moral considerations by suggesting that the law is made by judges who do draw upon considerations of social and moral advantage in making the law. One of the great problems for Holmes' philosophy of law, therefore, is the demonstration of the consistency of these two propositions.[269]

Thus writes White and it well captures the core of Hart's rejoinder to Howe. White elaborates this analysis by identifying a deeper paradox in Holmes's thought, one that White also found in Thorstein Veblen. "The paradox arises from the fact that they sharply separate science and value in some of their writings while in others they suggest the possibility of scientific valuation." White resolves the paradox by noting that for both of these social thinkers "not all empirical statements are statements of value" while, by the same token, "all statements of value are empirical."[270]

In the case of Holmes White finds the needed support for his analysis in "The Path of the Law." He believes Holmes's view of law "as a set of predictions" turns law into a "body of empirical statements."[271] What White means, I think, is that Holmes's emphasis on factual groupings – A takes B's property without A's permission; A petitions the court for redress; the court, because B is unable to restore the property to A, orders B to pay A the fair value of the property as assessed by a jury – reflects Holmes's effort to make law more scientific, that is, to turn law into statements that can be empirically verified (using the best techniques available for clarifying and then confirming or disconfirming statements of fact) or hypotheses that can be tested (one can check to see whether if B does x the court upon A's petition will do y to B) without any reference to morals as commonly understood.

In other words, Holmes for White was trying to find ways of connecting cases (individual groupings of facts called causes that connected with other individual groupings of facts called consequences) that did not require the connecting rods of authority (called precedent) or the deductive chains of morality (what seemed or felt right based upon limited and unrefined internal reference).

The assembled sequences that inquiry isolates, once analytically scrubbed, might reveal – beyond the clearly evident careers of laws in action – a hidden direction.

[268] Hart, *supra* note 262, at 931–32.
[269] White, *supra* note 265, at 69–70 (emphasis in original).
[270] *Id.* at 209–10.
[271] *Id.* at 63.

That direction might demonstrate an evident propensity that had little in common with circulating notions of rights and wrongs or commonly mouthed legal justifications. Various and repeated instances of cases involving redress for the unpermitted takings of property might reveal, for example, that legal officials, without ever quite realizing it, made decisions that, while seeming to side with possessors against disseisors, also showed a tendency to privilege the perceived efficient use of available resources. That use trumped the putative moral prohibition against knowingly taking something that belonged exclusively to someone else. The empirical marshaling and correlating of legal events thus performed a double function.[272]

White argued, correctly, that Holmes oriented his exposition of law toward the practical, the practitioner, toward what Holmes termed a "business-like" understanding of the legal enterprise. Sound predictive ability would, more often than not, engender professional success. A well-founded perception could be a legal game changer. For this reason White understood the bad man as emblematic of the relationship between lawyer and client.[273] Though he did not quite draw this inference, consideration of his point regarding the bad man's purpose suggests that chicanery and the effort to check chicanery created its own feedback loop. At times that loop might generate a brilliant winning legal insight that drew energy from the cumulative but dimly perceived effects of prior legal practice.

White also invoked Holmes's wartime experience to explain Holmes's general orientation but for a different purpose than Howe. It did not inculcate a flinty skepticism but a fierce loyalty: "The business of a lawyer is to defend his client, just as it is the business of a soldier to defend his country, and Holmes' attitude toward his client was not unlike Stephen Decatur's toward his country: he hoped that his client would always be right, but *his* client, right or wrong!"[274]

By invoking Decatur – of "my country right or wrong" fame – White takes us back to Fuller's charge of authoritarianism. It also takes us to Hart's argument that once one begins taking the path that Holmes took in the first part of "The Path of the Law" one inevitably ends up in the bog of behaviorism. To the behaviorists, thoughts, ideas, arguments, moral aspirations mattered little; talk was cheap; identifiable patterns of stimulus and response, on the other hand, potentially revelatory. White did not take such a surly view. But White was not a lawyer. He was not being tarred with the brush of belonging to an amoral profession operating under the

[272] If I am correct in my reading of Morton White then he understood Holmes on this point in a manner similar to some of the most prominent legal realists. *See* Mark Steven Mendell, Pragmatism and Legal Reasoning 186–87 (1989) (unpublished Ph.D. dissertation, University of Pennsylvania) (on file with the University of Pennsylvania repository); Karl Llewellyn, *Some Realism about Realism*, 44 Harv. L. Rev. 1222, 1241 n.46 (1931) (noting that correlations of fact-situations and outcomes may bring out a hidden factor in past uncertainty).

[273] White, *supra* note 265, at 64–68.

[274] *Id.* at 66 (emphasis in original).

state's blessing. Yet at the same time he understood very well the root problem that underlay Fuller and Hart's concerns: could one derive the *ought* from the *is*?

White contended that Holmes's apparent belief that one could do so guided the famous opening passages of *The Common Law* and what Hart called the second part of "The Path of the Law." But White found that Holmes stopped short in explaining how it could be done. He was not alone in this shortcoming. Veblen also stopped short and even the great Dewey, who did recognize the problem and did not stop short, faltered in his explanation.

White summarized the matter through three propositions. The first, that not all empirical statements are statements of value, showed that the domain of the empirical was far greater than the domain of value. The second, that all statements of value are empirical, pointed toward the substance of (legal) study, how one could begin to isolate specific statements of value based upon the "characteristic of being liked, desired, wanted, satisfying." And the third, that no ethical statement is empirical, pointed up the immense difficulty – White did not think it impossible – of deriving an *ought* (in the sense of an ethical obligation) from empirical statements of value.[275]

To the extent that Hart followed Fuller he overcame the problem by bypassing it. The *ought* was already baked into the *is* and vice versa. This response might not satisfy analytical purists but it had the advantage of reflecting the actualities of purpose-driven human action or conduct (*not* behavior). Purposive activity is the common denominator for Hart. For that reason he did not think it possible to fit together the two parts of "The Path of the Law." "For if law is the purposive pursuit of ends, Holmes' 'cart' is the horse and his 'horse' is the cart."[276]

That reference, to remind the reader, comes from "The Path of the Law"'s opening section:

> The primary rights and duties with which jurisprudence busies itself again are nothing but prophecies. One of the many evil effects of the confusion between legal and moral ideas, . . . is that theory is apt to get the cart before the horse, and to consider the right or duty as something existing apart from and independent of the consequences of its breach, to which certain sanctions are added afterwards.[277]

Hart believed this way of looking at law – centering as it does on sanctions – prioritized conflict over cooperation, means of repair over modes of operation. The purpose of law was to enable people to live better lives, just as the purpose of a car was to facilitate transportation. To focus attention on legal consequences and call that the essence of law was no different than saying that people primarily drove cars to avoid being injured in a car accident.[278]

[275] *Id.* at 211–12.
[276] Hart, *supra* note 262, at 935.
[277] Holmes, *The Path of the Law*, *supra* note 14, at 391.
[278] *See* Michal Alberstein, Pragmatism and Law 125–26 (2002).

Unsurprisingly, Hart could not fathom the point of the bad man. "Why that helps [to look at the law the way the bad man does], unless to make us more effective counsellors [*sic*] of evil, I have never understood . . . . Is a lawyer serving either his client or his profession well if he predicates his advice simply on the likelihood of the client's being caught, and on what would happen if he were?"[279]

Hart here states an opinion that probably had a number of adherents in the 1950s legal community. He may not have described the relation between the bad man and the law with the same logical subtlety as Fred Rodell – who explained away Holmes's "shocker" that all "law really amounts to is what a bad man cannot get away with" as justifiably expressing Holmes's hatred of humbug[280] – but he was as firmly convinced as Fuller that Holmes's effort to isolate law from morals would only work ill on the legal community.

ii *Howe's Short Reply to Henry Hart*

Like Hart, Howe does not mention Morton White, either in his initial article or his brief rejoinder to Hart. It's a bit odd given that White also taught at Harvard (in the Philosophy Department) and *Social Thought in America* made somewhat of a splash when it came out. Isaiah Berlin gave it a rave review in *Mind* and Arthur O. Lovejoy sent White a complimentary letter.[281] Yet despite White's artful showing of why Holmes deserved to be included in the early twentieth-century liberal pantheon, Howe makes no reference.

I find it especially curious because White clearly had a sense of the infighting within the legal community over Holmes's legacy. "Those who cite his demand for a purge of the legal vocabulary claim him as a brutal positivist who would eliminate all interest in morals, a stern advocate of (legal) justice under a falling heaven."[282]

White's reference to a "falling heaven" seems quite in keeping with Howe's insistence – which he reiterates in his reply to Hart – that much of the animus directed against Holmes arose from Holmes's refusal to believe in, or countenance, a "morality laden with the implications of the absolute."[283] Fred Rodell made a similar argument against Holmes's hecklers, as did, more distantly, a then unchastened Jerome Frank in his 1930 *Law and the Modern Mind*.[284]

The absence of any acknowledgment of White's work may have been due, I speculate, to Howe's aversion to the style in which White wrote. Despite its evident virtues – historical sensitivity and analytical sophistication and lucid exposition – *Social Thought in America* presented a peculiarly placid rendition of the thinking of

[279] Hart, *supra* note 262, at 932.
[280] Rodell, *supra* note 226, at 623.
[281] Morton White, A Philosopher's Story 72–73 (1999).
[282] White, *supra* note 265, at 68.
[283] Mark DeWolfe Howe, *Holmes' Positivism – A Brief Rejoinder*, 64 Harv. L. Rev. 938 (1951).
[284] Rodell, *supra* note 226, at 622–24; Jerome Frank, Law and the Modern Mind 253–60 (1930).

its leading characters. If Holmes, Dewey, Veblen, and historians Charles Beard and John Harvey Robinson were *revolting* against formalism, how White told that tale was, ironically, fairly phlegmatic. For Howe, possessed as he was in 1951 with a pressing sense of the magnitude of the loss of faith that Holmes underwent, White might just as well have written the book in a neighboring dialect instead of from a neighboring discipline.

It is truly an occasion for regret that Howe died before finishing the Holmes biography. Howe's inherent and acquired intellectual virtues, his interest in the course of this civilization called America, his sense of place and of times, his moral commitment, his finesse and courtesy, distinctly mark him as a representative scholar of a prior generation. Howe may have unduly amplified the extent to which Holmes believed in the promise of American life. Yet he shared Holmes's strong loyalty to their forerunners. If he did not quite have Holmes's spiritual range that is no slight against Howe. Even Holmes was not always sure of what he heard or saw or what it meant.

11 THE PRAGMATIST VIEW: THE BAD MAN AS HEURISTIC

Published in a Canadian journal, philosopher Moses J. Aronson's 1941 overview of modern American jurisprudence identifies Holmes as a watershed. Holmes inspired a multitude of jurisprudential streams. He was a genius of many intellectual moods; these moods, Aronson notes, reflected "a temperament too rich to permit itself to be constricted by the bonds of scholastic logic, and perhaps in a deeper sense mirroring the spiritual disintegration of his times."[285] Read with some latitude (both semantically and chronologically), this characterization of Holmes brings into greater balance Howe's strong feel for Holmes's deep-seated skepticism and Henry Hart's decided opinion that Holmes was one of the people most responsible for teaching his generation to see that "[l]aw as it *is* is a continuous process of *becoming*."[286]

Hart's claim brings to mind this quote from *The Common Law*: "However much we may codify law into a series of seemingly self-sufficient propositions, those propositions will be but a phase in a continuous growth."[287]

Quite apart from whether Holmes's separating – or, less strongly, distinguishing[288] – law from morality was either warranted or wise, lay a somewhat more pedestrian question: how do you teach something that is in a continuous process of becoming? Language is tricky when dealing with such recondite matters. It may be that analytically most definitions of "is" and "becoming" will end in paradox, but

285 Moses J. Aronson, *Tendencies in American Jurisprudence*, 4 U. Toronto L.J. 90, 92–93 (1941).

286 Hart, *supra* note 262, at 930 (emphasis in original).

287 Holmes, *The Common Law*, *supra* note 14, at 133.

288 *See* Wilfred E. Rumble, American Legal Realism: Skepticism, Reform, and the Judicial Process 42 (1968).

practicing lawyers still have the mundane task, after explaining to the Court why they are standing there, to respond to the slightly raised eyebrow – "what is the law?"

Alongside the fact that most lawyers will answer this question by stating the law in a way favorable to their cause, lies the less frequent occurrence (or more frequent depending on the type of court) of the individual appearing *pro se* who typically cannot tell the court what the law is but can quite emphatically answer that other raised eyebrow question: "What do you want the court to do?"

Separating these two questions for the dual purpose of both clarifying the applicable law, if any, and clarifying the pressing desire may help in understanding what is a dominant motif in the scholarly commentary on Holmes's bad man.

It is a heuristic many scholars say. And as far as I can tell, Aronson was the first to put it exactly that way. Holmes, "propelled by a sort of atavistic reversion to the Austinianism of his youth," according to Aronson, invented "the ingenious methodological device of the 'bad man'[.]"

> Interpreted as it should be in the spirit in which it was formulated and in the light of the total context of Holmes's thought, this observation reveals a profound insight – the insight namely that no good can come from confusing the body of rules formulated by the legislature and the judiciary which alone deserves to be called law, with the ethical, religious, temperamental, or other motives which entered into the purely legal pronouncement.[289]

Aronson calls this ingenious methodological device the "heuristic bad man,"[290] and thus initiates a distinctive line of commentary.

Aronson's description of the bad man's purpose as a methodological device – preventing confusion of law as formulated in legislative or judicial rules with "the other motives that enter into the purely legal pronouncement" – is, as stated, difficult to understand. It begs the issue of the criteria one must use to separate out the "law" aspect of a rule from the "other motives" that have entered into the pronouncement. He seems to want to emphasize the Austinian idea of the use of sovereign force as the sine qua non of law but that provides little methodological guidance.

But this notion of the bad man as a heuristic has gotten a tremendous amount of play over the decades. Even when the word is not used, many commentators have understood Holmes's point in introducing the bad man as in some sense pedagogical. Tufts thought the bad man might lead to clearer legal thinking; Fuller thought not. Frank thought it would help focus attention where the legal action really took place, the specific lawsuit that meted out specific sanctions for specific words or deeds. Zane believed for that very reason Holmes showed beyond a shadow of a doubt he had no grasp of law. Yntema drew the inference that the bad man

289 Aronson, *supra* note 285, at 95–96.
290 *Id.*

helped create the needed objectivity for legal study to take place – it helped create the right frame of mind, the necessary objective outlook – and Cook seemed to agree since it, as an essential aspect of the scientific method, would help the law student turn law into a living system.

Howe held Holmes made a poor rhetorical choice by using the bad man to convey a deeply important point, namely that terms common to both morality and law frequently confuse legal thinking. The meaning of terms once exclusive to the moral domain had shifted to another domain, the legal. Moral standards had evolved into legal standards. The legal meaning no longer perfectly corresponded with the moral one. Henry Hart didn't see much use for the bad man. Perhaps on a different day, in a more charitable mood, he might have agreed with Aronson's point that the bad man expressed Holmes's positivism, either in the Austinian sense or in the more generalized sense that sought to keep statements of fact separated from statements of value, but that, of course, was no cause for celebration.

Morton White inferred Holmes used the bad man to emphasize the professional or businesslike aspect of the lawyer–client relationship. He did not connect that specifically with a heuristic intent but it seems to be lurking in the background. On the other hand, in his famous book published a dozen or so years after White's, H. L. A. Hart pooh-poohed the whole "bad man as heuristic" idea. He seemed to suggest that if that was the best Holmes could do then he did Harvard a favor by resigning his professorial post after a few short months to take a judgeship. Why the bad man?, this Hart asked. Why wouldn't the law be more open or accessible to the "puzzled man" or the "ignorant man" or the "prudent let-me-get-my-affairs-in-order man"? Why all this focus on sanctions when the essence of law as a form of social control lies in how it helps people plan their lives?[291]

The list of commentators who have in one manner or another referred to the bad man as heuristic could go on for many paragraphs. Often missing is any detailed discussion of how Holmes meant it to work. A heuristic, before it became a mainstay of behavioral economics, typically meant, in an educational context, something that enabled a person to discover or learn something for him or herself.[292] Using this definition as a test, we can eliminate those just discussed – who haven't already, by dismissing or damning the idea, eliminated themselves – except for Morton White.

The notion that the bad man invokes the lawyer–client relationship seems to capture well the emphases of the first few paragraphs of "The Path of the Law." The emphasis on law as a business ("the business of a lawyer is to know law"), that a lawyer is selling professional judgment, that the study of law has a strong practical side, that studying or determining the law's reach is a constant, never-ending

[291] H. L. A. Hart, The Concept of Law 40 (2d ed. 1994).

[292] *See, e.g., Heuristic*, American Heritage Dictionary of the English Language (5th ed. 2011) ("Of or constituting an educational method in which learning takes place through discoveries that result from investigations made by the student.").

professional endeavor, all these points and others give credence to the idea that the central institutional relationship in law – at least for heuristic purposes – is the lawyer–client one. It gives the law student a specific frame of reference and implicitly poses the question – how can I best help my client? – that serves to guide study and distill legal knowledge from legal learning.

Given White's dedication to pragmatism, it comes as no surprise that other commentators with pragmatist leanings tend to see the bad man's purpose in a similar way. The basic interpretive gambit is to connect the bad man's concern with state action with the idea of prediction of what the courts will do and to put the law student in the middle, between the bad man and the court. Thus, to learn the law, and to escape the dangers to legal virtue and competence that improperly superimposed moral frames of reference represent, the law student must look at the law as if she or he had a bad man (or a bad woman) as a client. That seems clear enough. It is an approach law students can use to effectively integrate themselves into the vast body of the living law. The emphasis on discerning conceivable consequences, that the meaning of the law lies in its conceivable sanctions under conceivably pertinent circumstances, makes this particular approach conceivable pragmatically. Or at least it seems to.

Even before White, renowned Peirce scholar Max Fisch considered Holmes's prediction theory "to be the only systematic application of pragmatism that has yet been made."[293] Fisch wrote this in 1942. He believed "the most striking fact about it . . . is that it clearly conceives the law not from the legislator's or judge's point of view but from that of the practicing lawyer."[294] Fisch initially strongly connected Holmes with the founders of pragmatism via the Metaphysical Club – which has since become a time-honored article of faith even though Fisch ultimately had doubts[295] – and even ventured to suggest, unexpectedly, that Peirce's formulation of the core tenet of pragmatism had as much to do "with the methods of practicing lawyers" as those of the experimental sciences.[296]

Being unusually historically minded Fisch also wondered: "The historian would like to know out of what need pragmatism grew?" His answer, also surprising, is really quite important.

> The only application of the doctrine put into print during the Club's lifetime was Holmes's first formulation of the prediction theory of law. In 1871, Holmes was appointed University Lecturer on Jurisprudence for the following school year. For the first time he thus had need to define not only the fundamental legal concepts

[293] PEIRCE, SEMEIOTIC, AND PRAGMATISM: ESSAYS BY MAX H. FISCH 8 (Kenneth Laine Ketner & Christian J. W. Kloesel eds., 1986).

[294] *Id.*

[295] *Id.* at 293.

[296] *Id.* at 9.

> but the concept of law itself. This, I suggest, was the need under pressure of which both the prediction theory and pragmatism took form.[297]

At this point we note without elaboration that Fisch's thesis reminds one of what William Gardiner Hammond wrote to Holmes in an 1879 letter. "I have long been convinced that the growth of our law schools, and the marked change of the method of professional training from mere office-work to systematic instruction must logically involve a re-formulation of the law itself."[298]

The resurgent interest in pragmatism in the 1980s did much to draw scholarly attention to the resemblances between Holmes's thought and that of the leading American pragmatists, especially Peirce and Dewey. No one, however, directly followed up on Fisch's argument that the formulation and extension of pragmatism's leading methodological idea – Peirce's conception of meaning – had as much to do with the practices of lawyers and the emergent needs of law school professors as with the methods of the experimental sciences. Nor did anyone take very seriously Howe's corollary contribution. He had suggested that how Holmes and Nicholas St. John Green viewed the function of evidence – to foster working beliefs in the jury – contained the first semblance of what eventually became the pragmatic outlook.[299]

But on the plus side the then persistent opinion, despite repeated objections, that pictured Holmes as an unregenerate positivist in the stereotypically Austinian mode – as Aronson had indicated in his survey – began to finally liquefy under the glare of strong scrutiny. Holmes the pragmatist, or the founder of legal pragmatism, came back into vogue. It thus behooves us to take a closer look at a few scholars (Frederic R. Kellogg, Thomas C. Grey, Catharine Pierce Wells, and Susan Haack) who have taken this perspective to see what we can learn from them about the bad man.

[297] *Id.* at 9–12.

[298] *See* David M. Rabban, Law's History: American Legal Thought and the Transatlantic Turn to History 225 (2013); *see also* Thomas C. Grey, *Holmes and Legal Pragmatism*, 41 Stan. L. Rev. 787, 825 (1989) ("The spread of university-based legal education had created new demand for an intelligible curriculum and courses, and as members of a new full-time professoriate, with the time and the incentive to do scholarship, Holmes's contemporaries saw meeting that demand as their primary task and opportunity.").

[299] Howe, *supra* note 166, at 268–69 ("In those gatherings of lawyers and philosophers Holmes and Nicholas St. John Green brought a common attitude towards law to bear on the problems of philosophy. They exposed their philosopher friends to the common-law lawyer's distrust of general principles and by the vigor of their challenge drove the philosophers towards pragmatism."). *See also* Jerome Frank, *A Conflict with Oblivion: Some Observations on the Founders of Legal Pragmatism*, 9 Rutgers L. Rev. 425, 434–52 (1954).

i *Frederic R. Kellogg*

The first notable effort in the pragmatist resurgence belongs to Frederic Kellogg. In his 1984 *The Formative Essays of Justice Holmes*, the first of his three published books on Holmes, Kellogg developed Fisch's point that Holmes's prediction theory reflected Peirce's pragmatic maxim of meaning.[300] But what makes Kellogg's study important, and distinct from predecessors, is his concern to show the path that led Holmes from his early preoccupation with legal categorization to one that emphasized instead the operative quality of law.

Kellogg focuses on what he calls "the formative essays" – selected articles Holmes wrote prior to *The Common Law* – because he finds there the needed steps to adequately appraise Holmes's achievement in *The Common Law* and after. Though Holmes from the start dissented from Austin's emphasis on the priority of rights over duties – Holmes believed the opposite – he retained Austin's conviction that law should be a science. This requirement meant, at minimum, that law should be organized into a body of knowledge. But how? Austin suggested the use of sovereign command as a way of scoring the legal from the nonlegal, and the use of legal right as the controlling concept for categorizing positive laws and showing how distinct areas of law related to one another.

Holmes, Kellogg argues, did not think it possible to demarcate definitively the legal from the nonlegal. More important, he believed duties more basic than rights because the existent law showed various instances of operative duties without any correlating rights. The two were not coextensive. Second, duties as ordinarily conceived in the law were not coextensive with sanctions. One could face a sanction (such as a tax) and yet have no duty to not perform the act that led to the sanction.[301]

Beyond the evident logical problems with Austin's analytic approach lay latent issues with the law itself as a subject of knowledge. On this point Kellogg first discusses Nicholas St. John Green. In his article entitled "Slander and Libel" Green undertook to show, using the same combination of analytic and historical methods that Holmes would ultimately use in *The Common Law*, that what was generally referred to as the law of slander and libel was not law at all, at least in the sense of arising from a general principle or group of principles. In fact just the opposite: "The latest decided cases upon this subject *make the law*."[302]

Green was led to conclude that no general principles existed in this branch of the law through painstaking historical investigation. What appeared to be general

[300] Kellogg, *supra* note 267, at 48–57. One could also find the same basic argument in Frank, *id.* at 428–29 and Edwin W. Patterson, Jurisprudence: Men and Ideas of the Law 12–121, 465–508 (1951). These in turn relied partly on Philip P. Wiener, Evolution and the Founders of Pragmatism 152–89 (1949) as well as on Fisch. Kellogg's other books are Frederick Kellogg, Oliver Wendell Holmes, Jr., Legal Theory, and Judicial Restraint (2007) and Oliver Wendell Holmes Jr. and Legal Logic (2018).

[301] Kellogg, *supra* note 267, at 23–41.

[302] *Id.* at 15–17; Nicholas St John Green, *Slander and Libel*, 6 Am. L. Rev. 593, 612 (1872) (emphasis in original).

principles were, upon close historical inspection and analytical criticism, predicated upon an "unessential similarity." Kellogg believed Green's proposition, if extended to other areas of the law, could "threaten the legitimacy of the entire pure analytical approach to law."[303]

Holmes employed the same methods as Green and came to a similar conclusion, that nonlogical origins lay behind the supposedly logical substantive content of the law. Holmes put it even more strongly: the nonlogical played a fundamental part in both the origin *and* the development of law. Kellogg observes that once Holmes realized this view's full implications, he rejected the Austinian mode of demarcating a boundary for law through a preestablished empirical base (the sovereign's verifiable commands).[304]

The deficiencies in the Austinian approach to organizing existing law (Kellogg includes utilitarianism in this approach) eventually led Holmes to conceptualize legal phenomena in terms of action (susceptibility to liability) instead of thought (logical categorization). This was the key move that Kellogg says cannot be rightly appreciated unless placed within the trajectory of Holmes's thinking during the formative period (1872–80). Holmes retained two intertwined goals from his Austinian period, making law a "scientific" body of knowledge and excising false conceptual essences from the methods of legal inquiry. But after his epiphany of how law worked historically (that is, in my words, how legal participants sought to achieve external results that satisfied pressing needs with a minimum of internal dislocation), Holmes, Kellogg says, moved toward a hermeneutic that understood fundamental legal concepts primarily in terms of their effects instead of their intensive structure or their logical relationship with other leading conceptions.[305] Or in less freighted words, Holmes came to the epiphany that law, in itself, is a process of inquiry.[306]

Holmes thus developed a way of analyzing legal concepts – such as possession – that mirrored the way Peirce employed his pragmatic maxim. "[W]hat the law *does* is what the law conceptually *is*. This is extremely close to the Peircean precept[.]"[307] Kellogg uses Holmes's analysis of the legal concept of possession – how the concept is intellectually justified or why the concept is legally sound – to illustrate how Holmes searched in the past for certain triggers (what caused the court to act) that eventually became abstracted and formalized in the common law (as causes of action). Thus in the case of possession what recurred as an essential similarity across the cases was the court's recognition that the holder of property's intent to exclude others deserved the law's protection. It was a recognition that depended as much on the enforcement procedures that had historically arisen and developed as on any conscious rationale.[308]

303 Kellogg, *supra* note 267, at 17.
304 *Id.* at 22.
305 *Id.* at 42–57.
306 *Id.* at xi.
307 *Id.* at 56.
308 *Id.* at 54–57.

Kellogg thus reorients the understanding of Holmes as a theorist of law away from the "positivism" of Austin or subsequent legal realists to one that emphasizes the common law's historical practices and developed (and developing) causes of action. Kellogg sees a connection between common law ways of reasoning and the pragmatic maxim of meaning. The linchpin is Holmes. Kellogg does not directly address Fisch's suggestion that the origin of Peirce's maxim might have had much to do with the methods of practicing lawyers. That's unfortunate because Kellogg is a practitioner and worked as one when he wrote the book. His take on Fisch's thesis might have led to some interesting insights.

But perhaps I am being too shortsighted. Kellogg does, after all, single out Fisch's "prescient suggestion" that "Holmes's prediction theory of law was a trademark of the pragmatic reduction of concepts to effects."[309] He also develops the connections between Holmes's prediction theory and what John Dewey called the method of "extensive abstraction." That method, inspired by Peirce, defined concepts in terms of the observable relations between objects (their noted effects upon each other). It compactly provided a formula to the whole of Holmes's legal philosophy: it reduced "legal categories to their operations and the law itself from a logical system of doctrine to a developing set of causes of action."[310]

Where does the lawyer–client relationship, or the bad man heuristic, fit in Kellogg's interpretation? That is not an easy question to answer. Kellogg does not mention the bad man. He seems to purposefully avoid doing so. He does, however, respond to the Fuller–Hart criticism that Holmes merely extended Austin's separation of law and morals. Kellogg believes that criticism failed to recognize that Holmes, unlike Austin, did not see a "real boundary" between law and morals but rather a "pedagogical one." Neither did Holmes see law as in some sense a substantive entity. Kellogg accordingly maintains that the prediction theory is "less a definition of law than a tendency to abstain from defining it."[311]

This statement is paradoxical, especially given how Holmes describes in "Path" his definition of "law" (what the courts will do in fact). Kellogg undoubtedly knows this but is trying, valiantly one might add, to refocus the prediction theory in a way that does justice to what he believes to be its overriding virtue (that is, its directing attention to *inquiry*).

The prediction theory corresponds to Peirce's focus on effects. That is the first point. The second, following Dewey's "extensive abstraction," is that the relevant effects – strictly for the purpose of identifying law apart from morals or other forms of social control – are those existing and developing causes of action that reflect entrenched manifestations of legal liability. Like Green, Holmes used analytical and historical methods to tease out the operative legal concepts (like intent to

309 *Id.* at 69.
310 *Id.* at 65.
311 *Id.* at 67, 72.

exclude) from nonlogical origins or extraneous nonlegal phenomena or events. Both men recognized that operative legal concepts rested at all times on more than logic. Once it is discovered that the same method of restricting legal concepts to their effects or operations both clarifies the past (separates the legal from the nonlegal) and illuminates the present (by preventing prevailing moral or political notions from occluding the actual operations of law), then, and this is the third main point, existing law or proposed law is ready to undergo evaluation and testing.

To be fair, Kellogg does not expressly take this last step. He believes that Holmes's method optimally clarifies existing law (enforced values) and best articulates the relevant legal choices when the court is facing a hard case. But it is not solely up to the court, institutionally speaking, to make the final decision, to make the law. Kellogg might agree with Holmes that at times judges have the sovereign prerogative of choice but he thinks that prerogative ought to be used sparingly.[312]

In the end, Kellogg believes Holmes never relinquished the hope he shared with Austin to establish law as a scientific discipline. He just took a radically different route. In his formative essays he developed a method identifiably pragmatic, one that sought to clarify existing law in light of its historic antecedents and through a logic that reduced legal conceptions to their realized and realizable effects. He would further burnish this fundamental insight that law is best understood as a process of (social) inquiry in the pages of *The Common Law*.

ii *Thomas C. Grey*

In his 1996 keynote address at Brooklyn Law School's symposium, "*The Path of the Law* 100 Years Later: Holmes's Influence on Modern Jurisprudence," Judge Posner identified Thomas Grey as the foremost student of Holmes's thought.[313] Grey's reputation as a Holmes scholar rested largely on his classic 1989 article, "Holmes and Legal Pragmatism."[314] Yet his earlier piece on Langdell ("Langdell's Orthodoxy"[315]) also helped to establish his reputation as a serious student of American legal theory.

Grey also participated in the Brooklyn Law School symposium. His contribution, "Plotting the Path of the Law,"[316] represents his analysis after many years of studying and teaching the essay. It well serves as an entry point into a complex analysis of Holmes and the bad man.

[312] He develops this theme in his OLIVER WENDELL HOLMES, JR., LEGAL THEORY, AND JUDICIAL RESTRAINT, *supra* note 300. On Holmes's view see Thomas C. Grey, *Molecular Motions: The Holmesian Judge in Theory and Practice*, 37 WM. & MARY L. REV. 19, 33–37 (1995).

[313] Richard A. Posner, *Foreword: Holmes*, 63 BROOK. L. REV. 7, 9 (1997).

[314] Grey, *supra* note 298.

[315] Thomas C. Grey, *Langdell's Orthodoxy*, 45 U. PITT. L. REV. 1 (1983).

[316] Thomas C. Grey, *Plotting the Path of the Law*, 63 BROOK. L. REV. 19 (1997).

"Plotting the Path of the Law" shows what happens when an interpreter, even one as thorough, conscientious, sophisticated, and nuanced as Grey, attempts to open up "The Path of the Law" without first appreciating Holmes's use of backsight or hindsight – that is to say, Holmes's acquired habit of taking a longitudinal look into events, of seeking in the law's past the needed reference points from which to triangulate into the future.

Instead, Grey's approach is to superimpose a literary trope upon "Path," one he calls a quest narrative. At first glance the use of the quest trope seems a bit contrived, but a careful reading of the article in light of Grey's other published works on Holmes shows how Grey ingeniously uses it to integrate into his interpretation all the most important elements that make up for him Holmes's legal pragmatism.

Grey justifies his interpretive use of the quest narrative by pointing out that the strongest clue Holmes intended to employ the "descent–ascent" structure intrinsic to the quest narrative is "the stark contrast between the way law is portrayed at the beginning and the end of the essay." Instead of dividing "Path" into two main sections, as did Henry Hart, Grey divides it into three principal parts, along with an introduction and a conclusion. These divisions, Grey argues, reveal an intrinsic structure that takes the hearer or reader through an intellectual journey into law that Holmes probably meant to mimic in form the standard account of scientific progress. That account, loosely speaking, represented the growth of science as equivalent to the growth of enlightenment, an account of how the mind, with reason's aid, pulled itself out of the mire of convention and superstition and, again through reason's continued assistance and direction, reached that high plateau from which it could catch sight of the universal law.[317]

In a manner reminiscent of postmodern literary critics, Grey's suspicions that there may be more to "Path" than meets the eye were first aroused by the evident cracks in the surface reading. Of these he notes three prominent incongruities. The first and most pronounced is the dramatic shift in tone from the introduction to the conclusion.[318] Somehow we go from the opening sentence, "When we study law we are not studying a mystery but a well-known profession[,]" to the closing ones thirty-three paragraphs later: "The remoter and more general aspects of the law are those which give it universal interest. It is through them that you not only become a great master in your calling, but connect your subject with the universe and catch an echo of the infinite, a glimpse of its unfathomable process, a hint of the universal law."[319]

"Nowhere," says Grey, "does he [Holmes] say how a single phenomenon can be at once so reduced and so exalted."[320] Indeed, he does not.

[317] *Id.* at 19–29.
[318] *Id.* at 25–27.
[319] Holmes, *The Path of the Law, supra* note 14, at 391, 406.
[320] Grey, *supra* note 316, at 25.

The second and third incongruities arise from how part I, which Grey describes as encapsulating Holmes's thesis on the limits of the law, fails to connect to part II, which reiterates the famous not-logic-but-experience theme, and even appears to contradict part III in which Holmes advances his ideal of the law as instrumental reason. In the nomenclature of American legal theory, part I is formalist or positivist (law as autonomous), part II realist in a historical and sociological sense (law as functional), and part III reflects what would become a Progressive utilitarianism (law as instrumental) that belies the evident moral skepticism of part I.[321]

Grey in his own pithy manner has summarized almost a century's worth of interpretations of "Path." The essay's incongruities, breaks, stark contrasts, and abrupt movements from part to part without much if any transition Grey attributes to Holmes's conscious rhetorical design. The quest narrative's structure and Holmes's free use of hyperbole and paradox (Grey provides many examples)[322] cast an aura of retrospective romance around Holmes's portrayal of an American lawyer's picaresque course from neophyte grasshopper to weathered practitioner. Holmes's literary craftsmanship made an otherwise random and potentially devitalizing sequence of events into a journey that became meaningful, that invigorated. The seeming incongruities between the different parts exist more as rhetorical devices than irreconcilable jurisprudential positions. The parts taken together actually reflect Holmes's mature jurisprudence, his legal pragmatism. But in reading "Path" Grey insists one must keep in mind that Holmes wanted much more to be remembered than to be understood. Grey grants that he succeeded; that people like me over a 120 years later are still reading and writing about "The Path of the Law" is Holmes's "unjust reward for writing well, a meretricious immortality won by mastery of rhetorical tricks."[323]

The more I think about this particular assessment of both "Path" and Holmes the more it astounds me. It brings to mind how a Catholic writer from Virginia I once met described Thomas Merton, the celebrated Trappist monk who wrote a bestselling twentieth-century memoir about his odyssey to Catholicism. Merton, he said, was 50 percent holiness and 50 percent phoniness. Fifty percent holiness, he added after a sip, was an awful lot of holiness.

In a strange way Grey functions as an intellectual transformer in how his mature opinion on Holmes brings together various historical currents. We see something of Frank's admiration, Zane's disgruntlement, Yntema's insight, Cook's analytical clarity, Fuller's sweeping present-mindedness, Howe's textual fidelity, and Lucey's knowing, self-assured moral abhorrence.[324] It all coalesces in how Grey treats "The

[321] *Id.* at 25–27.
[322] *Id.* at 29–35.
[323] *Id.* at 57.
[324] On the last point see Grey, *supra* note 298, at 792 ("It is easy to list the man's repulsive aspects").

Path of the Law": not – as one might expect – as a jurisprudential masterpiece, but as a piece of (jurisprudential) performance art, equal emphasis on the performance and on the art.

The conclusion should be inescapable that if "Path" narratively emplots a quest, it is Holmes's own youthful quest for assurance that he had not wasted his talents in choosing the sordid practice of law as his profession. And Grey does make that connection. But he does not stop there nor does he collapse the art into the performance. The art is still important, very important. It lies in Holmes's concentrated attention to how the practice of law, sordid or otherwise, established the best perspective from which to fathom, understand, critique, and frame the law's guiding conceptions.

In seeing the significance of the practice of law as the fundamental theme of "Path," one would expect Grey to address in his articles how prior scholars who also saw strong connections between America's only indigenous philosophy and its common law practice or its leading legal theorist had developed those points. But there is very little of that. Beyond obligatory footnotes, he does not discuss how Philip P. Wiener laid out the all-important scientific, evolutionary framework, or Max Fisch's suggestion that legal practices may have influenced Peirce's formulation of his maxim of meaning as much as the experimental sciences. He does not refer to Morton White's idea that the bad man is emblematic of the lawyer–client relationship. Nor does he, surprisingly, engage with Frederic Kellogg, who had traveled if not the same then at least on a parallel path of inquiry in the early eighties.

Grey is not alone in his lack of overt, sustained engagement with the work of others. It is probably a defining characteristic of modern American legal scholarship. That is to say, the practice of modern American legal scholarship requires in most cases only a cursory interaction with the work of other scholars – usually through a footnote acknowledgement – unless there is a very specific, usually political, dispute to be threshed out or a position to be attacked or defended. In articulating one's own views the unspoken rule seems to be to ignore, distinguish, or damn with faint praise what came before unless the circumstances require one to straightforwardly criticize. We have seen plenty of examples of this tendency in our own chronicle of the different perspectives taken on the bad man. Fuller never really discusses Yntema or Cook, they don't say much about Zane, Howe brushes off the Jesuits, the Jesuits ignore Tufts and ridicule Frank, Frank insults and then ignores Zane, Zane has his own axe to grind, and the hard thinking everyone has undertaken to understand and communicate something important about American law typically gets lost in the standard drill of scholarly or not-so-scholarly legal argument.

It's an intellectually wasteful, unproductive state of affairs. It's also sad. If we are feeling unkind we can pin the blame on Holmes. In his own scholarly work he set a bad example. I am sure it is no news to the law professors that the practice of academic law can in its own way be as empty and as sordid as everyday legal practice.

Even so, I did not digress to the topic of modern legal scholarship because I think Grey has somehow fallen below the workaday ethic of academic lawyers – I don't – but because Grey's focus on the centrality of practice implicates what lawyers do in their studies and offices, in courtrooms and classrooms. And in the pages of law reviews.[325]

The manner in which Grey introduces the bad man makes for an interesting comparison to Frank and Yntema. The bad man's chief value for Frank lay in how Holmes's metaphor widened the scope of the student's vision. All actual legal events and the processes and sub-processes that constitute those events are the proper subject matter of legal study. "Actual" in this sense includes those actions or behaviors that have been typically ignored or slighted or just not seen because of social proclivities or blinding preferences. Something of the expose exists in Frank's use, something that ties into the traditions of journalistic muckraking and literary naturalism. He took special satisfaction in pointing out, repeatedly, how the sausage was made.[326]

Yntema, on the other hand, sees the bad man's primary use as the means for narrowing and sharpening the student's vision. For him the bad man objectifies the domain needed for scientific legal analysis. It marks that domain off from the subjective world, that of habit, custom, history, prejudice, morals. Isolating and demarcating the objective domain is the primary move one must make before engaging in the investigation and subsequent evaluation of legal phenomena.

If Yntema sees the bad man as an artificial heuristic for taking one outside the bounds of existing, operative law for the purpose of study and analysis, Grey sees the bad man as essentially functioning in the same way but going in the opposite direction. The bad man, for Grey, is the means Holmes chose for taking the student *into* the bounds, into the theater of existing, operative law; it ushers the student, albeit brusquely, into the practice.[327]

Grey makes the argument in an intriguing way. He initially points out how the opening section of "Path" reduces law. By "reduce" he means that it is "clarified; its sediment of pretense precipitates out[.]"[328] Holmes precipitates out the sediment of pretense by emphasizing the law is not a mystery but a profession and a business. Holmes glosses this deflationary account of law with three "novelties" to the English

[325] *See* Thomas C. Grey, *Freestanding Legal Pragmatism*, 18 CARDOZO L. REV. 21, 24 (1996) ("Legal thought issues as commentary, heuristic and critical reflection upon practice and administration, and upon prior commentary . . . . And legal theorizing is simply the more general and abstract kind of commentary, neither supreme over nor epiphenomenal to but coordinate with the other practices that make up the law.").

[326] *See* RUMBLE, *supra* note 288, 107–36.

[327] Grey, *supra* note 316, at 36–40. *See also* Grey, *supra* note 298, at 787, 836 ("Holmes was the first writer to base a jurisprudential theory on a perspective derived from the practice of law.").

[328] Grey, *supra* note 316, at 36.

positivist tradition: first, he uses the bad man to shift the focus to the remedies the courts will employ ("the real language of the law is the language of remedies"); second, the bad man's emphasis on prediction serves to emphasize what the courts *will* do, not *have* done; and, third, the emphasis on the courts, not the legislature, indicates the extent to which the legal center of gravity has moved when one compares the American legal context to the historic English one.[329]

Grey then declares that most of what Holmes says about the bad man and prediction are just further examples of Holmes's tendency toward hyperbole and paradox. Holmes enjoyed playing the provocateur, shocking intellectual complacency. This opinion is another version of what we first saw in Tufts, that Holmes couldn't *really* have meant it when he suggested that students look at the law like his friend the bad man. Similarly, Grey doubts Holmes meant the prediction theory as an "all-purpose definition of law."[330] He cites the most common objection – which David Luban had once most forcefully advanced – that judges of courts of last resort are not in the business of predicting their own behavior.[331] True. But Holmes said court not judge. And Holmes as a member of the highest court of Massachusetts, where decisions take place by majority vote, may well have engaged in predicting the actions of his colleagues from time to time.

The latter point we will further discuss in the next part. In regard to Grey's main argument in "Plotting the Path of the Law" it is but a cavil. Grey's argument is that ultimately much of what Holmes said – or is remembered to have said – in "Path" is overblown rhetoric. Stripped down, and put alongside what Holmes said or wrote at other times, "Path"'s main contentions simply develop Holmes's basic notion that law is a sustained effort to communicate and consummate judicial remedies. The bad man, the stress on courts and prediction – indeed the entire formalist part I – is but an elaborately conceived heuristic. It brings to the fore what Holmes learned as a budding practitioner:

> Reflection upon the more sordid aspects of legal work had actually helped him to a more scientific understanding of his subject. He had learned from Bad Men, (or from morally indifferent business clients) that the law's central operation is the granting of judicial remedies, and that its dogmas are formulated for the most part to help its practitioners predict judicial action for the benefit of those who purchased their services.[332]

Though for Grey the heuristic intent of "Path" may begin with the bad man, it does not end there. It was not enough for Holmes to prepare students mentally for

[329] *Id.* at 36–37.

[330] *Id.* at 38.

[331] *Id. See* David Luban, *The Bad Man and the Good Lawyer: A Centennial Essay on Holmes's The Path of the Law*, 72 N.Y.U. L. REV. 1547, 1577–80 (1997). In this article, Luban actually steps back from his previous position and finds it meaningful to describe a judge, in certain sense, as predicting what the next judge will do.

[332] Grey, *supra* note 316, at 50.

the realities of practice that awaited them. Readying for practice was more than a matter of mental and emotional acculturation if one wanted to retain the capacity to grow as a lawyer, to become a master. That required cultivating a certain frame of mind. Grey believes the needed viewpoint occurs when the moral terminology is washed away and the "operational question of what judicial remedies will attach to what states of affairs" starkly emerges.[333]

Yet formulating in this manner Holmes's critical method for anchoring legal theory to legal practice deemphasizes the dynamic quality of Holmes's thinking, how he sees past law and present desires constantly interacting in a common law society (recall the judge's raised-eyebrow questions). Grey's formulation renders the past relatively inert. He does not fully appreciate the purpose of the cynical acid. One needs it to expose the lineaments of law that present perplexities etch upon the less malleable parts of the past. New dilemmas accentuate old devotions. Grey does recognize, though, that the cynical acid wash is only a first step, in the same way that for many Protestants the revelation of sin is the needed first step to salvation or, for some philosophers, the brace of doubt the tentative first step toward knowledge.

In Grey's rendition of the course Holmes took in "Path" the necessity of practice – representing the client – by its own logic led eventually to the perception of law's social dimensions (anthropology and history) and its normative dimensions (political economy, theories of legislation, ethics). The quest narrative provides the mimetic device for conveying the sequence of awakenings but it does little to explain how they connect intelligibly.

How Grey resolves this problem explains why he treats judicial remedies as fundamental. He turns first to Holmes's pragmatism. He states bluntly that he believes Holmes "was the primary founder of legal pragmatism."[334] Grey takes this position to counteract the opinion that Holmes merely had a knack for uttering well-dressed shibboleths. Grey declines to enter the fray on that issue, however. He merely states his position and then uses the version of pragmatism that John Dewey articulated – which Grey suggests owes a lot to Holmes – to reveal the legal theory that, ironically, he believes Holmes did his best to hide in "Path" for the sake of literary immortality.[335]

Legal pragmatism, as Grey explains it, recognizes that law is both a social activity (people in their interactions make "law" for themselves) and a specific way of thinking (what Dewey would call a "logic") about that activity. What makes legal pragmatism "legal" lies in the intended audience: lawyers. That is to say, those who participate in the practice of law are given both a map of the relevant terrain and the

[333] *Id.* at 53. *See also* Grey, *supra* note 298, at 832–33.

[334] Grey, *supra* note 298, at 51.

[335] *Id.*

tools for using the map most effectively. In short, legal pragmatism, like the law itself, is for lawyers.[336]

Grey finds the essence of legal pragmatism in the word "practice." On the one side, law is a set of collocated practices. These practices are situated, entrenched; they arise from shared expectations; they also form in their various conjunctions recognizable professional contexts that manifest path dependency and an inescapable tacit dimension. On the other side, law is practical. It seeks to accomplish certain ends. It is purposive and instrumental. The catch is that these ends must be accomplished within the set of ongoing practices that form the grounds for law in its active, instrumental mode.[337]

In other words, to use an analogy, the lawyer proceeds with map in hand of the legal terrain in which the lawyer happens to be operating. The map, though complex, is intelligible to the lawyer and provides real assistance as the lawyer seeks to navigate the terrain, to get from point A to point B to do either X or Y.

The problem, however, is that the terrain keeps shifting in ways small, large, and in between. And some of these shifts are partly in response to what the lawyer is doing. Some of these changes also, occasionally in very minute ways, begin to reveal aspects or features of the terrain that had not been seen or noted before and when finally included in the map may significantly reconfigure it. The mapmakers, who also participate in the legal community but do so from the mountains ranging the terrain, (a) cannot keep up in real time with the changes within the terrain, (b) cannot always agree among themselves whether a change actually occurred or how to depict it, and (c) do not realize that at very rare moments the mountain has slightly moved rather than the terrain below.

Given that the lawyer is committed to continuing to operate as a lawyer in the terrain, what are the lawyer's options when the mapmaking community disagrees about existing maps and provides different versions? Option one, ignore all the new maps and just proceed on acquired know-how (intuition) and expediency. Option two, use those parts of the map which the mapmakers and other lawyers more or less agree are accurate and useful and for those other areas of the terrain that are effectively unmapped because there is no consensus, go back to option one and rely on intuition and expediency. Option three, find a map from among the competing mapmakers that seems accurate, useful, and reliable, in the sense that further changes will also probably be accurate and useful, and stick with it. Option four, find a new type of map. New mapmaking techniques and new principles of mapmaking, say from a point of view from within the terrain itself, have produced maps drastically limited in scope but much more accurate in detail. To the extent the lawyer relies on these types of maps the lawyer is going back to option two.

[336] Grey, *supra* note 325, at 37–38.

[337] *See* Grey, *supra* note 298, at 793–805; Grey, *supra* note 325, at 22–31; THOMAS C. GREY, FORMALISM AND PRAGMATISM IN AMERICAN LAW 1–3 (2014).

Legal pragmatism for Grey encompasses all four of these options. He, however, categorizes them into two sets, what he calls the formalist tendency and the pragmatic one.[338] This categorization may make for some confusion given that the formalist and pragmatic tendencies are typically counterpoised to one another. But he sees legal pragmatism comprising both because, in his hands, both are primarily types. Types of what? Mental habits; that is, accustomed ways of grouping and dividing legal phenomena that correlate with discrete social needs and wants. American society during the formative period of modern American law had a pressing need for legal predictability and certainty. It needed stable legal principles (formalist tendency). It also needed law to be flexible and responsive to emerging social problems and dislocations. Law had to be instrumental (pragmatic tendency).

Grey sees the formalist tendency operating in Holmes when Holmes speaks of legal principles as being few in number and articulated for the purpose of making law easier to be understood and remembered (a map-using function). Langdell also believed legal principles to be few in number and probably developed his case method as a way to help students identify them and learn how to reason with them. He also thought they existed, in some sense, apart from human belief. Beyond this conceptualist feature, formalism for Langdell also included a mandated series of logical steps (reasoning deductively from premises to conclusion) that struck Holmes as lamentably inadequate and specious.[339]

Part of the reason Holmes found Langdell's justification for legal conclusions spurious is because Langdell did not recognize the hidden determinants of context and interest that underlay lawmaking. Holmes did more than any prior legal thinker – with the exception perhaps of Nicholas St. John Green – to bring out these hidden determinants. These were the unconscious elements, the felt necessities, and the operative theories of legislation contained in Holmes's use of the word experience.[340]

Grey argues that Holmes synthesized the formalist and pragmatic aspects of American jurisprudence in his legal pragmatism. It combined the best of the historical and analytical schools, bringing together in one swoop the insight that law is "both guided by past practice and looking forward in a practical spirit to future consequences."[341] Grey finds the same synthesis in Dewey. It is programmatically revealed in the combined and essential methods of analytical clarification, historical investigation, and utilitarian assessment.

338 Grey, Formalism and Pragmatism, *supra* note 337, at 1–3.

339 Grey, *supra* note 315, at 39–46.

340 Grey, *supra* note 298, at 805–14; Thomas C. Grey, *Bad Man from Olympus*, 42 N.Y. Times Rev. Books 4 (July 13, 1995) ("His skepticism was of the Wordsworthian kind that revels in the sublimity of the unknown, and when he said law had been and likely always would be based largely in 'experience,' he was invoking the Romantic historicist idea of a collective unconscious made up of custom and tradition that could never be fully captured by articulate reason.").

341 Grey, Formalism and Pragmatism, *supra* note 337, at 2.

From this big picture presentation Grey draws a corollary. He calls it perspectivism. Perspectivism initially arose from the reality that beliefs emerge from "a complex of already existing beliefs that can never be made fully conscious and explicit."[342] This intrinsic opaqueness of origins Grey tends to view as part of the historicist, romantic tradition to which Holmes was an heir. And that certainly may be the case. One wishes Grey were clearer in identifying these "romantic" elements (whether as the organic outgrowth of spirit or an ordained developmental pattern or a manifold of distinctive folkways). Yet it may also be the case that the presence of a welter of partly unconscious, partly opaque background beliefs fits with the Darwinian thesis of natural selection. As Nicholas St. John Green demonstrated in his classic article on "Proximate and Remote Cause," the interlocking elements of experience fated to become legal causes are those selected out of the total situation, which always includes the purposes of those seeking to discover causes.[343] Those purposes have an instrumental quality and what we might call a prophylactic quality. The prophylactic quality is intended to minimize the risk of change or alteration to those things in the total situation (other purposes, protected values, for example) that the selectors don't want changed. It is intended to guard, among other things, against the boomerang effect of the instrumental purpose.

That effects or consequences may go in unwanted or untoward directions leads Grey to identify a second important feature to perspectivism, its fallibilism.[344] Review of consequences and self-adjustment creates a constant feedback loop. That observation, along with the recognition that beliefs, given their hidden origins, can never be made entirely to cohere, gives perspectivism its saliency as a way of expressing the insight that ideas have limited purposes and limited life spans.

While Grey's corollary of perspectivism does a good job in distinguishing limits, it is less successful in conveying the features of interaction or interchange that exist within the total situation. It doesn't quite seem to recognize, to loosely paraphrase Nietzsche, that when we stare into the abyss the abyss – and the abyss behind the abyss – stares back. In the context of Grey's extensive writings on Holmes this cashes out in how Grey subtly but unmistakably drains the dynamism (though not the tension) from Holmes's thought. We see this most clearly in how Grey treats the bad man, which, under his analysis, is a heuristic used to vivify a particular perspective (the lawyer–client relationship) in and upon law (that is, a perspective upon the beliefs and practices we call law that is also embedded in those same beliefs and practices).

The telltale sign lies in Grey's focus on judicial remedies. Holmes, Grey says, intended the bad man as a way to focus "attention on the operative aspect of law, the

[342] Grey, *supra* note 298, at 804–05.
[343] Nicholas St. John Green, *Proximate and Remote Cause*, 5 KAN. CITY L. REV. 114, 125–29 (1937) (orig. pub. 1870).
[344] Grey, *supra* note 298, at 804–05.

remedy[.]"[345] Thus explained, the bad man plays a different heuristic role than legal conceptions, which, in Grey's interpretation, also have a pedagogical function in Holmes's thought. Legal conceptions are handy summaries, making it easier for students and practitioners to remember and understand the law. Let's call them heuristics of the first grade. A heuristic of the second grade, such as the bad man, seeks to deepen legal knowledge by reorienting the student's focus to effects and consequences, law in its operative mode. Now, the focus on effects and consequences can go in two directions, backwards and forwards. We saw earlier that Fred Kellogg used Peirce's maxim to connect the law's present with its past. It distinguished persistent effects (the effect of doing X has been, and will continue to be Y and Z). Kellogg also highlighted persistence by focusing, not on judicial remedies, which tend to be more forward looking, but on causes of action, which tend to use the past to gauge the present.

Grey, in contrast to Kellogg, has less concern to keep live and centered in the mind the connections between present and past, the persistent effects. He tilts the scale forward. For him Holmes's bad man deepens legal knowledge by drawing attention to the operation of law in terms of future risk. This insight is certainly valuable. Grey emphasizes – as did Howe – that to understand the bad man one must first comprehend Holmes's leading conception of duty. Grey believes Holmes uses judicial remedies to gradate duties. The judicial remedies themselves are then translated into the language of incentives. Law becomes a way of allocating risk, and Grey finds Holmes's emphasis on the risks of action (perils Holmes generally said) and on the options private law often affords to the risk-taker to sum up the bad man's heuristic purpose.[346]

In short, Grey finds ensconced in the bad man and in the prediction theory the rudiments of what Mark Mendell refers to as the insurance theory of law. Mendell wrote a dissertation on "Pragmatism and Legal Reasoning" during the same time period that Grey wrote his "Holmes and Legal Pragmatism."[347] Both authors seem to agree that one of the great bequests of pragmatism to legal thinking lies in drawing out the social policy consequences of incentive and risk, transforming law into a risk-allocating tool, operating on the same general principles as liability insurance.

But this emphasis on judicial remedies shortchanges law's capacity to become more than a risk-allocating tool. It also has the capacity to measure the wants and ideals that correlate with specific risks, or that give rise to new loss–reward ratios. For Holmes this requires recognition that the persistence of events as much as the persistence of effects had hidden costs. Peirce's maxim, as Kellogg employs it, essentially swallows up the past into surviving causes of action. Or, alternately, it

[345] *Id.* at 832.
[346] *Id.* 830–33.
[347] Mendell, *supra* note 272, at 155–235.

grades the past by leveling it, not recognizing or caring about the geologic multiformity of its terrain.

Grey in principle recognizes the historicist aspects in Holmes's thought: "He was also a historicist, who believed that people were not solely driven by a universal desire for pleasure and aversion to pain, nor even by a small number of biologically given wants, but also by ideals and tastes that varied widely according to culture and history."[348] But his exposition of Holmes's pragmatism does not identify the necessary techniques for identifying or negotiating those historically varied "ideals and tastes." Grey – and Kellogg too – sees legal pragmatism as primarily an analytical, clarificatory tool. Kellogg views it as adding to the positivist's semantic analysis toolkit without losing the positivist's emphasis on making law scientific; Grey as combining various heuristics for meeting competing social demands. Yet both are still present-minded in a way Holmes was not. Neither is as sensitive as he to how the pressures of the past or pasts – varied "ideals and tastes" (as relatively hidden lines of cumulative wants and their wakes) – have the potential to implode the felt values of the present. This point will become clearer when in Part V we discuss how the bad man's point of view arises from the realization that certain reticulated lines of law intersect – and thereby create forced choices (options) – and not vice versa.

For these reasons Grey's bad man has a limited function once one wrings out Holmes's rhetoric. The bad man ties into how Grey understands the purpose of perspectives, and it also explains why for him legal pragmatism has a defining eclectic, freestanding quality. Grey traces legal pragmatism's roots more to Holmes's democratic faith than to Holmes's historicist sensibility (that we are in history as a fish is in water).[349] Unsurprisingly, he tends to pay more attention to contending maps, mapmakers, and mapmaking techniques, and to the different purposes of the users, than to the geological movements shifting the terrain.

iii *Catharine Pierce Wells*

Catharine Pierce Wells is the modernist poet among our group of pragmatists. She, like Kellogg, uses Peirce's thought to denote what she believes to be the philosophic wellsprings of Holmes's jurisprudence. For this task she finds Peirce's concepts of abduction and perceptual judgment just as important as Peirce's pragmatic maxim.[350]

348 Thomas C. Grey, *Holmes on the Logic of the Law*, *in* THE PATH OF THE LAW AND ITS INFLUENCE: THE LEGACY OF OLIVER WENDELL HOLMES, JR. 136 (Steven J. Burton ed., 2000). Though this admittedly shorthand statement of historicism does not seem to mesh well with his previous statements. *See, e.g.*, Grey, *supra* note 340.

349 Thomas C. Grey, *Holmes, Pragmatism, and Democracy*, 71 OR. L. REV. 521, 538–39 (1992).

350 In this section I have relied on the following articles or essays: Catharine Wells Hantzis (now Catharine Pierce Wells), *Legal Innovation within the Wider Intellectual Tradition: The Pragmatism of Oliver Wendell Holmes, Jr.*, 82 NW. U. L. REV. 541 (1988); Catharine Pierce Wells, *Holmes on Legal Method: The Predictive Theory of Law As an Instance of Scientific Method*, 18

We already quoted Wells's most extensive discussion of the bad man in the above section on Francis Lucey (Section 8). Though she does not use it, the currently fashionable term "disruptor" works well to describe the role that for her the bad man plays in relation to any specific legal regime or the broader social mores in which it is anchored. She realizes the point of the bad man is to clarify the distinction between law and morals. But the novice's ability to understand the distinction thus clarified may at times demand much finer grades of perception than typically available to the untutored mind.[351]

For this reason she finds it essential to illuminate the specifically philosophical presuppositions of Holmes's thought. And these she finds best articulated in Peirce's pragmatism. As her scholarship progresses she also puts more weight on the Emersonian antecedents, but the basic categories for denoting and depicting remain Peircean.

That means, in this context, understanding that human beings do not have special access to the "thing-in-itself." We begin in experience (perception). All experience is mediated by and through signs. For Peirce, humans interpret present cognitions in reference to previous cognitions that seem to fall within the same type. The pragmatic maxim is a rule of interpretation that is meant to improve the mechanisms (the mental habits) we use in interpreting the thoughts that occur to us. But the act of interpreting must begin somewhere (it does, with perceptual judgments) and it must end somewhere (it does, with a perceptual judgment that often informs action). Between the initial and ending perceptual judgment lie different types of inferences; some of these the pragmatic maxim unifies into a clarificatory tool. But there is one type of inference that has the potential to lead to a reorganized, more vibrant understanding of the matters that hold our attention. This type of inference Peirce at various points called "abduction."

Abduction is an act of insight. It plays a necessary role in the mind's purposive activity as it seeks to maintain or establish habit, alleviate doubt, and bring into greater unity the multiplicity of drives, feelings, images, and thoughts that form the stream of experiences in which the mind lives and moves. Mind is properly designated an "it" because mind is not primarily individual. Mind, like language,

S. Ill. U. L.J., 329 (1994); *Old-Fashioned Postmodernism and the Legal Theories of Oliver Wendell Holmes, Jr.*, 63 Brook. L. Rev. 59 (1997); *Why Pragmatism Works for Me*, Boston College Law School Legal Studies Research Paper Series, No. 2000–12 (2000) (available at http://ssrn.com/abstract=753569); *Oliver Wendell Holmes, Jr., and William James: The Bad Man and the Moral Life, in* The Path of the Law and Its Influence: The Legacy of Oliver Wendell Holmes, Jr., 211–30 (Steven J. Burton ed., 2000); *Oliver Wendell Holmes, Jr., and the American Civil War*, 40 J. Sup. Ct. Hist. 282 (2015). Long after this section was drafted, Professor Wells graciously forwarded the manuscript of her Oliver Wendell Holmes: A Willing Servant to an Unknown God, which I have read with interest. *See* Catharine Pierce Wells, Oliver Wendell Holmes: A Willing Servant to an Unknown God (2020).

[351] Wells, *Old-Fashioned Postmodernism*, *supra* note 350, at 60 n.5.

is chiefly social. Peirce emphasized the sociality of mind, he believed signs to be the mind's basic constituents, and he did not think that all signs could be treated as chemists tended to treat chemical compounds, analyzing them into their specific elements, without destroying their intrinsic quality as signs.

That is to say, Peirce believed some signs to be irreducibly composite. At one and the same time this type of sign presented itself to an interpreter as a discrete, individual thing in experience, having its own intrinsic, material quality, *and* as related to something else, another sign or group of signs, its representational quality. Wells argues that a certain type of sign or cognition – for Peirce believed all thinking occurred through signs – functions in legal discourse as a certain kind of perceptual judgment. We generally call them facts. A perceptual judgment is "perceptual" due to how it affects the person who holds the judgment – "that individual is unable to believe that the judgment is false."[352] The complement to a perceptual judgment is a theoretical judgment. Of this kind of judgment one can be genuinely doubtful.

Wells uses Peirce's distinction between perceptual and theoretical judgments to undermine the traditional empiricist distinction between fact and theory. Peirce developed the idea of abduction to supplement the standard logical canon of induction and deduction. These traditional methods were necessary but not sufficient to account for the actual way in which the thinking summarized as "scientific" actually operated. Peirce wanted to tease out from his study of the history of science, and his own considerable scientific work, the logic of scientific methods. And this meant bypassing the traditional account that emphasized both "induction" and "facts."

Wells believes Holmes wanted to do the same thing in law. She finds a number of overlaps in how each man formulated the issues and relevant approaches in their respective areas of inquiry. Of these overlaps one of the most important is how each thinker conceived the formation of generalizations. Peirce used abduction to describe the thinking process through which one draws up a beforehand un-thought explanatory hypothesis that unifies otherwise discordant features of experience into a workable sequence. Since it is a hypothesis the contemplated sequence can be tested. But that is not its most critical attribute. Abduction's significance rests on its status as "the only logical operation which introduces any new idea."[353]

Wells's notion that Peirce's description of abduction's role in scientific thought parallels Holmes's view of the role generalizations played in law is very valuable.

Wells's early work is difficult to follow, however, because she insists on grafting Holmes's thought onto Peirce's. Kellogg did something similar in his first book, *The Formative Essays of Justice Holmes*. In later studies he took more care to use

[352] Wells, *Legal Innovation within the Wider Intellectual Tradition*, *supra* note 350, at 571.

[353] Wells, *Holmes on Legal Method*, *supra* note 350, at 337 n.21 (quoting Charles S. Peirce, *Three Types of Reasoning*, *in* V The Collected Papers of Charles Sanders Peirce 94, 105 (C. Hartshorne & P. Weiss eds., 1934)).

traditional common law thought and practice as a way to center his interpretations of Holmes.[354] Wells, though clearly aware that Holmes drew his everyday intellectual sustenance from the common law, has a difficult time distinguishing Holmes's positions because she wants to key everything to Peirce. For that reason we end up with paragraphs written in a more philosophical vein than a legal one:

> To put it in simple terms, Holmes denies that there is a distinction between fact and law. He is striking deep at the formalist view that judges apply *rules* to the *facts* of individual cases. Holmes sees no real distinction between the case as a particular collection of factual circumstances and the legal interpretation of those circumstances. This is because our legal theories are embedded in our apprehension of the case, in ways that cannot be rooted out. Legal generalizations do not merely sum up past cases; they also determine to a large degree the appearance of future ones.[355]

These statements are not easy to follow; they are written more to emphasize an important philosophical point, of which Holmes was no doubt aware, than to give a full-fledged accounting of how Holmes worked and thought as a legal professional or jurist. This quote concentrates into Holmes's jurisprudence the three Peircean ideas discussed: abduction, the pragmatic maxim, and, perceptual judgments.

To take the latter first, Peirce's idea of perceptual judgment, given how Wells has defined it, ranges from a strong version (Holmes's "can't help") to a weak version (when the perceptual judgment's surd element is more pronounced than its relation or relations to other classes of facts). In law, as Wells notes, perceptual judgments are embedded in legal practice, most explicitly in legal doctrine.[356] And because they are embedded in legal practice and doctrine they have the capacity to direct legal action by providing subtle or not-so-subtle pointers. The subtle pointers are the ones Holmes sought to master in his jurisprudence (these he sometimes called "remote conceptions"). The not-so-subtle ones, of overwhelming intensity, he could never master: they were his "can't helps." They mastered him.

Wells may very well recognize these distinctions but she has not shown how perceptual judgments or legal pointers can be organized or arrayed into any kind of rational or intelligent order. In fact, she ultimately consigns them to the ongoing living traditions of common law practice.[357] Philosophically, given her Peircean premises, there ought to be a way to rationalize them, even if only through categorization. But even though she talks about "categorizing the cases" it is not

[354] *See, e.g.*, KELLOGG, LEGAL THEORY, AND JUDICIAL RESTRAINT, *supra* note 300, at 26–60 (2007).

[355] Wells, *Legal Innovation within the Wider Intellectual Tradition*, *supra* note 350, at 572 (emphasis in original).

[356] *Id.* at 570–75.

[357] Wells, *Holmes on Legal Method*, *supra* note 350, at 342–45; Wells, *Old-Fashioned Postmodernism*, *supra* note 350, at 72–75.

persuasive because she has not shown how perceptual judgments (which include normative evaluations) connect to the pragmatic maxim (which she redescribes as a legal method). For Kellogg the pragmatic maxim worked by integrating persistent effects through existing and developing causes of action. Wells does not take this step and because she doesn't she is left with the disarray of strongly embedded perceptual judgments and, at times, a somewhat free-floating pragmatic maxim.[358] We have effectively gone back to the chaos of the cases but with a somewhat more sophisticated if not fuller index.

The pragmatic maxim's relative inutility in Wells's hands is inversely proportional to the emphasis she places on abduction. The emphasis on abduction, in turn, links to her stress on the weight pragmatism places on viewpoints or perspectives. Pragmatism's openness to new perspectives, new viewpoints, new insights that elicit new meanings or new colligations finds its formal expression in legal doctrine's centrality to legal practice and legal education. Developed doctrine always contains a heuristic feature, ballast for the new developments that may come.[359]

This openness to new and different viewpoints, or what Wells also calls the "external viewpoint," becomes for her the hallmark of Holmes's mature jurisprudence: "The recognition of the legitimacy of an 'external' perspective in legal and moral theory is the most distinctive feature of Holmes' legal philosophy. It is perhaps ironic that Holmes, the archetypical insider, should insist so strongly that the legal system be viewed through the eyes of an outsider."[360]

We noted above Wells's suggestion that the bad man is a "lawbreaker" and nothing more. That is, the bad man is one who does not share the lawmaking majority's ideals or tastes. Wells believes Holmes used him ironically, as way to convey the historical lesson "that there were long periods in its [the common law's] history when the substance of law was chiefly determined by the movement of armies." For her, the bad man served as a constant reminder that despite contemporary aspirations to make law democratic and just, what makes law *law* is that it embodies the organized force of the community. Consequently, the bad man, as a change agent, as the outsider par excellence, is not always "bad" in the conventional sense. He (or she) could be a Moonie or a psychopathic murderer or, heaven forbid, both.[361]

Wells makes these observations in the closing sections of an essay that uses William James's moral philosophy, especially as articulated in his "The Moral

[358] Though she is aware of how Kellogg ties the pragmatic maxim to historical antecedents. *See* Wells, *Legal Innovation within the Wider Intellectual Tradition*, note 350, at 563–64. In her A Willing Servant to an Unknown God she takes greater pains to put Holmes himself in a carefully limned cultural setting, but still does not quite do it through the law itself. *See* Wells, A Willing Servant to an Unknown God, *supra* note 350.

[359] Wells, *Holmes on Legal Method*, *supra* note 350, at 341–42.

[360] Wells, *Legal Innovation within the Wider Intellectual Tradition*, *supra* note 350, at 589.

[361] Wells, *Oliver Wendell Holmes, Jr., and William James*, *supra* note 350, at 224–27.

Philosopher and the Moral Life," to illuminate "The Path of the Law." James on most accounts is much easier to follow and understand than Peirce. One may still have reservations about this tactic of using the vocabulary of one thinker to illuminate the thought of another. Especially when it comes to Holmes the best advice still seems to be a version of what he got from Shattuck: the business of a Holmes scholar is to know Holmes. It may be that Wells, like so many other law professors, does not particularly like Holmes's métier, law proper. But she does seem to like, or at least admire, Holmes, and finds herself curious as to, "What was it in his character that enabled him to withstand the crisis [of the Civil War] without losing himself?"[362] A careful reading of her work, especially her later pieces, where the prose relaxes, leaves one with the strong impression that she has a savvy, well-informed even sagacious take on Holmes's thought, one that leads her in various ways to highlight repeatedly what Perry Miller called Holmes's "prodigious open-mindedness, his hospitality to all ideas[.]"[363]

iv *Susan Haack*

Susan Haack takes us back directly to the theme of the bad man heuristic. Haack, like Wells, recurs to Peirce's thought in her main pieces on Holmes, but in an unexpectedly low-key way. She refers to James and Dewey as well, but the references to Peirce tend to come at critical junctures.[364]

Haack is a devotee of the classical pragmatist tradition. She refuses to truck with neo-pragmatists (à la Richard Rorty) or economic wolves disguised in pragmatist wool (Judge Posner).[365] Max Fish's thesis that Holmes's prediction theory was the first notable effort to work out the central idea instilled in Peirce's pragmatic maxim she finds plausible; his suggestion that Peirce may have extrapolated the pragmatic maxim from Holmes's 1872 iteration of the prediction theory she does not. Fisch's other suggestion that common law practices may be as responsible for how Peirce articulated the pragmatic maxim as the methods of the experimental sciences she ignores.[366]

[362] Wells, *Oliver Wendell Holmes, Jr., and the American Civil War*, *supra* note 350, at 310. I think she took it upon herself to answer that question in A WILLING SERVANT TO AN UNKNOWN GOD.

[363] Perry Miller, *Introduction*, *in* AMERICAN THOUGHT: CIVIL WAR TO WORLD WAR I xxxvii (Perry Miller ed., 1954).

[364] In this subsection I have relied on the following articles: Susan Haack, *On Legal Pragmatism: Where Does the Path of the Law Lead Us?*, 3 PRAGMATISM TODAY: J. CTR.-EUR. PRAG. F. 8–31 (2012) (updated version of article originally published in 50 AM. J. JURIS. 71–105 (2005)); *On Logic in the Law: "Something, but not All"*, 20 RATIO JUR. 1–31 (2007); *The Pragmatist Tradition: Lessons for Legal Theorists*, 95 WASH. U. L. REV. 1–34 (2018); *The Pragmatist*, *in* PRAGMATISM AND PREJUDICE: THE PHILOSOPHY OF OLIVER WENDELL HOLMES, JR. 169–89 (Seth Vannatta ed., 2019).

[365] Haack, *The Pragmatist Tradition*, *supra* note 364, at 19–24.

[366] Haack, *On Legal Pragmatism*, *supra* note 364, at 13–14; Haack, *The Pragmatist*, *supra* note 364, at 169–74.

One quickly realizes three things about Haack. She has definite opinions; she will discuss only what she thinks is worth discussing; she will not linger too long over any one detail. She is both sober-minded and impassioned. It makes for an interesting combination.

Her take on Holmes breaks into two parts. She does agree with Fisch that Holmes embodied the pragmatist spirit. In the way he approached intellectual problems, how he articulated his concerns, the manner his mind made or refused to make certain connections evinced characteristic pragmatic attitudes. That is to say, he demonstrates an intellectual taste, a cluster of predilections, that she believes also unifies such thinkers as Peirce, James, Dewey, and Dewey's onetime colleague, George Herbert Mead. What are these predilections and attitudes? She helpfully lists them:

- an approach to meaning in terms of consequences and, especially in Peirce, a conception of meaning as in constant evolution, shifting and growing "in use and in experience";
- a disinclination to philosophize in an a priori way, and an understanding of philosophy as about the world, not exclusively about our concepts or our language;
- a distaste for dogmatism, and correspondingly, a robust and thoroughgoing fallibilism;
- a repudiation of false dichotomies, and a corresponding stress on continuity – to borrow Peirce's word, "synechism";
- a concern with the social character of both language and inquiry;
- an acknowledgement of contingency, of the role of chance, both in the cosmos and in human affairs;
- a willingness to draw on results from the sciences and, in particular, to take evolution seriously; and
- an inclination to look to the future, and a distinctive way of knitting future and past.[367]

Haack illustrates each of these bullet points with one or two examples from Holmes's work. Most examples succeed; some don't. Take the last bullet point. From the perspective of this study, Haack's view on how Holmes knits past and future presents a previously unimagined opportunity to further clarify Holmes's ideas on this important topic.

"The need to balance past and future is, in a way, built into the job-description of a common law judge[,]" she begins. "He must apply the law to the case at hand in a way that is consistent with how it is written and with how it has been interpreted in

[367] Haack, *The Pragmatist Tradition*, *supra* note 364, at 7–8; *The Pragmatist*, *supra* note 364, at 171–73.

the past, but also with an eye to future consequences of interpreting this way or that."[368]

The terms Haack uses to describe the juristic endeavor – "balance," "apply," "the law," "consistent," "written," "interpreted," "consequences" – are all, of course, freighted with semantic, technical difficulties. The sentence, as a whole, suggests Haack sees judicial activity in a mode that is common in the United States today, when constitutional provisions and statutes and administrative rules set the tone for the judicial enterprise, especially at the federal level, and not how the enterprise would probably have looked or felt to a Massachusetts state court judge in 1895 or a US Supreme Court justice a decade later, when the job of discerning the law that pulsated in the decided cases still effectively defined the judge's role.

She then turns to Holmes's 1895 speech, "Learning and Science." She notes that Holmes in this speech brought to his hearers' attention the necessary connections between present and past. It is here we first encounter the famous admonition "that historic continuity with the past is not a duty, it is only a necessity."[369]

To say, as Holmes does, that continuity with the past is both "historic" and a "necessity" is to bring to mind at least two of the modes by which the past bears upon the present. The "historic" is the past as conceived by inquirers, sometimes trained and disciplined, sometimes not. It denotes histories of various types, qualities, and ranges. "Necessity," on the other hand, refers to the past's inexorable qualities; the dictates we cannot but help but follow; the vocabulary we use to express our insights; the limits pressed, unawares, upon our imagination. Superimposed upon these embedded structures and strictures is what Holmes singles out as the "peculiar logical pleasure in making manifest the continuity between what we are doing and what has been done before."[370]

To these impediments Haack counterpoises Holmes's call that "the present has the right to govern itself so far as it can." Even so, given the embedded structures and strictures, and the distinctive intellectual pleasures of revealing a coiling continuity, the declaration that the present has a "right" to govern itself – arrayed as it is against the "duty" to maintain continuity – seems to strike a pleading, almost desultory note.[371]

Haack doesn't quite see it that way. For her the declaration that the present – some unidentified we, here, now – has a right to govern itself as far as it can sets the stage for what she calls "a remarkable expression of the pragmatist style of knitting past and future." She then quotes the last line of the speech, interlineating the needed references:

[368] Haack, *The Pragmatist*, *supra* note 364, at 178.
[369] *Id.*; *see* Oliver Wendell Holmes, *Learning and Science*, *in* III CW 492.
[370] *Id.*
[371] *Id.*

> [T]he eternal procession [of many generations of lawyers, judges, and legal thinkers] moves on, we in front for the moment; and stretching away against the unattainable sky, the black spearheads of the army that has been passing in unbroken line already for over a thousand years.[372]

This mini peroration – the entire speech, in fact, concentrates the call to modulate time's ravages – sums up Holmes's sense of law's thematic persistence, as a practice and as an ideal, despite abrupt changes in melody or the unmistakable lack of background harmony. In terms of modern American pop culture: Forrest Gump's feather.

Is the source of the resonance truth or its search? Haack believes it is. She follows up the Holmes quote with one from Peirce, believing Holmes's passage to bear "more than a passing resemblance to Peirce's metaphor of inquirers as 'storming the stronghold of truth'[.]" She also thinks the passage well expresses Peirce's synechism, his stress on continuity.[373]

Missing from her adroit comparison is any detailed description of how the pragmatic knitting actually works. How is the past and future knit? She doesn't say. This silence is a bit surprising from a pragmatist philosopher. The stress on continuity, à la Peirce, seems to draw attention away from efficient causes. I'm not sure I'm phrasing this the right way; I'm not enough of a logician or a Peirce scholar to wrangle with Haack over this point.

I am deeply puzzled, however. More so because she qualifies her interpretation of Holmes as exemplifying the pragmatist spirit by claiming – and this is the second main point of her take on Holmes – that he was too much imbued with the conviction that "the history of law is the history of moral progress."[374]

Most Holmes scholars would be taken aback by this claim. I too am taken aback, given my own belief that Howe got it more-or-less right on Holmes's moral skepticism. Haack anticipates that reaction and modifies the claim to emphasize what she calls Holmes's moral fallibilism. This modification certainly makes sense; perhaps Howe himself would have chosen the word given the chance. But at the end of the day Haack still sees a "real tension" in Holmes's thought "between his insistence on the distinctness of law and morality and his conviction that the history of law is a history of moral progress."[375]

This incongruity she finds most clearly expressed in the opening and closing sections of "The Path of the Law." Similar to Grey, who sought to use the literary device of the narrative quest to render comprehensible two outlooks so seemingly at odds, Haack takes the tack of organizing "The Path of the Law" around the steps that

[372] Haack, *The Pragmatist*, *supra* note 364, at 178 (quoting Holmes, *supra* note 369, at 492).
[373] Haack, *The Pragmatist*, *supra* note 364, at 178.
[374] Haack, *On Legal Pragmatism*, *supra* note 364, at 22–23.
[375] Haack, *The Pragmatist*, *supra* note 364, at 181.

Holmes projected as necessary for obtaining the final grade of clarity in law, in seeing law as simultaneously particular and general, local and universal.[376]

Haack understands the bad man as key to Holmes's algorithm because the bad man provides the necessary first grade distinction, the one between law and morality. It is a distinction based upon a defined negation (morality $\neq$ law). She sees the bad man and what later came to be called the "prediction theory" as working hand-in-hand, as bringing to bear the "perspective of a working attorney advising a hypothetical client who doesn't give a damn what's right, but just wants to know what's legal." The value of this perspective lies in bringing into a single focus two different points. First, it draws attention to a specific legal regime, say, Massachusetts 1897. Second, from that mass of law existing at that time and in that place – from the "statutes, rules, and precedents" – it brings into view the judge's expected interpretation.[377]

Or, in conventional Peircean language (which Haack does not use), the bad man's point of view brings together a sign and its interpretant. This relation invokes two further questions. What is the sign (any combination of statutes, rules, or precedents) ultimately suggesting to the interpretant (judge)? And, what will the judge do in light of what the sign suggests and what the client (the bad man) has done or is proposing to do?

Historically, notes Haack, the heavy focus on the second question led to the mistake of calling Holmes a proto-realist. He was not. His jurisprudence is more complex. One expects Haack at this juncture to identify the bad man's point of view – which really begins with that of the working attorney – as the interpreter who is in a triangular relationship with both the sign and the interpretant, a relationship in which the dynamics of interpretation go in each and every direction. But Haack does not take this step. Instead, she proceeds to the second major point of negation, that law is not solely logic nor does it inhere in solely logical form (law $\neq$ logic).[378]

Having dispensed with these two major negations, Haack quickly explains that the following sections of "Path" – on the uses of history and science – are part of Holmes's "positive" account of law, the growth or development of law that goes "far beyond the-law-in-England-in-1215 or the-law-in-Masschusetts-in-1897." The clearest signpost that he seeks to head in this direction is his criticism of Sir James Fitzjames Stephen's "striving for a useless quintessence of all systems, instead of an accurate analysis of one." Here in clearest terms is Holmes's averment that all legal systems are local, specific to time and place. "The idea of 'law-in-itself' is an illusion."

376 Haack, *On Legal Pragmatism*, *supra* note 364, at 14–24.

377 *Id.*

378 *Id.*

> Moreover, every legal system is an artifact of history; all have evolved, grown, adapted (and many have died away) in response to changing circumstances, pressures, and needs.
>
> And this means that from the very broadest perspective the law – now understood as referring to the whole accumulated history and ongoing evolution of the myriad legal systems of the world – encompasses both the past and the future of the social organization of humanity; in short, of civilization.[379]

Thus Haack summarizes what she takes to be a central theme of "Path"; indeed, of much of Holmes's writings. What is still missing though is any clear sense of how Holmes (or anyone) gets to this point. The assertion that law ≠ morality does not seem especially helpful as a heuristic – Haack uses the word – for achieving this global perspective, especially when she interprets this same perspective as the epiphany that the history of law is the history of moral progress.

Yet in other passages she makes a slightly different claim. There she describes the culmination as "civilized social life." In those passages she emphasizes Holmes's keen sense for law's range, its locality, its flexibility, its adaptability, its gestation in snarled, often unhappy circumstances. Law evolves.[380]

It is a nice question whether saying that law evolves is synonymous with saying that the history of law is the history of moral progress or that the latter is just another way of expressing the rise of civilized social life. Perhaps moral ≠ civilized; perhaps that is a distinction that made a big difference to Holmes and led him to insist on pointing out his friend the bad man's way of seeing things.

Haack does not follow up this lead. She ultimately provides no clear account of how, for Holmes, law evolves or how he, in the pragmatic spirit, knits past and future.

She recommends, instead, that legal scholars and theorists recognize that systems of social norms (of which law is one) form a continuum and from that hypothesis seek the salient similarities and dissimilarities across and between systems. This reminds one of Holmes's early efforts to categorize law according to duties. Her second recommendation is for legal theorists to take heed of Peirce's insight of how meanings grow in time, become richer, shed old, useless extensions, and in the process become transformed into a new vitality.[381] Peirce's maxim, when properly understood, directs attention to the vitality of meaning through its emphasis, not on what is or will be, but on what could have been. It's beauty lies in in its subjunctive quality; how it tests the limits of imagination, how it brings together a term's potential meanings.[382] Perhaps this subjunctive quality is what Haack had in mind when she spoke of pragmatism's knitting ability, but she doesn't expressly say so.

379 *Id.* at 17.
380 *Id.* at 19.
381 *Id.* at 19–21.
382 *Id.* at 11.

Peirce's confidence in the power of inquirers to storm successfully the stronghold of truth arises from his belief in the object of truth's drawing power. Peirce's Real exerts its own gravitational pull on the entire community of inquirers; it orders them in relation to each other and to the truth, the Final Opinion concerning the Real. In Holmes Haack sees the same confidence, but finds nothing substantive to back it up.[383]

What she does find is a gifted jurist who had great insight but not sufficient philosophical clarity. The bad man for her becomes a way to obtain a wider, more expansive view of law qua law (similar to Frank), and not a means for honing one's wits before being thrown into the game (Grey).

Yet what is perhaps most puzzling about Haack's take on Holmes is the complete lack of attention to the question – which she is eminently qualified to address – whether there is any significant *logical* function associated with Holmes's introduction of the bad man. That is to say, whether the bad man's entire significance as a marker in the logic of inquiry is merely to stand as a wrong way sign, or whether the bad man, as a pointer to those norms that have not obtained legal expression, draws attention to those circumstances of life, or to those meanings of good and bad, that have either lost out in the game of legal approbation (rendered secondary or criminal) or have not yet challenged the fundamental tenets of civilized life.[384] Or to say it in the way Holmes did at the close of the first chapter of *The Common Law*: "If truth were not often suggested by error, if old implements could not be adjusted to new uses, human progress would be slow."[385]

Our review of four pragmatists who have tackled, either directly or indirectly, the idea that the bad man is a heuristic, that he offers to a law student seeking to learn the law the useful perspective of a practicing attorney with an amoral client, or a client with dispositions contrary to the dominant taste, leads to two overarching conclusions. They all believe the bad man is a device that Holmes concocted for primarily rhetorical purposes (in both the positive and negative sense of rhetorical). None of them sees the bad man heuristic directly arising from the premises of Holmes's jurisprudential thinking.

Second, the interplay, the dynamism, between the judge's two queries with which we began this section (to the attorney: "what is the law?" and to the individual appearing *pro se*: "what do you want the court to do?") is ignored or downplayed. Not only is the interplay between these two questions slighted, their ability prick out the subtle cultural gradations of what is inside the law's boundary, or identify what lies completely outside its walls at a given time, finds little comment.

[383] *Id.* at 21.

[384] *See* Haack, *On Logic in the Law*, *supra* note 364, at 1–9 (discussing Langdell and Holmes's use of logic but not commenting in this respect on the bad man).

[385] Holmes, *The Common Law*, *supra* note 14, at 133.

Pedagogy served as a favored Holmes approach ("I too am, or at least have been, a pedagogue[,]")[386] for bringing into view the intersection of past and future from within the body of the law. That Holmes understood the law as a "body" is well brought out by Michal Alberstein in her perceptive book *Law and Pragmatism.*[387] She finds it something to criticize. Our take is different. Holmes turned to the law, gave it a signification not previously had, gave it a body, personified it as beholden to a command and a calling, because time does not stop. The moral sensibilities of the present had little innate power to penetrate the hidden reaches of the pressing, still vibrant past. The hidden reaches of the past could be living, personified, on the other side of the river or up the hill. Or found, un-personified, in the practices of the courts. Only the bad man would know that. Only the bad man would recognize at first or second sight the past's skiagraphs on the present.

12 YOSAL ROGAT

Probably no single article on Holmes since the Howe–Hart exchange has exerted as much influence on how subsequent commentators have perceived Holmes as Yosal Rogat's "The Judge As Spectator."[388]

It came out in the winter of 1964. Rogat contributed it to a symposium that the *University of Chicago Law Review* organized to mark the 1963 publication of both the second volume of Howe's Holmes biography and Howe's edition of *The Common Law*. One assumes the organizers invited Rogat to participate because he had, in the previous academic year, published a lengthy two-part article entitled, "Mr. Justice Holmes: A Dissenting Opinion."[389]

Only the historian as imp would dare ask whether the dissenting opinion sought to defend Holmes from the assaults of the Jesuits and their ilk. Of course not. The majority opinion from which Rogat demurs seems to be the same dominant liberal opinion about Holmes in many law schools that drove Lucey into a vituperative orgasm in the early forties. At least one assumes Rogat is referring to the same general outlook when he says in the first sentence: "This Article is one of a series which will attempt to prove that Mr. Justice Holmes was not, as is widely believed, uniquely responsive to the claims of civil liberties; that he was, in fact, quite often indifferent to them."[390]

[386] Holmes, *supra* note 369, at 491.

[387] Michal Alberstein, Pragmatism and Law 55–91 (2002).

[388] Yosal Rogat, *The Judge As Spectator*, 31 U. Chi. L. Rev. 213 (1964).

[389] Yosal Rogat, *Mr. Justice Holmes: A Dissenting Opinion* (part 1), 15 Stan. L. Rev. 3 (1962); Yosal Rogat, *Mr. Justice Holmes: A Dissenting Opinion* (part 2), 15 Stan. L. Rev. 254 (1963). After Rogat's death in 1980 James M. O'Fallon published the third part, Yosal Rogat and James M. O'Fallon, *Mr. Justice Holmes: A Dissenting Opinion – The Speech Cases*, 36 Stan. L. Rev. 1349 (1984).

[390] Rogat, *A Dissenting Opinion* (part 1), *supra* note 389, at 3.

How we go from that declaration to "The Judge As Spectator"'s opening line – "To think about Mr. Justice Holmes is to fall under the spell of a favorite of the gods [,]"[391] – presents a real curiosity unless we recall the recurring misgiving about Holmes's alleged tendency to employ sleight-of-mind. Much of it comes down to the justice's masterful use of language. Even so, one wonders whether Rogat himself fell under Holmes's "spell" or whether he, with his own bit of art, is only pretending that thoughts about Holmes have this occult power to take possession of one's self unawares as part of his strategy to undercut Holmes's authority in the profession.

The "Dissenting Opinion" articles certainly amount to an attempted bouleversement of Holmes's reputation as a great liberal. That Rogat's efforts, combined with others, have had measurable success can hardly be doubted. Few today would call Holmes a liberal without the use of an asterisk. Yet what makes "The Judge As Spectator" stand out from other critiques – both Rogat's and those of the other "dissenters" – is the skill with which Rogat develops, in the idiom of stated liberal values (civil rights, equal protection, free speech), the argument that how Holmes pursued law as a vocation would, if imitated, corrode the classical republican ideals – especially the rule of law – that had a strong hand in the founding of the country.

Putting the matter in this way draws attention to the similarity between Rogat's view and the opinion that the way of Holmes led to fascism. Rogat demurs from this judgment as well. He distinguishes between authoritarianism and totalitarianism and argues that Holmes's brand of authoritarianism was, in a sense, "the very opposite of 'totalitarian' thought."[392] Holmes's emphasis on self-interest, his skepticism regarding people's ability to identify the general good, his emphasis on freedom as lack of restraint, his insistence that morals should be separated from law would make his opinions repugnant to those committed to the "one soul" ideal in politics.

The same would be true of Holmes's image of the operative legal system. It "comes close to a bill of fare on which a price has been attached to each act by an impersonal management almost indifferent to what the customer himself decides; totalitarianism sees law as a system of prophylaxis based on knowledge and anticipation of what and how the patients are likely to decide."[393]

The relevant force of this contrast comes from Rogat's suggestion that totalitarianism takes as its starting point that which Holmes refused to accept, the motivation and nature of the actor. It views crime as a disease, the task of the legal system to prevent antisocial potentialities, and assumes humans are fully malleable. Holmes, in contrast, harkens solely to the common law. He may have, in Rogat's view, exaggerated its toughness and amorality and unduly acquiesced to the commands

[391] Rogat, *The Judge As Spectator, supra* note 388, at 213 *supra*.

[392] Rogat and O'Fallon, *A Dissenting Opinion – The Speech Cases, supra* note 389, at 1366.

[393] *Id.* at 1366–67.

of the perceived sovereign, but these failings did not turn him into a nascent totalitarian.[394]

How then to understand Holmes? After arduously analyzing more than thirty-five non-unanimous opinions – those Holmes wrote or in which he specially joined – on such topics as the legal status of aliens, civil rights, and free speech, Rogat strongly supports his main contention that Holmes had no special concern for individual liberty and did not, on that score (and probably no other), deserve the profession's adulation. He makes a number of surprising contentions along the way. For example, he sees the justice as strongly ideological, uninterested in the consequences of his decisions, opposed to thinking professionally about social problems ("we believe that the single most pervasive feature of Holmes's entire outlook was its tendency to cut off, at every level, the application of intelligence to social problems"),[395] and exceptionally uninterested in any perspective other than his own.

He ultimately concludes, as is well known, that Holmes's vaunted judicial restraint and detachment did not arise because of some deep-seated intellectual, moral, or political commitment but because, "[t]o a remarkable degree, Holmes simply did not care."[396]

Indifference may seem to put an end to the examination but in Rogat's hands it turns into a trope that leverages further thought. From one angle it illuminates how Holmes conceived the practice of law as a vocation. From another it puts Holmes's perspective on the law into a wider compass; it emphasizes Holmes's submission to the fate that would render him, Holmes the jurist, immaterial to the point of vanishing.

First, Holmes's perspective on the law. Rogat argues that perspective took strength or force as its starting point. In essence, Holmes exhibited a "tendency to assimilate a distinctively legal method of control to a crude system of social control resting on absolute power."[397] And: "Holmes's account of legal phenomena was fundamentally impoverished; it suffered from a failure to distinguish a crude system of social control resting on naked force from a distinctively legal method of control."[398]

Given Holmes's habitual obeisance to the will of the dominant power within the society, Rogat maintains Holmes never forsook any opportunity to clear the way, legally speaking, for the dominant power to act. Take Holmes's vaunted external standard. Its energy manifests itself precisely in how it steamrolls over actual intentions and in its cardinal principle that the consideration of legal rules must be dissociated from moral notions. This latter point was "closely related to the overriding importance Holmes attached to the elimination of obstacles to the will of the dominant class."[399]

394 *Id.*
395 Rogat, *A Dissenting Opinion* (part 1), *supra* note 389, at 9 n.27.
396 Rogat, *The Judge As Spectator*, *supra* note 388, at 255.
397 Rogat, *A Dissenting Opinion* (part 1), *supra* note 389, at 12.
398 Rogat and O'Fallon, *A Dissenting Opinion – The Speech Cases*, *supra* note 389, at 1361.
399 Rogat, *A Dissenting Opinion* (part 1), *supra* note 389, at 40 n.184.

Because Holmes collapsed the distinctive features of legality – appeal to reason, articulation of reasons for decisions, recognized moral limits to political power – into his version of social control, he conceived legal method as mechanistically as he did the legal system. The bad man, in Rogat's view, simply served as a device for eradicating obstreperous moral notions, those that attempted to impede the dominant power from having its way. The dominant power, the sovereign, expressed its desires through duly appointed legal means. Moral ideas – meaning morally inspired notions outside the law that lead to political and legal action – disrupt the flow of the sovereign will and must be banished.[400]

The bad man, then, brought into the equation the malevolence necessary to neutralize pressing moral feelings of goodwill that posed the risk of acquiring "legal relevance" without, in effect, having gone through the proper legal channels.[401] Rogat does not quite put it this way. It does seem, however, to be implied in his claim that Holmes stressed "acts" rather than "thoughts" because "acts" fit more easily into Holmes's belief that the law is nothing more than a crude method of social control. Law puts into motion the will of the sovereign. The will of the sovereign always carries the strong presumption of correctness whether it speaks through the medium of the common law or more directly through statute. The bad man helps one see the grounds upon which this strong presumption rests; his perspective, taken seriously, counteracts both the sense of moral obligation and that of moral indignation that might, jointly or severally, distort an otherwise professional view.[402]

Rogat, aghast at this manner of conceiving law and the judge's role, forewarns, "Holmes's prediction as well as his 'bad man' theory stands in the same peculiar relation [as Holmes's theory of contract stands in relation to the institution of contract] to a legal system. In each case Holmes's success in securing adoption of his theory might substantially eliminate the institution he seeks to understand."[403]

This prophecy is extreme; one might well chalk it up to the fervent advocacy common in the Warren Court era. But it also reminds one of the note sounded by Zane, amplified by Lucey and his supporters, hinted at by Fuller, and, looking ahead, repeated but accentuated in their own way by Grant Gilmore (1977), Louise Weinberg (1997), and Albert W. Alschuler (2000).[404] But after Rogat it takes on a new inflection. He, distinctly, attributes Holmes's deference to the

[400] Rogat, *The Judge As Spectator*, *supra* note 388, at 225–26; Rogat and O'Fallon, *A Dissenting Opinion – The Speech Cases*, *supra* note 389, at 1362–63.

[401] Rogat, *The Judge As Spectator*, *supra* note 388, at 225–26.

[402] *Id.* at 223–27.

[403] *Id.* at 226.

[404] Grant Gilmore, The Ages of American Law 44 (2d ed., new foreword and final chapter by Phillip Bobbitt 2014) (orig. ed. 1977) ("The real Holmes was savage, harsh, and cruel, a bitter and lifelong pessimist who saw in the course of human life nothing but a continuing struggle in which the rich and powerful impose their will on the weak and poor."); Louise Weinberg, *Holmes' Failure*, 96 Mich. L. Rev. 691, 692, 713 (1997) (emphasizing the "littleness" in Holmes's work and the pusillanimity that led him to focus mainly on private law instead of

dominant power not to a character flaw or misguided ideas but to an instinctive indifference exacerbated by social and cultural dislocation.

The basic story line that emerges from Rogat's articles is that Holmes's character inclined him, by the turn of the century, to the belief that the way of life he had fought to protect, as had his ancestors, did not have universal significance; he believed it would not last given the current social and cultural conditions in the United States. The one joy left to him lay in perfecting the legal intelligence to which he had committed his life. Rogat does not quite end the story with that flourish but I think it fits. I also think it fair to say, though Rogat would disagree, that Holmes dared to hope that a constantly improved legal intelligence would, in the long run, best govern the country he loved.

Before proceeding let us take a moment to recall what Holmes wrote in 1918: "If I may quote myself again, property, friendship, and truth have a common root in time. One can not be wrenched from the rocky crevices into which one has grown for many years without feeling that one is attacked in one's life. What we most love and revere generally is determined by early associations."[405]

Rogat most likely sensed the pathos lodged in these words like a spent bullet but he did not let that deter him from his mission of ending the Holmesian contagion. He hoped to starve the ferment that Emerson had first excited in the 1860s.[406] It posed a vital threat to the legal profession in the 1960s. He took a different tack than his predecessors, however; he took the view that Holmes developed his legal style in the same manner as his friends Henry Adams and Henry James had perfected, respectively, their historical and literary styles. Working from the unstated premise that "the style is the man," Rogat, not yet sensitized to the malapropism of over-inclusive gendered language, extended the concept of style to include the distinctively sincere insincerity of these three American Anglophiles circa 1900.[407]

public law and to bypass the importance of equity); ALBERT W. ALSCHULER, LAW WITHOUT VALUES: THE LIFE, WORK, AND LEGACY OF JUSTICE HOLMES 194 (2000) ("For Holmes to retreat to sneers and 'can't helps' because he lacked a clear vision of the universe was a cop-out. Arresting though his iconoclastic views of moral issues often were, these views were more adolescent than profound."). However, in fairness to Gilmore, who had a more sophisticated understanding of Holmes than either Weinberg or Alschuler, we must note that he also, to the extent he "could follow the dark outlines of his thought," recognized that Holmes "was both a greater man and a more profound thinker than the mythical Holmes ever was." THE AGES OF AMERICAN LAW at 167 n.13; *see also* Grant Gilmore, *Some Reflections on Oliver Wendell Holmes*, 2 GREEN BAG 2d 379 (1999).

[405] Holmes, *Natural Law*, *supra* note 11, at 446.

[406] *See* letter from Oliver Wendell Holmes, Jr. to Ralph Waldo Emerson (April 16, 1876) (on file with the Harvard Digital Suite, Mark DeWolfe Howe research materials on Holmes, 1858–1968. Finding Aid, General Correspondence, General, Group II: Box 14, Folder 32, Emerson, Ralph Waldo, correspondent, 1876).

[407] Rogat, *The Judge As Spectator*, *supra* note 388, at 230–43.

The argument in "The Judge As Spectator" is subtle, evocative, and at the same time blunt and over the top. Presumably written after much time and effort reviewing Holmes's opinions on the legal status of aliens, civil rights, and free speech – and maybe even whatever he could find on defendants' rights – "The Judge As Spectator" leads one through various byways and circumlocutions to the feet of this one fateful sentence: "Holmes did not have to exert effort to attain the condition of disinterestedness that, in at least one sense of the word, is the paramount judicial requisite; he started with a kind of primal, organically grounded equivalent of that condition."[408]

Most people immersed in Holmes's writing to the degree that Rogat immersed himself would, upon reading that sentence, involuntarily recall these lines from "The Path of the Law": "If the typical criminal is a degenerate, bound to swindle or to murder by as deep seated an organic necessity as that which makes the rattlesnake bite, it is idle to talk of deterring him by the classical method of imprisonment. He must be gotten rid of; he cannot be improved, or frightened out of his structural reaction."[409]

Rogat does not come out and call Holmes a "legal sociopath," but he comes as close as good manners permit.[410] A certain refinement of usage characterizes Rogat's style, one that transforms his antipathy to this man Holmes into one self-consciously clinical. The turn to Adams and James serves to lessen the instinctive aversion because Rogat, in keeping with his refinement, knows that there must be more at work than simply a literate pen and a regal face to account for Holmes's prominence in legal circles and the adulation accorded him. The first Justice Harlan also filed powerful dissents, most notably in *Plessy* v. *Ferguson*. But he, a Christian fundamentalist, never garnered the same praise from, nor rose to the same stature among, the people who hoisted Holmes.[411]

That "more" is the modernist sensibility that Holmes, along with Adams and James, manifested in their work. Rogat takes the unusual step of treating legal opinions as cultural products on par with histories and novels. Though forming a specialized, technical genre, case decisions may as effectively as traditional literary expression expose the shattering of want, the fragmentation of viewpoint, the gossamer qualities of sympathy, the very brittleness of logic that confrontation with

[408] *Id.* at 246.

[409] Holmes, *The Path of the Law*, *supra* note 14, at 400.

[410] I have taken the term "legal sociopath" from Anthony Kronman. ANTHONY T. KRONMAN, MAX WEBER 13 (1983) ("Only the behavior of a person who himself has no normative commitments to the law and is wholly uninfluenced by the commitments of anyone else – a kind of legal sociopath – necessarily falls outside the domain of the sociology of law."). Albert W. Alschuler also never went so far as to call Holmes a "legal sociopath" but he did title the published results of almost an almost decade-long project, *Law without Values: The Life, Work, and Legacy of Justice Holmes*. *See* ALSCHULER, *supra* note 404.

[411] *See* G. EDWARD WHITE, THE AMERICAN JUDICIAL TRADITION: PROFILES OF LEADING AMERICAN JUDGES 105–20 (3d ed., 2007).

a mighty tide of temperament leaves in its path. The man civilized by inclination, aspiration, and inheritance stands bereft, alone. A wave of something more obdurate than democratic feeling mowed across the American landscape and, after it had passed, three of the finest intellects in the nation decided they could no longer in good conscience call their country home.

James decamped to England; Adams internally exiled himself to the study of medieval Catholicism and modern American runes; and Holmes? Holmes, says Rogat, retreated into participation, he withdrew into public responsibilities. Thus begins the line of argument that ultimately leads to the fateful sentence on the primal, organic nature of Holmes's detachment. The inspiration for this supposed insight into Holmes's character comes, perhaps unsurprisingly, from Holmes's father, the author of *The Poet at the Breakfast Table*, who, in that volume of parlor pleasantries, called him "The Young Astronomer" and described him to interested readers as a "spectator," too much inclined "to looking at life as at a solemn show."[412]

From this gratuitous point of (undoubtedly) constructive paternal criticism Rogat begins to draw out the terms of his argument. Leaving as little as possible to the vagaries of inference and interpretation, as single-minded as Lucey but approaching Fuller's polish, he puts forward his fundamental supposition that "Holmes can best be understood by seeing the importance of that characterization. For his unusual distance from the life of his time led him to define his judicial role in a manner that was equally unusual. Ultimately, Holmes was set apart by the way in which he conceived his vocation."[413]

By this route Rogat introduces the main point of his article. Holmes's indifference may have its source in the organic necessity of his being, but for his detachment to take on greater social and cultural proportions one had to view the detachment itself as a sociological event, as a purposeful response to social and cultural changes, as, in part, a rearguard effort to stem the rising tide of the benighted. That was one reason for drawing extended comparisons to Adams and James and not to other contemporary Bostonians, say, John Chipman Gray or Moorfield Storey.

The second reason had to do with writing style. The manner in which each man chose to communicate or to conceal or to communicate by concealing through his favored form of expression betokened a double- or triple-mindedness that, from Rogat's perspective, led in Holmes's case to the articulation of a false choice, do or die. Learned Hand may have been momentarily silenced by Holmes's invocation of the sacred right to kill but Rogat was not.

[412] Rogat, *The Judge As Spectator*, *supra* note 388, at 243. Rogat's student Douglas Baird continues the comparison into this century. He entitles the introduction of his book *Reconstructing Contracts*, "The Young Astronomer." Douglas Baird, Reconstructing Contracts 1–8 (2013).

[413] Rogat, *The Judge As Spectator*, *supra* note 388, at 243.

Holmes's way of writing he does admire though; he finds his style "more alive, enjoyable, and immediately effective than that of any other common-law judge."[414] But he buries this praise in a content-less footnote. He mainly argues Holmes's style of writing projects a false objectivity, an artful conceit that fosters the feeling of utter impassivity while simultaneously inviting the cognoscenti to find the hidden key. The seduced, if still game to keep seeking for further enlightenment after crossing the threshold, ultimately discover no there there, a bewildering emptiness and utter coldness that turns the rattlesnake, by comparison, into a cozy tribble.

If Lucey taught us that jurisprudence has a use for horror, Rogat introduces us to how the surreal works itself into law.

It may not be completely fair to Rogat to compare "The Judge As Spectator" to Max Weber's classic vocational essays, "Politics As a Vocation," and "Science As a Vocation."[415] But the comparison is apt to the extent each is understood as an effort to depict, not an idea or an ideology, but the concrete constellations relevant normative ends have assumed in their respective societies. While Weber brings to his remarks on the German scene an almost unmatched erudition as to how societies have traditionally organized their forms of political leadership and their institutions of learning, Rogat's delineation of law as a vocation in the United States rests on the unarticulated premise that the vocation has yet to be established and the unstated conclusion it should not be established.

Both the premise and the conclusion depend, in turn, on the disestablishment of Holmes as America's representative jurist, its one genius in the law, on deprogramming those many members of the profession who, seduced by his distinguished background, intellectual sophistication, and literary charm, tend to look upon Holmes as a paragon.

Admittedly, it is bizarre to claim that Rogat sought to show that law as a vocation existed in the United States only through negation. But that is what he has done. He offers none of the concrete prescriptions that Weber did, even through he employed a similar type of sociological analysis. Rogat's emphases on personal liberty and social equality draw their energy from morality, not law. The reader is left to infer that what Holmes saw as his vocation was, upon close analysis, not a vocation at all, at least not in any modern or classical sense of the term. The deference to majority will was in essence deference to amoral power. One cannot draw out a professional ethic, much less a vocation, from an ultimately nonnormative end. That was Rogat's fundamental contention.

Yet he layered his argument with the observation that Holmes made it appear he had done nothing but simply, stoically, devoted his life and his art to his job, to serving his fellow citizens, the archetypical jobbist. Holmes described himself as

[414] Rogat, A *Dissenting Opinion* (part 1), *supra* note 389, at 9 n.31.

[415] *See* Max Weber, *Politics As a Vocation* and *Science As a Vocation*, *in* FROM MAX WEBER: ESSAYS IN SOCIOLOGY 77–156 (H. H. Gerth and C. Wright Mills trans. and eds., 1946).

merely the "supple tool of power."[416] Holmes was sincere in his insincerity because no one knew to what kind of life that power would ultimately lead (not even Holmes). Or how he understood the meaning of his job. To maintain, as Rogat essentially did, that the most famous judge in modern America – and a former practitioner, legal scholar, and law professor – a judge who pursued his legal work with the utmost passion and dedication, who dearly loved the law, who appeared to be imbued with the relish and drive befitting a dignified calling, that this judge could not under any circumstances be trusted to serve as a role model for the profession, despite the great esteem in which he was held, because this same judge happened also to be an utter legal sociopath would surely throw one for a huge loop if one was not already accustomed to purple crocodiles dropping out of the clear blue sky. I live in Miami after all.

Of course, those inclined to agree with Rogat would say the way I have put the matter is rather perverse. Louis Menand, for example, takes the view that Holmes is the "Emerson of professionalism."[417] He emphasizes the aesthetic insularity within which Holmes worked and that grounded his self-conception. Rogat would be dissatisfied with ending the analysis there because the whole point of "The Judge As Spectator" is to argue against any model of judicial detachment that takes one out of "life." A judge should be impartial, yes; but Rogat says Holmes presents for our consideration a very different question: "Whether a minimum of involvement is not also required."[418]

Rogat clearly believes the answer is yes but he does not work out the degree of involvement required or state exactly why within the pages of "The Judge As Spectator." Neither does he elaborate how law as a vocation should be understood because, as I suggested above, he does not give any indication that he believes the practice of law in any capacity to be a vocation in the sense of something especially dignified and set apart from other social roles in the United States.

But do not lawyers have a special contribution to make to the common weal? Rogat would probably say yes but demur from any effort to christen it a calling. He seems more reluctant than his predecessors in dissent to bring down a higher power on Holmes's head. His diagnosis of Holmes's innate indifference he believes sufficient to counter conventional efforts, like Howe's, to find in Holmes's skepticism sufficient bona fides for calling him a liberal. Nor does he find it fitting to call Holmes a pragmatist à la Dewey.[419] Holmes stood at the outer limits of disenchantment. It took a scholar like Rogat – one willing and able to cast an absurdly cold, unblinking sociological eye – to insist that the pace of events had outdone even the exceptional culture-creating powers of Holmes and his peers.

[416] Rogat, *The Judge As Spectator*, *supra* note 388 at 249–50.

[417] Louis Menand, The Metaphysical Club: A Story of Ideas in America 59 (2001).

[418] Rogat, *The Judge As Spectator*, *supra* note 388, at 243.

[419] *Id.* at 249–56.

13 LAW AS A VOCATION

In speaking of strictly scientific work Weber poses this question in "Science As a Vocation": "Why does one engage in doing something that in reality never comes, and never can come, to an end?"[420] The accomplishment that took years, took hard intensive, consuming work, will also wane with the years, become outdated, antiquated, outmoded. The beat goes on. This transitoriness comprises the law of scientific progress. His question broaches the *meaning* of science Weber explains because, "after all, it is not self-evident that something subordinate to such a law is sensible and meaningful in itself."[421]

He acknowledges the pressing practical purposes, which he understands as aligning the expectations that science creates with contemporary goals and techniques. But Weber wonders about the personal attitude of the academic type, the one who does not work mainly for specific, practical ends. Even though the academic claims to pursue "science for science's sake," this person allows himself to be integrated into an ongoing scientific enterprise that has no known conclusion and which renders every accomplishment relative and relatively insignificant.

Unending scientific progress, part of modern rationalization and disenchantment, brings to the fore the problem of value in a unique way. Weber finds that Leo Tolstoi formulated the problem trenchantly. Is death meaningful? Tolstoi asked. No, he answered, because "the individual life of civilized man, placed into an infinite 'progress,' according to its own imminent meaning should never come to an end; for there is always a further step ahead of one who stands in the march of progress. And no man who comes to die stands upon the peak which lies in infinity."[422] Unlike their ancestors, a modern person may tire of life – but be satiated never; they will never die ensconced in the belief that the grail that last touched their lips was holy.

On a Sunday in March 1931 at 10:30 p.m., Eastern Standard Time, the nation celebrated Justice Holmes's birthday via a live radio broadcast.[423] Justice Holmes was singularly honored for his many accomplishments. He was also the nation's first active Supreme Court justice to reach ninety. The temperature hovered in the low forties that night in Washington, DC. It was cold but not bitter cold.[424] After remarks by Charles Evans Hughes, the chief justice of the United States Supreme Court, Charles E. Clark, dean of the Yale Law School, and Charles A. Boston, president of

[420] Weber, *Science As a Vocation*, *supra* note 415, at 138.
[421] *Id.*
[422] *Id.* at 139–40.
[423] For a good discussion of this event see LIVA BAKER, THE JUSTICE FROM BEACON HILL: THE LIFE AND TIMES OF OLIVER WENDELL HOLMES 3–7 (1991).
[424] *The Evening Star*, Washington D.C., Mar. 8, 1931, part one, A-7.

the American Bar Association, Holmes, seated in his study, cleared his throat and spoke into the microphone:

> In this symposium my part is only to sit in silence. To express one's feelings as the end draws near is too intimate a task.
>
> But I may mention one thought that comes to me as a listener in. The riders in a race do not stop short when they reach the goal. There is a little finishing canter before coming to a stand still. There is time to hear the kind voice of friends and to say to oneself: 'The work is done.'
>
> But just as one says that, the answer comes: 'The race is over, but the work never is done while the power to work remains.'
>
> The canter that brings you to a stand still need not be only coming to rest. It cannot be, while you still live. For to live is to function. That is all there is to living.
>
> And so I end with a line from a Latin poet who uttered the message more than fifteen hundred years ago – "Death plucks my ear and says, 'Live – I am coming.'"[425]

Read in a certain light, Holmes's radio address appears to support Rogat's charge that the judge entombed himself in Olympian indifference: only the horse's ending flourish, the canter, draws his attention. That the race had been long and hard, that the prize had been worthy, that other riders in other races could use a bit of encouragement goes unsaid. Perhaps there was a moral somewhere in those words for those willing to find it, but probably not. The sincere insincerity was patent. The oracular pronouncement, "to live is to function and that is all there is to living," takes on an astrological shimmer when the country is deep in the throes of what came to be called the Great Depression.

Even as the final end approaches the will to not care stays unbroken.

To live is to function. That is the gist. We should expect no other lesson from this ninety-year-old man who spent over half his life using the law to partially unravel the tightly tangled skein of human affairs. His use of the word "function" is determinately odd in this context, giving one pause, jolting in its sudden change of register. The word "function" seems to me at first blush decidedly unsentimental, un-lyrical, denuded, social-scientific, somewhat reptilian. One of the country's most honored judges and gifted writers declares to those Americans listening in that to function is all there is to living. He does not talk about commitment, the privilege of service, or the rule of law. He says nothing about a life's calling.

The perplexity immediately arises whether Holmes would have agreed with Tolstoi. Death has no meaning because life has no meaning and a life spent in the service of the law has no special value because no individual decision or collection of decisions that a judge makes ever has any long-lasting saliency.

[425] Oliver Wendell Holmes, *Radio Address*, *in* III CW 541.

Achievement is anonymous, to recur to a phrase that Mark Howe once used.[426] The trick is to continue, to exalt in the performance, accept gracefully the applause when the applause comes ... and if not, carry on. Thus speaks the spectator.

Rogat never really understood how a man he believed so indifferent in his outlook on life could become, for so many members of the legal profession and beyond, the visible manifestation of American liberal hope and enlightenment. Even the great literary critic Edmund Wilson, from whom Rogat apparently drew much inspiration, finds the sequence unfathomable albeit comic.[427] Wilson concludes his 1962 book, *Patriotic Gore*, with a well-known lengthy chapter on the justice. He, as would Rogat, emphasizes the justice's "carapace of impenetrable indifference," but attributes it "partly to the impregnable security of belonging to the Boston 'Brahmin' caste."[428]

But being part of the Brahmin caste did not in itself suffice to draw out the lineaments distinctive to a personality that had, like the legendary figures in the Book of Daniel, come out of the fiery furnace alive. This is how Wilson posed the problem in 1962:

> Of his generation that fought in the Civil War and among the really gifted men whose characters and subsequent careers were profoundly modified by it, Holmes the younger perhaps stands alone as one who was never corrupted, never discouraged or broken, by the alien conditions that the war had prepared. How was it that he managed to survive, to function as a first-rate intellect, to escape the democratic erosion?[429]

Wilson finds his answer not only in Holmes's Brahminism; Holmes's "high-minded egoism and his philosophic temper of mind" also worked jointly with his Brahminism to submerge events into that netherworld Holmes's forebears called God's will. The articulated major premise for understanding Holmes lay for Wilson in Holmes's Puritan ancestry, in the abiding Calvinist temper, the underlying disposition that found little dignity and much shame in contemplating who might not be damned.[430]

Wilson's assessments carry a judiciousness one finds lacking in Rogat. But then again Wilson was not a law professor, he found *The Common Law* practically impenetrable, and it goes almost without saying – except it must be said because few today know much about Wilson – that he did not appear to share Rogat's sense of moral urgency. Wilson viewed Holmes within the fissured panorama of

[426] *See* The Occasional Speeches of Oliver Wendell Holmes 61 (Mark DeWolfe Howe ed., 1962).

[427] Edmund Wilson, Patriotic Gore: Studies in the Literature of the American Civil War 766–67 (1962).

[428] *Id.* at 782–83.

[429] *Id.* at 782.

[430] *Id.* at 782–95.

the American past, just as he did Henry James and Henry Adams. It was he who first saw that Adams and James had taken up the roles of spectators, those who stand and watch. "The men of action," said Wilson, "make history, but the spectators make most of the histories, and these histories may influence action."[431]

i *The Bad Man As a Projection*

With these considerations in mind we take up the thirteenth way of looking at the bad man. He is a projection. As we noted in Part III, he first appears in lecture IX of *The Common Law*. In discussing the difference between conditions subsequent and precedent, Holmes adds:

> On the other hand, every condition subsequent is precedent to the incidence of the burden of the law. If we look at the law as it would be regarded by one who had no scruples against doing anything which he could do without incurring legal consequences, it is obvious the main consequence attached by the law to a contract is a greater or lesser possibility of having to pay money. The only question from a purely legal point of view is whether the promisor will be compelled to pay. And the important moment is that at which that point is settled. All conditions are precedent to that.[432]

Holmes admits this way of formulating the existence of conditions precedent is extreme. But it is no less extreme than how he stipulated the existence of a condition subsequent: "All are subsequent to the first stage of the obligation."[433] And thus we find ourselves again in the midst of another Holmes-contrived polarity, between the obligation and the incidence of the burden of the law.

To be clear, the burden of the law according to Holmes is not when the man without scruples becomes liable in one sense of that word – say due to nonperformance or shoddy performance – but when he is compelled to pay. That, Holmes emphasizes, is the "important moment."[434]

Something curious happened between 1881 and 1897. During that interval, between *The Common Law* and "The Path of the Law," a shrewd observation regarding the moment of truth in a legal event grew larger, more encompassing, and became for Holmes the basis for understanding law. "The prophecies of what the courts will do in fact, and nothing more pretentious, are what I mean by the law."[435] We cannot pretend to know exactly how or why this happened. But we do know that what characterizes both the man with no scruples and the man who is bad

[431] *Id.* at 668–69.
[432] Oliver Wendell Holmes, *The Common Law*, *supra* note 14, at 277.
[433] *Id.*
[434] *Id.*
[435] Holmes, *The Path of the Law*, *supra* note 14, at 393.

is the propensity to see which deeds or misdeeds will lead to the moment of lawful compulsion – and which will not.

At some point Holmes also realized that this insight into how law(yers) worked in his society provided an invaluable pedagogical tool. It enabled students to navigate the complexity of legal materials – the body of reports, of treatises, and of statutes – through the adoption of a viewpoint that emphasized that what the courts had done, or would do, had, in fact, intrinsically only a little to do with morals or logic. It seems in Holmes's opinion that neither the thread of logic nor the string of moral principle would be enough to tie a present situation with past decisions and future outcomes. His insight – presumably one shared by other practicing members of the profession – that the essence of law lay in court action, in the specifically legal consequences a deed or misdeed incurred, took what may have been the most myopic, self-serving attitude possible, one unthinkingly adopted by those lawyers given to sneering or hustling or pontificating, and transformed it into the basis for a new legal framework.

In other words, Holmes, through the force of his rhetoric, projected the bad man from his common law origins onto a new plane of social existence. The bad man is a remote conception. That the bad man originated in Holmes's common law jurisprudence is one thesis of this study. A second is that in magnifying a personality type that presumably many legal professionals knew and know, either through direct acquaintance or through hearsay, by making this personality type the focal image of legal learning and investigation, Holmes brought to a head as pedagogically formative a legal question that had not quite existed before with the same potency: What do we allow the bad man to get away with?

Fred Rodell made a similar observation in 1951 but he put it in the negative (all "law really amounts to is what a bad man cannot get away with").[436] Legally speaking, Rodell's formulation is better. It draws attention to the habit of creating a zone of prohibition and working outward. But for pedagogical purposes it lacks the needed structure for truly learning the inner workings of a common law jurisdiction. For to begin the study of law by adopting the point of view of the bad man – that is, to take the steps required to enter fully into the purely legal point of view – one cannot begin from either endpoint, from conduct already denoted as lawful or unlawful. One must begin off-center, from what Holmes at times called the penumbra.

To put it another way: to learn law as an effective practitioner knows it, one must not begin, according to Holmes, with established dogma. Dogma is a necessary preliminary but not the proper starting point. Nor should one begin with the presumption that a specific consequence will ensue from a given set of circumstances. One should begin with the prophecies of what the courts of a given jurisdiction will do in fact. Note the plural: prophecies not prophecy, courts not court. The distinction is important and we will address it further in the next part. For

[436] Fred Rodell, *supra* note 226, at 623.

now, let's keep delving deeper into the stance that Holmes presses upon us, that of the bad man who must prophesy.

The effective practitioner knows not only how to read the existing prophecies but can, when the moment comes, prophesy in turn. One wonders whether through his varied use of "prophecy," as a noun or verb, Holmes has in mind a definite shade of meaning he wishes to convey. In the published address that came to be known as "The Path of the Law" he uses the word "prophecy" in some fashion nine times. "Prediction" is used seven times. Scott Brewer has commented on how Holmes moves easily between "the more scientific term and the more biblical term for prognostication" several times within the essay's opening pages.[437] The question is why.

My best guess is that he uses the two words almost interchangeably to capture something distinctive about the law, two distinct, interrelated pressure points: its antiquity and its futurity. The antiquity Holmes identifies early in the essay with his comment about the "sibylline leaves"[438] in which "are gathered the scattered prophecies of the past upon the cases in which the axe will fall. These are what properly have been called the oracles of the law."[439] The futurity he expresses in the very next sentence: "Far the most important and pretty nearly the whole meaning of every new effort of legal thought is to make these prophecies more precise, and to generalize them into a thoroughly connected system."[440]

At first reading, the law's futurity appears to be at odds with its antiquity. The futurity lies in the *newness* of the effort of legal thought. That part is clear enough. The discordance disappears when we ask how the prophecies are to be made "more precise." It's a separate and preliminary issue from generalization and systematiza-

[437] Scott Brewer, *A Jurisprudence of Logical Form*, *in* THE LEGACY OF OLIVER WENDELL HOLMES, JR. 127 n.8 (Steven J. Burton ed., 2000).

[438] In the Greek tradition a sibyl is an old woman who utters ecstatic predictions of woe. At one time, sibyls were thought to wander through the world and to attain an extraordinary age – as much as 1,000 years. But Delphi, Samos, Erythrae in Ionia, Marpessus in Troas, and Cumae and Tibur in Italy each had their own resident sibyl. Certain collections of oracles were attributed to individual sibyls. These oracles were seen as relevant, and able to be applied, to certain situations, especially when an emergency arose. Interestingly, some early oracles were written in Greek hexameters, and their content protected through the use of acrostics.

The Romans, for example, claimed to have received a partial collection of the prophecies of the Cumean Sibyl under one of the two Tarquinian kings in the sixth century BCE. What is certain is that a collection of such books existed in Rome and was preserved in the temple of Jupiter Capitolinus during the Republic. These books were entrusted to a special priestly commission composed first of two, then of ten, then of fifteen members who could consult only when ordered to do so by the Senate in times of recognized emergency. Arnaldo Momigliano and Emilio Suarez de la Torre, *Sibylline Oracles* in 12 THE ENCYCLOPEDIA OF RELIGION 8382–86 (2d ed., Lindsay Jones ed., 2005).

[439] Holmes, *The Path of the Law*, *supra* note 14, at 391.

[440] *Id.*

tion. The bad man is needed for increasing precision because that effort in the legal context is more like synthesis not analysis. It is the effort to unify more knowledge and more perspectives and bring them to bear on a single point. That same effort to coalesce and to apply constitutes the single most important cause in what is commonly called professional judgment.

Holmes says as much when he points out that "[t]he process is one, from a lawyer's statement of a case, eliminating as it does all dramatic elements with which his client's story has clothed it, and retaining only the facts of legal import, up to the final analyses and abstract universals of theoretic jurisprudence."[441]

To say this "process" is more like synthesis than analysis seems counterintuitive. Certainly, the primary skill a young lawyer is taught and judged upon is the ability to analyze facts, to eliminate what Holmes calls the "dramatic elements," and to analyze legal concepts, to pass them through successive grades of clarity.

Many commentators, some discussed in previous sections of this part, have added to the traditional tests of clarity a pragmatic one and see Holmes as a forerunner in this respect. According to this argument, the bad man functions as a heuristic for reifying such legal concepts as "duty" and seeing how the most pressing of its meanings function in specific contexts. But if left unexamined this approach leaves unanalyzed a ubiquitous feature of operative legal concepts. That feature is persistence. The matter for much thought then becomes whether and if so, how, a legal concept has accumulated by successive degrees a persistent vitality.

Vitality – used as Karl Llewellyn used the word, to designate a concept that vigorously has influenced action[442] – points toward a concept's power to influence action and its ability to sustain that power. Vitality has both a diachronic and a synchronic dimension. Yet if legal concepts have no independent, metaphysical reality as Holmes believed, then what, exactly, is the subject matter of study? Is it the working life of the judges and other members of the legal profession? Is it their technical language and institutionalized habits of thought? Is it the rationalized environment in which members of the profession act, the functioning interconnected institutions, or the broader political dynamics in which the institutions themselves interact? These were certainly options Holmes could have chosen in 1897. But he didn't.

According to "The Path of the Law" the subject matter of study is the law and the law is the prophecies of what the courts of England or Massachusetts will do in fact. That much everyone can agree upon. The bad man is presented as unscrupulous, self-interested, and not given to vague sanctions of conscience. That too everyone can agree upon. The single-minded concern for material consequences seems to be the bad man's

[441] *Id.*

[442] Karl N. Llewellyn, *What Price Contract? – An Essay in Perspective*, 40 YALE L.J. 728 (1931) (stating that "by 'vital' I mean a concept which had vigorously influenced men's actions").

most defining trait. But that concern has to be connected with the bad man's task of prophesying, through studying the sibylline leaves, what the courts will do in fact.

On the other side of the coin, the courts are the instruments of the public force. The bad man's concern is not with the public force per se but with the public force as mediated through the instrumentality of the courts. Holmes has carefully arranged his terms. "The object of our study, then, is prediction, the prediction of the incidence of the public force through the instrumentality of the courts."[443]

Thus, we have arrayed on one side the self-interest of the bad man and on the other the self-interest of the public force. The opposition immediately brings to mind Holmes's metaphorical use of the Plank of Carneades in *The Common Law*: "If a man is on a plank in the deep sea which will only float one, and a stranger lays hold of it, he will thrust him off if he can. When the state finds itself in a similar position, it does the same thing."[444] Taking the "state" as equivalent to the "public force through the instrumentality of the courts" leads to the realization that in constructing this opposition Holmes is laying the grounds for a new, and vital, way of seeing the law.

Holmes describes law as predictions or prophecies of court action that the bad man must study because the public force is not always constant or consistent. Its self-interest warbles. The bad man, because he has no spiritual, moral, or social concerns, clearly sees that the public force's self-interest varies and shifts and whatever seemingly unified expression law may possess at any given moment has been achieved through the intercession of the courts.

The self-interest of the bad man becomes then a projected point of present stability, the artificial ground from which one can begin to draw lines. Once a line is connected to a specific act that the public force has taken in its own self-interest (again, through the courts), either in favor or against the bad man, one has begun to satisfy the necessary initial conditions to understand the law from within – its boundaries and inner dynamics, its breadth, its length and depth. Perspective arises. The bad man by establishing a relation between his self-interest and that of the public force as expressed through the courts makes it possible for the law to be known, not as a theoretic datum of existence or through direct acquaintance, but as a discipline of power.

ii *The Law from Within*

In the opening pages of *Justice Holmes on Legal History* James Willard Hurst explains, in his careful analytic way, that the phrase "roles of law in the United States" as used in his discussion of Justice Holmes and legal history refers to one or more of four factors: (1) the legitimate monopoly of violence and, as a corollary, the

[443] *Id.*

[444] Holmes, *The Common Law*, *supra* note 14, at 137.

power to oversee other forms of compulsion that people within the jurisdiction impose on others; (2) the ideal of constitutionalism, that there should be "no center of public or private power not subject to some check outside itself," that such power be used in a manner consistent with individual or common welfare, and that the power holders themselves should not determine the relevant criteria; (3) the use of law to define values and allocate resources to implement defined values, mainly through regular and rational procedure; and, (4) the use of law to govern, along with the market, the economy; meaning, the use of law as a "principal means to affect allocations of manpower and material means among competing objects of use[.]"[445]

Hurst acknowledges he cannot invoke Holmes's support for the pattern and weighting of the list, but he finds in these "four salient combinations of value and function" the distinctive indicia that mark off law's roles in American history.[446]

To some people keyed into the prevailing literatures surveying American political, legal, and economic development Hurst's list appears relatively unobjectionable, even if truncated. From another angle, it appears woefully, no violently, one-sided, as it makes no mention of law's role in effectuating morally reprehensible ends. Hurst makes no mention of how some Americans used law to oppress, dehumanize, victimize, harass, and intimidate other Americans or indigenous peoples, to enslave a race, or to pillage and plunder the land and its nonhuman inhabitants. These two points of view do not so much impose different opinions on Hurst's schema as articulate present strong meanings or evaluative reactions comprised, in varying proportions, of what Hurst calls reason and will.

History, given how Hurst interprets Holmes, is part of the human or cultural sciences because it partakes in the development of meaning. "For Holmes there is no abstract legal order; so, too, for him there existed no legal history apart from the questions which men put to the record."[447] Present meaning creates its own corridor into the ascertained past, and for both Hurst and Holmes the task of inquiry lay in bringing to realization the relative strengths of the reasons and wills that composed that corridor. Take one more step and the idea dawns that "inquiry" is itself a corridor, also comprised of reasons and wills. Since further thinking along the same lines becomes self-defeating, the option to turn toward concrete eventualities, consequences, becomes very attractive.

Seen from the future, the present meaning if sufficiently pressing becomes, by degrees, instituted into life as a "combination of value and function."[448] This combination is not, in actuality, primarily an organic or mechanical contrivance. It is a manifold that connects reason, understood as logic and other forms of rationality, and will, that which subsumes emotion, attitude, desire, and drive. Meaning, in one sense, is a complex of various perceptual conduits, inhibitors, and accelerators that when

[445] James Willard Hurst, Justice Holmes on Legal History 5–6 (1964).
[446] *Id.* at 5.
[447] *Id.* at 6.
[448] *Id.* at 3–17.

united into a functioning, impermeable manifold project a strong sense of actuality. One may view it, meaning, as a node, a junction of mechanism and purpose; what Holmes brilliantly described as a ganglion; it occurs at different levels in the various interactive processes of life, including the historical.

Viewing "meaning" in this manner helps me understand Hurst's use of the word "living" in such phrases as "the living reality of a particular legal system" or the "living law" or the "living legal order."[449] Hurst uses his four factors as indicia to demarcate the living legal order from the greater and more encompassing ambit of human experience. They become nodes – points of vitality – of legal meaning. Unquestionably he had blind spots. Even so, a living legal order, again for Hurst as for Holmes, does not exist in a timeless or space-less dimension – especially one to which logic has special access – but within the dynamic of space and time or what Hurst terms context and sequence.

Hurst believed the dimension of time best revealed the dynamic of the law in experience. It created perspective. As indicated in Part III, sequence he analogized to length and depth and context to breadth. Stated this abstractly, it is difficult to appreciate how insightfully Hurst interprets Holmes's life work. The law no longer is seen as a series of systematic propositions or a fixed algorithm for directing the use of hard state power. Neither does Hurst reify "law" into a single monolith that takes on a life of its own. Rather it becomes a dynamic network of usages, customs, practices, prohibitions, rules, decisions, declarations, and commands that come together at various points to create, gradate, enforce, or eliminate duties. In a court case the full panoply of law – and for Holmes "law" primarily meant the common law – agglomerates for an instant into a single surgical point, the point of decision. Viewed against its relevant backgrounds and in light of its realized and realizable effects that single decision acquires its unique legal meaning.

Hurst summarized this line of thinking in the phrase "value and function." On the one hand, value referred to those aspects of life believed worthwhile that the activity of law itself generated and that revealed themselves through cumulation, change, or commitment. "For the law itself grew to be a massive and complex social institution. As such it tended to generate out of its sequential experience its own values and ranking of values."[450] Function on the other hand pointed to coexistence and interaction, a grouping of phenomena ranging from grounds articulately understood and inarticulately felt, to events, patterns of behavior, beliefs, which, if they did not all intermesh, created a determinate field of interests. Function found "its own balance-of-power problems out of the context of its evolving existence."[451]

[449] *See, e.g., id.* at 6, 11, 13.
[450] *Id.* at 89.
[451] *Id.*

Value and function interpenetrate in what Hurst calls "events, ideas, and attitudes," but present themselves as distinct depending on the viewpoint taken.[452]

Parenthetically, one may note that once law is circumscribed as an activity, the issue of which point of view predominates – the internal or external (typically seen as internal or external to the legal order or, more restrictively, the legal profession) – comes to the fore.

In a previous part we commented very briefly on H. L. A. Hart's critique of the idea that the prediction of what the court or law enforcement officials would do in fact provides a satisfactory description, if not definition, of law. Hart illustrated his disagreement through the use of a traffic light. Treating a red traffic light as a sign in the same way one sees a certain type of cloud as a sign that rain is coming – the traffic light and the cloud become indicative of associated happenings – led, Hart contended, the student of law to "miss out on a whole dimension of social life." That dimension is one in which the red traffic light is not a sign but rather a signal for drivers to stop, that is, it has meaning within a social convention that recognizes rules and standards of the road. For these drivers, Hart adds, the violation of the rule that one should stop at a red light "is not merely a basis for the prediction that a hostile reaction will follow but a *reason* for the hostility."[453]

Hart's italicizing the word "reason" presumably signified the dimension of social life he believed legal thinkers like Holmes and Karl Llewellyn missed. Hart's "reason" incorporated a disposition and a feeling (aspects of will in Hurst's language) that also played a part in melding rules into habits, habits into actions, and actions into events. While Hart certainly had reason to criticize excessive focus on certain behavioral features (those reactive, repetitive, and relatively mindless) of social life as the exclusive material for legal study, he failed to realize that the dimension of social life in which law has its meaning – or innermost meaning as Holmes might say – recognized no intrinsic distinction between that which he denoted sign and signal.

Thus in pondering Hurst's notion of "value and function" and how he uses it as an analytic to expound the twin topics of Holmes's thinking on legal history and the roles of law in the development of the United States, we conclude that while it tremendously helps in laying the necessary groundwork for a perspectival view of law proper it does not quite get us to the requisite three-dimensionality. Hurst superimposes his own well-developed sense of historical perspective upon Holmes's work, but missing is what Holmes calls the "purely legal point of view." That point of view is dynamic; it adds a moving current to an otherwise static but electrified perspective. The bad man never mounts the platform in *Justice Holmes on Legal History*. Hurst gets us into the museum but we have yet to step into a working installation.

[452] *Id.* at 12–17.

[453] H. L. A. Hart, The Concept of Law 88–90 (2d ed. 1994) (emphasis in original).

iii *None Dare Call It Wise*

Much of our criticism of Hurst amounts to the nagging worry that he unduly foreshortened the present, that the length, breadth, and depth needed for the purely legal point of view to take hold and to become operative lacks the necessary extensions. It seems that a promise made at the beginning of *Justice Holmes on Legal History*, that the approach Holmes advocated for studying law would lead to "more than mere increase in technical capacity; it promises understanding[,]" has yet to be brought to fulfillment.[454]

In the opening pages of his book Hurst quotes a selection from the following passage. It is taken from Holmes's 1886 oration to the Harvard Law School Association at its first general meeting, which coincided with the 250th anniversary of Harvard University:

> For whatever reason, the Professors of this School have said to themselves more definitely than ever before, We will not be contented to send forth students with nothing but a rag-bag full of general principles, – a throng of glittering generalities, like a swarm of little bodiless cherubs fluttering at the top of one of Corregio's pictures. They have said that to make general principles worth anything you must give it a body; you must show in what way and how far it would be applied actually in an actual system; you must show how it has gradually emerged as the felt reconciliation of concrete instances no one of which established it in terms. Finally, you must show its historic relations to other principles, often of very different date and origin, and thus set it in the perspective without which its proportions will never be truly judged.[455]

For Hurst Holmes's approach exemplified in the field of law the thought patterns "by which modern man has advanced his general knowledge."[456] William LaPiana adds that this oration ("The Use of Law Schools") is prime evidence of the growing movement in the late nineteenth century among legal educators and a certain class of practitioners to upgrade the standards of the profession. "The Use of Law Schools," LaPiana argues, "illustrates the nature of the relationship between the new model of legal education [the Harvard Law School model under Langdell and James Barr Ames] and professional aspirations."[457]

Hurst and LaPiana's interpretive approaches, singly or jointly, draw attention to how many lawyers, as an increasingly cohesive group, reshaped themselves, legal institutions, and the law in the United States during the late nineteenth century. LaPiana brings to the fore the active part legal educators played in crafting the

[454] Hurst, *supra* note 445, at 4–5.

[455] *Id.* at 4 (quoting Oliver Wendell Holmes, *The Use of Law Schools*, *in* III CW 477).

[456] Hurst, *supra* note 445, at 5.

[457] William P. LaPiana, Logic & Experience: The Origin of Modern American Legal Education 89 (1994).

emerging professional ideal and ensuring that those who established the tenor of the profession did so under the auspices of academic instruction.[458] That instruction, at least for Langdell and his followers, focusing as it did on the case method, had the virtue of being both practical and theoretical. That is, to put the best possible spin on their aspirations, law students would, after duly completing the required three-year curriculum, know how to treat actual legal problems because they had been trained in the operative common law regimen. They would, in short, know how to use case law to make legal arguments and how to justify the arguments made.

The passage from "The Use of Law Schools" quoted above certainly appears, at first blush, to support the idea, hinted at by Hurst and developed by LaPiana, that Langdell's case method was none other than the inductive method of the sciences applied to law (understood in this context as the reported decisions).[459] Holmes claimed that the Harvard Law School professors' pedagogical creed required:

1. That general legal principles be given a body so that they could acquire value;
2. Understanding that general legal principles become embodied when one shows how the propounded legal principles work or function in an actual legal system;
3. Seeing that legal principles work or function by how they change the existing situation and to what extent they do so (i.e., how the changes due to the employment of these legal principles in an actual situation are delimited by other principles or other factors in the actual situation);
4. Understanding that the function of legal principles is not enough, however, for appreciating their value or how that value was acquired. In other words, understanding how a legal principle functions in an actual situation (law in action) is necessary but not sufficient for comprehending its worth. One must also understand how the principle arose historically. That means realizing that principles arise, (a) in time, (b) as the felt reconciliation of, (c) concrete instances, and, (d) that no single concrete instance established the exact principle under review;
5. And, lastly, once one understands (a) how principles function within a living body of law, and (b) that their value arose from both their function and their satisfaction of prior, sometimes presently unrecognized or no longer pressing needs (felt reconciliations), one must then place them within a broader schema. That schema is made up of the principles under review, joined with other principles that have been vetted in the same way, and the whole is then organized according to recognized,

[458] *Id.* at 79–109.
[459] *See id.* at 110–31.

> relative persistence (vitality) so that various proportions become evident; or, as Holmes succinctly stated, set in perspective.[460]

It is worth noting that Holmes's description of the Harvard pedagogical creed introduces the second major part of "The Use of Law Schools" – a discussion of Langdell's innovation in teaching law, the case method. The case method, which comprises both a method of study and a method of teaching that centers on reported appellate cases, inculcates legal principles "through the cases which have developed and established them."[461] As a method of teaching, it is incomparable says Holmes. "I am certain that when your object is not to make a bouquet of the law for the public, nor to prune and graft it by legislation, but to plant its roots where they will grow, in minds devoted henceforth to that one end, there is no way to be compared to Mr. Langdell's way."[462]

Holmes's unusually high praise of Langdell's teaching method is oddly missing from LaPiana's otherwise deeply informed 1994 study of the origins of modern American legal education. On the other hand, stepping back in time, though William Keener does not quote the specific sentence just quoted from "The Use of Law Schools" in his 1894 article, "The Inductive Method in Legal Education," he does use other passages, including the one summarizing the Harvard professors' pedagogical creed, as primary evidence for why the case method bests its competitors.[463]

"The Use of Law Schools" was also cited in two important early twentieth-century historical studies of legal education in the United States. Josef Redlich's classic 1914 assessment referred to how Holmes described his success in using the case method while a professor at the Harvard Law School.[464] Alfred Z. Reed in his remarkably thorough *Training for the Public Profession of the Law*, done, as Redlich's study, under the auspices of the Carnegie Foundation for the Advancement of Teaching, adverted to two key sentences in "The Use of Law Schools" to buttress his assessment of how growing sophistication in philosophical analysis and historical understanding had transformed taught law. This is what Reed wrote:

> [U]nder the influence of the school of historical jurisprudence, the conception of a changing and developing law, gradually ridding itself of obsolescent features, also came to the fore. The law to be analyzed and classified was no longer regarded as a

[460] Oliver Wendell Holmes, *The Use of Law Schools*, *in* III CW 477.

[461] *Id.* at 478.

[462] *Id.*

[463] William A. Keener, *The Inductive Method in Legal Education*, 17 ANN. REP. A.B.A. 473, 480–81, 485–86 (1894); G. Edward White quotes Keener quoting Holmes without overtly recognizing that fact or apparently realizing that Keener and Holmes were moving in different directions. Josef Redlich in his analysis recognized the important difference between the two. *See* G. EDWARD WHITE, TORT LAW IN AMERICA: AN INTELLECTUAL HISTORY 32–33 (Expand. ed., 2003); JOSEF REDLICH, THE COMMON LAW AND THE CASE METHOD 48–51 (1914).

[464] REDLICH, *supra* note 463, at 29–30.

> flat field, to be studied as it exists to-day. Time was recognized as an element that must be considered in gauging the authority of decisions of other days. The field of law became as it were a body of three dimensions.[465]

In support of this claim, Reed referenced both Pound and Holmes. From Holmes's speech he pointed to these two sentences:

> But Story's simple philosophizing has ceased to satisfy men's minds. I think it might be said with safety, that no man of his or the succeeding generation could have stated the law in a form that deserved to abide, because neither his nor the succeeding generation possessed or could have possessed the historical knowledge, had made or could have made the analyses of principles, which are necessary before the cardinal doctrines of the law can be known and understood in their precise contours and in their innermost meanings.[466]

Reed's insight into how the pressing social and intellectual needs of the last quarter of the nineteenth century added a third dimension, that of time, to what had been a "flat field" of study advanced, in its own way, Redlich's perception of how German-inspired historical learning had helped transform law into a science.[467]

That is to say, Redlich criticized the much-lauded argument that the case method employed in law the same inductive approach employed in the natural sciences. Redlich thought Keener mistaken. The case method was an empirical method, not an inductive one.[468] Redlich effectively elaborates on Holmes's basic point – that prior to the development of certain modes of learned investigation and analysis law could not truly be discerned. He adds to it the important observation that the conjoining of these techniques and modes of thought permitted the study of law to become a full-fledged science.[469]

In his book on Langdell and the inception of modern professional education, Bruce Kimball contends that much of the credit Holmes has amassed over the years for his historical insight of "paradox of substance and form" rightfully belongs to Langdell.[470] Langdell, not Holmes, first articulated to his students at Harvard the notion that declarations formal and logical masked substantive historical changes. Kimball further maintains that Holmes in his reviews of Langdell's books

[465] Alfred Zantzinger Reed, Training for the Public Profession of Law 351 (1921).

[466] *Id.* (citing Holmes, *The Use of Law Schools*, *supra* note 460, at 477).

[467] Redlich, *supra* note 463, at 43. *See also* Harold J. Laski, *Mr. Justice Holmes: For His Eighty-Ninth Birthday*, *in* Mr. Justice Holmes 147–48 (Felix Frankfurter ed., 1931) ("He can claim, in a sense, to have been the first of American judges with a grasp of history sufficiently profound, and philosophic principles sufficiently articulate, to have made the law an incisive expression of social life.").

[468] Redlich, *supra* note 463, at 55–59.

[469] *Id.* at 48–51.

[470] Bruce A. Kimball, The Inception of Modern Professional Education: C.C. Langdell, 1826–1906 124–29 (2009).

caricatured Langdell's thought. He did not realize that Langdell employed a mode of legal analysis that was demonstrably, if not always consistently, three-dimensional.

What Kimball means by three-dimensional is not the same as what Reed meant or the idea that I am trying to develop in this book. For Kimball, the three-dimensionality of Langdell's thought consisted of (1) induction from authority, (2) deduction from principle, and (3) analysis of justice and policy or what Kimball refers to as "acceptability."[471] Kimball glides over the temporal feature in Langdell's thought. This aspect, as Redlich and others have pointed out, played an important role in anchoring the case method to law conceived as a body of principles. It also differentiated Langdell's method from the case method that successors like Ames and Keener developed. In their hands it lost its overt chronological, synthetic quality and became a relatively disembodied mode of analytic reasoning. Thinking like a lawyer became its own catchphrase. It seems law students were no longer expected to learn the development of the cardinal doctrines of the two main legal systems in the United States, common law and equity. Instead, analytical and logical facility truncated from any sense of overt measure or proportion, other than exigency of the moment, became the leading indicator of legal talent and ability.[472]

With these observations in mind, we return to "The Use of Law Schools" with a better understanding of the lurking issues that Holmes adroitly sought to address.

His praise of Langdell's teaching method appears genuine even if he perhaps added an extra oomph to soothe feelings still raw over his abrupt departure from the Law School in 1882.[473] But before turning to Langdell's method of instruction he wants to discuss "the use and meaning of law schools."[474] Holmes carefully specifies what he takes to be the chief use of a law school – "So I say the business of a law school is not sufficiently described when you merely say that it is to teach law, or to make lawyers. It is to teach law in the grand manner, and to make great lawyers." And how does a law school do that, teach law in the grand manner and make great lawyers? By teaching its students to become specialists, "specialists who have taken all law to be their province," who have "undertaken to master a special branch of human knowledge."[475]

The specialist, as a social type, serves in Holmes's mind to inculcate certain virtues necessary to a democratic polity. "Modesty and reverence," says Holmes, "are no less virtues of freemen than the democratic feeling which will submit neither to arrogance or servility."[476] The need for the specialist has arisen because the "effervescence of democratic negation" has gone beyond external distinction

[471] *Id.*

[472] Redlich, *supra* note 463, at 23–25; *see also* Robert Stevens, Law School: Legal Education in America from the 1850s to the 1980s 54–57 (1983); White, *supra* note 463, at 26–29.

[473] Kimball, *supra* note 470, at 327.

[474] Holmes, *supra* note 460, at 474.

[475] *Id.* at 475.

[476] *Id.*

and breached what Holmes calls "the lines of Nature which establish orders and degrees among souls of men."[477]

Quite apart from the hackles this passage has probably raised among many twentieth-century American legal scholars unsympathetic to, or un-seduced by, Holmes, lies the outline of a still half-hidden question: why does Holmes believe that learning, especially learning in the law, will contain the effervescence of democratic negation? Why does he further claim that specialists in the intellectual world furnish "a perfect type of the union of democracy with discipline"?[478]

Though we may be a long way from understanding the intricacies of Holmes's comment, a tentative answer would bring back into the picture the mid-nineteenth-century dispute over whether "legal learnin'" played havoc with the social order or coordinated beneficially its various interests and dimensions. That issue had resurfaced in a roundabout way at the end of the century as the march toward professionalization increased apace. The use of a law school, especially one as well favored as Harvard's, lay for Holmes in how it upheld the "dignity of moral feeling and profundity of knowledge."[479] That was the first important point. The second arose from Holmes's expectation that high accomplishment, what he calls "quiet genius and serene mastery," would exert its own natural orbital pull and compel "obedience and respect" on the part of those who require assistance or need help.[480]

Holmes's ideal may seem naïve or unrealistic or too intimately tied to the social conditions of his time and place, but it certainly forces a change in the interpretation that the way of legal study simply mimicked in form that of the natural sciences, that it induced from cases the basic principles of law.[481] "The main part of intellectual education is not the acquisition of facts, but learning how to make facts live."[482] That was an individual enterprise, one dependent largely on native genius, but one for which law schools provided both the necessary workshop and nursery. On this reading, law schools should exist not merely to create a meritocracy but to establish the necessary institutional space for the future master to grow and to work and to develop. To function properly democracy needed such masters, devoted to their calling, respected for their sagacity, honored for their principled bearing, ever ready to prove themselves against all comers, to do their job, to function.

It took a genius of Holmes's caliber to see that American democracy as it existed in the late nineteenth century presented no less a cost of individual supersession than did scientific progress. He did not need Tolstoi to deliver the message. Holmes had already recognized in "The Soldier's Faith" that death had no meaning in the

[477] *Id.*
[478] *Id.*
[479] *Id.* at 476.
[480] *Id.* at 475–76.
[481] *See, e.g.*, William P. LaPiana, *Victorian from Beacon Hill: Oliver Wendell Holmes's Early Legal Scholarship*, 90 Colum. L. Rev. 809, 811–17 (1990); LaPiana, *supra* note 457, at 110–22.
[482] Holmes, *supra* note 460, at 475.

modern world. If the Civil War embodied for Holmes Emerson's lament that grief could teach him nothing,[483] it would not be too much of a stretch to think that for him, Holmes, the legal profession should find fit to include within its ranks those few individuals Emerson identified as "plastic and permeable to principles[.]"[484]

Langdell's method, then, had its uses. It brought students into direct contact with operative legal principles – such as those governing offer, acceptance, and consideration in contract law – and it did so through the medium of the cases. Langdell had articulated in his original 1871 casebook his pedagogical goal and procedure. The goal was mastery of legal principles or doctrines: "To have such mastery of these as to be able to apply them with constant facility and certainty to the ever-tangled skein of human affairs, is what constitutes a true lawyer; and hence to acquire that mastery should be the business of every earnest student of the law."[485] The procedure depended on recognizing that legal doctrines came into their present state slowly ("by slow degrees"). In some instances that growth took centuries. From this observation Langdell made an astounding pedagogical leap: "This growth is to be traced in the main through a series of cases; and *much the shortest and the best, if not the only way of mastering the doctrine effectually is by studying the cases in which it is embodied.*"[486]

We learn from Langdell's much later 1886 speech to the Harvard Law School alumni – at the same event where Holmes delivered "The Use of Law Schools" – that the most important qualification for a law teacher was not legal practice or trial advocacy or experience in managing affairs – "not experience, in short, in using law but experience in learning law; not the experience of the Roman advocate or of the Roman prætor, still less of the Roman procurator, but the experience of the Roman juris-consult [*sic*]."[487] With this in mind we look back at Langdell's 1871 statement and find these two sentences:

> I entered upon the duties of my present position, a year and a half ago, with a settled conviction that law could only be taught or learned effectively by means of cases in some form. I had entertained such an opinion ever since I knew anything of the

[483] Ralph Waldo Emerson, *Experience*, *in* Essays and Poems by Ralph Waldo Emerson 236 (Peter Norberg ed., 2004).

[484] Ralph Waldo Emerson, *Self-Reliance*, *in* Essays and Poems by Ralph Waldo Emerson 125–26 (Peter Norberg ed., 2004).

[485] Christopher Columbus Langdell, A Selection of Cases on the Law of Contracts vi (1871).

[486] *Id.* (emphasis added).

[487] *Professor Langdell's Address*, *in* Report of the Organization and First Meeting at Cambridge, November 5, 1886, Harvard Law School Association, 48, 50 (1887). According to Roscoe Pound, the jurisconsult originated as one who provided legal advice for wills, conveyances, and other formal transactions as well as on existing or available legal rights and duties. The role ultimately became formalized as law writers and law teachers. Roscoe Pound, The Lawyer from Antiquity to Modern Times 55–58 (1953).

> nature of law or of legal study; but it was chiefly through my experience as a learner that it was first formed, as well as subsequently strengthened and confirmed.[488]

From his own vital experience in learning law, in legal study, Langdell drew out a robust program for training young lawyers.

As is well known, Holmes reviewed the various iterations of Langdell's casebook on Contracts, or the supplementary expository material, in the pages of the *American Law Review*. Bruce Kimball claims to have discovered other reviews that Holmes wrote on Langdell's works on Sales and Equity Pleading.[489] Be that as it may, we find Holmes in 1871 making points similar to those he would make in 1886. He finds of especial interest the chronological arrangement of the cases. "Tracing the growth of a doctrine in this way not only fixes it in the mind, but shows its meaning, extent, and limits as nothing else can."[490] He called the plan of the book "original and instructive" and mentioned, offhandedly, that he was struck by how Langdell's work confirmed the first sentence of "Codes, and the Arrangement of Law" – "It is the merit of the common law that it decides the case first and determines the principle afterwards."[491]

Holmes's next review, also in 1871, added a few minor criticisms. He again noted the originality of Langdell's casebook. It forced the "student to find out the principle and trace the connection between case and case for himself."[492] Holmes understood, as many subsequent commentators have emphasized, that Langdell's technique required the student's persistent attention and active, intensive intellectual involvement. Learning the law was hard work and Langdell's method made it even harder.[493]

Skipping over the reviews of Langdell's volumes on Sales and Equity Pleading that Kimball believes Holmes authored – I am not convinced – we come to the oft-cited 1880 review of the second edition of Langdell's contract casebook. By 1880 Holmes's criticisms have gone from minor to major. While he continues to acknowledge Langdell's gifts as a legal scholar he finds his flaws proportional to his merits. In the utter *consistency* of Langdell's interpretation of diverse and conflicting cases Holmes finds what he deems to be "the weak point in Mr. Langdell's habit of mind."[494] Where does the weakness lie? What flaw has become glaring to Holmes in

[488] LANGDELL, *supra* note 485, at v. *See also* Catharine Pierce Wells, *Langdell and the Invention of Legal Doctrine*, 58 BUFF. L. REV. 551, 599 (2010) ("Langdell was first and foremost a teacher of law.").

[489] Bruce A. Kimball, *Langdell on Contracts and Legal Reasoning: Correcting the Holmesian Caricature*, 25 LAW & HIST. REV. 345, 397–99 (2007).

[490] Oliver Wendell Holmes, *Review of* A Selection of Cases on the Law of Contracts (Part I), *in* I CW 243.

[491] *Id.*

[492] Holmes, *Review of* A Selection of Cases on the Law of Contracts, *in* I CW 273.

[493] *See, e.g.*, LAPIANA, *supra* note 457, at 26–28.

[494] Oliver Wendell Holmes, A *Review of* A Selection of Cases on The Law of Contracts, with a Summary of the Topics covered by the Cases, *in* III CW 102–04.

1880, when he is on the cusp of finishing *The Common Law*, that was not obvious in 1871?

Kimball attributes Holmes's criticisms to his need to discredit those who had achieved what he most desired – recognition of intellectual powers – but that explanation seems to me unhelpful when better alternatives exist.[495] The question is, what changed in Holmes's outlook between 1871 and 1880 that would lead to such a drastically different evaluation of Langdell's casebook?

As we have argued, the most dramatic change in Holmes's thinking, the one that had led him to write and inform Emerson that the period of probation had ended – he was no longer a student but had become a thinker – was the realization that much of existing law (legal doctrines) had arisen not exclusively through progressive ratiocination – either as an exercise of independent reason or as the articulated rationale, the practical reasoning, arising from social development – but as a "felt reconciliation" that took on the translucence of necessity. The manner in which Langdell presented contract law obscured the unresolvable intellectual antinomies and those nonintellectual grounds or elements that had played a role in shaping the ultimate decision. One could blandly refer to Langdell's mode of presenting contract law as excessively formalistic or conceptualistic, but the real problem for Holmes lay in how Langdell ignored the "the feelings which make the content of logic, and which have actually shaped the substance of the law."[496] Holmes did not deny the major role of logic or, more broadly, of reason. He does not even deny that the lucidity of clear thinking still works its compelling magic in the adumbration of legal propositions. But he did not think it wise or beneficial to separate the egg white from the yolk and then pretend that the inner part of the egg consisted of the white only. In the yolk lay life! . . . and, we now know, cholesterol.

Langdell's genius for learning the law has indelibly impressed itself on American law schools. In the hands of his students, especially Ames and Keener, the case method got transformed from a propaedeutic to its own objective end, from a guide to legal principles to a professional technique. Robert Stevens said it best when he commented that Langdell, perhaps inadvertently, "set the style" that "ensured American law would take the atomistic rather than the unitary approach that distinguishes it from other common-law systems[.]"[497]

Holmes, on the other hand, encouraged a mode of teaching law that led to neither the atomistic nor the unitary approach. Professional technique had its place. The systematization of doctrine had its place. Lawyering in the United States for Holmes was not so much a manner of thinking as a mode of being. We think back to Chief Justice Lemuel Shaw. He stood for Holmes as the greatest magistrate the country had yet produced. As a great magistrate Shaw would not have, presumably,

495 KIMBALL, *supra* note 470, at 325–29.

496 Holmes, *supra* note 494, at 103.

497 STEVENS, *supra* note 472, at 55–56.

eschewed learning. But he also would not have shunned what had not yet been reduced to learning or only begun the gauntlet of criticism, informed or uninformed. Though Holmes did not use the word it appears Chief Justice Shaw possessed one very important characteristic, he had perspective.

The word perspective in this context is hard to define. But it will help us to get a better sense of its meaning if we take one more look at how Holmes summarized the Harvard professors' pedagogical creed.

Holmes agreed and supported Langdell's substantive point that the principles or doctrines of the law have grown and developed. He also thought Langdell achieved a real innovation in perceiving that one major methodological tool for discerning the life history of a legal principle – the study of reported cases – could also serve as a unique pedagogical tool. How a common notion such as quid pro quo became embodied and acquired value(s) in law through transformation into the doctrine of consideration, and how the doctrine itself became refined over time, provided an important lesson in legal embryology.[498] At this level of study no substantive difference existed between the anthropologist and the legal scholar. The difference between the two only became evident when the legal scholar sought to tease out from the available cases and other relevant materials (extant treatises, guidebooks, general or institutional histories, etc.) the gist of the decisions or the specific values the courts had sought to enforce and protect.

Even at this level of inquiry Holmes and Langdell are not far apart. It is intrinsic to the common law's way of operating as a legal system that judges listen to counsel's argument as to how other judges have determined or elicited the value or values to be safeguarded or promoted. Increased sophistication in projecting the circumstances in which decisions took place and deliberately relating those circumstances to the present moment – when another decision must be made – constituted a major part of the effort in the nineteenth century to make law scientific. Langdell's program for legal study combined the science of law (a distinct subject matter and method) with the effort to professionalize the practice – to elevate among practitioners what Holmes called the "dignity of moral feeling and the profundity of knowledge." No reason to think Holmes dissented from this goal.

But Langdell took the wrong turn for Holmes when he sought to unify the results of his scientific labors and his pedagogical ones into a single systematic statement of legal principles. In turning the common law into a Roman style *elegantia juris* Langdell had, effectively, short-circuited the *learning* of law in favor of the *teaching* of law. In other words, Langdell was "less concerned with his postulates than to show that the conclusions from them hang together."[499]

[498] *See, e.g.*, Oliver Wendell Holmes, *English Equity*, *in* III CW 335–36.

[499] Holmes, supra note 494, at 103. *See also* DANIEL KORNSTEIN, THE SECOND GREATEST AMERICAN loc. 1072–85 (2017) (ebook).

At this point we must be extremely careful so as not to miss the importance of Holmes's argument. Holmes's 1876 breakthrough had led him to appreciate how formulated legal doctrine did not represent either the articulation of a natural legal principle or the outcome of exclusively casuistic analysis. Doctrine, as a generalization, did not simply represent the result of a discrete, insulated process of ratiocination. Charles Eliot notwithstanding, the study and practice of law bore few formal similarities to the study and practice of chemistry.[500] That analogy, of course, posed greater allure in the late nineteenth century that it does today. Langdell had taken a good thing too far because his insistence on consistency unduly favored context over sequence, exposition over exegesis, logic over rhetoric.

Holmes believed one should begin at the point Langdell slighted, with the postulates, and end with a *perspective* that arose from the relative historic distances between articulated legal principles. He does not maintain that either teaching or learning law should culminate in the systematic grasp of doctrine. That is to say, it seems to me that Holmes's recapitulation of the Harvard professors' pedagogical creed is not so much a summary as a restatement. One does not run across in Langdell or Ames or Gray or Thayer much mention of instilling perspective as a pedagogical goal. Holmes effectively put his own spin on what an institution dedicated to teaching law, especially teaching law in the grand manner, ought to do.

"The aim of a law school should be, the aim of Harvard Law School has been, not to make men smart, but to make them wise in their calling, – to start them on a road which will lead them to the abode of masters."[501] The abode of masters we glean from another of Holmes's speeches is "that other bench reserved for the masters of those who know."[502] I think that "other bench" probably refers to the bench where the English serjeants of law sat. That exclusive body, historian J. H. Baker tells us, "in over six centuries of history, numbered less than one thousand members[.]"[503]

Baker further informs us that the ties of this "elite body of judges and advocates" to the much "larger profession" beneath them arose mainly from the institutional strength and character of the Inns of Court and Chancery. It "explain[s] how the reasoning of a small group of men in Westminster Hall grew into one of the world's two greatest systems of law."[504] One need not infer that Holmes desired to return his profession to its modus operandi in England circa 1400 to appreciate that he aspired to see, and believed Harvard Law School had the opportunity to create, a collegium

[500] On Eliot's critical role see LaPiana, *supra* note 457, at 7–28; *see also* Anthony Chase, *The Birth of the Modern Law School*, 23 J. Legal Hist. 329–48 (1979).

[501] Holmes, *supra* note 460, at 476.

[502] Oliver Wendell Holmes, *Law and the Court*, *in* III CW 505.

[503] J. H. Baker, An Introduction to English Legal History 155 (2007). Holmes could also be referring to the masters who sat on the bench or "benchers" at the Inns of Court, that is, the barristers who sat on the bench at moots as judges. *Id.* at 159–62.

[504] *Id.* at 155.

of law, a place where those more experienced and those less experienced in the law could come together to advance its study.

That study, contrary to the taxidermal tendencies of Langdell vis-à-vis legal principles or of Ames vis-à-vis legal method, took as its basic intuition the three-dimensionality of law. That is to say, the study of law sought to bring together two important elements, the principles and the method. It sought to unify them so that precedent and argument and decision correlated in a manner that simultaneously illuminated the specific legal event at hand, and related that event to other basic legal doctrines, even from other epochs, that it did not directly implicate. This objective was grand; I don't think Holmes would have denied that assessment. But he thought it worth pursuing because he saw no other way to bring together what theorists like Langdell had slighted: the postulates at one end and the felt reconciliation at the other.

Logic as traditionally understood could not connect these two points. Holmes perceived one to occur at the beginning and the other at the end of legal reasoning. But "reasoning" for him did not simply mean a logical sequence, one that prized consistency or noncontradiction. It always included practical considerations, both in terms of ends and in terms of means. Practical considerations meant taking one route out of the possibilities presented. Too exclusive a focus on the route chosen, however, on the specific practical considerations sought to be achieved and the means to accomplish them, leads to an undue emphasis on law's instrumental use. For Holmes the whole always comprised more than its parts because the whole always contained within it a "can't help," an element of the atemporal present, where the sense of congruity between cause and effect is overpowering. No breach exists between subjective (personal/inward) and objective (impersonal/outward) viewpoints.[505]

When a breach has occurred, when the outward and inward fail to align, the natural recourse is to seek realignment. That insight informed Peirce's pragmatism as he expressed it in 1878. Despite the great weight of authority that finds the genesis of Holmes's ideas in Peirce's insight I am inclined to think otherwise.[506] I think Holmes independently became aware of the multifactorial, time-conditioned, and

[505] Kunal Parker perceptively singles out those elements of experience that for Holmes seem to be impervious to historical critique but does not connect them, as I would, to his "can't helps." *See* Kunal Parker, *The History of Experience: The Historical Imagination of Oliver Wendell Holmes, Jr.*, 26 Pol. and Legal Anthrop. Rev. 60, 73–77 (2003).

[506] To some extent at least, Frederic Kellogg in his most recent book backs away from his earlier assumption that Holmes's legal method simply was a working out of Peirce's pragmatic maxim. *See* Frederic R. Kellogg, Oliver Wendell Holmes Jr. and Legal Logic 18 ("Holmes's social induction, which bears a genetic but not identical relation to the philosophy now known as pragmatism, informs many claims and opinions that he advanced in his long career."). *But see* Herbert Hovenkamp, The Opening of American Law: Neoclassical Legal Thought 1870–1970 138–144 (2015) (maintaining the line of thought that finds in Peirce and the so-called Metaphysical Club the fountainhead for many of Green and Holmes's distinctive ideas on causation in law).

purposive nature of thinking through his deep study of the common law and its history. He also benefitted tremendously from the work of such colleagues as Nicholas St. John Green. The law as an act of practical reason and physical force musters – arranges or composes – in the same way as does a clear idea a whole array of beliefs or what Peirce called perceptual judgments. It does not combine, in the sense of melding, but coordinates actualities and imaginaries for the sake of specific ends-in-view and, to the extent feasible, seeks to minimize unwanted effects, ends-not-in-view. In this sense the law is pragmatic, in one use of that unwieldy term.

The ability to understand law, then, when broken down, means the ability to comprehend, at-and-for a given time, the ends-in-view the law sought to obtain and how. Threats of physical force always played a part but so did other tools of sanction and incentive. It also means learning to measure how that action affected ends-not-in-view but which at a later date become all-too-evident, sometimes as unintended consequences. Lastly, one must learn to ascertain and evaluate the costs the ends sought exact or exacted. In this endeavor to obtain perspective the point of view of the present does not comprehend itself. The phrase ("point of view of the present") is mainly an abstraction, a covering term, which draws attention away from the fact that the present's point of the view cannot be fully articulated. It is nascent, primarily felt. Acknowledging feeling as a source of law is of course problematic; it threatens to take us back to the blandishments of the emperor's wife.

To this danger Holmes counterpoised the common law's great merit. To decide before being able to articulate fully the principle that governed the decision did not, as an achievement, belong to any single common law judge. As Holmes made clear in his many eulogies of departed members, it was, within the context of law, a unique virtue that belonged to the profession as a corporate body. It dignified the calling. To hone the ability, to inculcate the virtue, to refine the procedures, to bring to awareness the inner mechanisms of the magistrate's intuition necessitated, as Holmes constantly maintained, increased effort, "To see so far as one may, and to feel, the great forces that are behind every detail[.]"[507]

General propositions of law by themselves do not carry one very far in this endeavor. Nor do brilliant insights. The calling required both a passion for law, for its trajectories, and a respect for those present commitments that kept lit the lights of knowledge. As Holmes put it at the end of his "Learning and Science," the very short speech he delivered at the celebration honoring Langdell's twenty-five years of service to the Harvard Law School: "The Italians have begun to work on the notion that the foundations of the law ought to be scientific, and, if our civilization does not collapse, I feel pretty sure that the regiment or division that follows us will carry that flag."[508] Law, as an "ideal system," would "draw its postulates and its legislative

[507] Oliver Wendell Holmes, *The Class of '61*, *in* III CW 504.

[508] Holmes, *supra* note 369, at 492.

justification from science."[509] In other words, the feelings and beliefs that had hitherto formed postulates or justified legislative acts would find greater articulation in the language of science. The great forces behind every detail would slowly reveal, through patient investigation, the feelings and thoughts that made them great.

iv *The Bad Man Lives*

During the time I have spent working on this book newly published pieces on the bad man and "The Path of the Law" have continued apace. In 2016 appeared two new ones. The first, Christoph Bezemek's "Bad for Good: Perspectives on Law and Force," was part of a session devoted to Frederick Schauer's *The Force of Law*.[510] In his contribution Bezemek guides us on a trolley tour through the theme park of Western jurisprudence. He points out the sundry characters that have been associated with the bad man, or that existed prior to the bad man, such as Kant's "Race of Devils." A goodly number are sighted; the most prominent one missed is Hume's knave.[511] As befitting a good tour guide, Bezemek moves briskly but manages a breezy, informative tone and drops his fair share of snazzy one-liners.

I had a hard time reading Bezemek's piece. At one point, midway through, I began to wonder if he had conceived it as an academic hoax or slyly intended to spoof the idiocy of jurisprudential thinking. But, no. I believe he intended his contribution as serious scholarship. I was the problem.

The style in "Bad for Good" – the pastiche of names and concepts and propositions topically arranged with only a scintilla of interpretive finesse or explication – reveals in magnification, because of the piece's brevity, a dominant mode of contemporary legal scholarship. That mode brings to mind passages from Herman Hesse's novel *Magister Ludi*, which I read when young. One can now find it under the title, *The Glass Bead Game*. From what I remember of the book, which I'm sure I did not understand when I read it, is that the Glass Bead Game, in its less optimal form, is played with glass counters, representing unified bits of recognizable cultural knowledge (like today's memes) that are then arranged and rearranged in complex patterns. Acknowledged success in manipulating cultural symbols leads to advancement in the game (in its more pristine form) until one attains the elite rank of master of the game or of play. Hence, Magister Ludi.

Given my efforts in this very long part to bring into relief, accurately and thoughtfully, some of the prevalent ways of looking at the bad man and at Holmes

[509] *Id.*

[510] Christoph Bezemek, *Bad for Good: Perspectives on Law and Force, in* The Force of Law Reaffirmed: Frederick Schauer Meets His Critics 15–16 (Christoph Bezemek and Nicoletta Ladaure eds., 2016).

[511] *See* David Hume, *Of the Independency of Parliament, in* David Hume, Essays Moral, Political, and Literary 42–46 (Eugene F. Miller ed., rev. ed. 1987). I owe thanks to Gary Chartier for bringing Hume's knave to my attention.

since the turn of the twentieth century, I find myself ill equipped to handle a nifty piece like Bezemek's. Holmes denounced in "The Use of Law Schools" what he called "the most hateful of American words and ideals" – smartness. Smartness stood against the unified ideal of learning and science. "It is from within the bar, not from outside, that I have heard the new gospel that learning is out of date, and that the man for the times is no longer the thinker and the scholar, but the smart man, unencumbered with other artillery than the latest edition of the Digest and the latest revision of the Statutes."[512]

The ideal that guided Holmes in law contrasts starkly to the working ideal that guides much of contemporary legal scholarship in the United States. This working ideal appears to prize moral originality, advocacy, intellectual horsepower and dexterity, and a certain type of formal organization. Exposition marches in outline and to the beat of citations. It does not favor rudimentary exegesis or plain vanilla understanding, or the more advanced goal of establishing a parallax for our knowledge of the law. It prizes smartness, that is, analytically sophisticated categories and distinctions that prove proficient at marshaling and organizing supporting materials for the thesis advocated.[513] Because Bezemek's contribution does not use the formal apparatus typically found in longer pieces it reveals the lack of sustained engagement that a more systematic approach typically conceals. Bezemek's discussion syncopates, in relation to Holmes and the bad man, from Aquinas, Hobbes, and Kant to H. L. A. Hart to Henry Hart to Lon Fuller to Hans Kelsen to Joseph Raz to William Twining to Robert Gordon to David Luban to Scott Schapiro to Duncan Kennedy to Albert Alschuler to quite a few others. This syncopated movement permits Bezemek to gloss over or ignore differences in approaches, outlooks, intellectual commitments, or objectives that do not directly touch his primary concern (to argue that the bad man's perspective can turn one into a "formidable doctrinal scholar").[514] What results is the scholarly version of a jazzed-up PowerPoint marketing presentation.

The second piece published in 2016 was Dan Priel's "Holmes's 'Path of the Law' As Non-Analytic Jurisprudence."[515] Priel's discussion is easier to understand than Bezemek's – we are not simply herded from bullet point to bullet point – and it certainly bears marks of sophisticated jurisprudential thinking. Take, for example, how Priel concludes his article, which defends the view that "The Path of the Law" exemplifies in its structure a grand narrative, an evolutionary account of law:

[512] Holmes, *supra* note 460, at 476.

[513] Though I doubt he would agree with what I have written, I have learned much from Judge Posner's reflections on legal scholarship. *See, e.g.*, RICHARD A. POSNER, THE PROBLEMATICS OF MORAL AND LEGAL THEORY 38–90 (1999); RICHARD A. POSNER, DIVERGENT PATHS: THE ACADEMY AND THE JUDICIARY 1–50 (2016).

[514] Bezemek, *supra* note 510, at 16–24.

[515] Dan Priel, *Holmes's "Path of the Law" As Non-Analytic Jurisprudence*, 35 U. QUEENSLAND L.J. 57 (2016).

> Such a positive, optimistic, view of the law is not obvious. It is quite an understatement to say that lawyers do not enjoy the best of reputations, that they exert a negative influence on society. And with barely an exception, lawyers do not make up the best individual human minds. [!!!] And yet the combined efforts of middling individuals have created 'one of the vastest products of the human mind'. It is easy (and necessary!) to decry the law for all its complexity, pomposity, confusions, and mediocrity, until one sees what happens to complex societies whose legal institutions break down. This too, I think, is part of the message of 'The Path of the Law'.[516]

Priel poses a question in this paragraph that goes to the very core of "The Path of the Law." How have the combined efforts of "middling individuals" created, if that is the correct word, "one of the vastest products of the human mind"? In other words, how has the common law in the United States – comprising ongoing institutions, a network of social practices, distinctive habits of mind, a developed and developing ethos – leveraged the combined talents and interests of innumerable participants since the thirteenth century? And, more important, through what instrument or instruments may current-day participants improve and refashion this vast artifact so that it is more effective, less unwieldy, more in tune with the best aspirations that our thinking has to offer us?

Seen in the right light these questions deserve top billing. Moving backward through Priel's article, the reader tries to understand how Priel's argument that Holmes's essay has a coherent thesis, that it is an exercise in historical jurisprudence writ large, ties into his conclusion that the common law as a whole is much greater than the sum of its middling parts. One wants to know the mechanism or mechanisms that make this possible.

Priel contends "The Path of the Law" presents "an evolutionary account of law."[517] He identifies three ages of law that correspond to what he believes to be the three main parts of the essay. In his focus on the structure of the essay he treads ground already trod by quite a few others, most prominently Thomas Grey. Although Priel proceeds in a different manner and with a different end in view, one will not find any mention of Grey's idea that "Path" emplots a quest narrative. Priel too notes the tonal clash between the opening and closing passages of "The Path of the Law" but he does not pause to consider how Grey or Susan Haack or Robert Gordon, for instance, handled that very same issue. He does indicate (in a footnote) Henry Hart's position that "The Path of the Law" consists of two incompatible parts, but that is the extent of the reference. No discussion, no comparison, no tacking, no evaluation.[518]

516 *Id.* at 73.
517 *Id.* at 70.
518 On this issue of how so many academic lawyers lack a professional ethic or awareness when it comes to prior scholarship *see* E. Donald Elliott, *Holmes and Evolution: Legal Process As Artificial Intelligence*, 13 J. LEGAL STUD. 113, 114 (1984) ("The absence of a strong sense of its

Why put this burden on Priel? Why not simply allow him to develop his thesis as he sees fit?

The ground of my criticism is the same ground that has impelled me to create these focused and linked forays into how some people before me viewed Holmes and the bad man. The best articulation of the intuition that guided me comes from that gray eminence of modern American thought, Chauncey Wright. Wright's statement came to me by way of Thomas Grey in his "Holmes and Legal Pragmatism."[519] Grey quotes it as part of his defense for the length and reach of his study on Holmes's thought. Grey cites Philip P. Wiener's book *Evolution and the Founders of Pragmatism* as the source.[520] Wiener, in turn, found it in one of Wright's letters to Francis Abbot, dated 1867, contained in the collection of Wright's letters that his longtime friend James Bradley Thayer edited and privately printed after Wright's death in 1875. Wiener says that Wright's statement "has been the guiding principle of our own study of the minds of the founders of pragmatism. It may well serve as a pragmatic formulation of the essential aim and method of all intellectual history[.]"[521]

Wright opens his correspondence by thanking Abbot for his most recent letter. He acknowledges Abbot's commitment to philosophical debate. Even in the midst of personal difficulties, Abbot still found the time and energy to continue their mutual give-and-take on philosophical issues. Wright praises Abbot for the letter's intellectual richness and for how it "affords so much light on the real grounds of our differences, that I hardly feel able in the limited space of a letter to say all I wish on its various topics."[522]

> The most profitable discussion is, after all, a study of other minds, – seeing how others see, rather than the dissection of mere propositions. The restatement of fundamental doctrines in new connections affords a parallax of their philosophical stand-points (unless these be buried in the infinite depths), which adds much to our knowledge of one another's thought.[523]

How Wright articulated his point reminded me, for some reason, of the chapter entitled "Harvard College" in *The Education of Henry Adams*. Toward that chapter's end Adams comments on the slight bit of education he was ever conscious of

own past is a distinctive feature of legal scholarship."); E. Donald Elliott, *The Dis-Integration of Administrative Law: A Comment on Shapiro*, 92 Yale L.J. 1523, 1524 n.10 (1982) (making the "modest proposal" that "law review editors impose the requirement that scholars express their ideas as improvements or corrections to the paradigms that already exist in the literature, rather than each scholar proposing his or her own new model and inventing his or her own private language.").

519 Grey, *supra* note 298, at 791.

520 Wiener, *supra* note 300, at 30.

521 *Id.*

522 James Bradley Thayer, The Letters of Chauncey Wright 123–24 (1877).

523 *Id.* at 124.

receiving while a student at Harvard. It lay in self-possession. "If Harvard College gave nothing else, it gave calm. For four years each student had been obliged to figure daily before dozens of young men who knew each other to the last fibre . . . no audience in future life would ever be so intimately and terribly intelligent as these."[524]

Scholarship as a mode of interrogation and self-discipline cannot be expected to replicate in present circumstances the tempered honesty, somewhat personal, somewhat unfeeling and brutal, that according to Adams characterized the society of schoolboys at Harvard College in the mid-nineteenth century. But simulation is possible. Something similar tinctures Wright's desideratum to know the real degree of difference between his mind and another's. And it is, I am sure, only by happy coincidence that the old English serjeants, who contained the law in their breasts, likewise did debate and calibrate, before Harvard came into existence, the matters before them, perhaps more courteously than Harvard schoolboys, but no less intimately and terribly.[525]

So we return to Daniel Priel's "Holmes's 'Path of the Law' As Non-Analytic Jurisprudence." Given that his article appears almost 120 years after the Boston University audience listened to Holmes's address, one anticipates some acknowledgement of, even if not sustained overt engagement with, the preceding reams of commentary. And Priel obliges. After his fleeting mention of Henry Hart's article, he states that, "'The Path of the Law' has been the object of extensive (and widely divergent) commentary, and I don't expect this essay to end the conversation about it."[526] He cites symposia held to celebrate "The Path of the Law"'s 100th anniversary and the many articles those events produced, as well as the most recognized prior commentary (Rogat is duly mentioned),[527] but in no one case does Priel attempt to consciously integrate his analytic efforts into those of others, even if only through disjunction and contrast.

The one minor exception, at least in regard to the bad man, is his response to Marco Jimenez's 2011 "Finding the Good in Holmes's Bad Man."[528] He takes this long law review article to be representative of those many commentaries that miss Holmes's point in introducing the bad man.

Jimenez, Priel contends, goes off track when he attempts to bring the bad man and the good man into synergy.[529] A look at Jimenez's article shows an effort to argue, first, that Holmes concocted the bad man as an instrument for inculcating

[524] Henry Adams, The Education of Henry Adams 782 (Lib. of Am. ed. 1983). For a summary of pedagogical reforms that sought to overcome undergraduate education's bankruptcy of purpose in that era see G. Edward White, Tort Law in America: An Intellectual History 20–26, 345 n.6 (Expand. ed., 2003).

[525] *See also* Oliver Wendell Holmes, *Middlesex Bar Association Address, in* III CW 535–36 ("I am associated on the bench with men, every one of whom is my personal friend, with men whose varied abilities, single-heartedness, and devotion to their task I admire, and we meet on terms of unrestrained mutual criticism in a common effort to develop the law in a worthy way – in a way worthy of the great traditions of the state.").

[526] Priel, *supra* note 515, at 58.

[527] *Id.* at n.6.

[528] Marco Jimenez, *Finding the Good in Holmes's Bad Man*, 79 Ford. L. Rev. 2069 (2010).

[529] Priel, *supra* note 515, at 62 n.24.

virtue. Second, the bad man point of view accomplishes this end by illuminating the incentive structures required to contain through legal means actual bad women and men and/or, through the same means, to slowly transform – through the interplay of sanction and habit – the internal structure of these actually bad people. Viewing law as the bad man views law, externally, outside the vague sanctions of conscience, provides the best entrée for beginners, and those more experienced, to engage in the Aristotelian virtue of justice (just practices oriented toward just ends).[530]

For Jimenez Holmes's use of both the bad man and the good man in "The Path of the Law" provides a descriptively and normatively satisfying theory of law. Jimenez believes the most important and most overlooked sentence in "Path" to be this one: "The practice of it [law], in spite of popular jests, tends to make good citizens and good men."[531] It is through the proper practice of law – that is, understanding that one part of the practice involves containing (taming) the "calculating man" (the bad man)[532] and the other part reforming him (killing the bad part) through incentive structures embedded in ongoing usages and institutions – that one can unite law and morals at a deeper level of practice.[533]

Priel will not have it. He picks out a couple of sentences from Jimenez's long article and critiques them in a phrase or two. Priel may be right. At some critical junctures Jimenez's argument seems forced.[534] But that is not the point. How Priel proceeds in the argument, his utter lack of direct, sustained engagement with the thought of a colleague, I find both amiss and deleterious to a worthwhile jurisprudence. That is not to say Jimenez does much better. Though demonstrating vigorous and diligent learning, Jimenez seems to use both Holmes's work and that of others to showcase his not inconsiderable ingenuity. He has clearly written a smart piece. It taught me interesting things I did not know. But he shows little understanding or respect for the canons of learning. These, parenthetically, should not be confused with the law review directive that one must provide the reader with an overabundance of exhaustive, and, at times, exhausting, citations.

But back to the bad man. Despite his criticisms of Jimenez, Priel too sees the main use of the bad man as an instrument or device for clear legal thinking.[535] Jimenez shows why on this score the bad man is a better tool for that purpose than

[530] Jimenez, *supra* note 528, at 2103–120. A clear precursor to Jimenez in argument, though not cited by him, is William H. Wilcox, *Taking a Good Look at the Bad Man's Point of View*, 66 CORNELL L. REV. 1058 (1981) (arguing that both the bad man and the good man are defined by prudential concerns, that is, both are instances of the prudent man).

[531] Jimenez, *supra* note 528, at 2106–109 (quoting Holmes, *Path of the Law*, *supra* note 14, at 392).

[532] *Id.* at 2113–114.

[533] *Id.* at 2117.

[534] Take, for example, his use of the passage Holmes wrote about getting the dragon out of his cave. Jimenez uses that passage to support his interpretation of the role of law vis- à-vis the bad man even though it is clear from the text that Holmes is writing about the use of history. *Id.* at 2105.

[535] Priel, *supra* note 515, at 60–61.

the good man. Through the practice of law, how the law in effect tames the bad man, we can see, from the internal point of view, how the law actually works. That is Jimenez's main argument.[536] The relevant contrast for Priel consists in *not* seeing the bad man as a guide for action. He is merely what Priel calls an "epistemic device."[537] How the bad man as an epistemic device differs from seeing the bad man as a heuristic Priel does not say. He does not acknowledge the longstanding commentary that has taken that position. Since he does not acknowledge it he has no self-imposed responsibility to distinguish his idea or his view of the bad man from, say, Aronson's or Fisch's or White's or Grey's or Haack's.

I was certainly intrigued by this idea that the bad man is an epistemic device. I wish Priel had done more to differentiate the notion; to give it shape and texture, in light of both Holmes's oeuvre and existing commentary; that he had done more, in effect, to individuate his idea.

We learn from Priel's discussion that Holmes invoked the bad man for two reasons. The first Priel calls substantive. "[I]t does not matter what lawyers say or even believe about the law, if those beliefs are not accompanied by action."[538] The law, to be law, must be enforced. This point is fairly clear and well grounded. Thus said Holmes to Laski: "When I talk of law I talk as a cynic. I don't care a damn if twenty professors tell me that a decision is not law if I know the courts will enforce it. (Of course – when I speak of the lawmaking power I mean concurrence of all the necessary organs in putting the enactment into execution.)"[539]

The second reason is one Priel calls "more subtle." Using "Holmes's notorious claim that a contract is to perform or pay damages" as an example, Priel argues that the implementation of the bad man forces an awareness or cognizance of those specific norms, among the many that play a role in legal institutions and in the law broadly conceived, that have an unambiguous legal effect.[540] Priel extracts from "The Path of the Law" a very specific idea – that the bad man directs and focuses the desire to "know what the law requires." His point is similar to our argument that the bad man, through an acknowledged and heightened sense of self-interest, has the clarity of vision to see what the self-interest of the state requires.[541]

The difference, though, between our argument and his has to do with how we see this specific analytic point connecting to Holmes's overall jurisprudence. Take the example Priel uses, whether entering into a contract is, in effect, obtaining an option to perform or pay damages. Despite Priel's assertion, Holmes never expressly says in "The Path of the Law" that one has an option when one commits a contract even

[536] Jimenez, *supra* note 528, at 2117.

[537] Priel, *supra* note 515, at 60.

[538] *Id.* at 59.

[539] I Holmes–Laski Letters: The Correspondence of Mr. Justice Holmes and Harold J. Laski, 1916–1925 115 (Mark DeWolfe Howe ed., 1953).

[540] Priel, *supra* note 515, at 59–60.

[541] *Id.* at 60.

though that is a possible inference. As pointed out in Section 7, in his 1919 letter to Walter Cook Holmes agrees with Cook's objection, "it is not the theory of the common law that he [the contractor] has an option. I dare say it even might be proper to describe the breach as illegal[.]"[542]

So, if it is not an option what is it? I would say it is a forced choice. What's the difference? The difference arises from the recognition that the power to bind one's self to a future event, whether or not that event is under one's control, has its own provenance and trajectory within the common law, one partly based upon the difference between threatened state action (a duty) and actual state action (physical compulsion). Actual state action is not, in one sense, law. It may be lawfully regarded and legally justified if challenged but it is not, in itself, law. Law for Holmes is always prospective or subjunctive. Law operates in the domain of culture, not as brute fact.

We will explore this idea further in the next part. Enough for now to suggest that when Holmes says one is liable for a compensatory sum when one commits a contract unless the promised event comes to pass he is *condensing* into a legal formula the cumulative effect (felt reconciliation) of various historical sequences in the common law. In this particular case, the condensed legal formula was recognized as long ago as the seventeenth century. At this particular junction Holmes tells us he is content to abide with Lord Coke.[543]

Priel, as do many others, treats a formula condensing common law experience as a stand-alone proposition regarding law's determinate effects. That proposition then, somehow, converts into an analytic statement encapsulating a salient property of contracts. Once that transformation is complete the argument then devolves into a wide-ranging discussion of how, or whether, this distinctive, isolated property affects (or infects) the entire legal regime.

For this reason Priel devotes quite a few paragraphs to explaining, and defending, his argument that the bad man is an epistemic device.[544] He probably does not call the bad man a heuristic because for him the bad man as an epistemic device need not expressly connect to legal practice. He appears to have more of a jurisprudential function.

That function Priel does not detail other than to say, in a manner reminiscent of Frank or Yntema or Cook, that the bad man serves to open one's eyes and clear one's mind apropos the operations of the law. The point is well taken but, from an informed perspective, fails, without further elaboration, to advance our knowledge about either Holmes or "The Path of the Law." Nor does it, as expressly argued, illuminate Priel's thesis that "The Path of the Law" is an exercise in historical jurisprudence.

Drawing on the so-called three stages of the development of the (social) mind that Auguste Comte made popular in the nineteenth century, Priel sees Holmes tracing in

[542] *See* Letter from Oliver Wendell Holmes, Jr. to Walter Wheeler Cook (Feb. 25, 1919), *supra* note 111.

[543] Holmes, *The Path of the Law*, *supra* note 14, at 394.

[544] Priel, *supra* note 515, at 59–61.

"Path" a historical movement from a legal mind naïve and untutored to one increasingly sophisticated and artificial. The key term for Priel appears to be "artificial," though he does not dwell on it. He supports his interpretation of "Path" by pointing to the prevalence, in the late nineteenth century, of evolutionary discourses and modes of explanation. The movement from the first stage, from a natural, intuitive sense of law, to the stage where law is "increasingly rationalized in the sense that legal justification is no longer emotive but rather based on elaborate doctrines[,]" receives, I take it, analytical expression in the bad man (though Priel never actually says this). The bad man, then, is an epistemic device because it functions as a jurisprudential brace: to direct and assist the individual mind's transition from a natural, intuitive, subjectively certain sense of law to one more variegated and complex and self-consciously self-questioning (fallible). This latter stage is the second in the ages of law, corresponding somewhat to the one Comte called metaphysical. And since each stage has its own mode of legal justification – "the justification at this stage [the second] is historicist and imitative" – the content and form of law replicates the originating mentality.[545]

The movement from the second to the third stage, called scientific, is one Holmes projected into the future. Priel believes that Holmes saw this movement as law's great metamorphosis, "for it is at this point that law will cease to be natural and become fully artificial – and all the better for that. It is at this stage that societies use law to shape their fate with an eye to improving their lot."[546]

Priel maintains that for Holmes issues of the relative worth of ends or values define the third stage. The stages in which underlying values were unthinkingly accepted were "giving way to the law that, inevitably, passes judgment on what counts as the good life."

Priel offers a strong, intelligent reading of "The Path of the Law," but the lack of historical depth (ironically given his thesis) hamstrings it.[547]

The newly fashioned legal technique that he believes should be implemented, which, perhaps following the lead of E. Donald Elliott,[548] he describes as primarily artificial, must somehow raise the average tone of professional practice (comprised of Priel's "middling individuals"). Professional practice, it should be clear by now to readers of this book – even if Priel heads in a different direction – includes felt law, decided law, enacted law, practiced law, taught law, systematized law, and thought law. Each has its own provenance. Many of them overlap. Holmes hoped legal professionals would one day create from within the intersections an informed

[545] *Id.* at 69–72.

[546] *Id.* at 71.

[547] Given his focus on Comte, Priel would have benefitted from an informed dialogue with Patrick J. Kelley's lengthy article on Holmes and contract law. Kelley in his many articles also interprets Holmes as a Comtean Positivist. *See, e.g.*, Patrick J. Kelley, *Critical Analysis of Holmes's Theory of Contract*, 75 Notre Dame Law Rev. 1681, 1684–689 (2000).

[548] *See* Elliott, *supra* note 518, at 113. Priel does not cite this article but he does cite Elliott's subsequent longer article on evolution, E. Donald Elliott, *The Evolutionary Tradition in Jurisprudence*, 85 Colum. L. Rev. 38 (1985).

perspective that would array into a unified sequence these various lines of law and their associated vanishing points.

CODA

These thirteen ways of looking at the bad man do not include all the ways one may find in the historical record. As early as 1910 one finds the idea that the bad man functions mainly to make the law accessible to the common man.[549] More recently, in 2013, a very prominent scholar claimed almost the opposite, that the bad man could just as easily – because Holmes uses him to suggest a parsimonious, more elegant theory about contracts – been called a "physicist."[550] The instances and variations are overwhelming. We have not discussed, for example, most of the articles and essays contributed to the three symposia that celebrated "The Path of the Law's" 100th anniversary.[551] With respect to the pieces we have discussed, we have tried to arrange them in a manner conducive to obtaining perspective on the reception of "The Path of the Law" since 1900.

Beyond that, we have brought together various opinions and outlooks, not for the purpose of creating an overarching synthesis, but to bring into full view the various underlying sensibilities, styles of thought, and modes of argumentation that have achieved currency regarding Holmes and the bad man. What stands out is the lack of dimensionality in most approaches. Most of them, to use Hurst's terms, have a better sense of context than of sequence. If they have a sense of sequence, then context by comparison tends to suffer. And as for a coordinated depth to the offered analysis of Holmes or of "The Path of the Law," that too tends to be absent.

On the positive side, these deficiencies have enabled us to bring the purely legal point of view into the round. If law is for lawyers as Simpson maintained, then the purely legal point of view becomes an invaluable means for developing a better-honed sense of what the directives or pointers are telling us lawyers to do. "When we study law we are not studying a mystery but a well known profession." It bears quoting that sentence again. The job, or function, of the profession, for Holmes, was to study, to understand, when legal duties would be enforced, and how, and why.

Our retrospective has brought into view what is half-hidden, half-understood, half-perceived. The part not hidden, not opaque, fully transparent is the dignity many legal scholars have believed law has, should have, need not have, or lacks. Investigating the bad man becomes then a query into the sources of law's dignity as an ideal and a practice. The question extends beyond the much discussed separation thesis and comes to rest on what Holmes called the "dignity of moral feeling and the

[549] Herbert Pope, *The Common Law and the Common Man*, 5 ILL. L. REV. 22, 26–27 (1910).

[550] DOUGLAS G. BAIRD, RECONSTRUCTING CONTRACTS 49 (2013).

[551] *See* Symposium, *The Path of the Law after One Hundred Years*, 110 HARV. L. REV. 989 (1997); Symposium, *The Path of the Law 100 Years Later: Holmes's Influence on Modern Jurisprudence*, 63 BROOK. L. REV. 1 (1997); Symposium, *The Path of the Law Today*, 78 B.U. L. REV. 78 (1998).

profundity of knowledge."[552] He does not tell us the source of this "dignity," or whether the "dignity of moral feeling" is self-validating, but he does tell us it belongs to the thinker and the scholar, not the smart man, who believes the learning and study to which the thinker and the scholar devote their lives pointless.[553]

Less transparent are certain commitments or sensibilities that often render participants unprepared or unsuited for handling law as a social and cultural power in a democratic society. They are ill fitted to work in a setting where pigs sometimes forget to be polite and take their hooves out of the trough. Jerome Frank, I venture to speculate, is a good example of a smart, committed, realist legal scholar who ultimately could not control his nausea. The daily scenes he witnessed in the courtroom, involving either the parties or their lawyers – most likely their lawyers – probably got the better of him. He ultimately took refuge in some version of natural law.[554]

But the strength of our depiction does not depend on whether Frank could stand to eat the sausage after seeing how it was made. Nor does it depend on the personal proclivities or tastes or intellectual vigor of any one person. Its strength lies in the arrangement of the whole, in how it shows the interactions (or their lack) between the different people and ideas depicted. Its strength rests on its effort to bring the purely legal point of view into 3D. The purely legal point of view, as a point of view, converges on that remote conception that Holmes called the bad man. The dimensionality we have sought to portray ranges into the present. It is simply a matter of learning to "see as."

Speaking philosophically, the fundamental theorem of the law must inform how law is taught and studied. That is the topic of the next part. The goal is further integration, further clarity how law as an idea and an ideal musters force in the service of experience. From what Hurst called reason and will, we look to triangulate, as we believe Holmes also did, to a point from which law's present falls into sequence with its past and future. This act of projecting into the future has its own duration, its own history, its own way of adding breath and body to what otherwise would be a reiteration of elemental forces. The bad man understood as a projection provides much-needed dimension and dynamism to the study of law. Law becomes what Holmes described as a magic mirror – in which "we see reflected, not only our own lives, but the lives of all men that have been!"[555] It is the calling of thinkers.[556]

Holmes died on March 6, 1935, two days before his ninety-fourth birthday. On his birthday he was buried in Arlington National Cemetery (section 5, #7004).[557]

[552] Holmes, *supra* note 460, at 476.
[553] *Id.*
[554] PURCELL, THE CRISIS OF DEMOCRATIC THEORY, *supra* note 31, at 173.
[555] Holmes, *supra* note 5, at 469.
[556] Oliver Wendell Holmes, *The Profession of the Law*, *in* III CW 472.
[557] ARLINGTON NAT'L CEMETERY, www.arlingtoncemetery.mil/Explore/Notable-Graves/US-Supreme-Court (last accessed Oct. 23, 2019).

PART V

The Theory of Legal Study

SYNOPSIS

This part works on two levels that more or less correspond to its subdivisions. At one level this part zooms in again on Holmes's thought. It seeks to examine how his basic idea of the legal set-up in his society differed from that of Langdell's and to discuss the consequences of the differences in conception for legal pedagogy. And as legal pedagogy primarily meant preparing a person for legal practice, we take the time to inquire deeply into Holmes's own thoughts and feelings about law as a profession, on the qualities one might need to succeed and the kind of life one might expect to live; and, at a more philosophical level, on law as a subject for study, as an art of reflection, as a means to accomplish personal and social ends.

Section 1 ("Procedure and the Development of Legal Doctrine") and Section 2 ("A Well-Known Profession") work out the view that law as a professional activity ought not to be separated from the professionals who undertake it. In both these sections the primary goal is to reveal both the intricacy and reach of Holmes's thinking about the law. What is the role of procedure? How does legal doctrine develop? Where did Langdell go wrong? And, more directly in regard to the profession, who should become a lawyer? What qualities must or should that person have? What qualities, gifts, and goals should one find in a law teacher or in the consummate professional? What is the use and meaning of law schools? All these questions and others are touched upon, examined, discussed, compared, and expounded as an effort to present Holmes's thought on the subjects that concern us as carefully and accurately as possible.

At the second level, this part tilts more in the direction of legal theory than intellectual history. Sections 3 and 4 reflect this change. The scope is widened to bring back in larger issues or the opinions of other commentators on Holmes, but this time for the purpose of laying down markers for thinking about or imagining law; further clearing of the ground that Holmes first laid out. We also show why the "systematized generalizations" he sometimes said or hinted that he thought someday achievable in the law were actually not achievable. It was an inherently unworkable goal.

Section 3, "The Legal Profession and Law," is where we finally tackle head-on the many ramifications, some quite complex, of the pronouncement that "law is for lawyers." We take a closer look at Bryan Simpson's *Invitation to Law*, we look more directly at William Twining's two articles on Holmes and legal education, and take another glance at Hessel Yntema's insightful article on "The Path of the Law." We also address head-on many of the outstanding criticisms directed at Holmes's work over the years regarding his notions of law writ large – as a statement of the circumstances in which the public force through the courts will act – and writ small (*e.g.*, "commit a contract").

We return to the bad man in this part, to provide a final, culminating explanation on how Holmes intended the bad man to help law students learn law. We emphasize the importance that "professional judgments" have to the ethos of the profession. Understanding how "professional judgments" come into being justifies legal pedagogy in the same way that perfecting them serves as the only real justification for the existence of the profession as a profession in a democratic society. This interpretation binds the seemingly dispersed and disconnected parts of "The Path of the Law" to each other and to Holmes's work as a whole.

There is a real faith working in Holmes, one he never tried to hide. So in Section 4 ("The Lawyer's Faith") we make our best effort to draw it out and give it the solidity of form it deserves. We then work from the faith we have quarried to, and from the combined effect of Holmes's two great moral experiences, to provide further shape and direction to Holmes's overriding ambition: to bring into the legal profession a new discipline and, as it were, to finally make it a discipline, to make it both the ends and means of knowledge. Fundamental to Holmes's jurisprudence is the notion that any conduct may be judged either lawful or unlawful. Why and how professional judgments of "lawful" and "unlawful" take the form they do, and how to improve them, is the curiosity, and the hope, that kept Holmes working at his desk even into his nineties.

INTRODUCTION

Many legal writers have been led astray, as has Sir James Stephens, "by striving for a useless quintessence of all systems, instead of accurate anatomy of one." Holmes makes this observation almost offhandedly in the latter part of "The Path of the Law," in the beginning of the section in which he wants to put in a "good word" for the study of jurisprudence. James Fitzjames Stephens was a force to be reckoned with in English legal circles, especially in matters related to the criminal law. How familiar his name was to those in attendance for Holmes's address is hard to say but certainly, one assumes, the law professors from Boston and Harvard knew about him. Holmes contrasts unfavorably Stephens's writings on the law of possession to Frederick Pollack and R. S. Wright's then recent book on the topic. Holmes calls the volume "enlightened." That high praise must somehow relate, one infers, to the work's power to help the reader obtain a clear-eyed view of how the common law so often brought together through its judgments a time-tested ground of experience, like the instinct to fight dispossession or to try to recover what has been taken through force or fraud, and the reasoning that would convert such a "tendency" in the facts into a recognized basis for civilized life.

Holmes then repeats what he said at the beginning of his talk: "If a man goes into law it pays to be a master of it, and to be a master of it means to look straight through all the dramatic incidents and to discern the true basis for prophecy."[1]

How a student should develop both the needed awareness and the necessary skills to master the subject was really "The Path of the Law"'s overriding theme. It is also, with some necessary exposition and extension, the theme of this part. All that has come before is in one sense prelude; the diverse elements one must have at hand

[1] Oliver Wendell Holmes, *The Path of the Law, in* III The Collected Works of Justice Holmes: Complete Public Writings and Selected Judicial Opinions of Oliver Wendell Holmes 391 (Sheldon Novick ed., 1995) [hereinafter CW].

to assemble and shape the apparatus (technology) required for advancing law as a discipline.

The actual legal system Americans inherited began in what we call procedure. We begin at the same point, looking carefully at how Langdell and Holmes worked from their contrasting understanding of the development of procedural and doctrinal forms to reach their distinctive conclusions and prescriptions. From there we look more closely at how Holmes understood the profession of which he was a part. The main texts for analysis will first be taken from his published *Speeches* and, second, from a mid-brow periodical of that era, *The Youth's Companion*. In that magazine Holmes provided his considered thoughts on the ingredients for success the legal profession in America required, first in a short piece entitled "Just the Boy Wanted," and then in two contributions to a series on "The Bar As a Profession" in which he pointedly demurred from the more ponderous advice of England's Lord Chief Justice. The Lord Chief Justice did not take kindly to Holmes's disagreement.

In the third section of this part, "The Legal Profession and the Law," we turn back to themes introduced in earlier parts. Three in particular merit further attention. First is Simpson's summation in the opening pages of *Invitation to Law* that "Law is for lawyers." We look closely at that pronouncement in light of Holmes's enjoinder that to properly learn the law one must study an actual system. We find that the brilliance of Simpson's formulation does not quite manage to frame a legal pedagogy mainly because Simpson does not provide a way to organize and scale all the different and distinct directives (pointers and their arrangements) that in theory constitute law.

The second and third subsections turn back to the role of history and the use of the bad man as a way to inculcate the purely legal point of view. These two subsections lay out the essentials of Holmes's program for legal study as he expressed it in "The Path of the Law" and "Law in Science and Science in Law." That program begins with the recognition that the law's antiquity and futurity are, and ought to be seen as, in constant tension. The profession's task is to bring them into equilibrium. Another way of making the same point is to see the interlaced inquiry "what is (the) law?" as providing the necessary means, through its focus on professional judgments, for coordinating three activities (succinctly – history, philosophy, economics) that Holmes believed vital to the development of the profession but which he never could quite manage to make cohere.

Holmes's use of the bad man was a way to break the unseen hold of the past, to bring into full view as much as possible certain background assumptions or inclinations to present legal action; and to help the student understand that the law that was taught, the dogma of the law schools, had a present usefulness that was both needed and arbitrary though not capricious. Holmes wanted the law taught in such a way that students understood that they must work outward, that is, begin with present dogma, law already distilled of its dramatic incidents, and from there proceed, recursively, backwards through history and forwards through economics and other social scientific studies.

Holmes's suggestions were not always clear or congruent with one another. We suggest the problem arises from his inability to find the right vocabulary to express how the multidimensional endeavor he advocated fit together. On the other hand, the problem with how many commentators have attempted to make sense of Holmes's many and varied prescriptions arises, mainly, from their lack of appreciation for how Holmes sought to build-out the discipline of law from within its ongoing practice. This part concludes with an exposition of one such attempt, that involving "temporal harm" and its justifications in the context of torts.

1 PROCEDURE AND THE DEVELOPMENT OF LEGAL DOCTRINE

In his entertaining, informative but by no means streamlined presentation of how the American legal system evolved, Charles Rembar remarks that contemporary historians frequently give the wrong impression that ancestors – say, those who predated thirteenth-century Angles, Saxons, or Normans – were not significantly different from the people who happen to be reading their, the history writers', articles and books. They were. Even so, he says, there is one point in which they are much closer than often suggested: "they are closer to us in legal procedure than in other modes of thought. They differ in their insistence that the proof be left to magic, not in their idea of the proper sequence of the steps of litigation."[2]

That legal procedure has played an often underappreciated role in shaping the content of black letter law – fundamental and settled legal doctrines – is one of the more important lessons that the lawyer who most contributed to the founding of modern American legal education sought to teach. William LaPiana has argued that Langdell's concern with procedure, with the interplay between court practice and pressing issues that called for legal resolution, differentiated Langdell's approach to legal education from that of his immediate predecessors. LaPiana sums up his thesis this way: "Langdell's legal science exemplifies the shift from the idea of legal order based on principles inherent in the constitution of a divinely created universe to one based on proper understanding and arrangement of technical principles inherent in the historically produced legal system."[3]

The phrase "historically produced legal system" encapsulates LaPiana's argument that Langdell viewed the law as a "system" that judges and other formal court participants in old England had somehow brought into being under the constraints of their occupations and through the employment of reason. Reason, one gathers,

[2] Charles Rembar, The Law of the Land: The Evolution of Our Legal System 233 (1980).

[3] William P. LaPiana, Logic and Experience: The Origin of Modern American Legal Education 70 (1994).

played a critical role in rationalizing and regulating those social activities that had once found their home in custom. To the skeptics who doubted whether the existing multitudinous reports of decisions spanning 600 years could be organized into a teachable system that went beyond tradecraft, LaPiana's Langdell responded by developing his famed case method.

The strength of LaPiana's history lies in how he presents Langdell as a cultural nucleus. That is to say, LaPiana sees in Langdell's innovations – not just the case method as a mode of teaching and studying law, but in raising entrance and graduation requirements, in developing and ordering a more stringent curriculum, in the introduction of regularly administered examinations, in instituting the vocation of the American law professor, in his Austinian approach to law and his groundbreaking legal scholarship – a de facto point of convergence for various social desires and recognized social needs (in short: for quality men qualified to practice quality law in a quality legal system) that, in retrospect, seem almost indissolubly linked. But these interconnections are more probably the result of artful historical presentation and a current willingness to accept as given certain juxtapositions.

Take, for example, the biggest point of contrast LaPiana develops early in *Logic and Experience*. It is between those who took the narrow way of legal pedagogy and those who took the broad. It is between those who saw law primarily as a "science of principles" (the broad) and those who emphasized, sometimes exclusively, law as the "practical science of procedure" (the narrow).[4]

LaPiana contends that in nineteenth-century America those who advocated law as a "science of principles" did so under the auspices of Francis Bacon. At the time that meant, LaPiana explains, one of three things: (1) empiricism, (2) avoidance of hypotheses, or (3) classification. It was, as another commentator expressed it, "a naïve rationalistic empiricism – a belief that the method of pure empiricism consistently pursued would lead to a rational understanding of the universe."[5]

To understand LaPiana's point consider the following. An intelligent and rational understanding of the universe strongly implied the existence of stationary objects of attention. These objects focused the mind of those who inquired through

[4] *Id.* at 55–58.

[5] *Id.* at 30 (*quoting* GEORGE H. DANIELS, AMERICAN SCIENCE IN THE AGE OF JACKSON 65 (1968)). On "Protestant Baconianism" and legal science specifically *see* Howard Schweber, *The "Science" of Legal Science: The Model of the Natural Sciences in Nineteenth-Century American Legal Education*, 17 LAW AND HIST. REV. 421, 441–55 (1999); but *see* Catharine Piece Wells, *Langdell and the Invention of Legal Doctrine*, 58 BUFF. L. REV. 551, 596–99 (2010) (arguing that Langdell did not employ a "Baconian" method). Though not referenced by LaPiana, a remarkably concise and thorough summary of the efforts to make legal pedagogy more "scientific" during this era, especially as those efforts related to the broader endeavor to make higher education more "scientific," is to be found in G. Edward White's *Tort Law in America*. G. EDWARD WHITE, TORT LAW IN AMERICA: AN INTELLECTUAL HISTORY 20–62 (Expand. ed. 2003) (orig. pub. 1980); *see also* G. EDWARD WHITE, II LAW IN AMERICAN HISTORY: FROM RECONSTRUCTION THROUGH THE 1920S 312–48 (2016).

recognizably empirical techniques. Empirical means the habit of looking outside one's intuitive understanding for explanatory frameworks; one does not rely solely or primarily on the wellsprings of one's own reason. If we work off the presumption that the learned people of that era also pretty much accepted that societies and cultures changed over time – bracketing the question whether and, if so, to what extent people themselves fundamentally changed – the issue then became how to halt and fix opinion and turn it into knowledge. In other words, how one could achieve conformity between opinion and the stationary object.

One favored nineteenth-century approach took the shape of a large stepladder. One began at the bottom, with what we might call facts. These were things, objects (phenomena), and features of experience that had certain observable properties. One characteristic of facts so conceived, and one often overlooked, is their multitude. Multitude is not limited to quantity only; it included increasingly refined qualitative descriptions of phenomena (which includes human acts or behaviors). From sheer plenitude one takes the steps needed to reduce the manifold of phenomena, whether individual features or sense impressions, into something relatively abstract and comprehensible to the mind, something that could ultimately be thought of without explicit reference to the endless facts themselves. One might then call this something a principle. Principles set the terms and often indicated the content of an explanation (as in the principle of mutuality brings together and explains the elements of contract formation). A principle, seen as the end and justification of reasoning, the top cap of the ladder, became, in turn, that relatively stationary object that focused the mind's attention.

LaPiana does not lard his history with these kinds of miniature commentaries. He seems to take for granted that his readers will understand his use of words like "science," "empirical," "facts," "inductive," and "principle." Thus, when he writes about law as a "science of principles," he selects out of the historical record various renditions that fit the fact-principle prototype (as I have described it). If that prototype does not work, then the alternate, the fact-classification prototype, will usually fill the bill. Classification indexes phenomena according to salient characteristics. The fact-classification prototype seems to me to be the less affluent cousin to the fact-principle prototype; if one can't reach a principle then mid-rung classification become the next best available alternative.

LaPiana's inattentiveness to the vagaries of language almost manages to submerge the value of his most significant insight, that Langdell shifted the relatively stationary object used to focus the mind from the realm of moral or philosophical principles to that of legal technique. Legal practice provided the needed structure for legal principles. In keeping with our imagery, Langdell set the large stepladder on its side, legs open and pointing outward from where he stood. He turned it into a mechanical instrument that effectively encompassed his community's legal experience (legal premises and practices). To modify the metaphor: his position became the dominant benchmark or control point by which past legal experience would be surveyed and measured.

LaPiana seems to suggest that Langdell treated the "historically produced legal system" as a given – that is, as a bequeathal from prior generations of common law practitioners – and sought in his teaching and scholarship to draw out from the multitude of reports its lineaments as a logically coherent, closed system of legal doctrine founded upon, and still sustained by, procedure. This new conception of the nature of a legal principle, or a legal doctrine, superseded the false and pernicious – pernicious for the study of law and for the quality of legal institutions – opposition between law as a science of principles and law as the practical science of procedure.

"What content, then, can be found in the statement that law is a science?" asks LaPiana. He responds:

> The importance of the case method of teaching to the definition of the new model law school provides at least a partial answer. Only full-time scientists can properly pursue legal science. Their task is to find principles in the original sources of the law, which are the cases. Understanding the opinions of the courts will reveal the true basis of the law. That basis is not grand principles related to the ultimate ordering of society, but the narrow, technical principles that make up the real work of the lawyer, which courts use to decide real cases.[6]

LaPiana then amplifies this point on the importance of technical principles by recounting a debate between Samuel Williston and Langdell over a contract law issue. Sidestepping the substance of the dispute, LaPiana draws attention to *how* Langdell argued: by using both "principles of contract law and pleading, he showed that the question, if properly isolated for decision [*i.e.*, put into issue and tried], would be decided in accord with his views."[7]

With this discussion LaPiana illustrates the key steps in Langdell's approach. First, one must have access to the reported cases, hence the huge role of a well-stocked library in Langdell's vision. The library serves primarily as a resource for the professors, only secondarily for students. Second, cases the professors select become the materials from which students through their own strenuous mental exertion (but under the guidance of the professor) draw out the leading principles in a certain area of the law. Third, once "induced" these legal principles should be applied deductively (they form the major premise) to issues arising in practice and tested "experimentally" against the reports to see if the established decisions support the expected outcome. This third step in LaPiana's rendition is a bit blurry. Given the context, I think he wants to emphasize how for Langdell the interplay between an existing legal question, the applicable precedents, and the procedural postures underlying

[6] *Id.* at 57–58.
[7] *Id.* at 58.

the applicable precedents and the current question, gave an articulated legal doctrine (principle) its distinctive content. One could then test whether the principle one has refined fits the decided cases by working out its application through the stages of pleading and proof.

It is Langdell's manner of using the cases to loop together the discerned principle and the applicable procedure that most impresses LaPiana. Together they narrowed the facts into an issue, just as the forms of action had traditionally done in the common law. He finds in Langdell's approach a technical proficiency that at one and the same time serves to frame the historical emergence of the legal system – points of law slowly being bound together to create fundamental legal doctrines or rules – and illustrates the type of reasoning (logical) that bound those points of law into a solid legal principle (such as the doctrine of mutuality). The principle, once identified, can be traced, articulated, and taught. Probably for this reason LaPiana does not seem too impressed with the oft-repeated arguments that overemphasize the conceptual or formal elements in Langdell's method without giving due weight to its technical (procedural) grounding. LaPiana summarizes his discussion by concluding, after reviewing Langdell's notable studies in equity jurisdiction, that those studies and his efforts in contract law bear striking similarities. "In both cases his explanations of the workings of the law are intimately tied to the peculiarities and technicalities of procedure."[8]

Langdell makes for an interesting comparison to Holmes precisely because both men understood the significant role procedure played in the formation of substantive legal doctrine. One need not recur to Maine's famous remark – "So great is the ascendency of the Law of Actions in the infancy of the Courts of Justice, that substantive law has at first the look of being gradually secreted in the interstices of procedure"[9] – to establish the solidity of a perception that had probably achieved contemporary currency. A couple of years earlier Holmes in his lecture on the history of contract in *The Common Law* said pretty much the same thing: "whenever we trace a leading doctrine of substantive law far enough back, we are very likely to find some forgotten circumstance of procedure at its source."[10]

If one grants that both Holmes and Langdell recognized the fundamental role procedure played as a generator of legal doctrine in the history of the common law, and grants also, as both men said in different ways, that the "growth and development" of legal principles took time, sometimes even centuries, one must ask what made each think that by investigating the cases in a certain order the doctrine or rule or principle (using these words synonymously) being sought could be ascertained.

The question is clearly complex and I don't pretend to have a full answer. But for our purposes it is instructive to see how Holmes distinguished his approach from

8 *Id.* at 69.

9 Henry Sumner Maine, Dissertations on Early Law and Custom 389 (1883).

10 Oliver Wendell Holmes, *The Common Law*, *in* III CW 244.

Langdell's. Holmes saw both extraordinary merit and extraordinary limitation in what he called Langdell's "habit of mind."[11] Langdell's exemplary diligence, carefulness, patience; his "profound intellect working out original theory through a mass of detail, and evolving consistency out of what seemed a chaos of conflicting atoms[;]" his desire to assume the role of the jurisconsult all struck Holmes as a particularly clear instance of impressive intellectual virtues gone awry.[12] In depicting what he called Langdell's "ideal in the law, the end of all his striving," as "the *elegantia juris*, or *logical* integrity of the system as a system,"[13] Holmes drew attention to a particular habit of mind that sought to impress itself on how the teachings from the cases regarding the law of contracts ought to be understood.

Most scholars have taken Holmes's use of the words "logical" or "logic" or the phrase "formal connection of things" to convey the substance of his critique and have overlooked that Holmes used these terms primarily to *indicate* the habit of mind he found objectionable. This habit of mind Holmes saw as the main problem. Logic was merely a symptom. In its press for consistency this habit of mind might utilize the techniques of traditional logic or search for new strictures. Holmes had no controversy with the traditionally conceived logical powers unless or until they sought to supplant, on the one side, the required powers of observation and investigation (traditional empiricism) or, on the other, the innovative philosophical power to join newly elicited facts to each other and to facts already accepted (the hallmark of advanced social thought).

Holmes refers to Langdell's undue confidence in his own ability to coordinate the cases, tease out the principles, adjust part to part, in sum, to create an integrated legal system as *theological*. "He is, perhaps, the greatest living legal theologian."[14] The phrase borders on a jeer. Some commentators – Gerald Postema, for instance – appear to delight that A. V. Dicey threw the same word, theologian, back at Holmes when he reviewed *The Common Law*.[15]

> Mr. Holmes, in short, deals with the texts of the common law in the same way in which speculative but orthodox theologians deal with the texts of Scripture. They devote a great deal of ability to showing that certain doctrines are in themselves true, and at the same time labour, with equal assiduity, to prove that these doctrines may be deduced from, or are consistent with, a mass of texts . . . quoted in its support.[16]

[11] Oliver Wendell Holmes, *Review of* A Selection of Cases on the Law of Contracts, with a Summary of the Topics covered by the Cases, *in* III CW 103.

[12] *Id.*

[13] *Id.* (emphasis in original).

[14] *Id.*

[15] Gerald Postema, Legal Philosophy in the Twentieth Century: The Common Law World 50 n.15 and 65 n.25 (2011).

[16] Albert Venn Dicey, *Review of* The Common Law, *The Spectator, Literary Supplement*, June 3, 1882, reprinted as appendix II in Saul Touster, *Holmes a Hundred Years Ago:* The Common Law *and Legal Theory*, 10 Hofstra L. Rev. 673, 714 (1981).

Dicey's critique singles out a style of argument frequently denounced in theological circles as proof texting, that is, amassing Biblical texts – appropriately cited by book, chapter, and verse – to support a doctrinal proposition to which the text offered has little, if any, innate connection. The alleged lack of innate connection depends of course on the critic's own premises. A similar criticism would in ensuing years be launched against the case method and its ghastly creation, the case lawyer.[17] Sidebar: even to this day colleagues comment ruefully that a lawyer so inclined can find some case from some jurisdiction and spin it to support almost any position no matter how patently ludicrous or outlandish.[18]

Holmes's criticism points in a different direction. He found troubling how Langdell's incisive intellect imposed itself on both the materials and the method. Given his own deep learning in the cases – Dicey believed it easily surpassed that of any English lawyer[19] – Holmes recognized the value of the legal insights Langdell had mined and brought to the surface but balked when he realized how Langdell sought to implement them. Langdell's attempts at systemization brought out Holmes's orneriness; the question is why.

This question brings us to an impasse; or better if more pretentiously stated, an aporia. What do we really explain if we say that Holmes thought Langdell's approach would invariably distort the materials and pervert a method – the historical – they both valued? Is it merely the thesis that law is something more than logic? The scholars have taken sides: some thinking Holmes got it more or less right; others, like Kimball, constructing an imposing scholarly rampart to reinforce Langdell's achievements against repeated onslaughts that he thinks find their genesis in Holmes's petulance.[20] Yet even Kimball, following LaPiana's lead, concedes that Holmes and Langdell shared more commonalities than the generation whose sentiments Morton White expressed in his *Social Thought in America: The Revolt against Formalism* let on.[21] Instead of logic vs. experience we have *Logic and Experience*.

LaPiana's formulation appears to resolve the impasse but it does not. The impasse arises from an irresolvable difference in mindset that Holmes perceived between himself and Langdell regarding how a lawyer should respond to the unified query we discussed in previous parts: "what is the law? – what is law?" In calling Langdell "perhaps the greatest living legal theologian" Holmes took aim at a certain noetic temper, one that, in its drive for specificity, cogency, and integration, persistently

[17] *See* LaPiana, *supra* note 3 at 132–38.

[18] After I wrote this sentence, I found that Frederick Pollock said the same thing over 100 years ago: "Any man who knows how to handle the professional apparatus of reference can find, with moderate industry, something like a show of authority for almost anything: and it is the delight of a certain class of advocates to snatch an advantage (though it is apt to be a fleeting one) by this method." Frederick Pollock, The Genius of the Common Law 114 (1911).

[19] Dicey, *Review of* The Common Law, *supra* note 16, at 713.

[20] Bruce Kimball, The Inception of Modern Professional Education 325–38 (2009).

[21] *Id.*

ignored the hidden biases and undersides of doctrinal formation.[22] In seeking to make law the epitome of reason, it did not – could not – recognize the many circumstances by which reason itself had been channeled. For Holmes the epitome of law is law.

Holmes's use of the term "theologian" in 1880s Boston is hard to understand. No one comparable to Princeton Theological Seminary's B. B. Warfield occupied a chair at the liberal Harvard Divinity School. We may not know whom, or what theological school, Holmes may have had in mind when he called Langdell a theologian, but given the gist of Holmes's pronouncement I venture to speculate that the most prominent person equipped to fit the bill in that anglophone era was John Henry Cardinal Newman. That Holmes knew about and read Newman his reading list shows.[23] Whether he knew about Newman's 1845 *An Essay on the Development of Christian Doctrine* the particular list consulted does not disclose. Newman's historical investigations upheld the primacy of Catholic dogma and constituted a well-wrought brief in support of his notorious conversion from Anglican orders to the apostolic Church of Rome. Of especial interest – to help us appreciate the force of Holmes's comparison – is Newman's disquisition on the concept of development.

Development in the sense in which Newman wants to use it must first be distinguished from other kinds of developments, say, mathematical, physical, or material, that do not involve a clear line of identity between those endpoints demarcated as beginning and end. From defects in language, the word "development" has taken on, Newman says, three distinct meanings. It stands for the process of development, or the result, or is used to describe a result that is "true or not true (that is, faithful or unfaithful to the idea from which it started)[.]"[24] It is the latter that he believes is a "development" deserving the name. One test for development in this sense is whether the possibility of an outcome not faithful or true to the initiating idea exists. Newman calls a false or unfaithful development a corruption.[25]

Because one does not ordinarily call a particular line of mathematical reasoning corrupt (rather, it is erroneous), Newman does not think mathematical developments – "the system of truths drawn out from mathematical definitions or equations"[26] – fall within his use of the term, though he concedes they are

[22] Gerald Postema has provided a succinct description of what he describes as the dominant "jurisprudential temperament" in the anglophone world from the mid-nineteenth century to the middle of the twentieth. Postema's description of this dominant jurisprudential temperament illuminates what I have called a noetic temper. *See* Postema, *supra* note 15, at 25–32.

[23] Eleanor Little, *The Early Reading of Justice Oliver Wendell Holmes*, 8 Harv. Libr. Bull. 163, 190 (1954).

[24] John Henry Cardinal Newman, An Essay on the Development of Christian Doctrine 41 (6th ed. 1989) (orig. pub. 1878).

[25] *Id.*

[26] *Id.*

analogous. Mathematical conclusions proceed on the basis of strict demonstration; for that reason those conclusions "cannot be declensions from the original idea."[27]

Newman further distinguishes his version of development from its physical or material cognates. Physical refers to what we would today call organic. He again concedes these kinds of changes bear analogies to what he has in mind but they are not the same. He makes the same point for what he calls material developments, that is, improvement of resources through human contrivance (economic development) which, he points out, fall under the heading "art," understood as the adaptation of nature to "the purposes of utility and beauty, the human intellect being the developing power."[28]

Having gone through the exercise of stating what his use of "development" does not mean, Newman proceeds to identify five types of development that fall within his use of the term. It bears keeping in mind that in all cases faithfulness is the dominant leitmotif. To use an image, one has found and followed the thread (Ariadne's) upon which the changes ring.

"The development then of an idea is not like an investigation worked out on paper, in which each successive advance is a pure evolution from a foregoing, but it is carried on through and by means of communities of men and their leaders and guides; and it employs their minds as its instruments, and depends on them, while it uses them."[29] What makes a "change" a "development" for Newman is the working out of an idea. The various "aspects of an idea are brought into consistency and form." It is "the germination and maturation of some truth or apparent truth on a large mental field."[30] The actual movements understood retrospectively as developments are invariably aggressive. Ideas push to establish *jurisdiction* (Newman's word, not mine) over all relations of life, and what cannot be assimilated is sidelined.[31]

The first type is political. The development is political when the subject matter of the ideas is "society and its various classes and interests."[32] How discordant ideas are trussed up to look harmonious for the sake of presenting a unified front or quelling dissent presents one manifestation of political development. Or, less obviously, when the ideas put forward are rationalizations of decisions made under the pressure of events or unacknowledged principles. Newman's main point seems to be that the political context illuminates the saltation of feelings and thoughts and interests and motives into ideas proper that then, in turn, undergo in the same context further morphological changes. The political context illustrates quite well why Newman entitled the chapter "Development in Ideas" and not "Development of Ideas."[33]

[27] *Id.*
[28] *Id.* at 42.
[29] *Id.* at 38.
[30] *Id.*
[31] *Id.* at 38–39 (emphasis added).
[32] *Id.* at 42–44.
[33] *Id.* at 33–54.

The second kind of development in ideas that Newman discusses is the logical. These are developments in which what he calls the "intellectual character" predominates. These developments properly work off the consistency between a major premise and its various conclusions. Logic, whether in religious doctrine or law, works out its distinctive chains of reasons in specific settings, and a chain of reasoning initiated may very easily acquire a life of its own.[34]

Third are historical developments. These Newman describes as "the gradual formation of opinion concerning persons, facts, and events."[35] This particular type of development recurs to one of Newman's fundamental beliefs, "that, from the nature of the human mind, time is necessary for the full comprehension and perfection of great ideas."[36] This temporal context is the beating heart of development; the other contexts arrange themselves as necessary to support or amplify it.

The ethical aspect of development is the hardest to explain. Newman begins by saying that these developments "are not properly matter for argument and controversy, but are natural and personal, substituting what is congruous, desirable, pious, appropriate, generous, for strictly logical inference."[37] Ethical development introduces – though Newman does not use the word – *scale* into the mix. Newman begins his discussion by referring to Bishop Joseph Butler's observation that "certain relations imply correlative duties and certain objects demand certain acts and feelings." And the converse is true as well: certain "sentiments imply objects and duties."[38]

Newman cites the theological example Butler uses to support his first observation. The relation between the First Person of the Holy Trinity and the Second and Third leads to the inference that the Second and Third are due the same reverence as the First, even though no express scriptural command enjoins it. This analogy illustrates how a relation may have correlative duties as invariable accompaniments, or how an object of veneration may demand certain acts and feelings that extend beyond the initial requirements of reverence. An example of the converse, how a sentiment can instill its own idea, is conscience. Conscience assumes in Newman's hands status as an antecedent warrant, based only in probability to be sure, for the doctrine of a Moral Governor. In such manner sentiments and feelings become the grounds for subsequent conceptions.[39]

Newman's assertions and style of argument might strike us as problematic and unpersuasive, but his overall point regarding ethical development is worth considering. He is arguing that an idea's moral implication has its own interior dimension, apart from its logical amplification. It works out its own ever-enlarging trajectory.

34 *Id.* at 45–46.
35 *Id.* at 46.
36 *Id.* at 29.
37 *Id.* at 47.
38 *Id.* at 47–48 (internal citations omitted).
39 *Id.* (internal citations omitted).

An idea's moral development after a certain level requires connection to means other than reason (wealth, friends, political power) to further structure itself, to increase in scale, to grow. By this route Newman brings into view broader vistas of social formation – how the inward development of an idea's moral aspects help societies take shape, cohere, and mature. In its stylized progression, Newman's depiction bears many similarities to how earlier eighteenth-century Scottish philosophers of history conjectured the course of what they called civilization.[40]

The final way in which ideas develop Newman calls metaphysical. The motive power of this development is a concentrated love. An idea has developed metaphysically when through focused attention (scrutiny) one has achieved "its exact and complete delineation."[41] Newman provides a brief phenomenological sketch of how this works. The mind "habituated" to a particular object of thought turns with "curiosity" to contemplate further the object and "begins to form statements concerning it, before it knows whither, or how far, it will be carried." In hindsight one can clearly perceive the process.

> One proposition necessarily leads to another, and a second to a third; then some limitation is required; and the combination of these opposites occasions fresh evolutions from the original idea, which indeed can never be said to be entirely exhausted. This process is development, and results in a series, or rather body, of dogmatic statements, till what was an impression on the Imagination has become a system or creed in Reason.[42]

Despite his keen sensitivity to development and its modes, Newman does not doubt the final outcome. He is much impressed by how the resulting doctrines are necessarily consistent with each other and form an integrated whole.[43] Very probably a similar conviction that law, properly understood, would display the same type of cogency, coherence, and consistency; a similar unreflective confidence in his ability to surmise principles and formulate general propositions; a similar display of the intellectual power to order them into a self-referencing and mutually reinforcing intellectual complex prompted Holmes to label Langdell a theologian. This borderline slight assumes Langdell saw the common law as some kind of revelation. And as the implicit comparison to someone like Newman indicated, Holmes knew that Langdell perfectly understood, as did the Cardinal, that ideas develop. But as a theorist (theologian) of the common law Langdell, from Holmes's standpoint, primarily limited that development to what Newman called the "intellectual character" of ideas.

[40] *See* J. W. Burrow, Evolution and Society: A Study in Victorian Social Theory 10–23 (1966).

[41] Newman, *supra* note 24, at 52–53.

[42] *Id.* (internal citations omitted).

[43] *Id.* at 96.

The important difference, though, from Holmes's perspective between a first-class theologian like Newman and someone like Langdell, who operated in a discernibly theological mode but without the ability to get past third gear, was the latter's failure to give sufficient attention to the postulates from which he worked. "But as a theologian he is less concerned with his postulates than to show that his conclusions from them hang together."[44] Much of what is distinctive and valuable in Holmes's thought lies in his focus on postulates. Langdell's lack of concern with how the postulates upon which he predicated his legal analyses came into being and persisted revealed his lack of historical sensitivity or anthropological awareness. Langdell's mode of thought had a no-nonsense, padlock-snapping character. Holmes found this habit of mind, this mode of thinking – probably as typical then as it is today – both unphilosophical and unscientific even if highly effective. Unphilosophical – because it pre-selected and logically systematized the propositions that describe the circumstances that called for law and the specific enactments of public force which such statements authorized. Unscientific – because Holmes believed Langdell oversimplified his postulates to ensure the success of his logical analysis – to create dogma, in other words. And this mode of thinking proved itself effective because it produced in the unaware an ersatz certitude.

Holmes made his point sarcastically. He goes from comparing Langdell to a theologian to comparing him to Hegel. That is, "If Mr. Langdell could be suspected of ever having troubled himself about Hegel[.]"[45] We again see reflected in this clause Holmes's disparagement and dissatisfaction, impatience even, with a certain habit of mind. Though Holmes pinpoints Langdell's penchant for attending exclusively to "the formal connection of things, or logic," his real quarrel with Langdell lies in how the latter avoids including in his analyses the "content of logic."[46] With this statement Holmes broaches his famed paradox of substance and form. We learn that in Holmes's opinion the content of logic – logic understood as the "formal condition of things" – is *feelings*. And feelings in Holmes's opinion have "actually shaped the substance of the law."[47]

Though Holmes may not have been aware of it, Newman no less than he focused intently on the nature of postulates and their formation. Newman had in fact drawn parallels in *An Essay on the Development of Christian Doctrine* between how the law in England worked and how certain Catholic dogma had come into being. "It is a common occurrence for a quarrel and a lawsuit to bring out the state of the law, and then the most unexpected results often follow."[48] Specifically in reference to the Pope's infallibility he observes: "The *regalia Petri* might sleep, as the power of a Chancellor has slept; not as an obsolete, for they never had been carried into effect,

[44] Holmes, *supra* note 11, at 103.
[45] *Id.*
[46] *Id.*
[47] *Id.*
[48] Newman, *supra* note 24, at 149–50.

but as a mysterious privilege, which was not understood; as an unfulfilled prophecy."[49]

Of equal interest is how Newman uses terminology most often, at least in our day, associated with law and lawyers to frame his arguments against both skeptics and Protestants. He puts into question fundamental propositions of the famed Baconian method when applied to subjects other than the hard sciences. In fact, part I of his *Essay* may be viewed as a sophisticated critique of such placeholder terms as "presumption" and "burden of proof." This leads directly to Newman's master concept of "antecedent probability":

> Moreover, in subjects which belong to moral proof, such, I mean, as history, antiquities, political science, ethics, metaphysics, and theology, which are pre-eminently such, and especially in theology and ethics, antecedent probability may have a real weight and cogency which it cannot have in experimental science; and a mature politician or divine may have a power of reaching matters of fact in consequence of his *peculiar habits of mind*, which is seldom given in the same degree to physical inquirers, who, for the purposes of this particular pursuit, are very much on the level.[50]

His use of the phrase "on the level" is not self-explanatory. But as ever Newman takes great pains to make sure his meaning is not lost: "And this last remark at least is confirmed by Lord Bacon, who confesses, 'Our method of discovering the sciences does not much depend on subtlety and strength of genius, but lies level to almost every capacity and understanding;' though surely sciences there are, in which genius is everything, and rules all but nothing."[51] Lord Bacon's method subsumed into the common law would eventually bring into existence the very "middling individuals" that Dan Priel observed in 2016 overwhelmingly populate the legal profession.[52]

To the extent that law falls within the subjects that Newman identified as belonging to "moral proof,"[53] the question arises as to the means or method of

[49] *Id.*

[50] *Id.* at 112–13 (emphasis added).

[51] *Id.* (internal citations omitted).

[52] Dan Priel, *Holmes's "Path of the Law" As Non-Analytic Jurisprudence*, 35 U. QUEENSLAND L.J. 57, 73 (2016).

[53] Newman explains "moral proof" as follows:

> Further, let it be considered, that, even as regards what are commonly called Evidences, that is, arguments à posteriori; conviction for the most part follows, not upon any one great and decisive proof or token of the point in debate, but upon a number of very minute circumstances together, which the mind is quite unable to count up and methodize in an argumentative form. Let a person only call to mind the clear impression he has about matters of every day's occurrence, that this man is bent on a certain object, or that that man was displeased, or another suspicious; or that one is happy, and another unhappy; and how much depends in such impressions on manner, voice, accent, words uttered, silence instead of words, and all the many subtle symptoms which are felt by the mind, but cannot be contemplated; and let him consider how very poor an account he is able to give of his impression, if he avows it, and is called upon to justify it. This, indeed, is meant by what is

reasoning that validates the proof. For Newman that method is one that self-consciously seeks to connect the reasoning employed with the postulate upon which it rests. The postulate and the reasoning in their separate ways support and enhance the conclusion obtained. Newman often used the term "antecedent probability" to characterize the postulate. Antecedent probabilities took different forms; they partook in a style of reasoning that Newman thought Bacon unjustly condemned. "It will be a great mistake," said Newman, "to suppose that because this eminent philosopher condemned presumption and prescription in inquiries into facts which are external to us, present with us, and common to us all, therefore authority, tradition, verisimilitude, analogy, and the like are mere 'idols of the den' or 'of the theatre' in history or ethics."[54]

To counteract the great authority of Bacon, Newman cited Barthold Georg Niebuhr, a renowned nineteenth-century German historian who specialized in Roman history. In Niebuhr's concept of "instances" Newman found a style far more congruent to reasoning in matters historical or ethical than Bacon's vaunted empiricism. As Newman quotes Niebuhr, "instances are not arguments, but in history are scarcely of less force; above all, where the parallel they exhibit is in the progressive development of institutions." For Newman the ultimate lesson was clear: "In all matters of human life, presumption verified by instances, is our ordinary instrument of proof, and, if the antecedent probability is very great it almost supersedes instances."[55]

In discussing Newman's idea of antecedent probability I am, emphatically, *not* suggesting that Newman influenced Holmes in how he understood or treated postulates. Newman's ideas provide a convenient comparison because in both cases – Newman's antecedent probability and Holmes's postulate – what is recognized as necessarily existing in the present – what makes continuity with the past a necessity – is something vital, something that orients an inquiring mind in its inquiries. Vitality for a religious consciousness existed mainly in presumption and prescription. These manifested the work of God in the world through designated and still active means. For Holmes, on the other hand, vitality in law lay in the feelings "which make up the content of logic, and which have actually shaped the substance of the law."[56] That is to say, vitality for what Duncan Kennedy calls a "legal consciousness"[57] lay in the strong and weak feelings that have shaped law in

> called moral proof, in opposition to legal. We speak of an accused person being guilty without any doubt, even though the evidences of his guilt are none of them broad and definite enough in themselves to admit of being forced upon the notice of those who will not exert themselves to see them.

John Henry Newman, Fifteen Sermons Preached before the University of Oxford 187 (James David Earnest and Gerard Tracey eds., 2006).

54 Newman, *supra* note 24, at 113 (internal citations omitted).

55 *Id.*

56 Holmes, *supra* note 11, at 103.

57 Duncan Kennedy, The Rise & Fall of Classical Legal Thought 27 (2006).

the recognizable past and which, through patient inquiry, increase in the inquirer the formative capacity or range of perception and sensibility needed to advance law in the future. If one accepts this premise, then as one inquired into the reaches of the past (that is, into the cases) to understand any single point of law one had to be open to subtle changes in form, which – if one got past the logical overlay – registered changes in feeling, which also, if well understood, would increase one's power to shape current law (that is, find an acceptable or needed point of convergence among competing social desires and draw the needed boundary demarcating unacceptability).

To oversimplify Holmes's point: a postulate in some sense unified feeling and form. It had provided much needed structure to a nascent or emerging legal mind; it engendered a habit of thought. It also provided orientation for present inquirers. A postulate existed as an indissoluble, inseparable unity, a felt necessity.

In the attention Holmes devoted to postulates we find a clue to why Holmes thought that investigating the cases in the right order would reveal the development of legal doctrine. For him, in contrast to Langdell, development did not have a primarily logical character (understood as both the logic of discovery and the logic of justification). Oddly, neither the logical form nor the temporal form (temporal understood as succession) sufficiently distinguished development for Holmes. The distinguishing feature lay in the mode in which feelings supervened onto brute force, and eventually assumed a noetic form that took its prevailing meaning from the dominant temper. The movement of feelings required, in turn, the right mindset to be understood. Development required the right endpoint. Signification had qualitative aspects that exclusively noetic articulation (in the form of logical propositions) could not capture or express. Holmes would not have put it that way but it seems to me to capture his mature idea that any statement of law could be rewritten as a statement of the circumstances in which the public force would act through the courts. He somewhat confused the matter in 1880 when he said, "The important phenomenon is the man underneath it, not the coat; the justice and reasonableness of the decision and not its consistency with previously held views."[58] Understanding the man underneath did require the ability to evaluate the "justice and reasonableness of a decision" according to precedent. But it also required the capacity to develop the tools to differentiate and, when needed, reintegrate the feelings that had shaped the logical form. Logic was not the only way to connect one decision to another.

The "growth and development" of postulates lay in patterns of sentiment and sense primarily recursive, not linear. For this reason a postulate and a perspective from which it could be comprehended and set in proportion, when one approached the postulate self-consciously and through the proper avenues of inquiry, served to

[58] Holmes, *supra* note 11, at 103.

inform each other. Joined together they add to their individual depths a shared luster and vibrancy. Dimension comes into being.

On the one side, Holmes's comments on Langdell's casebook leave us with a series of instructions. A legal scholar seeking to do justice to the common law of contract must recognize that the law did not grow mainly through one form (logic) but through and against many forms, including the logical, shaped by feeling (experience). To recognize and comprehend this mode of growth and development the legal scholar must engage in the appropriate style of inquiry and in the right frame of mind. That frame of mind must be scientific and that included for Holmes recognizing the omnipresence of feelings, mindsets, temperaments and the choices, or their lack, by which they (the feelings, mindsets, and temperaments) manifested themselves in the ambit of law as conveniences and expedients. The ambit of law does not exclude arbitrariness or random accumulations, or what Hurst called drift. It enmeshes these within the course of change, which sometimes may slow down to a swamplike stasis. It also includes due attention to the logical form or, better yet, the rationality, that exists in the law. In ancient law one found a distinctive unity of feeling and form in procedure. Procedure encapsulated and expressed-in-action an arrangement of values. That is still true today. Karl Llewellyn made the same point in *The Bramble Bush* when he noted that procedural regulations are "the door, and the only door, to make *real* what is laid down by substantive law. Procedural regulations enter into and condition all substantive law's becoming *actual* when there is a dispute."[59] And by this long and winding road we come back to where we began this section, Charles Rembar's observation regarding the relative lack of historical distance between ancient- and modern-style legal procedure.

On the other side, Holmes, without ever quite explaining what he was doing, took a word, "postulate," typically associated with geometry, one that signified a proposition accepted as true without proof, and used it to organize into a functioning whole what many anglophone legal thinkers believed separate, logic and feeling. It may seem we are moving back in the direction of LaPiana's *Logic and Experience*, but the difference lies in how the style of Holmes's thinking is understood.

LaPiana views Holmes in the tradition of Baconian empiricism; he argues that Holmes participated in the same inductive style of reasoning that Langdell carried over from his predecessors.[60] The main difference between them and their predecessors lay in their greater awareness of the overarching procedural context. They sought through their study of the law to formulate expressly legal principles, not merely to illustrate moral or political ones. But in saying that Langdell and Holmes saw the relevant "facts" (the cases) in the same way, LaPiana fails to appreciate how

[59] Karl Llewellyn, The Bramble Bush: On Our Law and Its Study 9 (1930) (emphasis added).

[60] *See* William P. LaPiana, *Victorian from Beacon Hill: Oliver Wendell Holmes's Early Legal Scholarship*, 90 Colum. L. Rev. 809, 810–17 (1990); LaPiana, *supra* note 3, at 110–22.

Holmes brooded over the postulates that Langdell took at face value. Holmes, in sum, had a much more profound awareness than did Langdell of how a legal form that appeared to be self-evident became instantiated, its original function(s), and its transformations.[61]

The nub of the discussion turns on what Holmes probably meant by "feelings," how an inquirer could understand and communicate those feelings ensconced in the common law as it existed in Massachusetts circa 1880. We must first recall Holmes's 1876 intellectual breakthrough, when he came to realize that the suppositions his contemporaries and predecessors had used to explain or justify legal doctrine were just that, suppositions; they had little warrant or probability of being true other than the fact that they had arrived in thought and could, like a modern-day Lego brick, be somewhat arbitrarily connected to other thoughts, existing ideas, ongoing practices.[62]

We might at this point be tempted to say that Holmes was simply transposing Newman, that presumptions and burdens of proof had shifted, that the Past had to justify itself to the Present and not vice versa. One cannot deny this Emersonian strain in Holmes's writings. But it is not really his main point. His main point, as his tremendous efforts in unearthing postulates and obtaining perspective suggest,[63] was to bring what his predecessors had done and his contemporaries were doing, and what successors might do, into a state of dynamic equilibrium. That required a new way of seeing the law, a new understanding of the operative legal consciousness.[64] The dominant late nineteenth-century emphases on development or stasis, history or reason, were one-sided, deeply unintellectual even, because there existed no overriding legal calculus, or what I have called a metric of the law, to serve as a fundamental organizing schema.

Holmes believed this might one day be done on a large scale because he had so often in his historical research found it done in miniature. We turn back to the opening salvo of *The Common Law*:

> The law embodies the story of a nation's development through many centuries, and it cannot be dealt with as if it contained only axioms and corollaries of a book of

[61] Perhaps for similar reasons John Henry Schlegel found much merit in Grant Gilmore's comment that Langdell was "essentially a stupid man." John Henry Schlegel, *Langdell's Auto-da-fé*, 17 LAW AND HIST. REV. 149–54 (1999).

[62] For a fuller discussion of this point *see* Alexander Lian, *The Jobbist, in* THE PRAGMATISM AND PREJUDICE OF OLIVER WENDELL HOLMES, JR. 9–30 (Seth Vannatta ed., 2019).

[63] *See, e.g.*, Oliver Wendell Holmes, *Early English Equity, in* III CW 327–38; *Executors, in* III CW 381–86.

[64] This way of looking at legal consciousness is certainly at odds with Duncan Kennedy's structuralist approach as he worked it out in *The Rise & Fall of Classical Legal Thought*. That approach – looking at the conceptual apparatus, the reasoning techniques, the legal ideals, and key images that the elite bar used to ascertain operative structural homologies – bypasses the dynamic, interactive, historical conscientiousness, and self-reflexivity one finds in Holmes. Perhaps for that reason Kennedy did not find Holmes's *The Common Law* to be a useful model for his own project. *See* KENNEDY, *supra* note 57, at vii–xlii.

> mathematics. In order to know what it is, we must know what it has been, and what it tends to become. We must alternately consult history and existing theories of legislation. *But the most difficult labor will be to understand the combination of the two into new products at every stage*. The substance of the law at any given time pretty nearly corresponds, so far as it goes, with what is then understood to be convenient; but its form and machinery, and the degree which it is able to work out the desired results, depend very much on its past.[65]

Given the reference points we have been able to build up since first discussing this passage in Part II, we are now in a better position to appreciate the most famous of Holmes's many iterations that, sometimes, effectively, 1+1=3.[66] Granted, that equation leads technically to a sum and not a product, but the underlying point remains. "But the most difficult labor will be to understand the combination of the two [history and existing theories of legislation] into new products at every stage." It may have been Nicholas St. John Green who first put this insight into words. According to Philip P. Wiener, Green viewed the "details" of the common law "as not simply the mass of law but its shifting historical contexts with its diverse expression of the public will."[67] In this phrase we see a differentiation of the law. It is not simply a mass of cases; it is a mass of cases plus cases fashioned into groupings that reveal different expressions (perhaps incompatible) of the public will. The contextualized cases function as an individual whole. The public will or sentiment that they express is as much part of the material or "facts" of the law as any single decision.

Coming from a similar angle, Holmes scaled down Green's insight to the level of the postulate. It too formed or configured into an array a series of particulars and wholes. The array took on legal form by virtue of the social power that found the arrangement satisfactory, or as Holmes said, expedient or convenient.

It is difficult to see at the level of the postulate the various individual particulars and wholes because Holmes lumped them together into the term feelings. He did not elucidate how the form itself expressed, even as it organized, feeling. Perhaps in this sense law did begin as aesthetic phenomena. Our thesis also suffers because of Holmes's relative imprecision in his use of language. Feelings could at one and the same time signify (a) certain perennial and recognizable emotional states and dispositions, such as revenge; (b) the experience of a particular person in a particular circumstance struck by revenge; or (c) the opinions or feelings of others immediately attuned to the struck person's intense feeling and who responded accordingly. The postulate that the thing that did the harm must be destroyed organized the array of different feelings into an operational order. Holmes often underfunded the value of this insight by turning to psychology as the explicans. Even so, the postulate

65 Holmes, *supra* note 10, at 115 (emphasis added).

66 Touched with Fire: Civil War Letters and Diary of Oliver Wendell Holmes, Jr. 1861–1864 95–97 (Mark DeWolfe Howe ed., 1946); *see also* Philip P. Wiener, Evolution and the Founders of Pragmatism 174 (1949).

67 Wiener, *supra* note 66, at 155.

provided sufficient grounds for what must be done even if it did not expressly dictate how. When the "how" within a particular community became formalized into a procedure we have recognizable law coming into being.

Holmes does not tell us how the postulate that grouped together durable feeling, individual circumstance (the particular hurt), and community sentiment (the social response) took on a specific form or led to a specific rule. But the postulate and rule are one; two unified and interconnected strands of experience. We are, nevertheless, left with the impression from the opening sections of *The Common Law* that at a certain point the requirement to constrain and direct the use of organized social power brought into play increased scrutiny of the existing form. Common law lawyers scrutinized and argued with each other when problems arose that did not mesh easily into the accustomed forms or procedures (foreseen but unintended harms, for instance).[68]

A social problem became a legal problem because it represented competing, legally cognizable interests. Holmes would probably have not disagreed with that characterization but would have made the important qualification that different interests carried different weights. The weights were not merely social or political; in many instances custom or habituated modes of thought brought to bear the tremendous weight of past, cumulative sentiment. The previously unseen felt resolution of a conflict – or the new "product" as Holmes called it – took on the trappings of a felt resolution precisely because the resulting judgment – putting an old form to a new use, for example, to accomplish a certain end and leave as much as possible undisturbed – felt right, it mostly solved the pressing problem; it presented, by and large, a socially acceptable decision. It, in other words, arranged or organized dominant and perhaps even dormant feelings – including feelings regarding the use of sovereign power – into a socially productive form.

Parenthetically, if we look at the matter philosophically, we see that the pragmatic grade of clearness for ideas that Peirce articulated and the use of the common law power in a community as Holmes depicted it work identically, though at different scales.[69] This commonality may explain why many see deep connections between Holmes and Peirce. But I don't think there was much direct influence. They both saw, independently, how the effect of an idea or of social power inhered in its form, how under the circumstances an idea or judge-sanctioned state force sought to muster conceptions or feelings or beliefs (using these words compendiously) to accomplish certain ends and to push toward equilibrium.

If the foregoing suggestions are on point we obtain a deeper insight into why Holmes's 1880 review of Langdell's contracts casebook, which included the *Summary*, struck an exasperated tone one does not find in his reviews of earlier versions.

[68] Holmes, *supra* note 10, at 116–17.

[69] *See* Charles Sanders Peirce, *How to Make Our Ideas Clear, in* 1 The Essential Peirce 124–41 (Nathan Houser and Christian Kloesel eds., 1992).

In the first review, he specifically praised the arrangement of cases, how that arrangement helped to instill a doctrine's "meaning, extent, and limits," and he saw in Langdell's unique approach confirmation of his own remark "that judges know how to decide a good deal sooner than they know why."[70] The second continues the compliments of the first. Both reviews were published in 1871. By the time the third is published in 1880, Holmes has undergone his intellectual awakening. He agrees with Langdell that for a lawyer to achieve competency the lawyer must become intellectually enmeshed in both the substantive doctrines and the procedures that sustain and bind them and which, in turn, the substantive doctrines reinforce. He believes, as does Langdell, that the common law presents itself to an inquiring lawyer as something *sui generis*.

I think LaPiana right in emphasizing how the focus on procedure facilitated the alignment in late nineteenth-century America between the common law as a hoary practice and a new academic discipline. I think Robert Gordon wrong in his general criticism of LaPiana's thesis (Gordon generally favors making law a function of policy studies).[71] Gordon is correct, though, in criticizing LaPiana's thin conception of "fact."[72] LaPiana, to support his thesis of how Langdell reshaped law into a discipline, argues that Langdell was more keenly aware than his predecessors of the range of legal facts and the power of such facts, especially those denoted procedural, to structure and support distinctively legal principles. But in LaPiana's hands the facts are all brought to a single level, sitting on a bookshelf or library table. He interprets the overriding problem in the spirit of Langdell. It becomes clear from LaPiana's rendition that Langdell used procedure as an instrument, a level, to keep the shelf or table straight and true. For this reason, procedure takes on primary importance for him and becomes, as it were, a Procrustean bed from which substantive legal principles emerge.

LaPiana mistakenly lumps in Green and Holmes with Langdell. He does not quite realize that Green and Holmes had a much stronger consciousness of history (understood both as a deep sense of social change and of the forms used to bring the past into alignment with the present), and a more vibrant, ranging, many-sided feel for the workings of law than did Langdell. Langdell did not share their capacities or sensibilities. Langdell was an incredibly gifted legal technician, but Green and Holmes had gone a step or two beyond (not around) technics.

For Holmes Langdell's Procrustean bed of procedure essentially represented Langdell's own habit of mind; it revealed the man's basic temperament; it sought to structure the past in service of the present instead of seeking to engage intelligently with it (that is, with the past's artifacts, modes of temporal representation,

70 Oliver Wendell Holmes, *Review of* A Selection of Cases on the Law of Contracts (Part I), *in* I CW 243.

71 Robert Gordon, *The Case for (and against) Harvard*, 93 MICH. L. REV. 1231 (1995).

72 *Id.* at 1236–40.

narrative embodiments, sequences and contexts). Langdell turned "growth and development" into its own rigid formula – much as Newman had done in his *Essay*, though Newman did it with dramatically more finesse – because both men were ultimately seeking to establish or prove dogma. Fallibilism held no charms for either of them. Holmes, in contrast, found in a self-conscious fallibilism the true seedbed for legal principles. Speaking wryly, as Holmes often spoke to his father, in the fallibilist (or fabulist) dimension of being it did not seem so strange to find that at times 1+1=3.

A less wry, more serious exposition of this point is found in Holmes's essay on Montesquieu:

> It [the wit which deals with the daily aspects of life and offers trenchant solutions in two or three lines] is no less dangerous to great thinking, to that profound and sustained insight which distrusts the dilemma as an instrument of logic, and discerns that a thing may be neither A nor not-A, but the perpendicular, or more plainly, that the truth may escape from the limitations of a given plane of thought to a higher one.[73]

The big drawback to that clever pronouncement lay in its evident inhospitality to pedagogy. It is not often remarked that in his 1880 review Holmes ended on two distinct notes. First, he clarified that his "preceding criticism is addressed to the ideal of the final methods of legal reasoning which this [Langdell's] Summary seems to disclose."[74] With this sentence Holmes seems to suggest that Langdell began well but ended badly. He began well with the cases, he began well with the notion that by tracing the development of a legal doctrine, through the mechanisms of approval, disapproval, extension, and retraction, the student of law would learn its meaning and application, but he ended badly, in Holmes's view, because he did not attempt to put his findings into an overall perspective (that is, put them into relation with doctrines from other times and origins to determine their true proportion). Instead, Langdell took one aspect of a legal postulate and converted it into a defined proposition, an articulated major premise. He ignored its inner history and emotional makeup. Thus the successive changes in a legal principle or doctrine took on the rigorous and exclusive intellectual character that Newman identified as logical.

Holmes recognized that for the purposes of legal education in a law school – and in the 1880s legal education took place as often in law offices as in law

73 Oliver Wendell Holmes, *Montesquieu, in* III CW 424. Fred Kellogg provides a helpful explanation of Holmes's position in terms of formal logic. The originality of Holmes's approach, he says, lies in how he treated the principle of bivalence, "that of 'p or not-p': a proposition must either be true or false. . . . Holmes's idea of logical uncertainty rests on the notion of degrees, but not of semantic degrees, and rather degrees of completeness in the process finding similarity in the succession of experience or experiments. Bivalence is a quality of the successful completion of inquiry resulting in settled propositions." Frederic R. Kellogg, Oliver Wendell Holmes Jr. and Legal Logic 13 n.23 (2018).

74 Holmes, *supra* note 11, at 103.

schools – Langdell's approach found sufficient justification. The limited time in any given law school course made "dogmatic teaching" a necessity. Holmes said: "A professor must start with a system as an arbitrary fact" – using the word "fact" compendiously and in a very un-Baconian manner – "and the most which can be hoped for is to make the student see how it hangs together, and thus send him into practice with something more than a rag-bag of details." For this reason, he believed "Mr. Langdell's teachings, published and unpublished, [to have] been of unequal value."[75]

In his concluding note Holmes pointed out that what Langdell had done for the law of contracts could not be ignored. Langdell's arguments must either be "adopted or refuted." He here displayed his own belief in the importance of experience – including the determinate if passive role played by the undersides of beliefs and actions – by stressing that a conclusion "based upon refutation of its opposite is very different from the same opinion based on ignorance of the arguments by which such an opposite could be maintained."[76] In these words we hear the powerful opening bars of *The Common Law*.

But the basic problem that legal study presented – to devise canons for learning how to understand, and work within, a legal system that has both static and dynamic elements, that is both continuous and emerging, that displays both purposiveness and listlessness, and that depends on the sustained interaction of different parts – Holmes would not fully address or settle in his own mind until the mid-1890s. By that time he had shifted his attention and the emphasis of his thought, roughly speaking, from the past to the present. But he never totally left behind his preoccupation with the past or deemphasized his concern for the future. Holmes mainly sought to resolve the basic pedagogical problem he had identified in 1880 through a series of important canons to govern the teaching of the dogmatic core that Langdell had refined. He saw, as had William G. Hammond, that how law was taught and learned would have a disproportionate if not fully recognized role in operationalizing law and setting the tone for a democratic society that found its raison d'être in the rule of law. Nothing was more important than education – how one started the journey toward professional competence.

As he said in a speech to a group of Harvard undergraduates (all men) in 1886:

> Your education begins when what is called your education is over, – when you no longer are stringing together the pregnant thoughts, the "jewels five words long," which great men have given their lives to cut from the raw material, but have begun yourselves to work upon the raw material for results you do not see, cannot predict, and which may be long in coming, – when you take the fact that life offers you for your appointed task.[77]

75 *Id.* at 103–04.
76 *Id.* at 104.
77 Oliver Wendell Holmes, *The Profession of Law*, *in* III CW 472.

2 A WELL-KNOWN PROFESSION

i *Speeches*

In the same year that a few lit sticks of dynamite hurled at the police in Chicago's Haymarket Square ignited the first of many national post–Civil War xenophobic scares, Holmes delivered four addresses, three in his home state and one in nearby Connecticut:[78] in chronological order, from February to November 1886, "The Puritan," "The Profession of Law," "On Receiving the Degree of Doctor of Laws," and "The Use of Law Schools." Holmes included them in the first edition of his *Speeches* published in 1891. On the flyleaf he referred to these talks as "chance utterances of faith and doubt." They were, he added, "printed for a few friends who will care to keep them."[79]

In the 1880s and 90s the only Holmes that most Americans knew was Oliver Wendell Holmes (Senior). He would die in 1894. But in his heyday this gifted raconteur and literary stylist and man of science had charmed the nation's immense reading public with his breakfast-table stories. Brimming with conviviality, bon mots, learned allusions, sly observations, they also contained, in the true spirit of a writer for whom nothing is off limits, some half-curious, half-critical wonderments about his eldest son, whom he dubbed the Young Astronomer. The boy was sometimes given, the father explained, to a consuming, otherworldly philosophic passion that made him oddly oblivious to the flower lovely and fresh that bloomed in his presence.[80]

When many years later the Young Astronomer got appointed associate justice of the Massachusetts Supreme Judicial Court the father chortled to his dinner guests, after treating them to a poem composed in his son's honor, "To think of it – my little boy a Judge, and able to send me to jail if I don't behave myself."[81]

Perceptive literary commentators, including Edmund Wilson, have compared the writings of the two men, noting how the Civil War cut like a cleaver the curlicues that tended to adorn the father's florid style.[82] The war chastened American prose, Wilson noted.[83] It became the language of responsibility – terse, austere, and direct.

78 For a brief overview of the social unrest in that era *see* SUSAN-MARY GRANT, OLIVER WENDELL HOLMES: CIVIL WAR SOLDIER, SUPREME COURT JUSTICE 108–09 (2016).

79 Sheldon M. Novick, *Editor's Introduction to Speeches in* III CW 461; OLIVER WENDELL HOLMES, SPEECHES [vii] (1934).

80 MARK DEWOLFE HOWE, JUSTICE OLIVER WENDELL HOLMES: THE PROVING YEARS, 1870–1882 5–7 (1963).

81 SHELDON M. NOVICK, HONORABLE JUSTICE: THE LIFE OF OLIVER WENDELL HOLMES 169 (1989).

82 EDMUND WILSON, PATRIOTIC GORE: STUDIES IN THE LITERATURE OF THE AMERICAN CIVIL WAR 635–69, 743–96 (1962); *see also* Peter Gibian, *Opening and Closing the Conversation: Style and Stance from Holmes Senior to Holmes Junior, in* THE LEGACY OF OLIVER WENDELL HOLMES, JR. 186–215 (Robert W. Gordon ed., 1992).

83 WILSON, *supra* note 82.

It evaded common sentimentality. In Holmes's (Junior's) case what it lost in conversational fluidity and charm it gained in compactness. He sees the same austere style at work in the occasional pieces, like those in *Speeches*, as in the judicial opinions. Wilson believes Holmes worked very hard on the published addresses; he made them perfect; he gave them "a crystalline form as hard and as bright as Pater's flame."[84]

This is high praise coming from Wilson. The reference to Walter Pater, the master nineteenth-century English essayist and supreme spokesperson for aestheticism, the life of beauty, brings into play an interpretative gambit that has been repeated ever since. If the style is the man then Holmes, on this reading, has walled himself off from humanity, from the plaintive foibles of his uncaring fellows. He in the manner of a true Puritan has shunned their abiding indifference to the superlative. He entranced himself in the common law as others in that era might entrance themselves in Greek and Roman antiquities or the art and sculpture of the Renaissance.

We have already noted how much Yosal Rogat's declamations against Holmes seem to owe their inspiration to Wilson. The same emphasis on Holmes's remoteness, his insular aestheticism, distinguished the portrait that Louis Menand sketched in *The Metaphysical Club*.[85] On the other side of the coin, a young scholar, Allen Mendenhall, has taken the idea that Holmes worked within the tradition of an Emersonian aesthetic in a new direction.[86]

Mendenhall argues that Holmes in his dissents inaugurated a new type of jurisprudence, the jurisprudence of agon, in which the dissenting opinion writer self-consciously, through rhetorical means, seeks to go beyond simply showing that the majority opinion missed the boat. The dissenting opinion, as a literary subgenre, through its unique combination of imaginative sense and antagonistic style struggles to ground a new perspective, a new starting point from which to employ and emplot subsequent legal argumentation.[87] It is what Mendenhall calls a pragmatic aesthetic; one of transition, that is to say, one that takes its form within the recognition that, even in a world of unending flux, change, to be intelligible, must be directed and rhetorically engineered; one which recognizes that only through contest and struggle can new rooms be added to the mansions of legal experience.[88] At its most artful the finely crafted dissent points toward new registers of feeling and of meaning; and toward a new justification for legal action or inaction. As Holmes might say, at these rare moments the innermost meaning of law transforms itself.

[84] *Id.* at 781.
[85] Louis Menand, The Metaphysical Club: A Story of Ideas in America 23–69 (2001).
[86] Allen Mendenhall, Oliver Wendell Holmes Jr., Pragmatism, and the Jurisprudence of Agon (2017).
[87] *Id.* at 1–80.
[88] *Id.* at 43–80.

Mendenhall has written an intriguing book that deserves more attention than I can now afford. I have mentioned him mainly to provide an endpoint to Wilson (whom, regretfully, Mendenhall does not recognize as a predecessor or engage as an interlocutor). For Wilson the key aesthetic characteristic of Holmes's writing lies in its crystalline form. Wilson calls Holmes a "real concentrator of thought who specialized in law but who was trying to determine man's place, to define his satisfactions and duties, to try to understand what humanity is."[89] What stands out for Mendenhall is the "superfluity" in Holmes's dissenting opinions. Superfluity as Mendenhall uses it is a technical critical term that covers both the mode and manner of Holmes's public writing. The mode: one of bucking constraints – constraints of thought, feeling, value, and expression. The manner: poetic or rhetorical elements that the specific writing under consideration reveals.[90] Holmes's adroit use of poetic and rhetorical techniques sought to establish a sensibility through which he and his readers or listeners could meet. From my perspective he employs a voice that often appears to be bordering on the second person; it is dialogic. He is forever addressing his colleagues or those soon to become his colleagues. An odd openness, a fraternal formal-informality characterizes Holmes's most famous dissents. Judge Posner, as Mendenhall reminds us, commented that Holmes wrote with "a lightness of touch foreign to the legal temperament."[91] One may see its source in what Mendenhall identifies as Holmes's unceasing effort to stylize an emerging point of view, a new taking of experience.

These two dominant attributes of Holmes's mature style – the inert crystalline form and the ranging superfluity that gestures directly toward interlocutors – create their own aesthetic polarity. The impassivity is always there; but so is the longing. Unlike his father, Holmes did not find it so easy in his mature years to scudder the frozen pond of New England sentiment.

Speeches reflects this aesthetic polarity. The four I have mentioned, three chosen simply because of their contemporaneity with "The Use of Law Schools," serve to foreground "The Path of the Law" as an exercise in pedagogy. But it is perhaps an 1895 speech, the very short "Learning and Science," that best sets the tone.

Given at the celebration honoring Langdell's twenty-five years at the Harvard Law School, "Learning and Science" typically draws attention because Holmes managed to avoid mentioning Langdell's name or praising him in any way. This neglect may have arisen from pique on Holmes's part, as some commentators suggest, or for reasons less sullen.[92] It is hard to know, much is guesswork. It bears mentioning that the keynote speaker at this event, Frederick Pollock, who spoke on the "The Vocation of the Common Law," identified Holmes and Langdell as

[89] WILSON, *supra* note 82, at 781.

[90] MENDENHALL, *supra* note 86, at 22–29.

[91] *Id.* at 12–13 (quoting Richard A. Posner, *Introduction*, *in* THE ESSENTIAL HOLMES xiii (Richard A. Posner ed., 1992)).

[92] *See e.g.*, KIMBALL, *supra* note 20, at 327.

brothers-in-arms, united in their efforts to use original sources to detect the still beating hoary principles of the common law.[93]

Pollock made sure to emphasize that Langdell's contribution to the science of the law went beyond Austinian positivism.

> If, on the other hand, our traditions, our professional habits of thought, and our judicial practice are not foolishness, *it would seem to be because the law is not an affair of bare literal precepts, as the mechanical school would make it, but is the sense of justice taking form in peoples and races*. The law of our English-speaking commonwealths, on which the sun never sets, is one law in many varieties, not many laws which happen to resemble one another in several particulars.[94]

It was this "essential unity of the common law" that most impressed Pollock.[95] From it Langdell's contribution to legal pedagogy garnered its deeper utility and significance. Pollock further believed that the will to make the common law even greater than it already was would drive its practitioners toward developing a philosophical statement of its leading principles. He also hoped for an Anglo-American jurisprudence that would develop from and in turn further the formal cooperation of Anglo-American legal institutions. This anticipated philosophical development of principles and formal cooperation of institutions set the groundwork for a new calling, what Pollock called the vocation of the common law.[96]

Holmes reported to Lady Pollock that her husband's oration was well received.[97] He said nothing of his own contribution; perhaps there was little he could add to the little that was there. One or two of the dinner addresses were as short as or shorter than his contribution. But none, shorter or longer, approached his in quality or in the solemnity of tone. Before he stood, Justice Henry B. Brown, of the United States Supreme Court, grandly remarked how Massachusetts's associate justice, "though comparatively young in years, has already thrown 'gladsome light' upon certain dark

[93] Frederick Pollock, *The Vocation of the Common Law*, *in* Report of the Ninth Annual Meeting, June 25, 1895, in Especial Honor of Christopher Columbus Langdell 1870–1895, Harvard Law School Association 18 (1895). One also infers from his "open letter" to Holmes in the preface to his *Law of Torts* that Pollock had found the approach and mode of study at Harvard, with its emphasis on the original historical sources, quite congenial. *See* Frederick Pollock, The Law of Torts v–viii (1887) ("Of Harvard and its Law School I will say only this, that I have endeavored to turn to practical account the lessons of what I saw and heard there, and that this present book is in some measure the outcome of that endeavor.").

[94] Pollock, *The Vocation of the Common Law*, *supra* note 93, at 14 (emphasis added).

[95] *Id.* at 13–14.

[96] *Id.* at 13–19. For a fuller discussion of Pollock's veneration of the common law *see* Richard A. Cosgrove, Our Lady the Common Law: An Anglo-American Legal Community, 1870–1930 134–60 (1987).

[97] 1 Holmes–Pollock Letters: The Correspondence of Mr. Justice Holmes and Sir Frederick Pollock, 1874–1932 57–58 (Mark DeWolfe Howe ed., 2d ed. 1961).

corners of our jurisprudence."[98] James C. Carter, who as president of the Harvard Law School Association presided over the event, pointed out in his brief introduction that "[w]e have always looked to him with pride as one of the best representatives of the teaching at this School[.]"[99] Even the last scheduled speaker, Gustavus H. Wald, who would prove instrumental in setting up a law school in Cincinnati along the Harvard line, observed how much the zeitgeist yoked the two men together.[100] He recalled that in 1882 Pollock had written to him exclaiming in disbelief that the Benchers of Lincoln's Inn had refused, even after Pollock had provided them courtesy copies for review, to purchase for their library either Holmes's *The Common Law* or Langdell's *Summary of Contracts*![101]

One wonders if as he arose to speak – perhaps from memory as he often did – Holmes felt the odd discomfort of being lauded for what he was not. Was he really "one of the best representatives" of Harvard's teaching as Carter said? Were *The Common Law* and *The Summary of Contracts* really two books from the same intellectual patch? The problem seems to be not lack of recognition but something even more despairing to the philosophical mind, misrecognition.

"Learning and Science" is a chance utterance that begins in doubt. It begins as so many of Holmes's pieces begin, with a nod to the Civil War, but not without first acknowledging that he must be "in the presence of very learned men."[102] He assumes learned men fill his audience since most of them have graduated from Harvard Law School within the last twenty-five years, that is to say, during Langdell's tenure.

One familiar with Holmes's speeches immediately thinks back to the last time he addressed this same group, the Harvard Law School Association, at its inaugural meeting in 1886, when he, not Pollock, had given the keynote address. In that address, "The Use of Law Schools," he had praised the Law School's professors for not sending their students into the profession "with nothing but a rag-bag of general

[98] Henry B. Brown, *Mr. Justice Henry B. Brown's Address*, *in* Report of the Ninth Annual Meeting, June 25, 1895, in Especial Honor of Christopher Columbus Langdell 1870–1895, Harvard Law School Association 57 (1895). The reference to "gladsome light" may be alluding to Sir Edward Coke. *See* Postema, *supra* note 15, at 583.

[99] James C. Carter, "Introductory Remarks to Mr. Justice Oliver Wendell Holmes's Address" in Report of the Ninth Annual Meeting, June 25, 1895, in Especial Honor of Christopher Columbus Langdell 1870–1895, Harvard Law School Association 59 (1895).

[100] Charles Wilby, *Memorial on Gustavus H. Wald*, *in* Proceedings of the Annual Meeting of the Ohio State Bar Association 178–84 (1902).

[101] Gustavus A. Wald, "Mr. Gustavus A. Wald's Address," in Report of the Ninth Annual Meeting, June 25, 1895, in Especial Honor of Christopher Columbus Langdell 1870–1895, Harvard Law School Association 80 (1895). Wald did not get a chance to deliver his address because of the lateness of the hour. Pollock also refers to what may have been the same refusal to buy *The Common Law* in his tribute to Holmes in the March 1931 edition of the *Harvard Law Review*. *Mr. Justice Holmes – Tributes*, 44 Harv. L. Rev. 677, 694 (1931) (tribute by Frederick Pollock).

[102] Oliver Wendell Holmes, *Learning and Science*, *in* III CW 491.

principles, – a throng of glittering generalities, like a swarm of little bodiless cherubs fluttering at the top of one of Correggio's pictures."[103] Learning in the law gave the "bodiless cherubs" their bodies.

The excitement Holmes had expressed in an earlier speech "The Law," his exultation in how devoted and reverential learning brought law to life, is conspicuously missing from "Law and Science" opening.[104] When in doubt, one does not exult. When in doubt, one does not revere. A moment that typically called for commendation and reflection found Holmes at a loss. He quotes two lines from Wordsworth's poem, "The Solitary Reaper" ("old, unhappy, far-off things, / And battles long ago;") and reports to his audience that "once the ghosts of the dead fifers of thirty years since begin to play in my head, the laws are silent."[105]

The allusions in this simple clause are tiered. Five years before Langdell set the Law School on a new course the Civil War had officially ended, the dead and dying waiting, patiently, to be reckoned. Holmes was undergoing his initiation into the profession, which he would later describe as perhaps the greatest moral experience of his life. The fife brings to mind one of Holmes's favorite symbols, the pipe. He calls it the lonely pipe of death. Holmes uses it to close his first Memorial Day speech (1884) ("there comes a pause, and through silence we hear the lonely pipe of death")[106] and to begin his second ("The Soldier's Faith" 1895) ("Any day in Washington Street, when the throng is greatest and busiest, you may see a blind man playing a flute. I suppose that someone hears him. Perhaps also my pipe may reach the heart of some passer in the crowd.")[107] The clean, far-off call of the pipe turns learning into naught. He reports to his colleagues that in such moments the laws fall silent. His colleagues, learned as they are, probably could not help but think of the well-known maxim: *Inter arma silent leges* (amid the arms of war the laws are silent).[108]

In just a few words spangled with sorrow, the speaker inverts a celebratory moment into a memento mori. The ebullience, the bluff camaraderie, the dignified mien, the glad-handing and curt smiles take a reprieve. If we are still for an instant, we might catch the distant echo: "Live – I am coming."

Inversion is undoubtedly one of those rhetorical devices that support both Wilson's attention to crystalline form and Mendenhall's thesis on superfluity. If audience members caught the reference to Wordsworth's "The Solitary Reaper" they might have also remembered that the solitary reaper in that ballad is a young

[103] Oliver Wendell Holmes, *The Use of Law Schools*, *in* III CW 477.
[104] *See* Oliver Wendell Holmes, *The Law*, *in* III CW 468–70.
[105] Holmes, *supra* note 102, at 491.
[106] Oliver Wendell Holmes, *Memorial Day*, *in* III CW 467.
[107] Oliver Wendell Holmes, *The Soldier's Faith*, *in* III CW 486.
[108] Black's Law Dictionary 1924 (Bryan A. Garner ed., 10th ed. 2014).

girl – a "Highland lass," the poet says – not a gaunt faceless man.[109] The justice, unlike his father, does not look to froth the event with bonhomie and charm; he expresses rather openly private, personal thoughts that seem, at least from our vantage, somewhat out of place. But then we hear in the background Wilson gruffly reminding us about Holmes's Puritan ancestry and his quasi-Calvinist temperament. If the man spoke in keeping with the lingering custom of reproof, one wonders whether this particular company of lawyers recalled the unspoken social code.

Inversions abound. We all know, as Yeats intoned, that the center cannot hold. But the locus ought really be Wilson's *Patriotic Gore*. Holmes somehow held it together and Wilson is not quite sure why. He was a Boston Brahman; he was philosophical and had a peacock's ego. All true. But Holmes also loved the law. It's a point that Wilson missed. In the surfeit of this feeling, Holmes sometimes felt estranged, perhaps a bit rankled, that those he thought ought to share the passion and the thirst didn't. A jeremiad beats in the wings but the time for jeremiads has passed. So he says:

> And yet as I look around me, I think to myself, like Correggio, "I too am, or at least have been, a pedagogue." And as such I will venture a reflection.[110]

The Harvard Law School pedagogues most likely in the audience (Langdell, James Barr Ames, James Bradley Thayer, John Chipman Gray) who recalled first-hand Holmes's abrupt departure from the faculty thirteen years earlier might have silently demurred at the self-description. He had taught for less than a semester. Granted, Holmes could point to various courses he had taught for Harvard College or the Law School prior to his 1882 appointment. But that hardly qualifies one to assume the pedagogue's mantle.

True to form, Holmes's self-revelation conceals more than it reveals. From Holmes's own writings we may infer, from his repeated references to Correggio, that this sixteenth-century Renaissance painter, known for the novel use of light and shade and illusionistic depth perspective, had impressed him both as an artist and as a man. In the latter respect, the dint of attraction lay in how Correggio embodies the qualities that Mendenhall gathered up in the term superfluity. The point is best made by Holmes but in an unusual manner. In his Introduction to Montesquieu's *The Spirit of the Laws*, published in 1900, Holmes uncharacteristically ends his thoughtful exposition by quoting the last few sentences of Montesquieu's preface:

> If this work meets with success, I shall owe it largely to the majesty of my subject. However, I do not think that I have been wholly wanting in genius. When I have seen what so many great men in France, England, and Germany have written

[109] William Wordsworth, *The Solitary Reaper*, www.poets.org/poetsorg/poem/solitary-reaper (last accessed October 28, 2019).

[110] Holmes, *supra* note 102, at 491.

> before me, I have been lost in admiration, but I have not lost my courage. 'And I too am a painter,' I have said with Correggio.'[111]

"I too am, or at least have been, a pedagogue." The feint is slight. To the far side lies the war like a cold slab; the pale fifer faces it and lifts his dusty instrument; on the near side sits an audience of lawyers, judges, and law professors listening, waiting. In the intervening hesitancy the man whom they face speaks to them, not as a working jurist, but as a self-proclaimed teacher of law teachers. That is his authority. "And as such I will venture a reflection."[112]

I tend to think the specific moment I have sought to sketch made little impression on the attendees. As an individual instance it probably fell among the scattered pebbles littering the hall's entranceway. In writing about it I run the risk of unduly magnifying its tiny proportions. Yet the text of "Learning and Science" when read alongside the other contributions to the Langdell celebration clearly strikes a deeper, perhaps more odious chord. In this four-paragraph address one finds it easier to recount the prescriptions in paragraphs two through four than to explain how the inversions found in the first relate to the rest.

My best guess falls back on the idea of perspective, on coordinated position and contrast. And on the idea that in composing into a new arrangement the existing panoply of social life found in the law one does the work of a pedagogue. In keeping with the motif of self-creation that Holmes frequently draws upon, the work must be begun before one knows where it will lead or how it will end. The principles have yet to be surmised that will order a society that is still in the process of coming into its own. Yet without law – that is, without the instituted and measured say of many different voices, present and past – society enters into a state approaching war. The clash of cymbals stills the onlookers. And then the player arises slowly and strikes a sinking melody.

It is not easy, I imagine, for anyone devoted wholeheartedly to the life of the mind to tell a group of strong-willed learned men that the learning they all prize and have gathered to celebrate will in time fall into oblivion. But that is the first part of the message we find in "Learning and Science." It is not a new one for Holmes. He has repeated the same theme in various speeches and in various ways since the mid-1880s. It almost does not matter where one begins. Most assuredly, the greatest, most memorable rendition is "The Soldier's Faith." In the 1886 series we have pulled out from *Speeches*, "The Puritan" condenses into vivid imagery two important insights that relate to this theme. The first concerns how memorialization works to mark out a cultural field. The second is how the ineluctable effacement of time works to give the marked field its requisite depth. A culture requires depth of meaning to develop

[111] Holmes, *Montesquieu, supra* note 73, at 431–32 (quoting MONTESQUIEU, THE SPIRIT OF THE LAWS xlv (Anne M. Cohler, Basia Carolyn Miller, and Harold Samuel Stone eds. and trans., Cambridge University Press 1989)).

[112] Holmes, *supra* note 102, at 491.

(culture understood as a more or less integrated system of ongoing, shared meanings).

Holmes delivered "The Puritan" to commemorate the 250th anniversary of the First Church of Cambridge (where his grandfather, Rev. Abiel Holmes, had served as a minister). The most important sentences come in the middle of the address:

> When the citizens of Cambridge forget that they too tread a sacred soil, that Massachusetts also has its traditions, which grow more venerable and inspiring as they fade, – when Harvard College is no longer dedicated to truth, and America to democratic freedom, – then perhaps, but not till then, will the blood of martyrs be swallowed in the sand, and the Puritan have lived in vain. *Until that time he will grow greater, even after he has vanished from our view.*[113]

Considered beyond its rhetorical effects, the paradox that Holmes has articulated is difficult to understand. The passage certainly embosses on the attentive reader's mind the two ideals to which Holmes gave ultimate obeisance – truth and democratic freedom. But how does the power that brought these ideals to life, what Holmes calls "the cold Puritan passion," "the Puritan ferment," manage to retain its power, its vitality, long after its human embodiment, the Puritan, has disappeared from the scene?

Holmes does not directly answer this question. Instead, he takes the tack – as he often did in *The Common Law* – of depicting two types of artifacts, those that are still living (that is, shown to be vital and meaningful) and those that are survivals. We see again another instance of a Holmes contrived polarity. Some artifacts, however, such as the knight militant with whom Holmes begins the address, are neither obviously living (as is Harvard College or the First Church of Cambridge) nor an out-and-out survival. These types of artifacts have an almost Sphinx-like quality that enables them to continue to organize and direct perceptions long after they and the environments in which they once lived and moved and had their being have receded from view. In the language of Part II, they essentially become vanishing points. Though Holmes does not quite say it, the inference is evident that those artifacts that fade with time, that become less particular, more universal, that retain their power to inspire depend, in some sense, on the absence of anything strong enough to eradicate their unseen impress upon the present.

Memorialization and effacement work hand-in-hand to give cultural meaning extension and depth; "The Puritan" provides a figurative rendition of what Holmes says more prosaically in "Learning and Science": "The past gives us our vocabulary and fixes the limits of our imagination; we cannot get away from it."[114] That is memorialization and effacement. He also says: "But the present has a right to govern itself so far as it can; and it ought always be remembered that historic continuity with

[113] Oliver Wendell Holmes, *The Puritan, in* III CW 470–71 (emphasis added).

[114] Holmes, *supra* note 102, at 492.

the past is not a duty, it is only a necessity."[115] This sentence is justly famous. It compresses into a single coherence, into a single string of words, ideas seemingly incompatible and at war. If continuity with the past is a necessity how could one ever exert the right to countermand its dictates? And, what is the source of this nonlegal right?

One possibility presents itself in "The Profession of Law." This February 17, 1886, address, delivered just five days after "The Puritan," comes to us as the truncated end of a longer speech delivered to undergraduates at Harvard. It contains some of Holmes's most striking language about his chosen profession. It marks a pivotal point in American history, the turn away from a Puritan God-fearing past toward a secular, humanistic, law-fearing future. American law has begun to understand itself as law. Think back to LaPiana's thesis on the importance of Langdell. But Holmes had access to reaches of experience that Langdell did not.

In "The Profession of Law" we once again hear Holmes utter words that are both familiar and strange. The best example of the familiar: "How can the laborious study of a dry and technical system, the greedy watch for clients and practice of shopkeepers' arts, the mannerless conflicts over often sordid interests, make out a life?"[116] The sentiment expressed, one that still has a strong currency in the United States, took on a specific coloration in Holmes's hands. To the common dissatisfactions heard today he added one more pressing to him; one, I venture to say, as uncommon then as it is now. That leads us to the strange.

> But to those who believe with me that not the least godlike of man's activities is the large survey of causes, that to know is not less than to feel, I say – and I say no longer any doubt – that a man may live greatly in the law as well as elsewhere; that there as well as elsewhere his thought may find unity in an infinite perspective; that there as well as elsewhere he may wreak himself upon life, may drink the bitter cup of heroism, may wear his heart out after the unattainable.[117]

These words, even after discounting for the differences between a late nineteenth-century American sensibility and an early twenty-first-century one, still seem so unfamiliar and strange as to become positively foreign, especially when one keeps in mind that he is talking about the legal profession. As phrased, the passage makes it hard to pinpoint the source of the unspoken dissatisfaction that led to these difficult-to-understand locutions. The opening of "The Profession of Law" and the first clause of the passage quoted provide the best clue.

"The Profession of Law" opens with an unnamed undergraduate, who, after hearing what has been said, asks: "What is all this to my soul?" But Holmes does not identify the undergraduate posing the question as an undergraduate or even a student. He is "some spirit of fire." Then comes a Biblical allusion to Jacob's

[115] *Id.*
[116] Holmes, *supra* note 77, at 471.
[117] *Id.* at 472.

purchase of Esau's birthright for a mess of pottage.[118] The question "What is all this to my soul?" becomes rephrased as a query whether through the law ("such a door as this") the "spirit of fire" can reach his own "spiritual possibilities." The dissatisfaction we seek to understand partly arises from wariness and discontent; it also finds its source in the barely constrained grandiosity of youth. Holmes deliberately caters to this feeling in the opening clause of the passage quoted above – "But to those who believe with me that not the least godlike of man's activities is the large survey of causes[.]"[119]

Let's stop right here and retrace the last few steps. "The Puritan" brings to our attention a dynamic that Holmes believes works in human history. I called it the dynamic of memorialization and effacement. I also suggested that the following sentence from "Learning and Science" encapsulates that dynamic: "The past gives us our vocabulary and fixes the limits of our imagination; we cannot get away from it." That is to say, the past works in ways seen and unseen, through means of which we are conscious and of which we not conscious. It works through articulated thoughts and inchoate feelings and everything in between. It sets limits to what we can conceive. Whether we agree with Holmes's position or not, it is at least understandable. But then we turn into a cul-de-sac. "[H]istoric continuity with the past is not a duty, it is only a necessity."

To tackle this aphorism we turned to "The Profession of Law." There a different dynamic is at work. Instead of memorialization and effacement, we find a dynamic less rarefied, one dramatically scaled down, more clear-eyed as to costs because less unwilling to blink away the personal. The personal interest in safeguarding "spiritual possibilities" creates its own strange loop; to "not the least godlike of man's activities" Holmes counterpoises a "fact," which he also describes as the "fact" that "life offers you for your appointed task." The movement (to say it another way and to draw from another of Holmes's speeches) goes from an individual will that exerts "all the faculties by which man is likest to a god" to that which is dense, opaque, both pressing and fleeting, inscrutable, enigmatic, enticing, filled with blandishments and false comforts, and yet unmovable – to the fateful fact.[120] The actual movement between dedicated will and enfolding fact Emerson described presciently as education ("The world exists for the education of each man.").[121] Holmes calls it "the democracy of self-devotion."[122]

[118] *Genesis* 25:29–34.

[119] Holmes, *supra* note 77, at 471–72.

[120] Holmes, *supra* note 104, at 469.

[121] Ralph Waldo Emerson, *History*, *in* Ralph Waldo Emerson: Selected Essays, Lectures and Poems 130 (Robert D. Richardson, Jr. ed., 1990).

[122] Holmes, *supra* note 106, at 466. *See also* William G. Weaver, *The "Democracy of Self Devotion": Oliver Wendell Holmes, Jr., and Pragmatism*, *in* Renascent Pragmatism: Studies in Law and Social Science 23 (Alonso Morales ed., 2003) ("Holmes did not see law as something that needed refinement relative to a particular goal, as something that has a particular path of progress embedded in its history that would be perverted if turned away

This latter point constitutes the kernel of the short message Holmes delivered at Yale's commencement ceremony, where he was awarded an honorary doctor of laws degree in June of 1886. There he explicitly drew upon the love of honor he believed inherent in self-devotion, though he called it "self-seeking" in the address, and affirmed his belief that if it did not take a man to the transcendent heights that the Puritan once reached, it at least "carries him above the earth and teaches him those high and secret pathways across the branches of the forest the travellers on which are only less than winged."[123] This locution is also difficult to understand. But we come closer to its meaning by attending to its spatial imagery. The love of honor may not "lift a man on the wings to the sky" – as once did the Puritan's exalted joy, but it does raise him high above the earth where the air circulates among the topmost branches of the forest. And the power of honor "to bind men's lives," he hopes to make the young men in the audience understand, "is not less now than it was in the Middle Ages."[124]

The love of honor becomes for Holmes the only working engine of cultural survival left. It enabled him to survive the Civil War and to endure the initial immersion into his chosen profession. Honor connects the paltry to the puissant. It becomes a lifeline for the spiritually bereaved. We come to understand that while historic continuity with the past may be a necessity, that necessity – whatever its logical or normative significance – is not fully determinative of the present. It is mainly a cultural necessity, most evident in the law as "learning."[125] The two dynamics discussed (memorialization – effacement, spiritual possibilities – enfolding fact) cut across each other, similar in operation to how Hurst described sequence and context. Yet Holmes gave more attention than Hurst to the different tonalities and registers evident in present experience, the different abiding temperaments, mindsets, dispositions, and cultural colorations – from polychrome to monochrome – because, I speculate, as a judge he witnessed their display many a working day.

I am inclined to believe that there was much Holmes could not say openly and straightforwardly because he was a sitting judge. And some things he would not say, even in private correspondence, because they would sound too odd, far-flung, and perhaps half-baked. He was not above protecting his reputation. He saw red when he found out in 1902 that other members of the Boston legal community thought of

from. Holmes judged with the belief that the law was one of the greatest public conversations in our culture.").

123 Oliver Wendell Holmes, *On Receiving the Degree of Doctor of Laws*, *in* III CW 473–74.

124 *Id.*

125 Gerald Postema argues that for Holmes logic as form functioned as one of the two ineradicable normative demands in the law, substance (policy/good sense) being the second. For that reason Postema is unable to take Holmes's adage that "continuity with the past is only a necessity and not a duty" as anything more than a "*bon mot*," a further indicator of Holmes's inability to think long and hard about philosophical problems. He does surprisingly little with Holmes's *Speeches*, which is where one finds the pulse of Holmes's thought. POSTEMA, *supra* note 15, 68 n.28.

him as merely a "literary fellow."[126] He had more than pulled his weight as a jurist he complained to Pollock.[127] Still, he felt intellectually lonely and isolated. Pollock was a lifelong friend, somewhat of a kindred spirit, but not one fully in sync. Holmes's loneliness probably explains his occasional spasms of delight upon reading anything that appeared to abut upon his deepest beliefs. On the other hand, he excessively worried the temptation to withdraw into the citadel, either inwardly or outwardly. He stayed put where he was and sought to keep up his courage. His "chance utterances" were probably meant as much for him as for his friends, to bolster his faith and give free rein to his doubts. Their style of composition, the delicate transitions from superfluity to forms crystalline and back again, derived its aesthetic energy from a circuit that included his two greatest ideals, democratic freedom and truth.

In the current between these two ideals we find the source of the "right" of "the present to govern itself as much as it can." Holmes's use of the word "right" in this context is of course vague. But its vagueness cannot be eradicated without materially changing its meaning. Its meaning, in turn, depends in part on the perceived necessity that continuity with the past entails. What happens when one realizes that the past has prescribed one's vocabulary and limited the reach of one's imagination?

From one viewpoint, it would seem that no matter how much one twists and turns and pulls one cannot disentangle one's self from this particular net. Or to use Nietzsche's imagery, the chain of the past stays attached to your ankle no matter how far or fast you run.[128] Yet from another standpoint, one less constrained, an opportunity for mastery presents itself. The past as Holmes describes it is a fundamental power of nature; so is self-exertion. The means (vocabularies, imaginaries) may be continuities but self-exertion is not. It is unique. This self-exertion is the primary source of Holmes's vague term "right." It is the irrefragable sense of power active or agent. Within the confines of a literary exposition it brings to mind the pulsating vibrato of an actualized and living phrase. Deliberately embedded in the present the resulting interaction – between the past and self-exertion – produces its own distinct and distinctive feel. The situation then summons its own doppelganger (a discernible array of elicited feelings, inclinations, and thoughts). The present is thus *presented* and *re-presented*.

That, at least, is my take on Holmes's position on the source of the present's right to govern itself to the extent possible. It is part of his broader understanding of how self-exertion fuses belief and will. It is part of his sense of how the common law unwittingly sought ever-higher planes of resolution. This analysis of Holmes's

[126] Liva Baker, The Justice from Beacon Hill: The Life and Times of Oliver Wendell Holmes 354–55 (1991); G. Edward White, Oliver Wendell Holmes: Law and the Inner Self 305–06 (1993).

[127] I Holmes–Pollock Letters, *supra* note 97, at 106.

[128] Friedrich Nietzsche, Untimely Meditations 61 (R. J. Hollingdale trans., Cambridge University Press 1983).

position skirts both traditional conservative or romantic interpretations. In the same manner it flanks progressive and liberal ones. This position's attraction for Holmes lay in how it submerged self-seeking into a deeper, longer-lasting series or sequence. It turned continuity into a means of self-improvement and that can only be done through deliberate self-submission to the truths of professional inquiry.

But in America the truths of professional legal inquiry could no longer be had without reference to democratic freedom. In the late nineteenth century, as many people and not just Holmes realized, democratic freedom partly meant unending tumult. Here one found the sources of that social change that often went by the name, history. These sources were as much political as economic, cultural as social, spiritual as temporal. Democratic freedom radically enlarged the range of inquiry. It did so both horizontally and vertically. Holmes viewed his present with depth because he intuitively understood – probably because of the many years spent in painstaking historical inquiry – that only when the past is dechronologized can the present acquire the requisite depth needed for genuine inquiry to take place. It takes a while to understand that dignity and depth are correlates. So are their opposites.

To say it another way, Holmes took Emerson's view of history and applied it to law. He understood, as did well-known English social theorists, that the present – in the guise of so-called civilized people and primitive populations, posh and less-than-posh habits and practices, barbaric and civilized modes of thinking, the entire range of living mentalities, from the most ridiculous suppositions and superstitions to the most refined scientific theories and facts, from approved to disapproved patterns of thought – had to be accounted for and negotiated. They all had empirical status. They were all, in one sense, sources of law. John Burrow formulated best the overriding issue when he noted that in the Victorian era, social thought was beset with "a tension between English positivistic attitudes to science on the one hand and, on the other, a more profound reading of history, coming to a large extent from German romanticism, which made the older form of positivistic social theory, philosophic radicalism [of the Jeremy Bentham and James Mill variety], seem inadequate."[129]

To see education as the mode of hurrying up the pace of social evolution, as many at that time conceived it, could easily make one susceptible to pretty panaceas. Meliorism and Social Darwinism were all of one cloth in this respect. Progression was not foreordained. On the other hand, quietism betrayed self-exertion. It lacked toughness. It was unmanly.[130] That left exactly one viable alternative: an intense effort to establish new lines of communication between the present and the past and the future. A new mode of integration had to be invented. A new sensibility breathed into life.

[129] Burrow, *supra* note 40, at xv, 30.

[130] *See* John M. Kang, Oliver Wendell Holmes and Fixations of Manliness 62–77 (2018).

Accepting the past's hold on the present did not invariably lead to passivity but posed new opportunities to organize social energy. On the one side, that goal required critical history. Critical or emancipatory history would lead to the release of social energy. That part of the story is well understood.[131] On the other, it required the slow reworking of old behavioral patterns and the creation of new cultural ideals, new organizational forms that would subsume and rework the old; social energy somehow made socially productive in the broadened ambit of democratic freedom. That part of the story has not been well understood or told. Law as power inhered in its organizational form. Apparent differences in form were mainly differences of scale. We see most clearly this meaning of law for Holmes in the various formal Answers to Resolutions he gave, on behalf of the court, for departed colleagues. He included these in his *Speeches*. In these brief remarks he searched for ways to extrapolate from current practice, from the felt working traditions that invoked a heritage and a race, a new dignity that would henceforth mark the legal profession in the United States.

Before discussing that topic, let me head off a common misunderstanding. Succinctly put, it holds that Holmes primarily sought to supplant learning with science.[132] This misunderstanding finds much justification in the text of "Learning and Science." Not many words after proclaiming that the "present has a right to govern itself so far as it can[,]" he says: "An ideal system of law should draw its postulates and its legislative justification from science. As it is now, we rely upon tradition, or vague sentiment, or the fact that we never thought of any other way of doing things, as our only warrant for rules which we enforce with as much confidence as if they embodied revealed wisdom."[133]

Read in isolation this passage supports the view that Holmes turned his back on the past, that he thought it would somehow be feasible to escape the inescapable continuity. The call to turn to "science" as the source of postulates and justifications for governing rules inspired subsequent generations of American legal scholars. But this call to science, as typically understood, is only half, a single part of the helix, of the DNA strand operative in the common law as Holmes conceived it. It bears recalling at this juncture that in "The Profession of Law" Holmes noted that when it came to law scientific study directed the student to three cognate subjects: "to anthropology, the science of man, to political economy, the theory of legislation, [and] ethics."[134] If these three disciplines laid out the path to properly understand law, once the student has learned the substantive law and procedure (the prevailing legal dogma), it is because these three areas of study operated within the folds of the past, inside the historical continuity as it were, temporal or atemporal beachheads

[131] *See, e.g.*, Robert W. Gordon, Taming the Past: Essays on Law in History and History in Law (2017).

[132] *See, e.g.*, David H. Burton, Oliver Wendell Holmes, Jr. 71 (1980).

[133] Holmes, *supra* note 102, at 492.

[134] Holmes, *supra* note 77, at 472.

notwithstanding.[135] Direct engagement with the feelings that made or make law living and vital, or to understand why survivals became survivals, or to evaluate courses of conduct taken and undergone, required a mode of interrogation in which the interrogator also became the interrogated; the mode is self-reflexive; in this setting questioning abjures indifference.

Again, Holmes believed one had to work through the continuity, to find ways to turn necessities into working mechanisms. He would build a race.[136] This endeavor required greater focus and self-determination than existed at the time within the Boston legal community. It required an attitude fundamentally more self-aware and open than Langdell displayed in his best-known works. Science would not simply supplant learning; instead, as Holmes had come to see things, learning and science when pressed hard, very hard, against each other would lead to something else, something unforeseen. 1+1=3.

The end result would be that learning as his generation knew it would pass from the earth. Holmes, unbeliever that he was, still tended to think in biblical terms. It was the Puritan in him. But the secular, learned humanist also had to have his say. The same audience that listened to Frederick Pollock orate on the glories of the common law that bound to one another the English-speaking commonwealths heard this man Holmes tell them that the future of (their) law lay with the Italians. Keep in mind this was 1895, and, as the New Yorkers in the audience probably knew, Ellis Island was hopping with immigrants from the Italian peninsula. The Italian jurisprudes at the time mainly followed the French tradition of codification. I don't know whom Holmes had in mind, or if he merely intended to divert his audience's attention from the unction of race, probably not, but it is a revealing remark all the same.

"The Italians have begun to work upon the notion that the foundation of the law ought to be scientific, and, if our civilization does not collapse, I feel pretty sure that the regiment or division that follows us will carry that flag."[137] Priceless asides like the one in this quote manifest beautifully the rhythmic flow of Holmes's mind. Absent a catastrophic breakdown, memorialization and effacement continue. Rightly understood, the current word will not be taken as the last or final word. He ends with a plea for constancy. Will the pedagogues of today so thoroughly train the pedagogues of tomorrow that they will be able to detect that "change of emphasis from an argument in Plowden [1518–1585] to one in the time of Lord

[135] Kunal Parker has conceived "temporality" as the competing temporal modes, other than the unreflective present, from which nineteenth-century American legal thinkers sought to counterbalance or direct the movements of events – or the rule of law itself – from within an expanding democratic republic. Kunal M. Parker, Common Law, History, and Democracy in America, 1790–1900 25–66, 219–78 (2011).

[136] Oliver Wendell Holmes, *Ideals and Doubts, in* III CW 443.

[137] Holmes, *supra* note 102, at 492.

Ellenborough [1750–1818], or even from that to one in our own day[?]"[138] That difference in emphasis, says Holmes, "is as marked as the difference between Cowley's [1618–1687] poetry and Shelley's [1792–1822]."[139] The law teacher must above all others be a devoted listener to the law's warbles.

This same theme of constancy Holmes approached from a different direction in the Answers to Resolutions he gave honoring departed colleagues. Some of the departed he did not know or barely knew. Others he knew well; and at least one, George Shattuck, he knew quite well. Shattuck had been one of the organizers of the Harvard Law School Association. He was in the audience when Holmes delivered "The Use of Law Schools" in 1886. I don't know if he attended the twenty-fifth anniversary celebration honoring Langdell in 1895. It's possible, since he and Langdell had been classmates at Harvard College and had known each other a long time.[140] Shattuck had also recommended Langdell to President Eliot of Harvard for a position at the law school.[141] Shattuck passed away in 1897, a few short months after Holmes presented his most considered ideas on legal study to the assembled students, professors, and honored guests at the Boston University School of Law.

Holmes opens by recounting all the good Shattuck did for him, principally as a benefactor and educator. His pedagogy came via example. In this tribute Holmes expands a bit upon the observation he made in "The Use of Law Schools" – "It seems to me that nearly all the education which men can get from others is moral, not intellectual .... [it] lies mainly in the shaping of men's interests and aims."[142] Shattuck, we learn, impressed the young Holmes with "his sweeping, all-compelling force, his might of temperament, his swiftness (rarely found with such might), his insight, tact, and subtlety[.]"[143] Holmes does not explicitly mention Shattuck's learning or intelligence. Granted, keenness of thought certainly may be taken to reside in insight, tact, and subtlety; learning appears cumbersome in comparison, and intelligence per se lacks the necessary nuance.

It pays to ponder the kind of mind Holmes admired and believed would, if fortunate, wax in the law. Shattuck, if we read Holmes aright, had a tremendous personality – "sweeping, all-compelling force" – and a temperament strong and well

[138] *Id.*

[139] *Id.*

[140] Kimball, *supra* note 20, at 24–32. *See also* the memoir that Holmes included, and to which he contributed the final three paragraphs, in the bound proceedings reprinted from the Massachusetts Historical Society, Oliver Wendell Holmes, Memoir of George Otis Shattuck 3–11 (1900). It appears from an off-hand comment by Mark A. DeWolfe Howe that Holmes's cousin, John T. Morse, Jr., wrote the main part of the memoir. *See* Mark A. DeWolfe Howe, A Partial (and Not Impartial) Semi-Centennial History of the Tavern Club 1884–1932 136 (1934).

[141] LaPiana, *supra* note 3, at 12.

[142] Holmes, *supra* note 103, at 475.

[143] Oliver Wendell Holmes, *George Otis Shattuck, in* III CW 492–94.

grounded. It's hard to know what that means exactly – "might of temperament" – but I take it Holmes is referring to Shattuck's ability to remain calm, unflappable, and undeterred. Shattuck's swiftness, which Holmes found surprising in one not easily unsettled, stands out enough for Holmes to mention it twice. He refers to it again when speaking of Shattuck's consummate skill in cross-examination. There may even be a third reference when Holmes comments on Shattuck's uncanny ability to bring "out deeply hidden truths by some invisible radiance that searched things to their bones."[144]

What stands out from his portrait of Shattuck, especially the first few paragraphs, are the qualities Holmes saw fit to emphasize. Eulogistic conventions and personal affection aside, Shattuck emerges as a man unscholarly but astute and decisive. He was well equipped to use the apparatuses of legal scholarship when needed but that was not his forte. Given Holmes's own scholarly bent, one wonders to what extent that factor played a part in Shattuck first mentoring then hiring him.

Holmes also points to what we today would call Shattuck's charisma. Shattuck was a big man in the Suffolk Bar; he had qualities that Holmes did not. On the other hand, Holmes had vision. Looking back from the distance of thirty years Holmes could easily acknowledge that without Shattuck in his young life his education would have been sorely impoverished. In Shattuck he got a glimpse of the law as lawyering; law not so much in action as in motion. The qualities that Shattuck had at his command – the persuasive force of his personality, his assertiveness, his all-important sense of tact – combined with his specific noetic skills – astuteness, subtlety, quick thinking, imagination – and further combined with his purposiveness served to transport the will of others to his ends. His ends became theirs. I think this display of forensic and rhetorical power fascinated Holmes. It fascinated him because Shattuck somehow knew how to connect the tools of his trade and the knowledge at his fingertips with the sentiment or sentiments that governed his audience. He knew how to direct the flow.

Success appeared to come from knowing how to work with the currents of life, not against them. Knowledge of what Holmes called the here-and-now was indispensable. We come back to Shattuck's swiftness of mind. Part of what may have induced Holmes to refer to Shattuck's "might of temperament" is the contrast that it provided to Shattuck's agility of thought. He saw things in a flash; he had an immediate multidimensional view of the situation. Holmes believed it an unusual ability in someone with the temperament that Shattuck had. Given how Holmes uses the word, temperament does not primarily mean temperamental. Shattuck was not moody, though we cannot rule out moments of melancholy. Nor does he appear prone to anger nor do Holmes's descriptions suggest he was coldly unemotional,

[144] *Id.*; *see also* HOLMES, MEMOIR *supra* note 140, at 10 ("He was fertile in resource and very quick in seeing all the bearings of a fact or of a piece of testimony, a matter in which most men of weighty ability are slow.").

phlegmatic. The standard descriptors do little to help us understand what Holmes is driving at by this word, temperament. We have suggested that by "might of temperament" Holmes adverted to Shattuck's ability to stay calm and focused no matter what came his way mainly because that quality is still very much lauded and prized by attorneys, especially litigators. As the specific meaning of Holmes's usage eluded me, I unthinkingly reverted to the general tenor of the term in a context that seems to work and with which I am familiar. I may have in fact missed the mark.

Swiftness contrasts to stolidity. Stolidity itself contrasts to heightened emotion. Seeing deeply hidden truths at a glance, X-ray style, contrasts to a patient or a plodding accumulation of facts, or obliviousness to pressing but hidden elements. Temperament, considered without an adjective, has no relevant contrasts. It takes its hue from the prevailing tone. It seems more and more to be like the physical base upon which the pyramid of personality is built. Emerson likened it to an iron wire. For Holmes it becomes the natural mold through which education must work. It is a matter of aims and interests, reshaping the mold from within. The mold itself is part of the historic continuity – determinism of habit, not of cause.

So perhaps I did not completely miss the mark after all. Perhaps Holmes meant by "might of temperament" what I took him to mean. And perhaps he also meant by it something else, something connected and closely related but slightly different. Law, culturally speaking, arises out of power self-confident. It has behind it, within it, the force of what Hurst called will. These words – temperament, will, law, power – are treacherous, the "things" (the arranged objects, activities, patterns of behavior, sequences of thought, the imbuing or circulating feelings) to which they point hard to think. A word-symbol reverse-engineered does not necessarily disclose its operative significance. Analysis at the border often hits a wall (a.k.a. a steel barrier). All that is left is a disarray of determined objects and feelings, configurations of meaning excised from their living matrix. That realization leads to the most important insight of Holmes's career: democratic freedom and legal truth put each other to the test and that test cuts both ways across time.

Swift thinking and a mighty temperament jointly give length and breadth to the immediate ends of the moment, the here-and-now. What is missing is a sense of height. At the beginning of a single long paragraph in his Shattuck remembrance, Holmes hints at how the test might work. "People often speak of correcting the judgment of the time by that of posterity. I think it quite as true to say that we must correct the judgment of posterity by that of the time."[145] What a remarkable thing for Holmes to say! One might easily hold up this sentence as just another typical Holmesian aperçu, well phrased and suggestive, but opaque. That only delays the hard thinking about its meaning. Read one way, Holmes's aphorism inverts the traditional view on the role of effects. The traditional view is that one generation uses the consequences – foreseen and unforeseen – to judge the decisions or actions

[145] Holmes, *supra* note 143, at 494.

of a prior one. This judging, as an objective of historical reflection, is often more critical than edificatory or antiquarian (by antiquarian I mean exhibiting piety towards the past). It takes the ambit of present circumstance as the benchmark by which to evaluate past actors.

For some reason, reflecting on Shattuck's life as a lawyer led Holmes to look for a way to connect the actual life of a man he knew and admired to certain superlatives of human achievement. That nexus may be an intrinsic part of memorialization, of remembrance, at least in Western culture, but it does not fully account for Holmes's willingness to create a magnetic polarity between future generations and those whom they succeeded.

Posterity in Holmes's usage is ambiguous; it may or may not include descendants apart from those who could trace their stock back to the British or related migrations. Also unclear is *whose* future judgments on the past would have the greatest impact in the culture or would stand most in need of correction. Holmes knows that America's northeastern ports are teeming with immigrants, that women are politicking for the vote, that the push for civil rights for African Americans has not petered out, that there are voices crying out for the Seminole, the Cherokee, the Apache, and even the much-abused Chinese laborer. Despite these possibilities, no evidence jumps out that Holmes had the descendants of these people in mind as the posterity whose judgments might find reproof from his present or another past. Yet we cannot categorically exclude the possibility.

Shattuck was part of a subculture that Holmes believed great but fragile. For convenience we can call it the culture of achievement. That culture included such representative figures as the explorer Nansen, the poet Wordsworth, and the philosopher Kant. The best measure of greatness for Holmes was "the total of human energy which they embody."[146] Allowing for differences in quality, he pointed to Nansen's remarkable physical powers ("to digest blubber or to resist cold") as well as his astounding physical courage. Wordsworth possessed an inimitable capacity to "express the unutterable." Kant had tremendous speculative reach.

Interpreted charitably, Holmes is not saying that a society's culture finds its highest justification in great individuals. For Holmes, the justification of a culture does not lie in what some have called aesthetic phenomena. We must be careful of that misunderstanding. Its justification lies in its ability to function. A functioning culture serves as its own justification.[147] At its best it preserves existing and opens new avenues of vitality. In the first part of the same long paragraph in which he described the potential of the past and the present to become polarities for each other, but before he lists examples of men who possessed great qualities (Nansen, Wordsworth, Kant),

146 *Id.*

147 *See* Oliver Wendell Holmes, *Speech to Bar Association of Boston, in* III CW 499.

he introduced the "small man" who is able to please his companions by virtue of "some little felicity."[148] The difference between the great and those who do not achieve greatness is that the great are willing to put the raw talent they have nourished or cultivated, or maintained deliberately uncultivated, to the test. The "total human energy" which has found its most rewarding outlet cannot obtain permanency, it cannot endure, unless it can fight its way into the very tissue of being. That is true greatness; its success for the most part unseen.

Studied analysis, furthermore, will not reveal *how* an idea, a thought, a mood, a disposition, a mode or pattern of thinking or of acting became instilled in the very tissue of being. It is hard to catch the propagation of ideas or ideals in action. By "instilled in the very tissue of being" I mean that the phenomenon under consideration has become integrated into an organized cultural pattern, a distinct pattern of meaning, or has refashioned the very form in which existing meaning expresses itself and which enables it to maintain its vitality.

This notion of integration, or the ability and willingness to fight for an outcome against significant counterpressure, is what for Holmes separates risk-taking greatness from self-protective small-mindedness. It's an odd way of seeing things, but essentially one has not lived well until one has taken one's little truth (be it the expression of a felicity, quality, talent, capacity, or skill) and made it great through combat.

The warlike imagery sometimes gets in the way of Holmes's message. In plain terms, it seems to me that what Holmes is saying is that one's private cornucopia, which one prizes and adorns and perhaps take great spiritual pride in, means relatively little unless one takes it out of one's inward garden, where only lovers and friends are allowed to visit, and brings it into a public forum, the market or the court or the battlefield or an equivalent. One must come down from one's cave high in the mountain. One must radiate one's special gift into the body public through constant and unremitting and unrewarding toil. It must be translated. It must undergo testing. One exerts influence on others through example and ideal more than through censoriousness. One must recognize that "experience," in one use of that word, embodies the ever-present counterpressures that function in social life. Experience gives social life its resilience. It is the power of what exists and persists to shape in its own image what might come-into-being. Holmes's genius led him to see how this power worked at different scales, from brute fact to heightened speculation. It became an essential aspect of the new dialectic between democracy and truth. Without the constraints of democracy, the poetic freedom to broach truth would amount to little more than poetic larceny. Without that poetic freedom, democracy would degenerate. There would be no forthcoming truth-formed ideals, arising from what he beautifully called the "truthful imagination," to withstand the democratic

[148] Holmes, *supra* note 143, at 494.

effervescence.[149] For Holmes it came down to the binding power of a professional conscience. That explains the added twist not typically noticed, that he broadened democracy's reach – it explicitly includes the dead as well as the living.

The dead may have reached a judgment that puts into question one of posterity's. How does that work? For Holmes – and he makes this argument to explain why he believes Shattuck a great man – the judgment of a prior time that we can fathom by utilizing all the historical and analytical resources at our command, that is, understanding the great problems of a prior here-and-now and how they were formally addressed, lies, in the context of law, in the particular legal decision or structure put into place to resolve the pressing issues. That is the "judgment" of which Holmes speaks. It embodies the felt actuality of a particular time. It is abstract in this usage and so hard to understand. But that "judgment" (or, as we will call it below, "practical judgment" or "professional judgment") represents for Holmes not just reason but reason made effective, a theoretic–practical power (pragmatic, in one use), that collates and organizes various competing interests and wants, many obvious, many hidden. And it does it at the appropriate scale. If a viable judicial ordering, and if necessary, and if the conditions are propitious, it would increase in scale until it reaches its natural limit. If significant and strong enough, a "judgment" (legal or nonlegal) creates a tenor or tone that reaches far into the future. Or, more common in our less controlled era, present judgments (legal or nonlegal) seek to sabotage the past. Judgments work in both directions. Holmes believed that for American society and its culture to gain further strength and cohesion, posterity had to recognize that its reaction against a prior generation or generations would always be one-sided and unbalanced until posterity finds in itself the capacity to withstand correction by its predecessors. And vice versa. Neither the present nor the past should be subject to a scorched earth policy. The critiques at their best go in both directions and lead to unanticipated resolutions.

Shattuck's temperament and mental agility enabled him to impress himself upon events, to shape them, sometimes minutely, according to his taste and desires. By extension, this ability to impress and form power-enhancing or power-distributing events constitutes the chief function of the legal profession in a democratic society. It arises because legal professionals, due to their role in American democracy, are in a privileged position to understand and appreciate the historic, multivalent complexity of their society. American democracy, as seen through law, enfolds its legal professionals. Lawyers function in and through the "tissue" of this society's "organic structure." To law, in Holmes's conception, had fallen the task of keeping this organic structure intact, of providing direction to human wants within the body politic. Those lawyers who did more than practice a trade and look to short-term ends soon realized their actions had long-range consequences on what those who came after them might do or think or even feel.

[149] Oliver Wendell Holmes, *William Allen*, *in* III CW 485.

It's not so much hard to comprehend what Holmes is saying as to understand what it means. Take, for example, these sentences with which he closes the long paragraph we have been discussing:

> The great problems are questions of here and now. Questions of here and now occupy nine hundred and ninety-nine thousandths [999/1000] of the ability of the world; and when the now has passed and has given place to another now, the heads and hands that build the organic structure of society are forgotten from the speech of their fellows, and live only in the tissue of their work.[150]

The great problems of the here-and-now called for much more than legal intervention. They also call, in Holmes's opinion, for greater and greater organizational ability. The capability to organize and productively employ larger and larger swaths of human energy stands as the ultimate desideratum; if the effort is fortunate it becomes a testament to the human power to withstand and surmount the consequences of its own successes. For an effort less than fortunate, the potential implosion of a culture becomes as much a danger to be feared as the social and economic predictions of a pessimistic Malthusian.

If that is the big picture then the smaller one, the one that most directly concerned the legal profession, had to do with the legal ability to address the problems of the here-and-now that fell within its purview. This "legal ability" at the level of practice brings into focus attributes that Holmes recognized as Shattuck's "might of temperament" and "swiftness." Redescribed as perseverance and insight, these providential attributes, combined, made Shattuck count for much, enabled him to add his two bits to the "organic structure of society."

As is evident from his other encomia, Holmes had long since come to the conclusion that what lawyers and judges did in a common law jurisdiction had far-reaching effect. He repeats the point often enough to make one take notice. Consider the following instances (in order of the subject's disappearance).[151] *Sydney Bartlett* (1889) ("But remotely what the lawyer does is to establish, develop, or illuminate rules which are to govern the conduct of men for centuries; to set in motion principles and influences which shape the thought and action of generations which know not by whose command they move. The man of action has the

[150] Holmes, *supra* note 143, at 494.

[151] In his remarks involving many of these same addresses, and *Speeches* as a whole, G. Edward White emphasizes what he calls a "dissonance between the propositions Holmes advanced in his extrajudicial addresses and his own experience as a lawyer." White further sees Holmes implementing two far-reaching analogies, that of chivalry (service) and quest for glory (ego gratification), to negotiate the dissonance and assuage his guilt over how he fell short in his performance as a soldier in the Civil War. I think the "dissonance" as White frames it is a formulation Holmes would have rejected. Indeed, his own intellectual struggles were to overcome the perceived dissonance or incompatibility between the life of the mind and the life of the practitioner. And in that endeavor he was more successful than not. White, *supra* note 126, at 210–15 (1993).

present, but the thinker controls the future; his is the most subtile [*sic*], the most far-reaching power.").[152] *Daniel S. Richardson* (1890) ("Their [the great lawyers of the past] true monument is the body of our jurisprudence, – that vast cenotaph shaped by the genius of our race, and by powers greater than the greatest individual, yet to which the least may make their contribution and inscribe it with their names. The glory of lawyers, like that of men of science, is more corporate than individual.").[153] *William Allen* (1891) ("Unless we are to accept decadence as the necessary end of civilization, we should be grateful to all men like William Allen, whose ambition, if it can be called so, looks only to remote and mediated command; who do not ask to say to any one, Go, and he goeth, so long as in truthful imagination they wield, according to their degree, the most subtile [*sic*] and intoxicating authority which controls the future from within by shaping the thoughts and speech of a later time.").[154] *George Shattuck* (1897) ("Sooner or later the race of men will die; but we demand an eternal record. We have it. What we have done is woven forever into the great vibrating web of the world. The eye that can read the import of its motion can decipher the story of all our deeds, of all our thoughts. To that eye I am content to leave the recognition and the memory of this great hand and heart.").[155]

The ability to read even a minuscule section of the great vibrating web of the world may easily take a lifetime to acquire. The pressing here-and-now does not typically permit such a luxury unless that here-and-now is but a thin, elongated, mesmerizing sliver of space–time in an otherwise tremendous, long-lasting, slow-moving event (for instance, Nietzsche's "death of God"[156]). In the realm of American law, here-and-nows are generally much more pressing and transitory; resolutions of current problems require much energy, thought, and will. Of the three, thought seemed to Holmes the most important. Remember, law is the calling of thinkers. Thought also provided the most viable way to consciously connect the present with the past and vice versa. Historical reason – that is, historical knowledge combined with astute analysis of vital legal principles – brought past and present together in a clear-headed, mutually determinative manner. What had previously happened beyond normal human awareness could now be investigated and made to serve well-formulated ends. Professional judgment on larger scales becomes possible. That is the main point upon which Holmes insists. This endeavor required the dedicated and *joint* effort of the entire profession, from the most experienced judges and advocates to tyros fresh from law school working on their first client matter.

[152] Oliver Wendell Holmes, *Sidney Bartlett*, *in* III CW 481.
[153] Oliver Wendell Holmes, *Daniel S. Richardson*, *in* III CW 482–83.
[154] Holmes, *supra* note 149, at 485–86.
[155] Holmes, *supra* note 143, at 494.
[156] FRIEDRICH NIETZSCHE, THE GAY SCIENCE 119–20 (Bernard Williams ed., Josefine Nauckhoff and Adrian Del Caro trans., Cambridge University Press 2001).

ii *Just the Boy Wanted*

Who should join this well-known profession? That is a hard question to answer. William LaPiana has pointed to the mix of prejudices (ethnic, racial, class) that subtly, and oftentimes not so subtly, worked to shape the turn-of-the-century (nineteenth to twentieth) meritocratic ideal.[157] In earlier parts we intermittently asked, "What kind of person do we want the study of law to create?" These two questions are perhaps not unrelated. Though Holmes, to my knowledge, never directly addressed the second question, he did provide some guidance on the first, and as for the second we may surmise that the short answer would point to his portrayals of Shattuck, Bartlett, and Richardson as exemplary attorneys and Allen as an exemplary judge. The longer answer would require a more thorough canvassing than we can now afford of the professional ethos or culture that informed, both positively and negatively, his opinions.

Suffice to say that for much of his professional life Holmes lived and moved within the ambit of Boston lawyers and judges (mainly members of the Suffolk and Middlesex Bars). It bears mentioning in this connection that a leading Boston practitioner of the generation born in the *fin de siècle*, F. W. Grinnell, would in 1923 reference selected addresses in *Speeches* as evidence that the great Holmes fully understood what apparently many of his contemporaries did not, that law is for lawyers.

In "The 'Functioning' of the Judicial Intellect," Grinnell used the discussion surrounding the publication of Benjamin N. Cardozo's *The Nature of the Judicial Process* to examine broadly the question whether judges "make" or "find" law.[158] His article makes for fascinating reading because it brings together in a nontechnical way some of the themes we have touched upon in this and previous sections. Grinnell is concerned that a new fiction, that judges "make" law, will replace the old fiction that they simply "find" it. This opposition is manufactured, Grinnell contends. "What," he asks, "is the answer, without referring to European jurists or learned works, in simple language to the question whether judges 'find' law or 'make' law?"[159]

"[T]he intellectual processes of a court," he explains, "necessarily involve both the process of 'finding' and of 'making'."[160] In his own way Grinnell has rephrased the operative double helix ("What is the law?" – "What is law?") essential to the

[157] LaPiana, *supra* note 3, at 79–92. *See also* William W. Fisher III, *Legal Theory and Legal Education, 1920–2000*, *in* III The Cambridge History of Law in America: The Twentieth Century and After (1920–) 59–61 (Michael Grossberg and Christopher Tomlins eds., 2008); Jerold S. Auerbach, *Enmity and Amity: Law Teachers and Practitioners, 1900–1922*, *in* Law in American History 584–99 (Donald Fleming and Bernard Bailyn eds., 1971).

[158] F. W. Grinnell, *The 'Functioning' of the Judicial Intellect*, 8 Mass. L.Q. 29 (1923).

[159] *Id.* at 30.

[160] *Id.*

profession. The bar, he further points out, also employs the same processes of "making" and "finding" that the courts employ when the bar provides advice on various issues (through formal publications, informal opinions, or considerations of leading practitioners). In addition, individual practitioners, in their capacity as advisers, may informally help to develop or orient practices that may eventually find formal enunciation as law.

Grinnell provides examples of how what ultimately became law was suggested by practitioners or arose due to circumstances. Lord Mansfield, as is well known, "found" the law merchant before it became formalized and appended to the common law. But in many other instances "judge-made" law arose partly from the "arguments of counsel and the intellectual work of declaring and explaining the principles and their application." To individual judicial labor must be added the work of counsel "who convince the mind of the court by their care in 'finding,' their intellectual force and imagination in conceiving, and their skill and power of statement in explaining and demonstrating, the principle or rule involved and its application."[161]

Grinnell is keen on the importance of judges but dispels the myth they are juristically self-sufficient. Grinnell's phraseology in making this point, commenting as he does on the "suggestive minds of the profession," takes us back to the young Holmes. In his "The Theory of Torts," he provided a multilayered description and analysis of how the many and various "suggestive" sources of law (customs, evidence, opinions of jurors, for instance) worked in and through the practice and the courts and culminated in decided law.[162]

Perhaps most intriguing is how Grinnell develops his point. Drawing on the opening paragraph of Holmes's "John Marshall" address – also included in *Speeches* – Grinnell quotes Holmes's description of how in Boston's Old State House James Otis, a lawyer, "argued the case of the Writs of Assistance, and in that argument laid one of the foundations for American constitutional law."[163] Grinnell notes how Otis in that speech "stirred the imagination and enthusiasm of the young John Adams, who became the draftsman of the Constitution of Massachusetts in 1779." As a draftsman Adams had, despite his faults, "the balance of character and intellect, which gave him power of statement that convinced not only the convention and the people of his day, but the influence of which is still a living force and has more to do with the foundations of American constitutional law than the law-making of most judges."[164] Grinnell in this sentence may simply be repeating in different words what Holmes said in his *Speeches* – Shattuck becomes Adams – or both may be reflecting a powerful conviction among dedicated practitioners in

[161] *Id.* at 31.
[162] Oliver Wendell Holmes, *The Theory of Torts*, *in* I CW 328–31.
[163] Grinnell, *supra* note 158, at 32 (quoting Holmes, *John Marshall*, *in* III CW 500).
[164] *Id.*

late nineteenth-, early twentieth-century Boston about the lawyer's role in determining the direction of the American way of life.

Grinnell offers additional examples of how other professional participants in the American legal system (legislators, Supreme Court justices, treatise writers) both "made" and "found" law, the strength of the making and finding itself often proportional to participants' "intellectual grasp and power of statement" of what had come before in light of current circumstances. He concludes his examples by noting how even legal educators such as Langdell "helped make law by changing the methods of studying it in America." New methods of study "made" law because they changed the manner of "finding" it and transforming the accompanying sense that one had succeeded in the search.[165]

Grinnell ends by invoking Holmes's tribute to Daniel Richardson as one of the finest statements available on how the common law system in America actually works. One draws the inference that lawyers like Grinnell felt there was something fundamentally unique about the American system of law, even distinct from that of the English. In America, he summarized,

> neither courts nor legislatures have a monopoly of law-making under our system, that they are both engaged in "finding" as well as "making" the law, and that they are both assisted by unnumbered members of the bar, past and present, as well as many laymen, who often contribute their brains and skill as well as their business sense and customs to the development of the law.[166]

This sense of how law worked in this country, as a constant interplay between "finding" and "making," between the entwined queries, "What is the law?" – "What is law?," led Grinnell to the conclusion that the then current emphasis on judges as "law-makers" would impoverish perception of the profession, not enhance it. He concluded by observing that "most judges probably make much less than they find and less than is made for them to find by the accumulated efforts of the bar, the law faculties and text writers and, in the background by the life of the community."[167]

One may easily draw the lesson from Grinnell's piece that each part of the profession must play its designated part for the "judicial intellect" to function properly. It was a matter of remaining vigilant, constant, to what in the law's past could be assayed and understood (Holmes's "the change of emphasis"[168]), and that which seemed relatively impervious to intellectual recovery or analysis (*e.g.*, the hidden pressure points, the undetected flow of sentiment). It's hard to know from this one piece whether Grinnell shared Holmes's sense that history provided an invaluable tool for aligning present and past. Holmes believed it had the power to link together images from different points in time. With some luck, finesse,

165 *Id.* at 32–33.
166 *Id.* at 33.
167 *Id.* at 34.
168 Holmes, *supra* note 102, at 492.

imagination, empathy and acuity, these images, collated and connected, could bring a workable past into the ambit of a working present.

Condensing the relation into a formula, procedure is to the legal profession what the legal profession is to the broader society. For these relations to hold, procedure must be seen as LaPiana indicated, as central to the professional viewpoint, and the legal profession must be seen as Holmes indicated, as a well-known subject for study ("When we study law we are not studying a mystery but a well known profession."). That study took its dominant tone from how one conceived – or failed to conceive – the connections between the subject, law, and the modes and methods of instruction, the purposes of instruction, and, how one viewed the principal participant in the pedagogical endeavor, the student.

Apart from the biases prevailing at the time about who was fit to study law – prejudices of gender, race, ethnicity, and class – the question of what type of endowments, intrinsic or acquired, best suited an aspirant for its study arose from time to time. Arguments raged over whether students needed the "right stuff" to study law. People like Langdell had no doubts that the right stuff was absolutely needed. LaPiana says Langdell sought to make legal study difficult: "the institutional reforms made it more difficult to get in and stay in; then his new method of study made things more difficult once you were in."[169] LaPiana's word choice in this instance is impeccable because "difficult" captures so many relevant nuances and ranges of meaning. Not only had the study of law at Harvard become difficult, one who desired to practice law in Boston had the added challenges of seeking entry among a group of men convinced of their position as gatekeepers of the profession. Some of these men were extremely able. Many of them, I assume, would not suffer fools gladly.[170]

Studying, learning, practicing, and succeeding in an environment where the "bar" was both high and fierce, and good clients scarce, led Holmes to emphasize the hardships associated with law more than its glamour or monetary rewards. In two pieces for *The Youth's Companion*, a national weekly periodical for young adults and families published in Boston, Holmes shared with its readers the qualities one member of Massachusetts's highest court thought important in aspirants.

The first piece, published in 1889, seems to have been written in response to a general question of who would be "Just the Boy Wanted" in the law. Perhaps other responses came as well from prominent physicians or clergy. Holmes opens with

[169] LAPIANA, *supra* note 3, at 26.

[170] Though I cannot cite anything directly on point to support this impression about the Suffolk Bar, I have learned a great deal about the emergence of the profession in Massachusetts from Gerard W. Gawalt's work. *See* GERARD W. GAWALT, THE PROMISE OF POWER: THE EMERGENCE OF THE LEGAL PROFESSION IN MASSACHUSETTS 1760–1840 (1979); Gerard W. Gawalt, *The Impact of Industrialization on the Legal Profession in Massachusetts, 1870–1900*, *in* THE NEW HIGH PRIESTS: LAWYERS IN POST-CIVIL WAR AMERICA 97–123 (Gerard W. Gawalt ed., 1984); Gerard W. Gawalt, *Massachusetts Legal Education, 1766–1840*, 17 AM. J. LEGAL HIST. 27 (1973).

another instance of what we now recognize as his trademark inversions, especially when he is speaking or writing as one contributor among many.

> A boy who wants to succeed in the law will probably do so. An encouraging thought, as far as it goes. But the power to want to do a thing is as much a talent as the power to do it well, and the two are very apt to go together. So that I am not offering encouragement, but stating the first inborn gift which the boy born for the law must have.[171]

The "want" is primary; Holmes doubly emphasizes the point. "The boy who is wanted in the law must be able himself to want something very hard all the time, and for a long time." This quality, Holmes grants, is a precondition for success in every endeavor of life and not peculiar to law. He then proceeds to enumerate the talents specific to law. But before addressing those it bears mentioning that the "want" Holmes says a boy must have – and, of course, today we would not be so descriptive or exclusive – is the same motive force that, in the legal profession, connected Richardson to Bartlett connected Shattuck to Richardson connected Holmes to Shattuck. Achievement is anonymous. The "want" ultimately takes shape in the guise of an ideal. The "thinker" is an ideal as much as the "boy wanted" … "the boy wanted in the law [law is the calling of thinkers]."

What qualities does the profession demand? Holmes begins his answer in the same way he would begin his most considered statement on legal education eight years later, by first succinctly stating what he believes law to be: "The law is a great mass of rules, showing when and how far a man is liable to be punished, or to be made to hand over money or property to his neighbors, and so forth." As these rules are contained in books, Holmes proceeds to the obvious point: "A lawyer learns them in the main by reading books."[172]

Addressed to teens or pre-teens the obvious is worth stating. Maybe it's worth stating regardless of the audience. Close reading is essential, even after three years of initial study, because "all his life long and almost every day he will be looking into books to read a little more than he already knows about some new question which he has got to answer." That is to say, the question "What is the law?" never goes away. Holmes considers the power to use books essential. The aspirant, he says, "ought to have enough flexibility and fineness of mental fibre [*sic*] to make it easy for him to collect ideas from printed words."[173]

If Holmes had stopped right at this point, his message would be relevant in almost any common law jurisdiction, whether Massachusetts or England, or beyond the common law, in Scotland or France. Books and reading are central to understanding and practicing law in the modern world. To put it in more ambitious terms, in

[171] Oliver Wendell Holmes, *Just the Boy Wanted, in* III CW 338.
[172] *Id.*
[173] *Id.* at 338–39.

keeping with the ambition of the boy who wants, learning is a good thing and the more flexible and fine the mental fiber the more robust the resulting network.

But then Holmes takes the next step, the one that takes the boy out of Scotland or France and puts him squarely in London or Boston circa 1889. The lawyer does not study law to recite it but "to use it and to act upon the rules he has learned in real life." He then says what he would repeat a few years later: "His business is to try cases in court, and to advise men what to do in order to keep out or get out of trouble. He studies his books in order to advise and to try his cases in the right way." The practical aspects of the profession begin to emerge and the book learning begins to recede. "A man may be clumsy with his books, but if he can tell another man in distress what to do, he has the better half of the ability."[174]

Holmes is now preparing to drive home the needful quality everyone agrees is crucial to the successful practice of law, practical judgment. Book learning is essential, but only as preparation to practice. Practice lies in knowing how to take what is in the books and turn it into good advice. The talent for converting book learning into good advice depends upon the ability to extract the "important facts" from the "sea of dramatic circumstances." But what makes good advice "good" is practical judgment. Holmes describes it as a "sense of the relative importance of things with reference to the accomplishment of some desired end." It is, he adds, "what commands the world."

> The lawyer's judgment is a sense of the relative importance of facts with reference to the rules of law, and a sense also, – the more the better, – of their relative importance with regard to business, because law and business are bound together very closely, and in advising a man what to do the lawyer often needs to consider business consequences as well as law.[175]

Thus are the talents and skills that one who wants success in the bar, especially as an adviser, must seek to perfect. But the practice of law involves more than consulting and advising; it often includes advocacy, persuading both judges and juries. In dealing with the former, judges, the would-be lawyer, according to Holmes, must master the ability to think analytically – to clearly state facts and issues – and, interestingly, must also learn to handle ideas "with ease and familiarity." This latter skill is one of the "marks of a civilized man" and mainly "the result of training still comparatively rare in this country."[176]

Different skills are involved in dealing with juries or legislators, that is to say, with those who are not experts, who have not received training to handle questions typically confronted in the law. He then states the point that he would later make central in his eulogy of Shattuck: "You may convince a lawyer of a proposition of law by reasoning alone, but to carry an untrained man upon a question of conduct or of

[174] *Id.* at 339.
[175] *Id.*
[176] *Id.*

life, takes all the powers of your nature at once." To lead a man to act, to bring about a "fighting belief," to "set in motion the predetermined drift of his nature," one "must be able to paint transporting pictures" so that the untrained man "finds himself arrived at the desired conclusion by an act of vision."[177]

By this step Holmes has taken the boy wanted out of London. He is wanted in Boston alone. He is an American. This point is difficult to understand unless one keeps in mind this homage to American democracy from "The Puritan": "Whether they [the Puritans] knew it or not, they planted the democratic spirit in the heart of man. It is to them we owe the deepest cause we have to love our country, – that instinct, that spark that makes the American unable to meet his fellow man otherwise than simply as a man, eye to eye, hand to hand, and foot to foot, wrestling naked on the sand."[178]

The qualities that an aspirant lawyer should have are qualities that correspond to an ideal that suffuses American life, that each person meets every other on an equal social footing. Equal social footing did not, however, mean for Holmes a corresponding equality in spiritual dignity. Remember what he said in "The Use of Law Schools" – "When the effervescence of democratic negation extends its workings beyond the abolition of external distinctions of rank to spiritual things ... they are not only wrong, but ignobly wrong."[179] But equal social footing did put the onus on the advocate to combine whatever native and acquired skills she or he has to instill in her or his audience a "vision" that would enable them, through their own volition, to reach the conclusion the advocate desires.

Holmes based his recommendation on the premise that every man's "deepest beliefs are the product of all his powers and passions[.]" On any important question that is "mixed and practical" – when the question presented is both debatable and pressing – "in some degree the whole man goes into his belief." That is to say, strong beliefs bring into play the entire panoply of experience. The skilled advocate will have some sense how that particular panoply is arranged, what values take precedence and give vitality to the rest. Holmes called it "the predetermined drift" of a man's nature.

The thought immediately occurs that Holmes's prescriptions in this respect reek of manipulation. The person with the greater skill of persuasion, in directing the flow of sentiment, will thrive in a democratic polity. Holmes is not blind to this reality; indeed it appears he sees no other possibility should one accept the democratic premise of social equality. But he does say this: "A bad man will awaken in his hearers whatever class prejudice, or mean envy, or base unbelief, will make it easy for them to side with him." This explicit reference to the "bad man" is the first, as far as I know, in Holmes's public writings. The "bad man" in this context contrasts to

177 *Id.*
178 Holmes, *supra* note 113, at 470–71.
179 Holmes, *supra* note 103, at 475.

the "noble man," one who uses the skills of advocacy to awaken in others "unsuspected powers of aspiration," and whose rhetoric will "carry them on wings over the gulfs that cross his path."[180]

Without pressing the point too hard, we see in these words an important clue to how Holmes understood the basic setup of his society. It's also an important clue to his constant references to such phrases as "in the air" or words like "ferment" or similar language. Democracy at its best encourages openness; openness to ideas, moods, attitudes, whatever their source; ideals, or their opposite, can be catching. But that same openness can act as a solvent, it can create a gulf. Shared conviction can take one over and past "the gulfs that cross" the path. This latter phrase reminds us of the difficult locution Holmes used in "On Receiving the Degree of Doctor of Laws" in reference to honor – "If it does not lift a man on wings to the sky, at least it carries him above the earth and teaches him those high and secret pathways across the branches of the forest the travellers on which are only less than winged."[181] It also brings to mind this sentence from *The Common Law* – "It will readily be imagined that such a system as has been described [*noxae deditio*] could not last when civilization had advanced to any considerable height."[182]

The inference dawns that for Holmes cultural-spatial location is significant. It may augur realities untapped by poetic expression. The relative "height" of a civilization has a direct bearing on the ability of its laws to function, to shape social wants and their satisfactions. Meanness or idealism may strive to take control; dignity must learn to navigate between and beyond both. The successful advocate, whether as a bad man or a good one, is the one who possesses the all-important tact, that is, the ability to "discern the kinds of natures with which he has to deal, and to feel, by a sort of instinct, in what directions they will follow easily, and from what they will turn away."[183]

Holmes concludes "Just the Boy Wanted" with some good homespun advice, even after 120 years. He recommends a "tough constitution," since many an advocate, more so than an adviser, must "undergo great stretches of prolonged intellectual sport, often joined with bodily exertion, and sometimes great excitement and anxiety." Still true. He adds: "The pace is killing."[184] Also still true.

But in the end, the wanting is what counts. He says striving is a means by which the inevitable comes to pass. This is Puritan talk; this is Emerson, and behind him

[180] Holmes, *supra* note 171, at 339–40.

[181] Holmes, *supra* note 123, at 474. Dean Clark of the Yale Law School quoted this passage in his tribute to Holmes on the nationwide radio address that celebrated Holmes's ninetieth birthday. *See* https://sds.lib.harvard.edu/sds/audio/454933120 (last accessed November 13, 2019).

[182] Holmes, *supra* note 10, at 122.

[183] Holmes, *supra* note 171, at 340.

[184] *Id.*

Jonathan Edwards, talk.[185] But then Holmes closes with his own distinctive, modern twist: "The desire of his [the boy's] soul is the prophecy of his fate."[186]

Holmes's second contribution to *The Youth's Companion* came out a year before he delivered the address that came to be known as "The Path of the Law." This contribution comprises two parts. The first is Holmes's response to a submission on the topic of "The Bar As a Profession" that *The Youth's Companion* apparently solicited from the Lord Chief Justice of England, Charles Russell, Baron Russell of Killowen. The second is a very brief surreply to the good Baron's rejoinder.[187]

The Youth Companion's teaser in the February 13, 1896, edition, which contained the Lord Chief Justice's piece, informed its readers that the next issue, "the Washington's Birthday Double Number," would contain the American viewpoint by "the able inheritor of a great name." The editor characterized Holmes's contribution as "a most interesting supplement."[188]

The Lord Chief Justice begins by drawing a line of descent. The line is not one of inheritance but of aptitude. In English life the bar had long been the home for intellectual talent. He then quotes Burke. Burke praised the law as "one of the first and most noblest human sciences[.]"[189] But Burke also wondered, as many did, whether its study posed its own unique dangers to the mind. In his remarks to the graduating class at Brown University in June of the following year (1897), a few months after he delivered "The Path of the Law," Holmes would also quote Burke.[190] He recounted to his audience the vocational struggles he underwent as a young man intent on the law.

> Voices of authority warned that in the crush of that ice any craft might sink. One heard Burke saying that law sharpens the mind by narrowing it. One heard in Thackeray of a lawyer bending all the powers of a great mind to a mean profession. One saw that artists and poets shrank from it as from an alien world. One doubted how it could be worthy of the interest of an intelligent mind.[191]

185 *See also* Oliver Wendell Holmes, *Remarks at Dinner of Boston University Law School Alumni*, *in* III CW 511 ("These were all matters of evolution if you choose, but not evolved without human effort – and one man or many, the makers of the very framework and tissue of our lives are unknown."). For the cultural antecedents to this remark *see* Paul K. Conkin, Puritans and Pragmatists: Eight Eminent American Thinkers v, 1–35 (1968); Perry Miller, *From Edwards to Emerson*, *in* Perry Miller, Errand into the Wilderness 184–203 (1956); Edward A. Purcell, Jr., *On the Complexity of Ideas in America: Origins and Achievements of the Classical Age of Pragmatism*, 27 Law & Soc. Inquiry 967, 968 (2002).

186 Holmes, *supra* note 171, at 340.

187 *See* Lord Chief Justice of England [Charles Russell], *The Bar As a Profession*, 70 The Youth's Companion 77, 79–80 (1896); Oliver Wendell Holmes, *The Bar As a Profession*, *in* III CW 386–89; Lord Chief Justice of England [Charles Russell], *A Rejoinder*, *in* III CW 389–90; Oliver Wendell Holmes, *A Postscript*, *in* III CW 390.

188 Editor, *Washington's Birthday*, 70 The Youth's Companion 77, 82 (1896).

189 Lord Chief Justice, *The Bar As a Profession*, *supra* note 187, at 79 (no source provided for the Edmund Burke quote).

190 Baker, The Justice from Beacon Hill, *supra* note 126, at 321.

191 Oliver Wendell Holmes, *Address at Brown University Commencement*, *in* III CW 517–18.

One does not get the impression that the Lord Chief Justice was ever wracked with such (namby-pamby?) doubts. He does not single out the cautions that Burke uttered. He focuses instead on what the profession promises: not great wealth but "[social] distinctions and adequate means in store[.]" These promises are for those who possess real talent, not merely book smarts and a glib tongue. Its promises are for those who say in the right way what is worth saying. For the benefit of his American audience he quotes the words Daniel Webster used to celebrate John Adams – "Clearness, force and earnestness are the qualities which produce conviction."[192]

As one reads the Lord Chief Justice's comments on the type of man his profession wants, the conviction begins to form – undoubtedly influenced by his bewigged visage planted in the center of the article – that the Lord Chief Justice himself was a man of conviction. His was undoubtedly a mighty temperament; and he evinces this might by describing very early in the article the sort of men the profession does not want. It does not want men who are only smooth talkers. It does not want men without strong brains. It does not want men who are "unfit." By "unfit" the Lord Chief Justice means those men who possess talent but not of the right kind. "[T]here is at the bar, as I know it, a greater amount of talent unfitted for that profession than any other calling of life."[193] The unfit includes, he adds, men better suited to careers in journalism, science, music, and business than law.

The message given to young readers, or their aspiring parents, is that professional misery, not professional success, awaits the unsuited child – boys typically – who seeks a life in the law. The Lord Chief Justice then provides a few additional thoughts for the reader's consideration. As did Holmes in "Just the Boy Wanted," he first stresses the wanting. Loving the law is the most important qualification for entering it. The second is possessing "physical health and energy." Few men of "weak physique" achieve success. "No man of weak health ought to be advised to go to the bar."[194] It's a point he repeats. Third, one must possess what he calls "common sense." Common sense or clear-headedness seems similar to what Holmes called practical judgment. It is connected to understanding business, or, perhaps better stated, it refers to the ability to unify legal learning with business understanding. Common sense is eminently practical. That's the gist.

After these considerations – to which the Lord Chief Justice also adds patience and the financial means to wait, sometimes a long while, for clients to show up – he moves to the topic of schooling. He makes three important points. First, that university training is preferable, almost essential. Second, that in the law, unlike other professions or occupations, "there is no such thing as knowledge that

[192] Lord Chief Justice, *The Bar As a Profession*, *supra* note 187, at 79.
[193] *Id.*
[194] *Id.*

is useless[.]"[195] Any knowledge may become relevant at any time. He has in mind the usefulness to a barrister, who is the lawyer permitted in England to present the case on the client's behalf to the court, of any scrap of information that may at any moment be pressed into service to explain, to illustrate, or to analogize.

The third suggestion is the one that Holmes would find most regrettable. The Lord Chief Justice strongly recommended the study of the "Corpus Juris" or the systematized body of Roman civil law. He recalled how he and other students, both at university and in the Inns of Court, had the privilege of reading "no inconsiderable part of the civil law" under the tutelage of Sir Henry Maine. He maintained much of the common law found its source in the Roman. Concentrating on the Corpus Juris would, he contended, give "the attentive student a knowledge and a grasp of principle hardly otherwise attainable, which he will always find useful throughout his life."[196]

The Lord Chief Justice closes by doing what so many distinguished members of the bar, past and present, have done. He tags onto his distinctly un-perfumed advice the platitudinous reminder that theirs is a higher calling: "Lastly, he [the aspiring lawyer] must remember that he is engaged in a profession which may well engage the noblest faculties of heart and of mind – that he is engaged in the practical administration of that law whose voice is the 'Harmony of the World.'"[197]

I consider Holmes's response to the Lord Chief Justice to be one of his hidden gems. Holmes adapted his style to the occasion. His paragraphs are brief, the writing a bit more journalistic than essayistic or scholarly. Holmes increases slightly the degrees of difference between the practice of law in England and the United States. He begins politely, saying that perhaps the variations are a bit more pronounced than the Lord Chief Justice realizes. In the United States there's very little danger that the attractions of a career in business will be undervalued. In the United States there's also less danger that the historic professions – ministry, law, or medicine – will be overvalued compared to a life spent making money in trade or industry.[198]

The lawyer with a scholarly bent will probably fare much better in the British Isles than the United States. The top men in the US are "usually the hard fighters." Accordingly, the mental refinement one may obtain through a university education matters less to the lawyer in the United States. He would not go so far, Holmes adds, as a "jesting friend of mine once did and say that the main use of a university education is to learn the humbug of it." He thinks it "very useful and very important to a man as a man. But in this country I do not think it quite so important to a lawyer as a lawyer."[199]

[195] *Id.*
[196] *Id.*
[197] *Id.* at 79–80.
[198] Holmes, *The Bar As a Profession*, *supra* note 187, at 386.
[199] *Id.*

One is not quite sure what to make of this comment. On the one hand, England did not have a strong tradition of university education for its solicitors and attorneys. The majority apprenticed or attended the Inns of Courts. The barristers often did attend university and then enrolled in "cram" courses to pass the bar examination. The legal knowledge thus obtained was typically more superficial than solid. On the other hand, Langdell's reform efforts at Cambridge – as Harvard's law school was then usually called – to modernize legal education and make it both professionally and academically respectable included the prerequisite of a college degree.[200]

Since Holmes is usually understood to have supported the reform efforts at Cambridge, his comment presents a puzzle. Perhaps he was merely making a sociological observation. Perhaps he was being more clear-eyed than the Lord Chief Justice (and the reformers at Harvard) regarding the actual qualities and attainments one needed for professional success. Perhaps he was simply acknowledging the powerful sentiment at large in the country, specifically among the many practitioners who opposed increased institutionalized demands and barriers to practice. After all, as the common so-called "Lincoln Objection" went, Abraham Lincoln had not attended a university or a law school and he became both a great lawyer and a very great man.[201]

It may be useful at this point to pause and get our bearings. It helps to keep in mind that Holmes's contribution to the topic of "The Bar As a Profession" comes to us hard on the heels of "Learning and Science." He believes some of the distinguished professors at Harvard, such as Langdell and James Barr Ames, emphasize too much historical study; stress too much learning per se. From a broader angle, we can see that by 1896 Holmes's ideas on law and its study have taken a definite turn. In the following year he will attempt to articulate and arrange them with care in "The Path of the Law." In essence, and to paraphrase Alexander Pope, they amount to this: The proper study of American law is American law.[202]

Though much is guesswork, we can catch various glimpses of the path that led Holmes to this opinion.

We start in 1870. In the year that Langdell assumed his duties at Cambridge, Holmes and Arthur Sedgwick took over the editorial responsibilities at the *American Law Review*. Holmes, a recent graduate of the Law School, took it upon himself to publish a comment in the pages of the *Review* regarding its current condition. "For a long time," he wrote, "the condition of the Harvard Law School has been almost a disgrace to the Commonwealth of Massachusetts." That assessment left little ambiguity. He continued. "We say 'almost a disgrace,' because, undoubtedly, some of its

[200] Kimball, *supra* note 20, at 210–19.

[201] Susan K. Boyd, The ABA's First Section: Assuring a Qualified Bar 14 (1993).

[202] Pope's original couplet: "Know then thyself, presume not God to scan; / The proper study of mankind is man." Alexander Pope, *An Essay on Man: Epistle II*, www.poetryfoundation.org/poems/44900/an-essay-on-man-epistle-ii (last accessed April 4, 2019).

courses of lectures have been good, and no law school of which this can be said is hopelessly bad."[203]

One can readily imagine the reaction of Harvard's faculty to this bit of impertinence. Professor Joel Parker, who had taught at the law school both before and during Holmes's student years, thought the comment not only disrespectful but also "rather bumptious."[204] Harvard professors in those unfettered days had a knack for selecting choice words to knock down the brash conceit of former students!

The problem, it turned out, was Harvard's lackadaisical approach to preparing its students for the profession. Competence was not obligatory, subject to examination. The school mainly cared about attendance and tuition. "[A] school which undertook to confer degrees without any preliminary examination whatever was doing something every year to injure the profession throughout the country, and to discourage real students."[205]

Even accounting for the vehemence of youth, the remark is notable for its double-sidedness. On the one side, the school's leniency was hurting the profession. Here Holmes is gesturing to what later scholars, such as Anthony Chase, William LaPiana, and Bruce Kimball, have, in their various ways, identified as the pressing need many educators and lawyers felt at the time to institutionalize professional discipline and implement professional standards. On the other side, Harvard's borderline disgrace lies as much in how the current system "discouraged real students."

As noted above regarding his references to Burke and Thackeray, in later life Holmes would often tell audiences that during his early years in law he was much wracked with doubt whether this profession was a fit enterprise for an intelligent man, for that young "spirit of fire" who wanted to make good on his spiritual possibilities. One filled with such drive would likely find the facile patter of an inert law school disheartening. Even more, the nonchalant success of the less able but more adaptable undoubtedly left a bad lingering taste.

The young Holmes had no qualms in letting his dissatisfaction be known. Yet he may also have timed his comment to support the newly installed Langdell in his reforms. The comment also notes that the faculty had finally begun to remedy the problem. It quotes a recently issued circular informing the public that the Law School would not confer the Bachelor of Laws degree upon students unless they "pass satisfactory examinations in all required subjects, and, in at least seven elective subjects, after having been at the school not less than one year."[206] The comment applauds these curriculum changes. They should, along with a rejuvenated faculty, encourage those "real students" who want to master the law.

[203] [Oliver Wendell Holmes], *Note*, 5 AM. L. REV. 177 (1870) (unsigned note).

[204] As quoted in WHITE, *supra* note 5, at 316; *see also* MARK DEWOLFE HOWE, JUSTICE OLIVER WENDELL HOLMES: THE SHAPING YEARS, 1841–1870 205–06 (1957).

[205] [Holmes], *Note, supra* note 203.

[206] *Id.*

The comment ends by observing that the pedagogical goal of Harvard Law School ought to be the same as that proposed to the trustees of Northwestern University. The Law School's objective must not be limited only to preparing students for practice. For those "students who desire," it ought also to provide "the same facilities to investigate the science of human law, theoretically, historically, and thoroughly, as they have to investigate mathematics, natural sciences, or any other branch of thought."[207]

Thus, from early on, we see the beginnings of two trajectories in Holmes's thinking on legal education that start from the same point but would move in different directions. The modern law school should ensure that its students who wish to learn the practice are properly trained in both procedure and substantive law – what Holmes later calls dogma – and it should also provide the needed facilities for those "real students" who sought to master their subject.

The following year, 1871, Holmes had the opportunity to express further his opinion on how the subject matter ought be taught. The occasion was a review of his friend James Bryce's *The Academical Study of the Civil Law*. Bryce had argued in his inaugural lecture as Regius Professor of Civil Law, University of Oxford, that the study of Roman law would cultivate a young mind – introduce it to vital and pertinent antecedents to European history as well as to classical philology and ethics – and provide a sure grounding for professional legal study. Specifically, in regard to the latter purpose, the study of Justinian's Digest would provide excellent training in understanding key organizing legal principles and how systematic deduction from them worked.[208]

In essence, Bryce wanted to turn Roman law into a propaedeutic for English law. He was largely updating in 1871 an argument that Maine had originally made in 1856. Maine had urged the acceptance of the Roman law as the grammar for all advanced legal systems.[209] In truncated form the Lord Chief Justice made the same point forty years later in "The Bar As a Profession."

That Holmes did not buy into this project is surprising. He certainly understood the main problem that Bryce sought to address: the chaos of the cases and statutes. English law was not a system but a huge mass of isolated rules. As Bryce noted, some of these rules were laid down without a sufficient statement of supporting reasons. Other rules judges deduced from principles they dimly understood. Others statutes created; these rules ended up traversing the established rules in irregular ways.

207 *Id.*

208 James Bryce, The Academical Study of the Civil Law 10–11 (1871).

209 *See* H. J. S. Maine, *Roman Law and Legal Education*, *in* Cambridge Essays 1–29 (Contributed by Members of the University, 1856); *see also* Peter Stein, *Maine and Legal Education*, *in* The Victorian Achievement of Sir Henry Maine: A Centennial Reappraisal 195–208 (Alan Diamond ed., 1991); William Twining, *Maine and Legal Education: A Comment*, *in* The Victorian Achievement of Sir Henry Maine 209–16 (Alan Diamond ed., 1991).

In short, Bryce concluded his diagnosis by observing that Acts of Parliament paid no respect to the symmetry, "such as it was," of the common law.[210]

But Holmes did not agree with Bryce's main argument. In many respects following Friedrich Karl von Savigny, Bryce asserted that in the Roman law one found the "forms" – the legal principles, their grounds, and an implicated style of systematic reasoning – needed to bring increased order and symmetry to the operative law of Englishmen. "Englishmen" for Bryce included Americans.[211] The surprise we feel at Holmes's disagreement arises from the many indicators that he possessed a passion for philosophical understanding. That is to say, one would expect a person intellectually constituted as Holmes to support the effort to inject into the common law the Roman's jurisprudential sophistication. Bryce argued that many of the defects of the common law arose from "a want of that feeling for the symmetry and simplicity of the law which a scientific conception of it would be certain to produce in the profession."[212]

But Holmes resists all such reform efforts. He thinks Bryce's idea of including the study of Roman law in the professional curriculum unworkable in the United States. Why? Because in the US, unlike in England, the problem is not aversion to general principles but the temptation to be too easily content with them. Nor is what Bryce called "the case lawyer" a problem for the American bar. "Our practice," says Holmes, "is too general and unspecialized for that."[213]

Holmes then makes a distinction that would surface again in his "The Bar As a Profession." It is between the practitioner and the jurist. He notes that the practice of "the common law begins and ends with the solution of the particular case." The best training to help students learn how to resolve the particular case "is found in our moot courts and the offices of older lawyers." For those students who wish to "study law philosophically from the beginning[,]" Holmes would direct them to Maine and to Austin, to English legal history, before sending them to the great Roman jurist Ulpian. At any event, reading Ulpian would undoubtedly be useful but only "after our own [law] is pretty well mastered."[214]

We should take a moment to compare this statement to Holmes's comment on the state of Harvard's law school. There he criticized the complete lack, at least before 1870, of formal tests to determine if a student understood the essentials before being unleashed on an unsuspecting world. He also thought a law school worthy of its name should offer the right kind of facilities for those "real students" who wanted to do more than learn the rudiments of practice. A little less than a year later, he is objecting to Bryce's proposal to include the study of Roman jurisprudence as part of the professional curriculum in law. He thinks it won't work in the US because the

[210] Bryce, The Academical Study of the Civil Law, *supra* note 208, at 20–22.
[211] *Id.* at 21.
[212] *Id.* at 35.
[213] Oliver Wendell Holmes, *Review of* The Academical Study of the Civil Law, *in* I CW 250–51.
[214] *Id.*

problem with US practitioners is what he calls elsewhere "glittering generalities," and not that they are walking "case lawyers," filled with facts and rules but having no hint that a principle may be hovering on the horizon. US lawyers in contrast loved to toss around principles.

Read in a certain light, Holmes's review of *The Academical Study of the Civil Law* fits well with the stereotypical English and American view that legal study ought mainly to be practical, that is, it ought to prepare the law student for assisting others in society with their concrete legal problems. We find this same point of view superbly updated and articulated in Brian Simpson's *Invitation to Law*. In his review, Holmes says nothing about sequenced courses and graded examinations, or viewing law as a discipline worthy of sustained inquiry. In terms of teaching the purely practical aspects of law, what existing schools such as Harvard's had been doing – running moot courts – was on the right track. That training in presentation and disputation, plus a brief turn at the office of an experienced lawyer (as Holmes had studied in the law office of Robert Morse),[215] would adequately prepare students for the realities of practice.

The perceived inconsistencies in these two early pieces are mainly due, I think, to their differing emphases given their different contexts. We must also factor in Holmes's professional inexperience. He had, as of 1871, only been engaged in the practice of law and in serious legal scholarship for just a few years. He was still learning and thinking. Beyond any discrepancies of opinion, what stands out are two important points. First, legal education should teach law students how to resolve concrete cases. In that respect, it needed to be practical. Second, he insisted that the Roman law did not have the wherewithal to provide the necessary grounds or principles for a proper philosophical grasp of American law.[216] The "forms" that would organize one's understanding of American law could not be imported from a foreign jurisprudence. He had not yet formulated his mature argument that these "forms" must arise from intense, self-reflexive historical study, sustained philosophical analysis, and well-honed, dedicated inquiry into present circumstances, but he was headed in that direction. Again, the proper study of American law is American law.

Between his review of Bryce's *The Academical Study of the Civil Law* and "The Bar As a Profession," Holmes made a number of observations regarding the purposes

[215] Howe, *supra* note 80, at 204.

[216] He reiterates this same opposition again in 1873. *See* Oliver Wendell Holmes, *Review of* Outlines of Roman Law, *in* I CW 321 ("We have several times expressed our opinion that to study the Institutes is not the easiest way to learn either law or jurisprudence, and that any one intending to be a lawyer ought to acquire the habit of thinking in terms of his own system before dallying with another."); Oliver Wendell Holmes, *Note Regarding the* American Civil Law Journal, *in* I CW 322–23 ("We have repeatedly expressed our conviction that the Roman law, as a philosophical *result*, is vastly inferior to modern law. . . . But for the philosophy of law the "Fragment on Government" [by Bentham] and Austin's lecture are worth the whole *Corpus*.") (emphasis in original).

or best modes of legal study. "The Use of Law Schools" stands out in almost full relief for its concentration on the topic. But in many other writings Holmes made many interesting off-hand comments. Yet through them all he remained firm in his opinion that neither the Roman law, nor the habit of mind it inculcated, served as a fit tool for the philosophical comprehension of American law.

He did, though, agree with Bryce that the chaos of the common law had to be superseded. We saw in Part I how he attempted to work out through the categorization of duties his suggestion in "Codes, and the Arrangement of Law" that a "well-arranged body of law would train the mind of the student to sound legal thought and remove obstacles from his path which he now only overcomes after years of experience and reflection."[217] If what results after "years of experience and reflection" is greater confidence, greater understanding, more sophisticated means of employing the *techne* of the law, then we are only a few shorts steps away from saying the journeyman has grown in professional judgment.

Holmes perceived the categorization he developed in "Codes, and the Arrangement of Law," and refined in subsequent articles, to have a pedagogical use because it arose from close attention to the dynamics of the common law, not from the *elegantia juris* of the Roman. It pointed up what seems to have been the main objective of practitioners-cum-scholars like Langdell and Holmes when they broached the topic of legal education: to reduce the amount of time a budding lawyer needed to develop a working sense of the common law as an operative system. In other words, how could the professional learning curve be shortened? And more pertinently: how could it be shortened in such a way so as not to retard the emergence of law as a well-founded discipline?[218]

But we must also keep in mind that Holmes's opposition to the Roman law's pedagogical uses arose too from his deeper opposition to the imposition onto legal issues of so-called transcendent principles. The problem with practitioners in the United States was their too easy, too glib use of abstractions and generalities. They loved their natural law talk. Using Roman law as a propaedeutic would only further enable this intellectually debilitating propensity. Yet Roman law had its edificatory

[217] Oliver Wendell Holmes, *Codes, and the Arrangement of the Law, in* I CW 214.

[218] Gerald B. Finch in his inaugural lecture at Queens' College, Cambridge, recounts that during his stay in Boston during the spring of 1885,

> Mr. Sidney Bartlett, the Father of the Massachusetts Bar, told me that the three years' course at Harvard was equal to seven years' work in an office. Mr. Justice Oliver Wendell Holmes and Dr. Eliot, President of the University, spoke to the same effect. Dr. Eliot related with pardonable pride that at a recent dinner of old Harvard men a prominent young advocate had declared that when a student he had often heard it said that the course at Harvard was equal to ten years' actual work; that he was then incredulous; but that after being in practice for ten years he came to know it as a fact.

GERARD B. FINCH, LEGAL EDUCATION, ITS AIM AND METHOD 10–11 (1885); *see also* John Tyler, *Methods of Legal Education*, 34 ALBANY L.J. 84–85 (1887) (praising Cambridge University for establishing a law school that looks to America and not the Continent for its model).

uses. For lawyers already well versed in the common law the study of the Roman might prove a useful clarificatory tool. Holmes explained this point in his "Misunderstandings of the Civil Law."

He began by reiterating what he had said in his review of Bryce's book, that the study of the civil law ill-served the beginner who intended to "practice at a common-law bar." It would, he averred, encourage a dangerous reliance on "glittering generalities." It would also foster "distaste for the exhaustive analysis of a particular case, with which the common law begins and ends."[219] And then he adds this remark supporting the notion that for seasoned lawyers study of the Roman law has something to offer.

> Nobody doubts, nowadays, that a large part at least of the common law is founded on that of Rome. Bracton made no secret of what he owed to it. But Coke, when he used Bracton, did not go behind the text; and Coke is the modern starting-point. The consequence must be that in other cases, as in this, doctrines get swerved from their true meaning and extent, because we do not remember their history and origin. A rule of law that has been gradually developed can only be understood by knowing the course of its development; and that is more or less known by good lawyers, if the rule took its rise in England. So far as our jurisprudence reaches back to an earlier date, these are the same reasons for tracing it to its source.[220]

We have in this passage one of Holmes's first statements on the power of honed historical study to "un-swerve" the past and to clarify legal doctrine as it exists in the present. He also brings into his critique the idea of learning to trace the development of a legal rule, or to recognize the slow articulation of a legal doctrine, through a line of cases. One can only understand the "meaning and extent" of a rule of law "by knowing the course of its development." That, he says, is more or less known by "good lawyers."[221] It bears keeping in mind that "Misunderstandings of the Civil Law" appeared in the *American Law Review* only a short time after his review of the first edition of Langdell's casebook. As mentioned earlier, in that piece he praised Langdell's decision to order the cases chronologically. "Tracing the growth of a doctrine in this way not only fixes it in the mind, but shows its meaning, extent, and limits as nothing else can."[222]

In Part IV, Section 13, we provided a lengthy analysis of Holmes's restatement in "The Use of Law Schools" of the Harvard Law School professors' pedagogical creed. We saw that Holmes restated the creed to include the all-important idea of perspective. It was perspective that organized and proportioned the whole. In a previous section of this part we also analyzed at length Holmes's 1880 criticisms of Langdell, that he was too much the "legal theologian," more concerned to show that "conclusions from them hang together" than to understand the postulates themselves.

[219] Oliver Wendell Holmes, *Misunderstandings of the Civil Law*, *in* I CW 260.
[220] *Id.*
[221] *Id.*
[222] Oliver Wendell Holmes, *Review of* A Selection of Cases on the Law of Contracts, *in* I CW 243.

Holmes prefaced these criticisms with the observation that Langdell labored under the ideal of *elegantia juris*. We might also recall at this point that Langdell himself described his work as comparable to that of the Roman jurisconsult. It thus becomes unmistakably clear that Holmes's criticisms of Langdell fit into his broader critique of his contemporaries' constant efforts to superimpose upon the common law, or, more specifically, the American common law, a grand conceptual design, whether arising from Roman law or so-called Natural Law. He opposed the enjoinder that students of the common law use Roman law or Natural Law as the necessary comparator, the essential magic mirror, to bring certain lessons home. Such grand conceptual designs or extraneous standards ill-suited the dynamism of a society that sought to remove gratuitous social barriers and allow inborn gifts to fructify. Roman law, as did history more broadly, might serve as an important resource for understanding the shape of operative law but not for developing a distinctive American jurisprudence. To treat Roman law as a propaedeutic would stifle the nascent and essential habit of inquiry upon which a well-functioning legal regime and a vital jurisprudence would depend.[223]

We come back now to Holmes's comment in "The Bar As a Profession" that questioned the importance of a university education to the aspiring lawyer. It bears repeating that he believed it "very useful and very important to a man as a man" but not to the "lawyer as a lawyer."[224] It is a good question whether this statement represents Holmes's repudiation of the position he seems to have taken in his 1870 comment on Harvard Law School. But if we look more closely at the comment we can see that Holmes has been more or less consistent in his relative emphases:

> The learning and ability of these gentlemen [the faculty] warrant us in predicting that their labors will make Harvard Law School what it ought to be. What it ought to be we find well expressed in a late report of Dr. E. O. Haven to the trustees of Northwestern University: "The object of a law department is not precisely and only to educate young men to be practicing lawyers, though it will be largely used for that purpose. It is to furnish all students who desire it the same facilities to investigate the science of human law, theoretically, historically, and thoroughly, as they have to investigate mathematics, natural sciences, or any other branch of thought."[225]

[223] Legal historian M. H. Hoeflich has consistently argued that the Roman and civil law more profoundly affected American law in its formative period than has been realized. To what extent it did, and to what extent legal thinkers at the time thought it ought to, are questions that require careful differentiation. *See* M. H. Hoeflich, *Roman and Civil Law in American Legal Education and Research Prior to 1930: A Preliminary Survey*, 1984 U. Ill. L. Rev. 719 (1984); M. H. Hoeflich, *Law & Geometry: Legal Science from Leibniz to Langdell*, 30 Am. J. Legal. Hist. 95 (1986); M. H. Hoeflich, *The Americanization of British Legal Education in the Nineteenth Century*, 8 J. Legal Hist. 244 (1987); M. H. Hoeflich, Roman & Civil Law and the Development of Anglo-American Jurisprudence in the Nineteenth Century (1997).

[224] Holmes, *supra* note 187, at 386.

[225] [Holmes], *Note, supra* note 203.

We can't say how the young Holmes understood the implications of Mr. Haven's educational ideal as stated, but the mature Holmes still maintains that the primary purpose of a law school is to educate lawyers to practice law. He thus demurs from the Lord Chief Justice's stress on the preliminary necessity of a university education.

The reasons he gives for demurring are worth stating. They reflect many of the social and economic realities of American life, Holmes's own disinclination to correlate a specific educational path with a specific ideal of human attainment, and his own developed opinion that law itself, rightly studied, opened the vistas of the mind as well as any other branch of human knowledge.

Holmes begins by reiterating what he said in "Just the Boy Wanted," that the practice of law involves a good amount of reading. Having some ability to get around the written word certainly helped, but he added, "a man may sweep juries before him, command the attention of judges, counsel sagely in great affairs, or be a leader in any senate of the country with nothing of the scholarly about him."[226] He makes this observation, "not to make light of the good of going to college," but to encourage those many young men who might think the highest reaches of a legal career foreclosed to them because they lacked the wherewithal to attend. He then says: "I have had letters from young men beset with this doubt, and always have told them that it is no ground for despair."[227]

In Holmes's words of encouragement to the young men who took it upon themselves to write to the associate justice of the Massachusetts Supreme Judicial Court with the famous name we glimpse, I think, Holmes's faith in the distinctive virtues of American life. He lived in a society that in its dominant cultural self-understanding placed a premium on a person's inborn qualities. Later generations have certainly contested that self-understanding or pointed out its many hypocrisies. But there it is, all the same. We don't typically associate kind gestures with Holmes. And maybe he didn't encourage those anxious, confused young men out of kindness. Then again, maybe he did.

The lack of a college education also did not carry the same consequence as it might in England – among the barristers at least – because the manner in which law was taught in the US law schools partly made up for the deficiency. Law teaching in the US also differed in important respects from that which prevailed in the UK. "I think all the lawyers I know hereabouts [Boston] would agree that the place for a young man to study law is a law school, not a lawyer's office."[228]

What did a law school provide that a lawyer's office did not? From Holmes's perspective, given his experience with and focus on Harvard, it provided both an educational method and a setting for the development of forensic skills. I think he still believed such student tournaments as moot courts quite useful. He also still

[226] Holmes, *supra* note 187 at 386–87.
[227] *Id.* at 387.
[228] *Id.*

thought that a short stint at a lawyer's office after graduation "to see how things are done" would provide sufficient exposure to the essentials of practice to "perhaps to get a little of the usual law student's conceit rubbed off."[229]

Practice in Massachusetts, he said, is very easily understood. What requires time "is not to learn the routine of clerk's offices or what a writ looks like, but to master profoundly and in detail the great body of the law." Law school provided a much better venue for such learning than did the "listless solitude of the office." No less vital were "the companionship and intellectual excitement" often found in a law school. For those who lacked a university education, this companionship would "take the place ... of the experience which they missed at an earlier stage."[230] In these words, Holmes clues us in that for him certain qualitative, formative experiences stand out in one's life because of how they have structured interests and defined aims. The law school at Cambridge fostered intellectual excitement, a "catching enthusiasm." Law as much as Emerson's grand orations had the capacity to catalyze the philosophical ferment in one's mind. From Holmes's mature standpoint, the way law was taught at Harvard had the capacity to link together two overriding pedagogical goals. It prepared the student for practice. It also enlarged and honed the mind, not through the weighty shibboleths of truth and justice, but, paradoxically, through meticulous study and cautious thinking.

Law rightly understood and rightly taught and studied formed its own pathway to the higher reaches of the mind. As Holmes eloquently put it: "The law may lead to high things those who stay in it as well as those who pass beyond but not above it to other forms of command."[231]

He then takes direct aim at the Lord Chief Justice's paean to the glories of the Roman law. "In a law school the lines of study are marked out, of course, and the student will not be likely to find much time for the Roman law. If he studies that, it will be in his months of waiting for clients. But in spite of the very great authority by which the study of it is recommended I have never been able to believe that it has the value so often supposed."[232]

As to be expected, the Lord Chief Justice took umbrage at this slight. In his "Rejoinder" he makes special mention of his "surprise" – read: incredulity and disbelief – that Holmes should so deprecate both university training and study of the Corpus Juris. The dispute had not yet come to issue but lines were being drawn. Ever the consummate barrister, the Lord Chief Justice first qualified what "Roman law" meant – the Corpus Juris included German emendations and glosses – and then pointed out how much Holmes's illustrious predecessors (Marshall, Story, Kent) owed to the study of Roman law. He granted that the American law schools

229 *Id.*
230 *Id.*
231 *Id.* at 389.
232 *Id.* at 387.

had surpassed the British; that superiority consisted in its "systematic teaching of the historical and scientific aspects of law before the actual, practical, workaday law is dealt with."[233]

He did not see how it would be possible to teach law historically and systematically, or even comparatively, without recurring to the Roman law. He registered a few more disagreements, all in various ways reemphasizing his fundamental position that the Roman law was still a "living voice," but drew to a close in good lawyerly fashion. He brought down the weight of contemporary expertise on Holmes's head. He cited the 1894 Gresham Commission report, a report that included curriculum recommendations for the establishment of a law faculty at the newly reconstituted University of London. All the distinguished men that the Commission examined, including the esteemed James Bryce and even "Professor E. H. Emmott of the Johns Hopkins University, Baltimore[,]" were "emphatic as to the importance of the study of Roman law in any high system of legal training."[234]

It comes as no surprise that a quick look at the Gresham Commission report does not indicate that those who testified in favor of a law faculty expressed the same fervor for the study of Roman law as the Lord Chief Justice.[235] In its section on "Law" it says nothing at all about the testimony that the Commission received. But, then again, a careful rereading of the Lord Chief Justice's "Rejoinder" reveals that it doesn't actually say that the report itself either strongly endorsed the study of Roman law, or that the testimony to which he refers is found in it. It only states that a slough of prominent persons whose opinion the Commission solicited so advocated. Clever. The Lord Chief Justice made his point in such an artful way that even with the most careful reading of the report it could not be refuted without the transcripts of what the identified examinees said. And even then what counts as "emphatic" is not at all clear-cut.

Holmes, of course, was no fool. His surreply, entitled "Postscript," was polite but forceful. He clarified that he did not undervalue the moral or even intellectual advantage of a university education. He was only evaluating its "importance for what I may call a fighting success."[236] In that respect, university education took second place to solid professional training. To appreciate why Holmes refused to budge on this point takes us to the fundamentals of Holmes's thought. Let's turn back for a moment to his "The Bar As a Profession." He states his basic beliefs in two short paragraphs. They total three sentences. These paragraphs immediately followed his confession of skepticism regarding the pedagogical value of the Roman law that "surprised" the Lord Chief Justice. He, in turn, barely addresses these two short paragraphs. He only alludes to the second when he politely suggests that the

[233] Lord Chief Justice, A *Rejoinder*, *supra* note 187, at 389.

[234] *Id.*

[235] *See* Gresham University Commission, The Report of the Commissioners xlii–xlvi (1894).

[236] Holmes, A *Postscript*, *supra* note 187, at 390.

"learned judge" open his ears to the Roman law's "living voice." Otherwise, he ignores them. He probably did not quite comprehend them. I doubt anyone who read them at the time actually understood fully what Holmes was driving at.

> A system of law at any time is the resultant of present needs and present notions of what is wise and right on the one hand, and, on the other, of rules handed down from earlier states of society and embodying needs and notions which more or less have passed away.
>
> To get to the bottom of any system, therefore, a good deal of history has to be studied, and this is true of the law under which we live now. But our law has reached broader and more profound generalizations than the Roman law, and at the same time far surpasses it in the detail with which it has been worked out.[237]

Holmes follows these two paragraphs with this observation: "One who is master of our own will master any civilized body of law with ease."[238]

I fear few today could claim mastery in the same manner as Holmes. I certainly cannot. With much tentativeness, then, I suggest a possible reading of these two key paragraphs fully aware that, compared to Holmes's, my frame of reference in regard to the common law is deficient and in respect to the Roman nonexistent.

Let's begin with the word "resultant." I am aware of two other times that Holmes used that same word. In the lectures on "Agency" that he gave at the Law School while still a professor, subsequently published in the *Harvard Law Review* as a two-part article, Holmes ended the introduction by saying: "Finally I shall give my reasons for thinking that the whole outline of the law is the *resultant* of a conflict at every point between logic and good sense – the one striving to work fiction out to consistent results, the other restraining and at last overcoming that effort when the results become too manifestly unjust."[239] In his valedictory address to the Middlesex Bar Association, before heading to Washington to assume the post of associate justice of the United States Supreme Court, he provided in a single paragraph of average length a summation of his life's work that included this sentence: "I have considered the present tendencies and desires of society and have tried to realize that its different portions want different things, and that my business was to express not my personal wish, but the *resultant*, as nearly as I could guess, of the pressure of the past and the conflicting wills of the present."[240]

By the late nineteenth century, the word resultant had two meanings, one nontechnical, the other technical. The nontechnical – the consequence or result – is the older meaning. The technical meaning, "a force, velocity, or other vector quantity that is equivalent to the combined effect of two or more component vectors

[237] Holmes, *The Bar As a Profession*, *supra* note 187, at 387.
[238] *Id.*
[239] Oliver Wendell Holmes, *Agency I*, *in* III CW 341 (emphasis added).
[240] Oliver Wendell Holmes, *Address to Middlesex Bar Association*, *in* III CW 536 (emphasis added).

TABLE 1 *Resultants in time*

Past	Moment in Time	Present
Rules Embodying Past Needs		Present Needs (social, economic, cultural, political, etc.)
Rules Embodying Past Notions		Present Notions (current conceptions of what is wise and right)
No longer vital, have passed away		Still vital or becoming vital, strong
Logic (the persistent valuations and thought patterns of existing rules)		Good Sense (the opposition to persistent valuations and thought patterns in favor of alternate valuations and thought patterns)
Pressure of the Past		Conflicting Wills of the Present
	Resultant	

acting at the same point[,]" is the more recent.[241] It originated in the nineteenth century. Without pushing the point too hard, I think we have in Holmes's use of resultant in 1896 another way of pointing to his earlier insight that, at times, 1+1=3. That is to say, the upshot of combined social needs and notions may lead in unanticipated directions and to new articulated legal forms (see Table 1).

Between his initial use of "resultant" in the early 1880s and his use in 1896 and later, I suspect Holmes kept searching for the right combination and ordering of ideas to express the multidimensionality of American law. And also to express his view that any single legal rule or doctrine, substantive or procedural, was the resultant, as was a vector, of certain culturally operative forces acting at a specific point and moving in a specific direction. These culturally operative forces were both positive (seeking a certain end) and negative (passively resilient or passively indifferent to other existing states of affairs). Without dimensionality it would be impossible to determine the prevailing direction(s) of legal action. One would have only a scalar quantity, not a vector, or, in more complicated (contested) matters, what we now call a tensor.

The dimensions themselves had to provide the reference by which the legal rules could both be understood in their function (context) and in their development (sequence). But those dimensions would only converge into a lifelike 3D through the directed will or attention of present purpose. Perspective took on greater form and definition, had a greater orienting capacity, when deliberately tied to purpose. It is at this point that we see the identifiable instrumental element in Holmes's thought. Subsequent generations of legal scholars latched onto this emphasis.[242]

[241] *Resultant*, THE AMERICAN HERITAGE DICTIONARY OF THE ENGLISH LANGUAGE (5th ed., 2011).

[242] *See* ROBERT SAMUEL SUMMERS, INSTRUMENTALISM AND AMERICAN LEGAL THEORY 19–38, 60–80 (1982).

But by itself it lacked sustainability. Present notions of what is just, or wise, or right – using these words with the recognition that they do not all align – added depth to function and lineage. Such self-conscious purposive activity introduced into the active legal mind a new plane of verisimilitude, it made possible a different ordering and proportionality than what had been available through exclusively analytical or historical terms.

Or, in the language of Part IV, it led to another way of looking at the bad man.

Still another way of saying the same thing is to say that Holmes sought to vivify legal practice. But to vivify the practice in an era when cultural foundations are disintegrating, or, less strongly, are evidently unstable, required two things. First, one had to deliberately employ the legal event as an operative concept. It served as the fundamental unit needed for projecting a nuanced understanding of the law that circumscribes present circumstances. Second, in terms of philosophical analysis, the concept of a legal duty played the same constitutive role. These two intertwined concepts – the legal event and the legal duty – together created a sufficiently strong base to integrate further investigations into the value and validity of existing law. From another angle, however, these same intertwined concepts provided the foundation needed for a three-dimensional view of law.

It might seem at this point in the discussion that Holmes is merely, in language unique to him, redescribing the role of tradition in classic conservative thought. Under this reading, the primary beginning point of legal education is to presume that existing legal rules had a good and sufficient reason for their existence. Any proposed changes must be put forth gingerly. The Past effectively governs the Present. The focus for Holmes, though, is not on abiding by time-honored truths, or searching through cultural debris for the holy grails of goodness and beauty. Remember, the present has a right to govern itself as much as it can.

Holmes looked to perform an essentially godlike providential task, to control both past and present, by redirecting the motive force of each. One must invariably occupy an elevated standpoint to perform such a task. Holmes believed he found that standpoint through his disciplined focus on the means and modes by which the use of power had been justified and developed in the common law. It is my own feeling that in this respect he was working out his idea of self-devotion or Emerson's notion of self-reliance in the context of American legal institutions. The primary text thus becomes this sentence of Emerson's: "We do not yet see that virtue is Height, and that a man or a company of men plastic and permeable to principles, by the law of nature must overpower and ride all cities, nations, kings, rich men, poets, who are not."[243] All the rest, as Justice Cardozo said in another context, is commentary.[244]

[243] Ralph Waldo Emerson, *Self-Reliance*, *in* Essays and Poems by Ralph Waldo Emerson 125–26 (Peter Norberg ed., 2004).

[244] Benjamin N. Cardozo, *Introduction: Mr. Justice Holmes*, *in* Mr. Justice Holmes 3 (Felix Frankfurter ed., 1931).

Holmes's second paragraph made what the Lord Chief Justice took as a bold claim. Compared to the Roman, the common law had "reached broader and more profound generalizations."[245] A few paragraphs later we learn that broader and more profound generalizations belong to the study of jurisprudence. That study is distinct from, though related to, the study needed to learn how to practice effectively. The difference between the practitioner and the jurist is a matter of degrees. At bottom, it is similar to how Holmes described the difference between gossip and philosophy. It "lies only in one's way of taking a fact."[246] It lies in the range and depth of perceptions brought to bear on the law that is learned and the issues lawyers use that learning to resolve.

Holmes explains that jurisprudence, "when properly taught," means

> the broadest generalizations of the principles and the deepest analysis of the ideas at the bottom of an actual system. *It is the same process, carried further, by which the law is carried out from particular cases into general rules.* A young man who has understood John Austin's tedious and often mistaken book has taken a real step forward, while Sir Henry Maine makes him feel as if his whole road were strewn with diamonds.[247]

To clarify these comments it helps to connect them with what Holmes had said before in "The Use of Law Schools" and what he would say the following year in "The Path of the Law." In "The Use of Law Schools," Holmes had pointed out that Story's "simple philosophizing has ceased to satisfy men's minds." The fault did not lie with Story. "I think it might be said with safety," Holmes continued,

> that no man of his or the succeeding generation could have stated the law in a form that deserved to abide, because neither his nor the succeeding generation possessed or could have possessed the historical knowledge, had made or could have made the analyses of principles, which are necessary before the cardinal doctrines of the law can be known and understood in their precise contours and in their innermost meanings.[248]

These words are forceful. They imply that Holmes's generation has found the necessary formula for restatement. Maine and Austin stand for methods of thought (historical and analytical) developed and improved in the nineteenth century. The jurisprudence that results is a jurisprudence that envisions the common law as a uniquely meaningful cultural creation. It is uniquely meaningful because its enlightened practice encourages its practitioners – law students, lawyers, judges,

[245] Holmes, *supra* note 187, at 387. This was not a new position for Holmes. In *The Common Law* he wrote: "Hence I say that it is important to show that a far more developed, more rational, and mightier body of law than the Roman gives no sanction to either premise or conclusion as held by Kant and his successors." Holmes, *supra* note 10, at 222.

[246] Holmes, *supra* note 187, at 389.

[247] *Id.* at 388 (emphasis added).

[248] Holmes, *supra* note 103, at 477.

and legal scholars – to think carefully about law as a discipline of power. It leads to the realization that law, understood as a certain type of power functioning as the public force or legal authority, exists in a predominantly differentiated form in a common law jurisdiction. But it comes together or rallies when needed at the point of effective application. These movements between differentiation and integration are the distinctive type of cultural flux that the operative concepts of the legal event and the legal duty, working together, are meant to capture. The notion of present purpose describes the standpoint from which a shared apperceptive judgment binds together legal facts with legal consequences.

Early in "The Path of the Law" Holmes returns to this idea that one and the same "process" is at work when a lawyer or a judge seeks to determine the general rule from particular cases as when the jurist seeks to extract from an actual legal system its deepest principles and broadest generalizations. Holmes argued that the "most important and pretty nearly the whole meaning of every new effort of legal thought is to make these prophecies [the cases upon which the axe would fall] more precise, and to generalize them into a thoroughly connected system." He then elaborates:

> The *process* is one, from a lawyer's statement of a case, eliminating as it does all the dramatic elements with which his client's story has clothed it, and retaining only the facts of legal import, up to the final analyses and abstract universals of theoretic jurisprudence.[249]

As Holmes is not always clear and precise, I think it best *not* to view this "process" as some version of the large stepladder we described earlier in this part, either standing upright or laying on its side. The key words are not "analysis" or "abstraction." Using terms that the nineteenth-century English polymath William Whewell made prominent, perhaps the best descriptors are "colligation" and "consilience." The key intellectual ability is the ability to correlate (muster) and to find new correlations (assemblages or orderings).

Frederic Kellogg has noted the similarities in logical method between the position that Whewell advocated and Holmes's mature opinion.[250] Kellogg sees the "process" that Holmes described in "The Path of the Law" as reflecting an original philosophical and logical stance, what he calls social inductivism.[251] Kellogg's insight is an important one because he notes, as we do here, that Holmes saw the "process" as a continuum, one that Kellogg calls, following John Dewey, the continuum of inquiry. That is to say, the practitioner and the jurist are engaged – as are others directly participating in the finding and making of the law – in the same "process" though at different points and for slightly different reasons. We would add to Kellogg's insight the corollary of scale. It is not just that the practitioner and the

[249] Holmes, *supra* note 1, at 391 (emphasis added).
[250] Kellogg, Legal Logic, *supra* note 73, at 48–53.
[251] *Id.* at 18.

jurist, as Holmes portrays them, operate at different points in the continuum of inquiry; they do so at different levels of specificity that reference distinct assemblages or colligations of events.

Part of the job of pedagogy, then, is to induct law students into this "process" and show them how it works at different levels. Because Holmes sees a unified "process" at work he states with the utmost confidence in "The Bar As a Profession" that "our law has reached broader and more profound generalizations than the Roman[.]" The Roman law is not a "living voice" for those well versed in American life. The "process" of eliciting and inquiring into and testing social values that marks the common law has had greater and more profound effect when working in the American context than in the English.

Though Holmes does not come right out and say it, it appears that for him the efficacy of the common law as a method of proving the use of the public force took on a richer, more extensive meaning in the tumult of American life than it did elsewhere. Perhaps he felt the English social and class divisions and the corresponding sensibilities more strongly constricted that "process" than did the constraints it faced in the United States. The democratic ethos prevalent in the US permitted more and varied interests, past and present, to be included, accounted, and reckoned.

Holmes concludes his exchange with the Lord Chief Justice by calling upon his own group of witnesses. The men who allegedly testified to the Gresham Commission in support of the Roman law as a pedagogical tool found their opposing compurgators in the great English scholars Frederick Pollock and Frederic Maitland. Holmes also called upon his own not inconsiderable scholarship in support. But as lawyers often do he emphasized those aspects of the debate – in this case, Roman influences in the history of the common law – which he knew played to his strengths and, correspondingly, to his opponent's weaknesses.

3 THE LEGAL PROFESSION AND LAW

i *Law is for Lawyers Redux*

A striking image on the dark blue cover of Brian Simpson's *Invitation to Law* draws the eye. It is a reproduction of French artist Jean-Louis Forain's 1909 oil painting *A Court Scene*. Slightly off-center, the defendant stands elevated behind a wooden partition. The top of her bent head forms the tip of an imaginary triangle that puts her in the focal point. The painting's ambience is murky, the tones unwelcoming. The woman wears a heavy, dark rust-orange dress, long-sleeved. Head bowed, shoulders hunched, arms drawn in and pulled up, her face folds into the dusky kerchief her hands had nervously clutched just minutes before. The news is bad. Sobs wrack within.

The poignancy arises not so much from her evident distress as from the reactions of those arrayed around her. To her right sits an older woman, also behind the wooden partition, whose hands rest on its top, one with palm flat down, the other's fingers clinging to a white handkerchief. She is probably the defendant's aunt or mother. The partition she grasped initially to steady herself now bears her lifeless hands as she absorbs misfortune's latest blow. Her dimly lit face is tight, distraught, resigned, cast in pale, the light emitting from an unseen part of the courtroom, most likely where sits the judge. The three men sitting on the other side of the divider, in front of her and her sobbing niece or daughter, presumably lawyers, also appear to be suffering intensely, not from physical pain or disastrous news but from boredom. Each one slouches or slumps indifferently, either across the table next to which they sit or behind it, in a chair; they look at neither the woman nor her mother nor the judge nor the viewer of the painting. Eyes unfocused, minds adrift, they are proverbially bored to tears as they wait for their cases to be called.

I wish I could ask Simpson whether he chose the cover, and if so why, or whether the publisher picked it. I wondered about it because how the artist depicts this particular courtroom scene renders, visibly and unforgettably, those currents of distrust and derision that often influence how the public perceives its lawyers.

Simpson certainly understood the distrust lawyers generated among members of the public. He entitles one section of his book, "Social Workers or Social Parasites?," and lists there nine complaints frequently lodged against members of the bar.[252] But, interestingly, he measures those complaints against ideals also interwoven into the very fabric of the profession, the cardinal thread being the rule of law. Simpson's position is that society needs its lawyers, just as it needs its plumbers, sailors, and surgeons, since

> [a]s the people most directly involved in operating the legal system they are in a good position to make the reality of that system conform to the ideal; this is particularly true of judges. They also, through the practice of law, help to make the law, and therefore the rule of law, actually available to people. There is no point having the rule of law but not letting people get at it.[253]

Simpson has no problem admitting the profession has its share of misshapen tomatoes. "There are crooked lawyers, just as there are crooked accountants,

[252] These are that (1) lawyers create the legal technicalities that make their existence necessary; (2) they pursue their own interests at the expense of their clients; (3) they charge excessive fees because they are greedy; (4) they are two-faced, selling justice but perpetuating injustice (inequality); (5) they are pettifoggers, that is they cavil and quibble to gain advantage, not to illuminate the law or maintain good faith positions; (6) they treat truth with contempt by defending the guilty and prosecuting meritless claims; (7) they use their privileged profession to ride herd over the common decencies of everyday life; (8) they are excessively conservative and resistant to change; and (9) they profit from other people's misfortunes. A. W. B. Simpson, Invitation to Law 165–66 (1988).

[253] *Id.* at 45, 142–44.

cowardly soldiers and promiscuous priests." To emphasize the point he recounts a harrowing experience with a sadistic Italian doctor.[254]

The gist is that lawyers are probably no more venial than other people. They are tasked, however, with an unusually difficult mandate: to play a special role in fostering the rule of law. Given Simpson's willingness to acknowledge the profession's many failings and yet praise the enduring strength of its leading ideal, I found the book's cover mystifying. I wonder if he approved as cover art the use of a painting so derisive of lawyers for a book entitled, without any smoldering sarcasm as far as I could tell, *Invitation to Law*.

That invitation is to join a group of people who have a special relationship with the law. Law is for lawyers. We return to Simpson's notion of the primary way lawyers think about law: it "is to tell *them* how to behave in settling what people's rights and duties and obligations and liabilities are." He continues: "The elaborate body of general principles, the more detailed rules and exceptions to them, the definitions of terms and significant distinctions, the practices and conceptions which to lawyers constitute the law, are there to provide lawyers with ways of analyzing problems, and ways of rationally justifying decisions as to what is to be done by courts about them."[255]

Taking apart Simpson's conception that "law is for lawyers" reveals two components. One component is the idea that law comprises directions for the inquiring professional. In keeping with Simpson's terminology, when matters are unsettled, law tells the lawyer, upon inquiry, what to do to settle the problem according to preexisting, legally defined categories – "rights and duties and obligations and liabilities." These preexisting legally defined categories Simpson also describes as "the professional legal tradition."[256] We subsequently learn, when Simpson specifically discusses legislation, "that passing a law, just like writing a symphony, cannot be understood simply as giving a set of instructions."[257]

The strength of the offered analogy arises from Simpson's comparison of a statute to a musical composition. It is true that in the performance the score and the composer's "own intentions" will play a considerable, if unquantified, role. But so will contemporary practice and conventions, current notions of musical excellence, the available skill of the performers, and even technical changes in instrument design. "An acclaimed performance will be one which strikes contemporaries, not the ghost of Beethoven, as a valid interpretation."[258]

Simpson's comparison helps orient the mind toward the idea he wants to express, but the precise concept is still difficult to grasp. The view that law – somehow inhering in cases, statutes, regulations, or rules – is "something" that provides

[254] *Id.* at 28.
[255] *Id.* at 15 (emphasis added).
[256] *Id.* at 121.
[257] *Id.* at 117.
[258] *Id.*

directions to lawyers suffers from imprecision. The notion is analytically elusive. But as a practicing lawyer I think I know what he means because I can visualize the steps I typically take to understand and resolve a legal problem. The steps I take rely on what I have learned in the past and what the law tells me about the specific matter at hand. In other words, there are pointers that lay dormant and pointers that become active. It depends on my goal.

Earlier in the book I referred to Simpson's "directions" as "pointers" and even equated both terms to Roberta Kevelson's Peircean idea of the law as a "system of signs." In that connection I also wrote, "law as practiced, law as lived, law reasoned and reasoning, law as institution and as text, exists within, and for, the collective expertise of dedicated practitioners." This statement is more descriptive and aspirational than analytical. It was also incomplete. While it describes the landscape as it were, it does not exactly clarify what, exactly, law is or how, exactly, it functions by providing pointers. Or how it exists (and in what sense does it *exist*?) within the collective expertise of dedicated practitioners.

Simpson recognized a similar problem in how the English common law is often described. He knows it involves the use of judicial decisions as authorities, either based on what the decision *said*, or what the court *did*, or the purportedly underlying reason (the *ratio decidendi*). Other versions of the same convention – one regarding cases not statutes – viewed court decisions as illustrative of deeper principles that existed independently of the particular case or even of all cases. "A massive literature," says Simpson, "has attempted, with virtually no success, to give a crisp meaning to these ideas, which express and try to state formally the essentially imprecise notion that the law exists in the rational collective consciousness of expert lawyers, just as culture may be viewed in this understandable if also puzzling way."[259]

Due to the relative imprecision of the idea that law exists to provide directions or pointers to lawyers, Simpson appears to intend the second component of "law is for lawyers" to complement the first. As I understand the second half of Simpson's formulation, it seeks to append the needed amplification by bringing in (1) the body of general principles and the detailed rules connected to them; (2) an associated terminology or jargon; and (3) the working practices or professional customs and their associated rationales.

I doubt Simpson ever managed to explicate the notion that "law is for lawyers" to his own satisfaction. Looked at from one angle, the leading question appears to be: what is the law telling you (the lawyer or the prospective lawyer or the judge) to do or to consider? But the question is not exactly the same for each role. For the practicing litigator – usually taken in these contexts as paradigmatic – the question becomes, "What arguments is the law telling me I must or may put forward to achieve a result favorable to my client?" The decision maker might well ask, "What

[259] *Id.* at 125.

decision is the law telling me I must or may reach or that I am precluded from reaching?" For the law student the operative question is different. The law student wants to know the avenues the law provided, in each instance studied, to reach the result professional participants thought best, or the best achievable. Or, perhaps less ambitiously, which arguments or rhetorical strategies, among the evident options, proved successful? And which did not? And why?

The background determinants that made one option more viable than another in a particular circumstance are often not evident from the case studied. To bring those background determinants into relief demands that one turn what is all-too-familiar into a subject of study.[260] A certain type of noetic distance achieved through an enforced curiosity becomes necessary. One way to look at *Invitation to Law* is as Simpson's effort to objectify the "law" pervasive in an invitee's society into concrete institutions, practices, norms, and directives. These work together to resolve disputes and promote social order through the careful use and observance of rules. He amplifies and extends the subject in a manner he believes will be useful to someone thinking about entering the profession. How these institutions, practices, norms, and directives came to be as they are, and why they work together as they do, structure the book. Not by accident does Simpson begin with chapters entitled, "The Pervasiveness of Law," and "Legal Ideals and Sordid Realities," that is, with discussions meant to work off the invitee's likely social outlook and initial intuitions vis-à-vis law before progressing to more descriptive historical or sociological chapters.

That Simpson's *Invitation* is a superb specimen of its type goes without saying. Readable, witty, informative, learned, and at the same time, tightly constructed, the tone neither omniscient nor exploratory, the *Invitation* invites the invitee to care about the law. Simpson's concern for how the quality of law and of lawyers affects the overall quality of a society melds the book's prose into a working faith. Perhaps through a better sense of law's ideals, especially the rule of law, prospective lawyers will not become as jaded or as blasé as the slouching *avocats* in Forain's *A Court Scene*. So maybe the cover contained a concealed warning. Simpson's was primarily the faith of a committed law professor; deep and broad and nuanced. Yet for that very reason he fell short of explaining exactly how existing law provides directives or pointers to the practicing attorney.

The basic problem lies in the book's lack of an organizing scale. Simpson recognizes that the law *for* lawyers is the law developed *by* lawyers. "Under the guise of merely making more precise conceptions which exist in popular consciousness quite independently of the law, such as theft or robbery, the lawyers, and the law, are now specifying standards of right and wrong behavior … This leads to the

260 Simpson's own work provides some of the best examples in legal scholarship of how one reveals a case's background determinants. *See* A. W. BRIAN SIMPSON, CANNIBALISM AND THE COMMON LAW: THE STORY OF THE TRAGIC LAST VOYAGE OF THE *MIGNONETTE* AND THE STRANGE LEGAL PROCEEDINGS TO WHICH IT GAVE RISE (1984); A. W. BRIAN SIMPSON, LEADING CASES IN THE COMMON LAW (1995).

development of what are called legal concepts, concepts which differ from lay concepts in sharpness and scope." He recognizes the emergence in history of legal standards that are distinct from moral standards. The legal standards themselves, whether substantive or procedural, create "the artificial world of legal categories, into which disputes and quarrels may be translated and, so translated, authoritatively determined."[261]

Within the legal vista Simpson has created, the primary source of movement comes from the interaction between the legal system's two main ideals, justice and the rule of law. These ideals must continually contend with the ever-present "sordid realities" of social life. In a manner similar to Hurst, Simpson has erected his own *tableaux vivants* to represent the operations of law and lawyers in a modern commonwealth. He recognizes these *tableaux* as arising out of the past and as having a strong purchase on the present. He emphasizes how they may cabin and confine present purpose, the efforts to employ the rule of law or to seek justice. But he does not emphasize the multidimensionality of law or the qualities practitioners need to make the constant interactions between present purposes and past outcomes productive.

In other words, Simpson's directives or pointers tend to be immediate and isolate. He depends on existing legal categories and existing institutional practices to put them into a working order, to clarify them and to give them direction and meaning. He seems to depend on the ideals of justice and the rule of law to give them whatever organizational meaning they might possess. Essentially, Simpson takes the framework in which law and lawyers function for granted. He recognizes that there have been efforts to articulate theoretically that framework but thinks they have mainly come to naught. The common law muddles on.

The general manner in which Simpson presents the idea that law is for lawyers certainly helps orient the mind of the invitee, even of the seasoned practitioner. He focuses on an essential feature of legal practice in a common law jurisdiction. His directives or pointers pose the question, "what is the law?" in another form. What we don't get from Simpson in *Invitation to Law* is a sense of how one moves from understanding the pointers, or "what is the law?," to that other part of the legal double helix, "what is law?" Or the reverse: how one might go from "what is law?" to "what is the law?"

In "The Common Law and Legal Theory," Simpson provides some guidance on the latter issue. The common law, says Simpson, should not be identified with certain articulated rules or practices. Rather, the common law is best seen as a customary system of law in this sense: "that it consists of a body of practices observed and ideas received by a caste of lawyers, these ideas being used by them as providing guidance in what is conceived to be the rational determination of disputes litigated before them, or by them on behalf of clients, and in other contexts." "These ideas

[261] SIMPSON, *supra* note 252, at 14–16.

and practices," he adds, "exist only in the sense that they are accepted and acted upon within the legal profession[.]"[262] Because the common law comprises no more than those ideas and practices that the caste of lawyers receives and accepts as authoritative, it should not be confused with propositions or tests of legality that arise outside the working ambit of the profession.

To employ a phrase that Simpson does not use but which seems to me to capture his central point, law is the ethos of the profession. The ethos that makes this group of people in the commonwealth identifiable as a group, as *lawyers*, is "law" in a primary, generative sense. The terms "customary" and "traditional" become in Simpson's hands markers to locate the law in time, in the past, and to indicate how the constitutive ideas and practices are transmitted, "through time as a received body of knowledge and learning."[263] Law, then, is the ethos, the evident and dormant beliefs and aspirations, the evolved institutions, that bind this particular group of people together and that mysteriously self-perpetuate.

But the movement from "what is law?" to "what is the law?" is still opaque. How does the ethos become articulated or instantiated as an idea or practice at a specific point? And how do existing ideas and practices – "what is the law?" – connect to the environing ethos? These problems pose two overriding questions. First, how does one best account for the phenomena just described, the interconnections between "what is the law?" – "what is law?" (labeling it a "process" may prejudice the search for an answer). Second, how may one best induct an outsider into this particular ethos, the profession? And how may those already inducted into the profession mature as professionals, that is, continue to develop professional judgment? In short, how is this ethos best inculcated?

We noted earlier that *Invitation to Law* lacked an organizing scale. It invites the student to study law by presenting an extended slide show, as it were, of important topics. By informing the invitee of the profession's guiding ideals, its general history, its frequently used categorizations of topics (contracts, torts, property), the sources of its authoritative materials, the roles and functions of its members, the predominant mode of study utilized (formal academic instruction), the book hopes to slowly, more or less imperceptibly, change how the invitee begins to see and understand the "law" that pervades his or her society. The "law" of which the invitee had little awareness begins to take shape; at first foreshortened, it slowly becomes less immense and uniform, less conventionally a "fact" and more like an "artifact" as it recedes from familiarity; it becomes something increasingly distant, opaque, strange, requiring firsthand study and practice to understand. Pointing out how the law that is pervasive (and near) is also foreign (and far) begins to create the perspective needed to appreciate and understand the complexities of the subject.

[262] A. W. B. Simpson, *The Common Law and Legal Theory*, *in* Oxford Essays in Jurisprudence, Second Series 93–94 (A. W. B. Simpson ed., 1973).

[263] *Id.*

But without an organizing scale the different activities and approaches, the range of working ideas and settled practices, fail to mesh.

Simpson certainly seems to suggest, both in *Invitation to Law* and in "The Common Law and Legal Theory," that the common law does mesh in a manner that positivists, such as John Austin or H. L. A. Hart, could not explain.[264] One may infer from his writings that it meshes through an ethos that connects doctrine with practice, both with institutions, and all three with active members who are seeking to employ their best judgment to accomplish a specific end. But that still leaves open the problem of how that "ethos" should be rendered, if for no other purpose than to guide practitioners and to teach beginners. Because the common law is immense in reach and scope how it is reduced into teachable form will undoubtedly affect its subsequent implementation. Learning affects practice. But that is not all. Learning also affects the temper or tone of the enterprise. To minimize counter-productivity, the enterprise (lawyering, advising, judging, administering, teaching) as presented and the learning as taught ought also to mesh with each other and with the ethos they help define.

Holmes provides the organizing scale for depicting the common law that Simpson could not quite find. For Holmes "prediction" (what the court will do in fact) functions as the needed organizing element. It organizes the common law from the standpoint of directed, present inquiry. It brings into unified view the various dimensions of the common law. Alternately, it reveals the "mesh" that connects one part of the prevailing ethos to another because, from the standpoint of inquiry, the strands in view serve a double function: as enacted judgments (understood broadly) and as potential grounds for subsequent prediction. Predictions revealed which strands or patterns had scaled and become pronounced. Predictions could be minute or sweeping. Predictions could drive a single decision in a single case or condense the history of an entire jurisprudence. Predictions interconnected doctrines and practices, procedure and substantive law, institutional operations with societal pressures. Prediction enabled an expansive view of the common law, both vertically and horizontally.

We come back yet again to the first sentence of the first paragraph of "The Path of the Law": "When we study law we are not studying a mystery but a well known profession." Once we connect this sentence with the last sentence of the paragraph – "The object of our study, then, is prediction, the prediction of the incidence of the public force through the instrumentality of the courts." – we realize Holmes is mainly redescribing as "prediction" what he, in "Just the Boy Wanted," first described as that ability which "commands the world" – practical judgment. Prediction is a practical or professional judgment in active mode. Prediction of the incidence of the public force through the instrumentality of the courts is, for working lawyers, the paradigmatic instance of professional judgment in the United

264 *Id.* at 80–88.

States. It must be studied, analyzed, taught, and mastered. Holmes laid out the essentials of such a program in "The Path of the Law" and "Law in Science and Science in Law."

ii *The Theory of Legal History Redux*

The first essential takes us to history. On Holmes's own terms, comprehending the interplay between past and future would provide much-needed insight into the present. In Parts I and II we presented the idea that the conjoined query, "what is (the) law?," had both static and dynamic features. The notion of duty focused the static, synchronic side of the query. Apart from the specific mode of communication used, duty signified an initial disparity, potentially, between the outcome one wanted (or did not want) and what the agents of the sovereign wanted. The test for determining a "true" duty lay in the associated penalty. If the penalty directly or indirectly led to a loss of legal status then one knew that the specific "command" in this instance had not presented an option to accept liability and pay but a true legal duty.

We also suggested in Part I that Holmes qualified Austin's notion of the sovereign – it did not necessarily inhere in the seat of a determinate authority – by giving it a sociological orientation. For the purposes of law, concentrated legal authority had dispersed to the courts. The courts, as the dominant enforcement power, took guidance from what they understood the "law" to require. The enforcement power itself did not exist as a discrete entity, unbegotten, without its own institutionalized pressures, antecedents, commitments, traditions, and designated modes of operation. More pertinently it existed, as argued in earlier sections of this part, as an integral part of a "well known profession."

The main point is that the query, "What is (the) law?," seen statically, provides at any given moment a picture of which groupings of fact may have legal consequences. Law does not arise in the absence of particular groupings of fact and the stated desires of the enforcement power. Pressed hard enough in one direction law liquefies into tissues of experience (basic iteration: unreflective custom plus social needs plus nascent cultural conceptions and feelings). Pushed in another direction it congeals into what Holmes calls dogma.

The importance of the question "what is (the) law?" lies in how it directs attention to the outer crust of existing law *and* to its tissue-like interior. It also points up the realization that law transforms, that it takes shape both in reference to what it has been and what it will be. This dynamism is not simply dyadic; it may be triadic or even more complicated. Part II sought to describe the modes of movement and transformation through the use of such terms as "apperception" and "triangulation."

In his later writings Holmes struggled to find the right way to express his leading ideas. He did not quite see their connections as an interlaced query, as we have expressed it, but at various times championed one part or the other. For the mature

Holmes "what is law?" took precedence. As he explained it, "Every one instinctively recognizes that in these days the justification of a law for us cannot be found in the fact that our fathers have always followed it. It must be found in some help which the law brings toward reaching a social end which the governing power of the community has made up its mind that it wants."[265]

This statement supports those who see Holmes as a proto-realist. The use of history is clearly secondary – "but of course I think, as other people do, that the main ends of the subject are practical, and from a practical point of view, history with which I have been dealing thus far, is only a means, and one of the least of means, for mastering a tool." Its main purpose is to "burst inflated explanations," and to put the brake on the lawyer who is "apt to invent, if he does not find, some ground of policy for its base."[266]

Yet those who see Holmes as a proto-realist typically do not pause to consider Holmes's odd turn in the very same paragraph: "Notwithstanding the contrasts which I have been making [that is, between abstractly scientific historical explanation and historical explanation used for practical ends], the practical study of the law ought also to be scientific."[267] This sentence, lying almost dead center in "Law in Science and Science in Law," serves as a tiny introit to what one might call The Lawyer's Faith.

It pays to be clear on the contours of Holmes's thinking before confronting that topic in the last section of this part. The "contrasts" to which he refers are between law seen as "a great anthropological document" that stands in need of scientific historical explanation (mainly in terms of morphology and transformation), and law understood as a practical subject in which the use of history as an explanatory mechanism is less pronounced. As he put it: "From a practical point of view, as I have illustrated upon another occasion, its use is mainly negative and skeptical."[268] That other occasion was probably when he delivered the unnamed Boston University Law School address that has come down to us as "The Path of the Law."

If we compare the discussion of history and its uses in both "The Path of the Law" and "Law in Science and Science in Law," a certain pattern to Holmes's thought begins to emerge. To appreciate its movement it helps to benchmark Holmes's position in these two essays against his 1886 restatement of the Harvard Law School professors' pedagogical creed in "The Use of Law Schools." In that piece he congratulated the Harvard Law School professors upon their insistence that their students would not simply be taught a "rag-bag full of general principles." As we noted in Part IV, Section 13, Holmes restated the creed to ensure that "history" was used to give these general principles a body (extension), a corresponding lineage

[265] Oliver Wendell Holmes, *Law in Science and Science in Law, in* III CW 412.
[266] *Id.*
[267] *Id.*
[268] *Id.*

(emergence), and to reveal their patent and latent functions (specific operations in an actual system of law). He then ended by saying: "Finally, you must show its historic relations to other principles, often of very different date and origin, and thus set it in the perspective without which its proportions will never be truly judged."[269]

The use of history typically meant for practitioners the use of cases. The cases showed the extent and limit of a principle that served as their major premise. The cases that professors selected also introduced students to a principle's embryology, its lines of development and growth, and thereby increased understanding and facilitated its use.[270]

A decade later Holmes has shifted his rhetoric. He is less enamored with the Harvard-style pedagogy. We saw the first inklings of discontent in "Learning and Science." He probably had begun to realize that little had been done to advance the ultimate goal of setting legal principles in perspective – that is, proportioning the various historic legal principles in relation to each other. Without perspective a legal principle's ground and scope could never be truly judged. The concern to determine truly a legal principle's proportions did not traditionally preoccupy either the typical law student or practitioner. Before the rise of the modern law school it fell to magistrates like Lemuel Shaw if it fell anywhere. After 1870 and the rise of the legal professoriate the question becomes more difficult. It points up the issue whether for Holmes this task fell to those who exclusively taught law for a living.

Holmes closed "The Use of Law Schools" by hoping that the legal specialist upon whom the health of democracy depended would become cultivated; that the specialist would lay in the "outline of the other sciences, as well as the light and shade of his own." Holmes further desired this same specialist should be passionate and reasonable [that is, scientific]; that "he should be able not only to explain, but to feel;" that he would "see things in their proportion."[271]

By the time we get to "The Path of the Law" Holmes has solidified his reaction to what he sees happening at Harvard Law. Granted, this assertion is primarily supposition – I am not aware of correspondence or other documents that would provide direct support – but the supposition is worth making, even as an hypothesis, because it brings together various elements in Holmes's thought that have not been brought together before. The key passage in "The Path of the Law" that supports the supposition that Holmes's disenchantment with Harvard Law has grown serves as a transition paragraph. It takes us from Holmes's discussion of the initial canons – to use Hessel Yntema's word – of legal study (regarding morals and logic) to the one concerning the role of history. It begins with a lament.

> Now let us consider the present condition of the law as a subject for study, and the ideal toward which it tends. We are still far from the point of view which I desire to

[269] Holmes, *supra* note, at 477.
[270] *Id.*
[271] *Id.* at 479.

> see reached. No one has reached it or can reach it as yet. We are only at the beginning of a philosophical reaction, and of a reconsideration of the worth of doctrines which for the most part are still taken for granted without any deliberate, conscious, and systematic questioning of their grounds.[272]

The striking thing to note about this paragraph is how it compares to a paragraph that we have already discussed twice. That is the paragraph from "The Use of Law Schools" in which Holmes began by observing that "Story's simple philosophizing has ceased to satisfy men's minds." He did not lay the blame upon Story but pointed out, as already commented, that Story's generation did not have the historical or philosophical sophistication needed to understand the leading legal doctrines "in their precise contours and in their innermost meanings."[273]

What Holmes's generation possessed that Story's did not is a more scientific and philosophical approach to law. As he put it, "The facts are being scrutinized by eyes microscopic in intensity and panoramic in scope." The intensity and the scope must work together to reveal precise contours and innermost meanings. That takes us to history and related disciplines. On the philosophical front, "a thousand heads are analyzing and generalizing the rules of law and the grounds on which they stand." Holmes did not pause to explain how these two activities should work together. We are merely given to understand that there is a syncretism, as it were, between *what* is being studied and *how* it ought to be thought about (identified and analyzed). Holmes proceeds to brandish the pennant and exclaim:

> The law has got to be stated over again; and I venture to say that in fifty years [1936] we shall have it in a form of which no man could have dreamed fifty years ago [1836]. And now I venture to add my hope and belief that, when that day comes which I predict, the Professors of the Harvard Law School will be found to have had a hand in the change not less important than that which Story has had in determining the form of the text-books of the last half-century.[274]

How different the tone we find eleven years later. The rider still hoists the pennant but obstacles chastened him in his path. He is aggrieved but resolute.

The question that fairly jumps out from a careful reading of both "The Use of Law Schools" and "The Path of the Law" is this: what has delayed the philosophic reaction, the reconsideration of the worth of doctrines, the deliberate, conscious, systematic questioning of their grounds?

The easy answer is tradition. This is the answer that Holmes gives after describing the development of law – "our law," he says – that has gone on for nearly a thousand years. He compares that development to the development of a plant, but then singles out its distinctiveness – "mind, like matter, simply obeying a law of spontaneous

[272] Holmes, *supra* note 1, at 398.
[273] Holmes, *supra* note 103, at 477.
[274] *Id.*

growth." That "obeying" is an instance of imitation. Imitation is a necessity of human life since, as Hurst following Holmes pointed out, life is short and wants and needs are many. But "because we are all compelled to take on faith at second hand most of the rules on which we base our action and thought," does not mean "that each of us may not try to set some corner of his world in the order of reason, or that all collectively should not aspire to carry reason as far as it will go throughout the whole domain."[275]

In these latter quoted clauses we hear again the refrain from "Learning and Science": "But the present has a right to govern itself so far as it can; and it ought always to be remembered that historic continuity with the past is not a duty; it is only a necessity."[276] He would repeat it again in the opening paragraphs of "Law in Science and Science in Law."[277] We have argued that the denoted "right" lies in self-exertion and self-exertion in the context of law consists primarily in the effort to think.[278] The present's right to govern itself as far as it can somehow connects to the reconsideration of the worth of legal doctrines, the deliberate, conscious, systematic questioning of their grounds.

Holmes, fully aware of the prejudices of his audience, then proceeds in "The Path of the Law" to clarify the stance from which the activity of thinking must be undertaken. "An evolutionist," he says, "will hesitate to affirm the universal validity of his social ideals, or for the principles which he thinks should be embodied in legislation. He is content if he can prove them best for here and now." The approach may be piecemeal but for that reason no less urgent or valid. "Still it is true that a body of law is more rational and more civilized when every rule it contains is referred articulately and definitely to an end which it subserves, and when the grounds for desiring that end are stated or are ready to be stated in words."[279]

If tradition has effectively blocked the road to a more rational and civilized body of law – note the use of the two adjectives – then the question arises how that "tradition" ought to be dealt with in the course of inquiry. At this point we confront the ancient dragon cornered in its cave, the second most remembered image after the bad man from "The Path of the Law." "When you get the dragon out of his cave on to the plain and in the daylight, you can count his teeth and claws, and see just what is his strength. But to get him out is only the first step. The next is either to kill

[275] Holmes, *supra* note 1, at 398–99.

[276] Holmes, *supra* note 102, at 492.

[277] Holmes, *supra* note 265, at 406.

[278] In a broader sense, Holmes categorized "thinking" as an instance of "the one great pleasure and end of life." *See* Oliver Wendell Holmes, *Remarks at a Tavern Club Dinner for Albert Venn Dicey, in* III CW 523 ("The interest of men is not money or beauty or truth but the pursuit of money or beauty or truth. And all experience the same vital pleasure – the one great pleasure and end of life – that of realizing their own spontaneous energy through whatever channel they are best able to bring it out.").

[279] Holmes, *supra* note 1, at 399.

him, or to tame him and make him a useful animal." He then draws the moral: "For the rational study of the law the black-letter man may be the man of the present, but the man of the future is the man of statistics and the master of economics. It is revolting to have no better reason for a rule of law than that so it was laid down in the time of Henry IV [1399–1413]. *It is still more revolting if the grounds upon which it was laid have vanished long since, and the rule simply persists from blind imitation of the past.*"[280]

Because scholars often quote Holmes's "it is revolting" line in many different contexts the phrase has lost pungency. Keeping in mind the illustrious members of his audience, especially the legal historians, Holmes's strong expression of disgust at the evidently narrow way in which many lawyers and judges – broadly speaking, his colleagues – unthinkingly went about their business had what seems to be a double intent.

The first is to open the eyes of those who did not yet see how expansive and encompassing is the role of the past. The historic continuity is a necessity. Consciousness of this continuity has its own internal range, from relative lack of awareness ("blind imitation") to limited awareness ("laid down in the time of Henry IV") to morbid awareness ("the pitfall of antiquarianism."). In other writings, such as "Law in Science and Science in Law," Holmes would shadow the continuities with the equally evident if less pronounced discontinuities ("The law of fashion is a law of life."). Thus, without ever quite telling us what he is doing, Holmes sets up another polarity. On the one end is "tradition" (strong continuity) and on the other "fashion" (relative discontinuity).

It stands to reason that "fashion" or "discontinuity" also created its own internal range. The recognition that Story's simple philosophizing had a built-in lifespan exemplified one endpoint. The sense that a particular "fashion" fit into an overarching story, and many overarching stories were common in the nineteenth century, minimized discontinuity's felt effects. We are perhaps at the mid part of the range. At the other end, an intensive and encompassing intellectual or emotional "fashion" (as in a prevailing mode of analysis and explanation) might see itself, reflexively, as a conscious effort to break cleanly with tradition.

Holmes was in the unusual position of someone who was well aware of the relative discontinuities but did not believe it possible to sever all connections with the past and begin anew. He did not think that increased social and historical awareness – that is, awareness of how humans functioned in social groups and how their past actions and thoughts impinged on their present behavior – somehow provided an exalted position from which to issue social or political or economic directives. In regard to law the advantage of hindsight provided even less grounds for justifying an action or sequence of actions as the ultimate expedient. That was because "hindsight" might just be another supposition in disguise.

[280] *Id.* (emphasis added).

This latter point leads to Holmes's second reason for baring so openly his disgust. His "revolt" was not so much against something called "formalism" as against the unsophisticated "historicizing" of the legal historians. The risk of blindly imitating the past was not as great for Melville Bigelow, James Barr Ames, or James Bradley Thayer – notable legal historians – as it might be for less historically conscious and conscientious lawyers and judges. But the apparently excessive value placed on historical study at such law schools as Harvard's and Boston's could easily lead to mindsets similar to those that pushed Holmes to the edge of nausea. The problem lay in the abundance of relatively unreflective, uninspired historical research and analysis. "The man of science in the law is not merely a bookworm. To a microscopic eye for detail he must unite an insight which tells him what details are significant. Not every maker of exact investigation counts, but only he who directs his investigation to a crucial point."[281]

The difficulty in nailing down Holmes's specific complaint against the legal historians arises from the lack of any sustained explanation of how "learning" and "science" should work together. The main impression many scholars have gotten from the articles and speeches he wrote in the 1890s is that "science" should supplant "learning." We have already shown that it could not be that simple.

It fell to Holmes to articulate how three activities, broadly speaking, should work together. Historical study and philosophical analysis had taken American law past Story's simple philosophizing. That much was clear. Philosophical analysis did its work by helping to demarcate jurisprudential degrees and boundaries. It gave philosophical form to the notion of going "beyond the established lines."[282] It disentangled the legal point of view from competing viewpoints (moral, social, or spiritual). History, for its part, revealed specific morphological shapes (initially arrayed needs and purposes) that from greater distance took on the mirage of philosophical form. Hence his last great blast against "Natural Law" in 1918.[283] History also revealed that the role of experience far surpassed that of logic in the life (growth and development) of the law (the "actual system"). Philosophical analysis had helped single out the two key concepts needed to frame a well-wrought American jurisprudence: the legal duty and the legal event. Historical study had ultimately increased in importance because of the philosophical analysis. The third activity, which Holmes variously describes as economic or statistical analysis, or the study of political economy, concentrated the effort to clarify current choices. It did so by illuminating both present circumstances and future consequences.

The importance of these three activities led Holmes to advocate a new style of legal analysis. We have condensed that new style into the compound question,

281 Holmes, *supra* note 265, at 412.

282 Oliver Wendell Holmes, *Speech Prepared for Delivery at a Banquet for Admiral Dewey, in* III CW 524.

283 Oliver Wendell Holmes, *Natural Law, in* III CW 445–48.

"what is (the) law?" In our use it becomes an essential device (a stereoscope) for a 3D view of legal power. Holmes did not quite get to that point because he had difficulty in coordinating the three activities.

Both the problem and the solution become clearer if we take a closer look at how Holmes laid out the progression of legal thought and the dead ends he encountered. Story's philosophizing was simple because it relied on general moral convictions or arguments to carry the legal analysis and bridge the distance between the past and present. Holmes's academic colleagues engaged in simple historicizing because they neglected to elucidate how the historical "grounds" they uncovered directed, or failed to direct, present action in furtherance of well-formulated, well-understood social ends. Social ends, in turn, were not well understood because the needed preliminary investigation and assessment was still in its infancy. If historical research and understanding is preparatory – getting the dragon out of the cave – how does one decide whether to kill or tame? That seems to depend on perceived social ends and the power to convert the past to present use.

But, on Holmes's own terms, social ends could not be understood apart from history, which, since it was not self-revelatory, initially required the intelligent discrimination, gathering, and questioning of artifacts. On the other hand, other tools, like economics and statistics, could be used to clarify present circumstances and future consequences. Such studies might employ formal analyses, but the implementation of those analyses into existing law required fitting them into sequences and contexts that had definite, continuing histories. Thinking – the deliberate, conscious, systematic questioning and reconsideration of legislative grounds – had to begin from somewhere, however. Holmes's prescriptions seem uncoordinated, perhaps even unworkable as a whole. Starting from a single perspective – history, philosophy, or economics (or, more broadly, social scientific/empirical studies) – would invariably lead to a distorted assessment.[284] Because the dominant intellectual tenor at Boston and Cambridge favored the historical, he put his weight on the least favored side, the clarification of present circumstances and consequences for the purpose of intelligent legal action.

The essence of the problem lay in how to coordinate the dimensions of experience (sequence and context) and their study (via history, philosophy, and economics) through a single register, one that we call law.[285] We suggested earlier that

[284] David Rosenberg provides a similar description but does not see the same problems of coordination and workability as I do in Holmes's overall project. The reason may be that he puts less emphasis than I on the dialectic between present ideas and past realities in Holmes's thought. David Rosenberg, The Hidden Holmes: His Theory of Torts in History 42–68 (1995).

[285] As noted *supra* Part IV, Section 13, Bruce Kimball has argued that C. C. Langdell anticipated Holmes's "paradox of form and substance." But Kimball also notes that Langdell never managed to coherently articulate how the three dimensions (induction from authority, deduction from principle, and analysis of justice and policy) worked together. Kimball, *supra* note 20, at 337–38 ("He [Langdell] also employed his characteristic three-dimensional mode of reasoning, including an explicit commitment to formalist analysis and deduction from legal

present purpose – the problem one seeks to resolve intelligently, the question one wants to answer competently – had the potential to unify the various dimensions and bring into view three-dimensionality. But for that potential to be realized it must find a way to coordinate the various dimensions. What turns a two-dimensional view into a three-dimensional view is depth. As depth is hard to talk or think about in the abstract, it is best to begin with an example.

At the end of the paragraph in which Holmes both introduces the "man of the future" (man of statistics or master of economics), and vents his disgust at the blind imitation of the past that keeps alive empty, useless forms, he tells his audience that he is "thinking of the technical rule as to trespass *ab initio*[.]"[286] Holmes does not discuss the details of the rule in "The Path of the Law." Holmes had the opportunity to deal with it in an opinion he wrote and the court issued almost a year earlier, in March of 1896.[287]

He briskly begins that opinion by reviewing the case's procedural posture and facts. The defendants had been convicted, after a jury trial, of larceny. The defendants appealed. As the grounds for the appeal, they argued that the evidence put forward in the trial did not justify the conviction. The evidence showed that the agents of a man named Perkins had bought a horse from a stable in Boston. The agents then hired a boy to take the horse from Boston to Framingham, where Perkins lived. Along the way the boy met the defendants. The defendants told the boy they would deliver the horse to Perkins and paid him the money he would have received. The boy agreed, took the money, and left the horse with the defendants. Not long after the hand-off, the authorities found the horse on the defendants' property in Natick. The defendants were charged with a felony, larceny, for misappropriating Perkins's horse.[288]

Holmes begins the analysis in his trademark way. He establishes a polarity. If the boy had converted the horse the offense would not have been larceny. It would have been embezzlement. That comment leads one to wonder, if the boy could not have been charged with larceny why were the defendants? The reason lies in what Holmes calls "the ambiguous attitude of the law toward his [the boy's] custody, which prevents it from regarding his conversion as a trespass."[289] No such ambiguity exists, however, when a third person converts the chattel. "It is larceny equally whether he takes the thing from a bailee, from a servant, or from the owner

principles, inductive consideration of authorities, and sublimated consideration of policy and justice after denying its relevance to the legal issue. Despite the contradictory methodological standards, Langdell sought consistency and coherence among all three dimensions of his analysis."). What Kimball calls "dimensions" seem more like factors.

286 Holmes, *supra* note 1, at 399.

287 Commonwealth v. Rubin, 165 Mass. 453 (Mass. 1896) (per Holmes, J.).

288 *Id.* at 454.

289 *Id.*

himself."[290] Thus sufficient legal grounds existed for the defendants to be charged with larceny.

The difference between embezzlement and larceny under Massachusetts's law at the time depended on the defendant's intent at the moment the defendant received possession of the goods. If the defendant received possession honestly, and only afterwards contrived to deprive the owner of possession by converting them to his or her own use, then the defendant committed the crime of embezzlement. If, on the other hand, at the time of receipt the defendant harbored the intent to deprive the owner of possession and convert the goods to his or her own use, the defendant committed larceny.[291]

As it appeared before the Supreme Judicial Court, the legal question turned on whether prosecutors could prove the prima facie case of larceny against the defendants by employing a rule of evidence known as trespass *ab initio*. The law provided that larceny could be proved by either alleging the element of "a taking by a trespass" [that is, the use of force or violence] or by showing that an exception to that requirement could be met. One exception "is when the possession of a chattel, but not the title, is gained by a trick or fraud with the intent to convert it."[292] Assuming that one could prove the defendants' intent to convert the horse, it would fall within the trick or fraud exception.

Holmes then continues his analysis. "So that the question is narrowed to whether there was any evidence of intent at the time when the defendants received the horse, the only fact bearing upon the matter being what they did shortly afterwards."[293] The jury found that shortly after the defendants paid the sale price to the boy and received from him the horse they did not deliver it to Perkins but took it to their property in Natick. Conceivably, the defendants argued that what they did was not larceny because (1) the boy voluntarily gave them the horse and they paid for it, (2) they stepped into the boy's shoes and became agents (servants) of Perkins, or (3) they did not have the intent, at the time they received the horse, to keep it and *not* deliver it to Perkins. They apparently argued that the right charge, if any, should have been embezzlement not larceny. The legal issue, as Holmes phrased it, was whether the jury could permissibly infer from what the defendants did after receiving the horse their intent at the time they received the horse and thus find them guilty of larceny.

Holmes noted that the common law provided precedent for such a circumstance. The rule of trespass *ab initio* had originally applied to cases where intent mattered. The rule provided that intent could be presumed conclusively from subsequent conduct. But the original function of the rule, as a rule of evidence, had been lost in the maze of subsequent interpretations and holdings. Massachusetts's courts treated

[290] *Id.*

[291] *See* Commonwealth v. Ryan, 155 Mass. 523, 526–30 (Mass. 1892); Commonwealth v. Lannan, 153 Mass. 287, 288–89 (Mass. 1891); Commonwealth v. Barry, 124 Mass. 325 (Mass. 1878).

[292] Commonwealth v. Rubin, *supra* note 287, at 455.

[293] *Id.*

it as a technical, substantive rule regarding the proper use of official authority. The courts said it only applied in situations where a person acting under the color of law exceeded the limits of that person's authority. In such circumstances, the courts would presume – even without any direct proof – from the subsequent abuse an original intent to exceed lawful authority. The initial intent, shown by the subsequent abuse, turns the putatively lawful actor into a trespasser *ab initio* [from the beginning].

Holmes in this particular case takes us from (past) ground to (present) ground. The past ground is what underlay the evidentiary rule that "original intent was presumed conclusively from the subsequent conduct." The present ground, in his reformulation, is what supports, "the less extreme and more rational proposition which led to the technical rule, namely, that the subsequent conduct is *some evidence* of the original intent[.]"[294] Holmes has, in effect, taken a single rule and shown that its present use as a substantive point of law has little historical justification (it is a survival). He further shows that present policy arguments (suppositions) do not capture its true meaning (as historically revealed), and argues that any continued use must find its justification in a rational purpose that contributes to a clear social end. His analysis in *Commonwealth v. Rubin* is multilayered. For that reason the connection between the case's legal analysis and the point he wants to illustrate in "The Path of the Law" does not immediately stand out. It pays to retrace his reasoning in this instance. The goal is to better understand his aim and to grasp the difficulties – for him and for subsequent commentators – in putting his leading ideas into a coherent working order.

As his opinion affirmed the verdict, one could infer that he thought the jury, following the trial court's instructions, had determined that they could, based on the evidence presented, use the defendants' subsequent conduct to determine the defendants' original intent. The grounds upon which the jury rested their decision were partly factual (what the credible evidence showed the defendants did soon after receiving the horse) and partly legal (the rule of evidence that permits inference from subsequent conduct to prior intent). In regards to his discussion of the proper purpose of the doctrine of trespass *ab initio*, one could say Holmes simply removed the barnacles that encrusted this particular rule, he cleansed it of historical accretions and showed its initial use – an example of the critical historian at work.

Holmes argues that the original ground of the trespass *ab initio* rule was to handle an evidentiary issue that determining intent might pose when intent is material. It was originally a rule of evidence. Only in and through and after various circumstances did it take on the guise of a substantive rule of law that applied to a single class of cases. Since that class of cases (involving the abuse of official authority) did not include cases of either agency or bailment, it did not appear from current

[294] *Id.* at 456 (emphasis added).

precedent that it could be used to legally justify the evidentiary inference against the defendants. That position was wrong; it misunderstood the rule.

> But since it has been settled that the intent may be decisive as to larceny, the less extreme and more rational proposition which led to the technical rule, namely, that the subsequent conduct is some evidence of the original intent, has been acted on frequently in England by leaving the case to the jury when the whole evidence consisted of an ambiguous receipt and a subsequent conversion.[295]

Holmes uses a recent Massachusetts case regarding the trespass *ab initio* rule to illustrate what he finds revolting about professional practice. Remember, he finds it revolting "to have no better reason for a rule of law than that so it was laid down in the time of Henry IV." No doubt he had in mind such Supreme Judicial Court decisions as *Etsy v. Wilmot* (1860) and *Smith v. Pierce* (1872).[296] Both stated that the trespass *ab initio* rule only applied when the defendant exercised official authority. It did not pertain to bailments or other private relations. Thus a rule that could be applied to the horse-appropriating defendants – to establish their intent upon receipt of the horse – was in danger of being disregarded because it had been put into a slot presumably labeled with a policy justification (curtailing abuse of official authority). The prevailing conception of the rule had, in point of fact, no direct connection to its original grounds.

This latter observation leads to those situations that Holmes found even more revolting, "when the grounds upon which it was laid down have vanished long ago since, and the rule simply persists from blind imitation of the past." Holmes clearly thinks the trespasser *ab initio* rule is a survival. He brings it up again in "Law in Science and Science in Law." There he tells his audience, "I have tried to show that the doctrine of trespass *ab initio* in like manner was the survival in a particular class of cases of a primitive rule of evidence, which established intent by a presumption of law from subsequent conduct, after the rule had gone to pieces and had been forgotten as whole."[297]

Both the wording and the placement of this passage in "Law in Science and Science in Law" are instructive. It comes as the second example of instances in which the critical use of history has burst "inflated and unreal explanations." How do explanations become inflated and unreal? The answer to that question takes us back to Holmes's breakthrough 1876 article, "Primitive Notions in Modern Law, No. I." There he noted "that the various considerations of policy which are not infrequently supposed to have established those doctrines, have, in fact, been invented at a later period to account for what was already there, – a process familiar to all students of legal history."[298] He repeats the same idea at least twice in "Law in

[295] *Id.*
[296] Etsy v. Wilmot, 81 Mass. 168 (Mass. 1860); Smith v. Pierce, 110 Mass. 35 (Mass. 1872).
[297] Holmes, *supra* note 265, at 413.
[298] Oliver Wendell Holmes, *Primitive Notions in Modern Law, No. I*, *in* III CW 5.

Science and Science in Law": "And when a lawyer sees a rule of law in force he is very apt to invent, if he does not find, some ground of policy for its base."[299]

This common tendency led to a bevy of legal rules that had no clear rational basis. Beside trespass *ab initio* he uses as examples, (1) the rule regarding a fresh complaint in a proceeding involving the indictment of rape; (2) the presumption in a civil proceeding that a deaf and dumb person lacks legal competence; (3) the liability of a master for the torts of his servant in the course of employment; and (4) the liability of a common carrier for damage to goods during transit. All these instances are sufficient, he repeats, "to illustrate my meaning, and to point out the danger of inventing reasons offhand for whatever we find established in the law."[300]

These comments certainly illuminate how explanations become "unreal," but how do they also become "inflated"? One possibility: suppositions that occur and seem warranted are overfilled with certitude. They are inflated with conviction. Interests filled with much-too-much certitude distort judgment, that is, give disproportionate emphasis to certain present interests or wants at the expense of others, past or present. Holmes most famously put it this way: "These immediate interests exercise a kind of hydraulic pressure which makes what previously was clear seem doubtful, and before which even well-settled principles of law will bend."[301]

But if that is the case, Holmes seems to be criticizing what he in his eulogy of George Shattuck praised, the mighty temperament of the skilled advocate. Legal principles established through litigation are as much established by the force of personality as through insight, sheer intellect, and argumentation. Recall what he said in the first lecture of *The Common Law*: "Every important principle which is developed by litigation is in fact and at bottom the result of more or less definitely understood views of public policy; most generally, to be sure, under our practice and traditions, the unconscious result of instinctive preferences and inarticulate convictions, but none the less traceable to views of public policy in the last analysis."[302] Without historians doing their work there would be nothing to counteract the continuity of the past in the shape of survivals. On the other hand, critical history by itself provided no positive guidance; it mainly eliminated suppositions that could not be supported by the most sophisticated historical research and reasoning available. History separated what suppositions backed by a strong temperament unthinkingly joined – the established law and its rationale.

At the same time, Holmes believed that history had overstepped its bounds. As he put it in the opening section of "Law in Science and Science in Law": "This process of historical explanation has been applied to the matter of our profession, especially of recent years, with great success, and with so much eagerness, and with such a

[299] Holmes, *supra* note 265, at 412.

[300] *Id.* at 413–14.

[301] Northern Securities v. United States, 193 U.S. 197, 400–01 (1904) (Holmes, J. dissenting).

[302] Oliver Wendell Holmes, *supra* note 10, at 133.

feeling that when you had the true historic dogma you had the last word not only in the present but for the immediate future, that I have felt warranted heretofore in throwing out the caution that continuity with the past is only a necessity and not a duty."[303]

Looked at carefully, Holmes's trespass *ab initio* example reveals he was employing the very same type of analysis that one finds laid out in the first paragraph of *The Common Law*. There he asserted that, "In order to know what it [the rule of law] is, we must know what it has been, and what it tends to become. We must alternately consult history and existing theories of legislation."[304] If we look at a rule of law as providing directions or pointers to members of the profession, then in this particular case the rule of trespass *ab initio* tells its own story.

According to Holmes the rule of trespass *ab initio* had been originally, in the early stages of the common law, a rule of evidence to establish intent. It arose in a time when rules of evidence were few and far between. The rule stated, "if a man abuse an authority given him by the law, he becomes a trespasser *ab initio*." Over time the rule had "gone to pieces and had been forgotten as a whole." This colloquial phrase, pregnant with meaning, reminds us that what once was unified – the rule and the internal and external circumstances it arrayed – got broken up in time (through changing conditions) and the bits that still functioned in the law had lost their raison d'être. The rule's function in a previous time found its raison d'être in a particular array of conscious purposes, strong convictions, articulate and inarticulate feelings, desires understood and desires inchoate. This array found its voice in the rule's dictate: what could or must be done in a specific case. Turning to the present, Holmes found its use and policy justification – to curtail the abuse of legal authority – to be equally indicative of built up prejudices and conscious purposes but having little historical justification, little conscious connection to prior decisions regarding the rule and the values it conveyed. Accordingly, present purposes and rationales took on disproportionate meaning. They became inflated. If overinflated they begin to radically distort previous commitments and decisions – hence Holmes's reference to hydraulic pressure.

On this reading, one can readily see the difference between two conceptions of a rule that goes by the same name. But after pointing out that the limitation under which the presently understood rule labored found no justification in the rule's origin and purpose, Holmes singles out the "less extreme and more rational proposition that led to the technical rule." That proposition recognizes "subsequent conduct is some evidence of the original intent," especially in those cases "when the whole evidence consisted of an ambiguous receipt and a subsequent conversion." The proposition that Holmes isolates serves to justify legally the defendants' conviction. That is to say, Holmes transports the "rational proposition" from the past

[303] Holmes, *supra* note 265, at 406.
[304] Holmes, *supra* note 10, at 115.

to the present and he does so without any comment regarding the "grounds" of the proposition, whether in the primitive era of the common law or in 1896.

Holmes's main point, in both "The Path of the Law" and in "Law in Science and Science in Law," is that the rule trespass *ab initio* is a survival. He notes in "Law in Science and Science in Law" that Professor Ames had, since his decision in *Commonwealth v. Rubin*, suggested different originating circumstances for the rule. Regardless of its actual provenance, it "leave[s] the doctrine a survival, the reasons for which long have disappeared."[305]

As a survival the rule tends to foster inflated and unreal explanations. Why? In the heat of practice, legal professionals tend to treat the rule without any awareness of its historical trajectory, its depth. New circumstances have displaced its original meaning and purpose. Its obvious meaning and its scientifically ascertained meaning no longer coincide. Inflated and unreal explanations then step in. To say it more concretely: lawyers and judges provide inflated and unreal policy rationales to justify the use or disuse of a specific doctrine. Under such circumstances, understanding legal rules as historical artifacts with continuing effect correspondingly diminishes in importance.

Inflated and unreal explanations do not have the fortification of applied reason to sustain them. On the other side, social ends taken unthinkingly, especially those that support an existing legal doctrine or a legal regime, also lack the substance that applied reason provides. As the above discussion of the rule of trespass *ab initio* shows, Holmes found it difficult to coordinate three distinct aspects of his thought. First, any doctrine or rule of law had antecedents that, in turn, also had antecedents. These antecedents are often called "grounds." The regression sometimes ended abruptly in human psychology, or what Holmes variously referred to as human needs or instincts. But the use of history as a research tool to investigate and articulate those antecedents he believed indispensable. Second, viable legal doctrines – that is, those applicable to present-day circumstances – had to meet the test of intelligibility. Intelligibility, like psychology, usually restricted the range of conceivability. Holmes probably had a greater range than his contemporaries but he kept it in check because he believed, first and foremost, that law should be practical. Third, Holmes placed much importance in the rational determination of the social ends for which law existed. To this purpose he counseled the use of investigative tools for illuminating circumstances and consequences.

In addressing these three aspects, Holmes often began from the premise that his society had reached the point in human history from which it could deliberately remake existing laws or legislate new ones. Yet, as an evolutionist, he was ever conscious of fallibilism. His solution was not to move in a new direction unless it could be shown that the old way was unworkable, or that the benefits an alternate posed compensated for the risks. From his own historical investigations he had a

[305] Holmes, *supra* note 265, at 413.

strong sense of how conditions and circumstances had changed since the thirteenth century. He had an equally strong feel for the continuities. Trespass *ab initio* might still serve as a useful rule of evidence, at least as long as larceny and embezzlement existed as different causes of action, but its use should proceed intelligently – understanding its background, its trajectory, its fit within the overall scheme.

But that was the sticking point. Once Holmes identified the trespass *ab initio* rule as a survival – what next? Identifying it as a survival meant distinguishing between when form and substance cohered, and when form only survived, without the original substance. This same form proceeded to elicit from practicing professionals off-hand policy justifications (rationales) that often had no more to do with the rule's origination and purpose than the man on the moon. In *Commonwealth v. Rubin* Holmes provided a "less extreme more rational proposition" for the continued use of the rule – that subsequent conduct is some evidence of original intent – but nowhere grounds that so-called proposition. Of course, it may have been inappropriate for him as an opinion writer to venture outside the narrow confines the issue presented. But he does not use his decision in either "The Path of the Law" or "Law in Science and Science in Law" as an illustration or a starting point for how one would go about formulating the needed social end to justify the reshaped rule. Holmes certainly had a sense of the rule's relative viability. As a primitive rule of evidence it had no resonance with modern lawyering. As a disfigured survival it had too much impact; it crowded out more intelligent, effective guides. Holmes tells us that when used critically, "History sets us free and enables us to make up our minds dispassionately whether the survival we are enforcing answers any new purpose when it had ceased to answer the old."[306] But without saying anything more he leaves us in the lurch.

From Holmes's own effort in *Commonwealth v. Rubin* it appears he secures the rule to that catchall bucket of poured concrete, common sense. The very structure of Massachusetts law at the time created what he called a "slip corner" in the law governing the crimes of larceny and embezzlement. It may be that if Massachusetts rationalized its law, as Holmes desired, and got rid of the artificial distinction between the two – which mainly turned on whether the master had possession of the property before the servant's conversion – then Holmes would have found even less room for the delimited proposition that now backed the trespass *ab initio* rule. That is to say, a special rule of evidence regarding intent in these circumstances may no longer be needed because another, broader evidentiary rule – a rule covering more instances – would take its place.

In this scenario, intelligence has taken control of the situation and ousted tradition but not the past. Evidentiary rules ought not to turn on arbitrary distinctions that depend on when certain laws originated. Holmes wants the law to fashion itself in accordance with postulates established from within upon accurately

306 *Id.* at 412.

measured social desires instead of tradition. By "from within" Holmes means through the use of critical history, history done for the purpose of laying bare original purposes and functions and their transformation. It is history done at the behest of legal argumentation and decision-making. It arises in response to actual problems. It is a practical endeavor, and Holmes wants it to open the door to "science in law."

The challenge Holmes lays down, to accurately measure social desires, is immense. As stated, it is unapproachable. If, however, he was referring to those social desires strong enough to have found expression in law, then the task is still daunting but not quite as overwhelming. Anthropology and related disciplines that work out within their distinct purviews the implications of the proposition that "the law of fashion is the law of life," may thus, from their standpoints, inform a nascent "science in law." But the focus must remain on the law from within – the mediated intelligence and experience of practitioners. How knowledge acquired by those outside the working profession – by, for example, the dedicated sociolegal academic who studies law solely for anthropological or social scientific purposes – *converts* into knowledge that those within the profession, those busy in the hive, can employ in addressing actual legal problems is for Holmes the most pressing question of the day.

His ideal in this matter is John Chipman Gray. Gray was a man of prodigious learning. Yet, somehow, that learning "converted into the organic tissue of wisdom[.]" Moreover, Gray

> was a very wise man. So wise that those who met him in affairs would say that wisdom was the first thing to be mentioned with his name. He was able as no one else has been to unite practice in Boston, in which he was consulted and relied upon in matters of largest importance, with teaching at the Law School, where his subjects required study of subjects that seemed most remote from every day; and both with equal success.[307]

If Holmes wants to turn existing "law" into a matrix upon which, through emplotment, one could structure the future use of that concentrated social power also called "law" – giving "law" both a passive and an active side – then the language of rational propositions is confusing and misleading. If the phrase "rational proposition"[308] is meant to do more than demarcate the distance between a legal power's articulated, justified use and its passive, determinative capability, then Holmes runs the danger of isolating legal doctrine from its living sequence and context.

Holmes was certainly conscious of this danger and did all he could to avoid it. At the same time he kept trying to find a way to control the interaction between "history" on the one end and "theories of legislation" on the other. He sometimes thought the disciplines of statistics, economics, and political economy would

[307] Oliver Wendell Holmes, *John Chipman Gray, in* III CW 441–42.

[308] Commonwealth v. Rubin, *supra* note 287, at 456.

provide the necessary ballast but he was wrong. Without a conscious sense of depth – the relative distance and movement between present interests and those in the past that achieved legal expression – the policy or social sciences would further inflate the present. Critical history might bare the suppositions of the past and expose survivals, but it had little power to measure continuities not earmarked by survivals, that is, those principles of law that had not been sloughed off but which the body politic had absorbed even if unknowingly.[309] One needed another type of history, one that recognized – to use Hurst's terms – the cumulative sequence, the impetus and momentum of those social desires that had become so embedded in the social imaginary of the common law (present contexts) that they had the power to leap from mere legal expression to a new plane of experience. They had both the power to create depth *and* to form the needed grounds for future law.

Hessel Yntema commented in 1931 that Holmes's "formulation of legal evolution in terms of social ends is of itself a thesis, more profound and universal, more trenchant, than Maine's theorem 'from status to contract' or Tarde's law of imitation. And it has a range and vitality which avoids the formalism and *lack of perspective* in much historical work, such for instance as that of Ames."[310]

One could, as I did, sense the importance of Yntema's words and read them at least half-a-dozen times without fully understanding his meaning. But I think Yntema was on the right track. Yntema wrote his comment after quoting this passage from the concluding paragraph of "Law in Science and Science in Law."

> I have had in mind an ultimate dependence upon science because it is finally for science to determine, so far as it can, the relative worth of our different social ends, and, as I have tried to hint, it is our estimate of the proportion between these, now often blind and unconscious, that leads us to insist upon and to enlarge the sphere of one principle and to allow another gradually to dwindle into atrophy. Very likely it may be that with all the help that statistics and every modern appliance can bring us there never will be a commonwealth in which science is everywhere supreme. But it is an ideal, and without ideals what is life worth? They furnish us our perspective and open glimpses of the infinite.[311]

In a footnote Yntema ties that passage to this one from "The Path of the Law":

> I look forward to a time when the part played by history in the explanation of dogma shall be very small, and instead of ingenious research we shall spend our energy on a study of the ends sought to be attained and the reasons for desiring them. As a step

[309] *See* Holmes, *supra* note 10, at 133 ("The truth is, that the law is always approaching, and never reaching, consistency. It is forever adopting new principles from life at one end, and it always retains old ones from history at the other, which have not yet been *absorbed* or sloughed off. It will become entirely consistent only when it ceases to grow.") (emphasis added).

[310] Hessel Yntema, *Mr. Justice Holmes' View of Legal Science*, 40 YALE. L.J. 696, 702 (1931) (emphasis added).

[311] *Id.* at 701–02 (quoting Holmes, *supra* note 265, at 420).

> toward that ideal it seems to me that every lawyer ought to seek an understanding of economics. The present divorce between the schools of political economy and law seems to be evidence of how much progress in philosophical study still remains to be made.[312]

He then reinforces his argument by concluding that the "great virtue" of formulating legal evolution in terms of social ends "is to turn historical study upon tradition and thus to suggest the basis for a more rational consideration of legal problems."[313]

Yntema does not tell us exactly how turning historical study upon tradition will suggest the needed basis for greater rationality. If we turn back to the first section of "Mr. Justice Holmes' View of Legal Science," we obtain a better sense of Yntema's analysis and how it diverged from the basic problem that Holmes identified in "Law in Science and Science in Law." That is, how legal professionals might use the knowledge that an "abstract science" of the law provides to improve legal practice and judgment. The thought slowly dawns that for Holmes improving the law requires improving, bit by bit, the quality of the professional judgments constitutive of the practice.

Yntema in the beginning part of this article does not state the overriding problem in these terms because Yntema does not focus on the issue of how historical explanations that are "abstract" and those that are "practical" ought to work together. What Yntema labels "the theory of legal history" – an inartful expression – first directs attention to how Holmes distinguished two categories of historical explanation, the scientific and the practical. For Yntema historical explanations are meant to explain, in the loose sense, how certain beliefs and attitudes took on definite legal expression (their initial morphology) and how that structure, in turn, changed over time (the subsequent transformations). Yntema further seems to recognize that for Holmes the practical study of the morphology and transformations of legal doctrine always brings into the equation the actuality of present purpose.

Given this concern, Yntema tacks from the "theory of legal history" to the equally inartfully named "theory of legal evolution." The latter "theory" is the famed "paradox of form and substance in law": "The substance of the law at any given time pretty nearly corresponds, so far as it goes, with what is then understood to be convenient; but its form and machinery, and the degree to which it is able to work out its desired results, depend very much on its past."[314] For Yntema, the paradox of substance and form orients the task of using historical explanations for a practical purpose, for advancing the rationality of law. That is to say, the "paradox" provides the framework in which the explanatory endeavor takes place. He adds, "The implications which the hypothesis holds for legal history were explicitly set out in 1881."[315] That was the year when Holmes published *The Common Law*.

[312] *Id.* at n.39 (quoting Holmes, *supra* note 1, at 402–03).
[313] *Id.* at 702.
[314] *Id.* at 697 (quoting Holmes, *supra* note 10, at 115).
[315] *Id.* at 698.

Yntema sees Holmes from the very beginning of his career seeking to use historical study as a way to increase the rationality of current legal practice. Yntema sees the main objective as establishing the needed reference points for professional practice. They ought to be the best-available, best-understood, most "scientific" means and ends. This goal led Yntema "to an empirical conception of law." But for Yntema, as we noted in Part IV, Section 6, the "empirical" ties into the "actual." It becomes very tempting at this point to focus, as Yntema did, on the "actual" – the "legislative grounds" of the law – and ignore or minimize "its form and machinery." Many of the early realists went pretty far in this direction – most notably Jerome Frank – but Holmes himself never did. He never acted as if the "form and machinery" were solely vestigial, or had only been purposefully and cynically used to conceal the "secret root from which law draws all the juices of life."[316] That judges had used the "form and machinery" to clothe notions of expediency and convenience he was among the first to point out. But that did not mean he thought the "form and machinery" ought to be done away with.[317] He may have flirted at various points after the publication of *The Common Law* with the attractions of an overarching legal code – depending as he said on who put it together – but he never gave up his fundamental mistrust, for the reasons he laid out in "Codes, and the Arrangement of the Law."[318]

The interplay between the "form and machinery" and what is felt as expedient and convenient served as an early way of expressing the three elements of Holmes's thinking to which we have already drawn attention. How can history, philosophy, and economics – to give a shorthand description – be coordinated so that the resultant, enforceable law, unifies into a working array those means and ends still vital and those sought after? How can scientific history inform practical history and how can practical history itself help turn law – as a mode of inquiry and decision-making – into a full-fledged science? Yntema understood that any specific legal doctrine might instantiate or less strongly express and direct (point) attention toward an important social value, but he did not fully see the significance Holmes placed on determining proportionate value. Proportionate value depended largely on depth. Under the glare of Yntema's analysis, legal doctrine melted into those "grounds" that one could, from one's present, see and understand. Yntema, compared to Holmes, had little feel for the law's depth, its expanse and reach.

In our own day various intellectual categories serve as proxies for espied grounds – categories regarding race, or class, or gender, or sexual identity, or religion, or various other forms of social, political, cultural, or economic power for example. These categories are not solely artificial abstractions, nor are they untrue to events;

[316] Holmes, *supra* note 10, at 133.

[317] *But see* Richard A. Posner, The Problematics of Moral and Legal Theory 206–11 (1999) (interpreting "The Path of the Law" as laying the groundwork for the supersession of law).

[318] *See* Holmes, *supra* note 103, at 478; Holmes, *supra* note 217, at 212–15.

but as heuristics they do have the capacity to occlude those yet-to-be-seen tendencies that might, on occasion, modulate the ongoing Darwinian battle.

Yntema does not connect Holmes's articulation of his external standards, as in tort and contract, with Holmes's effort to press past and present conceptions and ongoing convictions and desires strongly against each other. When Holmes remarked on tendencies in the law, he did so because those tendencies became evident as he undertook the hard thinking needed to turn law into a discipline of power. He wanted to think more clearly and more profoundly about what mattered most to him. Tendencies espied in the past may often be revelatory of present interests. Holmes probably knew that. Yntema had an inkling something like this was occurring in Holmes's thought but did not fully comprehend the dynamics. That is why he writes that the great virtue of Holmes's thought was to "turn historical study upon tradition and thus suggest the basis for a more rational consideration of legal problems."[319] That was a great virtue. But for reasons other than the critical function of history that Yntema wants to emphasize.

Unsurprisingly, that great virtue takes us back to the bad man, to the purely legal point of view. Holmes's reflections on history in both "The Path of the Law" and "Law in Science and Science in Law" support the argument that history as a "practical" form of explanation in the law had to come into its own. It had to evolve; it had to acquire new characteristics and capacities; it had to work within its own framework. Holmes hated what he saw happening at law schools like Boston and Harvard. He took the argument straight to the historians seeking (successfully) to put them on the defensive. Ames and Holmes had gently crossed swords on occasion.[320] Holmes believed it had something to with his treatment of Langdell.[321] That might have been part of the story. But Holmes also seems to have been oblivious to how he at times came across. In both "The Path of the Law" and "Law in Science and Science in Law" he puts Ames, as he once did Langdell in *The Common Law*, under the microscope. It's all very subtle; yet neither Langdell nor Ames – the former and current dean of the Harvard Law School – ever comes out with an unqualified high-grade stamp of approval.

Holmes's longtime colleague and friend James Bradley Thayer filed an unofficial protest three days after Holmes delivered "The Path of the Law." He wrote this letter.

Cambridge, January 11, 1897

Dear Holmes

I heard your address the other day with delight. You speak as a master and a leader and have a right to.

[319] Yntema, *supra* note 310, at 702.

[320] *See* David M. Rabban, Law's History: American Legal Thought and the Transatlantic Turn to History 294–302 (2013); *see also* Hiller B. Zobel, *Ames v. Holmes: Ethics and the Legal Mind*, 1 Sup. Jud. Ct. Hist. Soc'y J. 18 (1995).

[321] Rabban, *supra* note 320.

I wish that in printing you might consider this one thing. You have a right to go ahead in the way that you suggest. But consider what would happen if the mob of judges who know so little of the groundwork should do the same thing. You know it all. But there are very few who do.

That being so I must believe that it is the first duty of this generation to clean up the history of the matter, – agreeing entirely with you that all this historical work has no other aim than to put solid ground under the feet of those who are to shape things for the future.

What I deprecate is that you who know how much there is to learn and how enormously it helps to [do] close and solid work, should seem to play into the hands of the [illegible] ignoramuses and should really do it.

Pray consider this danger and believe me,

Always truly yours,
J.B. Thayer[322]

In hindsight, Thayer's letter takes on a peculiar hue. Holmes at the beginning of his career had to overcome the slurs against legal learning, from both the unlearned and the learned. Now, near its apex, the dynamics have shifted. The contest no longer ranges to and fro between a Jacksonian propensity to slash the Gordian knot of legal niceties and the insistent efforts of the Storys and Kents in the population to promote order and wisdom through a developed, technical legal literature.[323] No, for Thayer it has become a contest between the "mob of judges" and the "[illegible] ignoramuses" on the one side, and those dedicated legal scholars who sought to clear the ground and lay a solid foundation for law on the other.

The English and American fixation on "the practical" inevitably hindered the working out of Thayer's ideal. As he had put it two years earlier in his speech, as its chairman, to the American Bar Association (ABA)'s Section on Legal Education:

> But as regards our law, those who press the importance of thorough and scientific study are not yet exempt from the duty of pointing out the use of it and its necessity. To say nothing of the widespread skepticism among a certain class of practical men, in and out of our profession, as to the advantages of anything of the sort, there is also, among the many who nominally admit it and even advocate it, a remarkable failure to appreciate what this admission means. *It is the simple truth that you cannot have a thorough and first-rate training in law, any more than in physical*

[322] Letter from James Bradley Thayer to Oliver Wendell Holmes (Jan. 11, 1897) (on file with Harvard University Holmes Digital Suite, Harvard University, Harvard Law School Library / The John G. Palfrey (1875–1945) collection of Oliver Wendell Holmes Jr. Papers, 1715–1938. General Correspondence, File Drawers: Box 22, Folder 30, Thayer, James Bradley, Correspondent, 1879–1900).

[323] *See, e.g.*, Michael Lobban, A History of the Philosophy of Law in the Common Law World, 1600–1900 145–53 (2007).

> *science, unless you have a body of learned teachers; and you cannot have a learned faculty of law unless, like other faculties, they give their lives to their work.*[324]

Thayer deemed necessary a corps of dedicated legal scholars to put American law on a rational footing. These dedicated legal scholars should follow the Harvard Law professors' pedagogical creed – explore and trace the development of legal doctrine, discern new connections, dispel false ones, clear away ambiguities, false theories, outworn and unintelligible phraseology, in short, dissolve and rationalize existing technicality – and thus provide the basis for an improved legal order. But what is missing from Thayer's rendition are two steps that Holmes included in his 1886 restatement, (1) showing how principles gradually emerged as the "felt reconciliation of concrete instances," and (2) setting legal principles in perspective and judging their proportions.[325]

Once one realizes that recognizing felt reconciliations requires, as much as does setting legal principles in perspective and judging their proportions, real perspicuity and insight, one of the more puzzling sections of "Law in Science and Science in Law" begins to take on new meaning.

Thayer, as the quote above shows, envisioned a special role for the legal scholar; he called upon the redoubtable authority of Langdell to support it.[326] He urged his hearers at the 1895 meeting of the ABA's Section on Legal Education to adopt the Langdellian spirit in the study of law: "our law must be studied and taught as other great sciences are studied and taught at the Universities, as deeply, by like methods, and with as thorough a concentration and life-long devotion of all the powers of a learned and studious faculty."[327] He further impressed the importance of this mission upon his hearers by noting that even Sir Frederick Pollock had recently come down from Oxford to take part in the twenty-fifth anniversary celebration of Langdell's tenure at Harvard. "He crossed the ocean for that mere purpose, and returned as soon as it was accomplished."[328]

Compared to Thayer, Holmes is reading from a very different playbook:

> But I doubt if there is any more exalted form of life than that of a great abstract thinker, wrapt in the successful study of problems to which he devotes himself, for an end which is neither unselfish nor selfish in the common sense of those words, but is simply to feed the deepest hunger and to use the greatest gifts of his soul.
>
> But after all the place for a man who is complete in all his powers is in the fight. The professor, the man of letters, gives up one-half of life that his protected talent

[324] James Bradley Thayer, *The Teaching of English Law at Universities*, 9 HARV. L. REV. 169, 174–75 (1895) (emphasis added).

[325] Holmes, *supra* note 103, at 477.

[326] On Langdell's role in creating a new "subspecies of lawyer – the full-time academic" – *see* John Henry Schlegel, *American Legal Theory and American Legal Education: A Snake Swallowing Its Tail?*, 12 GERMAN L.J. 67, 69–73 (2011).

[327] Thayer, *supra* note 324, at 173.

[328] *Id.*

may grow and flower in peace. But to make up your mind at your peril upon a living question, for purposes of action, calls upon your whole nature.[329]

These sentences bring the tribute to Shattuck back to mind. They lead to the inference that scientific law for Holmes demanded a more nuanced understanding of the interaction between the conscious articulations and unconscious supports underlying past judgments and those desires, feelings, inclinations, convictions, and articulations that spring to mind in the present. The relation extends beyond what is typically thought of as precedent. We come back to that fascinating sentence: "People often speak of correcting the judgment of the time by that of posterity. I think it quite as true to say that we must correct the judgment of posterity by that of the time."[330]

Brought together, Holmes's differentiation between the professor of law and the practicing legal professional and his sense that present and past judgments must correct each other draw attention to his primary concern: to improve the quality of the practical judgments that make up the law. Practical judgments are often nested, but no single, isolated practical judgment provides an analytical starting point or foundation for resolving legal issues apart from actual circumstances. Practical judgments always work in combination to further array conceptions, feelings, desires, and purposes for the sake of some specific end within a concrete setting. A better, more rigorous understanding of ends, Holmes believed, would lead to stronger judgments, which, in turn, would further the study and clarification of ends.

Given how often Holmes reiterates this desideratum, it comes as no surprise that after first politely responding to Thayer's January 11 letter – that when it came time to print the Boston University address he would most "certainly consider what you say[,]" since he agreed "most heartily" – he ultimately decided against any revisions.[331] It appears Holmes preferred to take his chances and be seen as supporting the ignoramuses and mob of judges than fall in, no matter how remotely, with a view that the best way to improve the law was to support the efforts of dedicated doctrinal historians. He desperately wanted to go in a different direction.

iii *The Bad Man and Legal Education*

William Twining is probably the leading writer and theorist in the anglophone world on legal education.[332] He has worked at the intersection of two disciplines,

[329] Holmes, *supra* note 265, at 412.

[330] Holmes, *supra* note 143, at 494.

[331] Letters from Oliver Wendell Holmes to James Bradley Thayer (Jan. 12, 1897 and Feb. 11, 1897) (on file with Harvard University Holmes Digital Suite, Harvard University, Harvard Law School Library / Mark DeWolfe Howe research materials relating to the life of Oliver Wendell Holmes, Jr., 1858–1968. General Correspondence, General Group II: Box 18, Folder 2, Thayer, James Bradley, correspondent, 1890–1900).

[332] For a good overview of the extent and nature of his interests see the collection of essays in William Twining, Law in Context: Enlarging a Discipline (1997).

education and law, that have not, historically, had a tremendous amount of interchange. As he points out in his engaging memoir, *Jurist in Context*, early in his career as a law professor he confronted the opinion that he did not have a proper job. Leading Law Lords in England boasted of their lack of formal legal education. They had attended university instead of the Inns of Court (*pace* the Lord Chief Justice's advice). Sneers from other professionals – lower court judges and practitioners, presumably – regarding his focus on legal education were, he wryly says, "more direct."[333]

For their part, professional educators in the United Kingdom did not consider legal education a proper area of research. Many law professors held the equally strong conviction "that specialists in education have little or nothing to teach legal educators and that Legal Education is not a respectable subject of study and research." Twining is not as unforgiving of such sentiments as one might think. On the whole, he believes, "the professionalisation of education is to be welcomed, but some skepticism behind resistance to these developments is healthy." Educational theory is important. But as long as it is too bound up with bureaucratization and managerialism, Twining thinks some skepticism is merited. He definitely does not think familiarity with educational theory and pedagogical technique is a substitute for being competent and enthusiastic about one's subject.[334]

Twining's general approach to issues in legal education falls somewhere along the spectrum between what Holmes called "the useless quintessence of all systems" and "the accurate anatomy of one."[335] Closer to the latter than the former, Twining's analyses take on a predominantly sociological flare as he attempts to bring into closer connection the various activities that constitute the practice of law and the instituted, formal educational curriculum or training used to prepare students for that practice.

Twining in his scholarship shifts the focus from learning rules to appreciating the various roles involved in law-related activity. He recounts in his memoir how R. G. Collingwood's idea that all history is the history of thought influenced how he began to conceive of the jurisprudential task. Ideas or events came into being in response to occasions and purposes. "[O]ne needs to put oneself in the writer's or actor's shoes and try to understand their situation, concerns, role, concepts, information and perceptions in order to reconstruct what they were thinking and what it meant."[336] He further recounts how one of Collingwood's articles began to help him differentiate the various "lenses" that different "specialists" use to understand an event and how those might differ from a nonspecialist's. For example, in ascertaining the "cause" of an accident in which a car skids while turning a corner, flips, and bursts

[333] William Twining, Jurist in Context: A Memoir 217 (2019).
[334] *Id.* at 221–22.
[335] Holmes, *supra* note 1, at 403.
[336] Twining, *supra* note 333, at 117.

into flames, the driver will think he turned the corner too quickly, the county surveyor will see the problem as the lack of skid-proof roads, and the auto manufacturer will (quietly) realize that the automobile's design was defective (it should have had a lower center of gravity).

From Collingwood and other influences, mainly literary, Twining began to develop his notion of standpoint. He introduced it formally in his 1973 article "The Bad Man Revisited." That was the same article in which he first observed that Holmes intended "The Path of the Law" as a discussion of legal education, not a contribution to general jurisprudence.

Contrary to the predominant understanding of the time, Twining did not see either "The Path of the Law" or Holmes himself advancing what was then usually called, "the prediction theory of law."[337] That is why he says upfront that Holmes did not intend this article as a contribution to general jurisprudence. H. L. A. Hart had subjected the prediction theory to scathing criticism in his 1961 book *The Concept of Law*. Implicitly Twining suggests that Hart had gone off track, at least concerning "The Path of the Law." Twining believes its significance – despite its lack of clear exposition at critical points – lay in how Holmes engineered an elementary, and effective, switch in standpoint. Holmes sought to introduce the law student to the functioning legal system not through an analysis of leading legal concepts, or through the explication of legal doctrine, or from the elevated perspective of an appellate judge, but through the point of view of a participant at the boundaries, one who only cares what other participants in the system will do in response to what she or he does.

Standpoint for Twining typically includes a certain vantage (in an observational sense), a certain task or objective, and, at times, the advocacy of an ideology or principle (Marxism or utility, for instance).[338] In regard to the bad man, Twining sees him as providing an entry point into the legal system understood as a system of roles, not a system of rules. Prediction becomes key, not as a theory of law, but as a way to focus on legal action, how various legal roles may interact under given conditions.

As do many legal scholars before and after him, Twining primarily understands the bad man as highlighting a certain aspect of the lawyer–client relation, where the client is seeking advice regarding proposed, potentially problematic conduct, and the lawyer providing it. He subsequently simultaneously expands and clarifies this interpretation. In a 1997 retrospective, he bemoans the lack of scholarly integrity in how so many scholars have treated Holmes and the bad man; the lack of nuance in the use of such words or phrases as vantage point, perspective (especially as

337 *Id.* at 120–21. *See also* William Twining, *Bad Man Revisited*, 58 Cornell L. Rev. 275, 276–80 (1973). For similar comments to Twining's *see* Martin P. Golding, Philosophy of Law 37–38 (1975) (noting that the prediction theory of law cannot stand as a general theory of law, even if Holmes meant it as such).

338 Twining, *supra* note 337, at 275, 285–87.

employed in the internal/external distinction), role, and purpose; the lack of conscientious exposition of "The Path of the Law." Twining concludes by calling for a more expansive and nuanced vocabulary for depicting those actions and events generally summarized as "law."[339]

As for the bad man himself, Twining reiterates in 1997 what he first said in 1971. Holmes put forward the bad man for two reasons. First, "to dramatize a distinction between law and morals – the badness or amoral aspect, and second, to focus attention on a more realistic standpoint for law students than that of appellate judges – the predictive aspect."[340] In these two respects the bad man is best seen as Holmes's effort to extend the positivist tradition. Twining correspondingly extends his initial argument to further argue that the bad man provides "an enduring symbol of a positivist view of law seen as other people's power."[341]

Twining's work is hard to summarize because he is simultaneously expansive and detailed. He moves in many directions and often finds trying the habitual lack of nuance and clarity in the jurisprudential thinking of his contemporaries. In the comparison that Isaiah Berlin made famous, Twining is the quintessential fox. Holmes, by contrast, is a veritable hedgehog.

Twining may have perceptively seen that Holmes did not intend "The Path of the Law" as a contribution to general jurisprudence (that is, as articulating a so-called prediction theory of law). But in emphasizing its pedagogical intent he, oddly, does little to explain how the distinction between law and morals that the bad man is meant to emphasize, and the "bottom-up" standpoint he is meant to represent, fit together to educate the aspiring law student. Standing in the wings is the unspoken assumption that these two pointers orient students and help them understand a complex, working profession. Seeing how various roles function and interact, how viewpoint and purpose operate together, how the actions of legal professionals may appear depending whether one is participating or observing, how legal reasoning works, and why, may be the needed parts of any pedagogical program. But in respect to Holmes one must ask whether they were the necessary parts of the program he advocated.

The answer to that question is no. Twining appears to have initially approached "The Path of the Law" in a manner similar to the early American realists, and then refined his original perceptions in keeping with the goals of a more expansive and nuanced jurisprudence. Twining the fox did not quite see how Holmes the hedgehog intended in "The Path of the Law" to explicate the single "process" that connected the lawyer's initial statement of the case to the final analyses and abstract universals of theoretic jurisprudence. Twining disaggregated and differentiated

339 William Twining, *Other People's Power: The Bad Man and English Positivism, 1897–1997*, 63 Brooklyn L. Rev. 189, 212–22 (1997)

340 *Id.* at 204.

341 *Id.* at 194.

many of the leading terms and functions of jurisprudence and of lawyering, he brought to bear a schematic view that showed how the various lines and connections operated at varying levels of generality, but he did little, in his discussions of Holmes and the bad man, to give the resulting schema the requisite depth. In other words, through philosophical, sociological, and historical analysis and depiction he extended his present but did not give it movement and direction. He stayed mainly in two dimensions.

To appreciate this criticism, one must entertain the idea that law comprises various pointers – professional judgments surmised and encapsulated – meant for lawyers, that these pointers exist in varying arrangements, and that these arrangements, along with the pointers themselves, possess differing magnitudes and directions. The terms, "pointers," "arrangements," "magnitudes," and "directions," need explication of course. But more than that, one must first see the pointers and their attributes as existing on a plane of verisimilitude made actual through the recognized feedback between present legal purpose and past court action. The query, "what is (the) law?," demarcates the ambit, or range, in which this feedback loop works.

One finds grounds for the foregoing criticism of Twining – but not its articulation – in "The Path of the Law"'s opening sections. In Part IV, Section 13, we wrote, "Holmes, through the force of his rhetoric, projected the bad man from his common law origins onto a new plane of social existence."[342] That sentence suggests that Holmes took a disposition or tendency he found in the English common law and personified it into a guide for legal inquiry. He did the same thing on a smaller scale with the prudent man. We might call both of these artificial devices, the bad man and the prudent man, "heuristics" if we use the word with some care. The important point is that in both cases the heuristic arises from and organizes the activity to which it is connected. It collates certain practices, ideas, and feelings into a new arrangement, and sometimes a new summation, that has the capacity to harness the relevant past and the anticipated future in support of present action.

The bad man as a learning tool introduced the student to a way of thinking that fit with the subject matter, law. In "Path" Holmes uses different terms to describe law, the most common being "body of dogma," "systematized prediction," and "the prophecies of what the courts will do in fact." Somehow, the mode and method of study had to fit the subject. In a passage from "Law in Science and Science in Law" which Yntema also quotes, Holmes writes,

> I sometimes tell students that law schools pursue an inspirational method combined with a logical method, that is, the postulates are taken for granted upon authority without inquiry into their worth, and then logic is used as the only tool to develop the results. It is a necessary method for the purpose of teaching dogma. But inasmuch as the real justification of a rule of law, if there be one, is that it helps

[342] *See supra* Part IV, Section 13.

> to bring about a social end which we desire, it is not less necessary that those who make and develop the law should have those ends articulately in their minds.[343]

We commented earlier on the incongruities this passage presented.[344] The inspirational and the logical methods somehow work together in teaching law derived from the cases. These combined methods directed the teaching of law in schools like Harvard's, and Holmes seems to chalk up their use to the time constraints imposed upon them. The alternative method Holmes proposes is as much a method for learning law as for teaching it. It inheres in instilling a viewpoint, the purely legal point of view; a point of view that brings into relief a new plane of verisimilitude, one essential for obtaining mastery over the subject matter.

Superimposing the above quoted passage onto the opening sections of "The Path of the Law" leads to the inference that to improve law – more specifically, to improve the practical judgments that form the tissue of law – one must add to history, philosophy, and economics (again, using these words compendiously) a necessary fourth element, a refined method for legal pedagogy. Taught law, Frederic Maitland once said, is tough law. Taught law was the law that had endured. Dean Pound in the 1930s thought that the tenacity of the taught legal tradition was much more significant to American legal history than the economic conditions of time and place.[345]

Holmes in the 1890s saw that the law that had endured and was taught at Harvard had taken on a peculiarly dogmatic form. That dogmatic form, he wryly hinted, combined two methods (the inspirational and the logical) that seemed very much at home in the theological camp of Cardinal Newman. He comes back to his concern with postulates. In the law schools the postulates "are taken for granted upon authority." Whose authority? Logic alone is then used to develop the postulates' implications. Again, by whom?

I think it pretty clear that Holmes is referring to the distinguished law professors at places like Boston University and Harvard. To call their approach "formalistic" does not really help clarify the exact nature of the problem because professors like Bigelow, Thayer, and Ames (not to mention Langdell) did quite a bit of spadework in unearthing the ancient reports and cases and putting them into some kind of working order. They certainly saw this time-consuming, difficult work as empirical and scholarly, not merely rote, justifying existing prejudices or mechanical in nature. The problem Holmes identified fell into two parts, (1) accepting blindly the worth of a governing postulate, and (2) using only logic to work out its implications. But a bigger related issue, unmentioned in "Law in Science and Science in Law," set up his discussion in "The Path of the Law." It did not involve the use of

343 Yntema, *supra* note 310, at 700 (quoting Holmes, *supra* note 265, at 418).

344 *See supra* Part IV, Section 6.

345 ROSCOE POUND, THE FORMATIVE ERA OF AMERICAN LAW 81–82 (1938); *see also* Roscoe Pound, *President's Address – Taught Law*, 3 AM. L. SCH. REV. 164, 165–66 (1912).

unexamined postulates or logic but the very character of the law used for teaching purposes. Holmes had once acknowledged that a "professor must start with a system as an arbitrary fact," but that pedagogical necessity did not entitle the professor to disguise the ineradicably arbitrary nature of the "dogmatic teaching" thus set up.[346]

Holmes may have believed the common law's true legal conceptions to be few in number, but that did not mean that the way those conceptions were currently understood or worked out or taught had a rational basis. Dogma was a necessary evil. The rise of university-based law schools in the late nineteenth century had, as William G. Hammond predicted, logically led to the law's reformulation. The resultant was not much to Holmes's liking. It masked all the nonlogical factors (desires, prejudices, unverified beliefs, conveniences and expedients, apathy, moral fervor, surreptitiousness) that bound and sustained existing dogma. It ignored the importance of vetting postulates. It created the wrong type of axiological framework. Even in using the language of authority (dogma) to describe it, Holmes lodges a quiet protest against its pretension as revealed wisdom. He seems to say to his student hearers: "The law presented to you, that you must study and learn and master has not been dropped from the heavens, nor has it the imprimatur of everlasting truth, but exists solely as a more-or-less arbitrary compendium, born in time and tainted by history, to help guide and instruct you as you take the steps you must take to join this well known profession."

That is why, when seen from one angle, law – presently enforceable rules and their justifications – stands as a living record of a profession that extends back hundreds of years. It has no inherent mystery; it invokes no occult science. Theoretically, each of the leaves of this mammoth palimpsest could be read, each paragraph, sentence, phrase, word, or mark traced back to some conjunction of desire, purpose, intelligence, and belief or to the interstices between them. Or, if Kunal Parker is to be believed, traced mostly to their opposites: agglomerations of mistakes, inversions, confusions, and unheralded survivals.[347]

Regardless of how one characterizes the collected assemblages, Holmes insists it must be studied in a manner adapted to its inherent composition. That is the first point. The second is that this "arbitrary fact" must be put back from whence its elements arose, into the stream of life. John Dewey thought the endeavor feasible as long as one kept in mind the practical standpoint. "[R]ecognition of the relatively slow rate of change on the part of certain constituents of social action is capable of accomplishing every useful, every *practically* needed, office that has led in the past

[346] Holmes, A *Review of* A Selection of Cases on the Law of Contracts, *supra* note 11, at 103–04.

[347] Kunal Parker, *The History of Experience: The Historical Imagination of Oliver Wendell Holmes, Jr.*, 26 Pol. and Legal Anthrop. Rev. 60, 71–72 (2003); *see also* Thomas C. Grey, *Accidental Torts*, 54 Vand. L. Rev. 1225 (2001). *But see* Brown v. United States, 256 U.S. 335, 343 (1921) ("The law has grown, and even if historical mistakes have contributed to its growth it has tended in the direction of rules consistent with human nature.") (per Holmes, J.).

and in other cultural climes to setting up external sources such as the Will or Reason of God, the Law of Nature . . . [.]"[348]

Dewey's prescription announced in less concentrated form and to a more dispersed audience what Holmes said to those who had dedicated, or might decide to dedicate, their lives to a profession he revered. Perhaps it would be stepping out of bounds to claim that Holmes wholeheartedly believed in law, had *faith* in the profession to which he had given his life. Perhaps the less risky course of action counsels taking refuge in quotation.

> I trust no one will understand me to be speaking with disrespect of the law, because I criticize it so freely. I venerate the law, and especially our system of law, as one of the vastest products of the human mind. No one knows better than I do the countless number of great intellects that have spent themselves in making some addition or improvement, the greatest of which is trifling when compared with the mighty whole. It has the final title to respect that it exists, that it is not a Hegelian dream, but a part of the lives of men.[349]

If the law was entitled to respect, that respect had to rest on reasons less inviolate than those that found their home in Natural Law, on the one hand, and more dignified and worthy of human attention, on the other, than the full-throated declaration that whatever is, is right. If law was the product of human intelligence, then that intelligence had to be queried. If law was the result of human wants, then those wants had to be scrutinized. If law arose mainly by accident, then rectification may be in order. If the law that demanded respect came bathed in the glory of past renown, of life curdled in horror and sustained by might, then into those mythy heaths the inquirer must cautiously venture.

In modern academic parlance one might say that Holmes faced a difficult hermeneutical problem. How does one bring to bear on the law of today the results of expansive scientific (empirical) inquiries without inducing what has been aptly called in another setting a reality distortion field?

The answer we find in Holmes – undoubtedly the same answer that impressed Dewey – lies in the practical.[350] It lies in the law's basic building blocks, practical judgments. Recall what he said in "Just the Boy Wanted": "Practical judgment, that is, a sense of the relative importance of things with reference to the accomplishment of some desired end, is what commands the world . . . . The lawyer's judgment is a sense of the relative importance of facts with reference to rules of law, and a sense also, – the more the better, – of their importance with regard to business[.]"[351]

[348] My Philosophy of Law: Credos of Sixteen American Scholars 81 (1941) (emphasis in original).

[349] Holmes, *The Path of the Law*, *supra* note 1, at 402.

[350] It was Dewey who, for reasons still not entirely clear, referred to Holmes in 1925 as "one of our greatest American philosophers." John Dewey, Experience and Nature 417 (Dover ed. 1958) (orig. pub. 1925).

[351] Holmes, *supra* note 171, at 339.

These practical judgments, when organized, reflected upon, and operationalized, become systematized predictions. Predictions are active, forward looking. In announcing in "The Path of the Law"'s opening paragraph that prediction is the object – as in the objective – of legal study, and then a few paragraphs later recharacterizing the "body of dogma" as "systematized prediction," Holmes is signaling his concern to prevent the calcification of the "dogma" that is taught.

In other words, for taught law to remain vital, responsive, and directive, it cannot separate itself from the ongoing fight and clash of interests as well as the abiding, unspoken bonds that stamp this profession as a profession. The upshot lies not in the perpetual jousting or jostling but in the habit of mind to which the practice leads. Lawyers do not pursue money directly, Holmes noted.[352] Instead of selling a good they offer services, mainly advice and representation. Advice and representation subtly tend to develop the habits of thinking about the interests of others and how those interests might be affected. Thus when opposing lawyers turn to the same sibylline leaves that record all the times the axe has fallen they do so, according to Holmes, to help them foresee those future instances when and where it might again strike. It is natural at this point in the sequence to fall into the mode of explanation that sees the "prophecies of the past" as, in some sense, the bases or grounds for the forthcoming prediction. But Holmes does not quite take this step. Instead, he interjects the hard-to-understand comment that "Far the most important and pretty nearly the whole meaning of every new effort of legal thought is to make these prophecies more precise, and to generalize them into a thoroughly connected system." This sentence precedes the one in which he characterizes this all-important "process" as a single one, going from the lawyer's statement of the case to the "final analyses and abstract universals of theoretic jurisprudence."[353]

The difficulties in connecting the dots lie in how Holmes seems to have gone from trying to prevent an essentially arbitrary, though not capricious, "body of dogma" from calcifying and reifying to seemingly encouraging that which he wants to prevent. It's hard to see how increasing precision and generalizing these more precise statements into a system does not lead us back to what it seemed Holmes wanted to get away from, a dogmatically structured and integrated legal corpus.

But then Holmes gives us a clue to the direction he wants to go. He says: "It is to make the prophecies easier to be remembered and to be understood that the teachings of the decisions of the past are put into general propositions and gathered into text-books, or that statutes are passed in a general form."[354] What, we are driven to ask, is the relation between a "general proposition" and the scattered prophecies/teachings of the past? In the same vein, what is the relation between a general form statute and the specific problems or issues that the legislature sought to address?

352 Holmes, *supra* note 187, at 386.

353 Holmes, *The Path of the Law*, *supra* note 1, at 391.

354 *Id.*

The initial response takes us back to Holmes's idea that law embodies the sequence of events that the governing authority wants to see happen or not happen. Prophecies – not one but many – are made "more precise" through every "new effort of legal thought." The most important word in this clause is "new." Every new effort of legal thought is an effort to increase the law's intelligibility, to make law more knowable. That requires philosophical acuity and imaginative insight if one hopes to escape the ill effects of policy or other rationalizations. The effort to think through the law to its generative conditions and ongoing consequences is an effort that takes place at a certain moment in time and space and unavoidably instantiates a certain constellation of values. Intelligibility organizes a lawyer's sense of what the courts will do in a specific circumstance, and the ability to express that judgment depends, Holmes seems to suggest, on the number or weight of instances that point in the same direction. One must find or uncover the feature or features in the legal landscape that will invariably or most likely induce the court to move in a certain way. Yet if pushed too hard in that direction the danger arises that the effort to increase law's intelligibility, its rationality, will falter. We end up where the common law lawyer began – in the chaos of the cases. The relevant descriptions would be different but the result would be the same. When Holmes says that the "number of predictions when generalized and reduced to a system is not unmanageably large[,]" he is expressing at one and the same time his confidence that once all the "dramatic elements" are eliminated from various cases the resulting operative facts can be restated as a generalized proposition which, in turn, can be systematized. That is to say, Holmes wants to use the existing "body of dogma," that which has no more entitlement to respect than the mere fact it has endured, that it is tough, and begin bit by bit to transform it into a body, not of dogma, but of "systematized prediction." Holmes is trying to redirect the most advanced understanding of law existing in the law schools away from justifying unexamined postulates and in the direction of greater awareness of grounds and better reasoned ends.

He does not tell us, though, how these general propositions should be systematized. The immediate assumption that logic exclusively should do the systematizing work finds little direct support in Holmes's writings. All we really know is that predictions when generalized into a thoroughly connected system result in a "finite body of dogma which may be mastered within a reasonable time."[355]

Without further trying to harmonize what may be incongruent statements, we can summarize the foregoing discussion as follows:

1. Taught law is tough law put into a body of dogma for the sake of teaching.
2. The dogma taught is not necessarily irrational or unreasonable but it is arbitrary (that is, there is no overwhelming, universal justification for it existing as it does).

[355] *Id.*

3. The dogma that is taught includes selected cases, the principles that the selected cases are meant to inculcate, and doctrinal summaries and explications that logically integrate decision with decision.
4. To prevent dogma from arresting thought as the Roman law so often had done in European or British history, Holmes emphasizes that the dogma taught or solidified only represents a working summation of professional legal opinion on the various topics addressed.
5. In other words, the dogma taught represents the articulate, reasoned opinion of the members of the profession that created it.
6. Dogma did not stand as the condensed proxy for all professional opinion, but as the measured reflection of those who had the task of educating and guiding the succeeding generations of lawyers. But for that very reason it had the capacity to influence strongly how other professionals thought about their tasks.
7. To prevent that existing dogma from suffocating future thought, Holmes wants to do two things, (a) improve the means by which the professors reason to and articulate the dogma that is taught, and (b) emphasize the dogma's practical, not sacerdotal, office.
8. Dogma's practical office serves to orient and guide lawyers and judges as controversies arise.
9. Dogma's practical office orients and guides lawyers and judges because dogma provides a point of continuity. Its teachings condense past experience, but those teachings have to be ferreted out with the right intellectual tools and made intelligible in contemporary circumstances. The inspirational and logical methods sidelined genuine inquiry and made dogma dogmatic. If viewed as a subject matter for further inquiry, however, dogma becomes interactive and involved, not passive and inert.
10. Thus the dogma that exists could be reshaped bit by bit so that its postulates (those past grounds espied from the context of current concerns) connected more clearly with the ends that dogma seeks, or should seek, to implement in the face of countervailing pressures.

We thus see that Holmes in "The Path of the Law" was trying, at one and the same time, to move in two seemingly opposite directions. He agreed with the oft-cited criticism that law professors like Langdell set up and taught a body of law that increasingly diverged from actual professional expectations because of its emphasis on logical integration. That emphasis may not have been exclusive, but it was pronounced. On the other side, Holmes wanted to keep insisting that one could find and articulate a rational order from the chaos of the cases – or the chaos of cases and statutes – without recurring to a jurisprudential style reminiscent of the Roman.

The axis of Holmes's thinking centers on a so-called single "process" that somehow governs and connects both the lawyer's statement of the case and the final analyses and abstract universals of theoretic jurisprudence. It was this "process" that both created the grounds upon which dogma rested and had the power to keep it alive to new circumstances and new thought. Holmes also believed this same "process" suggested a more direct method for thinking more clearly about law and understanding its unique office in a democratic society.

"Process" as Holmes uses it is by itself uninformative. What we learn from the second paragraph of "The Path of the Law" is that this "process" has a discrete beginning- and endpoint. The beginning point is "the lawyer's statement of the case, eliminating as it does all the dramatic elements in which his client's story clothed it, and retaining only the facts of legal import[.]" The endpoint is the "final analyses and abstract universals of theoretic jurisprudence." Later in the address Holmes describes jurisprudence as "simply law in its most generalized part. Every effort to reduce a case to a rule is an effort of jurisprudence, although the name as used in English is confined to the broadest rules and most fundamental conceptions. One mark of the great lawyer is that he sees the application of the broadest rules."[356]

Again: "If a man goes into law it pays to be a master of it, and to be a master of it means to look straight through all the dramatic incidents and to discern the true basis for prophecy."[357]

Jurisprudence for Holmes is certain kind of noetic ability, a type of insight. He describes it as the ability to discern the "facts of legal import," and thus arrive at the "true basis for prophecy." It appears to be comprised of two subsidiary skills. At its most sophisticated, the skill needed to discern the facts of legal import – that is, avoid getting tangled in merely dramatic facts – has a strong component of historical inquiry. In the trespass *ab initio* example we closely looked at it became evident that its application did not turn on whether or not the case involved government officials. That was irrelevant. It turned on when one could use subsequent conduct as evidence of prior intent. The fact of legal import was the close conjunction in time of an act inconsistent with honest intent.

The other ability Holmes often calls a skill is the ability to move to and fro from specific to general or from concrete to abstract. Such language has often led commentators to see the goal of reasoning for Holmes as in some sense conceptualistic or formalistic (both words are used). These descriptions suggest two very different types of intellectual operations. The first, from specific to general, suggests a logical taxonomy reminiscent of Austin (*infima species* – *summum genus*). The second, from concrete to abstract, is harder to describe but seems to depend on a deepening ability to perceive similarities or contrasts. For Holmes it depended on insight. Holmes clearly intends that one ought not to be satisfied with remaining at the level at which the "facts of legal import" are determined. And yet he also seems to say that through the effort of legal thought one moves from dramatic incidents to

[356] *Id.* at 403.
[357] *Id.*

facts of legal import to the broadest rules and most fundamental conceptions connected to an actual system of law. The question is how.

We suggested above, when discussing "The Bar As a Profession," that we do best not to see the "process" that Holmes describes as an actual "process" in the sense of an algorithm, or series of logical steps (abductive, inductive, deductive), or as descriptive of an ultimately indescribable effort to reduce things to their essence. On the other hand, while "synthesis" – as words like "colligation" and "consilience" suggest – may be more accurate than "analysis" in describing the style of thinking Holmes advocated, it still leaves room for misunderstanding. Each angle of vision seems to truncate in some fashion what Holmes wanted to keep connected – the generative facts and the resulting legal rule or guiding conception.

Holmes himself demonstrates how the jurisprudential ability works early in *The Common Law*. In discussing the criminal law of murder he goes through an analysis in which he keeps seeking a more fundamental term. He moves from malice to intent to foresight to knowledge. At every step he seeks what he calls a "lower term." The most fundamental term he finally adduces is not a "term" at all but the conjunction created by foreseeability, choice, and knowledge. "All foresight of the future, all choice with regard to any possible consequence of action, depends on what is known at the moment of choosing." Not only what the person actually knew but also what he or she should have known determine "what is known at the moment of choosing." "To make an act which causes death murder, then, the actor ought, on principle, to know, or have notice of the facts which make the act dangerous."[358]

Holmes's jurisprudential method actually relies on discerning certain continuities present in society that the law has taken up and used as signposts. That the inferences drawn are no less pressing today than they were yesterday – that a beam thrown from a great height onto a busy street below could easily cause death or grievous bodily harm – does not fully deprive them of their historical character. Holmes's jurisprudence largely works with those elements of experience that critical history has left untouched. They are part of what Hurst called sequence. These legal doctrines or principles are still vital and real and actively constitutive of the legal mind. They are the opposite of survivals; they are actual and meaningful.

But that does not make them rational. What makes them rational is a strong connection to a scientifically understood end. For example, the principle that one ought not to engage in conduct that has manifestly shown a tendency to cause temporal damage cannot be taken as all-encompassing. Such a principle is defeasible, dependent on acknowledged exceptions (*e.g.*, a former employer's right to say the truth about the employee's character and performance to a prospective employer) and further corroboration through the study of competing social ends. But here again we run into a problem. The study of social ends – through

[358] Holmes, *supra* note 10, at 143. *See also* Rosenberg, *supra* note 284, at 53–54 (1995).

economics, statistics, or broader policy studies – would certainly be an advance over spontaneous suppositions or ingenious on-the-spot policy rationales. The study of social ends is primarily a way to rationalize, at least in the minds of the inquirers, the circumstances of the present. But it also runs the risk of delinking what Holmes wanted to keep connected, the historically generative facts and the enunciated legal principle. In the same manner he never wanted the body of systematized predictions to be deracinated from the law's oracles, the prophecies of where the axe would fall. Holmes is constantly trying to keep what we called the law's antiquity and futurity in constant interaction because he knows that escaping the past is futile. It governs our actions and sets the terms in which we think and feel. Better to confront it and work within it as one triangulates to future – hopefully better understood – ends.[359]

Holmes's jurisprudence is unable to arrange the distinct methods he employed in investigating and understanding law (history, philosophy, economics, pedagogy) into a unified, functioning whole because that endeavor, as Holmes expresses it, wars with his own best intuitions regarding the need to discern degrees in the law, to determine relevant proportions. In the language of quantity, law is so much of this and so much of that and, at some scales, an unmeasured or unmeasurable mass of decisions. Holmes attempted to work from what already existed, whether the teaching dogma of a law school or the habitual understanding and practices of the profession, and use that existent as the portal for inquiry, reevaluation, restatement, and reconfiguration.

The "process" he advocated could not be understood on its own terms – it was unworkable – but it could be understood as an early effort to extend, in three dimensions, the purely legal point of view.

And thus we return to the bad man. In Part IV, Section 13, we argued that the bad man is best understood as a projection. We also referred to the bad man as a "remote conception." In doing so, we harkened back to the opening pages of *The Common*

[359] One good example of Holmes's approach is *Jackman v. Rosenbaum Co.* In this case involving party walls, Holmes's opinion upheld the lower court's judgment against the plaintiff and struck down the argument that the Pennsylvania statute that excluded damages without proof of negligence was contrary to the Fourteenth Amendment. Holmes noted that

> The Fourteenth Amendment, itself a historical product, did not destroy history for the States and substitute mechanical compartments of law all exactly alike. If a thing has been practiced for two hundred years by common consent, it will need a strong case for the Fourteenth Amendment to affect it ... Such words as "right" are a constant solicitation to fallacy. We say a man has a right to the land that he has bought and that to subject a strip six inches or a foot wide to liability to use for a party wall therefore takes his right to that extent. It might be so and we might be driven to the economic and social considerations that we have mentioned if the law were an innovation, now heard for the first time. But if, from what we may call time immemorial, it has been the understanding that the burden exists, the land owner does not have the right to that part of his land except as so qualified and the statute that embodies that understanding does not need to invoke the police power.

Jackman v. Rosenbaum Co., 260 U.S. 22, 31 (1922) (per Holmes, J.).

Law, to how Holmes understood and explored the desire for vengeance as a dynamic in primitive law and even afterwards, when the law did not seem so primitive. These descriptions, "remote conception" and "projection," work together to advance cognizance of the interconnections between law's antiquity and futurity. What connects the two diachronically is, at the risk of anachronism, the socially justified use of the public (sovereign) force. In the "Path of the Law" Holmes emphasized law's futurity – what the courts will do in fact – but necessarily lying in the background, as we have argued, was his deep awareness of law's antiquity and persistence, the slow, coasting, and at times unforeseeable way it adapted to changing social and cultural conditions.

By the time he delivered "The Path of the Law" Holmes had resolved to always begin with the present. By the "present" he did not intend solely or even mainly the results of empirical research and analysis into the daily workings of his society; he cared more about active or dormant symbols (organizers of perception). He focused attention on the legal significations (or what we have called pointers), visible and invisible, that organized and gave meaning to the facts that wound their way through the courts. To improve the law he wanted to open up the "present point of view." That is to say, to improve how one understood, gauged, and reorganized the law that directed the use of power. "Theory is my subject," he said, "not practical details." That attitude he carried across the board.

Holmes introduces the bad man as a device for students to study present-day law. He justifies the device on both practical and theoretical grounds. In terms of practice, the first thing a student must understand is the law's limits. The confusion between moral ideas and legal ideas – which leads to many "evil effects" – is primarily harmful because it blurs or erases the distinctions between the two viewpoints. He mentions, as an aside, that he does "not say that there is not a wider point of view from which the distinction between law and morals becomes of secondary or no importance, as all mathematical distinctions vanish in the presence of the infinite."[360]

The legal point of view, then, must be disentangled from the moral point of view, and, at the same time, loses its distinctiveness when seen from a wider perspective. Perhaps that wider point of view is the first iteration of what Holmes calls at the end of the address those "remoter and more general aspects of law" which give it "universal interest." The bad man is Holmes's preferred intellectual device for studying that "body of dogma" he recharacterized and reenergized as a "body of systematized prediction." In this latter phrase Holmes is effectively foreshadowing his ideal, how he wants to see the law thought about and studied. He wants to move away from a "body of dogma" established by authority, by postulates taken at face value, their worth unanalyzed and worked out through logic. Instead of "dogma" we have "prediction." That is to say, instead of using the inspirational method to

[360] Holmes, *The Path of the Law*, *supra* note 1, at 392.

establish the grounds that will justify legal action, he advocates the use of inquiry into both the historical rule and its justification (*e.g.*, the rule of trespass *ab initio*) and into the contemporary "grounds" – the policy justification, the spontaneous rational, the unarticulated but possibly irresistible feeling that one course of action is preferable to another. He then wants the results to be scrutinized in light of scientifically considered social ends and already-established law. Holmes ultimately wants to change the fundamental feedback mechanism by which the law is made and thereby increase the potential for directing with increased deliberation the law's future development.

The bad man is key to this endeavor. But because Holmes had no clear sense how his many-sided endeavor should work as a whole he presents his prescriptions as a series of disconnected steps that he calls a "process." As argued above, the endeavor as presented is unworkable because the use of insight and history and logic and philosophical analysis and social scientific research – all meant to work together to improve law, to improve the quality of the existing and forthcoming practical judgments that are the tissue of law – have no common conceptual elements that can unify them and create the needed reference points in a dynamic, ongoing system.

Holmes's prescriptions cannot be modeled as a "process" but they can be modeled topographically. The starting point is the bad man. Holmes intends the bad man as way to bring into view the legal contour lines of his society. The distinction between law and morals "is of the first importance for the object which we are here to consider, – a right study and mastery of the law as a business with well understood limits, a body of dogma enclosed within definite lines." The bad man and the student he is meant to guide begin in the present, in the here-and-now. Holmes first justifies the use of the bad man on a practical basis – to help a student understand the business of law, to "find out when this danger is to be feared." The danger, of course, being "under what circumstances and how far they [those seeking legal guidance] will run the risk of coming against what is so much stronger than themselves[.]"[361]

Even before Holmes mentions the "sibylline leaves" and the "oracles of the law" he has already in the language of "The Path of the Law"'s opening paragraph ever so faintly invoked a feeling reminiscent of a hoary past and evocative of an all-too-real present, the unease of coming up against something so much stronger than oneself. The fear (of fate, fortune, risks unknown) that once paved the way to the shrine of Apollo now leads to the well-heeled lawyer's foyer. Like most everything else, the ancient reverences have become everyday commonplaces.

Practicality is the first goal and the first step. The bad man (as a pedagogical tool) functions as the necessary starting point for turning law into an active register that can unite philosophy, history, and social science into a working dynamic. Though

[361] *Id.* at 391.

Holmes never put it in these terms, pedagogy, which begins with the bad man's point of view, slowly spirals upward and outward connecting the specific case in which the axe will or will not fall to the most universal generalizations of theoretic jurisprudence.

Early in this part we used the image of a large stepladder to convey the standard nineteenth-century Baconian view of how one moved from facts to principles. We also suggested that even if left open and turned on its side, as Langdell had effectively done, reflecting his view on the importance of starting with procedural facts and ending with legal principles, it would only – as Burke once observed – sharpen the mind by narrowing it. It would also encourage a false sense of certitude. Holmes does the opposite. He begins narrow; and step by circular step shows how one ought to proceed to obtain an increasingly wider, more encompassing 360-degree point of view.

If we pause for a moment and look at the larger picture, we realize the difficulty many have had in appreciating Holmes's singular effort to guide the students and to educate the educators[362] partly arises from "The Path of the Law"'s condensed form and partly because he attempts to express competing ideas and intuitions without a suitable framework. The other main reason for the difficulty is that so many subsequent commentators use a preestablished philosophical rubric (utilitarianism, pragmatism, structuralism, etc.) or the fixed single aperture of an intellectual-cum-political attitude (progressive, liberal, conservative, reactionary) to interpret the complexity and only end up creating more.[363]

Holmes spent most of his life working as a lawyer and a judge. That fact is where one must begin and end. In the 1890s, when he was in his fifties, he decided that he would put down more carefully than he had before his mature thoughts on how law should be studied and taught. The topic, one perennial if underdeveloped in the history of the common law, had resurfaced with fresh immediacy shortly before he delivered his address at Boston University. As already noted, James Bradley Thayer delivered what the *Harvard Law Review* would publish as "The Teaching of English Law at Universities" to the American Bar Association's Section on Legal Education. That section, the ABA's first, had been created in 1893. In the same year as his

362 Though undeveloped, William V. Badger in an early article noted the importance of pedagogy to Holmes's mindset. *See* William V. Badger, *Some Ideas of Mr. Justice Holmes Regarding Education*, PEABODY J. EDUC. 2, 6 (1950) (noting that "Oliver Wendell Holmes, Jr., was at the same time a great teacher – a teacher of judges, deans, and teachers in a larger community in which each plays his role."). *See also* JOHN T. NOONAN, JR. PERSONS AND MASKS OF THE LAW: CARDOZO, HOLMES, JEFFERSON, AND WYTHE AS MAKERS OF THE MASKS 12–13, 66–67 (2002 ed.) ("Holmes, like Blackstone and Wythe, had the great advantage of being a law professor who became a judge, so that his teaching could take the form of opinions in particular cases, and he could shape action by theory.").

363 For a discussion and various reflections on the intellectual chaos this tendency has created see the essays collected in THE PRAGMATISM AND PREJUDICE OF OLIVER WENDELL HOLMES, JR. (Seth Vannatta ed., 2019).

address, 1895, Thayer published his two-volume casebook on constitutional law. In the preface he lauded Langdell and his "case method," and expressed candidly his pleasure in publishing the work in the same year that Harvard was celebrating Langdell's twenty-fifth anniversary. He continued:

> The method of legal study with which his name is associated, regarded as a mere mode of investigation, was indeed no novelty at all; lawyers have always known well enough the necessity of following it in working out their problems. But Dean Langdell, early in life, had the sagacity to apply it to his own self-instruction in law, and in his greatly valued help of fellow-students; and when he came back to the school as a professor, he had the courage and the foresight to introduce here the same method of study, and lay down for himself a mode of instruction which rigorously drove his pupils to adopt it.[364]

Probably no better précis of the case method's genesis existed at the time. It was primarily a method of self-study, not of teaching. In the prior year William Keener, one of Langdell's former students, delivered his rousing defense of the case method before the ABA's Section on Legal Education. He called it "The Inductive Method in Legal Education,"[365] and thus began, as subsequent commentators noted, the migration from a method of study to a method of analysis – of thinking like a lawyer.

Holmes's longtime friend Frederick Pollock published his *First Book of Jurisprudence* in 1896; the title page announced he intended the book "For Students of the Common Law."[366] Holmes refers to it toward the end of "The Path of the Law." He gladly noted the little book was "wholly free of the perverting influence of Roman models."[367] His other good friend John Chipman Gray had had his say in the late 1880s and then again, more summarily, in the very first volume of the *Yale Law Journal*.[368] The issue with Gray's reflections on legal education came out in March 1892. It also included longer pieces by Keener, Edward J. Phelps, and Christopher G. Tiedeman.[369] The editors devoted the issue to "Methods in Legal Education" and disavowed any "desire to arouse controversy." They believed it high time for legal education to acquire a theoretical foundation – "A *science of pedagogy* begins to loom ominously at the horizon." Then some more fine student hyperbole: "the old-fashioned teacher staggered at the apparition to quietly withdraw. Bombshells are everywhere thrown into the queer structure of tradition. Will this movement pass quietly by the professional schools?"[370]

[364] James Bradley Thayer, I Cases on Constitutional Law vi (1895).
[365] William A. Keener, *The Inductive Method in Legal Education*, 17 Ann. Rep. A.B.A. 473 (1894).
[366] Frederick Pollock, The First Book of Jurisprudence (1896).
[367] Holmes, *The Path of the Law*, *supra* note 1, at 403.
[368] *See* John Chipman Gray, *Cases and Treatises*, 22 Am. L. Rev. 756 (1888); John Chipman Gray, *Methods of Legal Education*, 1 Yale L.J. 139, 159–61 (1892).
[369] 1 Yale L.J. 139, 139–61 (1892).
[370] *Id.*, *Editorials*, at 162–63.

"The Path of the Law"'s use of cases or real world examples to illustrate its main theses differentiates it from most contributions to the topic. It brims with concrete instances, as do most of Holmes's published writings on the law. Compared to most other oft-cited legal articles on law and legal education from the period, his are positively replete with instances and examples. Once combined with his favored analytical approach – to state an issue and to unravel it through the use of polarities or complementarities – one begins to acquire a sense for the rhythm of Holmes's thought. Its energy derives from his effort to elevate the tone of the common law through the common law's own habitual ways of working through legal issues.

If one diagrams the bad man's function as Holmes presents it in "The Path of the Law" the limits that demarcate "law" from other important viewpoints – the social, moral, and spiritual – come into view. One main opposition, as argued in Part IV, Section 13, is between the bad man and the power of the state as enacted through the instrumentality of the courts. As shown in Figure 1, the bad man and the state form the y-axis. It is a misunderstanding to think the relevant opposition is between the bad man and the good man, the one "who finds his reasons for conduct, whether inside the law or outside it, in the vaguer sanctions of conscience." The good man forms one end of the x-axis that has at the other end the outlaw. The outlaw, a survival from the antiquity of the common law, takes on new meaning in modern societies as a person who suffers a precipitous drop in legal status.[371] This drop in status, as argued in Part I, gave a manifestly concrete edge to Holmes's notion of legal duty.

The use of this diagram helps define the beginning reference points for understanding what the law is and how it works in a common law jurisdiction. The diagram is pegged to the American common law; it depends upon and works within it as an actual legal system. This diagram reveals Holmes's goal of helping beginners orient themselves in a system within which they will soon take their roles as practitioners. It finds justification on both practical and theoretical grounds. That both justifications should lead to the same result was important for Holmes. "The theoretical importance of the distinction [between morality and law] is no less, if you would reason on your subject aright."[372] The theoretical distinction is that the limits of morality are "prescribed by conscience, or by our ideal, however reached[,]" but those of law are primarily court prescribed determinants on the use of force. That there are many overlaps Holmes does not deny. Some commentators take one point of co-extension, prudence (acting lawfully, avoiding countervailing state power), as the needed foundation for building-out a legal theory, but without the necessary controls it invariably forsakes the practical in favor of the theoretical.[373] Prudence

[371] Frederick Pollock noted in 1896 that, "Outlawry, now all but obsolete even in name, was the formal expression of the archaic social rules by which law was gradually made supreme." POLLOCK, *supra* note 366, at 25.

[372] Holmes, *The Path of the Law*, *supra* note 1, at 392.

[373] *See, e.g.*, William H. Wilcox, *Taking a Good Look at the Bad Man's Point of View*, 66 CORNELL L. REV. 1058 (1981).

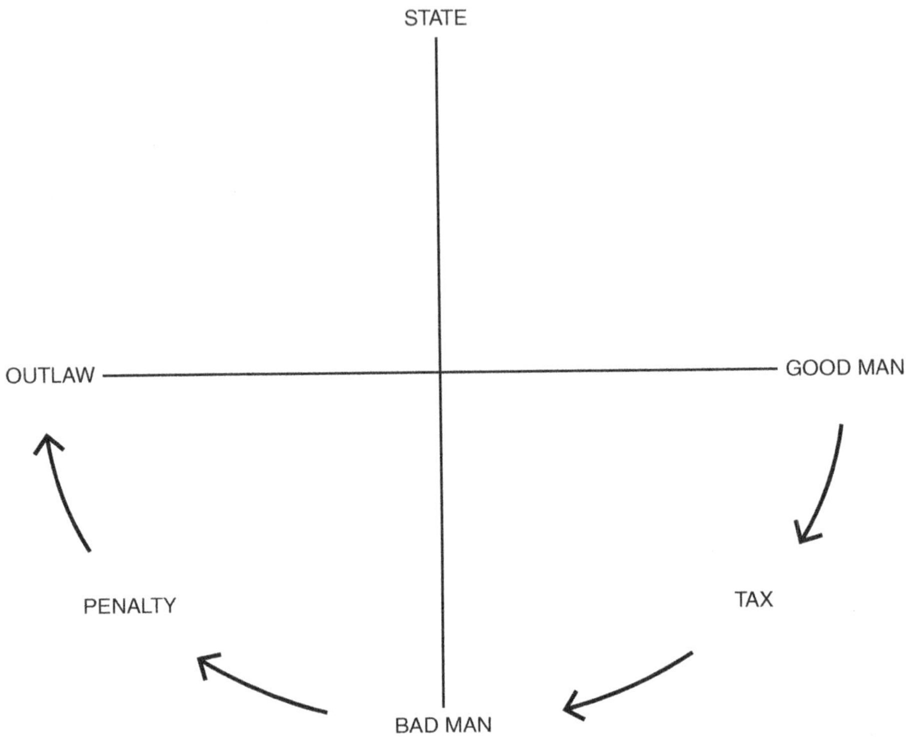

FIG. 1 "Bad man" diagram.

pitched at the right key becomes a practical judgment that can be investigated and correlated; pitched at the wrong key, it becomes moralistic, scholastic, and stifling.

Understanding that the bad man and the state are in constant opposition, neither able for long to get the march on the other, forms an elementary circuit of comprehension. For the novice who thinks the law is clear-cut, the bottom right and left-hand quadrants prove the most difficult. These are the areas in which the established correlations between what has been decided, what has happened (or may happen), and how the court will respond to the pointers called into play are less firm, the consequences ranging from a "tax" (right side) to a "penalty" (left side). On the other hand, the upper quadrants are zones of clear-cut safety or clear-cut disaster. On the right side, the overlaps between law and conventional conscience are strongest. On the left, conventional conscience is on holiday and law takes full command.

Not having the use of a diagram to clarify or convey his meaning, Holmes seeks to illustrate his first and most basic point – the overriding distinction between legal and moral duties – by focusing on the "notion which as popularly understood is the widest conception which the law contains, – the notion of legal duty[.]" People inflate the notion with all sorts of moral, social, or spiritual convictions or connotations that have not found distinct legal expression.[374] But from the point of view of the bad man it leads to a legal terminus (compulsory payment of money or imprisonment). Holmes uses the bad man's point of view as a way to explain the difference between a tax and penalty – all which hinge on the conception of legal duty that he worked out early in his career – and ends by pointing out that the *meanings* of the disagreeable consequence are found not solely in the penalty as stated but also in the collateral disadvantages or consequences that the law attaches to the act.

Though "Path"'s wording is more compressed and frankly more difficult, the main idea is no different in essentials than what he had written in his early articles. Penalties become a rule of construction to see if an absolute command was intended; collateral consequences bring into view the reach of duties not overtly prescribed.[375] To achieve this level of comprehension is pedagogically challenging, for both the teacher and the student. One obstacle to seeing the connecting threads between what Holmes wrote in the 1870s and "The Path of the Law" is Holmes's reformist impulse, which he cannot resist. He says: "The only other disadvantages [other than compulsory payment] thus attached to it which I have ever been able to think of are to be found in two somewhat insignificant legal doctrines, both of which might be abolished without much disturbance."[376] For reasons unexplained, Holmes thinks the doctrines of prohibiting the enforcement of illegal contracts and the inability of a wrongdoer to recover from his associates may be abolished without much loss to the legal regime. That may be true and that may make it easier to discern etched lines of a legal duty, but the rationalization of legal doctrine was not his primary purpose for introducing the bad man. It was, as he well put it, to shrink the vague circumference of this particular notion – that of legal duty – to make it more defined. Washed in cynical acid, this piece of worked-over metal loses the overlays that obscured the hard etchings of enacted power. Cynical acid is the counterpart to critical history – both reveal the true lines of operative force but from different temporal standpoints.

We know from a much later letter to John Chipman Gray that Holmes had begun to have doubts about the operative viability of legal duty as a working concept when he wrote "Path." Gray had written to Holmes in 1913 and reminded him that

> Some time ago I told you my sympathy with an article of yours . . . to the effect that the best classification of the law was on duties. You told me of a later palinode of yours in some article or address in which law was based on some other definition or

[374] Rosenberg makes a similar observation when he writes that for Holmes formalist scholars "tended to infuse language as well as history with *a priori* moral assumptions." ROSENBERG, *supra* note 374, at 46.

[375] Oliver Wendell Holmes, *Review of* The Law Magazine and Review, *in* I CW 296–97 [hereinafter, "1872 Jurisprudence Essay"].

[376] Holmes, *The Path of the Law*, *supra* note 1, at 394.

> idea. I wish you would tell me, if it is not too much trouble, where the two articles are to be found.[377]

Holmes replied:

> It delights my soul to hear from you again.
>
> The duty basis was the theme of my first article in the Law Rev. Oct. 1870 – Vol. 5 p. 1. "A long time ago, gentlemen," as old Parsons used to say in a melancholy voice, "a very long time ago." Later I became convinced that the machinery of rights and duties was a fifth wheel – and partially expressed it in an address to the Boston Law School Jan 8/97 that was printed in the Harv. Law Rev. My theme and present view is expressed in American Banana Co. v. United Fruit Co 213 U.S. 347, 356 'Law is a statement of the circumstances in which the public force will be brought to bear upon men through the Courts.'
>
> All that is told us about rights of property is in the books on torts – (I am not speaking of conveyancing of course).
>
> And our so called rights and duties are merely prophecies as to the incidence of this public force. As I said in my address we need to wash our conceptions with a solution of cynical acid to get rid of the moral associations attending our common legal language.[378]

Taking this letter from Holmes to Gray as an endpoint, it is possible to trace the changes in Holmes's thinking on the fundamentals even if the reasons for the changes remain opaque. In "Codes, and the Arrangement of the Law," he argued that "duty" not "right" functioned as the fundamental, generative conception in the law. Two years later, he wrote, "The test of a legal duty is the absolute nature of the command."[379] To determine if the command was "absolute" one did not so much look at the source of the command (the "sovereign") as its enforced effect. "The imposition of a penalty is therefore only evidence tending to show that an absolute command was intended (a rule of construction)."[380] The paradigmatic legal event under this conception is possession, operating upon and honing, as it does, the intent to exclude.

Holmes's next major statement is in "The Path of the Law." "The prophecies of what the courts will do in fact, and nothing more pretentious, are what I mean by

377 Letter from John Chipman Gray to Oliver Wendell Holmes (June 15, 1913) (on file with Harvard University Holmes Digital Suite, Harvard University, Harvard Law School Library / Holmes, Oliver Wendell, Jr. Addenda, 1818–1978 Correspondence: Box 1, Folder 8, Gray, John Chipman, Correspondent, 1877–1913).

378 Letter from Oliver Wendell Holmes to John Chipman Gray (Oct. 27, 1914) [It is possible the year should be listed as 1913 since otherwise it would mean Holmes waited over fourteen months to respond to Gray's June 15, 1913 letter.] (on file with Harvard University Holmes Digital Suite, Harvard University, Harvard Law School Library / Howe, Mark DeWolfe. Research materials relating to life of Oliver Wendell Holmes, Jr., 1858–1968. Major Correspondence: Box 3, Folder 10. Gray, John Chipman, Correspondent, Complete set 1877–1915).

379 Holmes, *supra* note 375, at 296.

380 *Id.*

law." The focus – from the purely legal point of view – is how a legal event will terminate. On the one side are the prophecies. The prophecies themselves are not univalent signs; they do not fully correspond with any one subsequent event. Prophecies are inherently figurative. The intelligence that makes a prophecy prophetic exists always in the present. That is the obverse side of the law, the one facing us, the inquirers. Present concerns, present inquiries transform the existing "body of reports, of treatises, and of statutes" into sibylline leaves, the source by which a prophetic utterance (a.k.a. a practical judgment refined and forecasted) comes into being.

The present mindset and know-how of the inquirer make the prophecies determinative for the here-and-now. The range of comprehension an inquirer should have is wide, but it's of little long-term use unless it can be arrayed into a workable form. The shape the form takes depends on preexisting grounds and the pressures exerted upon the inquiry and inquirers. While extralegal factors always play a part, the point of legal education is to help students understand the legal factors. What they are, how they work, how they shift and change depending upon how the legal event that will lead to a final outcome has taken shape. Holmes's use of the word "fact" has borne much weight it was never intended to bear because most commentators have not realized – nor did Holmes give them much reason to –that Holmes's use of the word is synecdochical.

Holmes's use of the word takes us back to his "The Theory of Torts." Following upon his "1872 Jurisprudence Essay" Holmes pointed out how a certain class of preliminary facts the court must determine – whether a statute was properly enacted, what it means, the applicable scope of the precedents – condense into the query, what is the law? He further explains:

> This class of facts, inasmuch as their function is only to suggest a rule of law, are investigated by the court in such a way as may be most convenient. The fundamental fiction of the law is that all are presumed to know it, and it follows that whatever facts are necessary preliminaries to such knowledge may not only be judicially noticed by the courts which declare the law, but must be found out at their peril by those who are called on to obey it. It is hard to see any distinction, whatever the nature of the fact may be; and, although not every fact judicially noticed is a source of law, the facts which are such are not confined to the example which has been mentioned. *They are not always to be found in any previous acts of any branch of the sovereign body.*[381]

The facts which function as the sources of law, which become the pointers that govern and guide the profession in a given case or matter, work dynamically with the interests brought together for resolution. Specific facts or questions materialize from these background facts. These background facts in Holmes's terms are not dramatic,

[381] Oliver Wendell Holmes, *The Theory of Torts*, *supra* note 162, at 328–29 (emphasis added).

not the kind of facts Mrs. Quickly would always notice, but they do often structure the "facts of legal import." They configure the features that make the legal landscape a landscape.

The preliminary facts, the sources of law, and the procedure in play set the typically unnoticed perimeters, or, to change the imagery, form the assumed backdrop, the oft-unnoticed facts that put into relief the issues in dispute. Holmes also saw that the common law was not solid, like granite, but porous, like coral. "Modifications of the law are recognized much sooner in the rules of evidence than in pleading, where precedents remain of record."[382] This insight directly leads to what he would say over twenty years later, that the law is the prophecies of what the courts will do in fact. The connecting point, the lesson that the bad man teaches, lies in the idea of defeasibility, one central to the common law and Holmes's own acquired habit of mind. Defeasibility joins presumption with action but leaves the door open to its own eventual dislocation or dissolution.

The word "fact" as Holmes uses it in "The Path of the Law" correlates procedure with background assumptions that govern unless questioned. These along with the substantive issues and interests brought into play form the emerging legal event. Legal events that fall into set molds are the easiest to resolve and when perfunctory become administrative. Not all prophecies are oracular; if they were legal dogma would be impossible. The "law" is equivalent to the "in fact" (singular) that the courts (plural) have done in light of the understood prophecies (plural).

Fact for Holmes is a tiny tapestry. What a court may do "in fact" may be under- or overdetermined. It depends on the number or type of courts that have given attention to the question at issue and concurred. The judgment a court gives alters the circumstances for somebody. As a "fact" it is made up of even more sub-facts – the law that applies, the controlling interpretations or precedents, the jury or judge's determinations of who to believe and what probably happened – that in turn are made up of even more sub-facts of various groupings and orders. At the bottom of the well are not individual stony Baconian facts but groupings. The pressure of the contest forces the legal mind to concentrate its resources and focus its attention on the groupings of fact that call to it.[383]

The trajectory in Holmes's thinking from the definition of legal duty in the "1872 Jurisprudence Essay" to his statement of law in *American Banana* indicates a maturing distrust of conceptual precision along with a more intense desire to

[382] *Id.* at 329; *see also* Donnelly v. U.S., 228 U.S. 243, 277–78 (1913) ("The rules of evidence in the main are based on experience, logic, and common sense, less hampered by history than some parts of the substantive law.") (per Holmes, J.).

[383] Coming from a compatible viewpoint, Daniel Kornstein insightfully comments that Holmes's breakthrough work, *The Common Law*, arose from his series of lectures on "the common law, that large pointillistic body of individual cases (as opposed to statutes) decided over time by judges." Kornstein's inspired use of the adjective "pointillistic" reveals an abiding essential of one facet of legal practice in a common law jurisdiction, both as science and as art. DANIEL KORNSTEIN, THE SECOND GREATEST AMERICAN loc. 232 (2017) (ebook).

rationalize existing law along the lines of least resistance, like that of a yacht. He had come to see rights and duties as a fifth wheel – unnecessary, superfluous – to what? One suggestion: to the sequence of facts found and the facts adjoined as the denoted enforcement response. He feared the language of prediction still encouraged and fed the need for dogmatic utterance. In reporting to Gray his "theme and present view" that "Law is a statement of the circumstances in which the public force will be brought to bear upon men through the Courts[,]" Holmes essentially conceded he did not know how to bring into theoretical unity history, philosophy, economics, and the demands of pedagogy but stubbornly held on to his sense that the lines the public force drew could be parleyed into philosophical insight.

Law had to be worked out of and into what he once called "actual forces."[384] If not, neither the law – which presumptively had some claim to be more intelligible and rational than the "actual forces" upon which it was founded – nor the "actual forces" themselves would derive any value from the other. Without that connection the operative legal intelligence would ultimately become brittle and dry, like the yellowed leaves of an un-cracked tome. It would, as Holmes memorably put it, "become a matter for pedagogues, wholly devoid of reality."[385] Yet without that connection those existent "actual forces" would lose something – hard to say what – something that only minds devoted to thinking about the actual could provide.

The section of *American Banana* in which Holmes thematized his most mature view of law is worth quoting as it serves as a small window into his thinking:

> Law is a statement of the circumstances in which the public force will be brought to bear upon men through the courts. But the word commonly is confined to such prophecies or threats when addressed to persons living within the power of the courts. A threat that depends upon the choice of the party affected to bring himself within that power hardly would be called law in the ordinary sense. We do not speak of blockade running by neutrals as unlawful. And the usages of speech correspond to the limit of the attempts of the lawmaker, except in extraordinary cases.[386]

John T. Noonan, Jr. did not take as harsh a view of Holmes's position as did our almost forgotten friend John Zane.[387] Zane considered Holmes's view of law barbaric. Noonan in his *Persons and Masks of the Law* took a more respectful tone, though one sorrowful that such a great legal mind as Holmes had taken refuge in the very mask of sovereignty he had as a young man justly condemned as a superannuated relic. Noonan found himself burdened with the thought that the justice in America who had the best claim to greatness deserved not laurels but wreaths.

[384] Holmes, *The Common Law*, *supra* note 10, at 224 ("Law, being a practical thing, must found itself on actual forces.").

[385] *Id.*

[386] American Banana Co. v. United Fruit Co., 280 U.S. 347, 356–57 (1909) (per Holmes, J.).

[387] *See supra* Part IV, Section 5.

Noonan assumes the paragraph quoted above is a précis of "The Path of the Law," which Noonan describes as a "small summa" of Holmes's judicial philosophy.[388] He takes the reference to the party who elects to bring himself within law's domain as a reference to the defendant, the United Fruit Company. Noonan comments: "He [Holmes] did not explain why it lay within the choice of United Fruit, a corporation incorporated in the United States with its affairs directed from Boston, to bring itself within the power of the United States."[389]

Indeed he did not because that was not his point. Noonan – who has written a most perceptive and informed commentary on the case and its decision – did not quite realize that Holmes had a habit of concertinaing his legal arguments, especially in court opinions.

The lead-up to Holmes's most considered definition of law starts from a discussion of the sovereign's reach through law, or what we might call jurisdiction. Holmes begins by establishing, in terms of territorial sovereignty (not sovereignty over the person), a polarity that has at the one end the sovereignty of the United States over its territory and at the other end the sovereignty of a foreign government over its territory. In between lay the penumbra of those "regions subject to no sovereign, like the high seas, or to no law that civilized countries would recognize as adequate[.]" In such circumstances the civilized countries may elect "to treat some relations between their citizens as governed by their own law, and keep to some extent the old notion of personal sovereignty alive."[390]

This old notion of personal sovereignty has been mainly superseded by the idea of territorial sovereignty but had not disappeared. In certain regions of the international order it remained alive and well. Civilized countries may declare "that they will punish anyone, subject or not, who shall do certain things, if they can catch him, as in the case of pirates on the high seas."[391] In other cases that directly affect the core of national interests they may fully disregard the limits of territorial sovereignty and declare that they will punish, if they can, acts done by their subject in a foreign jurisdiction. Holmes uses as an example a United States statute prohibiting as treason criminal correspondence with a foreign government. These pockets of jurisprudence in which the otherwise outdated notion of personal sovereignty still lives and breathes attest to its longevity; but its scope is small and, Holmes implies, shrinking. The era when British notions of personal sovereignty – "English statutes bind British subjects everywhere" – prevailed is receding and giving way to what Holmes describes as "the general and almost universal rule that the character of an act as lawful or unlawful must be determined wholly by the law of the country where the act is done."[392]

388 Noonan, *supra* note 362, at 102.
389 *Id.* at 103.
390 American Banana Co. v. United Fruit Co., *supra* note 386, at 355–56.
391 *Id.* at 356.
392 *Id.*

History and analysis have clarified the scope of a present rule of law and its relevant background. Holmes does it all so quickly and with such deft and masterful brushstrokes that one hardly realizes the genius at work. Just as one barely sees as slowly taking command the still emerging ideals of democracy and self-rule.

Holmes folds his exposition into a working definition: "Law is a statement of the circumstances in which the public force will be brought to bear upon men through the courts." He refers to the language he used in "The Path of the Law" – the word "law" is commonly "confined to such prophecies or threats when addressed to persons living within the power of the courts" – but doubts the power of a threat or prophecy to function as law in "the ordinary sense" if the party affected may choose whether or not to be subject to it. Noonan, for one, took the phrase in "the ordinary sense" as an allusion to how Holmes had defined law in "Path" – as the prophecies of what the courts will do in fact.

Given Holmes's subsequent letter to Gray, the shift in Holmes's thinking as reflected in *American Banana* lies in how the terms "rights" and "duties" should no longer function as the standard pin-and-socket connectors between existing and forthcoming law. He now states forthrightly what he only intimated partly in "Path," that "the machinery of rights and duties was a fifth wheel[.]" He adds that "Our so called rights and duties are merely prophecies as to the incidence of this public force. As I said in my address we need to wash our conceptions with a solution of cynical acid to get rid of the moral associations attending to our common legal language."[393]

It is hard, given these comments, not to concede that Noonan may be right, that *American Banana* essentially restated the position Holmes took in "Path." It's hard to see the difference Holmes had in mind. If law is not defined in terms of existing rights and duties then perhaps Holmes has simply taken one step closer toward his goal of disinfecting law language of its present-day extralegal moral connotations. It helps to recall what Holmes wrote to Walter Wheeler Cook in 1919, that to "know law one must be cynical and disregard ethics that find no legal expression."[394] If a "legal expression" is the "statement of the circumstances in which the public force will be brought to bear upon men through the Courts[,]" then in giving up on the language of duty Holmes is not giving up on his efforts to categorize legal relationships in terms of duty (in terms of actions subject to penalty, loss of legal status) but simply not using the word to describe the action because he does not think the benefit worth the cost. Too many other associations connected to the word "duty" make it impossible for his meaning to be fully appreciated.

[393] Letter from Holmes to Gray, Oct. 27, 1914, *supra* note 378.

[394] Letter from Oliver Wendell Holmes, Jr. to Walter Wheeler Cook (Feb. 25, 1919) (on file with Harvard University Holmes Digital Suite, Mark DeWolfe Howe's research materials on Holmes, 1858–1968. Finding Aid, General Correspondence, General Group II: Box 14, Folder 18, Cook, Walter Wheeler, correspondent, 1919–1931).

The obvious cost is that the word "duty" discourages clear thinking – thinking things not words. The word "duty" brings in too many moral connotations that impede the ability to trace the historical movement of a particular rule or doctrine. It occludes the vision necessary to recognize the pertinent continuities and discontinuities. Furthermore, it may foster a worrisome case of delusive exactness – consider how many have latched onto Wesley Hohfeld's "wondrous model" – when marshaled into an analytical scheme. The mind becomes mesmerized and the ability to listen to the stiller, smaller voices of experience correspondingly weakened. Law as a "statement of circumstances" is more neutral; it does not immediately call forth moral associations or inflate legal analysis with present-day predilections. Dispensing with the machinery of rights and duties also keeps the heavy hand of the past in check. The customary or common rights and duties of the community and its members lose their halo of inviolability. Translated into a "statement of circumstances" their defeasible (or, at the other end, "can't help") character becomes evident; the contest between interests becomes sharper and more defined.

Because Holmes wanted to forego the continued use of the word "duty" does not mean he also wanted to forego the notion of a jurisprudential boundary. Far from it. Duty took its meaning from the generative fact of banishment or exile. Holmes kept the notion that a person could still become a *caput lupinum* (a man [person] with the head of a wolf), that is, an outlaw, but sought to elaborate it into a more expansive formula. Holmes sought to scale the law to match the new scales that marked many areas of American life – social, cultural, economic, and political. He sought to torque the common law to a new height. The difficulty many have had and still have in seeing and understanding what Holmes was trying to do – even if his attempts miscarried – arises from the fateful fact he never found the right kind of language to express fully his ideas and his intent.

Dispensing with the machinery of rights and duties also meant letting go of the categories he had worked so hard to establish as a young man. To a large extent these categories had been subsumed into the flux of history – into the development or desuetude of legal principles – but once duties and rights fell away it became even harder to correlate the many instances and ways in which the public force had been brought to bear upon the more or less recalcitrant. Academic pedagogy on these new terms became well-nigh impossible as typically conceived. Holmes's continued migration from modes of expression that found their genesis in a system or network of concepts, that did not fathom how ideas arose from and melded back into thereby transformed circumstance, led him to explore the boundary between word and event, not as solely an intellectual endeavor, but to find the adequate means to instill in his colleagues a more profound curiosity and respect for this reification called the public force.

For this reason he found it of the utmost importance to emphasize territorial sovereignty. If that sovereignty was a mask or an impersonation as Noonan contends, its purpose was not to avoid persons but the contrary, to make possible a fuller rendition of the person. Holmes did not think of personhood and statehood as antagonistic ideals. Each complemented the other. But what still requires elucidation is his statement that "A threat that depends upon the choice of the party affected to bring himself within that power hardly would be called law in the ordinary sense. We do not speak of blockade running by neutrals as unlawful."[395] In plain terms, if an option exists then law does not.[396]

In many ways this passage takes us into the inner circuitry of Holmes's thought. Dropped as it is in the middle of a Supreme Court opinion one cannot blame Noonan for thinking it had something to do with the defendant in the case. As much as establishing polarities, concertinaing the universal into the particular and vice versa is a hallmark of Holmes's jurisprudence. In this instance he draws attention to the intimate connection between a people and their law. The intimacy of the connection energizes the reach and scope of law as a culture-making power. The correspondence of this power to a specific expanse of land – the territory under the control of the sovereign – may have no warrant other than self-determination. But it appears that such self-determination was not self-justifying for Holmes. It had to invoke the auspices of civilization for it to gain legitimacy in his eyes. On the other hand, civilization did not by itself justify new expansions that interfered with the comity of nations. It's hard to be more definite than these somewhat vague statements because Holmes does not give us much more to work with in the opinion.

But if we stay with the idea of territorial sovereignty as the sine qua non of a well-functioning legal system, we see that the first and foremost requirement is its mandatory character. Law is law. It is not fundamentally a policy suggestion or an option that carries a price. It is not up to the person to decide whether to submit to its threats. Holmes noted that people don't usually speak of law in such terms just as they don't typically refer to neutrals running a blockade as doing something unlawful. The force of the comparison arises from an intuitive sense that law somehow differs from raw power or wiliness, that which seeks to accomplish a specific end without much care or concern for extraneous consequences or potential ramifications. Law, unless one harkens back to mythical beginnings, works within and against established circumstances and events. Territorial sovereignty is the foundation upon which law builds and to which it must constantly recur as it develops.

Territoriality is not jurisdictionally absolute, though close. Its importance for Holmes lies in how it unifies legality with brute fact. Threats or predictions, to overcome the charge that law amounts to little more than a bandit with a cocked gun, must draw upon wants and intentions that supersede the specific event in view. Law is a matter of constantly arranging and rearranging social life in light of these

[395] American Banana Co. v. United Fruit Co., *supra* note 386, at 357.

[396] As he put it in a speech prepared for a dinner honoring Admiral George Dewey in 1899, "For the law does not mean sympathetic advice which you may neglect if you choose, but stern monition that the club and the bayonet are at hand ready to drive you to prison or the rope if you go beyond the established lines." Oliver Wendell Holmes, *supra* note 282, at 523–24.

superseding ideals. If a man has an option whether these arrangements shall encompass him or not, then, as Holmes noted, it can hardly be called law in the ordinary sense. Law has a temporal component – whether expressed in terms of history or psychology – that Holmes thinks ineradicable. As Hurst noted, that temporal component characterizes a sequential movement – impetus, momentum – that occurs in and through a specific spatial setting, summarily described as a context. Law like language has a pervasive, all-inclusive character. No one, not even the outlaw, within a specific territory is ultimately outside the control of the sovereign. The sovereign, for Holmes, ultimately becomes a stand-in for the leading offices of a democratic polity.

Holmes took two great bodies of nineteenth-century legal thought, the British and German, and refashioned them to work within an American setting.[397] On the one hand he believed in the virtues of democracy and the democratic spirit that recognized no artificial distinctions between persons. On the other, he believed in the virtues and values of truth-seeking. Truth-seeking means acknowledging the irreducible groupings of fact inherent in circumstances. And in terms of law that meant acknowledging the constant interplay between the self-interest of the state and that of the bad man, each seeking to shove the other off the one floating plank.

Acts occurring outside the territory of the United States, such as those of both the American Banana Company and the United Fruit Company, typically fell outside the subject matter of the courts because, absent territorial power, law loses its capacity to assimilate, discharge, and grow. Brute fact loses the specific taint and smell of its native soil. Noonan, for one, senses the broader reaches of Holmes's thinking even if he did not quite understand how it played out in *American Banana*. He begins the first chapter of *Persons and Masks of the Law* by noting how Holmes's most famous epigram – The life of the law has not been logic: it has been experience – "endowed impersonal rule with existence and memory, a power of assimilation, and the capacity to develop."[398] Holmes, adds Noonan, endowed the law with vitality and so personified it.

But Holmes did much more than personify a rule. He endowed the entire common law with the ethos of personality, or in more evocative terms, a tradition and a race. He saw the entire realm of legal action as another might see the personalities that people a judicial circuit. Holmes saw vividly the cases before him as well as those in the books; he viewed them stereoscopically. That is not to say he always viewed them perfectly; that is, how the most enlightened opinion of the day might view them. Law magnified certain traits and habits. Once one had achieved an expert eye and a certain level of insight, the details and their significations merged into certain well-known threads and patterns. Louis D. Brandeis swore

[397] G. Edward White likewise said that Holmes's early effort "can best be characterized as a search for a distinctive, indigenous methodology[.]" WHITE, *supra* note 126, at 599.

[398] NOONAN, *supra* note 362, at 3.

by the facts; Holmes never found a way to explain to Brandeis that the facts, no matter how well developed and organized, only carried one so far. The ability to bring into being the voice needed for those facts to tell a different story did not come from delusive diligence. The Puritan in Holmes still believed in grace.

That Holmes had a vivid perception of law[399] – law not understood as pointing toward a single referent but as an ambit of interrelated activities, as a developing discipline of self-reflexive social power – most likely explains, in part, his astonishing ability to draft quickly his opinions on matters cumbersome and complex. He wrote like a master, not solely because he used language superlatively but because he had mastered the intricacies of the common law. It's an elementary point that many commentators and critics forget.[400] Thus when he invites the students in his audience to begin the journey that may one day take them to the abode of masters, he is not speaking idle words or puffing up the pretense of the moment. The journey begins dimly and in faith, as do all journeys that promise self-supersession.

But this particular journey begins for most students in a curious way. One studies law to benefit oneself by benefitting the short- and long-term interests of another. Law may be a well-known profession but it is also a profession that often works in a medium semi-transparent or semi-opaque, between what is transparent and what is obscure. Holmes believed this reality of the profession to be the bequeathal of civilization, the heritage of 2,000 years of visible human experience.[401] Law is not an option as long as living together, as a person among a people or as a people among persons, is not an option. But the law is porous and complex, the past seeping in and creating chambers and dead-ends when least expected. To the arbitrary fact of dogma, one that presents law as a monolith of reason, good sense, and goodwill, Holmes counterpoised the man without scruples. To be without scruple meant one did not experience any doubt or hesitancy regarding the morality or propriety of a course of action. One's hand roamed freely, without conscience.

[399] This is the insight that informs John C. H. Wu's analysis of Holmes's jurisprudence. John C. H. Wu, *The Juristic Philosophy of Justice Holmes*, 21 MICH. L. REV. 523, 529–35 (1923).

[400] Justice Charles Evans Hughes made this very same point regarding the profundity of Holmes's knowledge of the common law to Mark DeWolfe Howe. *See* STEPHEN BUDIANSKY, OLIVER WENDELL HOLMES: A LIFE IN WAR, LAW, AND IDEAS 165–66 (2019). *See also Mr. Justice Holmes – Tributes*, 44 HARV. L. REV. 677, 677 (1931) ("To me, Mr. Justice Holmes is a prophet of the law.") (Tribute by Chief Justice Hughes).

[401] *See* Le Roy Fibre Co. v. Chicago, M. & S. P. Railway, 232 U.S. 340, 354 (1914) ("I do not think we need to trouble ourselves with the thought that my view depends on the differences of degree. The whole law does so as soon as it is civilized. Negligence is all degree – that of the defendant here degree of the nicest sort; and between the variations according to distance that I suppose to exist and the simple universality of the rules of the Twelve Tables or the Leges Barbarorum, there lies the culture of two thousand years.") (Holmes, J., concurring) (internal citations omitted); Hoeper v. Tax Com. of Wisconsin, 284 U.S. 206, 220 (1931) ("This case cannot be disposed of as an attempt to take one person's property to pay another person's debts. The statutes are the outcome of a thousand years of history .... They form a system with echoes of different moments, none of which is entitled to prevail over the other.") (per Holmes, J.).

But not without fear. The bad man may at times move gingerly and seek counsel; not because he pays obeisance to the virtues of prudence and good judgment but because he knows all too well that the coldblooded part of the common law's brain does not believe in options. Holmes expressed this thought in similar terms.

> Nowhere is the confusion between legal and moral ideas more manifest than in the law of contract. Among other things, here again the so called primary rights and duties are invested with a mystic significance beyond what can be assigned and explained. The duty to keep a contract at common law means a prediction that you must pay damages if you do not keep it, – and nothing else.

Stopping right at this point, reading these sentences in a flat uninflected tone, leads to some version of efficient breach theory, or to the idea that law for Holmes is a menu of a la carte items. But if we continue to the next sentences we read two parallel formulations in which Holmes took much pride and which he would not back away from even if he convinced no one else: "If you commit a tort, you are liable to pay a compensatory sum. If you commit a contract, you are liable to pay a compensatory sum unless the promised event comes to pass, and that is all the difference."[402]

In modern terms the difference is that one legal event is defeasible and the other is not. In both cases the word "commit" embeds a legal conclusion (liability to sanction). Whether some person and/or entity has committed a tort may take years of litigation to resolve. Whether a contract has been committed typically requires much less judicial energy. That is because contract as a body of law forms a different part of the legal topography than does tort. It brings into the present traces of an ancient understanding of being bound, of being liable to an assumed risk (to use a modern phrase). Common law scholars of Holmes's era often referred to Tacitus' *Germania* when singling out this longstanding feature of the Anglo-Saxon tradition.

Pound in *The Spirit of the Common Law* and Pollock in *The Genius of the Common Law* both cite Tacitus' description of Germans playing dice. Pound in his retelling uses it to depict the stage of strict law:

> The stock argument of the strict law for the many harsh rules it enforces is that the situation was produced by the party's own folly and he must abide it. The whole point of view is that of primitive society and recalls the story in Tacitus of how the Germans played dice. They played, he tells us, as a serious business, even staking their own liberty; and if one lost in such a case, he voluntarily went into slavery and patiently allowed himself to be sold.[403]

Likewise, Pollock pointed to Tacitus' *Germania* as an early source for understanding the "permanent mind and temper of the Common Law[.]"[404] Among other things,

[402] Holmes, *The Path of the Law*, *supra* note 1, at 394.
[403] Roscoe Pound, The Spirit of the Common Law 19 (1921).
[404] Frederick Pollock, The Genius of the Common Law 8 (1911).

these tribal people called Germans "encouraged adventurousness" and were unrestrained in their gambling.[405] Holmes too referred to Tacitus' description of how "Germans would gamble their personal liberty and pay with their persons if they lost[,]" to buttress his argument that modern contract arose from the merging of dominant streams, that of barter and sale – characterized by the quid pro quo – and that of the giving of hostages, understood as the factual antecedent to suretyship.[406]

In describing a contract as a legal act, as the intentional acceptance of legal consequences, Holmes is portraying his understanding how these two main sources, as well as a third, that of oaths, syncretized with what became known as assumpsit into a new resultant. He brings them into conjunction first in *The Common Law* then in later articles, "Early English Equity" and "Law in Science and Science in Law."[407] Modern-day contract as a social device is a complex artifact; it sets in unison various customs and beliefs from different historical epochs and provenances.[408] In "Law in Science and Science in Law" he used the evolution of general conceptions involving what are now called contracts as an example of evolution in the "sphere of conscious thought and action." He takes issue with the contemporaneous never-fully-expressed assumption "that there must have been some theory of contract from the beginning, if you can only find what it was."[409]

There was no such theory. It is not clear from Holmes's published writings how he teased out the conclusion from his study and analysis of contract's heterogeneous prehistory that when one commits a contract one is, in part, taking the path first laid out by dice-playing Germans and ancient hostagetaking. Holmes's consistent mode of historical analysis alternates between what E. Donald Elliott identified as two different strands of nineteenth-century evolutionary theory. The first is Darwinian natural selection. Darwinian natural selection is subtractive. The second relies on

[405] *Id.*

[406] Holmes, *Early English Equity*, *supra* note 63, at 336.

[407] Holmes, *The Common Law*, *supra* note 10, at 241–63; Holmes, *Early English Equity*, *supra* note 63, at 335–38; Holmes, *supra* note 265, at 409–11.

[408] J. G. A. Pocock argues that this form of historical analysis originated in the English-speaking world in the work of Sir Henry Spelman. J. G. A. Pocock, The Ancient Constitution and the Feudal Law: A Study of English Historical Thought in the Seventeenth Century 103–04 (1987, A Reissue with a Retrospect, originally published in 1957) ("He [Spelman] recognized, however, that it was now theoretically possible to construct a completely new historical analysis of the law by distinguishing the elements of various origin which it contained." And: "There was nothing in the common law which Spelman need regard as immemorial, and he had dissolved the notion of custom into a series of influences of diverse origin.").

[409] Holmes, *supra* note 265, at 409–11. This tendency to assume an originative theory of contract was still alive and well even into the next century according to Grant Gilmore. In *The Death of Contract* he utters a mea culpa and points out this notion has subtly affected much of twentieth-century scholarship on contracts. Grant Gilmore, The Death of Contract 12–13, 117 n.17 (1974).

Herbert Spencer's idea of integration.[410] Holmes's use of these modes of differentiating and integrating social phenomena is unmistakable in the first part of "Law in Science and Science in Law." What is obscure is how he drew out from this sophisticated analysis the notion that when one commits a contract one is bound, as long as the contract stays in force, to pay damages unless one performs.

Equally opaque is why legal scholars persist in tagging Holmes as the originator of the idea that a contract provides the contractor an option – a promise to perform or pay damages – when he consistently and emphatically rejected the notion.[411] Noted contract scholar Joseph M. Perillo pointed out in detail how Holmes has been misinterpreted on this issue, but that has not stopped other scholars from continuing to misrepresent Holmes's position.[412] Nor have they accepted the burden to explain why Holmes should be seen as fathering the notion that a contract provides an option despite his unambiguous protests.[413]

Holmes's view of contract exemplifies his notion of how law enacts, extends, and deepens sovereignty within a territory. But enactment and extension are not purely episodic. Contract, like tort, derives its force from the impetus or momentum of previous cultural pathways that have been merged – through perhaps legal thought and/or through drift of circumstance – to reinforce each other. One could use a quasi-moral term, like "wrong," as Perillo did, to describe the same phenomena, but without the needed qualifications it becomes misleading.[414] Holmes's historical investigations showed him that in the modern, generalized term "contract" inhered features of greater or lesser antiquity. Raoul Berger in his "From Hostage to Contract" enlarges upon this Holmesian insight and painstakingly shows how the ancient features of the "pledge-idea," depicted in the historical records as hostage,

[410] E. Donald Elliott, *Holmes and Evolution: Legal Process As Artificial Intelligence*, 13 J. LEGAL STUD. 113, 139–45 (1984).

[411] *See, e.g.*, DOUGLAS G. BAIRD, RECONSTRUCTING CONTRACTS 46–56 (2013); Douglas G. Baird, *The Holmesian Bad Man's First Critic*, 44 TULSA L. REV. 739 (2008); P. S. Atiyah, *The Legacy of Holmes through English Eyes*, 63 B.U. L. REV. 341, 365–76 (1983). Richard Posner provides a good further example. He writes: "We have seen that Oliver Wendell Holmes argued, in the spirit of positive economics, that when you sign a contract ... You are promising that you will either perform or pay the amount specified in the clause." But Holmes complained to Pollock that one of Pollock's comments "shows the persistence of the impression that I say a man *promises* either X or *to pay damages*. I don't think a man promises to pay damages in contract any more than in tort." RICHARD A. POSNER, ECONOMIC ANALYSIS OF LAW 152 (9th ed. 2014); II HOLMES–POLLOCK LETTERS, *supra* note 97, at 233 (emphasis in original).

[412] Joseph M. Perillo, *Misreading Oliver Wendell Holmes on Efficient Breach and Tortious Interference*, 68 FORDHAM L. REV. 1085, 1086–90 (2000); BAIRD, RECONSTRUCTING CONTRACTS, *supra* note 411, at 46–56; Baird, *The Holmesian Bad Man's First Critic*, *supra* note 411, at 742–45.

[413] Patrick Atiyah acknowledges in a footnote that Holmes protested this common misreading in his 1919 letter to Cook, and showed concern about the broader effect his insistence on the technical legal point may have, but never directly confronts Holmes's multiple statements to Pollock denying that Holmes thought the common law of contracts expressly provided an option. Atiyah, *supra* note 411, at 372 n.163.

[414] Perillo, *supra* note 412, at 1087.

pawn, and surety, began to coalesce into forms resembling that of modern contract when two distinct elements, the debtor's moral duty to pay and the surety's legal duty to pay (that is, the surety's liability subject to sanction) combined in the same person once that person could, in effect, self-guarantee. As Berger noted, "'Liability' is therefore the coercive element, describing the status of a person or thing placed in the power of a creditor in order to secure a promise. As such it is initially identified with the pledge of a pawn or surety, and then it becomes by way of *self-guarantee* the sanctional element for the debtor's own 'moral duty'."[415]

From the various historical antecedents he most succinctly described in "Law in Science and Science in Law" Holmes drew out what he took to be the defining features of contract. As law, contract like tort pointed to what the enforcement power would do, the consequences it would enforce once the actor had acted in a way that bound it into a legal event (an incurred liability). One commits a tort; similarly, one commits a contract. Tort and contract are words that subsume the actor's action into a preexisting regime of measured force dedicated to ensuring outcomes. The difference, in regard to contract, between the ancient German who wagered his freedom on a throw of the dice and a modern-day contractor is that the modern-day contractor has the advantages of drawing upon centuries of differentiated legal experience. The grounds (conditions) for determining damages and for defeasibility have achieved both greater latitude and greater definition; they have become an integral part of the legal landscape.

For these reasons, to speak of a contract as presenting an option is to fundamentally misunderstand Holmes's notion of law. The "option" that a contract is said to present is formally no different from the coercive choice of one who is said to be laboring under duress. The ancient German had no option once he wagered and the dice began to roll. He was bound to slavery if he lost. The common law as it came into the nineteenth century, as Holmes read it, provided the contractor not with a freewheeling option but with the same kind of forced, momentous, and coercive choice as offered to a person under duress.[416] The key difference being that the choice forced upon the contractor has behind it the force – and pedigree – of law.

The best clue to understanding Holmes's position lies in one of the many reiterations he made of his view to Pollock. This particular one he made in 1927. Pollock had over the years thrown up many objections; the one overriding all others centered on the moment liability is incurred. Pollock thought it perverse to take the moment of inception, when the contract comes into being, and not the moment of

[415] Raoul Berger, *From Hostage to Contract*, 35 ILL. L. REV. 154, 162–63 (1940–41). *See also* Karl N. Llewellyn, *What Price Contract? – An Essay in Perspective*, 40 YALE L.J. 704, 714–16 (1931).

[416] *See* Union P.R. Co. v. Public Serv. Co., 248 U.S. 67, 70 (1918) ("It always is for the interest of a party under duress to choose the lesser of two evils. But the fact that a choice was made according to interest does not exclude duress. It is a characteristic of duress properly so called.") (per Holmes, J.).

breach as the governing instance when liability attaches. Holmes stuck gamely to his intuition that a contract at common law – that is, according to his view of how its predominant feature (loss of control) had coalesced and given present, practical viability to a welter of past cases – meant that liability arose at the moment one met the prevailing legal test for contracting.

> You always have regarded my notion of contract as a pardonable eccentricity (that when you commit a tort you incur a liability to damages *simpliciter*. When you commit a contract you incur a liability to damages *nisi*, illustrated by the fact that in most contracts if not in all you have only a limited, and it may be no, power over the event). It is a particular case of my general definition of a right as the hypostasis of a prophecy – like gravitation.[417]

Beyond the fact that liability is incurred at the moment of contracting, Holmes's formulation points up the relative certainty of liability to damages compared to the promised-for event. That the balance of certainty tilts toward the sovereign reveals the power the lawful authority has within a jurisdiction. The relative certainty of enforcement demarcates law from other mandated duties (moral, social, spiritual). The range of enforcement may extend from money damages to – through a concatenation of consequences – imprisonment.[418]

Yet when Holmes says that his view of contract is only a particular case of his general definition of right as the hypostasis of a prophecy – "hypostasis" being the imagined underlying substance or reality that gives the prophecy its prophetic character – he tips his hand as to the indomitable persistence of the past (habit, custom, tradition, ongoing dynamics of feeling and value). He denies the existence of moral or legal entities apart from the actual course of events. As he put it in "Natural Law," a right – and by extension a duty – understood as a "hypostasis of a prophecy" is just like the phrase "force of gravitation" in relation to the actual movements of bodies in physical space. "One phrase adds no more than the other to what we know about it." He then adds this all-important qualifier: "No doubt behind these legal rights is the fighting will of the subject to maintain them, and the spread of his emotions to the general rules by which they are maintained; but that does not seem to me the same thing as the supposed *a priori* discernment of a duty or the assertion of a preexisting right."[419]

In Holmes's use, hypostasis as a word mainly refers to what Hurst used the more social scientific words "sequence" and "context" to describe. The salient difference between Holmes and Hurst on this issue is Holmes's keener awareness of how the present conjunction of sequence and context has collated distinctly discernible historical trajectories with present-day proclivities. The promisor's technical election at common law to perform or pay damages – which was good enough for Lord

[417] II THE HOLMES–POLLOCK LETTERS, *supra* note 97, at 200.

[418] *See* Bailey v. Alabama, 219 U.S. 219, 246 (1911) (Holmes, J. dissenting).

[419] Holmes, *supra* note 283, at 447.

Coke – was, on Holmes's own terms, not so much a resultant as a logical byproduct of how the modern notion of "contract" had come together. Contract as a legal generalization harmonized and arranged into a single strand various and distinct developed habits and expectations: quid pro quo, formal covenants under seal, the freedom to wager one's destiny on a dice throw, hostage (pledge) taking, the spiritual regime of oaths, and the undertaking of a task or promise.

That the so-called option to perform or pay damages is not a live, morally neutral, and free-floating condition outside the carefully arranged features of a contract is shown by a case in which Holmes's dissenting opinion has been heavily and uniformly criticized. In *Bailey v. Alabama* Holmes disagreed that a black man in Alabama who was found liable for intending to defraud his employer could not be fined, imprisoned, and forced into hard labor. The majority saw the relevant Alabama statute as a tool to maintain peonage in the state. Holmes strongly protested this conclusion, and he did so on the basis of his theory of contract. He points out early in his dissent that "any legal liability for breach of a contract is a disagreeable consequence which tends to make the contractor do as he said he would."[420] This focus on motives is not new, it takes us back to Holmes's early scholarship. "Law as law is an agent, influencing conduct by motives, and applying consequences."[421]

In the case of *Bailey* he draws the pertinent lesson. "Breach of a legal contract without excuse is *wrong conduct*, even if the contract is for labor, and if a State adds to civil liability a criminal liability to fine, it simply intensifies the legal motive for doing right, it does not make the laborer a slave."[422]

In describing the breach without excuse as "wrong conduct" Holmes is not somehow looking for a way to bring moral evaluations that have found no legal expression back into the equation. He takes it for granted that in the common law's point of view the contractor could choose to ensure that the promised event would not happen – if the contractor had sufficient control over the event – and pay damages. He also takes it for granted that the state can add on further civil and criminal liability. It is one way in which the dominant opinion in the community that the conduct under consideration (purportedly opportunistic behavior) is morally wrong achieves legal expression.

It may help to keep in mind, for the purpose of understanding Holmes's position in *Bailey*, that he was mainly repeating in a different way what he first said in 1872: legal liability has nothing intrinsically to do with a preexisting moral duty – the goodness or badness of a specific act, whether seen as right or wrong conduct. That is, lawfulness or unlawfulness does not in every instance enact a moral assessment (even though lawfulness may have itself originated as a moral or pre-moral category). Committing a contract and thus incurring liability does not mean that the liability

[420] Bailey v. Alabama, *supra* note 418, at 246.
[421] Holmes, *The Theory of Torts*, *supra* note 162, at 328.
[422] Bailey v. Alabama, *supra* note 418, at 246 (emphasis added).

incurred turns the act of contracting into wrongful conduct. In *Bailey*, the wrongful conduct lay in *breaching* the contract and that became legally probative because it led to extra-contractual penalties. Holmes believed the state had the inherent power to put its thumb on the scales.

A charitable reading of Holmes's position in *Bailey* throws light on what he said regarding contracts in "The Path of the Law" and in other writings because it highlights the oftentimes hidden cost that comes with the freedom to contract. Holmes appears to have looked at all the instances of proto-contractual behavior – debt, covenant, surety, oath, and assumpsit – in English legal history and found that they featured acts in which the actor voluntarily agrees to place himself under an event over which he has less than full control. Just as torts forced those under the control of the sovereign to bear in certain circumstances the social consequences of their intended or unintended acts, contract as a mechanism of sovereignty forced contractors to bear the consequences of their voluntary decision to contract.[423] The greater the range of freedom to contract, the more situations over which the contractor had less than full control; a paradox no doubt but one indicative of a society in which the passive and active sides of law had become increasingly interconnected.[424]

Robert Hale is the scholar most responsible for bringing into view these many interconnections through terms his colleagues could appreciate. Hale took a good look at *Bailey* in his influential 1935 article *Force and the State: A Comparison of "Political" and "Economic" Compulsion*. Hale's article is a complex bit of reasoning. It represents one way of working out, in economic and political terms, the implications of Hohfeld's legal correlation of privilege/no-right.[425] Hale believes the dissenting opinion of the 69-year old justice differs "strikingly in its reasoning from that of the 55-year old Holmes who wrote *The Path of the Law* in 1897 and of the 31-year old editor of the *American Law Review* in 1872."[426] The striking difference apparently

[423] For a contrasting view of the origin and development of Holmes's theory of contract, one that emphasizes its radical break with the past and its use as a "monstrous machine" to limit liability as much as possible *see* GILMORE, *supra* note 409, at 15–37.

[424] By a different route, through a discussion of the ramifications of implying conditions into a contract, Morton J. Horwitz ends in a similar place. He argues that Holmes's thinking on contracts in "The Path of the Law" expressed "how the institution of contract itself was subordinate to social and political goals." It was a not an oasis of voluntarism or simply part of the neutral machinery of the market. MORTON J. HORWITZ, THE TRANSFORMATION OF AMERICAN LAW 1870–1960: THE CRISIS OF LEGAL ORTHODOXY 49 (1992).

[425] *See* Wesley Hohfeld, *Some Fundamental Legal Conceptions As Applied in Judicial Reasoning*, 23 YALE L.J. 16 (1913). Horwitz suggests that Holmes provided the original inspiration for Hohfeld's article. HORWITZ, *supra* note 424, at 129, 153–55.

[426] Robert Hale, *Force and the State: A Comparison of "Political" and "Economic" Compulsion*, 35 COLUM. L. REV.149, 158 (1935). For assistance in helping me understand the intricacies of Hale's complex work I am much indebted to, BARBARA H. FRIED, THE PROGRESSIVE ASSAULT ON LAISSEZ FAIRE: ROBERT HALE AND THE FIRST LAW AND ECONOMICS MOVEMENT 1–107 (1998); Neil Duxbury, *Robert Hale and the Economy of Legal Force*, 53 MODERN L. REV. 421 (1990); and Nicholas Mercuro, Steven G. Medema, and Warren J. Samuels, *Robert Lee Hale*

lies in Holmes investing Bailey's duty to perform his labor contract with more "mystic significance" than a younger Holmes would have found warranted. Hale's critique rests on a thin, ahistorical reading of contract, on the idea that Holmes's bad man supports a distinction between primary duties and secondary, sanctioning ones. For Hale the best gauge of the law's compulsory quality lies in the extent to which law removes the ability to *not* perform. For that reason he finds problematic Holmes's discussion in "The Path of the Law" of the difference between a tax and a penalty. "It will be noted that from the bad man's point of view little remains to differentiate a penalty from a tax; and that the notion of duty in the last paragraph [the one where Holmes discusses the formal similarity between tort and contract] throws overboard the absolute intent to forbid, so emphasized in 1872, and relies solely on the compulsory payment of money."[427]

Hale's critique brings to the fore the problematic nature of the bad man's point of view when stripped of its pedagogic function. To understand law – that meant for Holmes understanding what a people actually held most dear. It was a way of reading the ongoing record of the common law in light of the American people's newly discovered democratic sovereignty. One could read, and law professors have read, that record in any number of ways. But the way or ways that mattered most to Holmes were those that facilitated mastery, those that increased the capacity of the legal community to convert knowledge into wisdom. In his bad man conceit Holmes tested an approach that, in effect, brought the legal features of the social landscape into relief. At one and the same time it enabled a fledgling practitioner to learn what mattered to the more experienced members of the legal community, to become self-conscious of unacknowledged or untutored moral intuitions, and to realize that growth in law meant maturing the ability to make sound practical judgments.

The bad man conceit also took an ambitious student beyond the rudiments, beyond the initial efforts to obtain competence in working within a system that recognized lawyers as representative of other people's wants and interests. Holmes believed the training one received in law school should prepare one for practice. By directing the student's attention to concrete consequences the bad man did just that. But as consequences are not always direct and certain, the slip that allows for wiliness also provides opportunity for improvisation. At larger scales the opportunities for informed improvisation – what some like to call bricolage – led to a more sophisticated jurisprudence, a fuller recognition of those long-lasting features of experience that gave definition to an existing legal tableau. A general jurisprudence worthy of the name took root in law, in those many, many practical judgments that

(1884–1969) – Legal Economist, in The Elgar Companion to Law and Economics 531–44 (Jurgen G. Backhaus ed., 2d ed. 2005).

[427] Hale, *supra* note 426, at 153–54.

collated into workable form those desires sufficiently enticing and intense to capture and direct human vigor.

But then always one has the troublesome fire of the present. The tableaux of law undulate in the fiery air that spirits seeking their own possibilities ignite. The prosaic language of the law – the statement of circumstances in which the public force will be brought to bear upon you or me through the courts – seems devoid of depth and adventure unless the persons discerning and bringing the circumstances together into a single declaration of legal intent are like Holmes.

4 THE LAWYER'S FAITH

i *Book of Holmes*

Holmes was surprisingly contemporary in his willingness to reveal in print and word sentiments quite personal. He expressed these revelations in certain settings; they were tied to certain occasions. Only when he knew he stood near the edge did he demur from overtly expressing more than the occasion nominally demanded. "To express one's feelings as the end draws near is too intimate a task."[428] G. Edward White comments apropos this newfound timidity that it was fully in keeping with Holmes's structured version of intimacy.[429] Though White does not use this language, we come back to the aesthetic currents we identified earlier between Holmes's impassivity and his longing. His public addresses to his colleagues – which "he put his heart into," as White also notes – suggest Holmes recognized a bond between himself and his colleagues that obligated him when the occasion demanded to account for his actions.[430] Neither a nationwide radio address in 1931 honoring his ninetieth birthday nor the solitary piper's faint but increasingly distinguishable strains carried the same weight. He felt freer to speak allegorically.

That was not the case when one century had ended and the next one struck. After Theodore Roosevelt nominated Holmes for the US Supreme Court in 1902 and the printing presses began to clack, Holmes did not much like what he read. The soon to-depart chief justice of the Massachusetts Supreme Judicial Court went on a farewell tour. A sixty-one-year-old Holmes took the opportunity to account to his colleagues for a life spent at the bar.

His addresses at the end of 1902 added starkness to personal ruminations he had already made public prior to his nomination. The published addresses dating from after "Law in Science and Science in Law" (January 1899) until his move to Washington in December 1902 show an unusually pensive Holmes, a Holmes who feels strongly the need to communicate to his colleagues the leading ideas

[428] Oliver Wendell Holmes, *Radio Address*, *in* III CW 541.
[429] WHITE, *supra* note 126, at 464.
[430] *Id.*

upon which he has staked his professional life and reputation. Perhaps it had something to do with his being appointed chief justice in August of 1899. One gathers from the texts that even after that honor he felt to some extent unseen. He had to speak forthrightly.

The Bar Association of Boston held a dinner celebrating his appointment as chief justice on March 7, 1900, the day before his fifty-ninth birthday. His keynote for that time and place was unobjectionable. He proclaims the joy and glory of work. Hard, dedicated, controlled, persistent, unyielding effort – one would think this ethic so ingrained into the culture of New England that it would hardly require such emphatic proclamation. But so proclaim its virtues Holmes does, time and again, that his erstwhile close companion William James pointedly complained, after reading the speech, that Holmes was a one-trick pony. "I must say," reported an exasperated James, "I'm disappointed in O.W.H. for being unable to make any other than that one set speech which comes out on every occasion."[431] James found it exuberantly childish, its patronizing of those yearning to do good unbecoming in a chief justice.

James's criticism is often cited but seldom explored. James biographer Ralph Barton Perry, who included these snippets on Holmes's speech in the opening of the chapter "Ethics vs. Æsthetics," hints that perhaps James's moralism had gotten the better of him and he was perhaps being a tad unfair to the "stimulating and congenial" Holmes.[432] Perry published his acclaimed volumes on James in the mid-1930s near Holmes's death when the reverence for the justice stood at its peak.

Though one cannot know for certain, it appears these specific lines from the 1900 address lit the fuse of James's pen: "I confess that altruistic and cynically selfish talk seem to me about equally unreal. With all humility, I think 'Whatsoever thy hand findeth to do, do it with thy might,' infinitely more important than the vain attempt to love one's neighbor as one's self."[433]

Perry found it curious that James would sorely criticize one who in effect preached the same gospel as he did – "of action for the action's sake."[434] That concerted, dedicated activity could soothe the troubled soul and help make true what one believed had been one of the cardinal points of James's famed 1895 essay, "Is Life Worth Living?"[435] Evidently something in Holmes's tone, how he transposed courageous living into a minor key at a lower octave got under James's skin. Holmes contrasts a familiar biblical verse from Ecclesiastes to an equally familiar

[431] Ralph Barton Perry, II The Thought and Character of William James, 250–51 (1935).

[432] *Id.*

[433] Holmes, *supra* note 147, at 499.

[434] Perry, *supra* note 431.

[435] William James, Is Life Worth Living? 31–40 (1896) (first delivered in 1895 as a lecture and then reprinted in book form due to its popularity).

verse – at least to the audience he is addressing – from the Gospel of Matthew.[436] He finds the former "infinitely more important" than the latter. That claim given the time and place is certainly provocative, though apparently not controversial enough to disrupt the convivial assembly. Doubtlessly, the many judges and attorneys attending enjoyed an aperitif while listening ever more intently to the chief justice's unusual and engrossing after-dinner remarks.

But James evidently caught a top note in the address that to his ear had a disturbing adolescent ring. When Holmes recounts how that anxious curiosity whether one's "general point of view" will meet the test of fact fades, and the resulting gratification that one is right has waxed cold, and the work grows increasingly rote, each case entrusted becomes merely another "illustration of a universal principle," what remains is the thinker who faces "another case of the same old ennui, or the same sublime mystery, – for it does not matter what epithets you apply to the whole of things, they are merely judgments of yourself" – when Holmes says these things he is leading to something that James did not quite believe, that a stage of life had been reached, a stage of faith, when the pure vibrancy of living lies not in yearning but in doing one's work "irrespective of further aims." Then came the moment of quiet exultation. In this distinctly un-Tolstoyan credo Holmes believes he has identified the "triune formula of the joy, the duty, and the end of life."[437]

Evidently James did not see work – a display of dedicated, concentrated might – as in-and-of-itself the great joy and end of life. He saw in Holmes's exclamations childish exuberance, not the emerging beautification of a singular experience. In all likelihood he would have found even less to appreciate in the young Ernest Hemingway's much later bullfighting-inspired maxim, "the great thing is to last and get your work done[.]"[438] But Holmes would have applauded Hemingway's sentiment if not the exact wording as quoted.[439] For to last was not the great thing,

[436] Ecclesiastes 9:10 (King James) ("Whatsoever thy hand findeth to do, do it with thy might; for there is no work, nor device, nor knowledge, nor wisdom, in the grave, whither thou goest."); Matthew 22:35–40 (King James) ("Then one of them, which was a lawyer, asked him a question, tempting him, and saying, Master, which is the great commandment in the law? Jesus said unto him, thou shalt love the Lord thy God with all thy heart, and with all thy soul, and with all thy mind. This is the first and great commandment. And the second is like unto it, thou shalt love thy neighbour as thyself. On these two commandments hang all the law and the prophets.").

[437] Holmes, *supra* note 147, at 499.

[438] Ernest Hemingway, Death in the Afternoon loc. 3698 (1932) (ebook).

[439] About Hemingway Holmes had this to say to Laski:

> Hemingway must be a clever writer for he interests me when I can't see any reason for it (in *The Sun Also Rises*). Hemingway, I believe, is something of an athlete and [Owen] Wister writes to me has been hurt lately in a bull fight – which seems good. I am told that he is one of the heroes of the young – as T.S. Eliot has been. I don't yet see the need to get very excited about him – but it is well to keep one's mind open to the fashions of the day. Every fashion is beautiful while it is a fashion.

II Holmes–Laski Letters: The Correspondence of Mr. Justice Holmes and Harold J. Laski, 1916–1925 1205 (Mark DeWolfe Howe ed., 1953).

that he had made clear in his 1895 address, "The Soldier's Faith." For a man ultimately renowned for his skeptical talk he uttered in that candid, carefully constructed creed a number of strong affirmations that in unison sat as uneasily then as they do today.

This, he told the rising generation, we, your elders, still believe:

I. The joy of life is living.
II. The struggle for life is the order of the world.
III. The measure of power is obstacles overcome.
IV. The desire of your soul should not be for comfort but combat.
V. Honor lies in doing your duty and in loving your country.[440]

James no less than Holmes taught the vital importance of courageous living, of persisting in the unceasing, ongoing struggle. Of, as he once unforgettably put it, virtue grasping vice by the throat and not letting go.[441] He too spoke eloquently and knowingly of that "dumb region of the heart where we dwell along with our willingness and unwillingness, our faiths and fears."[442] That region warranted for James the out-sparking of belief, the reaching out toward God or gods, the guarantor(s) of the good and real.

Despite superficial similarities in how they treat that region of human experience underwritten solely by faith – a hard word to define or expound in this context – James's "Is Life Worth Living?" and Holmes's "The Soldier's Faith" are clearly pitched at different frequencies. In retrospect, 1895 conveniently marks an incipient coming-to-public-awareness that the firmament of a long-lasting spiritual subculture in the United States had been punctured. One could trace this subculture's beginnings to the arrival of those contentious Pilgrims and the subsequent migration of their more conventional co-religionists, the Puritans. Though both men are demonstrably modern, the sensibilities they express are at war. To use James's terms, the issue did not come down to believing too little or too much – Holmes was not really an agnostic in the English mold – but whether one could forthrightly feel assured, whether one could believe and proceed on no other grounds than one's aspirations and feelings. James thought the unseen dimension or dimensions of reality might one day provide the sought-after proof, that one would find a there there. He thought that an individual's acted-upon-faith would be instrumental in bringing that reality about. Holmes thought not. Assurance was a canard. It reflected too much self-importance. To him the God or gods of James were simply another instance of the individualist negations he complained of in "The Soldier's Faith." What mattered to Holmes was the uncombed, stumbling, sleepy civilization he saw and the roused, bespoke one he wanted to foresee.

[440] Holmes, *supra* note 107, 486–91.
[441] William James, The Will to Believe 169 (Dover ed. 1956) (orig. pub. 1897).
[442] James, *supra* note 435, at 61.

Civilization meant American civilization. Meditating on James's antipathy reveals something striking about the faith that Holmes proclaimed. It arises from self-devotion and self-exertion but depends fully for its realization upon the commensurate self-devotion and self-exertion of others. The stress on the joy of work and doing, on what James viewed as a symptom of adolescent exuberance, reflected Holmes's deepening awareness of a fundamental paradox: sometimes the best instance of superlative effort lies in gingerly giving in, not obstinately holding out. On rare occasions one might register a ringing dissent. The important thing is to function. Learning to live well meant learning to navigate within and through the awesome and less-than-awesome powers and forces that brought being into existence and made it real. At the deepest personal levels one could see and label such efforts as spiritual. At higher levels and at different scales they became something else entirely – they became law.

James's faith, his hopes in an unseen dimension of existence that would render the seen meaningful, his insistence on the right to believe, even on the slimmest of chances and at the greatest of risks, unduly, in Holmes's opinion, turned acute perceptions on the springs of human vitality into self-caused causes. Holmes once wrote to Morris Cohen that James's "will to believe," much like Cardinal Newman's famed "illative sense," subtly sought to disrupt the continuity of the universe and leave room for the "interstitial miracle."[443] To put it briefly, James's faith sought to limit the universe of cause in favor of chance; Holmes's to give itself entirely over to the endeavor to discern causes. James ultimately bet on chance, on those elements of existence still in play. Holmes's faith, in contrast, bottomed on cause because cause represented intelligence and intelligibility. But Holmes's faith is no spiritual exercise in deterministic passivity. It required one to deliberately actualize belief and create within one's own individuality a zone of vibrant living. Joy enlivens. That grand ambition one could not accomplish alone and by oneself; one needed others, one needed a community.

And so after his nomination in 1902 Holmes turned again toward his community, his Boston friends and colleagues, this time though to justify the legal work he had done since he began his career. What is the value of working with all one's might? To raise the bar of actualized potential, to hoist the heavy, battered flag a further quarter-inch up the weather-beaten pole. In the small world of the legal profession it meant an increased pressure – increased pressure on lawyers, judges, professors, and law students. This pressure is not the pressure of finding more clients or more creative ways to clear the docket, or of writing superlative critiques of existing legal regimes, or of achieving superlative marks of academic performance. Or of

[443] *See* Philip P. Wiener, Evolution and the Founders of Pragmatism 185 (1949) (quoting letter from Holmes to Morris Cohen, March 13, 1925, *in* Felix Cohen, *The Holmes–Cohen Correspondence*, 9 J. Hist. Ideas 3, 44 (1948)). *See also* John Henry Newman, An Essay in Aid of a Grammar of Assent 270–99 (1955) (orig. pub. 1870).

producing results regardless of the costs – that is, through guile, artful drafting, deceit or chicanery, or blinkered high-octane scholarship – but in improving the formulation and composition, the overall quality, of the professional judgments that the community accepts and implements. This desideratum, and this alone, gives the profession its unique meaning and dignity.

While Holmes did not put this desideratum in these exact terms, I believe he was heading in that direction and what he did say was very close. Two short speeches in late 1902, one given at a Tavern Club dinner in his honor and one to the Middlesex Bar, compress sixty years of life and more than thirty years in the law. To the Tavern Club he bids a "provisional adieu" as he waits for his nomination to work its way toward confirmation. It's an odd time for Holmes. As he puts it, "The roots of sixty years strike deep, and they cannot be tugged at or cut off without pain. The mere burning of old papers which have cumbered and annoyed one for thirty years, while it gives one for a moment a sigh of freedom, makes one feel a little later that it is the freedom of the cut flower – one little root in the past is gone."[444]

So begins the cinematic segue. He reminisces of the Boston of his youth, that half-Puritan Boston, the unutterable ennui of Sundays and the tolling of "the church bells which I still affectionately hate." He remembers that the Boston of that day had virtually no statutes. Once two figurines were erected he learned what he never forgot: "bad statutes are better than no statutes. They are points of interest, and give you something to think about." It's an interesting comment, made even more interesting when one thinks about it in relation to law.[445]

But the Boston of Holmes's adulthood was a Boston that had officially forsaken the aesthetic asceticism of its early days. One found public statutes and works of art aplenty; points of interest that, if one did not take due care, might do what the Puritan most feared, distract attention away from the Almighty. That Holmes survived temptation we must credit to what he called, apparently quoting Tennyson, "some divine, far-off event." For as he says:

> The event came. There was more than one. I am thinking now more of spiritual than of external changes. College gave one an atmosphere. The war was a great moral experience. The first five or ten years of one's profession was another, and perhaps a greater one. One had not all the aids that there are now to realizing why the subject was worthy of the interest of an intelligent man. I think I have done my share to make that plain.

And then:

> When I began it was not so easy as it is now to see that law, looked at through the stereoscope of history, is the story of our growth. It was not easy to put to oneself even the vaguer proposition that as the facts of the law are the facts of the universe

[444] Holmes, *Address at Tavern Club Dinner, in* III CW 533–34.
[445] *Id.*

> they are worthy of their share of the only intellectual interest there is, – the interest of being seen in their universal relations. As I look back to those periods of misery, the war and the beginning of one's profession, I cannot forbear saying, as I always say when I have any beginners within hearing, that it is true that you grow – that you must go through the trial of wretched doubt – doubt as to your own significance, ignorance of even what question you want to ask, – and that it is through faith and will – faith that there is a question and an answer – will to attain them – that one enters the door of life.[446]

The venue for this address, Boston's Tavern Club, stood as living proof that the old Puritans had been too unimaginative in their exultations; they had no inkling of the unique gravity gaiety could give to the life social. Through its worship of playful creativity and lively wit the Tavern Club had become a Boston institution. Howe's father, Mark A. DeWolfe Howe, had sketched a "partial and not impartial" semi-centennial history of the Club's personalities and high-minded antics in 1934.[447] Usefulness be damned was not the Club's motto but most of Holmes's addresses before the dinner in his honor took this old saw as his theme.

He first addressed the Club in 1893 at the dinner in honor of French writer Paul Bourget.[448] In 1895 he said a few words praising guest Rudyard Kipling, the famed journalist, novelist, and poet.[449] The next year the honored English versifier and parodist R. C. Lehman heard Holmes praise the pure waste of life as that uniquely male contribution to the common human stock.[450] In 1898 he recognized his friend Albert Venn Dicey.[451] And in 1900 he made a few remarks to honor Dr. S. Weir Mitchell, a noted contributor to the medical and literary arts, as had been Holmes Senior. Junior related his thought-out opinion that the artist and the thinker form two antagonistic endpoints of intellectual life. He praised Mitchell as that rare person who could unite the two without being splintered, who had the power "to disclose truth and the power to make it live in our hearts."[452]

Seen against the background of these remarks his 1902 address gains dimension. He is not talking directly to his colleagues but to the cream of Boston's creative class. Again we are struck by the personal nature of his remarks, how Holmes may to some extent be baring his soul. If this is "structured intimacy" then the structure is quite

[446] *Id.* at 534.

[447] Mark A. DeWolfe Howe, A Partial (and Not Impartial) Semi-Centennial History of the Tavern Club 1884–1934 (1934).

[448] Oliver Wendell Holmes, *Remarks at a Tavern Club Dinner for Paul Bourget*, *in* III CW 513–14.

[449] Oliver Wendell Holmes, *Remarks at a Tavern Club Dinner for Rudyard Kipling*, *in* III CW 514–15.

[450] Oliver Wendell Holmes, *Remarks at a Tavern Club Dinner for Rudolph C. Lehmann*, *in* III CW 516–17.

[451] Oliver Wendell Holmes, *Remarks at a Tavern Club Dinner for Albert Venn Dicey*, *in* III CW 522–23.

[452] Oliver Wendell Holmes, *Remarks at Tavern Club Dinner for Dr. S. Weir Mitchell*, *in* III CW 525–26.

intricate indeed. Holmes's harbored longing for a brief moment takes full control and stills his impassivity. Holmes searches for a way to make the perception that has ruled his mature life visible to a group of men who would never-ever imagine that law and its study could provide its own narrow path toward salvation.

What he said in general terms to the members of the Tavern Club he said more directly and concretely to his colleagues at the Middlesex Bar. We are now in early December 1902. On the third day of that month, the day before President Roosevelt officially nominated Holmes to the Supreme Court, he recounted many of the same things as he said a few months earlier. But this time one can detect an undertone of grievance. Evidently some of his colleagues did not think highly of his professional ability, at least according to the newspapers. He was merely a "literary fellow." "You are the judges," he says, "and even you are more likely to take your views from the accident of your professional needs than from a consideration of any general aspect of a man's work."[453]

What are those general aspects? In a single paragraph of medium length he gives an account of himself, as a thinker and as a judge.[454] In order of recitation here are the main points, Holmes's own words in bold, with my annotations.

1. **I have tried to see the law as an organic whole.** The word "organic" is not easy to understand in this context but we get a sense of the direction of the thought when we remember that oft-used description of the common law from Holmes's early days: a chaos with a full index. That sentiment is still alive and well among practitioners even if mostly unarticulated. Instead of an index we have search engines that use Boolean logic (commonly called "terms and connectors") to gather together the cases that match the search criteria. Interestingly, Holmes did not claim in this address that he spent his career trying to draw out from history and social life the law's most profound generalizations. In his earlier address to the Boston Bar, though, he did lament the lack of time to dig deeply into every legal problem and "generalize it all and write it in a continuous, logical, philosophical exposition, setting forth the whole corpus with its roots in history and its justifications of expedience real or supposed[.]"[455] We see here again the great tension in Holmes's thought, the same one we saw in "Path." In explaining how one should discern from the many lives the law has lived the direction in which power should flow in a specific instance he at times uses the language of "experience" and at times expresses the desire to make it "logical." Perhaps he meant that "experience" guided the inquiry, it determined the best method or methods to use in searching out the

[453] Holmes, *Address to Middlesex Bar, supra* note 240, at 536.
[454] *Id.*
[455] Holmes, *supra* note 147, at 498.

postulates, while "logic" dictated more the final form, the dogmatic packaging used to present the results so that others could understand and utilize them and have a basis for advancing understanding. Perhaps in that sense he meant to establish a type of metric that depends upon and uses more-or-less condensed summations of previously enacted law to further develop. It's hard to say. But as he stood and gave account of himself to his colleagues in 1902 he concentrated more on explaining what he had done and why and less on expounding the dream he hoped to see one day fulfilled. He says he tried to see the law as an "organic whole" – not that it *is* an organic whole – and to better understand that point we move to his next sentence.

2. **I also have tried to see it as a reaction between tradition on the one side and the changing desires and needs of the community on the other.** Here he transports us to the opening pages of *The Common Law*. The commentators have seldom appreciated his steadfastness of purpose. Holmes is a hedgehog. He knows only one thing and one thing only. If the law may be seen as an organic whole, if one can see that way, then one must learn also to see it as a living, reacting body. It is vital and ongoing, inert and resilient. The reactive elements are tradition and present needs and what in "Law in Science and Science in Law" he calls fashion. Fashion and present needs are often merged into one another but here we see Holmes noting a subtle distinction between changing wants and markers of value and those community needs that are or have become evident. To both he counterpoises tradition. But we do well to keep in mind that tradition, or more broadly the past, is, as he often said, only a necessity not a duty.
3. **I have studied tradition.** To understand the rules and practices that direct and command him and his community he has gone to the recognized sources. Through the prolonged study of artifacts and changing perceptions he hopes to reveal the intrinsic quality of each individual pointer, to understand the arrangements and combinations of pointers that have survived into the present. History as a program for research and thought and for harnessing time provides an excellent venue to meet and debate the law bequeathed by the past. Another way to say the same thing: Holmes uses historical research and analysis to put the legal tradition that he and his contemporaries had taken for granted on the dock. As he well put it, "my references to the Year Books often have had a skeptical end."
4. **I have considered the present tendencies and desires of society.** In this declaration we get as close as we ever do in the published Holmes corpus to Holmes tipping his hand on the role that current social conditions and their averments – what some call "politics" – played in

his judicial thinking. Because the quoted phrase can be so easily misunderstood it is important to draw attention to how he differentiates temporally those social features which he, as a judge, finds himself aware of and thinking about. Present tendencies may be less fashionable, less momentary, than present desires. Yet they are not anchored in the society like tradition. Even to make such preliminary distinctions requires that one well understand the present makeup and visible past of one's community. Perhaps Holmes is alluding to, and justifying, his articulated position on those labor-related cases that appeared before the Supreme Judicial Court in the mid-1890s. In deciding favorably to the cause of labor he was not promoting a political position but, as he noted in the next part of the above-quoted sentence, he "tried to realize that its [society's] different portions want different things[.]"

5. **My business was to express not my personal wish, but the resultant, as nearly as I could guess, of the pressure of the past and the conflicting wills of the present.** It is tempting to read this statement solely in terms of winners and losers, in light of the creedal article that the struggle for life is the order of the world. It also tempting to see it as merely a reiteration of what he said in "Path": "The prophecies of what the courts will do in fact, and nothing more pretentious, are what I mean by law." It includes both these elements and something more. This way of expressing the judicial task is actually quite curious given that it is being made by the Chief Justice of what was at the time the leading state supreme court in the country. But in line with our earlier comments on the fundamental significance of professional judgments we see here Holmes gesturing toward two realities. First, that the common law system as it exists is still a system predicated mainly on will not reason. Second, that the professional judgments to which this system gives rise, even when the system is increasingly supplemented by statutes, are still unavoidably limited and ineradicably marked by the predominance of a scientifically untutored will. Reason is still a mirage because reason is not grounded in scientifically vetted postulates. The result of justice in such a system is not, despite appearances, a decision founded upon untainted, morally certified reason. Once alerted to that fact a judge of last resort was placed in the position of trying to determine in the cases that came before the court the relative strengths of the actual forces in play. The law fashioned in such a crucible typically reflects in its composition the proportionality of those relative strengths. Most decisions of last resort are thus in this sense resultants, in that they arrange the past and sort out the presently competing wills through adroit, often morally or policy laden, formulations. Thus the intellectually alert judge committed to conducting his business in line with the highest

expectations of his profession and in keeping with his own hard-won insights could not really know – because reason in the form of science did not yet function as the primary predicate – but only guess at what formulations would assuage dominant opinion and keep the public in line. This was the system in which Holmes found himself working and moving, living and breathing; it was good as far as it went but it was not the best.

6. **I have considered the social and economic postulates on which we frame the conception of our needs, and I have seen them in a dry light. It has seemed to me that certainty is an illusion, that we have few scientific data on which to affirm that one rule rather than another has the sanction of the universe, that we rarely could be sure that one tends more distinctly than its opposite to the survival and welfare of a society where it is practiced, and that the wisest are but blind guides.** It bears reading these two sentences at least twice and keeping in mind that the person who uttered them is on the short road to a seat on the US Supreme Court. Perhaps it bears also mentioning that we should read them charitably. In other words, it is no devastating criticism of Holmes's position to contend that the commandment "Thou shalt not kill" in whatever guise it might appear in human societies reflects a universal, natural law. Holmes is beyond such platitudes. Holmes here is wondering out loud whether the postulates that have traditionally provided support and justification for the social and economic order of the society that he cares about are strong enough to sustain it as complexity and fragmentation increase apace. He will not sacrifice the good for the best but neither will he affix a halo atop the extant common law simply because it's the only body of law he happens to know intimately. One cannot help but wonder when the "dry light" dispelled the soft dreamlike glow of over-belief from venerated social and economic postulates. It is this skepticism, Holmes says, that makes him slow to overrule a decision. The great body of the law that he knows, the common law, has at least this sanction from the universe – it exists. Better to be slow to change what one knows but hardly understands.

The two provisional goodbyes from the latter half of 1902 bring us into contact with yet another Holmesian polarity. The aesthetics of impassivity and longing give way at some indeterminable, indefinable point to a pulse of feeling whose phases alternate between the peaks and troughs of sadness and joy. We see the same operative range in the 1900 speech before the Bar Association of Boston. Given James's famed powers of empathic perception it makes one wonder how he missed it. There, Holmes closes by telling his audience that he will but add a word: "We are all very near despair. The sheathing that floats us over its waves is compounded of hope, faith in the unexplainable worth and sure issue of effort, and the deep, subconscious content which comes from the exercise of our powers."[456] He does not then turn to declare abruptly the joyful dread of the bugle and the charge – as he did in his later address to the Middlesex Bar – but, unbelievably, quotes a stanza from an African American spiritual –

> Sometimes I's up, sometimes I's down,
> Sometimes I's almost to the groun'[.]

Here is a man, we only now begin to see even this far into the journey, who staggered for the greater part of his life under a burden of "doubt, self-distrust, and solitude."[457] Of these solitude proved most pernicious. It fed the doubt and harbored the self-distrust. He justified the digression by saying he hoped to encourage the young men in the audience who might suffer as once he did from a frightful, enervating intellectual loneliness but even as he said it one suspects he knew the offered rationale to be only partly true.

If effort itself is the object and source of faith, it implicates but does not privilege certain ends or means, unreachable ideals or unceasing struggle. It turns the focus inward; it trusts in the efficacy of action's internal rhythm and flow and its ever-widening scope. "For to live is to function. That is all there is in living." We now dimly perceive that by "function" Holmes intended to recalibrate the opening question of Emerson's "Nature," – "Why should not we also enjoy an original relation to the universe?"[458]

The authenticity of Holmes's faith, and of his doubt, arises from his belief that the dross of human experience is not meaningless. The meaning it may have, and the meaning it will have, one finds built up in-and-through law.[459] It requires a unique habit of mind to see law in this manner. Holmes's self-conscious beginning point lies not in daybreak meanderings on verdant summer morns, when it is a veritable soul-quenching pleasure to draw deeply the breath of life, when one may behold God face-to-face; but in the undisguised obverse – in that scarlet droplet of faith glistening on many blades green, brown, or steel in the killing field of Antietam or lit fleetingly by the blue line of fire radiating across the dark, soaked, splattered mud of Spotsylvania.

[456] *Id.*, at 500.

[457] *Id.*

[458] Ralph Waldo Emerson, *Nature, in* Essays and Poems by Ralph Waldo Emerson 9 (Peter Norberg ed., 2004). Probably because she relies too much on Stanley Cavell's interpretation of the Emersonian project, Michal Alberstein does not see how Holmes engineers this recalibration and brings it into law. *See* Michal Alberstein, Pragmatism and Law 1–99 (2002).

[459] As he put it to Morris Cohen: "But in general it requires tough fibre [*sic*] not to repine at spending one's energies on the transitory law when you fellows [mathematicians] are shaping the (relatively) eternal. But the transitory also shapes the eternal as Mons. Jourdain talked prose, without know it." Cohen, *supra* note 443, at 12.

Between the transcendental beauty of New England and the massive ugliness of killing for cause in regions south one finds the germination of something not quite foreseen but important enough to be called a moral experience. In "The Use of Law Schools," Holmes said, "nearly all the education which men can get from others is moral, not intellectual."[460] Holmes somehow found a way to tease a pilgrimage out of the endless sloughing through enemy soil in the unrelenting rain. Life lessons that had eluded his slightly older, better intellectually armored contemporary, Henry Adams, began to push up through the muck. The key was to look upon his compatriots with new eyes. Detractors hone in on his "I loathe the thick-fingered clowns we call the people[,]"[461] but hardly ever mention he wrote these words to his sister at the tender age of twenty-one while he and his friend Henry Abbot were snaking their way through "debatable land" in search of their regiment. Holmes had been in Boston recovering from his wound at Antietam.[462] It really lies beyond my comprehension why seasoned scholars would take this line as confirming a lifelong political conviction. Is it even worth mentioning that almost thirty years later no less a man-of-the-people than Walt Whitman sent Holmes a heartfelt note complimenting him on the publication of *Speeches*?[463] True, in that initial edition "A Soldier's Faith" had not yet made its appearance, but would Whitman have missed the critique of the "effervescence of democracy" in "The Use of Law Schools"? Or how Holmes urges law schools to raise up specialists to correct the ignoble excess of a noble feeling?

These questions are of course unanswerable. But we need not rest on Whitman's imprimatur to see that Holmes believed in the nobility of the democratic ethos. If the war had opened his eyes to the reality that men as valiant as Henry Abbot, who could not give a rat's ass for the plight of blacks in subjugation, that men such as he would throw away their lives to help a cause in which they did not believe, then can we say, as has been said with so much intellectual verve, that the war caused Holmes to lose his belief in beliefs?[464] Or did the war mark the beginning of his willingness to submerge himself into the ur-belief of effort? What he called faith?

The war became a great moral experience for him because Holmes found it shifted his interests and aims. Fanny Holmes said it best when she said that if not for the Civil War Holmes would have been a coxcomb.[465] His power of self-reflexivity

[460] Holmes, *The Use of Law Schools*, *supra* note 103, at 475.

[461] Touched with Fire: Civil War Letters and Diary of Oliver Wendell Holmes, Jr. 1861–1864 71 (Mark DeWolfe Howe ed., 1946).

[462] Budiansky, *supra* note 400, at 102.

[463] Sheldon M. Novick, Honorable Justice: The Life of Oliver Wendell Holmes 196 (1989). George M. Frederickson argued a long time ago that Whitman and Abraham Lincoln were "almost alone among the philosophers of Unionism in giving a strong democratic meaning to the conflict [the Civil War]." George M. Frederickson, The Inner Civil War: Northern Intellectuals and the Crisis of the Union 66 (1965).

[464] Louis Menand, The Metaphysical Club: A Story of Ideas in America 4 (2001).

[465] *See* Budiansky, *supra* note 400, at 128; Baker, *supra* note 126, at 105.

was strong and effectual. It helped him articulate what he said to the Harvard Law School alumni in 1886: "If you convince a man that another way of looking at things is more profound, another form of pleasure more subtile [*sic*] than that to which he has been accustomed, – if you make him really see it, – the very nature of man is such that he will desire the profounder thought and the subtiler [*sic*] joy."[466] This insight once voiced kindled a bright-blue hope that in time almost flamed out with disappointment – and may account for the greater proportion of pathos in his writings as one century ended and another began – but it also helps us immensely to understand the role of a law school as Holmes saw it in the mid-1880s.

It helps us understand because after the above quoted sentence Holmes says this: "So I say the business of a law school is not sufficiently described when you merely say that it is to teach law, or to make lawyers. It is to teach law in the grand manner, and to make great lawyers."[467] Other commentators have been content to merely quote this sentence, as if Holmes's aspirations were self-evident or self-executing, without attempting to carefully construe what it might mean to say that law must be taught in a "grand manner" or that the aim of the law school is "to make great lawyers."

These stated ideals take us, I suggest, to the metabolic core of Holmes's thought. To put it in personal terms, he taught himself law in the grand manner and he strove throughout his working life to be a great judge. And he sought to achieve these ideals under less than propitious circumstances, when, as he put it in 1902, "it was not so easy as it is now to see that law, looked at through the stereoscope of history, is the story of our growth." Even more to the point he adds: "It was not easy to put to oneself even the vaguer proposition that as the facts of the law are the facts of the universe they are worthy of their share of the only intellectual interest there is, – the interest of being seen in their universal relations."[468]

Holmes through these remarks amplifies the rather startling comment that the first five or ten years of his professional life made as great or an even greater moral impact on him than the three years he spent fighting the Confederacy. One must really stare at these sentences a long time, as one would stare at *Guernica*. Inevitably one must turn and walk away. The mural sits in memory, as sat the war, as sat the first decade of his professional life in Holmes's. Their combined education in misery prompted him at every opportunity to encourage those beginning in the practice of the profession with these words, "it is true that you grow – that you must go through that trial of wretched doubt – doubt as to your own significance, ignorance of even what question you want to ask, – and through faith and will – faith that there is a question and an answer – will to attain them – that one enters the door of life."[469]

466 Holmes, *The Use of Law Schools*, *supra* note 103, at 475.
467 *Id.*
468 Holmes, *supra* note 444, at 534.
469 *Id.* at 534–35. Holmes expressed these types of sentiments regarding "faith" constantly in the 1890s and beyond. *See, e.g.*, Oliver Wendell Holmes, *Address at Brown University*

Some commentators have taken this statement and others like them in Holmes's writings to be indicative of how Holmes rhapsodized law and turned it into an alternate dimension of fight and valor from which he could emerge with his courage and self-esteem intact. He could redeem himself in imagination from what he failed to do in life. Others, less acutely, but just as uncharitably, have simply seen them as part of Holmes's penchant for creating "a phantasy world of his own construction."[470] The truth is that it is hard to know what Holmes meant exactly. But the theme of solitude, loneliness, and hard work in learning the law, in seeing the law as something more than customary groupings and available utilities for resolving disputes or accomplishing client objectives, forces us to puzzle through the words. It seems to me that in making these statements Holmes leaves much unsaid, much that could be said if he were behind a pulpit expounding a verse. But there is no pulpit and there is no verse. It is not without interest that upon reading the first edition of *Speeches* Brandeis wrote to the author: "When the Lawyer's Bible comes to be made up – the book of Holmes will be its Job, and your Hymn of Praise will be the Te Deum of their service."[471] Brandeis may have simply found a way to be diplomatic as Novick suggests, but then from a different quarter we hear similar sentiments.

According to Paul R. Baier, longtime professor at the Louisiana State University Law Center and Holmes aficionado, one Colonel Frederick Bernays Wiener, "an old soldier of the law," told guests at a black-tie dinner that if not quite "a Bible, [*Speeches* is] still a book of most uncommon prayer." One speech in particular, he said, caught and held his attention through many days and months of great trial. It gave him much comfort. It was Holmes's address to the Bar Association of Boston in 1900, the same speech that threw James into an exasperated tizzy. Colonel Wiener further relates that he happened to meet a Boston lawyer who was present at the event. This was George R. Nutter, "one of the editors of Volume I of the Harvard Law Review" and sometime partner of the future Justice Brandeis (Brandeis, Nutter & McClennen). He asked Nutter, "What was the reaction of those present when the

Commencement, in III CW 518 ("The consummation to which I referred comes when he applies this knowledge to himself. He may put it in the theological form of justification by faith or in the philosophical one of the continuity of the universe. I care not very much for the form if in some way he has learned that he cannot set himself over against the universe as a rival god, to criticize it, or shake his fist at the skies, but that his meaning is its meaning, his only worth is as a part of it, as a humble instrument of the universal power. It seems to me that this is the key to intellectual salvation as the key to happiness is to accept a like faith into one's heart and to be not merely a necessary but a willing instrument in working out the inscrutable end.").

470 Mortimer J. Adler, *Legal Certainty, in Symposium*, Law and The Modern Mind, 31 COLUM. L. REV. 91, 97 (1931). *See also* Harold D. Lasswell, *Review of Howe*: Justice Oliver Wendell Holmes: The Proving Years 1870–1882, 73 YALE L.J. 532, 532 (1964) ("We sum up by saying that the scholar's role was a compromise between an intense craving for power and Holmes's continuing doubt of his adequacy as a man.").

471 Quoted in NOVICK, *supra* note 463, at 196.

Chief Justice's talk was concluded?" Nutter replied, "There really wasn't any. They were so moved and really too stunned even to applaud."[472]

How do we work our way back into this moment? We can't. But we can assemble the spatial–temporal fibers or bits remaining and use whatever means at our disposal to project a working image. We take as our starting point what Holmes calls a "moral experience." We take it to mean a dramatic reshaping of existing "interests and aims," a revision of wants, a move toward the profounder thought and the subtler joy. If a group of Boston lawyers found themselves at a loss when called upon to acknowledge that their legal practices and endeavors had potentialities separate from and beyond the instrumental or prophylactic, that they could also be seen and understood as part of the outreaching of the human spirit, and to acknowledge that in its wakes even the pervasive cynic force of common sense could be rendered inutile and powerless, then it behooves us to inquire whether this particular collocation of sentiment and event can be carded, combed, and woven into a tiny tapestry.

Or, in other words, can we find a way to turn this moment in time – the sentiment and the event, the event and the sentiment – into an object of inquiry, into that overriding "fact" which, as Holmes once told the young men at Harvard, "is all that life offers any man from which to start his thinking or his striving[.]"[473]

From this and related statements we gather that Holmes saw in retrospect that his search for meaning in the law in the decade after the Civil War had taken a greater psychological toll than he had ever realized. He had floundered a great long while, learning the rudiments, absorbing thousands of details, seeking to master an arcane and difficult subject that held no or little promise to realize or advance human understanding. It was the plight of one who single-mindedly thirsted for knowledge and insight but found himself caught in a mode of living that prized neither for its own sake. Instead, it was a mode of life often filled with utility, sophistry, combativeness, and chicanery. For Holmes to call his period of induction, apprenticeship, and grounding in the profession a "moral experience," one at least as intense as what he went through in the war, tells us, at minimum, that his interests and aims underwent a radical conversion, one at least as powerful as his war-induced revolt against the abolitionism of his youth and all that it represented.

From his battles as a young soldier and his intellectual struggles as a young lawyer he sought to identify and name the power that manifested itself in his life through persistence and commitment; it revealed that region of human experience which underlay emotion and passion but did not find its sole vitality or source in the instinct to survive. The will to survive had, like a strawberry plant, cast offshoots that

[472] Paul R. Baier, *Holmes and Honors Law at LSU – From Great Hall to La Maison Française*, 63 La. L. Rev. 53, 60–62 (2002).

[473] Holmes, *The Profession of the Law*, *supra* note 77, at 472.

in turn had also become primary centers and sources of vital attention.[474] He called these offshoots in-the-air "faith." Certainly he knew the word had religious overtones. He knew but didn't care because his purpose was not to overturn the ancestral gods but to direct the energies and hopes and loyalties they represented toward new ends. He would reunify and redirect the flow. He would do what Shattuck had done in the courtroom but he chose as his forum the whole country and its history. He called upon his America to believe in itself, to hold fast to the ideal of self-rule it represented among the nations, and he appealed, unabashedly, to the heritage of his people and his race to see that commitment through to the unseen perhaps unhappy end.

Put into modern terms, the motive force that kept Holmes going is a refusal to concede. Holmes did not concede during the fight that the course of the war defeated his ideals, and he would not concede defeat – though at times he may have come very, very close – in his unremitting efforts to make the rules by which Americans governed themselves more intelligent and intelligible. The fundamental theorem of the law we recall from "Law in Science and Science in Law" is that any action may be found lawful or unlawful. That theorem powerfully articulated Holmes's conviction that social meaning could become self-conscious and purposeful. The energy, the drive, the persistence to metamorphose that conviction into new social tissue, being, and form he revered as effort.

Between the conviction and its realization lies a large area of experience that traditional Protestant theology sometimes referred to as "justification." Justification has its own usages and rhythms, its own ranges of applicability, and we would be remiss in our analysis if we did not take a moment to see that at some indefinable point for Holmes justification has no language to express itself other than the language of honor and loyalty and obedience:

> I do not know what is true. I do not know the meaning of the universe. But in the midst of doubt, in the collapse of creeds, there is one thing I do not doubt, that no man who lives in the same world with most of us can doubt, and that is that the faith is true and adorable which leads a soldier to throw away his life in obedience to a blindly accepted duty, in a cause he little understands, in a plan of campaign of which he has no notion, under tactics of which does not see the use.

Or as he said a bit more plainly in 1884, partly to explain why Memorial Day might still mean something even to those born long after the Civil War: "It embodies in the most impressive form our belief that to act with enthusiasm and faith is the condition of acting greatly."[475] Left unsaid are the cumulative effects, presumably,

[474] *See* Cohen, *supra* note 443, at 23–25; *see also* Holmes, *Introduction to* Rational Basis of Legal Institutions, *in* III CW 449 ("Law is a plant that lives long before it throws out bulbs."). *But see* David Luban, Legal Modernism 146–50 (1994) (arguing that the "strawberry plant" analogy for the development of a vital mode of social inquiry is self-defeating).

[475] Holmes, *Memorial Day, supra* note 106, at 463.

that intelligence and judgment and past experience have on creating the other conditions necessary for acting greatly.

Over time Holmes joined and condensed the enthusiasm, the passion, the might, and a vital but never fully fathomed faith into a single impassive, unemotional, unattractive, unromantic, uninspiring, synthetic word – function. Undoubtedly he did so intentionally and it would probably take another lengthy analysis to figure out why.

ii *Stereoscopic Law*

But this study is already long enough and the time has come to move slowly upward and outward from the region of faith to that of belief. Belief in both institutional and propositional forms direct us away from the region of the "can't help" – which, as Francis Lucey, SJ, clearly saw, harkened back in phrase and sentiment to Martin Luther – to those mid-regions of the mind called discourse and debate. In terms of the institutions and propositions that concern us, those of American law, we find that Holmes rarely if ever jumps the brink from one legal regime or institution to another but always moves cautiously, deftly. He seems usually able to find the path he wants through the many uncharted realms.

Holmes's realization that paths could be made or found and that his faith was not unsound finds its grandest rendition in his 1885 address, "The Law." He delivered this address a year before "The Use of Law Schools." "The Law," the first address in *Speeches* delivered solely to members of the legal profession, the Suffolk Bar Association, finds Holmes at his most rapturous about the common work that they, the Court and the Bar, do. "The law is made by the Bar, even more than by the Bench[.]"[476] We saw earlier how F. W. Grinnell insightfully elaborated the same point some forty years later. But compared to Grinnell, even to the most articulate lawyers of that era I dare say, Holmes's language in "The Law" is self-consciously prophetic; a long resounding, rallying trumpet call. It ranges against incipient fragmentation a centripetal passion rarely encountered in the surviving legal literature.[477] It is profound and sublime and foretells a new dispensation in which legal actors do not lose themselves in their roles or in the ongoing drama but take heed of their charge.

[476] Holmes, *The Law*, *supra* note 104, at 469.

[477] Perry Miller's evocations of the competing pressures that the sentiment of a newfound spiritual sublimity put on nineteenth-century American jurisprudence remain unmatched, though Robert A. Ferguson has added important nuance and detail. Even so, Holmes does not seem to me to be the crabbed "specialist" that Ferguson describes. He is instead reaching out with a self-conscious, philosophically aware rhetoric that Miller found exceedingly rare in the American context. *See* Perry Miller, The Life of the Mind In America 99–265 (1965); Robert A. Ferguson, Law and Letters in American Culture 288–90 (1984); Perry Miller, Jonathan Edwards 310–11 (1949).

Holmes was by no means the first or only person in the late nineteenth century to sing the common law's praises. Indeed one legal historian, Richard A. Cosgrove, wrote an entire book, *Our Lady the Common Law*, dedicated to these hymns.[478] But Holmes is unique in how he brings into his rendition a self-conscious element of decision. He wants to raise the law that he knows and loves – which is to say the culture that he knows and loves – to a new height. This "abstraction called the Law," which unites the profession and which through its artifices plunges its members deeply into the stream of life – "its passions, its battles, its despair, its triumphs" – as both witnesses and actors, reflects, as does "a magic mirror," not only their lives but "the lives of all men that have been!"[479]

Holmes may have gotten a bit carried away in this utterance but read carefully and charitably we see at work sentiments similar in tone to those of leading seventeenth-century lawyers in England. Yet while Lord Coke spoke of how the common law was the "artificial perfection of reason," "fined and refined by an infinite number of grave and learned men," Holmes emphasized instead the vistas for the active mind that the law once seen as a "magic mirror" opened up. Holmes does not use the temporal tropes of "immemorial" or "insensible" in his paean because he sees his era as one that has opened up the extant law and provided the opportunity for inquiry.[480] As he would put it much later in his "Privilege, Malice, and Intent": "The time has gone by when law is only an unconscious embodiment of the common will. It has become a conscious reaction upon itself of organized society knowingly seeking to determine its own destinies."[481] In other words, "When we study law we are not studying a mystery but a well known profession."[482]

From the "Privilege, Malice, and Intent" quote it is worth highlighting the stated juxtaposition of unconscious and conscious and the unstated one of destiny and destinies. Facing these juxtapositions required a unique combination of fortitude and courage, of impassivity and longing, qualities often summed up in that era and for those people as "manly." It also must be said that the record of Holmes's writings as a whole, especially when read in connection with other similar expressions from the period, takes on the racial coloration – "race" used broadly and without any purported scientific or analytic exactness – of the self-proclaimed (white) Anglo-Saxon. There is no way to disentangle this element of "race" from Holmes's mature thought and still remain true to the record. But even if this element was at the forefront it did not function as the centerpiece that arranged the entire table of

478 Richard A. Cosgrove, Our Lady the Common Law: An Anglo-American Legal Community, 1870–1930 (1987). It is curious, though, that in his chapter on Holmes Cosgrove nowhere mentions "The Law."

479 Holmes, *The Law*, *supra* note 104, at 469.

480 *See* Lobban, *supra* note 323, at 33–40 (2016); Parker, *supra* note 135, at 28–43 (2011); Pocock, *supra* note 408, at 30–69.

481 Oliver Wendell Holmes, *Privilege, Malice, and Intent*, *in* III CW 377.

482 Holmes, *The Path of the Law*, *supra* note 1, at 391.

values; in time, I tend to think, Holmes became more willing to question its strong presumptive validity.[483] It partly explains his willingness in 1919 to let political radicals born in other countries but living in this one speak their minds, and to defend their political speech, even in somewhat fraught circumstances, as an allowable exercise of an American constitutional right.[484] Query: Would Henry Adams, or his brother Brooks, have done the same?

The willingness of Holmes to question the presumptive validity of the culture he loved and in which he found revealed the highest aspirations he yearned to fulfill accounts for much of his greatness. His refusal to lose himself in doubting those aspirations and to be willing to utter a simple "can't help" when the moment required accounts for the rest. He refused to diminish the actuality of his being, his values, and his commitments in the face of lustrous ideals or competing, compelling wants. At the same time, he refused to take his aspirations and discount them to present-day value to make them marketable. Holmes had a sense of time and of uncertainty that many of his contemporaries lacked. If his ideals survived intact they might form part of an economy of desires and destinies still unseen or unrecognized.

For these reasons, his declamation to "The Law" takes on a unique configuration. On the one side, it brings to mind the rhetorical force and passion that forerunners like Lord Coke lavished on the common law. And at the same time from another angle he recognized that "The Law" is where the present and past meet to hammer out their differences. Present and past being, of course, abstractions that point to the various elements of tradition, fashionable perception, and pressing needs and sensibilities that push up against each other, each seeking a desired outcome. The strange thing, though, is that in a common law jurisdiction the working lawyer is typically not relegated to a single role or part. In the great spell of feeling that surrounded the common law in seventeenth-century England this sociological fact may not have carried the same weight it would 300–400 years later. It was not unusual for proponents of the common law in the 1600s to see it supported by the great columns Nature and Custom:

> A Ground, Rule, or Principle, of the Law of *England* is a conclusion either of the Law of Nature, or derived from some general custom used within the Realm,

[483] *See* Oliver Wendell Holmes, *Law and the Court*, *in* III CW 307 ("I do not pin my dreams for the future to my country or even to my race.").

[484] *See* Abrams v. United States, 250 U.S. 616, 624–31 (1919) (Holmes, J. dissenting). *See also* John M. Kang, Oliver Wendell Holmes and Fixations of Manliness 78–129 (2018). I think Kang emphasizes an important point but his thesis would have benefitted from a more sustained interaction with the common law tradition in which Holmes moved. For an interesting alternate assessment of the dynamics at play see David A. Hollinger, *The 'Tough-Minded' Justice Holmes, Jewish Intellectuals, and the Making of an American Icon*, *in* The Legacy of Oliver Wendell Holmes, Jr. 216–28 (Robert W. Gordon ed., 1992).

> containing in a short Sum, the reason & direction of many particular & special occurrences.[485]

Holmes distanced himself from the hegemony of either Nature or Custom as traditionally conceived but held on to the notion that a ground, rule, or principle – taking these words without analytic precision – functioned as a pointer, an indicator, of "the reason & direction of many particular and special occurrences."[486] In a different vocabulary and mental frame these "short Sums" might be seen as arranging instances, and themselves as arrangements of those arrangements.

It is but a step from these "short Sums" to the famed legal maxims of Bacon. Scholars will often at this juncture cite Paul Kocher's article, "Francis Bacon on the Science of Jurisprudence," and specifically mention Kocher's claim that these maxims are not "legal rules of the very highest class of generality," but, rather, they are like the "middle axioms" of natural science.[487] According to Kocher some of these middle axioms – a term I do not fully understand – "establish practical ties between basic human rights and the ordinary court-room scene without which the former would remain mere un-instrumented airy platitudes."[488] We all of a sudden come face-to-face with Holmes's famed statement that, "General propositions do not decide concrete cases."[489] Kocher adds that others of these maxims "are themselves lesser substantive components leading up to the more broadly generalized statement of rights." He concludes: "So we must visualize some dimensional thickness within Bacon's concept of the law of nature to allow for different degrees of generality and instrumentation."[490]

With Kocher's suggestion that we "visualize some dimensional thickness" we take one step closer to seeing how the law could be seen stereoscopically. Formulations (substantive and procedural) that primarily played a heuristic role in seventeenth-century common law jurisprudence began to take on greater weight and proportionately more importance by the late nineteenth. We suggest tentatively – and it is only a suggestion since much would have to be done to make it something more – that one could construct a viable narrative connecting the "short Sums" from the above quotation to Austin's idea of utility to Holmes's notion of prophecy.

485 As quoted in LOBBAN, *supra* note 323, at 37 (emphasis in original) (internal citations omitted).

486 *Id.* On Holmes's distancing himself from Custom and Nature *see, e.g.*, LUBAN, *supra* note 474, at 28–31.

487 Paul H. Kocher, *Francis Bacon on the Science of Jurisprudence*, 18 J. HIST. IDEAS 3, 11 (1957); *see also* LOBBAN, *supra* note 323, at 39.

488 Kocher, *supra* note 487, at 11. Though I am not sure how Kocher is using the term, "middle axiom," Holmes interestingly used a similar phrase ("the middle axioms of experience") in describing the "realm of the ever old which also is ever new[.]" Holmes, *Montesquieu, supra* note 73, at 426.

489 Lochner v. New York, 198 U.S. 45, 76 (1905) (Holmes, J. dissenting).

490 Kocher, *supra* note 487, at 11.

It bears mentioning that no less an authority than H. L. A. Hart pointed out that for Austin utility functioned as an index to God's commands.[491] It provided a way to confer the dignity normally reserved for individual actions to acts taken from, and representing, a broader social viewpoint. Actions in terms of utility displayed movement – trajectories, a closer to or further away from supposedly optimal conduct. But with the growth of an increasingly historical consciousness (*homo faber*, humans as creators) the realization took hold that human limitations amidst the movements of life and culture had no backstop. The province of jurisprudence, to use Austin's phrase, began to overtake the once mighty empire of God's will, be it called Custom or Nature or Revelation.

These thoughts bring us back to Holmes's "The Law" and its unique configuration. Its exalted language might tempt us to forget that judges and lawyers spend much of their professional lives tamping down or diverting human indifference, overreaching, scheming, meanness, or just plain cruelty. Is Holmes merely giving us in "The Law" his own version of Mandeville's *Fable of the Bees*? Is it merely a reiteration of the lesson that private vices lead to public benefits? The evidence suggests otherwise. "If we are to speak of the law as our mistress," Holmes says, it is incumbent upon "we who are here [to] know that she is a mistress only to be wooed with sustained and lonely passions, – only to be won by straining all the faculties by which man is likest to a god."[492] The romantic figurations between wooer and wooed in the sentence are conspicuous, standing out in bas-relief because of their contrast to some powerful present-day sensibilities regarding the relations between various sexual and gendered identities. But what pops out like Andy Warhol's soup cans, making for an even more pronounced contrast, is his urging colleagues to exert those "faculties by which man is likest to a god." It is certainly not improbable that Holmes has again gotten carried away, taken to rhetorical extremes by the thrust of his own language and his passion for heightened literary expression.

But as so often is the case we confront in Holmes an aporia, not of Holmes's making but of our own, a cultural disjunction that cannot be resolved or dissolved through any formal means. We can take Holmes's directive as an exaggerated utterance, just as we took his comments regarding the "magic mirror," or we can take it as a sport of nature, a particle of possibility, a new emphasis that works its way unseen into that mesh of recognized obligations that is an evolving professional conscience. As we saw earlier in the case of his references to Correggio, Holmes is at times his own best interpreter. When he tells a group of undergraduates a year later in "The Profession of the Law" that, of course, the law is not the place for the artist or the poet we might expect some sage advice along the lines given by the Lord Chief Justice. But, no. He tells them the law "is the calling of thinkers." That sounds

[491] H. L. A. Hart, *Positivism and the Separation of Law and Morals*, 71 Harv. L. Rev. 593, 597 (1958).

[492] Holmes, *The Law*, *supra* note 104, at 469.

grand, if overblown and self-congratulatory. But then he adds, "to those who believe with me that not the least godlike of man's activities is the large survey of causes, that to know is not less than to feel, I say – and I say no longer with any doubt – that a man may live greatly in the law as elsewhere[.]"[493]

Can it be true that law through its thinkers has begun to take possession of providence, of attributes once thought exclusively divine? Does his assertion reveal anything more than an appeal to a youthful and immature grandiosity? We recall that Holmes suggested something similar in his tribute to Shattuck. If what he said has any potential merit then the inner path of American law occupies its own distinctive chronotope, to use a current academic locution.[494] Holmes may not have shared the simple moralizing of Story or Blackstone's sense that the common law manifested the mysterious, awesome providence of God, but he seems to have found a manner to express uniquely his sense of American sublimity.

He is thus unabashed in exhorting his hearers to exert to the utmost those "faculties by which man is likest to a god," that to fully employ the godlike ability to organize and arrange the social world depends on the "large survey of causes." Part of that large survey involves "a history of the moral life of his race."[495] The endeavor will not end "until, by the farthest stretch of human imagination, he [the thinker] has seen with his eyes the birth and growth of society, and by the farthest stretch of reason he has understood the philosophy of its being." Its goal, Holmes says more straightforwardly, is to see the very painful steps "by which mankind has worked and fought its way from savage isolation to organic social life."[496] The intellectual traits and skills required to meet these demands are not for the heavy-hearted or myopic. But no thinker thinks alone, just as no one practices law alone. We see in this rhetoric and in these demands a resurfacing of the same inclination to emphasize the "artificial reason of the law" that many scholars established as first appearing in seventeenth-century England and whose most imposing avatar was the imposing Sir Edward Coke. Here again, though on an issue more fundamental than that of contract law, Holmes takes his stand with Lord Coke. The main difference between the two being that Holmes sees this artificial reason registering the existing panoplies of thought and feeling at different and more varied scales than did Coke, who seemed to have limited the register to one or two dimensions (that of immanent reason and logic). Holmes begins to extend it to new levels and in new directions – up, down, and sideways. As a self-conscious American he could hardly do otherwise.

The continued rise of thinking and of the thinker as a self-conscious occupation since the seventeenth century also helps to explain this difference. J. G. A. Pocock puts it rather starkly when he says, "Coke's mind, it is clear, was nearly as insular as a

[493] Holmes, *The Profession of the Law*, *supra* note 77, at 472.

[494] *See, e.g.*, MARIANA VALVERDE, CHRONOTOPES OF LAW: JURISDICTION, SCALE AND GOVERNANCE 30–90 (2015); *see also* LUBAN, *supra* note 474, at 38–40.

[495] Holmes, *The Law*, *supra* note 104, at 469.

[496] *Id.*

human being's could be."[497] So perhaps the better comparison is between Coke and Langdell. Certainly in Coke's emphasis on the common law as immemorial we see something similar to what drove Langdell and upon which Holmes unerringly put his finger: the conviction that normative principles were immanent in a body of decisions. There was little awareness of how much present attitudes and concerns and purposes contributed to the manufacture and coloring of the viewing lenses. The focus on immanence in the West is typically theological, or, if transposed into a philosophical key, something similar to the Hegelian. Or, if further transposed into a lower key, one less ethereal or intellectualized, it partakes in the lifeblood, the *ethnos*, of a race.

What prevented Holmes from fully going down this road was the important philosophical lesson he told Pollock he had learned from Chauncey Wright. "Chauncey Wright, a nearly forgotten philosopher of real merit, taught me when young that I must not say *necessary* about the universe, that we don't know whether anything is necessary or not. So I describe myself as a *bet*tabilitarian. I believe we can *bet* on the universe in its contact with us."[498] Bettabilitarianism signified for Holmes a way of organizing knowledge; it relied on probability, which was one way of mapping out and assimilating possibilities to purpose. In relation to law it stripped away whatever immanence lawyers might ascribe to it when not fighting in the trenches and provided a means to do what Holmes most desired: to turn the practice of law itself into a discipline of knowledge.

We come back to those pivotal two sentences from the middle of "Law in Science and Science in Law."

> Notwithstanding the contrasts which I have been making, *the practical study of law ought also to be scientific*. The true science of the law does not consist mainly in the theological working out of dogma or a logical development as in mathematics, or only in a study of it as an anthropological document from the outside; *an even more important part consists in the establishment of its postulates from within upon accurately measured social desires instead of tradition*.[499]

The enjoinder to establish postulates "from within" must be understood as distinguishing this intellectual endeavor from applying to law knowledge acquired from external disciplines – anthropology, political science, and ethics, for instance – that Holmes believed had usefulness once aspiring lawyers got their bearings in the profession. The phrase, "from within," takes on added significance once we connect it to the purely legal point of view. One must learn to see how operative law ticks; one must get past the dramatic incidents. One must learn to visualize the combined grounds that gave the working rule the vitality it once had and may still have or else

497 Pocock, *supra* note 408, at 56.

498 II Holmes–Pollock Correspondence, *supra* note 97, at 252 (emphasis in original); *see also* Felix Cohen, *supra* note 443, at 34–35.

499 Holmes, *Law in Science*, *supra* note 265, at 413 (emphasis added).

conclude that it has become a shell, an archeological survival. The key point being that those who are practicing law, in whatever guise – practitioner, professor, legislator, or judge – must in some fashion self-consciously and purposefully connect what they are doing, and how, with what other working members of the profession have done. The voices to which Holmes most attends whether past or present are always the voices of colleagues. Historical investigation and philosophical analysis were mainly techniques he used to better hear and understand their voices; they were mainly means to that overriding end, the technologies available to him to make his colleagues' voices sharper, more distinctive, the varied emphases more meaningful. Holmes learned to hear, and to hear well, those who had gone before because he listened actively, dialogically. He wants his living colleagues and their successors to develop the same virtue.[500]

He also did his utmost to state very simply and comprehensively the theorem that underwrote the corporate activity in which they were all engaged. "But the theory of the law is that such lines exist, because the theory of the law as to any possible conduct is that it is either lawful or unlawful."[501]

Working directly from this theorem leads to the inference that legal study must begin in learning the lines that have been drawn and why – the actual legal system – and must end in mastering the difficult art of line drawing itself. This mastery is legal pedagogy's fundamental aim and purpose. It is a matter of perfecting the practical judgments that constitute the law. The fact that the entire endeavor often takes place within a distinctive rhetorical mode – often described as "thinking like a lawyer" – ought not be ignored. But neither should that mode become an end-in-itself, displacing the discipline it is meant to encase. The cocoon without the caterpillar becomes a dangling skull.

The directive that the practical study of law ought also be scientific sums up Holmes's preferred manner of making law more knowable, understood as manifesting a heightened intelligence and promoting intelligibility. The common denominator is how various threats of coercion should be justified through warranted knowledge. Normativity in the sense of morality does not play an expressly leading role unless one is willing to see knowledge and the effort to attain and bring it into being through action – through "fined and refined" practical judgments – as a moral good-in-the-having. Once historians have performed their critical task, and one understands how evolution works through the intertwined processes of elimination and integration, the work of structuring wants and similar imperatives – that is, other persistent social desires – remains. Clarifying those wants through language analysis ought not be underestimated; Holmes devoted almost the entire last part of "Law in

[500] *See* Holmes, *Learning and Science*, *supra* note 102, at 492; Holmes, *Introduction to* The General Survey, *in* III CW 439–40.

[501] Holmes, *Law in Science*, *supra* note 265, at 416. *See also* Oliver Wendell Holmes, *Trespass and Negligence*, *in* III CW 91 ("What the law really forbids, and the only thing it forbids, is the act on the wrong side of the line, be that act blameworthy or otherwise.").

Science and Science in Law" to that topic. There he expounds on his favorite mantra: think things not words. What he called "unreal formulas and inadequate generalizations" had a real effect, deleterious to be sure, in damming (and damning) up thought, critical inquiry, in preventing clearer alignments of wants and consequences.

As an interpretive rule of thumb, one should look to see if Holmes has put his own working prescriptions into action. It also helps to remember that sometimes he worked out the idea in practice before he worked it out in words. His "Privilege, Malice, and Intent" provides as good an example as any of how the practice of law itself ought to be scientific and seek its postulates from within, that is to say, from the working ambit of professional practice.

"Privilege, Malice, and Intent" is one of the more dense and intricate of Holmes's later pieces, reminiscent of his early work. The commentators have ranged across the board. Morton Horwitz most prominently sees it as modernism's first salvo in American jurisprudence, leading directly to that later outburst called "The Path of the Law." Horwitz believes that by introducing a balancing test in "Privilege, Malice, and Intent" Holmes had begun to realize that "there is no longer an organic customary principle" to negotiate or mediate between competing private rights, or between the state and the individual. That led to what Horwitz calls Holmes's "astonishing leap" in "The Path of the Law," the abandonment of the "conviction that common law categories were capable of providing neutral constraints on judicial decision making."[502] Horwitz's analysis has had a powerful impact among American legal historians.[503] It has also reinforced Duncan Kennedy's static, structuralist exposition of what he calls the classical legal consciousness.[504] It also lies in the background, as does Kennedy's work, to one of the most consistently perceptive if problematic books in American legal education, Kenneth J. Vandevelde's *Thinking Like a Lawyer*.[505]

In contrast, David Rosenberg thinks Horwitz is foisting upon Holmes's jurisprudence an intellectual construct that has no basis in Holmes's writings. Rosenberg argues that Holmes, from beginning to end, recognized that law in substance reflected politics (the "political nature of law-making"), and that that "legal reality" required its own methodological approach. In terms of torts, that "legal reality" mainly consisted of "the external rules of negligence and strict liability."[506] Rosenberg's study of Holmes's jurisprudence is better grounded than Horwitz's because Rosenberg recognizes Holmes's effort to focus on "legal reality." That leads

502 HORWITZ, *supra* note 424, at 109–43.

503 For indicators of Horwitz's influence see the assessments in PARKER, *supra* note 135, at 8–9, and WHITE, *supra* note 126, at 216–18. For a direct example *see* LOBBAN, *supra* note 323, at 218–20.

504 *See* KENNEDY, *supra* note 57.

505 KENNETH J. VANDEVELDE, THINKING LIKE A LAWYER: AN INTRODUCTION TO LEGAL REASONING (2011) (orig. pub. 1996).

506 ROSENBERG, *supra* note 374, at 64–68.

Rosenberg to a number of insights regarding Holmes's jurisprudential project, including his use of the "bad man" heuristic as a way to facilitate the testing of legal concepts and theories. He notes, for example, that the so-called transformation from "formalism" to "empiricism" that Horwitz and others claim to have occurred in Holmes's thought never happened; that Holmes never advocated the "separation thesis" that Lon Fuller and Henry Hart thrust upon him; that from the beginning of his career he was consistently concerned to approach existing law empirically, free from moral bias, but not to deracinate it from all "morality" (a decided impossibility).[507]

If Horwitz is relying on a sophisticated version of French structuralism to interpret Holmes's role in American legal history, Rosenberg in a manner reminiscent of the early realists interprets Holmes as bringing into law the methods and mindsets of empirical science. Rosenberg, however, often shifts without warning between emphasizing an internal perspective on "legal reality" – in which law grows through deliberate reflection on those judicially enacted intuitions that he calls "positive social morality" – to an external one, one that seeks to self-consciously test through experience observed legal outcomes.[508] For that reason, I speculate, he does not, in an otherwise comprehensive book on Holmes's tort jurisprudence, focus directly and at length on "Privilege, Malice, and Intent."

The importance of "Privilege, Malice, and Intent" lies in its attempts to structure the "legal reality" that Rosenberg rightly says focused Holmes's attention. Again, it is Holmes's own effort to work out his notion of "science in law" at the level of practice. Like any good pedagogue he must first teach himself before he can teach others. "Privilege, Malice, and Intent" shows Holmes grappling with the problem of how to tease out the implications of a legal insight so that both the insight and its ramifications may be used as a basis for further knowledge and action.

Holmes's goal in "Privilege" is to "analyze the general method by which law reaches its decisions."[509] As is often the case in Holmes's writing, there appears in

[507] *Id.* at 46–50, 196 n.48. *But see* ALBERT W. ALSCHULER, LAW WITHOUT VALUES: THE LIFE, WORK, AND LEGACY OF JUSTICE HOLMES 267 n.229 (2000) ("Rosenberg's central thesis – that Holmes endorsed foresight-based strict liability and that most modern torts scholars have not realized it – is correct, and the book [*Hidden Holmes*] displays impressive knowledge. Nevertheless, much of his Holmes-as-hero scholarship seems to be not only unconvincing but far-fetched. Not since Delphi has anyone gone as far as Rosenberg in projecting untold wisdom onto meaningless phrases."); *see also* A. W. Brian Simpson, *The Elusive Truth about Holmes*, 95 MICH. L. REV. 2027, 2042 (1997) ("What, if anything, Holmes meant by saying that the defendant was both "not to blame" yet "bound at his peril to know" that something he did not know was a peril to his neighbor nevertheless was a peril, is, to me, deeply obscure, and borders on the ultimate refuge of the scholar in trouble, the boldly meaningless.") (reviewing Rosenberg's *Hidden Holmes*). Alschuler is so caught up in shadow-boxing that he is not able, as I point out regarding Rosenberg in the next paragraph, to devote to "Privilege, Malice, and Intent" the attention it deserves.

[508] *Id.* at 50–51.

[509] Holmes, *supra* note 481, at 374.

this article a blurring, perhaps intentional, between descriptive and prescriptive objectives. That is to say, between describing the general method by which law (intraprofessionally) reaches its decisions and including in the description encouragement and directives to improve the method. But whatever the strength of Holmes's "should" it rests partly, one suspects, on his frustration that his colleagues seem to lack the will or wherewithal to follow through on a course of thought once begun. He decides to work out his argument by beginning from a point that he knows very well and that is established in Massachusetts practice, the theory of negligence.[510]

He begins as he often does by describing the type of damage that he believes the law seeks to redress or prevent. That damage is temporal damage. Language maven Bryan A. Garner correctly notes that temporal "was a favorite word of Justice Holmes." He used it in a specifically legal sense, which Garner defines as "nonecclesiastical."[511] Be that as it may, the word "temporal" describes legally recoverable damages in "Privilege, Malice, and Intent" and in "The Path of the Law." Its importance for Holmes lies in how it begins to organize and reshape the "legal reality" that Rosenberg saw as the essential subject of legal study. "Temporal" becomes a series of spotlights that direct and focus the law's attention and intelligence to certain types of alleged damages and ignores others. Temporal implies a type of recognition most often contrasted in Anglo-American legal history with "spiritual."[512] That is not to say that traditional English equity in its modern guise might not still have an important role. But as Holmes

[510] *See* William A. Lundquist, Oliver Wendell Holmes and External Standards of Criminal and Tort Liability: Application of Theory on the Massachusetts Bench, 28 *Buff. L. Rev.* 607, 616–22 (1979).

[511] Bryan A. Garner, A Dictionary of Modern Legal Usage 869 (2d ed. 1995). If temporal is only "nonecclesiastical," then "ecclesiastical" must condense an enormous variety of historical phenomena and modes of valuation pertinent to nontemporal harms in Anglo-American legal history. To take just one example, in *The Abuse of Casuistry* the authors note that in its judicial capacity the medieval Church reserved jurisdiction over certain classes of persons: (a) clergy, students, and crusaders, (b) the poor, widows, and orphans, (c) Jews in dealings with Christians, and (d) sailors, merchants, and other travelers. They infer that these people fell outside the local network of community members with whom the secular courts might be relied upon to deal fairly. In this example, the recipient of the harm matters more than the harm itself. Albert R. Jonsen and Stephen Toulmin, The Abuse of Casuistry: The History of Moral Reasoning 108 (1988). Other scholars have suggested that the word "temporal" means something like "tangible" as opposed to "intangible" harms like emotional ones. Kenneth S. Abraham and G. Edward White, *Torts without Names, New Torts, and the Future of Liability for Intangible Harm*, 20 n.48 (Mar. 27, 2019). Am. U. Law Rev. (forthcoming). Virginia Public Law and Legal Theory Research Paper No. 2019-12. Available at SSRN: https://ssrn.com/abstract=3361034. Thomas Grey, though, uses the word "secular" as a synonym for "temporal." Grey, *supra* note 347, at 1272–76.

[512] *See* Grey, *id.* Grey is almost alone among modern commentators in recognizing the vital importance that "temporal harm" or "temporal damage" had for Holmes as providing a substantive basis for the law of torts and its development.

observed in "Path," to learn how the common law works it is better to not treat an exception as the rule.

If temporal damage simultaneously reoriented and refocused the reach of the enforcement power in modern society by bringing into cognizance more kinds of hitherto nonexistent legal harms, then it also provided the needed grounds for the further development of a theory of torts. In the opening paragraph of "Privilege, Malice, and Intent" Holmes summed up a career of thinking about such a theory. He takes as foundational the idea that a person is legally responsible for acts done with notice of foreseeable consequences unless certain special exceptions apply. As we argued in Part II, the external standard of liability that Holmes consciously understood as articulating certain tendencies in the common law – meaning tendencies in argumentation and action – brought into a single, unanticipated formula persistent cultural values and new social concerns. From the point of view of theory it appeared as a well-wrought argument that justified a law of torts. From the point of view of practice, if that point of view had sufficient depth, it would appear as a new way of organizing social experience that had many resemblances to what had gone on before but was still, in some indefinable way, new.

That new way involved bringing into realization a new ideal, a new beginning point for what Holmes once called "the truthful imagination."[513] Again, without unduly laboring the point, the "reasonable man," like the "bad man," is a remote conception, a projection; meaning that like a vanishing point it has no intrinsic, defined content but, in the legal context, exists to organize perceptions and direct intelligence according to available understandings and pressing concerns. It is indicative, as Holmes would later say in "Privilege" and as quoted above, "of organized society knowingly seeking to determine its own destinies." That is to say, as an imaginative construct in the realm of torts the reasonable person brings into public view law's positive and negative capabilities.

The important point is that in "Privilege" Holmes is not backtracking from his earlier position on the viability of the external standard or the need to excise from the nomenclature of liability "actual fault" as people like John Austin had used the term. He is seeking to use his foundational insight that, all things being equal, liability attaches to an act done with notice of foreseeable harm to structure the grounds for further legal action. To make law productive (increasingly knowable), insights from one area of law must be brought into direct contact or at least juxtaposition with insights from other areas. Law must deliberately seek to cohere and mature. That was the larger goal. The more modest one at the level of torts involved bringing into juxtaposition the theory of negligence, built as it was on notice of foreseeable harm, with other insights or less clearly understood intuitions regarding the basis and scope of liability.

[513] Holmes, *William Allen*, *supra* note 149, at 485.

Thus the last two sentences of the first paragraph lay out the dimensions of the tableau Holmes intends to create:

> The standard applied is external, and the words malice, intent and negligence, as used in this connection, refer to an external standard. If the manifest probability of harm is very great, and the harm follows, we say that it is done maliciously or intentionally; if not so great, but still considerable, we say that the harm is done negligently; if there is no apparent danger, we call it mischance.[514]

Seen from an overly intellectualized viewpoint, as many commentators are wont to do, the standard becomes a discrete legal test. It begins to function solely as doctrine or dogma when one forgets its origin as an insight into judicial argumentation and action. It seeks to evoke and work out a tendency, and as that "tendency" becomes more established and secure as an ongoing conviction the danger arises that the originative insight will be lost amidst the plethora of detail and explication. There is a gap between an insight as formulated and its eventual scientific verification through experimentation. Rosenberg argues that Holmes sought to emulate within the scope of legal study the methods of empirical science.[515] That may be true. On the other hand, Rosenberg's argument may in its own way be unduly emphasizing "law in science" over "science in law."[516]

An alternative is to see Holmes's articulation of the external standard as a way of demarcating a legal landscape from the existing social terrain. The pertinent point of view on any act and circumstance is the one purely legal. The relevant measure is how near or far the actor was from foreseeable harm once the harm happened. Mischance, to use Holmes's term, sets the boundaries between probability and uncertainty. More fully dimensioned, less flat, is what Holmes calls negligence. That is where one draws the first and most evident dividing point. It bears repeating that a "legal object" understood as the specific temporal harm – which includes the act-and-its-circumstances – and that draws the enforcement power's attention only comes into view in this manner through a constellation, larger or smaller, of practical judgments. These in turn are conveyed to the present in "a body of reports,

[514] Holmes, *supra* note 481, at 371–72.

[515] Rosenberg, *supra* note 374, at 2–5.

[516] This tendency in the way Rosenberg analyzes Holmes's thought becomes most evident in Rosenberg's contribution to the *Harvard Law Review*'s centennial celebration of the publication of "The Path of the Law." In that piece Rosenberg clearly states his belief that Holmes wanted lawyers trained as "social engineers." He faults the then current law school curriculum for still being too caught up in "parsing the semantic logic of cases" and the dominance of such semantic parsing over policy analysis. The end result of Rosenberg's critique seems to be something not dissimilar to the urge prevalent in the nineteenth century to rationalize the law through codification. Instead of codification Rosenberg wants policy analysis and empirical studies and provides correspondingly little attention to the necessary dialogue between the continuities of the past and the self-reflexivity of the present. David Rosenberg, *The Path Not Taken*, 110 Harv. L. Rev. 1044, 1044–48 (1997).

of treatises, and of statutes," stretching back 600 years.[517] When one is arguing about whether a legal object exists or where it should be placed within the legal landscape then those same practical judgments function as pointers. Holmes does not use this type of language but it seems to me to fit the general tenor of his thought. His main point, so as to put his arguments about privilege, malice, and intent on the best footing, is that once action has become identifiable in the region of negligence liability attaches.

> To make out a *prima facie* case of trespass or libel [for example], if the likelihood of bringing force to bear on the plaintiff's person or of bringing him into contempt go to the height expressed by the word negligence, as above explained, it need not go higher.

As he wrote right before this quote: "In other words, for this purpose [reaching the level of liability required to make out a prima facie case] it does not matter whether the act is called malicious or negligent."[518]

To illustrate from civil procedure, pled in the alternative a claim for a tort sounding in negligence or for one in which malice is an element, each claim arising from the same cause of action, only makes a legal difference if a privilege is interposed as an affirmative defense (or in some cases on the applicable measure of damages). A legal privilege supports a justification for the complained of act. In the ordinary negligence case there is no way to overcome the privilege (*e.g.*, I have no duty to conduct my business in such a way as not to harm yours) because the so-called privilege is cast in terms of a non-duty. The inability to overcome the privilege typically manifests itself as the inability to impose a duty or in some cases to show legal causation.

Once Holmes has established the relevant control point, he observes that the "simple test of the degree of manifest danger does not exhaust the theory of torts."[519] Holmes begins working out the implications of this comment by designating a distinct class of cases that feature a certain kind of temporal harm. These types of cases arise when the actor engages in conduct that the actor knows, or should know, will damage the reputation or livelihood of the potential plaintiff. The harm is foreseeable. Not only is the harm foreseeable, it is more manifestly probable than the degree of foreseeability needed to support an action for negligence. It is important to keep in mind that in framing the analysis negligence sits in the background (or below, depending on the perspective) and beyond (beneath) negligence, mischance.

In the same way he laid negligence's foundation in the grounds of mischance, Holmes seeks to construct out of negligence a new special basis for legal action. For

[517] Holmes, *The Path of the Law*, *supra* note 1, at 391.
[518] Holmes, *supra* note 481, at 372.
[519] *Id.*

the most part he is using the same tool he used to develop his theory of negligence – foreseeability of harm based on notice – but this time foreseeability is not sufficient because foreseeability must itself be subjected to an external standard. One external standard becomes subject to another. In other words, in the cases Holmes has distinguished for special analysis, the actor "is not liable for a very manifest danger unless he actually intends to do the harm complained of . . . In some cases, he may even intend to do the harm and yet not have to answer for it."[520] And in this latter category, the actor may lose the privilege of not answering for the harm caused if the actor acted maliciously.

At this stage of the argument Holmes contends, as he would do two years later in his dissent in *Veleghan v. Gunter*,[521] that the reach of a justification or a justified privilege is a matter of policy, that is, these kinds of questions are "legislative questions, and judges are shy of reasoning from such grounds."[522] It is worth taking a moment to ponder why the existence and reach of privilege poses a legislative question instead of a judicial one. In other words, what for Holmes is the dividing point between a judicial question and a legislative one? Is it when a case lands in the penumbra between light and dark? In reading some commentators one comes away with the impression that Holmes gave up the ghost on expressly judicial reasoning and brought into the open the modern outlook that court cases were simply legislative (policy) battles by another name. Other commentators claim Holmes clung to the formalist gods. Others, many, say or imply that he was confused and incoherent. A good number of commentators write as if every case is or becomes penumbral. But practitioners know that is not true. Understood within Holmes's developed legal thought, a distinctively legislative (policy) question arises, I suggest, when the issue to be decided cannot be decided by recourse to any of the traditionally conceived sources of law including the jury. That most critical initial question, "what is the law?," has in these circumstances no easy answer.

To put it another way. New legally cognizable harms – temporal harms – emerge as both the complexity of American civilization increases apace and participants in this society become more and more cognizant of how much of their life-energy is absorbed by the here-and-now (999/1000). The law developed according to secular interests encompasses more and more aspects of social life. Perception of this dynamic underwrites the insight that we found in Holmes's tribute to George Shattuck. That tribute, written in the same time period as "Privilege, Malice, and Intent," the dissent in *Vegelan v. Gunter*, and "The Path of the Law," reveals the genesis of an insight, the larval stage, when all one can really do is blurt out the thought without much comprehension or inkling of its innermost meaning. Innermost meanings in this respect are always latecomers. And so when Holmes writes

[520] *Id.*
[521] Vegelahn v. Guntner, 167 Mass. 92, 104–09 (1896) (Holmes, J. dissenting).
[522] Holmes, *supra* note 481, at 373.

that "I think it quite as true to say that we must correct the judgment of posterity by that of the time[,]" he intimates at the law's immortality.[523] If James had read *Speeches* and caught this meaning he would not have agreed because it submerged the individual soul and its quest for some kind of being after death.[524] But belief in law's undying march was part of Holmes's faith in his chosen profession and in the law's developed capacity for giving shape and direction to contemporary interests and harms through the power of self-reflexivity.

Stated vaguely, self-reflexivity ("the conscious reaction upon itself of organized society knowingly seeking to determine its own destinies") in itself, apart from its specific manifestation in a genre of policy development (marginal utility, for example),[525] seems too amorphous and "in the air" to be a source of law, to take its place alongside the other traditional sources of law. We do well to recall the "1872 Jurisprudence Essay" and Holmes's remark that every source of law – as well as "a doctrine of political economy, or the political aspirations of the judge, or his gout, or the blandishments of the emperor's wife" – is solely a motive for decision until adopted. He further asks: "[W]hat more is the decision that adopts them [custom and mercantile usage] as to any future decision? What more indeed is a statute; and in what other sense law, than that we believe the motive which we think it offers the judge will prevail, and induce them to decide a case in a certain way, and so shape our conduct on that anticipation?"[526]

He later extended these same insights in both "The Theory of Torts" and in a gem of a note on negligence in his edition of *Kent's Commentaries*. In the latter he has this to say:

> When there is no definite fact, such as a statute, a precedent, a custom, or a rule of public policy, a belief in which determines the action of the judges, they sometimes accept what would be the conduct of the prudent man – meaning thereby of the jury – as their standard.[527]

In "Privilege" Holmes reaffirms his belief, especially given the widespread economic battles in the country and in the resulting cases coming before the court, that the old style of policy development, that which depended on the good sense and intuition of men like Chief Justice Shaw, no longer sufficed to move the law forward. The proportionate need for public policy decisions had become much greater to be sure.

[523] Holmes, *Shattuck*, *supra* note 143, at 494. *See also* Holmes, *Learning and Science*, *supra* note 102, at 492 ("And so the eternal procession moves on, we in front for the moment; and, stretching away against the unattainable sky, the black spearheads of the army that has been passing in unbroken line already for near a thousand years.").

[524] *See* William James, Human Immortality (Dover ed. 1956) (orig. pub. 1898).

[525] Herbert Hovenkamp shrinks all of Holmes's far-ranging insights and suggestions for improving American law into this one point. *See, e.g.*, Hovenkamp, The Opening of American Law 38–42 (2015).

[526] Holmes, *supra* note 375, at 295.

[527] Oliver Wendell Holmes, *Notes to* Kent's Commentaries, *in* II CW 197.

That is one reason he elevates these kinds of questions to the rank of "legislative." But that is not say such questions should exclusively determine the law or that all other sources of law must be stuffed into this one bulging box.

Self-reflexivity as a distinct source of law may take much time to develop, to become a more defined subject and mode of study. It may acquire sufficient definition by linking together other sources of law through a manner of reasoning that includes economic analysis and statistical formulations as well as other styles of studying social life and individual behavior. It's hard to say exactly what it will look like because Holmes never worked out the idea. But there is little warrant in limiting self-reflexivity to the economic viewpoint or to the features of social life that statistical language can describe.

Holmes struggled to discover how self-reflexivity might be brought into the legal landscape and take its role alongside law's traditional sources without tyrannizing them in truncated form as policy or expediency. He knew it required a change of mindset and the need to develop new mental habits for dealing with the existing law. In the "1872 Jurisprudence Essay" he first made clear that law is for lawyers. He called it lawyers' law.[528] By the time of "Privilege" he had attained much practical experience and had the benefit of years of reflection. His conclusion is that the effort to think self-reflexively – to not take "legislative considerations" as decisive without recognizing "their weight in an inarticulate form as unconscious prejudice or half conscious inclination" – requires "not only the highest powers of a judge and a training which the practice of law does not insure, but also a freedom from prepossessions which is very hard to attain."[529] Added to this latter requirement is something he first mentioned in "Just the Boy Wanted": "that sort of ease and familiarity in handling ideas which is one of the marks of a civilized man." That "ease and familiarity in handling ideas" may be partly a gift but it is, Holmes asserts, "more the result of training still comparatively rare in this country."[530] Still true.

Consequently, when Holmes focuses on the interrelations between privilege, malice, and intent two things are happening simultaneously. First, he is building out the law of torts; mischance and negligence are receding further into the background as the focus shifts to the foregrounded temporal harms. Second, he is adding a new source to those sources of law that traditionally functioned as the fundamental markers and had sanctioned socially acceptable motives for decision. The self-conscious creation of a new source of law, a new motive for legal decision, when viewed in combination with what had existed before, begins to add depth to the existing tableau. The tableau verges on the cinematic. It also becomes clearer that the space between mischance and negligence has been laid out through practical judgments, many of which may still be found in the extant "body of

[528] Holmes, *supra* note 375, at 295.
[529] Holmes, *supra* note 418, at 377.
[530] Holmes, *supra* note 171, at 339.

reports, of treatises, and of statutes[.]" These may indicate those legal grounds still fertile and vibrant and those unused or becoming fallow. What enables us to see the existing legal landscape in a new way is the emergence of self-reflexivity as a primary though not exclusive source of law. By and through self-reflexivity the legal landscape begins to transform into a cityscape.

Following this course of argument leads to the realization that Holmes is looking to lay out a new basis of liability for certain types of cases, one ultimately determined not by foreseeability – which is its necessary precondition – but by lack of justification for temporal harm. Holmes says plainly that the determination of justification lies in social policy but that phrase, upon which many commentators hang their entire analysis of Holmes's thought, conceals much more than it reveals. As a mode of self-reflexivity, it (social policy) demands finer discriminations, more detailed analyses and depiction of the relevant features of acts deemed lawful or unlawful than had hitherto been possible. Negligence environs the new, rising ground of justification. Lying further back (or below) is mischance. But such a broad-brush view depends on an elevated perspective. At eye-level the relative distances and dividing lines are not so easily discerned or demarcated.

It bears keeping in mind that Holmes in "Privilege" is working out the steps the practical study of law must take to be scientific. He is looking to establish "its postulates from within upon accurately measured social desires instead of tradition."[531] The key for Holmes is to find new ways to bring an operative but inchoate intuition into view; to solidify it; to develop new ways to measure existing lines and provide pointers for future ones to be drawn. And new ways, it must be said, to both surmise and instill the postulates that provide the sought-for coherence. The challenge, as Hurst noted, is not simply to find a more productive way to negotiate the past but to also maintain a relative balance or harmony between contemporary, still active and conflicting premises. Context matters. Privilege, formally speaking, is a necessary premise in any complex body of law. That is, there are times when the public power will forbear in a specific instance or instances from enacting its threat of force because of overriding considerations that owe their genesis to factual developments or pronounced wants. At times, the good traditionally protected takes second place to a new and different good. Privileges may often have a temporal component; they may rise or fall. For that reason critical history is a necessary preliminary. On the other hand, other existing premises may take on new shades of meaning because of the emergence of newly felt or recognized harms – harms which elicit the sensitivities of those with enough social clout to have their voices taken into account. In such circumstances the challenge is to rationally (scientifically) connect the new with the old. For Holmes an insight into the actual motives working in American society when generalized (that is, an insight extended and broadened, fined and refined) became the primary means to connect current

[531] Holmes, *Law in Science*, *supra* note 265, at 413.

decisions and legal practices with those that went before. He then sought to take those generalizations, each built on an operative insight (like that of the external standard), and organize them into a unified group of systematic propositions. That final turn seems to me unworkable for reasons already stated.

The first critical lesson we learn from "Privilege, Malice, and Intent" is that a privilege or a justification cannot be deduced from foreseeability. It must arise from grounds sufficient to overcome the presumption of liability. It has to arise from a conglomeration of specific circumstances that take into account the nature of the act, the type of harm caused, the relative social effect of each, its basic directionality (toward or away from the common weal), and any other relevant feature. The insight that might lead to a generalization applicable to all or many cases of justification is not possible at this stage (when Holmes is writing "Privilege") because the grounds for overcoming the presumption of liability are still congealing. What the question of justification does do, however, is to compel the inquirer to consider more carefully the instances when liability attaches to acts that have no recognizable motive other than harming another simply for the sake of the harm intended. Malice brings into relief distinct features of certain temporal harms society will not tolerate. It also compels more thought and more study on why certain temporal harms are permitted and others are not. The focus is not so much on the malice as it is on that quality or those qualities of temporal harm that malice and the means used to inflict it bring out of the penumbral shade into a stronger, harsher light.

Take for example *Rideout v. Knox*. That is the case in which Holmes, writing for the court, determined the constitutionality of a statute limiting the height of certain boundary fences. The statute prohibited what were commonly known as spite fences. Prohibited fences must be "maliciously erected or maintained for the purpose of annoying adjoining owners or occupiers."[532] It required an "actual malevolent motive as distinguished from merely technical malice."[533] The statute set out a height limit of six feet and permitted an owner to erect a higher fence if necessary. The defendants – husband and wife – had built along the edge between the wife's property and the plaintiff's a fence that rose eleven feet and extended seventy-five. The perfect trellis to trail a tangle of vines claimed one defendant, the husband. The case as it came before the Supreme Judicial Court presented two issues. First, whether the statute under review was constitutional. The opinion does not state whether the constitutional issue was brought under the US Constitution or that of the Commonwealth of Massachusetts, most likely both were involved. The second issue was whether the malice had to serve as the exclusive or dominant motive in building or maintaining the structure so as to bring it within the scope of the statute.

[532] Rideout v. Knox, 148 Mass. 368, 373 (1889) (per Holmes, J.).
[533] *Id.*

Unsurprisingly, Holmes begins his opinion by establishing a polarity. At the common law, he says, "a man has a right to build a fence on his own land as high as he pleases, however much it may obstruct his neighbor's light and air."[534] So far so good. When it comes to fences the common law does not limit what an owner may do on his or her land. But then he adds: "And the limit up to which a man may impair his neighbor's enjoyment of his estate by the mode of using his own is fixed by external standards only."[535] Read one way these two statements seem contradictory. On the one hand, an owner may build as high as she likes without worry that it will diminish the neighbor's enjoyment and use of his property. On the other, an external standard may limit that impairment. Seen as mainly discrete propositions – right to build as high as one likes, the law limiting the right to build when the impairment exceeds an applicable external standard – the resolution between them may take the form of logically clarifying the terms in each proposition and then organizing them under a well-known legal maxim. In cases like this one, as Holmes mentioned in "Privilege," the maxim *sic utere tuo ut alienum non laedas* (use your property so as not to damage another's) becomes a favored starting point.[536]

Another common way to resolve the tension between the two propositions is to search out a point of ambiguity in the terms and use that point to develop a resolution specific to the case. That style of problem-solving is mainly casuistic and one cannot say that its use in the common law has been rare. But given Holmes's primary objective to develop law's capacity to build on itself, law progressively more integrated, scientific, and more in line with what he takes to be the basic demands of human nature, the mode of casuistry may provide important and necessary techniques but it is not itself sufficient to accomplish the outcome he seeks.

The manner in which Holmes has set up his initial propositions points toward the type of resolution he favors. One property owner's "mode of using his own" is limited not by the neighbor's right to quiet enjoyment but by "external standards." In other words, the proper opposition is not between neighbor and neighbor but between neighbor and the state (or the governing authority, or the enforcement power, etc.). But it is not the state's authority directly that creates the opposition but an already developed enforceable standard that brings into the present a compressed array of prior instances. According to Holmes's citations, these prior instances involved the inducement of employees and prospective employees from a rival boot and shoe manufacturer, the digging of a well on one owner's land that cuts off the supply of water to another's, the diversion of an underground stream solely to prevent the plaintiff's continued use, and the intentional construction of a ditch or watercourse in front of the plaintiff's property that renders the plaintiff's ingress

534 *Id.* at 372.
535 *Id.*
536 Holmes, *supra* note 481, at 373.

and egress much more difficult.[537] In these cases malice as a motive was not sufficient to support a cause of action unless no legal right supported the action that led to the harm.

It becomes evident as Holmes proceeds in his analysis that he wants to shift the focus from the primary right at issue to the nature of the harm, or temporal harm as he liked to say, and the means used to inflict it. "But it is plain that the right to use one's property for the sole purpose of injuring others is not one of the immediate rights of ownership; it is not a right for the sake of which property is recognized by the law, but only a more or less necessary incident of rights which are established for very different ends."[538] It may appear that Holmes's focus in this sentence is solely on the defendants' right at issue, to build a fence on the property as they see fit. But further analysis suggests that the harm suffered by the plaintiff under the circumstances of this specific case seen *against* the background of prior decisions – the existing and developing "external standard" – led Holmes to more finely differentiate the nature of the defendants' right. The manifested harm, what Holmes called "aggressive annoyance," became a type of three-dimensional object that, like a prism, refracted the defendants' right of property at issue into its various component wavelengths.

One of those component wavelengths – or part of a stick in the bundle of rights to use the standard metaphor – Holmes identified as a "necessary incident" to the primary property right that the legal order had traditionally sought to protect. Even though he acknowledged that some common law authorities held that the right to use one's property as one saw fit might depend on one's motive, Holmes stated that the Supreme Judicial Court in 1889 viewed it otherwise. "[T]o a large extent the power to use one's property malevolently, in any way which would be lawful for other ends, is an incident of property which cannot be taken away by legislation."[539] Though this formulation seems traditional and unexceptional, the way that Holmes deploys it is quite radical. We must recall that in this part of the opinion Holmes is still addressing the issue of whether the statute prohibiting fences higher than six feet without a viable reason is constitutional. Even though he acknowledges that the motive of malice by itself cannot justify the use of the police power, the police power to a certain degree may be justified when the motive is connected to a recognized temporal harm. "Some small limitations of previously existing rights incident to property may be imposed for the sake of preventing a manifest evil; larger ones could not be, except by the exercise of the right of eminent domain."[540]

Thus, in four relatively short paragraphs, including citations, Holmes lays out the framework he thinks ought to be used to determine whether the statute at issue is

[537] Rideout v. Knox, *supra* note 532, at 372 (internal citations omitted).
[538] *Id.*
[539] *Id.*
[540] *Id.* at 372–73.

constitutional. He places the statute against a common law backdrop; he sets up the initial polarity between an absolute right and one limited by an external standard. He then uses the specific type of temporal harm at issue ("aggressive annoyance") as a third point to help differentiate both the defendants' property right in question and the reach of the external standard. He then notes that the reach of the external standard – through the police power – is itself subject to limitations and constraints but finds that its use in this instance is well within those limitations and constraints.

Once the initial conditions are set out, the case almost decides itself. Though he does not mention it, the working assumption seems to be that the legislature can formalize through statute an external standard operative in the common law. In this particular instance it involved the common law's treatment of malice, or "a malevolent motive for action, without reference to any hope of a remoter benefit to oneself to be accomplished by the intended harm to another."[541] The statute was confined to fences and structures in the nature of fences and only if they exceed unnecessarily six feet in height. "It is," says Holmes, "hard to imagine a more insignificant curtailment of the rights of property." He adds that it is "at least doubtful whether the act applies to fences not substantially adjoining the injured party's land."[542] The language of the statute clearly expresses that there must be "actual malevolent motive," however. Actual malevolent motive is malice distinct from what he calls "merely technical malice." And under the statute it must be the dominant motive. He understands "dominant motive" as the motive without which the fence would not have been built or maintained. As he would indicate in other writings, the malice must rise above a certain level, beyond technical pleading requirements or a discernible but not predominant motive of malevolence. It must be a fact of legal import that ties together a single overriding motive with a specific means for the sole purpose of inflicting temporal harm and the temporal harm must ensue; malice cannot simply be a dramatic element of the story.

Holmes held for the court that the statute as construed was constitutional. It was within the state's police power to regulate in the way that it did the erection and maintenance of fences on private property. "To that extent, it simply restrains a noxious use of the owner's premises, and although the use is not directly injurious to the public at large, there is a public interest to restrain this kind of aggressive annoyance of one neighbor by another, and to mark a definite limit beyond which it is not lawful to go."[543] The term "noxious use" in this sentence subtly points not to the limit of the right as traditionally understood (to use one's property as one sees fit) but to the extent of the *privilege* the law grants to inflict a certain kind of temporal harm. The law does not recognize a property owner's privilege to aggressively annoy one's neighbors through the means of a dastardly boundary fence. The privilege as

[541] Holmes, *supra* note 481, at 372.
[542] Rideout v. Knox, *supra* note 532, at 373.
[543] *Id.* at 373–74.

distinct from the right – using these words in a non-Hohfeldian sense – arises from a distinct array of individual and combined practical judgments that are susceptible to further arrangements and rearrangements. Noxious use begins to create its own distinct ground of liability, a ground that cannot really be properly seen or understood if isolated from the other grounds that the external standard had already put into place.

> On the whole, having regard to the smallness of the injury [to the defendant], the nature of the evil to be avoided [aggressive annoyance], the quasi accidental character of the defendant's right to put up a fence for malevolent purposes, and also to the fact that police regulations may limit the use of property in ways which greatly diminish its value, we are of the opinion that the act is constitutional to the full extent of its provisions.[544]

Taking this conclusion and subsuming it into the first part of "Privilege, Malice, and Intent" leads us to greater appreciation of how Holmes is seeking to establish law's governing postulates from within. The legal profession which represents society's various articulated interests – those of the individual, group, or state, or an inchoate body (Brandeis's "public interest") – through its own efforts begins to elicit and measure the competing social desires and thus brings into realization the needed mode for discerning the actual governing postulates at work. Once revealed the question arises whether they should be extended or curtailed or left unchanged. This activity of realizing, discerning, measuring, and establishing reveals one way in which self-reflexivity may work. It has, as mentioned above, the potential to become its own source of law.

On Holmes's preferred analysis the combined grounds for the court's decision in *Rideout v. Knox* could ultimately be generalized and cohered into systematic dogma. On the terms proposed in this study these same grounds, when juxtaposed and extended in the right way, acquire depth; a 3D view becomes possible. Each rationale supporting the opinion's conclusion reflects a practical judgment or set of practical judgments that when brought together create the necessary illusion, like Correggio's paintings, of depth. Each practical judgment, like a resultant (vector or tensor) in physics, has an overall magnitude and direction. Artificially brought together through a mode of inquiry they bring the temporal harm in focus into fuller view. The "smallness of the injury" to the defendants is not an empirical assessment in the sense of asking the defendant, either the property owner or her husband, whether the legislature curtailing the height of the fence they could build made them feel indignant, as if their legal status had dropped. Nor is it the formulated conclusion of statistical analysis of survey data depicting how the average property owner in the area might feel about it. Such an assessment introduced as

[544] *Id.* at 374.

evidence could become a factor for the court to consider. But that was not the norm when Holmes drafted the opinion.

The evil of aggressive annoyance may still be, in 1889, a temporal harm coming into its own, one necessarily dependent on a certain density of living and living arrangements. It too, no less than the smallness of injury, reflected a practical judgment not only as to the expedients of the moment but as to future needs and those pressing commitments from the past.

The quasi-accidental character of the right to use one's property for malicious purposes also exhibited an overall practical judgment that pits present needs against past commitments. In effect Holmes made the same point in *Rideout* that he made in *The Common Law* and would make in "Privilege": the external standard in torts brought into being a new plane of liability, what I have termed in keeping with the theme of this study as a new plane of verisimilitude. This is where what the law treats as real and actual – legal fault as the basis for liability for example – shifts ever closer to the actuality of American life and vice versa. Conduct that extends beyond the height of permissibility as malicious or malevolent conduct would be liable to state interference unless the good of the commonweal permitted on other distinct grounds (other than the alleged privilege of use) the means employed to inflict the temporal harm intended. The temporal harm when put into proper focus adds depth to an otherwise flat analysis. Contrary to the opinion of some commentators, Holmes was not backtracking from earlier positions when he stated that under certain circumstances a malicious motive could become probative. The malicious motive became relevant after the conduct in question exceeded a certain ceiling of permissibility and became legally cognizant in the shape of a temporal harm. Cognizance depended as much on the means utilized as the motive alleged.

I think Holmes's effort to develop the discipline of law becomes more understandable and rewarding when seen not in terms of propositions but stereoscopically. The stereoscope is to law what the microscope is to biology and the telescope to astronomy. It reveals in more minute and engrossing detail the composition and interactions of the objects in view. Legal objects under study may range from the molecular to the molar. The technology to view them stereoscopically may not yet be fully available but it does require a preliminary change in mindset. Holmes pinpointed the necessary focal point that unites distinct images into a stereoscopic frame: the nature of the temporal harm in question. Just as in *Rideout* the nature of the temporal harm refracted a supposedly unified property right into its component wavelengths so did the property right at issue differentiate the inflicted harm. One needed finer discriminations; it was all a matter of degrees as Holmes often said. Thus it rests on the state through its instrumentalities, in this instance the court, to give shape to and integrate through its own judicious use of power the hitherto unformed and unseen space between the privilege, the harm, and the duty. As he often did, Holmes reasoned in this instance from the greater power to the lesser. If the state through its police power could limit the use of property in ways that greatly diminished its value it could also limit the use in which the diminishment, from the external point of view, was marginal. Such use of the police power served to bring into relief the nature of the temporal harm by juxtaposing and measuring it against private right and public benefit.

Holmes employed the same type of analysis in the final topic he addressed in "Privilege," that of intent. Some commentators maintain that in the beginning of their careers Holmes and Pollock jointly articulated a new class of torts, the prima facie tort.[545] In formulating the prima facie tort – that the intentional infliction of temporal harm without justification is actionable – Holmes in particular, they further argue, began to sketch out a general theory of intentional torts, one that brought the so-called "classic intentional torts" and those of a more modern vintage (intentional infliction of emotional distress, wrongful interference with contract, and wrongful interference with prospective business advantage) into coherence. The chief importance of his endeavor did not lie in articulating a new class of torts but in distinguishing a new and independent ground of liability, however. This new, independent ground of liability not only depends, as did malice, on negligence for its objectification but also serves to bring negligence itself into greater clarity.

In his "Accidental Torts" Thomas Grey points out that the tripartite structure of tort law generally operative in the United States need not have taken the shape that it did. He credits Holmes's 1873 "Theory of Torts" for innovatively conceptualizing torts into a three-part schema: strict liability, negligence, and intentional torts. "Intentional torts," however, was not how Holmes described those causes of action that had as their gist acts malicious or fraudulent. It is a covering term imposed by later commentators that has become standard. Grey points out that Holmes's breakthrough in 1873 came when he recognized that "negligence" was not merely a catchall legal term for actions predicated on different substantive rules or an essential a state of mind that must be pled. It was

> [a] complex legal conclusion, a determination that a public standard of conduct existed, that it applied to a party's conduct, and that the conduct fell below the standard. The 'reasonable man' test was not a concession to the difficulties of proving individual capacities and states of mind, but rather a substantively distinct theory of liability.[546]

Grey uses the word "theory" to describe the external standard and that is probably the best word to use given Holmes's objective in 1873. Not yet had Holmes achieved the epiphany that he reported to Emerson in 1876, and which he described in "Law in Science" as the realization of a phenomenon pervasive in the law – "the paucity of original ideas in man, and the slow coasting way in which he works along from

[545] Kenneth J. Vandevelde, *A History of Prima Facie Tort: The Origins of a General Theory of Intentional Tort*, 19 HOFSTRA L. REV. 447, 447 (1990); Abraham and White, *supra* note 511, at 21–27.

[546] Grey, *supra* note 347, at 1266–67.

rudimentary beginnings to the complex and artificial conceptions of civilised [*sic*] life."[547] These "complex and artificial conceptions" could be put into a systematic framework – such as dogma for teaching purposes – or in the hands of later commentators they could be mapped out. Each mode of representation is best seen, however, as an effort to endue the visualization of law's many lines, their nodes of intersection, and their emerging or ending pathways.

In "Accidental Torts" Grey moves interestingly between these two types of representations, the ideational and diagrammatic. He writes of how Holmes sought to conceptualize a new theory of law that would apply to the large mass of cases arising out of industrial and other type of accidents. Yet he also frequently uses such words as "domain" and "map" or "mapping" to convey the significance of Holmes's innovations. He finds Holmes's objective theory of negligence to be a "compromise" between "true fault and strict liability," which is not inaccurate.[548] G. Edward White makes a similar point when he says it is preferable to see the defining characteristic of tort law in America as "being poised at the interface of those two variables [the individual and social dimensions of injury]."[549] But it would be better to see it as Holmes did, as a resultant, as a way of recognizing and delimiting a new basis of liability, of a certain kind of temporal harm, one that brought together and syncretized in a new way individual fault, individual freedom, and public policy concerns.

If his analysis of malice and privilege led Holmes to survey and develop a new ground of liability, one in which a specific kind of motive, malice, may to a greater or lesser degree delimit a privilege, his discussion of "intent" at the end of "Privilege, Malice, and Intent" led him to the same end but in a different direction. Holmes's analysis of intent like that of malice worked-off negligence; negligence stood as the existing ground, it helped demarcate these new bases for liability. Intent also showed the limits of the foreseeability standard when the "intent" at issue did not fit within the scope of the traditional direct action torts (assault, battery, etc.).

Holmes selects for analysis those cases in which liability for an intentional act is not understood solely in terms of foreseeability. How is it, he asks rhetorically, that a seller of firearms is not "answerable for assaults committed with pistols bought of him, since he must be taken to know the probability that, sooner or later, some one will buy a pistol of him for some unlawful end?" This question, as Holmes puts it, points up certain limitations to foreseeability as a ground for liability. "I do not think that the whole answer to such questions is to be found in the doctrine of privilege."[550]

If the complete answer is not to be found in privilege then some other type of justification must be in play. Holmes thus begins to elucidate an earlier passage in

[547] Holmes, *Law in Science*, *supra* note 265, at 408.
[548] Grey, *supra* note 347, at 1270–73.
[549] White, Tort Law in America, *supra* note 5, at 338.
[550] Holmes, *supra* note 481, at 378.

"Privilege" in which he mentions that privilege is only the most important category of justification for the infliction of temporal harm. We are led to infer that there is at least one other category of justification apart from privilege. To appreciate this second category of legal justification we must keep in mind Holmes's caveat that it does not depend on causal analysis, either in terms of factual cause or legal cause.

"The principle seems pretty well established, in this country at least, that every one has a right to rely upon his fellow-men acting lawfully, and, therefore is not answerable for himself acting upon the assumption that they will do so, however improbable it may be."[551] This principle supports the rule, in the case of defamation, that one who utters a slander is not liable for its wrongful repetition no matter how likely to happen if the repetition is done without the original perpetrator's authority or is not itself privileged.

This principle – that one may rely on the good conduct of others – ceases to provide a basis for justification for an indirect act that will foreseeably cause harm (such as the general selling of guns) when the actor takes one more step. Holmes describes it as when the actor not only realistically expects others to act unlawfully but also takes an extra step to bring about consequences that could not happen without that unlawful conduct. The classic illustration is the landowner who sets up traps to harm trespassers. In this case "he had contemplated expressly what he would have a right to assume would not happen, and the harm stands just as if he had been on the spot and had done it in person. His intent may be said to make him the last wrong-doer."[552]

In bringing to the fore the notion that reliance upon others' good conduct takes one out of the reach of foreseeability, Holmes is building upon the immunity that mischance provides. Expected good conduct like mischance is below the height (the range of common or specialized expectation) that foreseeability requires. This basis or ground of justification for an act to which temporal harm can be traced is separate from that of privilege. To appreciate its force we must also recognize that a harm that fell within mischance in Holmes's view also fell within the common law's general principle "that loss from accident must lie where it falls, and this principle is not affected by the fact that a human being is the instrument of misfortune."[553]

Scholars like Grant Gilmore have seen Holmes's articulation and use of this principle as a thinly disguised effort to promote an ideal legal regime where "no one should be liable to anyone for anything."[554] But Gilmore's well-known overstatement should not deter us from appreciating the effort Holmes undertook to extend the immunity that mischance provided to a level on par with intent. He was trying to demarcate and identify a certain basis for not finding liability that common law

[551] *Id.*
[552] *Id.*
[553] Holmes, *The Common Law*, *supra* note 10, at 163.
[554] GILMORE, *supra* note 409, at 15–17.

judges had historically relied upon. He does it by identifying this justification as that reliance one may have on the expected good conduct of others even though one engages in an act that *social experience* has shown to have the potential to eventuate in unlawfulness *due to* the conduct of others.

Holmes is doing what he can to bring the nature of "intent" into fuller relief, to give it more dimensionality. The justification he has identified lightens the dark shading of a potentially problematic act (selling guns). The actor loses this protection when the actor takes the fateful step of relying upon induced unlawful conduct to bring about the complained of harm. At that point, and only at that point, for this defendant the harm that has occurred becomes a temporal harm crying for redress.

A plaintiff in such a scenario is faced with the burden of showing that the defendant intended through the use of both indirect and unlawful means to cause the plaintiff harm. Even after the plaintiff has overcome the first hurdle – the protection that indirect action has in relying on the expected good conduct of intermediaries – it must still overcome the potential defense that the direct act was itself privileged. That is to say, where the indirect means is through a third party the question then becomes whether the direct action between the defendant and third party was privileged. For that reason Holmes returns to the topic of privilege in the final section of "Privilege, Malice, and Intent." "When the purpose of the defendant's act is to produce results complained of by means of illegal acts of third persons, his privilege will be narrower than when he intends to induce only legal acts." The use of such descriptors as "narrower" and "wider" are intended to illustrate that in questions of privilege "the nature of the defendant's act, the nature of the consequences, and the closeness of the bond between them, may vary indefinitely."[555]

To determine the relative width and scope of the grounds for liability, or the connected grounds in the legal tableau that liability does not reach (like relying on the expected good conduct of others), or those grounds for escaping liability altogether (privilege), what matters is whether the harm inflicted is a temporal harm and, if so, of what type. Holmes believed that by focusing on the temporal harm one would be better positioned to become more clearheaded on the method used to determine liability. That method demanded greater attention to the postulates that guided legal decision-making. And he was right. His bringing to the fore a hitherto unseen but functioning postulate – that one may in certain circumstances escape liability for foreseeable temporal harm because one has relied on the expected good conduct of others – perfectly exemplifies the type of careful, disciplined thinking he called for in "Law in Science and Science in Law."

But Holmes did not foresee how subsequent scholars would focus only on the role of policy ("legislative questions") and essentially disregard the other important dimensions that made temporal harms subjects of pressing legal concern. More to

[555] Holmes, *supra* note 481, at 379–80.

the point, subsequent scholars have not followed Holmes in turning the practice of law into a discipline that could build on itself. Because academic lawyers are further and further removed from the life of the typical practitioner the conjoining of theory and practice that Holmes proposed and spent a lifetime working out has never received the attention it merits. Moreover, the development of law as a discipline is also stymied because the representations typically employed in academic discourse do not sufficiently bring into view the constant interactions between past law and present concerns. Stereoscopic law, recognizing as it does the need for greater depth of perspective and detail in forming how law is taught, learned, practiced, declared, decided, and enforced – in short, arrayed into workable forms as professional judgments – has the potential to make legal pedagogy more vital, more germane, more sustaining of the dignity upon which the profession is or should be built.

Conclusion

Holmes's theory of legal study – "The Path of the Law" – fell victim to the enthusiasm subsequent generations of legal scholars felt at the prospect of bringing social life to heel at the feet of the "man of the future." Statistical analysis of incidents, the tools of marginal economics, greater attention to the realities of various social or institutional practices (in business, domestic life, or the courts, for example) competed for attention and resources with the continued unabashed compilation, categorization, and analysis of legal doctrine. By early in the twentieth century the legal academy had secured itself a permanent berth in the university. That drew a flippant remark from Thorstein Veblen.[1] But legal education, then and now, has never found its own foothold.[2] It lacks grounding in fact and articulation in theory.

[1] Thorstein Veblen, The Higher Learning in America: A Memorandum on the Conduct of Universities by Businessmen 211 (1918) ("The law school's inclusion in the university corporation has the countenance of ancient tradition, it comes down as an authentic usage from the medieval era of European education, and from the pre-history of the American universities. But in point of substantial merit the law school belongs in the modern university no more than a school of fencing or dancing."). Though Veblen put his finger on a real problem, he seems deficient in his knowledge regarding the history of American legal education. And, for the record, he denigrates much of what passes for higher education in early twentieth-century America, not just law schools, holding out instead for a "seminary of higher learning, as distinct from an assemblage of vocational schools [.]" *Id.* at 263. *See also* Gilbert Geis, *Thorstein Veblen on Legal Education*, 10 J. Legal Educ. 62 (1957). Herbert Hovenkamp takes pains to point out that no matter how much scholars love to cite Veblen, his actual influence seems to have been quite limited until the 1920s. Herbert Hovenkamp, The Opening of American Law: Neoclassical Legal Thought 1870–1970 84–86 (2015).

[2] In her discussion comments on Robert J. Kaczorowski's "Fordham University School of Law: A Case Study of Legal Education in Twentieth-Century America," Professor Robin West says, "It seems to me that law schools are still in search of their own independent mission and institutional identity." Robert J. Kaczorowski, *Fordham University School of Law: A Case Study of Legal Education in Twentieth-Century America*, 87 Fordham L. Rev. 861, 880 (2018).

Or as Holmes might now say, legal education in the United States is a chaos of classes and concerns with a full catalog.[3]

Holmes's theory of legal study had a more or less clear beginning point and endpoint. The endpoint lay in mastery. To achieve mastery the student had to begin by learning the lines already drawn between lawful and unlawful conduct and why. One began with the darkest perimeter lines, those that through artful framing slowly turned a large canvas, one filled with prejudices, moral or pre-moral inclinations, presumptions and prepossessions into the foundation needed for a three-dimensional legal tableau. One learned that conduct truly outside the perimeter turned a malefactor into an outlaw. In modern times that designation, outlaw, is mainly figurative, however.[4] The current-day loss of legal status and legal protection is still only relative – even for a convicted sex offender – compared to the absolute loss faced in the days when an outlaw could be killed on sight with impunity. Yet even to this day in certain states a prisoner may pay with his or her body; but until that point of carefully circumscribed direct action the law has not lowered fully its protective shield.

The student had to realize that the lines drawn were lines based on legal duties, not duties moral, social, or spiritual. In some instances the drawing of the line created the duty, or at least made it visible and commanding. Perhaps the law student or inexperienced practitioner would not even realize that duties other than the moral existed until face-to-face with the peculiar and intricate task that legal line-drawers faced: how to justify drawing the line here instead of there?

> When he has discovered that a difference is a difference of degree, that distinguished extremes have between them a penumbra in which one gradually shades into the other, a tyro thinks to puzzle you by asking where you are going to draw the line, and an advocate of more experience will show the arbitrariness of the line proposed by putting cases very near to it on one side or the other. But the theory of the law is that such lines exist, because the theory of the law as to any possible conduct is that it is either lawful or unlawful.[5]

Holmes went on to point out that regardless of how fine the intermixing between light and dark, at some point a line had to be drawn; it could not but help look somewhat arbitrary. The line drawers, the judges, often liked to disguise the

[3] *See, e.g.*, Martha Minow, *Marking 200 Years of Legal Education: Traditions of Change, Reasoned Debate, and Finding Differences and Commonalities*, 130 Harv. L. Rev. 2279 (2017).

[4] Interestingly, early in his career Howe wrote an article on outlawry. Mark DeWolfe Howe, *The Process of Outlawry in New York: A Study of the Selective Reception of English Law*, 23 Cornell L.Q. 559 (1937). It is most recently cited in a Note from the *Yale Law Journal* that takes as its topic the resources the historical process of outlawry provides for the killing of terrorists outside US territorial sovereignty, even if the terrorist is a US citizen. See J. Y. Chong, *Targeting the Twenty-First-Century Outlaw*, 122 Yale L.J. 724 (2012).

[5] Oliver Wendell Holmes, *Law in Science and Science in Law*, *in* III The Collected Works of Justice Holmes: Complete Public Writings and Selected Judicial Opinions of Oliver Wendell Holmes 416 (Sheldon Novick ed., 1995) [hereinafter CW].

arbitrariness and generally save themselves "the trouble of nice and doubtful discriminations."[6]

Holmes was not a judge who liked to save himself the trouble. He thought other judges and members of the profession ought to have the same attitude. Instead of being disguised, the arbitrariness, such as it was, ought to be justified and explained. One thus learned a professional judgment's composition, how it was meant to work, and how one might improve it. In this sense the external standard was only a start, a strong initial effort to bring law into full relief. Perhaps, from the perspective of the future, it might one day seem as exhibiting as primitive a legal mentality as that which permitted the stoning of an ox for goring to death a member of the community but letting its owner go free without liability.[7]

From the initial efforts to acquire a sense for the lines in play – the various points where conduct went from lawful to unlawful or vice versa – the student in Holmes's opinion had to begin to develop a deeper sense and feel for the subject of study. In one sense the standard categories – property, contract, or tort for example – were simply conveniences to mark out distinctive groupings of fact that the enforcement authority found dispositive, that is, tended strongly to lead to another group of facts. Holmes tried to find in each title of the law those central, distinctive features drawn from social life that unified the type of acts to which the title applied. In torts, for example, the central feature would ultimately become preventable temporal harm. In contracts, voluntarily subjecting oneself in a specific way – through reciprocally induced conventional consideration – to a future event over which one had less than full control.

One could learn how to distinguish and characterize the central features of lawful or unlawful action by applying specific criteria. These subsequently became "elements" in reference to claims alleging unlawful conduct or "indicia" or "tests" when applied to lawful means for accomplishing a lawful end. That is how much of modern law is currently taught, learned, and the learning evaluated. This approach makes it difficult to appreciate the importance Holmes placed on seeing the law, or at least the common law, as a working whole. Without a sense of the "whole" the various parts would be left stranded, lacking the necessary instrumentation to establish their relative dimensions and scope. One also became blind to many interconnections.

In "The Path of the Law" he argued that what made members of the profession members, that is, turned nonpractitioners into lawyers, was the single "process" in which all lawyers engaged with varying degrees of intensity – the effort to transmute the sources of law, the prophecies, into more precise formulations ("predictions") which, in turn, could be generalized and systematized. Even if that last step was unworkable, American law became meaningful for Holmes when he recognized

6 *Id.*

7 Oliver Wendell Holmes, *The Common Law*, *in* III CW 118 (citing *Exodus* 12:28).

how each little part played a role in crafting the whole and how the whole had the capacity to turn what was not a part into a part. One finds in "The Path of the Law" the same creed one finds in "The Soldier's Faith." But understanding and mastering the technicalities and mechanics also mattered because that is how lawyerly sensibility and skill both develop.

On the other hand Holmes did not think it desirable even if it were possible to turn every lawyer into a legal scholar. The one glaring weakness in Holmes's mature thinking on what law is and how it functions, or should function, in the United States is the limited attention he gives to the role of the law professor. His great address on "The Use of Law Schools" is in many ways more about the actual institution of a law school than about the professoriate. True, he mentions the weighty tomes of scholarship produced and Langdell's innovations in teaching methods, but clearly Holmes had doubts about the idea of people committing themselves exclusively to a life of legal scholarship and teaching without any, or with hardly any, active experience in what is typically understood as the practice of law. What would the creation of a class of jurisconsults portend for the American ideal of self-rule, the rule of law? He never directly addressed this question in his published writings.

Holmes was in the audience when Harvard President Charles W. Eliot spoke honoring Christopher Columbus Langdell's twenty-five years of service to the law school. He presumably listened to Eliot expand on what he called Langdell's second most important accomplishment after the introduction of the case method of instruction: that of commencing the practice of hiring as law professors people who had "no experience whatever in actual practice."[8] Upon mentioning the challenges in having that first such person, James Barr Ames, appointed to the faculty Eliot was interrupted by prolonged applause. The man who would soon become the second dean of Harvard Law School clearly had his many supporters. One wonders what went through Holmes's mind after the applause died down and Eliot had this to say:

> And what does it mean? What is to be the ultimate outcome of this courageous adventure? In due course, and in that no long term of years, there will be produced in this country a body of men learned in the law, who have never been on the bench or at the bar, but who nevertheless hold positions of great weight and influence as teachers of the law, as expounders, systematizers, and historians. This, I venture to predict, is one of the more far-reaching changes in the organization of the profession that has ever been made in our country.[9]

8 Charles W. Eliot, *President Charles W. Eliot's Address*, *in* Report of the Ninth Annual Meeting, June 25, 1895, in Especial Honor of Christopher Columbus Langdell 1870–1895, Harvard Law School Association 70 (1895).

9 *Id.* at 71. *See also* William G. Hammond, *American Law Schools, Past and Future*, 7 South. L. Rev. 400, 404 (1881) ("For almost three score and ten years the history of our law schools may be summed up in a very few words: They had little or no real influence on the life and work of the profession."); and *Id.* at 426 ("I have not attempted to conceal my belief, that to make the

Both the creation of a legal professoriate and the transformation of Langdell's case method from a method of investigation and assimilation into a method of analysis and argumentation – Ames and William Keener's "thinking like a lawyer" – began to stratify the profession in unforeseen ways.

Long ago Mark DeWolfe Howe said that the significance of *The Common Law* lay in how its "words had force and meaning not merely to philosophers but to practitioners and judges – to lawyers who cared little for history and less for philosophy but who sought for generality that was true to their own experience."[10] Howe does not mention how it might have affected people like him, those John Chipman Gray once called, in an 1883 letter to President Eliot, the "school bred lawyer."[11] People like Howe did not yet exist as a discernible group in the early 1880s. Gray was not alone in his skepticism; and he was no philistine. This is the same man who exactly thirty years later wrote Holmes, when they were both elderly, inquiring about a certain "palinode" of Holmes's regarding the law.[12]

Perhaps treatise writers like Joel Prentiss Bishop might be seen as paving the way. Bishop had practiced for less than a decade before turning with a sense of mission in 1852 to full-time legal scholarship. But Harvard pretty much ignored him.[13] One must assume that Langdell's decision with Eliot's support to give Ames a full-time job marks for historical purposes the emergence of this new social type.

One problem for those very few people who want to devote time to thinking about the foundations of legal education – assuming that one can talk intelligibly and intelligently about "foundations" – is whether there exists a "generality" that is true to the experience of American law professors as well as of American lawyers and judges. It may be that social fragmentation and division is much too advanced to even broach the idea of a "generality" that brings to light a common, recurring, and meaningful feature in professional experience. One may see a myriad of disconnected stars in the night sky or shimmering portentous constellations or one may hope to mark out dimensions and degrees across derived stellar distances. In this book we have followed Holmes in choosing the latter course.

schools all that they should be, we need in each school one or more teachers who can give their full time and strength to the work."); but *Id.* at 428 ("The analogy between judges and professors may not be complete, but it is strong enough to make me deprecate the thought of a body of law-teachers educated entirely for that purpose, without experience at the bar. I confess I do not see how any man could teach American law-students well without the experience of active practice.").

10 Mark DeWolfe Howe, Justice Oliver Wendell Holmes: The Proving Years 1870–1882 158 (1963).

11 *Id.* (quoting letter from John Chipman Gray to President Eliot (Jan. 8, 1883) (on file with the Harvard University Archives)).

12 Letter from John Chipman Gray to Oliver Wendell Holmes (June 15, 1913) (on file with Harvard University Holmes Digital Suite, Harvard University, Harvard Law School Library / Holmes, Oliver Wendell, Jr. Addenda, 1818–1978 Correspondence: Box 1, Folder 8, Gray, John Chipman, Correspondent, 1877–1913).

13 Stephen A. Siegel, *Joel Bishop's Orthodoxy*, 13 Law and Hist. Rev. 213, 216–19 (1995).

One way to chart the history of the American law since the Civil War is to see it as a series of repeated efforts by the producers of legal literature to depict and describe a lesser or greater "generality" that was true to their own experience. Before the legal professoriate became established, that experience and that generality most often found their home in a naïve, unreflective faith or a strong predisposition anchored in providence. The establishment of the legal professoriate in America coincided with an increasing awareness that the ancient verities had begun to crack and that, in one sense or another, "science" was both the cause and the consequence. "The present age is a critical one and interesting to live in," wrote George Santayana in 1913. "The civilisation characteristic of Christendom has not disappeared, yet another civilisation has begun to take its place."[14]

Direct involvement in legal practice – representing a client, deciding a case, framing a statute or court rule – began more and more to share office space with indirect involvement: teaching students, putting together casebooks, using both time-honored and relatively new techniques to sound out the actual situations in which law worked, or should work, in an effort to make both somewhat more congruent. A lot of that effort went by the name of legal scholarship. It's hard to provide a more precise description of the "peculiar jurisprudential phenomenon" Neil Duxbury described as a "mood" (a.k.a. "legal realism") that predominated among the people who began to man – for they were almost all men – the growing number of law schools that sprung up across the land right before and after the turn of the twentieth century.[15] That this mood did not govern every school, that some new law schools resolutely set their face against it, the history of the Fordham Law School bears witness.[16]

But, still. The "generality that was true to their own experience" that could not find its needed premises in the traditional, recognized pathways of head, heart, and tongue cast about for support. Hope in the guise of "social science" or the "spirit of reform" cleared and tilled a large expanse of ground that ultimately proved rocky. Some schools pioneered legal clinics to help those who had suffered inordinately under the onslaughts of outrageous fortune but could not afford legal services. Fittingly, we find one of the first begun in the city of Philadelphia. In these early clinics one historian finds the rudiments of a nascent "pedagogy of practice."[17] But, still. The generality was elusive; many doubted the viability of any experience that extended much beyond the confines of the concrete case. Jerome Frank gave up and turned to the ancient verities. And he was not alone. Outside law proper even as incisive an intellect as Walter Lippmann could no longer stomach the miasma of

[14] George Santayana, The Winds of Doctrine: Studies in Contemporary Opinion 1 (1913).

[15] Neil Duxbury, Patterns of American Jurisprudence 65–159 (1995).

[16] Kaczorowski, *supra* note 2, at 862–63.

[17] Robert J. Wilson, The Global Evolution of Clinical Legal Education: More Than a Method 88–103 (2018).

democratic power and ideals and headed for higher ground. Many legal educators followed; they had grown tired of the gnomic Holmes. Some of the best known, like Henry Hart, sought to reduce the generality to the refined techniques of a master legal goldsmith. Nature's ways seemed more inclined to processes than to outcomes. Even so, outside Harvard's heavily insulated workshop the siren song of nature and nature's God began to subside; in contrast, the sharp strains of the street corner pipers grew stronger bit by bit.

But, still. The search for a "generality that was true to their own experience" would not let Holmes go gently into the night. Richard Posner became a Holmes champion, as did some of the better-known Critical Legal Studies scholars. Others put their faith in ambitious policy development programs and cited Holmes rarely, only when needed. Yet the continuity of the past continued to hound their every step. The practitioners lumbered on, mostly uncaring and oblivious to what the academic lawyers were up to. Posner, at home both on the bench and behind the lectern, though never a foot soldier, heroically sought to bring the profession together as best he could, to find in the intricacies and scope of marginal economics, through the investigative techniques it favored, a mode of analysis that could put everyone on more-or-less the same page or at least in the same mirrored hall. Later in his career he broadened the techniques and enlarged the socioeconomic descriptions in an unyielding effort to awaken the profession, even former colleagues, from their dogmatic slumbers. Perhaps in his many, many naturalist's notes and texts one could find a generality that would resound with the experience of the American lawyer . . . Posner made converts . . . but, still.

For all of Posner's many virtues one does not find in his numerous writings the persistent drive to bring into deliberation the voice of dead colleagues. He is on record as advocating the supersession of law and believes in this he has Holmes's blessing.[18] I think Posner wrong. Holmes never ceased to be enraptured by the way the common law worked across the centuries. So perhaps somewhere in the rapture, in the sustained effort to hear the law's varying echoes across time, one might find a generality that rings true in and to the present.

The mindset needed for such a task is not likely to be found in today's law schools. They are too inflated with their own sense of good purpose, or at worst of professional pride. The path that Holmes suggested is not one that legal pedagogy ever took. But here and there we see glimpses of what might have been.

In this alternate reality educators who had a sense of what Holmes might have been driving at would not have been left alone to brood disconsolately, shut up in their own vocabulary. Or at least one such educator, Karl Llewellyn, might have been prevailed upon to keep writing commentary to his own unincubated verses until through persistent writing and persistent queries the shell cracked and the chick hatched. The allusiveness of Llewellyn's prose forces the rapids of analysis to

[18] Richard A. Posner, The Problematics of Moral and Legal Theory 206–11 (1999).

slow and even anodyne description to take pause. There is probably no greater educative experience in American law than reading both Posner and Llewellyn on Holmes – assuming one has taken pains to first read Holmes. Both are slightly closer in sensibility to each other than to Holmes but the contrast is enlightening.

Llewellyn may also have told himself at certain trying moments, "I too am a pedagogue." To his far side lies not the Civil War but the founding of modern American law. To a degree not yet fully examined or appreciated that founding took place in Boston, Massachusetts, nineteenth century, last quarter. To his near side lie the era of realism and its discontents that still forms and informs much of the law we see, hear, taste, and somewhat understand. Llewellyn's many writings are too far-reaching to easily characterize but what stands out to the student of Holmes and legal education is his article "What Price Contract? – An Essay in Perspective."

It is not obvious from its title that this piece is on Holmes. Llewellyn first prepared it as an entry on "Contract" for the *Encyclopedia of the Social Sciences*. Its editor, we are told, recognized the value of the piece but found it too impressionistic and "weak in its historical and comparative aspects."[19] By "historical and comparative aspects" the editor meant a conventional survey of the field in the standard scholarly style.[20] But instead Llewellyn provided a lengthy meditation on how one might begin to see the existing panorama of contract law with some perspective, if not yet stereoscopically.

"What Price Contract? – An Essay in Perspective" came out in the same March 1931 issue of the *Yale Law Journal* as did Hessel Yntema's "Mr. Justice Holmes' View of Legal Science." To celebrate the occasion of his ninetieth birthday, the caption facing the frontispiece photograph of the aged Justice announced that "The Editors of the YALE LAW JOURNAL, on the threshold of their legal careers, take especial pleasure in dedicating this issue to the dean of the profession."[21] Llewellyn in a subsequent review of Frankfurter's edited collection, *Mr. Justice Holmes*, described "Mr. Justice Holmes' View of Legal Science" as a "beautiful study" and lamented it was not included in the festschrift. Llewellyn thought Yntema's piece had been "touched with fire."[22]

Even four years later in his own distinctive, well-wrought tribute to Holmes published the month after the master's death, Llewellyn approvingly quoted Yntema's description of that mark that Holmes left, as "A valid but imperfectly realized ideal." He added: "For Holmes, Holmes almost alone, has cracked open the law of these United States. The time-deep calcine crust is burst forever."[23] Llewellyn's use of the phrase "time-deep calcine crust" is not easily understood but I gather it is his

[19] As quoted in N. E. H. HULL, ROSCOE POUND & KARL LLEWELLYN: SEARCHING FOR AN AMERICAN JURISPRUDENCE 186–87 (1997) (internal citations omitted).

[20] *Id.*

[21] Editors, Caption to Frontispiece, 40 YALE L.J. 681, 681–82 (1931).

[22] Karl N. Llewellyn, *Review of* Mr. Justice Holmes, 31 COLUM. L. REV. 902, 902 n.1 (1931).

[23] Karl N. Llewellyn, *Holmes*, 35 COLUM. L. REV. 485, 487 (1935).

way of pointing out how Holmes through his dedicated effort and hard thinking broke up into its various components the consolidated sediments of idea, will, feeling, and chance or accident that the passage of time, and human purposiveness and forgetfulness, had compacted into visible law. We would now describe these spatial–temporal strains or emphases of law under the rubric "judgments" – practical or professional.

But Karl Llewellyn was a man overcharged with ability. In "What Price Contract?," he sought to implement into his own scholarly activity some of the same prescriptions he had laid out to law students in *The Bramble Bush* regarding the study of court cases. When it came to contract law as a whole he sought to *visualize* its different parts, to understand their interconnections as both transactions and events, to make the operative facts no longer *flat*.[24] And to some degree he succeeded even if he never found a way to quite bring into the tableau he created the law that active lawyers and judges practiced.

It is not clear exactly how Llewellyn understood Holmes's approach; it is hard to say whether he appreciated Holmes's lifelong objective as found in *The Common Law* and extending through "The Path of the Law," "Law in Science and Science in Law," and beyond: to raise into existence through the common law's traditional techniques and goals of analysis, supplemented by modern modes of inquiry, a new plane for legal understanding and activity. Assuredly new habits of mind subsequently called "realism" had to be brought into play. More important, they and what had gone on before had to achieve a new level of coordination. Yet Llewellyn no less than Holmes understood that "perspective comes only through the perception of difference. To perceive difference differences must be presented."[25]

He intends "What Price Contract? – An Essay in Perspective," Llewellyn tells us, as an initial exploration into "role of contract in the social order, the part that contract plays in the life of men."[26] The whole paper builds on the sociological and institutional insights of such thinkers as Eugen Ehrlich, Max Weber, and Thorstein Veblen.[27] But here and there, in Llewellyn's initial effort to create perspective, though one not purely legal, one finds the hand of Holmes.

Llewellyn endeavors early in the article, as did Holmes in his chapters on contract in *The Common Law*, to establish a beginning from which he could coherently begin. Llewellyn finds it in the slow, cumulative interactions between what he calls "lay practice" and that practice which has an official character even in the absence of "officials" per se:

> As so often, all probability speaks here for interaction, with lay (or undifferentiated) practice initially in the foreground, later (as official practice comes to recognition as

[24] *See* Karl N. Llewellyn, The Bramble Bush: On Our Law and Its Study 59–76 (1930).

[25] *Id.* at 117.

[26] Karl N. Llewellyn, *What Price Contract? – An Essay in Perspective*, 40 Yale L.J. 704, 705 (1931).

[27] *Id.* at 706 n.6.

> such) moving into the background – though always present as a pressure toward official growth. The problem seems in any event to have been the determination of when that startling event, the forcible holding of a man (group) to a promise, was to occur; and it is vital to remember that law in its beginning is almost undifferentiated from other forms of social pressure.[28]

Yet if law in the beginning is "almost undifferentiated" from other forms of social pressure the course of events as seen from the present brings out a finer complexion. Those other forms of social pressure also begin to differentiate in response to law's increasing distinctiveness. Llewellyn, as does Holmes, understands the increasing differentiation or divergence taking form as an instance of the divergence of social or moral obligations from those legal. "There is the social or 'moral' obligation recognized at law not at all, or only indirectly[.]"[29] This description is Llewellyn's version of what we have described in this book as the differentiation and categorization of duties broadly understood: duties spiritual, moral, social, and legal. The bad man again takes center stage. The cynic view elbows its way to the front. "Holmes long ago noted that in the pinch the measure of what a contract means is its meaning to the evil-minded person."[30] Or: "that the true measure of law *to the man who is to be controlled* is: what, in particular, can or will anybody do about it, here and now?"[31] The student who begins to see law in this fashion certainly risks disillusionment, which Llewellyn readily admits. But as he put it in *The Bramble Bush*:

> ... I see in disillusionment no dampening of interest. *Rather I see all interest gaining in height and depth.* All that is lost is expectation of the unattainable. And the attainable becomes the more worthwhile, the more enthralling. Two things, and two things only, are the need; a will to understand, and a certain patience.[32]

And as did Yntema, Llewellyn repeatedly taps his finger as he emphasizes the importance of a collateral point. "The other aspect of the divergence, the difference in *content* between the running, flexible obligation understood in fact by the parties and the rigid, stereotyped obligation which the law will recognize, has had vastly less attention."[33]

Thus we learn that the law's form and content constantly diverge; rigidity and lived experience are constantly in tension; Llewellyn has in these phrases found a more concrete way to emphasize the reiterated point that the law is in flux. But

[28] *Id.* at 711.
[29] *Id.* at 712.
[30] *Id.* at 724.
[31] Llewellyn, *supra* note 22, at 488 (emphasis in original).
[32] Llewellyn, *supra* note 26, at 151 (emphasis added.)
[33] LLEWELLYN, *supra* note 24, at 712–13 (emphasis in original).

because Llewellyn has taken an expansive view he is able to focus on characteristics and traits that might have been otherwise invisible. He tells us for example:

> The feature of recurrence which I wish to pound on here is that *to the extent of* such divergence between non-legal obligation and the legal obligation officially recognized on the same facts, the legal obligation ceases to function merely as an extra insurance that engagements will be performed. That role, in essence, it need not lose. But it acquires another. It comes to function also as a *source of risk*.[34]

Legal obligation's function as a "source of risk" made possible the point of view of the man that Holmes called bad, that is, the purely legal point of view. Though Llewellyn does not quite make the point, the inference lies in Holmes's view that the actual, specific source(s) of the risk might not always be obvious.

From these efforts in the first part of the article to bring modern contract's parentage into focus, Llewellyn turns to a more sociological and institutional examination of the effects that contract itself, as a legal device and form, has had on modern society. That is to say, Llewellyn turns to techniques that are predominantly "law in science" and not those that might help build a "science in law." It is here we see the stereotypical "realist" habit of mind take hold of the subject and begin to layout the lineaments of ramification and expectation within a concrete social setting. We learn that as contract – as a bargaining device and an investment vehicle – scaled outwards it contributed to the increasing depersonalization of social relations. The "personal" element is unavoidably removed from the equation. Contract as a "legal form" takes precedence and largely displaces contract as "agreement-in-fact."[35]

From this observation Llewellyn proceeds to provide a series of naturalist-type socioeconomic vignettes of the then current scene. He reports not only on the myriad of forms "contract" has taken in modern twentieth-century America, but also provides ruminations on possible long-term effects. For example in a lengthy footnote he comments that probably the major effect of contract law is not so much in what "law officials" do as what they might do and the deterrent effect that has in keeping slackers in in line. "This work of the law-machine at the margin, in helping keep the level of social practice and expectation up to where it is, as against slow canker, is probably the most vital aspect of contract law."[36] Here again, Holmes redux.

But the sense of constant interplay between past and present that we find in Holmes is missing from Llewellyn's thoughtful and learned piece. So is the effort at two-way communication. So is the effort to turn the ongoing practice of law itself into its own discipline. Llewellyn primarily looked to the tools of sociology to provide the coherence he believed law lacked and needed. Yet he, like Holmes,

[34] *Id.* at 713 (emphasis in original).
[35] *Id.* at 722.
[36] *Id.* at 725 n.47.

could not find a way to make the coherence that he sought workable within the parameters that he set. The new sense and feel for law each hoped would take place within actual practice has not yet materialized. What has resulted instead, by and large, is a relatively new round of business as usual: (rule + policy) × [discounted by] (actual practice) = law.

In Holmes, in Llewellyn, in various other thinkers, we find many of the elements needed to see law in 3D yet they have not been coordinated. In terms of a broader pedagogy both the will and the materials are lacking to reveal that organizing focus, the sought-for-generality; that is, the ground that rings true to the experience of a well-known profession. The Holmes Stereoscope is a hand-held tool for combining existing images artificially and giving them not the same life and depth that do the eyes but an enhanced, higher-resolution definition and vibrancy. In the context of legal education the stereoscope as a tool for teaching and understanding the law can accomplish the same end. It organizes and makes possible greater perceptiveness. But one still needs the pedagogical equivalent of suitable viewers and suitable stereographs.

In one of his articles on legal education Llewellyn wrote in plain uninhibited words what he believed to be the most important quality in prospective law students: "I want every law student to be able to read and write."[37] Discounting for rhetorical effect, Llewellyn's admonition brings to mind what Holmes said in "Just the Boy Wanted": The aspirant "ought to have enough flexibility and fineness of mental fibre [*sic*] to make it easy for him to collect ideas from printed words."[38] Such flexibility and fineness may eventually lead to that "clearness of thought which makes clearness of statement, and that sort of ease and familiarity in handling ideas which is one of the marks of a civilized man. The former is a gift, the latter partly a gift, but more the result of training still comparatively rare in this country."[39]

The "handling of ideas" may be partly a gift but we have advanced sufficiently since Holmes's time to know that it is also a science and an art, a discipline that requires the taught ability, at the broadest levels, to tease out from the welter of circumstance and desire the filament of conception, or, in keeping with the terms we have suggested, the sequence of pointers aligned to resolve a question or problem or to advance the possibilities inherent in a suggestion. What we have not spent much time doing in this country, least of all in its law schools, is learning how to handle ideas with the greater refinement of perception they require, with less barbarity.

Holmes was probably not the first nineteenth-century jurist to point out the "serious legislative considerations" courts must weigh when deciding a nice case,

[37] Karl N. Llewellyn, *On What Is Wrong with So-Called Legal Education*, 35 COLUM. L. REV. 651, 660 (1935).

[38] Oliver Wendell Holmes, *Just the Boy Wanted*, *in* III CW 338–39.

[39] *Id.*

but he was probably one of the few to draw attention to how these legislative considerations had their "weight in inarticulate form as unconscious prejudice or half conscious inclination."[40] And he might have been alone in singling out what must be done: "To measure them justly needs not only the highest powers of a judge and a training the practice of law does not insure, but also a freedom from prepossessions which is very hard to attain."[41] Perhaps the training the practice of law does not insure and the required freedom from prepossession are linked; perhaps the link is a fine and flexible mental fiber, an acquired ease and familiarity in handling ideas.

Holmes provided an example of such fineness and flexibility in the last section of "The Path of the Law" when he recounted how he would have resolved the applicability of the statute of limitations in a case of prescription. The matter turns, Holmes said, not on the neglect or inadvertence of the owner but on the position of the possessor who has used the way openly and adversely for twenty years. The better argument for Holmes lies in "the nature of a man's mind. A thing which you have enjoyed and used as your own for a long time, whether property or an opinion, takes root in your being and cannot be torn away without your resenting the act and trying to defend yourself, however you came by it."[42] For Holmes an idea, a full-fledged idea that has become an individualized belief, is on no different footing, legally speaking, than a right of way one has used for over twenty years.

The equation Holmes makes is in many ways hard to understand. But if ideas become rooted in being then the path of the law must provide a way to decide when the cost of deracination is worth the perceived benefit. That analysis may require a casuistry of circumstance; but it also may require an increased, minute perceptiveness of and sensitivity to the ideas in question, and of their locations in being as it were.

The idea elicited and depicted may depend most of all on the quality of the effort spent in the eliciting and the depicting. We do well at this point to recall the basic guiding question of the profession, the legal double helix that we have periodically discussed throughout this book: "What is (the) law?" This environing question structures the working profession – we live, move, and breathe within its ambit – because at every point the initial question "what is the law?" sets the terms with which we begin. These are what Holmes called the motives for decision. Today it might be a trade practice, tomorrow the verdict of the jury, the day after the jury's verdict upheld on appeal. Often it's a line of cases that cannot be gainsaid. And as F. W. Grinnell so well reminded us, the first question leads ineluctably to the second, "what is law?," because of the constant interplay between the different members of the profession, the broader society, concrete problems, and the unending call in America for clearer, more powerful statements of what actual legal power

40 Oliver Wendell Holmes, *Privilege, Malice, and Intent*, *in* CW 377.

41 *Id.*

42 Oliver Wendell Holmes, *The Path of the Law*, *in* III CW 404–05.

is and what it should do. The most recondite and subtle philosophical articulation of "what is law?" means relatively little in the American context unless it can connect to, inform, and take sustenance from the more prosaic "what is the law?" And vice versa.

The point might become clearer if we turn our thoughts for a moment to the end of all law: better professional judgments. These types of judgments, which Holmes also called practical and which in that guise "commanded the world," give law as we know it its ability to scale. Holmes introduced the bad man in "The Path of the Law" so that his hearers would have an easier time distinguishing the salient features of the practical judgments that comprised the operative law at every range. They would learn where each line was drawn or could be drawn. They might even learn to more finely distinguish the various components of a particular line. From the individual breach of contract or tort case to a larger class of cases governed exclusively through statute (like workers' compensation), or through a mix of stated law and unstated custom, the focus on the practical judgments at work began to bring seemingly chaotic rulings and legal regimes into a discernible shape; certain features guided the eye and helped train the mind. Attention to the practical judgments embedded in experience might, as Hurst wisely suggested, help policymakers avert many of the pitfalls that policy implementation at the higher reaches experienced because the developed policy relied on too few variables.

But unearthing existing practical judgments is no easy task. It requires long-range critical history and for the shorter ranges a cynical attitude that refuses to inflate present-day legal events with distorting extralegal moral considerations. Law is law. And the business of a lawyer is to know law – an ideal well worth bringing back. It also means perceiving the beliefs and attitudes and proto-moral commitments that persist, even those that have not secured formal expression as a moral, social, or legal duty. Perhaps they persist in the background, not fully realized, perhaps they extend lines of perception that originated in yet unseen vanishing points. No one would know without some hard looking, hard thinking, and equally hard listening to the different emphases – past and present.

In one sense this meant learning to understand a profession that was in no sense mysterious but still unknown to itself in ways that mattered. The same stereoscope one might use to better grasp the nature and dynamics of a rule in contract or tort or property one could also use to bring into better focus the thoughts and opinions of colleagues.

In Part IV we looked for ways to collate, even into a finely configured arrangement, a series of perspectives, perspectives that different members of the profession, with different concerns and interests and goals, had on Holmes's controversial homunculus, the bad man, and the address in which he made his debut. That is to say, how can the thirteen ways be brought together so that they are more than just a string of vignettes or a lachrymose montage of misspent ingenuity or merely a lengthy succession of here-now, gone-now snapchats? The task seems impossible.

How to bring together the aggressive scientism of Walter Wheeler Cook with the imprecations of Francis Lucey and the other Jesuits? That such a resultant is not impossible Holmes demonstrated in his own work. Granted, Holmes did it at a more rudimentary level, elevating and building out the common law with macadam and asphalt. We today still build roads, streets, avenues, and also lanes, plazas, ways, and terraces, boulevards and drives, but these function better because of the technologically advanced composite materials used in their construction, traditions of zoning, and the developed system of traffic signs and signals we employ. We also build interstates and superhighways, in many cases overpassing the roads and highways built by prior generations. These have their complementary set of corresponding signals. It is a truism to say that law develops. But as Holmes noted in the last of his *Speeches*: "We too need education in the obvious[.]"[43]

What seemed revolutionary to Holmes when he first realized it but then seemed disturbingly obvious was how much of the law we lived and breathed was a composite of built-out feeling. These feelings became postulates when one took a cerebral approach; and at times gelled into conviction when one spoke plainly to the next-door neighbor. But the practicing lawyer knows law differently from the scholar or the layperson. Holmes had a real sense of each mode of knowing, and that multivalency, as much as anything, distinguishes his written work. In his 1876 breakthrough article, "Primitive Notions in Modern Law, No. I," he notes the disorientating nature of the agonizing pain that impels even a very intelligent person to beat the inanimate object seen as its cause. "Such a mental condition," he notes, "may be traced along the course of history, not merely in impulsive habit, but in formally enacted law."[44]

If we extend Holmes's insight, we realize that different "mental conditions" might be embedded not only in "formally enacted law" but in legal scholarship as well. In one sense this is a truism, since so much of legal scholarship is meant as advocacy or critique. But in another sense that insight might impel a more concerted effort to create, through the parallax of differences, a point, a line, a plane, an intricate, imbricated, multidimensional surface through which the question "What is (the) law?" might operate at a greater range, acquire even greater definition and depth.

To put it another way: legal scholarship might become the means by which and through which the very tissue of the law acquires greater differentiation and reflectivity; law through scholarship manifesting itself at a more self-consciously molecular level.

Or to say it yet another way, a new plane of verisimilitude might be in the offing, a plane where Rogat's sense of the surreal might be juxtaposed against Lucey's apperception of horror, where Tuft's moderation and disbelief abuts Zane's vehemence and cocksureness, where Hurst's historical reach and sensibility might bring into counterpoint the presentist mindsets of a Grey or a Haack, or where the logical acuity of a Wells or a Kellogg might press hard against a Yntema's subtle

43 Oliver Wendell Holmes, *Law and the Court*, *in* III CW 507.

44 Oliver Wendell Holmes, *Primitive Notions in the Law, No. I*, *in* III CW 9.

perceptiveness, and his ability against theirs. In such dedicated efforts to determine the real grounds of difference between one mind and another's, Howe's perseverance and talent for balanced judgment might itself be balanced by the tough-minded Cook's unerring sense for the jugular. Or perhaps the incipient dignity called spiritual that both Novick and Fuller saw crouching at the law's door might yet stand, unmastered, in full relief, unblemished.

On a base such as this the personalities of the future mighty Shattucks might one day be built.

But these dreams are wispy, future-laden. We live in an era when Chief Justice John Roberts's call for more "relevance" from legal scholarship mostly met indifference, defensiveness, or parody. These dreams arise from the hope that maybe one day we will learn to appreciate and better conserve the tremendous intellectual resources at our command and stop the indulgent waste. Cooperation, collaboration, patience – the willingness for the I to think through another and to have another think through the I might be how legal scholars will project a much-needed sense of movement, distance, and depth into American law. Holmes in this respect did not always set a good example but he had an inkling of the possibilities that greater openness and scrutiny of feeling, of the working postulates, might bring. And he well knew the profession's dire need for greater self-reflexivity.

For this reason no doubt, he was pleased to speak at the Boston University celebration, pleased to attend a new hall dedicated to the teaching of law. Toward the conclusion of his address, as mentioned above, he put forward, like any veteran pedagogue, a hypothetical. But unlike the typical hypothetical, his question about what ought to guide our thinking on whether a man should lose a right of way openly used for twenty years did not serve merely to test his audience's grasp of the law of possession or the boundaries of a statute of limitations. In the audience sat not only law students but also real heavyweights – Bigelow, Thayer, and Ames. Perhaps as much to them as to anyone in the audience he posed the question of how one might determine the grounds for decision. "The law," he maintained, "can ask no better justification than the deepest instincts of man."[45] These "deepest instincts," we assume, take us past the brute drive to survive. And in the society in which Holmes lived and moved, those same instincts warranted many contests that wound their way before the courts and even, in a different way, impelled a dog to fight for its bone. The struggle for life is the order of the world. But the instinct that led a dog to fight for its bone, or one person for a right of way and another for a dearly held belief, all worked at different scales and had behind them different resonances. In their varied forms they manifested continuity that Holmes thought a necessity, and necessity one must face forthrightly.

That these "deepest instincts" are not one-dimensional or absolutely controlling we learn from a footnote earlier in the address. In that part of the address Holmes is summing up his ideal: "I think that there is a general theory to be discovered,

[45] Holmes, *supra* note 42.

although resting in tendency rather than established and accepted." For example: "I think that the law regards the infliction of temporal damage by a responsible person as actionable, if under the circumstances known to him the danger of his act is manifest according to common experience, or according to his own experience if more than common, except in cases where upon special grounds of policy the law refuses to protect the plaintiff or grants a privilege to the defendant."[46]

And then the footnote:

> An example of the law's refusing to protect the plaintiff is when he is interrupted by a stranger in the use of a valuable way, which he has travelled adversely for a week less than the period of prescription. A week later he will have gained a right, but now he is only a trespasser.[47]

Why the "deepest instincts" do not protect the adverse possessor against a competing stranger when they justify a decision against an inattentive owner takes us straightaway to the lines that have been drawn, how risks and presumptions have been allocated, to the facts that law as the voice of the community has deemed most vital. The law of possession paradigmatically depicted for Holmes how the common law had not only the power to become a medium of human development but to incarnate it as well.

Questioning existing lines called for finer discriminations, more nuanced practical judgments. No one could match Holmes in tracing the ghostly provenances of opinions that ultimately found their culmination in the law. Holmes kept hoping to turn these lines into statements, turn the statements into broader propositions, and then order these propositions, systematically. Maybe he too, in his own way, had been unduly mesmerized by the translucence of knowledge in systematic form.

But Holmes was an American at heart. The great problem for any American who wants to perfect the law is mainly one of form. Holmes wanted the law to be a noble enterprise in the studied formation of a people. He aspired to systematize his findings but he never did. That form he was temperamentally unfit to handle. He possessed an extremely fine sensibility and well-developed powers of expression. His ideal form, in the law at least, warred with the natural bent of his powers. I venture to guess that Holmes did his most creative thinking by collating images and then working hard to discern the unseen but felt connections. But the effort to generalize and formulate law in the form of dogma did not provide, for him, an easy path from generative insight to systematic expression.

In 1912 Holmes complained that the "trouble with general or literary historical works is that they deal with premises or conclusions that are both unquantified." One never knows how much of this is needed to produce so much of that, or how much of either the record actually shows. Interestingly, he thought the situation was better in philosophy and economics. There, he said, one had more confidence in

[46] *Id.* at 401.
[47] *Id.* at n*.

tracing cause and effect. "The one shows the inward bond between successive stages of the thought of man; the other the sequence of outward events that have governed his action and (some believe) really have determined his thought. At all events the latter fits the former as the outside of a cathedral fits the inside, – although there are gargoyles and Mephistopheles without and angels and saints within."[48]

How do "gargoyles and Mephistopheles" become "angels and saints"? This question has in its lifeblood the angst that Holmes felt as a young man, when he was seeking to bring out of his legal studies an enterprise fit for the future. It was the alchemic sequence he spent a lifetime trying to divine, to draw out from the necessity called the past its workings and prospects.

Speaking of the cathedral he concluded: "There is no place for history of law in this metaphor; but, in plain prose, it is midway between the other two." He then delineates the various means by which the history that has been realized weaves its many works. It is a sight to behold. "We observe the illustrations, as striking here as in poetry or music, of the universal change of emphasis that each century brings along. An argument that would have prevailed in [Edmund] Plowden's time [1518–1585], and perhaps would have raised a difficulty to be got rid of in Lord Ellenborough's [1790–1871], now would only be answered with a smile."[49]

The inference he draws? The law will furnish philosophical food to philosophical minds. The further inference we have drawn is that the law must be seen in 3D, stereoscopically, as the first step toward establishing a metric by which and through which law can be further known, and made increasingly knowable.

I, for one, do not think Holmes was being melodramatic when he reported to a group of undergraduates at Harvard "in all sadness of conviction" that "to think great thoughts you must be heroes as well as idealists." The great thoughts in his opinion would not otherwise occur. Thinking in the law is a spiritual discipline. He added: "Only when you have worked alone, – when you have felt a black gulf of solitude more isolating than that which surrounds the dying man, and in hope and in despair have you trusted to your own unshaken will, – then only will you have achieved."[50] As he himself once thought he was a "dying man" after his chest wound at Ball's Bluff, the sense of isolation he felt in his legal studies must have been overpowering indeed. True moral experiences are soul-quenching.

How seemingly different the tone, then, we find in "The Use of Law Schools" delivered a few months later also at Harvard. There we find a more upbeat Holmes, one happy to take part in the celebration of Harvard's 250th anniversary. He is clearly proud of his alma mater. In a few words he brings together the past and future of his law school into a single, vibrant point of intersection. About twenty years had passed since his graduation. He went through a long period of probation, he mastered the

48 Oliver Wendell Holmes, *Introduction to the General Survey*, *in* III CW 439.
49 *Id.* at 439–40.
50 Oliver Wendell Holmes, *The Profession of the Law*, *in* III CW 472–73.

common law, and he was now a Justice in the highest court of his state. But his interest in legal education had not flagged. He wanted to take the opportunity, he said, "to say a few words about the use and meaning of law schools."[51]

In this book we have attempted to give some indication of what Holmes believed to be the "use and meaning" of law and of law schools. We spent many pages trying to crack the clues that Holmes left us in such writings as *The Common Law*, "The Use of Law Schools," "Learning and Science," "The Bar as a Profession," and, of course, "The Path of the Law." If "The Path of the Law" was Holmes's most considered statement on legal education it was because he had already laid the necessary groundwork in "The Use of Law Schools." Some of the implications hinted at in "The Path of the Law" he forcefully drew out in "Law in Science and Science in Law." But the *meaning* of law and law schools had not varied from his 1886 speech.

Unsurprisingly Holmes summed it up best. It lay in creating the right atmosphere. In 1929 Harold J. Laski wrote the Justice and reported on his latest endeavor to have the powers that be in England "set up a Royal Commission on Legal Education and see whether we cannot devote some of the immense funds of the Inns of Court to building a Harvard Law School in this country."[52] Mark DeWolfe Howe reports that the Commission was not actually created until 1932. Its mandate "was to consider the possibilities of closer coordination between the work done by the Universities and the professional bodies, and further provision for advanced research in legal studies."[53]

Holmes in his response recalled what he had said long ago, "that for most of the evil in the present state of the law I think the remedy is for us to grow more civilized. Your lawyers are educated in a more civilized *milieu* and whatever the system of teaching, they show it – judging from the decisions that from time to time I read. The atmosphere is more important that the specific contacts."[54] He wrote that in a letter to Laski dated June 21, 1929. By "civilized" he meant a person who knew the law but could also put the law itself into a broader context, who sought to be reasonable, who was willing to expand the range of understood feeling, who had, above all, the capacity "to see things in their proportion."[55]

He next wrote Laski on July 9. At the end of that letter, after his signature, he, in his typically courteous and understated way, appended a single sentence postscript. One gets the impression he wanted very much to tell the high-minded Laski something but didn't know exactly how. So he put it in a postscript. "I hope you took to heart my remarks about civilization apropos of your desired Commission on Legal Education."[56]

[51] Oliver Wendell Holmes, *The Use of Law Schools*, *in* III CW 474.

[52] II Holmes–Laski Letters: The Correspondence of Mr. Justice Holmes and Harold J. Laski, 1916–1925 1156 (Mark DeWolfe Howe ed., 1953).

[53] *Id.* at n.4.

[54] *Id.* at 1159 (emphasis in original).

[55] Holmes, *supra* note 51, at 479.

[56] Holmes–Laski Letters, *supra* note 52, at 1163.

Index

Made in the USA
Las Vegas, NV
28 October 2024

10598751R00295